"DREAMING THE MYTH ONWARDS"

C.G. JUNG ON CHRISTIANITY AND ON HEGEL

PART 2 OF *THE FLIGHT INTO THE UNCONSCIOUS*

The Collected English Papers of Wolfgang Giegerich

The Collected English Papers of Wolfgang Giegerich makes the work of one of archetypal psychology's most brilliant theorists available in one place. A practicing Jungian analyst and a long-time contributor to the field, Giegerich is renowned for his dedication to the substance of Jungian thought and for his unparalleled ability to think it through with both rigor and speculative strength. The product of over three decades of critical reflection, Giegerich's English papers are collected in six volumes: *The Neurosis of Psychology* (Vol. I). *Technology and the Soul* (Vol. 2), *Soul-Violence* (Vol. 3), and *The Soul Always Thinks* (Vol. 4), *The Flight into the Unconscious* (Vol. 5), and *Dreaming the Myth Onwards* (Vol. 6).

For a full list of titles in this series, please visit *www.routledge.com/The-Collected- English-Papers-of-Wolfgang-Giegerich/book-series/CEPWG*

Titles in this series:

The Neurosis of Psychology: Primary Papers Towards a Critical Psychology (Volume 1)
Technology and the Soul: From the Nuclear Bomb to the World Wide Web (Volume 2)
Soul-Violence (Volume 3)
The Soul Always Thinks (Volume 4)
The Flight into the Unconscious: An Analysis of C. G. Jung's Psychology Project (Volume 5)
"Dreaming the Myth Onwards": C. G. Jung on Christianity and on Hegel (Volume 6)

"DREAMING THE MYTH ONWARDS"
C.G. JUNG ON CHRISTIANITY AND ON HEGEL

PART 2 OF
THE FLIGHT INTO THE UNCONSCIOUS

COLLECTED ENGLISH PAPERS
VOLUME SIX

WOLFGANG GIEGERICH

Routledge
Taylor & Francis Group
LONDON AND NEW YORK

First published 2013 by Spring Journal Books

Published 2020 by Routledge
2 Park Square, Milton Park, Abingdon, Oxon OX14 4RN
52 Vanderbilt Avenue, New York, NY 10017

Routledge is an imprint of the Taylor & Francis Group, an informa business

British Library Cataloguing-in-Publication Data
A catalogue record for this book is available from the British Library

Library of Congress Cataloging-in-Publication Data
A catalog record has been requested for this book

ISBN: 978-0-367-48514-6 (hbk)
ISBN: 978-0-367-48516-0 (pbk)
ISBN: 978-1-003-04139-9 (ebk)

Cover design and typography by:
Northern Graphic Design & Publishing
info@ncarto.com

Contents

PART II.
HEGEL

PART III.
CODA TO
THE FLIGHT INTO THE UNCONSCIOUS

Acknowledgments

Versions of the following chapters have previously been published elsewhere:

Chapter 2, "The 'Patriarchal Neglect of the Feminine Principle': A Psychological Fallacy of Jung's" first appeared in *Harvest: Journal for Jungian Studies* 1999 vol. 45, no. 1, pp. 7–30.

Chapter 4, "God Must Not Die! C.G. Jung's Thesis of the One-Sidedness of Christianity" appeared in *Spring 2010, Vol. 84 (God Must Not Die! Or Must He?)*, Fall 2010, pp. 11–71.

Chapter 6, "Jung's Betrayal of His Truth. The Adoption of a Kant-Based Empiricism and the Rejection of Hegel's Speculative Thought" was first published in *Harvest. Journal for Jungian Studies* vol. 44, No.1, 1998, pp. 46–64.

Once again I want to express my sincere gratitude to Greg Mogenson, the series editor, for his engaged interest in the ideas presented in the following chapters as well as for his helpful comments.

W.G.

Sources and Abbreviations

For frequently cited sources, the following abbreviations have been used:

CW: Jung, C. G. *Collected Works.* 20 vols. Ed. Herbert Read, Michael Fordham, Gerhard Adler, and William McGuire. Trans. R. F. C. Hull. Princeton: Princeton University Press, 1957-1979. Cited by volume and, unless otherwise noted, by paragraph number.

GW: Jung, C. G. *Gesammelte Werke.* Zürich and Stuttgart (Rascher), now Olten and Freiburg i:Br: Walter-Verlag, 1958 ff. Cited by volume and, unless otherwise noted, by paragraph number.

Letters: Jung, C. G. *Letters.* 2 vols. Ed. Gerhard Adler. Bollingen Series XCV: 2. Princeton: Princeton University Press, 1975.

MDR: Jung, C. G. *Memories, Dreams, Reflections.* Rev. ed. Ed. Aniela Jaffé. Trans. Richard and Clara Winston. New York: Vintage Books, 1989. Cited by page number.

Preface

The phrase "to dream the myth onwards" comes from Jung's *Collected Works* 9i, § 271. This translation of the phrase—the sentence reads: "The best we can do is to dream the myth onwards"—gives rise to misunderstandings, and accordingly in Archetypal Psychology it has at times been misunderstood to mean an invitation to us by Jung to do just that, to dream myths onwards. But when we look at the context of this sentence and at Jung's German text we find that he tried to convey a different meaning. Warning against the illusion that archetypes could be explained or "translated" into precise conceptual meanings, he expressed his opinion that our explanations or interpretations of mythic or archetypal images *are* "at best" or "at most" a *dreaming* (Jung's emphasis!) the myth onwards by giving it a more modern form. Another time he used in a similar sense the word *Weiterdichtungen* (*GW* 8 § 152, a spinning-further of the yarn of the dream fantasy), here, however, not for our interpretations of dreams, but for the alterations that the dream as a *pure* product of the unconscious undergoes already in the dreamer in the process of its reaching consciousness. At any rate, no call to do anything, no program, but rather a warning against confusing our interpretations of archetypal images with explanations. In the best case, Jung thought, interpretations stay *within* the enclosure of the archetypal image itself to be interpreted, within the unbroken spell of its spirit and atmosphere, and that in all other cases they simply bypass it.

In using in the title of this book the phrase "dreaming the myth onwards," I am nevertheless precisely harking back to the misreading just outlined. I use it in the programmatic sense that Archetypal Psychology has given it. For two reasons I feel justified in doing this. First, I restrict the myth to which this phrase now, in my use of it, refers to a single one, that of Christianity, to "the

Christian myth" (Jung[1]). Secondly, with respect to this particular limited topic, the Christian myth, Jung himself did indeed have a clear *program*. Thus, in *Memories, Dreams, Reflections* we read, "The Christian nations have come to a sorry pass; their Christianity slumbers and has neglected to develop its myth further [Jung uses, very surprisingly, a word referring to the literal construction work of architects and masons: *weiter zu bauen*, to build further, which elsewhere is never used for myth] ..." (p. 331) "The fault lies ... solely in us, who have not developed it further ..." (p. 332). "The further development of the myth should probably carry on from the point where the Holy Ghost imparted itself to the apostles ..." (p. 333, transl. modif.) and where Christianity left off. When Jung speaks of the *Weiterbau des Mythus* (the continuation of the building up of the [Christian] myth, cf. p. 333f.), it becomes clear that the Christian myth is likened to a building the construction of which, according to Jung, was halted approximately two thousand years ago (halted through "our" neglect!) and needs to be picked up again today, similarly perhaps, we might say, to Cologne Cathedral whose construction was discontinued in 1473, but, after about 350 years of no building, was restarted and, on the basis of a great national effort, completed during the 19th century, in partly neo-Gothic style.[2]

The five essays of the first part of the present volume try to reconstruct essential aspects of Jung's attempt to develop the Christian myth further (in his sense of *Weiterbau* and *Weiterdichtung*) as well as his personal stance towards the Christian God in general. They examine critically Jung's religious ideas, his psychological "theology" (or "theosophy," as I prefer to call it): Jung's views about man's appropriate relation to God, his claims that the feminine requires to be anchored in the figure of a "divine" woman, that the Christian Trinity is fundamentally deficient and

[1] I need to emphasize that I am here quoting or citing Jung, not speaking on my own account. My own opinion is that it certainly can make sense to speak of a Christian *narrative*, but not of a Christian *myth*. We should avoid equivocations. The Christian story does not have the distinct logical and psychological form that distinguishes myth proper from other grand narratives. Myth is relative to an archaic, prephilosophical consciousness. Christianity has Greek philosophy as one of its roots. By the same token, with "dreaming the myth onwards" I do not give my, but point to Jung's program.

[2] Maybe any *Weiterbau*, even that of the Christian myth, if it begins after centuries or millennia of a neglect "to build its myth further," will inevitably have to be one in, figuratively speaking, "neo-Gothic" style.

needs to be expanded so as to turn into a quaternity, that Christianity as such is likewise deficient, namely one-sided, and that evil must be given the status of substantial reality (in contrast to the traditional conception of evil as a *privatio boni*).

The two papers that make up the second part of this book are devoted to Jung's attitude to Hegel as expressed in his relatively few and brief, but amazingly outspoken, radical, and rather emotional dicta about this philosopher. Although this—"Hegel"—is, at first glance, a subject far removed from and totally unrelated to the first topic, I hope that the deeper exploration presented in those papers will show that, in view of Jung's particular reaction to Hegel and the deeper, underlying motivation for his reaction, there is an intrinsic, even though indirect, connection between the two subjects. But even if this inner thematic connection did not exist, the two topics are at least externally connected through the fact that they equally *provoked* Jung to come forward from behind his professional scientific (empiricist) persona and his role as a true psychologist and to get involved in them with his deeply personal, very subjective, to some extent irrational *passion*.

Although the divers chapters each have their own different themes and start out from different textual bases, it is always not merely the particular issue but Jung's psychology project as a whole that is ultimately at stake. *It* is what is, as it were, circumambulated in each case from the particular point of view opened up by the specific theses under discussion.

This book represents the second half of my "Analysis of C.G. Jung's Psychology Project" which I placed under the title of *The Flight Into the Unconscious* (volume 5 of my *Collected English Papers*). Both halves were originally conceived as one book and completed at the same time. Since it would have become too voluminous, it became, however, necessary to divide the book into two volumes. But due to this common origin of the two books, what I stated in the Preface to the earlier volume about the motive, spirit, and focus of my efforts concerning the analysis of C.G. Jung's psychology project applies naturally just as much to the present volume 6. Inasmuch as this is a separate book, it may, however, be helpful to repeat a few major points made in the earlier Preface.

Rather than a critique from outside and in the name of principles or values external to it, what I present is a critical analysis of Jung's psychology from within the heart of Jung's psychology itself. Certain basic tenets of Jung's are being subjected to the alchemical *aqua fortis* and have to show whether they are gold or not. One essential critical question in this regard is: to what extent is Jung's psychology project responsive to the needs of the soul—the *concrete* soul in its historical setting at his time—deriving the views it entertains about the soul simply from how the soul in fact shows itself, and to what extent does it conversely come to the soul with preconceived ideas about what the soul *in abstracto* surely must be and want, thus—unwittingly—following an agenda of its own. And although the result of my analyses may in many cases appear to be devastating, the reader will not simply be left empty-handed with no more than ruins inasmuch as the critical destruction of a theoretical conception happens in the name of essential affirmative insights or principles and *ex negativo* supports them.

In my critiques, I usually speak of "Jung." But Jung the person is not my target. The word Jung functions merely as an abbreviation or stand-in for the body of work authored by Jung, that is, for the ideas and views contained in it. I am interested in the objective *psychology of* Jungian psychology as a general way of thinking and not in the man whose name it bears and his subjective psychology.

With the phrase "Jung's psychology project" I refer only to one single aspect of Jung's life-work as a whole, whereas all the other aspects (Jung's work on word association, on typology, his stance concerning the practice of therapy in the consulting room, his reflections on "psychology and modern physics," parapsychology, synchronicity, to mention only some of them) will be left out of consideration. With his "psychology project" I refer to the fact that Jung viewed his entire psychology, his life's work as a whole, as held together by one central concern—by one "dream" or "main project" that he felt had the status of an "*opus magnum* or *divinum*." He did not choose this as his "main project" but, according to his self-interpretation, had much rather been in its grip ever since his eleventh year or at least since those early experiences that he recorded in the *Red Book*. "It all began then; the later details are only supplements and clarifications of the material that burst forth from the unconscious ..." (*MDR* p. 199). This "main project" circles around such questions as those of Meaning, the Self and the nature of God, the ultimate significance of the individual, and the inner process, telos, and goal of life, but is also responsible, as I demonstrated in the previous volume, for some of his most basic theoretical tenets concerning the general structure of the psyche, above all his idea of "the unconscious," the fundamental difference between "the ego and the unconscious," and his concentration on the individual as "the makeweight that tips the scales."

My critique of Jung's "theosophy," of his treatment of Hegel, and of his "psychology project" at large in the precise sense outlined above is radical (above, I even called the result of my analyses "devastating"). Nevertheless this does by no means lead me to a lump-sum rejection of Jung and his work as such. On the contrary, I consider my own attempts to work out a rigorous notion of psychology as a discipline of interiority as inspired by Jung's deep insights about soul and psychology and remain very grateful to the impulses and understanding I received from "him," that is, his writings. They are full of wonderfully deep, admirably psychological interpretations of psychological phenomena as well as penetrating theoretical insights into the logic of psychology, a psychology that deserves its name ("logos of the soul").

But our admiration of and gratefulness to Jung in all these regards must not blind us to those other aspects addressed here in this (and already in the previous) volume, aspects that can only be considered as parts of an *ideological superstructure* and that despite their prominence in Jung's work are really an alien body within what is truly psychological in his *oeuvre*. Inasmuch as "the soul's" ultimate concern is with truth (not with people, with us, with our well-being or self-fulfillment) the Motto of the Academia Electoralis Theodoro-Palatina (1763) that I placed at the beginning of volume 5 applies to psychology in an even stricter sense than in life in general: "In everything, truth be your supreme commandment."

Berlin, April 2011
Wolfgang Giegerich

Part I
Christianity

CHAPTER ONE

Jung's Millimeter
Feigned Submission – Clandestine Defiance: Jung's Religious Psychology

Jung has written much about the religious dimension of the psyche and his interpretation of and relation to God. It is one thing to look at his explicit statements on the subject, and another to see how the religious question represents itself in Jung's own unconscious material and how this material is received and processed by Jung. One particular lengthy dream reported in *MDR* (pp. 217 ff.) is especially revealing in this connection. In this dream Jung paid his long-deceased father a visit. He was living in the country, in a house in the style of the eighteenth century, very roomy, with several large outbuildings. This house had originally been, in the dream, an inn at a spa where many great personages, famous people, princes had stopped. Several had died, and their sarcophagi were in a crypt belonging to the house. Jung's father guarded these sarcophagi as custodian. But he was also a distinguished private scholar. In a first part of the dream, Jung experienced his father interpreting a Bible passage with great intensity and with a mind flooded with profound ideas, of which, however, the dream-Jung and two other persons with him did not understand a thing. Then the scene changed.

> ... My father and I were in front of the house, facing a kind of shed where, apparently, wood was stacked, We heard loud thumps, as if large chunks of wood were being thrown down

> or tossed about. I had the impression that at least two workmen must be busy there, but my father indicated to me that the place was haunted. Some sort of poltergeists were making the racket, evidently.
>
> We then entered the house, and I saw that it had very thick walls. We climbed a narrow staircase to the second floor. There a strange sight presented itself: a large hall which was the exact replica of the *divan-i-kaas* (council hall) of Sultan Akbar at Fatehpur Sikri. It was a high, circular room with a gallery running along the wall, from which four bridges led to a basin-shaped center. The basin rested upon a huge column and formed the sultan's round seat. From this elevated place he spoke to his councilors and philosophers, who sat along the walls in the gallery. The whole was a gigantic mandala. It corresponded precisely to the real *divan-i-kaas*.
>
> In the dream I suddenly saw that from the center a steep flight of stairs ascended to a spot high up on the wall—which no longer corresponded to reality. At the top of the stairs was a small door, and my father said, "Now I will lead you into the highest presence." Then he knelt down and touched his forehead to the floor. I imitated him, likewise kneeling, with great emotion. For some reason I could not bring my forehead quite down to the floor—there was perhaps a millimeter to spare. But at least I had made the gesture with him. Suddenly I knew—perhaps my father had told me—that that upper door led to a solitary chamber where lived Uriah, King David's general, whom David had shamefully betrayed for the sake of his wife Bathsheba, by commanding his soldiers to abandon Uriah in the face of the enemy. (218f.)

The dream report is followed by "a few explanatory remarks concerning this dream" by Jung himself. He explains that what happened in the first part shows the unconscious task which he had left to his "father," that is, to the unconscious. But in the dream the dream-I and two shadow figures do not understand what is to be communicated to them. Jung then continues commenting on the part with which my citation of the dream began. He says (p. 219f.),

> After this defeat we cross the street to the "other side," where poltergeists are at work. Poltergeist phenomena usually take place

> in the vicinity of young people before puberty; that is to say, I am still immature and too unconscious. The Indian ambience illustrates the "other side." When I was in India, the mandala structure of the *divan-i-kaas* had in actual fact powerfully impressed me as the representation of a content related to a center. The center is the seat of Akbar the Great, who rules over a subcontinent, who is a "lord of this world," like David. But even higher than David stands his guiltless victim, his loyal general Uriah, whom he abandoned to the enemy. Uriah is a prefiguration of Christ, the god-man who was abandoned by God. "My God, my God, why hast thou forsaken me?" On top of that, David had "taken unto himself" Uriah's wife. Only later did I understand what this allusion to Uriah signified: not only was I forced to speak publicly, and very much to my detriment about the ambivalence of the God-image in the Old Testament; but also my wife would be taken from me by death.
>
> There were these things that awaited me, hidden in the unconscious. I had to submit to this fate, and ought really to have touched my forehead to the floor, so that my submission would be complete. But something prevented me from doing so entirely, and kept me just a millimeter away. Something in me was saying, "All very well, but not entirely." Something in me was defiant and determined not to be the dumb fish: and if there were not something of the sort in free man, no Book of Job would have been written several hundred years before the birth of Christ. Man always has some mental reservation, even in the face of divine decrees. Otherwise, where would be his freedom? And what would be the use of that freedom if it could not threaten Him who threatens it?
>
> Uriah, then, lives in a higher place than Akbar. He is even, as the dream said, the "highest presence," an expression which properly is used only of God, ... The dream discloses a thought and a premonition that have long been present in humanity: the idea of the creature that surpasses its creator by a small but decisive factor.

The idea toward which all these comments are heading, namely that the creature surpasses its creator by a small factor, is of great general importance and of central importance to Jung specifically. Leaving aside the question of the merit of this idea for the general thought about

God and man, I want, to begin with, to raise the more modest question whether this important thought can rightly be adduced to interpret the behavior of the dream-I in this dream.

Dumb fish versus human freedom?

I think not. First, as the dream text clearly states, the refusal of a total submission is here precisely not an act of human freedom. The dream-I simply *cannot* act differently without knowing why. Of course, we could still argue here that it is an autonomous unconscious impulse of freedom that forces itself upon the dream-I against that dream-I's consciousness. But even if we conceded this, we would have to realize that here it is not, as suggested by Jung, a question of a defiance on the part of the creature against its creator, of a human freedom threatening Him who threatens it; the dream neither indicates the presence of a threat nor introduces, as a vis-à-vis of the dream-I, the creator himself (or some thought of the creator). There is only the suggestion of Uriah, the image of a wronged, suffering man, an image evoking anything but a threat.

And then, is it really the psychological task set for the dream-I *not* to be a dumb fish by resorting to a mental reservation? Is not much rather the dream-I with its mental reservation precisely behaving as a dumb fish? It does not *demonstrate* its defiance. The dream-I does not own up to his resistance, but outwardly feigns total submission, while clandestinely refusing to go all the way with it. The millimeter distance between forehead and ground is small enough to go by unnoticed so that the dream-I can get away with it. And, at the same time, it is totally sufficient to amount, for the dream-I, to a full-fledged refusal out of principle.

What the dream presents us with here seems to me to be much rather a factual dodging or evading on the part of the subject and of a likewise factual deception than a noble standing up for human freedom. The dream-I cheats. It deceives both his father as well as "the highest presence"; the submission practiced here is a mock submission, one through which the conflict that might arise in the case of a true, i.e., an openly shown defiance is avoided, but the dream-I's (objective) stubbornness is nevertheless, although secretly, retained. It uses a dissociation: two truths that exclude each other (unrelenting submission – self-assertion through self-reservation) are supposed to be effective at the same time, however not as dialectically mediated, but as completely separate: The one as mere external appearance, the other as its true inner stance. Of course in practice, one might say, one millimeter does not make any difference—we do not have to be finicky. True, unless of course what is at stake is, as in the case of this millimeter, not a pragmatic question, but a question of *principle*, here the principle of refusing to submit, a refusal on principle, which ruins the whole apparent submission.

Another consideration is whether it is possible in the first place to submit if one is a dumb fish. Does *real* submission not precisely presuppose human freedom, in fact, *is* true submission not an act of freedom? The whole abstract alternative of freedom versus submission (the way submission is to be understood in the present context) is mistaken from the outset.

Unrelenting submission: The soul's most natural, spontaneous reaction to "the highest presence"

Furthermore, Jung himself taught us that in interpreting dreams we have to stick very closely to the concrete image and the precise wording. "... dream-images are important per se, inasmuch as they bear their meaning in themselves" (*CW* 8 § 471, transl. modif.); "To understand the dream's meaning I must stick as close as possible to the dream images. When someone dreams of a 'deal table,' it is not enough for him to associate with it his writing-desk, merely for the simple reason that his writing-desk does not happen to be made of deal." (*CW* 16 § 320, modif.) Rafael Lopez-Pedraza repeated this formula ("Stick to the image!") that since then has become very prominent especially in archetypal psychology. But here Jung in interpreting his dream does not stick to the dream motif of "the highest presence." We will have to ask what this motif involves.

One cannot choose the conditions set up at the onset of one's dream, such as, for example, if one is led by his father before "the highest presence" or not. But once one happens to have in fact been led before the "highest presence," then all that remains is to relentlessly prostrate oneself, because otherwise one simply has not understood what the nature of the situation is that one happens to be in. Submission is simply inherent in the *notion* of "highest presence," which comes with a distinct emotional valence, and inherent in the whole atmosphere of the dream itself. One simply has to prostrate oneself, not because one would have been forced by an external coercion or out of mere prudence, but out of one's own felt need, a spontaneous and thus free, natural response to the deep emotion, comparable to love, evoked in oneself by the experience of the highest presence. When there is this highest presence, then "all (one's) love and passion (would *normally*, so to speak *instinctively*) flow towards" it.[1] There is nobody here who exerts force and *demands* relentless prostration of Jung and his father. It is his father's own inner feeling that makes him prostrate himself. It is his completely voluntary act, an act making his deep emotion externally visible. In the Bible we read, "For out of the abundance of the heart the mouth speaketh." Here the abundance of the heart does not express itself through the mouth but through the whole body.

Apropos the topic of a "relentless prostrating oneself" we can also recall a relevant comment by Jung himself:

> Christians often ask why God does not speak to them, as he is believed to have done in former days. When I hear such questions, it always makes me think of the Rabbi who, when asked how it could be that God often showed himself to people in the olden days but that nowadays one no longer saw him, replied: "Nor is there anyone nowadays who could stoop so low." (*CW* 18 § 600, modif.)

In ordinary reality, it would of course be possible and probably the most natural thing that there is an external power that *assumes* the *title* of "highest presence" and thus lays claim to being this highest presence. So here we would have a claim, a demand for respect, which by the people subject to this demand might be seen as a usurpation. They would then want to prostrate themselves only perfunctorily and perforce, not out of their own inner conviction. It would be a show of respect merely because it is opportune or unavoidable. But in dreams, a notion such as "highest presence" *is* what it says it is. And because of this absolute identity of name and true reality, that which is said to be "the highest presence" *has* always-already won over the subject for

---

[1] I adopted the phrase in quotation marks from a letter of Jung's (to Herbert Read, 2 Sep. 1960, *Letters 2*, p. 591).

itself. A dissociation or duplicity between claim (or appearance or name) and truth cannot exist. Nor can the difference between the subject and the object exist. Such a reality as "the highest presence" is both intended meaning and true reality, inner and outer, subjective and objective at once, that is to say it is just as much objective, external reality as it is inner genuine feeling or conviction.

We see this relation in our dream in the behavior of Jung's dream father. His submission is obviously not opportunistic, but simply the honest expression of the feeling of his own heart. Only the dream-I can make a difference or insist on a discrepancy between subjective attitude and objective behavior, between official notion or title and personal conviction, explicit meaning and true being. But if it dissociates the two, then it can do this only because it is turning against or is dissociated *from its own soul.* It does not allow the soul to be the one that apperceives what the notion of "highest presence" says and it does not allow the soul to follow its own feelings. For if it were the soul in the dream-I that responded to the higher presence, it would have fallen to the ground out of its own inner need and desire.

I want to elucidate this point by means of passage by Jung himself. In a letter (to Hans Schmid, 6 Nov. 1915, *Letters 1*, p. 32, modif.), Jung wrote:

> True understanding seems to be something which one does not understand, but which nevertheless is alive and effective. When Ludwig the Saint once visited the holy Aegidius incognito, and when the two, who did not know each other, came face to face, they both fell to their knees before each other, embraced and kissed—and *spoke no word together*. Their gods recognized each other, and their human parts [*ihr Menschliches*] followed suit.

What Jung envisioned in this early letter was an immediate recognition of two people from soul to soul, unmediated by their conscious minds, and the immediate spontaneous bodily expression of the soul reaction to this recognition, the expression of the feelings of their heart, unmediated and unfiltered by any verbal exchange. "Their gods recognized each other, and their human parts followed suit," just like that. There is here a natural flow of feelings directly from the depth of the unconscious soul into real behavior. There is here neither a participation of the conscious mind nor any conscious resistance. The soul in its immediacy can live itself out unchecked.

It would of course be pretty utopian if we approached the encounter between two people in real social life with the expectation of a comparable immediacy. There is no reflection here, and the behavior of the two saints, if we conceived it as having occurred in everyday reality rather than in a legend, i.e., in a soul story, would even have to be criticized as "acting out." But in dreams, i.e., on the level and in the region of soul, this type of response is the standard by which the actual responses of a dream-I need to be measured. Is the dream-I, in how it views, feels and reacts, in tune with the reality and the course of events in the dream? In the present dream we see that the dream-I despite its great ego emotion is not immediately reached and touched in its soul by the notion of "highest presence" (not feeling compelled from within to fall to the ground; it merely externally imitates his father's *behavior*: "at least I had made the gesture with him"), nor do his "human parts" truly follow suit. They only go through the motion. On the contrary, something in him even prevents what would be the most spontaneous reaction *of the soul* to one's hearing that one has been led before the "highest presence." For it would have been the natural flow of feelings towards this Presence for the soul to directly show its appreciation and love through an honest wholehearted submission. The dream-I, if the soul would have had a chance in it, could not have helped throwing itself down and touching its forehead to the floor.

It would be a totally other story if in the dream it said that they were standing before a tyrant, a fiend, an unpredictable or evil god. There a desire to defy and to preserve human freedom might arise. But here it is "the highest presence," and every idea that does not belong to this designation and to the feeling that it entails must be omitted, according to the basic principle of dream interpretation expressed by Jung himself (*CW* 14 § 749, modif.): "Above all, don't let anything from outside, that does not belong, get into it, for the fantasy-image has 'everything it needs' [*omne quo indiget*] within itself." As much as his ideas of a defiance in the face of God, of the creature that surpasses its creator by a small but decisive factor, and of Him who threatens human freedom may be worth considering—by operating with them here Jung is, as it were, "in the wrong dream"; in his reflections he out of hand substitutes for "the highest presence" of the present dream the image, adduced from outside, of the unconscious-unjust God from his *Answer to Job* and thus brings completely inappropriate feeling-tones and associations into play.[2]

Furthermore, as matters stand in the dream, "the highest presence" does not refer to God in the first place, but to Uriah (the prefiguration of "the suffering *God-man* in the shape of a servant," him who has been wronged)—a completely different perspective! What sense would a refusal to perform the act of submission make in this case? The sincere submission would here have been that to "*suffering man*." With a submission to the image of suffering man the dream-I would thus have only taken its own suffering and its own humanness upon itself; it would have consciously placed itself *under* its humanness, under its truly *human* fate. Jung, condoning and ennobling the defiant behavior of the dream-I as its demonstration of freedom, is not ready to show the humility that would be a prerequisite for acknowledging the image of suffering man *as* "the highest presence."

But it is not even Uriah's presence as a positive fact: Uriah does not appear at all. He does not show himself. The highest presence appears in the form of absence, that is to say, in the logical status of absolute negativity!

It is very interesting that Jung had no difficulty to relentlessly submit in the sphere of power and the Will. In the "Basel cathedral" episode that he experienced during his twelfth year, Jung felt confronted with a "terrible will." "I don't want to, by God, that's sure. But *who* wants me to? Who wants to force me ...? Where does this terrible will come from? ... *I* haven't done this or wanted this ...." In this situation of brute force the boy Jung could, in the end, submit without resistance: "The wisdom and goodness of God had been revealed to me now that I had yielded to His inexorable command"

[2] By the same token, Jung's interpreting in retrospect the Uriah motif in his dream personalistically as a reference to the later fact that "my wife would be taken from me by death" and to the "detriment" he experienced from his publically speaking about the ambivalent God image, in other words, Jung's identifying himself with the suffering and wronged Uriah, is inappropriate. Uriah was the victim of a terrible betrayal and injustice by his king, even a real crime. That Jung lost his wife in old age through death is a very natural, normal event. Painful indeed. But nothing unfair about it. Jung was not wronged and betrayed by God. Jung's and Uriah's suffering are incommensurable.

(*MDR* pp. 37–40). But in our Uriah story, when it would have been a question of a deep feeling of love, of an inner soul movement in his own heart, and within the sphere of absolute negativity, Jung showed an attitude of defiance. Jung obviously needed the sense of compulsion, of being coerced, in order be able to submit without mental reservation, as in the Basel cathedral story: "I could not yield before I understood what God's will was and what He intended. For I was now certain that He was the author of this desperate problem." He needed to experience a literal Other as overpowering author and as a positive presence. A submission from out of his own heart, as an act of true freedom, was impossible. The "highest presence" as absolute-negative presence (as a literal absence) and the image of humiliated and wronged victim Uriah was not able to reach him inwardly, did not evoke a deep *feeling*,[3] but only his resistance: with this his reaction, Jung instead stayed in the sphere of the *Will*.

The modern situation and the counterfactual insistence on having a God

If it was *not* the ambivalent God who was refused the dream-I's total submission, why was the mental reservation expressed in a symbolic distance of one millimeter necessary in the dream? Presumably because Jung felt the need to hold on to the mythic world as a (seemingly) present reality and to wear the royal garment of the "age-old son of the mother."[4] This could not be reconciled with the figure of that Uriah who had been betrayed by his king and lord. By being betrayed, he lost, we might say in analogy to Jung's alchemical phrase, his status as "the 'son' of the king." He was expelled from this glorious position into the banality and misery of being nothing but a mortal. (Though admittedly, this "to wear the royal garment of the 'age-old son of the mother'" would in the case of Jung be one only in

---

[3] This dream scene could have served as an invitation to Jung to become initiated into the Christian logic of *kenôsis* and the way of absolute negativity. But Jung preferred to hold on to positivity. Concerning the *kenôsis* see my "'God Must Not Die!' C.G. Jung's Thesis of the One-Sidedness of Christianity," in: *Spring Journal*, Vol. 84, Fall 2010, pp. 11–73, now Chapter Four in the present volume.

[4] "In Bollingen I am in my truest nature ... Here I am, as it were, 'the age-old son of the mother,' ... the son of the maternal unconscious" (*MDR* p. 225). He is not just Mr. Jung. He has a higher dignity. And as "age-old," this dignity is indestructible; even if he dies as Mr. Jung, the glorious "age-old son of the mother" continues to exist.

the mode of its already having been retired: discharged and bracketed, suspended, namely only as relegated to "the *un*conscious," to "Bollingen," and only as personality No. 2.)

If it had not been Uriah but a majestic *God* who was the highest presence, then, I presume, Jung *could* have willingly touched his forehead to the ground without hesitation. But to sincerely bow to a "highest presence" that was in itself nothing but a suffering, wronged human being—this was out of the question, even when this was precisely the task that the dream, and Jung's father in the dream, set the dream-I. The lowly and pitiful image of human impotence and exposure to fate (Uriah), the prefiguration of Christ's absolute *kenôsis* at the cross,[5] was not exalted enough for the dream-I in the dream and for the Jung outside the dream. He wanted more: a real God in his absolutely overwhelming otherness.[6] He wanted true Transcendence, mythic numinosity. Clearly, Uriah is not even an image of the Jungian Self.

In his whole psychological thought Jung did not go the way of "Uriah." He went the way of the numinous God-image in the psyche, represented by mandalas and other splendid symbols. His is, to adopt a theological distinction of Luther's to our psychological needs, not a *psychologia crucis* (psychology of the cross), i.e., a psychology of logical absolute negativity in the spirit of *kenôsis*, but a *psychologia gloriae* (psychology of glory), a psychology with mythic meaning and with a God. The place of the Christian decisively kenotic movement is in Jung taken by a scheme of radical opposition and recalcitrance, i.e., egoic self-assertiveness.[7]

---

[5] Jung himself spoke of this prefiguration with specific reference to Christ's "My God, my God, why hast thou forsaken me?"

[6] For Jung, God was defined as "the name by which I designate all things which cross my wilful path violently and recklessly ..." (*Letters 2*, p. 525, to M. Leonard, 5 December 1959), as an "opposing will" (*CW* 11 § 290), "a powerful *vis-à-vis* (*MDR* p. 335), a "numinosity and the overwhelming force of that numinosity" (*MDR* p. 336).

[7] As indicated, Jung thinks the relation between God and man as that of opposing wills and hails man's "ability to 'will otherwise,'" ultimately even his "disobedience and rebellion," because they, he thinks, are required for "the necessary independence, without which individuation is unthinkable" (*CW* 11 § 292, transl. modif.). The "recalcitrance of the Fourth" plays a decisive role in Jung's essay on the Trinity (see Chapter Three below). That in a child's ego development a certain degree of recalcitrance is indispensable goes without saying. But a young child's and an adolescent's ego development should not be confused with the adult person's "individuation" in Jung's high sense, nor should the child's need to assert itself vis-à-vis its parents serve as the lense through which man's relation to God is to be imagined: it would be a childish theology.

Perhaps we could see it the following way. The psychological-historical development in Occidental history led to God's having come down to earth by becoming man and dying on the cross and to man's consequently having psychologically come of age, i.e., to man's now being devoid of a majestic God in the height to whom he could be upward-looking. Rather than submitting to the result of the history of the soul, Jung felt the need to hold on to the "God up there." And instead of himself submitting, he rather brought this, in his majesty unchallenged, God *logically* and *morally* down, namely in the *definition* of his (God's) *nature*, by resorting to the idea of "the creature that surpasses its creator by a small but decisive factor."

In both cases God comes down. But one time it is the *self-movement* of the God-idea in the soul from the status of substance to Spirit, from "object" to logical form. The other time, in Jung's case, it is the critical intellect's moral disqualification of God together with the equivalent declaration of human superiority. *With respect to God*, Jung practices "the depreciating, dissecting undermining-technique of 'psychoanalysis'" (*CW* 10 § 360, modif.) that he criticizes with respect to the treatment of neurotic patients.

Jung's move allows him two things. First, he can still pose as the proud *possessor* of a God and thus himself retain the splendid position of an upward-looking child of God. Secondly, he is able to relegate that humility that the dream-I was asked to show to God himself as God's humiliation in his essence, inasmuch as God was reduced to unconsciousness and natural instinctuality far beneath human consciousness and conscientiousness. Expressed in a rather colloquial way we could say that Jung still has a God, but that this God is pretty dumb and ruthless. As God he deserves our devotion, as dumb and ruthless we cannot really respect him—a clear dissociation between dignity and inferiority. Majesty, numinosity and natural power, on the one hand, and true dignity, on the other hand, part company. We get a chiasmus. With respect to numinous power God is up and we are down; with respect to conscious awareness and moral sense God is down and man is up. There is here neither a *homo totus* nor a *deus totus*. Both are split. The dissociation is perfectly reflected in the dream-I's gesture: with his prostration it shows human humility, and with the millimeter distance from the floor expressing its mental reservation it secretly insists on its superiority, thereby rescuing the principle of upward-looking and thus the idea of its proud possession of a God above.

The lowliness of "the highest presence" and one's submission to it as *self-relation*

This split is, however, not what the dream offers. In the dream itself we see Jung's father as the image of a *homo totus*: he relentlessly bows to that highest presence that is the image of suffering man; he truly bows, but what he bows to is no longer a God up in transcendence, no longer celestial. The highest presence has here come down from the level of gods and entered the human sphere with its suffering, which sphere is the new locus of "highest presence." Because Jung's father unreservedly falls to his knees before *this* highest presence, he fully bows to *his own* humanness and frailty. He is the image of one's no longer upward-looking. He is without a God (because Uriah as the highest presence cannot have anything higher above him). *This* his submitting to his being without a God is his true humility. Man is here entirely for himself, but for himself not in the flat positivistic sense, inasmuch as now the whole former *relation between* man as upward-looking being *and* God as the goal of this upward-looking has been inwardized, integrated into the one *relatum*, man, and reoccurs as the inner dialectical logic of what being-human in the fullest sense of the word means. The loss of God is thus not an amputation, not the elimination of the one half of the former man-God relation. No, "the highest presence" (formerly a designation for God) remains, and with it the necessity of our sincere submission. The difference, however, is that this submission is no longer to a positive Other, to God, and thus no longer religious. It is a logically negative submission, a self-contradictory self-relation. This shows that we are also dealing here with the successor-notion to the *deus totus*: Uriah is the undivided dream image of what is wholly human and as such, *only as such*, also "highest presence."

That the whole-hearted submission to Uriah as "the highest presence" has the character of a self-relation is highlighted if we compare what Jung said about Uriah, on the one hand, to what he said about his father, on the other. Uriah, we heard from Jung, was "shamefully betrayed" by his own king and "is a prefiguration of Christ, the god-man who was abandoned by God. 'My God, my God, why hast thou forsaken me?'" About his father Jung states, the Church and its theological thinking "had blocked all avenues by which he might have reached God directly, and then faithlessly abandoned him" (*MDR* p. 93). This "celebrated faith of his had played this deadly trick on him" (*ibid.* p. 94). "My memory of my father is of a sufferer stricken with an Amfortas wound, a 'fisher king' whose wound would not heal ... ... he had literally lived right up to his death the suffering prefigured and promised by Christ ... He wanted to rest content with faith, but faith broke faith with him" (*ibid.* p. 215).[8] Uriah and, allegedly, his father were both betrayed and forsaken. Just as Uriah is the prefiguration of Christ's suffering, so Jung's father lived the suffering prefigured by Christ. On both sides we have unjustly suffering man.

But interestingly enough, the dream father does not appear at all as a poor old blindly resigned man suffering from a wound that would not heal, as the man who, as Jung saw it, did not dare to think about religious matters (p. 215), the man "whose life had come to a standstill at his graduation. ... Once upon a time he too had been an enthusiastic student ...; the infinite treasures of knowledge had spread before him ... How can it have happened that everything was blighted for him, had turned to sourness and bitterness?" (p. 95). The dream father appeared as the exact opposite, as a distinguished scholar not only full of enthusiasm, but also full of intelligence and wisdom, as a religious teacher who dealt "with something extremely important which fascinated him. ... his mind was flooded with profound ideas." So the dream. Jung's dream father is intellectually rich; rather than pitiable he is a dignified model of

---

[8] We see here how powerful the ideas of "innocent victim," victim of a betrayal, and of the treacherous God as the metaphysical author behind ordinary human suffering were in Jung. It is at bottom the same inflationary interpretation as in the case of his own self-stylization as the innocent victim of his suffering from the death of his wife and from the criticism he received after his publishing his ideas about the ambivalent God-image. Betrayal, injustice! I suffer? It must be somebody's fault. Somebody must have wronged me. Who done it? Interestingly enough, the idea of "the suffering God-man in the shape of a servant" (Kierkegaard), the (implicit) identification of the proletarian with the Passion of Christ (Marx and Engels), the (literal) identification of insane Nietzsche with the Crucified, on the one hand, and the invention of the detective fiction, on the other hand, originated around the same time, during the 19th century.

deep religious insight. And Uriah at the other end also does not appear in his misery, but precisely high up there and honored with the most exalted title possible, the title of "the highest presence."

What the dream seems to want to suggest to the dreamer, Jung, is that his father or the psychological father image is healed, more than healed: unwounded to begin with. There is no need for Jung, the son, to take upon himself a psychological, spiritual task allegedly left unfinished by his forebear who had not been able to fulfill it. There is no wound, neither in his father nor on the side of Uriah. Everything about his dream father is fine, indeed, admirable.

What is it that brings this glory to his father and to Uriah, who outside the dream were both images of terrible woundedness? Is it not the total submission of the one to the other? By without reserve submitting to the prefiguration of suffering, Uriah, this suffering was overcome. Total humility and exaltation to the highest presence are the two sides of one and the same dream image, one and the same psychological truth. Both are strictly identical. *In* Jung's dream father it is Uriah himself who submits to himself as the prefiguration of suffering man, and conversely, by wholeheartedly prostrating himself Jung's father is himself the highest presence up there to whom he humbles himself. This is the intra-human self-relation I spoke about, a self-relation in the form of a self-abasement. Thus there is no glorious, majestic epiphany here, no coming "face to face with a psychically overwhelming Other" (*CW* 10 § 655). No divinity appears as a numinous presence before dwindling man. No, on both sides, down here as well as up there, there is the same: the humble image of man "betrayed" in his faith. The ultimate submission to the human loss of faith or loss of God ("My God, my God, why hast thou forsaken me?" referred to by Jung himself in connection with Uriah) is in itself its own exaltation to the highest presence.

All that the dream, or the soul, seems to want from the dream-I is that it follow his father's self-abasement and understand that the *wholehearted submission* to the loss of faith or loss of God *is itself* "the highest presence" (please note: not the loss of God, but the submission to this loss is the highest presence). The dream, I submit, wanted to teach Jung to understand that the loss of faith per se was not at all his real father's problem (as Jung saw him). *This* "problem" is shown in the dream not to be a problem. There is no not-healing wound here, not even a memory of a former wound. The dream father is in perfect harmony with himself and his lot. Compared to how Jung viewed his real father, the dream father is in a state of redemption. No, the problem of his real father (the real father in Jung's interpretation) had been that he had not done what the dream father does, namely that he had not unreservedly and out of his free will submitted to his loss of faith. He rather had experienced it as a terrible deprivation, a desperate loss, and remained stuck in this initial phase of his experience, apparently incapable of moving on with this experience by letting himself be taught by it, be initiated into it as his new truth. As if paralyzed by the change, he held on to his previous expectation of a fulfilling faith as the *sina qua non*, rather than letting himself now be also *psychologically* transported into the new *sine qua non* of that new stage of the soul's alchemical opus magnum in which he already *in fact* found himself. Owing to this fixation and inflexibility of mind a dissociation arose between what he insisted ought to be and what he felt to be actually the case. So he succumbed to "sourness and bitterness." His was a resignation (as a subjective emotional state), but not a re-signation, a being placed under a new sign, a new *truth*.

But the dream shows that the dream father was altogether different. He must have been able to lovingly go along with the soul's movement to a new stage or truth of itself, to go along with the change from "highest presence" as an overwhelming majestic God to man forsaken by God *as the new highest presence*. His submission to *this* highest presence, a submission not out of a sense of an imposed obligation, but coming from his own heart, testifies to the fact that *he*, other than the real father, is living under the new sign.

Remodeling Christianity in order to escape its further development

The real father of Jung's *Memories, Dreams, Reflections*, there can be no doubt, had a problem. The question is what precisely the problem was and therefore what the solution for it would have been. I said that it was his not going through with his loss of faith all the way so as to be initiated into its truth. Jung's view, by contrast, was that his father did not "pugnaciously" "quarrel" with God, "who was alone responsible for the sufferings of the world" (*MDR* p. 92). It is in the same line when Jung interprets his father's suffering in moralistic terms as being due to a betrayal, an injustice, when he speaks of his having been faithlessly abandoned and of the deadly trick that had been played on him. Jung's interpretation follows the pattern of innocent victim (his father) and guilty party (God, the Church, faith). In this whole area he subscribes to a psychology of blame and refuses to go the path of initiation deeper into what at first naturally appears as a "pathology."

Christianity, this is a frequently expressed criticism by Jung, "has neglected to develop its myth further in the course of the centuries" (*MDR* p. 331). But if anything was not allowed for Jung, then it was the *further* development of Christianity, and where he did meet with it, as in his father and in modernity at large in which it is approaching its form of fulfillment, he scornfully rejected it. What he did want when he spoke of the "further development" was something totally different: an improved, edited, corrected version of Christianity according to his own agenda, i.e., an *other* (alternate) Christianity, but by no means the *self*-movement of its "prime matter." Rather than continuing the alchemical-historical further-determination of the Christian truth, and rather than both intellectually and feelingly accompanying the soul's kenotic self-movement downwards beyond the glorious stage of our "*having* a God," Jung is guided and fired by a spirit of protest against the soul's movement. He insists on an ego move *contra animam*, on a decidedly anti-Christian program of his own. Psychologically, the historically real development to the point of the loss of God could be seen as part of the gradual historical self-realization of the Christian truth, as that moment when its deepest point (Jung cited "My God, my God, why hast thou forsaken me?") at long last *comes home* to the Christian soul itself (instead of being merely a content of its "myth" or teachings, merely something that happened two thousand years ago to one particular individual, Jesus Christ). But this home-coming was unacceptable for Jung.

To put it in the terms of our dream: formerly, "the highest presence" referred to God as a being, a substance in the metaphysical sense. But if it is now Uriah who is "the highest presence," then highest presence is no longer substantiated, inasmuch as Uriah is known to be no more than a humble human being and an absent being in the dream on top of it. He is not a God, not Christ, not even the Jungian Self. Rather, with him "the highest presence" has dissolved, become distilled, logically negative, vaporized, and as such it has taken lodgings in man himself as the *spirit* of man's being-in-the-world, the *constitution* of his consciousness. The soul's development—alchemically speaking—from substance or matter to mercurial spirit, or—in Christian terms—from a state where the Spirit is only the promise of a distant future to a state where it has already become actually present in consciousness was intolerable for Jung. For him God simply had to remain a substance, an entity, a personality—an overwhelming Other.

Why would Jung, who in so many ways was a true psychologist, truly open to the soul and its movements, in this one area refuse to follow the promptings of the soul? Why would the form of otherness be indispensable for him and the *sublimatio* and *evaporatio* of God, i.e., his becoming psychological, be intolerable? Why could Jung not even give to the Self itself (one of his central notions) the *form* of self, i.e., comprehend it as sheer fluid self-*relation*, but instead only the rigid form of otherness: *the* (substantiated) Self?! The question "why?" cannot be answered. We can only see *that*, when faced with the historical situation of religion that had been reached at his time and was vividly exemplified for him in his father, then his reaction—the decision of that whole person who is known as C.G. Jung—was to go the way of defiance and *ressentiment*, just as we see that when faced with this dream he made a virtue of the defiance on the part of the dream-I by making use of a far-fetched ideological theory, a clear "rationalization" in the psychoanalytic sense. One would have expected that a psychologist of his stature would have found fault with the resistence of the dream-I against what his father wanted him to do, his father, who after all functions in this dream as his psychopomp. And by interpreting a wholehearted submission as the act of a "dumb fish," Jung indirectly even denounces what his psychopomp is doing. Clearly, here Jung is going *contra animam*.

Jung's millimeter is the expression of a compromise formation. His behavior is extremely close to that of his dream father and at the same time it fundamentally, namely on principle, contradicts this behavior. This is an undialectical contradiction that can only maintain itself without self-destructing because its one side, the refusal, remains clandestine. Jung's behavior amounts to feigning a submission while in fact refusing it. This is significant. From early on Jung spoke out, with respect to the needs of the Western soul, against "going East," going to the wisdom of India for example. He felt that psychologically we have to stay faithfully within our own Western tradition. And in fact, his work gives the impression that his main effort is to struggle with the psychological predicament of the West and Christian truths. Not only his works that openly address Christian topics (the Trinity, the Catholic Mass, the suffering of Job, etc.), but also his whole work on alchemy belong here. Jung needed alchemy because he saw it as a correction of Christianity. But precisely this, that he wanted to correct Christianity, is where Jung's millimeter comes into play. In the spirit of defiance he did not want to further the development of the Christian soul from within it, but from without. Alchemy for him had the task of being a counterbalance or complement to what he said was the one-sidedness of Christianity. So here, too, we have a feigned devotion to Christianity. It is a devotion to it with the goal of altering it, *not* of letting it unfold its own inner logic. A dedication to it in the spirit of "defiance," a decidedly anti-Christian commitment to what for him was the Christian "myth."

JUNG'S RELIGIOUS DISCOURSE AS A GARB FOR VERY DIFFERENT PSYCHOLOGICAL CONCERNS

Jung's defiance or resentment comes from, or is directed against, the modern predicament as exemplified for Jung in the collapse of faith suffered by his father. Expressing it in mythological parlance we can say that Jung rebelled against the modern experience that "God is dead," that "God had forsaken us." This he could not forgive God. But in contrast to this religious parlance, we have to realize that this was not a genuinely *religious* problem for Jung (the way the problem that his father suffered from had indeed been), not a problem of *religious* psychology per se, but a *personal* existential or psychological problem merely in a religious guise. Other than his father he had already left the sphere of religion and saw his father's doubts from a standpoint outside. The issue for Jung was the creation of the *psychic (existential) feeling* of containment in and unbroken oneness with the world as in olden times, and for this feeling to *exist,* the world had to be "God's world," which in turn involved his psychology in the topic of God.

He felt he had a right to this containment and only in this sense the right to "have a God," just like children feel they have a right to have a good mother and father.

In refusing to go all the way *through* the experience of the loss of God, Jung really refused to go along with the soul's move into modernity, with modern man's "coming of age," with the Christian religion's self-movement to its own deepest point, its own absolute negativity. This threshold he did not want to cross under any circumstances, and at this point his efforts seem to have gotten fixated. All his later work on religious psychology tackles all the questions it raises while staying on this side of that threshold.

When Jung states that the Church had blocked all avenues by which his father might have reached God directly (p. 93), we see how he is begging the very question that his father was struggling with and missing the actual point of those doubts. For Jung, the basic result of one's direct experience is known from the outset: it will be the experience of God, however different its particular form might be. But the possibility that the authentic modern experience might lead into a true "God-forsakenness," into a true sublation and integration of God, is a priori excluded. If his father is suffering so much, it is in Jung's view on the one hand his father's own fault, *his* lack of courage to pugnaciously (i.e., defiantly?) come to terms with his situation, as well as, on the other hand, the fault of the Church with its stupefying theology. *Ultimately*, however, it is of course God's fault, who is responsible for all human suffering.

But Jung's primary concern in this whole area was not *God* as such, God in the sense of religion, God as the pious soul's object of infinite love and fear. Rather, his supreme need was for "*direct* experience" *in abstracto*, in other words, directness, immediacy, *the state of innocence* in the sense of a fundamental unbrokenness of one's world-relation. Jung, I submit, was not really and primarily a genuine *homo religiosus*. His interest in God and religion was ideological. He had clearly broken with religion as such, had dropped out. With a trace of contempt[9] he had turned his back on the religion of his fathers and the state in which

[9] See for example in what terms he described his first Communion, *MDR* pp. 53ff. ("this wretched memorial service with the flat bread and the sour wine," "a fatal experience for me. It had proved hollow; more than that, it had proved to be a total loss. ... the church is a place I should not go to. It is not life which is there, but death.")

he found real, objective religion to be in at his time, as exemplified by the religious crisis of his personal father.

JUNG'S SHORTCUT: "DIRECT EXPERIENCE"

In insisting on having a God as a substantiated Other, Jung could not simply go back to the faith of his fathers, back to the Church, because in his father he had had the living proof that this faith did not work anymore. It was a dead end. It was also impossible for him to go even further back to the polytheism of pre-Christian religions. They had long been obsolete, and Jung did not want anything that could only be had via obvious affectation. And of course, he could not simply invent a new religion either, because as man-made it would lack convincing authority. So where could he move?

Jung's wish was also not, as one might think under these circumstances, to "reform" his inherited religion as previous *homines religiosi* had done, most notably in the so-called "Reformation," by redressing its degeneracy and returning to *its* sources. No, he wanted a completely fresh beginning all of his own from a totally other source (which, as we all know, he was later to term "the unconscious"). If God could no longer be had with and through the official and public religious tradition, then the only way open to him was to cut corners by turning to what he called "direct experience." In connection with his father we hear from Jung that Jung could perhaps have helped his father in his religious doubts "had he been capable of understanding the direct experience of God," and further that the Church and its theological thinking "had blocked all avenues by which he might have reached God directly" (*MDR* p. 93). But maybe his father was simply too honest and upright to resort to a clever shortcut by which the real difficulty of the situation would merely be circumvented. Even if he could not go all the way through with it, he at least stuck to his difficulty, stayed faithful to the soul. *Chapeau bas*!

The point of the new source that Jung *opposed* to the religion of his father(s) was that it was not mediated through tradition and history. It had to be (at least appear to be) absolutely free from the society and culture in which one grew up, free from what was transmitted from outside through education and learning. This is why, Jung felt, one had to turn exclusively inward. Only there, only if the individual turned away from inherited culture and relied on his own inner and nothing else, could "direct experience" be gained, experience untouched by human thinking: pristine (and thus ultimately "*arche*typal"): *Urerfahrung* (primordial experience). (The fact that this "direct experience" is not unmediated at all, but draws on sunken and sedimented cultural history, Jung did not want to see.)

The fault of the "direct experience" is precisely that it bypasses the real psychological problem and merely offers an ersatz, a stopgap. To turn inward does not provide an answer to the predicament that the Christian soul is felt to be in. With this move, one merely deserts the alchemical retort of our opus magnum and devotes oneself to a private hobby instead, perhaps now trickily calling this hobby the actual opus magnum. The nicest dollhouse cannot make up for the brokenness of the family home in which a girl grows up. It is the state of our alchemical-psychological home that is the issue, not our personal dreams and experiences *in* a home that has gone to pieces. With his idea that his father could have been helped in his religious crisis if he had been capable of understanding the direct experience of God, Jung would have pulled the wool over his father's and his own eyes. His father would perhaps have had a consolation prize that might have taken his mind off his real problem. But this real problem itself, the state of the Christian truth, would have been left behind just as unresolved as Jung's psychology left it behind unchanged and untackled. His psychology merely distracts from the real issue.

At first glance Jung's "direct experience" seems to come very close to the deep visionary and dream experiences gained by individuals in ancient societies in those institutions that we call initiation rites. But a comparison between these two (seemingly near-identical) phenomena reveals their fundamental difference. For Jung the "direct experience" had to be *Urerfahrung*, which means that it had to be the source of its own authority, validity, and truth. The mere fact that it had been directly experienced was *ipso facto* supposed to guarantee its authenticity as a truth. But truth and authority of the experience was not what personal experience in the initiation rites had to provide for those to be initiated. Initiatory experiences had the verification and authentication of their contents outside of themselves, namely (1) in the myths and tales about the gods, nature spirits, ghosts, about the underworld and rebirth, the beginning and end of the world, the culture heroes and their inventions, with which the initiates had been familiarized from early on; (2) in the actual lived life of their community with its rituals, social organization and institutions, the practical management of daily life. On the one hand, life as it was in fact lived gave expression to those myths, but, on the other hand and more importantly, myth was the articulation of the inner truth and logic of the real life of the tribe.

The semantic *content* of visionary experiences and dreams was thus nothing new. Initiation experiences were not experiences in the sense of expeditions into unknown spiritual continents. It was all known from the outset and familiar to the initiate. The initiatory experience was a priori validated by the general traditional *knowledge* of the whole tribe. No intrusion of ideas and images that were absolutely alien to the consciousness of the initiate and to what he himself already believed and knew to be true and how he thought anyway. The *truth* of what he experienced was no question. So what purpose did the initiations have? What did they provide? They provided the initiate's personal appropriation of those truths, their instillation, incorporation into himself. The purpose of initiations was *individuation*—not individuation in Jung's personalistic sense (*our* individuation), but the individuation of the general truths of the community themselves, their enfleshment, incarnation, in real persons. What initiation is concerned with is the *logical* relation of the Universal and the Individual (as singularity), which is altogether different from the question of validation and authentication. (In Christianity the individuation of the general Christian truth is called "faith.")

But here the question arises what "installation of the general public truths in the individual" could possibly mean if, as I claimed, the semantic contents of the tribe's general knowledge had already been long familiar to the person to be initiated. What is the change brought by initiation? Here we can draw upon an adage from the *Kena Upanishad*: "Not *what* the eyes can see, but what *opens* the eyes, that is the Brahman." This sentence introduces the difference between what in our terminology is the contents of consciousness and the constitution or logical form of consciousness. Instead of merely bringing home to the person to be initiated certain contents or experiences ("what"), initiation opened the eyes, taught to see, on one's own, the world and the events of life *from* the point of view or in the light of the respective contents. Initiation is initiation into the logic or syntax of a truth. And only if this logic of the relevant truth has become one's own form of consciousness and the logical form of one's experiencing reality has one been initiated into it and has it become personally appropriated.

What is special about initiation is, however, that this opening the eyes to see in the light of a truth did not happen as a mental, intellectual, conscious learning, but as an essentially unconscious, subliminal, preverbal experiential event on the level of intuition and almost physical (body) experience. It was not active acquisition of a new frame of mind by an ego. It was a passive *being* "informed" as if from behind. One had to literally *undergo* and suffer an initiation.

We don't know this type of initiation anymore, because we have culturally substituted academic instruction and discursive learning for it. We have replaced initiation by information in the modern sense, which is the opposite of the old sense of informing (of giving form, formative principle, of impregnating, impressing). Our kind of learning is that kind of personal and active appropriation of general knowledge that does precisely not individuate this general knowledge, but retains it in the form of universal knowledge (of semantic contents as well as technical skills and methodical approaches) even in the individual mind. This knowledge remains in the status of ideality "up there." Initiation, by contrast, as "incorporation" and enfleshment was essentially experiential, deeply intuitive, emotionally gripping, involving not merely the intellect, but the whole person, and indeed unconscious bodily experience, and thus it indeed individuated and realized the Universal.

Much like ancient initiation experiences, Jung's "direct experience" can be emotionally gripping, too ("numinosity"). However, it lacks the authority of the backing of the community's or culture's general knowledge. Jung's shortcut is that he tried to get away with one's personal experience just like that, without any external backing. The direct experience was supposed to provide *immediate* access to truth, to what Jung called the archetypal. But the archetypes were free-floating. They were not rooted in the actual lived life and the real convictions of the community. Jung was keenly aware of this deficiency and personally deeply disturbed by his existential sense of being on shaky ground; in his student years he was, as he states, filled with "a secret fear that I might perhaps be like him [Nietzsche]," namely a "*lusus naturae* [a whim of nature], which I did not want to be under any circumstances" (*MDR* p. 102, modif.). Jung felt he needed proof "that I was not a leaf whirled about by the wind of the spirit, like Nietzsche. Nietzsche ... possessed nothing else than the inner world of his thoughts ... For me such irreality was the quintessence of horror ..." (*MDR* p. 189, modif.). "Was my No. 2 also morbid? This possibility filled me with a terror which for a long time I refused to admit ..." (*MDR* p. 102). This is why he wanted to show "—and this would demand the most intensive effort—that the contents of psychic experience are real, and real not only as my own personal experiences, but as collective experiences which others also have" (*MDR* p. 194). "I myself had to undergo the primordial experience [*Urerfahrung*], and, moreover, try to give to the content of my experiences a footing in reality; otherwise they would have remained subjective assumptions without validity" (*MDR* p. 192, modif.).

This is why Jung needed to invent *his* "the unconscious" *as* "the collective unconscious." In this way he tried to get through the backdoor after all a kind of collective backing after having expelled through the front door the real, official collective belief of his community, because this belief had become (vide his father) desperate and as such intolerable for him.

The collective unconscious is defined as the sum-total of *quod semper et ubique et ab omnibus creditur* (that which is believed always, everywhere, and by everybody). So far so good. As such it would provide authentication to one's subjective "direct experience." The only problem is that this so-defined unconscious is a counterfactual modern *fantasy* that is precisely belied by modern *reality*, inasmuch as the contents that make up the archetypes of the collective unconscious are *not* "believed everywhere, and by everybody," they are not the general belief-system of the modern world; on the contrary, they are truly foreign to it, if not even disparaged as superstitions. The problem of this kind of backing is already inherent in the logic of the notion of the collective unconscious itself, which amounts to a *petitio principii*:

one and the same thing, the collective unconscious, is the content of the experience, i.e., that which is in need of a backing, and it is itself supposed to be the backing for this experience.

The backing remains inaccessible: itself yonder, on the other side, in the *un*conscious and as such itself fundamentally questionable as to its truth; it is precisely not our conscious knowledge. And conversely, "direct experience" does not individuate the public knowledge and the logic of actually lived life, but remains split off from it as a private experience parallel to the truths of modern life. So in both directions, a union, a true joining together, of the two sides does not take place. Jung substitutes two separate unions on each side for it: on the one side the union of the image from the unconscious with the archetype, on the other side one's "direct experience" with the teachings of "the psychology of the unconscious" (a body of thought which has real lived life, the public convictions and the practice of social, economic, political, scientific, cultural life systematically outside of itself, defamed as the sphere of mere "collective consciousness" and ego hubris, as an aberration and untruth).

The mere assertion of the collectiveness of the archetypes of the collective unconscious through Jung's naming and defining the unconscious as "collective" was not really convincing and thus not sufficient. Another backing was needed. It had, however, to be a backing that was internal to "direct experience" itself, a backing through its own ultimate content—this because a confirmation from the real knowledge and belief of society at large was a priori excluded since as this public belief ("collective consciousness") it was totally incompatible with the type of images coming from the unconscious. We could also say: for its backing "direct experience" had to exclusively take recourse to something from *its own semantic inventory* (what Jung would call the archetypes) because, being a counter-program to the real situation and a deviation from truth, it could not rely on the only real backing there is, the logical or syntactical union of the Individual with the Universal. In fact, it was vital for it to blind itself to anything like the dimension of syntax and logical form. It was, after all, the psychology of the *unconscious*. "The unconscious" means, among other things, exclusive focus on the semantic (cf. for example Jung's "The content of psychosis," "the content of neurosis." What the logical *status* of these contents was did not interest Jung).

This is where, first, God and, secondly, evil, the evil shadow-side of God, come in.

"God": authenticator of "direct experience"

"God" came in only as a kind of "functionary," as a means to an end in this scheme of Jung's. He came in because "direct experience" qua experience requires otherness, a relation to an object vis-à-vis oneself. Without this countering other, one's direct experience might appear to be totally idiosyncratic, one's own concoction, a merely subjective state or an ego-trip,[10] rather than a real *experience*, i.e., the experience *of* something *real*. The object vis-à-vis oneself had to be *an overwhelming subject* that thwarts the human subject's will, and this is Jung's definition of God. "God" is the epitome of "the Other" and as such the guarantor of the true *autonomy*, "objectivity," and non-ego quality of the content of experience. It is overwhelmingness that proves experience's truly being an experience and at the same time turns the experience into one of God. These two statements are, so to speak, tautological (tautegorical): the direct experience proves that it is (ultimately) God and "God" proves that it is a real experience. "God" in Jung's sense is already inherent in the definition of "direct experience" from the outset. We could also say, "God" is "analytically" contained in the concept of direct experience itself and not "synthetically" a new addition to it. When for Jung God is "the most evident of all experiences ... in no more need of proof than the beauty of a sunset or the terrors of the night" (*MDR* p. 92), we see that God is not just a particular content of experience like all the others, but the experience of the very ground and authentication of experience itself.

However, this overwhelming other could not be someone or something that was totally alienated from us humans, such as blind fate, or the workings of a materialistically perceived nature. On the contrary, it had to have the character of what Jung would later call "the Self." Otherwise, it could not have provided that "directness" that

[10] Here we have to keep in mind what Jung had said in the passages about Nietzsche quoted above.

the direct experience was supposed to guarantee: directness in the sense of an existential state of unbroken oneness. The direct experience had to confront us with what was our own overwhelming other, an other with some human trait and "personality." This is a second aspect of the theoretical need for "God."

If the ultimate content of experience is God as the Other in the sense of overwhelming subject, the experience comes with its own backing. As overpowering it is unquestionably convincing, even literally so. But still, a problem remains: the unquestionable convincingness is only the convincingness of *facts*: psychic *reality*, which for Jung, here not being very demanding, was as such synonymous with truth in the sense of meaningfulness ("The idea is psychologically true inasmuch as it exists" *CW* 11 § 4). But of course, an overwhelming power, as "cogent" as it may be, is per se not really a sufficient candidate for truth. Facts are positivities. They have no soul meaning. Something else is needed.

From here a light is shed on Jung's fixation on the question of God's irrational injustice, his responsibility for human suffering, and on "the terrible question of evil" at large (*MDR* p. 331).

The functionality of "Evil"

To begin with, it is good to be very clear about one point: The question of evil in Jung's work receives its importance and urgency from Jung's "personal" existential and theoretical needs (the needs of *his* project) and not because it would be a pressing question for the *soul of today*. The past century has long taught us to see the "banality of evil," the human, all-too-humanness of all the incredible horrors that happened during the last century (and throughout history). And especially if one stays within (and faithful to) the particular dream of Jung's that we have been discussing one sees that the whole issue of good vs. evil is here completely out of place, both with respect to the dream motifs (submission to Uriah as "the highest presence") and the dream atmosphere. This dream may thus underline the general fact that the Christian soul has already left the issue of good vs. evil behind, because it is has gone beyond that psychological stage that gave rise to and needed this abstract opposition. The ambivalent God, whom Jung excavated out of the Old Testament, but presented as a future task for us to come to terms with, is the God who has psycho-historically long been overcome. What belongs to the archeology of the soul, was given immediate relevance for today.

To speak, in view of the suffering from all the horrors in history, of *a God* who is alone responsible for it amounts psychologically to a mystification. This is not what the soul says in our age. It is an ego statement. The soul does not believe anything like this anymore, just as there is for the soul no devil anymore (who once had been a vivid, serious psychological reality). The soul really does not reckon with God anymore. Is Jung's statement not a little bit like an assertion that Santa Claus is responsible for our Christmas presents?

The good-evil opposition is by no means a Universal, an eternal and inevitable theme for the soul to struggle with. It is relative to a distinct stage in the history of the soul, and it existed in this stage not for its own sake (as an eminent truth), but only for a psychological *purpose* and as one extremely important and powerful *instrument* for the further development of consciousness, namely for driving consciousness out of and beyond its mythological-ritualistic stage. But this instrument has done its job. The development it was supposed to bring about has already been fully accomplished long ago. There is nothing more for it to do, and the soul is now somewhere else and confronted with truly other tasks.

Nevertheless, "evil" plays an extremely important role in Jung's psychological thinking. We can see that Jung's fixation on human suffering and on the reality of evil is not only, negatively, due to Jung's refusal to let himself in for the modern experience of suffering from the loss of mythic containment. It has also, positively, a decisive instrumental function, namely as a necessary load-bearing structural component of his insistence on having a God. A first aspect of this is the (more formal and external) function of distraction. Jung *needed* the topics of suffering and evil in his psychological "theology" because only by having them for "pugnaciously" *quarreling* with God about could the idea of God be given the impression of being an unquestioned and unquestionable reality *at a time when* the reality of God was no longer supported and authenticated by the soul.

The religious experience that was truly authenticated by the soul at Jung's time was his father's experience. But this Jung had rejected, and by rejecting it he had landed himself (his psychology) with the problem of God's reality and truth. Horace (*Epistulae* 1. 10,24) wrote,

Naturam expellas furca, tamen usque recurret (even if you throw out nature with a pitchfork, it will always return). But truth is different. Once you have turned your back on it, it is gone and leaves a void—(psycho)logically unrest and a need, emotionally a yearning.

Teenagers and some neurotic adults who feel quite distinctly that they have outgrown or are outgrowing their parents need constant fights with their parents to create in themselves, against their better knowledge, the impression that they still *have* parents in a psychological sense and themselves are psychologically still their children. Blaming the parents is in those cases the psychological instrument for holding on to the parents precisely when the time of the parent-child relationship is long known to be over.

Analogously, the topic of suffering and the blown-up question of evil are in the service of resurrecting, under the conditions of modernity, a notion of God as a self-evident fact and authenticator of "direct experience." In this way the modern soul's truly religious experience concerning God, namely the experience that it had become fundamentally questionable whether there is a God or not, could simply be circumvented. By embroiling all our energies and interests in the other question whether God is only good, or not rather both good and evil, the existence of God is tacitly presupposed, a priori taken for granted; and the real and pressing question of the modern mind about his existence or nonexistence is scotomized. If we can say, as Jung does, that God is "alone responsible for the sufferings of the world" (*MDR* p. 92), how marvelous: we can still feel as God's children in "the boundlessness of 'God's world'" (*MDR* p. 72). We then have, to be sure, given up the idea of the only-good, loving God of our traditional religion—this is the tribute to be paid to our own modern age characterized by the loss of containment—but in return we rescued the logic of "metaphysical" childhood beyond its factual demise (although of course only seemingly).

The second function of the idea of "evil" is that it transcends the mere positive-factualness of the overwhelming character of God. The idea of unjust suffering, of justice and injustice, of right and wrong, of betrayal, guilt, responsibility, and victimization has nothing to do anymore with the sphere of natural facts. It introduces precisely the missing category of values and meaning and thus catapults us from the level of brute force to that of ideality, on which the full sense of "convincingness" is reached.

You cannot quarrel with facts of nature. By *quarreling* with God, assigning to him a brutal ruthlessness interpreted as his unconsciousness, and by conversely conceiving man as "the creature that surpasses its creator by a small but decisive factor," namely by his higher awareness, sense of responsibility and compassionate feeling, Jung could account not only for reality (unconscious overwhelming power), but after all also for truth/meaning (conscious awareness and feeling). But of course, since God's overwhelmingness was indispensable for backing up individual "direct experience" from within itself and for freeing it from the stigma of pure subjectivity (spuriousness, *lusus naturae*), the idea of justice could only be reconciled with the overwhelmingness if God was precisely conceived as *unjust* (betrayer) and fundamentally unconscious, while conversely justice and considerateness as well as consciousness were reserved for man, thus claiming a *human* superiority for a capacity (ultimately love) of which no one and nothing else but this very theory had systematically *dispossessed* God.

Consciousness and unconsciousness, justice and injustice had to be dissociated: kept separate and neatly allocated each to one side. Naturally so, because God had to authenticate "*the* unconscious." He had to be the unconscious party in this relation. Jung could not allow for an undissociated view, for which God would have been *the truth* of man *as homo totus* (so that the history of the changing God images would merely *reflect* the respective logical status reached by man.[11] Jung had to set up the relation between God and man in terms of radical otherness (vis-à-vis) and human superiority.

"Evil": Necessary prop for the soul's form of otherness and for the innocence of consciousness

It is a mystification when Jung adamantly substantiates evil *in its abstractness* (as if it were an archetypal, mythic reality, even a demonic force) over against the "privatio boni" definition of evil and when he,

---

[11] Thus no inferiority of the one and no superiority of the other. Consciousness and unconsciousness would be on both sides in exactly equivalent degrees, and any increase in consciousness would happen on both sides at once since they are not literally two, but the one is merely the reflection of the inner (logical) truth of the other.

e.g., states, "Evil today has become a visible Great Power" (*MDR* p. 331). For Jung, evil is not an adjective (an attribute of a noun or substance), but a noun (in itself an essence, a substance). This substantiation is a mystification, true. *But the substantiation is exactly the point*: Here we come to the topic of what the third *function* is that the idea of "evil" in its positive reality has for Jung's psychology-project. The idea of evil is needed to underpin the substantiality (positive reality) that Jung wished to claim not only for the God-image specifically, but for the whole sphere of unconscious images or the imaginal, i.e., for "direct experience." But why an underpinning for "God" in the first place? Did we not see that it is precisely God who has the function in Jung's psychology of underpinning and authenticating "direct experience" from within itself through his overwhelmingness and through the evidence of his experience that needed no proof?

Even if the experience of God could indeed provide this service to "direct experience," the idea that the experience of being overwhelmed from within was indeed the experience of *God* was no more than an assertion that was itself in need of authentication and "proof." Such overwhelming experiences may be common, but that they are experiences *of God* is something that the modern mind is not willing, indeed not capable, to concede. So the authenticator of "direct experience" is himself in need of an underpinning for the substantial reality attributed to him because this substantiality, basically the substantiality of the Old Testament God, has psychologically and historically long been obsolete and is for this reason in desperate need of an underpinning to give it some conviction that it does not have by itself.

The absolute reality of evil (ultimately the notion of "the Fiend" or "Adversary") supports the substantiality of God and the imaginal world ("direct experience") because it sustains the notion of ruthless otherness and thus tension, conflict, opposition. It has a psycho-logical effect. "The Fiend" and "evil" mobilize emotional energies in the subject. (To avoid misunderstandings, I must emphasize that I am speaking on a psychological level, i.e., on the soul level, the level of the soul's *logical* life, and not on an empirical or behavioral level. So even if it may sound so, I am not referring to subjective emotions in people, in the ego-personality.) The soul is—logically—upset, wants to protest against it. Thus on (a deep logical level) "emotionally" involving and arousing the subject with respect to "God" (who otherwise would leave the subject totally cold in our time), "the Fiend" and evil contribute to a kind of equivalent to "individuation" (in the sense explained above: "incorporation of the Universal in the Individual"), i.e., to the individuation/realization of God himself.

But I had to say "kind of equivalent" because what in the initiation rites in ancient cultures was indeed the *logical crossing-over* from the Universal to the Individual or, the other way around, the union of the individual (the person) with the Universal (god, totem animal, ancestor spirit, etc.) in a (*real*: experientially lived) *syllogism* or *coniunctio*, in Jung's scheme was something very different: a *semantic* or *content* change solely on the one side of the Universal itself. For Jung the *image* of the Godhead (or also one's self-*image*), in order to become *real*, had to be complemented, completed, by the addition to it of "the Fourth," Evil, the Shadow,[12] i.e., another archetypal element. The completion had to happen yonder, on the archetypal image side or to the content of experience in the unconscious. A logical or "syntactical" event in the sense of a real crossing-over as in initiation, by contrast, was prohibited. It would have meant inflation, if not psychosis. This was the tribute Jung had to pay to the logic of modernity, which, other than the metaphysical, reflexive logic of the copula (or the alchemical *vinculum* or *ligamentum*), does not permit a union of the individual with the universal in a (real) conclusion (syllogism). For it, the logical hiatus, the unbridgeable gap, the lacuna, lack, difference and *différance*, dissociation are constitutive. Therefore, if one wanted a psychology *with* God at a time when God was no longer, by himself and a priori, real for the soul, but only an idea or image *in* the soul, a sublated God, then one could only hope to bring about the real-ization of God by substituting Jung's semantic addition of a special archetypal *reality-providing content* (the Fourth) for the syntactical or logical union—unless, of course, one would have been willing to take recourse to a purely subjective solution: dogmatic

[12] For a closer examination of "the Fourth" in Jung see Chapter Three below. "The Fourth" for Jung had also the guise of the feminine. I discussed this latter aspect in my "The 'Patriarchal Neglect of the Feminine Principle': A Psychological Fallacy in Jungian Theory," in: *Harvest: Journal for Jungian Studies* 1999, vol. 45, no. 1, pp. 7–30. Now Chapter Two in the present volume.

fundamentalism, assertions backed up by the sheer power of the personality's will, which, however, was absolutely out of the question for Jung. Jung wanted an "objective" solution.

Conversely, the fact that God had to be supplied with a Shadow to give him reality clearly shows that psychologically the God-experience for Jung as a modern person, other than the God of tradition, was not real and true from the outset and by itself. To begin with, it was—much like the "horrible irreality" of "the inner world of his thoughts" that (according to Jung, *MDR* p. 189) was the only thing Nietzsche possessed—fundamentally unreal, just an idea, just an image, and therefore essentially in need of something to *make* it real.

We heard earlier that Jung felt he needed to show "—and this would demand the most intensive effort—that the contents of psychic experience are real ..." (*MDR* p. 194). We see this most intensive effort for example in his contorted attempts, in his work on the Trinity, to read his theory of quaternity—of the "Other" as "the Fourth," "whose nature it is to be the 'adversary' and to resist harmony"—already into Plato, where, however, it can only be found through a misconstrual of the relevant Plato passage and by Jung's lightly brushing aside the explanation of the best commentary to the text available at his time (Cornford).[13] "But the fourth, as the text [allegedly!] says, is intimately connected with Plato's desire for 'being'" (*CW* 11 § 188). This is not Plato; it is Jung, who as a *modern* man needs to substantiate or rematerialize the already sublimated, dissolved, evaporated God-idea, thereby trying to undo the soul's alchemical-historical work; and Jung felt the need to back up his exclusively modern *semantic* solution to the reality problem by supplying it with an ancient genealogy, thereby at least by implication providing it with archetypal timelessness and absolute necessity.

Furthermore, if God is alone responsible for human suffering, he appears as the perpetrator vis-à-vis the innocent human victim. As a perpetrator, a *Täter*, he is the true active element, whereas man is only a passive recipient. Both aspects are central: the first guarantees the full autonomy and absolute reality (overwhelmingness) of the content of experience, while the other—a fourth function—grants

[13] See Chapter Three below.

psychological innocence to the human person. And this innocence (the immunity to the modern experience) is after all what Jung's whole project is ultimately about. It is the innocence of direct experience, primarily in the existential sense as man's existence in the "boundlessness of 'God's world'" as a child of God, but also in a methodological sense: the ego (the psychologist or analysand) as the innocent observer of totally autonomous psychic facts (dreams as pristine nature). The dream images had to be *radically* unconscious (truly other, opposite). They were not allowed to be conceived as the subject's own (although subliminal) thoughts (in imaginal form). A reflexive union, the I's return to *itself in* its looking at its other, was not allowed. At bottom Jung's psychology in its logical constitution itself posits and confirms the unbridgeable gap or dissociation which is the law of modernity—that very gap that the semantics of his psychology is striving so hard to overcome (*mysterium coniunctionis*, etc.). And the dissociation between the syntax or logic and the semantic message is that same unbridgeable gap once more on a more subtle level.

The telos of Jung's dream: negativity

The dream about "the highest presence," however, does not support the need for substantiality and otherness, nor for the distribution of unconsciousness and consciousness each to another being or realm. Human suffering is on both sides (the dream-father *and* Uriah), as are humility and exaltation. And as to substantiality, "the highest presence" does precisely not become positively, literally present. Uriah does not appear, he is only intimated, only a mental idea in the dream-I; he is supposed to be secluded behind a *closed* door in a solitary chamber. Nor does anyone else embody, in the sense of an epiphany, "the highest presence." The latter does not become an image, a semantic content. It remains invisible, incorporeal, which shows that it is present only in its logical negativity: in the absolute negativity of the soul. Least of all does the dream point to God. He does not appear nor is he alluded to in the dream itself. In it, there are only the dream-father, the dream-I and Uriah (who however, as indicated, does not appear in person) and of course the *relation* prevailing between the father and Uriah.

In his reflections about the dream, however, Jung uses the idea that Uriah is behind the door for going off on his own associations, first going from Uriah to *King David*, then from the idea that Uriah is a prefiguration of the suffering God-man to *Christ*, and further from David as betrayer to *God* as betrayer. With his commentary on his own dream Jung creates the impression as if the dream talked about God and as if the highest presence were really this unfairly abandoning God. Jung did not stick to the absence of God in the dream and not to the logical negativity of "the highest presence." He obviously felt the need to fill *the empty space* that the dream presents with a personified image, substituting a positive substance ("God") for what is decidedly negative (*absent* Uriah).

Jung demanded the *present reality* of God and the archetypes, the mythic images. But "the highest presence" is precisely shown not to be this present reality, but an absence. And the dream-father who totally submits to "the highest presence" is at the same time the custodian guarding the crypt with the sarcophagi of the *deceased* "great personages" who had once upon a time lived there. The archetypal truths are no longer present realities. They had died. Their immediate presence (their substantiated form, their "flesh," *sarx*) has once and for all been eaten up or devoured (*phagein*) by the sarcophagi. Only custodian, not priest, believer, enthusiast. What the custodian is guarding and as private scholar studies is not "the great personages'" (the archetypes') present reality, but "their sarcophagi," i.e., their *historical* presence in Mnemosyne, their memory, *Erinnerung*: their presence in the inwardness of the mind. This presence is, according to our dream, "higher" than the immediate presence in the external form of otherness.

I spoke of the absence of "the highest presence" and the empty space. In connection with the notion of inwardization or interiorization, I would like to remind us of the exact dream text. Jung's "father said, 'Now I will lead you into the highest presence.' Then he knelt down ..." The father acts as psychopomp, guide of the soul. After his announcement ("I will *lead* you into ...") one would of course have expected that he would have taken the dream I and gone somewhere else with him where the highest presence was to be found. But instead of going anywhere he instantaneously kneels down and touches his forehead to the ground. Does this mean that he does not follow up on his word? Or does it not rather indicate that his total submission *is* the very way in which he leads into the highest presence, the one and only way how to get into the highest presence? Not through a literal movement in space from here to there, but through a soul movement, a change of attitude, an initiatory movement into *a state of mind as* the highest presence. The highest presence is not the title *of* a God or potentate and thus, only-objectively, *their* presence. Jung's father does not lead the dream-I *before* "the highest presence." He leads *into* it. This presence is a reality in its own right, rather than the presence of some other, and this is probably why it is the *highest* presence. Therefore, in order to get into it you have to, as it were, *yourself* become that into which you want to be led. You can be transported into another country, into a desert, into a temple or sanctuary, into outer space while staying who and how you had been before. But the highest presence cannot be reached the same way. It does not even exist if you have not arrived there[14]: if you have not produced it as your own logical form of consciousness. Even if guided by a psychopomp, he who wants to get there nevertheless has to bring *himself*, his own mind, into the logical condition of being in the highest presence. The latter is subjective-objective. This is why the movement into it must have the form of an initiation rather than locomotion. And this initiatory-productive moving into the state of the highest presence is in our dream shown to consist in nothing else than one's unrelenting submission in the context of the idea of Uriah as prototype of unjustly suffering man.

Is it not thus the case that the dream father is the true psychopomp because, other than the mythological soul-guides, he no longer leads in a naturalistic way to other literal-imaginal locations such as into the underworld or before highest presences? He leads *negatively*, in the distilled, sublimated form of one's own going under, one's *kenôsis*. His leading is no longer one in the *form* of otherness; it takes the *form* of self. It is guidance inwardized into itself, initiation come home to itself. And this is also why the highest presence that he is leading into is absolute negativity itself ("the soul"). He guides *out of* the mode of a thinking in terms of the semantics of

[14] It is not a positivity in the first place.

the imaginal (naturalistic-mythical places, objects, presences, and actions) *into* the mode of syntax and logical form.

At any rate, we now have to realize that Jung's refusal to bow all the way is not so much a defiance against unrelentingly submitting *to* the highest presence as much rather a refusal to *get into* "the highest presence" in the first place, into logical negativity. There *is* here nothing to bow *to*. There are not two things: a highest presence before which you can be led and then in addition your possible submission to it. Rather, both are one and the same thing: your absolute submission *is* itself the highest presence produced by your submission. No otherness. And that, it seems, was precisely the problem for Jung. I said earlier that if it had been a majestic God who was the highest presence, then Jung would presumably have willingly touched his forehead to the ground. His defiance was not really against (the ruthless) God (as also the Basel cathedral incidence shows). It was against the alchemical dissolution or evaporation of God, against God's presence only in Mnemosyne or in the interiority of the mind, a presence in the *form* of self (rather than a presence *as* Jung's "*the* Self"!).

Nevertheless, the interiority of the mind was not, and could not be, altogether ignored by Jung. That God and the archetypes did not have a present reality in the modern world was too obvious. There was no way around inwardness as the only place where gods might possibly still be found. But with his millimeter of defiance, Jung helped himself out by simply giving even to inwardness itself the external form of otherness.[15] Archetypal psychology would say here he literalized it. We could also say: he positivized it. In this way (the way of a compromise formation), he did pay tribute to the inevitable inwardness of the mind prescribed by his historical locus, while nevertheless holding on to his goal of otherness. Thus he was literally very close to this inwardness and yet kept an absolute distance, a distance on principle.

His crypt was therefore positivized (substantiated) as a segregated ontological realm or region: "our inner," "*the* unconscious," "*the* psyche." And because this crypt was the *literalized, positivized, substantiated* form

[15] This sentence is a description or analysis of what happened (what happened on the level of theory and *its* internal necessities). It is not to be read as ego moves motivated by ego intentions on the part of Jung as person.

of what in truth was the interiority of the mind, what he believed to find there was not the sarcophagi of the deceased and bygone, but rather the immediate presence of true life, the highest form and indeed the very source of life: "*Psyche ist das allerrealste Wesen, weil es das einzig Unmittelbare ist*" (*GW* 8 § 680; "Psyche is the ultimate reality [lit.: the most real entity (or being) of all], because it is the sole immediate [reality]," my translation). Immediacy contra the dream's sarcophagi (as mediating phenomena). *Literal* crypt ("the unconscious") contra the dream's absolute-negative interiority of Mnemosyne. Positive dissociation of reality into two ("psychic reality, which has at least the same dignity as physical reality" *GW* 15 § 148, my transl.) contra the absolute-negative inwardization of positive reality into itself, i.e., the negative as "the *soul*" *of* the world of positivity.

In insisting on "direct experience" Jung showed that he did not want to be merely a custodian and scholar of Mnemosyne. But inasmuch as his psychology is fundamentally the psychology of "the *un*conscious," he also shows that he is not priest, believer, enthusiast, founder of a sect, either. Jung stayed sober. Without question, *experientially* or *empirically* his "direct experience" *is* immediate experience. But it is the experience *of* that which *logically* is irredeemably entombed and sealed in the crypt of "the unconscious," in which each archetypal image is a priori enclosed in a sarcophagus. Logically, it could never come out into the open. Jung's "direct experience" *is* in itself the dissociation between empirical experience and inherent logic, and thus between "ego" and "soul." It is the opposite of itself. Jung's famous dictum in answer to the interview question whether he believed in God, "I do not believe, I know," points to a knowing that could on principle not come forward and openly declare itself (as also the equivocations with respect to that statement in his subsequent letters show[16]). It thus reveals itself to have been a knowing that did not have, was not allowed to have, the *form* of knowing. The form of otherness prevails here, too. This is the inescapable predicament of the psychology of the *un*conscious.

The same predicament recurs in the idea of the higher degree of consciousness as the "small but decisive factor" by which the creature surpasses the creator. The notion of "surpassing" enforces dissociation

---

[16] E.g., *Letters 2*, p. 525, to M. Leonard, 5 December 1959.

and alienation. The higher man rises to awareness, the more this God is relegated to unconsciousness. But for a truly psychological understanding "God" is consciousness's own highest content, indeed, "God" is the name for the principle of consciousness. By believing to have surpassed its highest content, this consciousness leaves its own principle behind in darkness. It establishes "the unconscious" within itself. But an advanced consciousness that does not manage to bring its own highest content and principle along in its development, shows itself to be, and to want to be, the very unconscious that it talks about as its own other. Not surpassing, not otherness, but self (the mutual having gone under of God and man into each other) is the mode of becoming more conscious.

Love

Staying only with the dream itself, we have to ask: What do Uriah as unjustly suffering man and total submission (in the context of the idea of human suffering) *as* "the highest presence" point to? Do they not point to the reality of the Spirit *as* the reality of Love, that Love which "beareth all things" and "endureth all things"—beareth and endureth (without defiance!) even Jung's (real) father's, even Uriah's, suffering and even all the horrors of history? Is the highest presence (which is present *only* through complete submission and not positively as something in its own right)—is the highest presence not the presence of this Love?

In the sphere of this Love, God has disappeared. Why? Because he has completely gone under as a positively imagined imaginal "entity" or person *into* his own true nature as Love, Love per se! (Not to be confused with the love that a being shows or feels!). God has not only left behind the particular archaic Old Testament form of himself that Jung could not let go of. He has also left behind the substantiated form of himself as a supreme being altogether, *the form of otherness*; he has self-sublated and interiorized himself into his Concept; he has undergone the further-determination of himself into what has traditionally been imagined as the third "person" of the Trinity, who, however, is not a person at all, but living spirit. God as "*the* overwhelming Other," as "semantic content" has become "syntactical," has dissolved into the fluidity, or logical negativity, of this Love. This Love is, as indicated, not to be understood as a positive subjective feeling, attitude, or behavior of people, but quite impersonally as an "objective" logical status, a particular logical form of the soul's world-relation and world-apperception in which people may find themselves. It is a relation without beings *who* relate. Ontology gives way to logic (logical life).

This Love is the self *as real*, the self *as* self—rather than as an other. And it is the self as *all* reality.

In order for Love to be, God *has* to have gone under into it. Absolute "God-forsakenness" is the condition of the possibility (and of the real emergence) of Love.

This Love is a real power, the ultimate objective reality. *But* it is only really present as that which it is if there is a *real* "subjective awareness" of it in the sense of a mind having been "initiated" into it, that is to say, having itself, by going under, attained the logical form of what in the dream is called "the highest presence."

It is one millimeter that separates Jung from this understanding of his dream and, apart from this dream, makes him interpret, so astounding for a soul-scholar of his caliber, his own century in terms of evil (on account of its many horrors), rather than as part of an *objective* historical initiation into Love. But whether a mile or a millimeter: the separation and the corresponding hardening of the heart are just as fundamental in the one as in the other case. With his one millimeter the dream-I as well as the interpreting Jung outside the dream insist on the inalienable otherness of *his* path and on the unbridgeable gap to his forebears' religion, even where this real religion—and *only it* was psychologically real; everything else is "ideology"—is creatively further-developed beyond his real father's religious impasse. Alternatives to what is psychologically real never exist (unless as simulations). This is why I said above that by turning his back on his father's religion Jung had dropped out of religion (in the psychological sense) altogether. There is no choice. We have to go all the way through with our real psychological situation, even if it appears as an impasse or as a dragon obstructing the way to the water of life. With his view that it was *his* task to solve, with his own psychology project, his (real) *father's* unsolved religious problem via the shortcut of "direct experience," Jung underpinned and ennobled for himself, and at the same time concealed, his *defection* from it.

It is the spirit of defiance and haughtiness—a spirit that is not only expressed in this one personal dream, but also on the objective level of theory in Jung's selective fascination with the Book of Job of all Biblical books and his penchant particularly for the Gnostics—that gives birth in Jung to his general insistence on "the reality of evil" and blocks the way to an openness to Love, Love in its absolute logical negativity, as pure logical form. We could express the same thing by saying that the necessity to insist on the reality of evil is a reflection of this subjective spirit of defiance; the preoccupation with evil and the shadow of God *is* the objectified subjective refusal to initiatorily *himself* enter into "the highest presence." "Evil" is the positivized psychological precipitate of the avoided logical negativity. It is this same spirit that makes Jung see this particular dream as the disclosure of the premonition of the idea of "the creature that *surpasses* [*überragt*] its creator by a small but decisive factor"—although there is not the least hint of any such competitive relation, just as there is no hint of the idea of the creator in the dream itself (but we already know that the pugnacious attitude towards God was the way in which God as some kind of entity could still be posited, i.e., pre-sub-posed, at a time when "God" had already gone under, become logically negative). What was ultimately at stake for Jung in all these regards was the form of otherness.

Everything in this part of the dream, even "the highest presence above," points downwards. Uriah is that highest presence that in itself has already gone under and for this reason does not literally appear in the dream as if it were and could still be an object of worship, of man's upward-looking. To the extent that Uriah can be considered the absent symbol of this highest presence, the latter is, to be sure, shown to be exalted (high up behind a small door to which a steep flight of stairs ascends), but exalted precisely and only *as* this having gone under all the way and *as* this not having a positive presence. Uriah is also not Jung's unconscious good-and-evil God, and the (not literally present) figure of Uriah does not lay claim to "surpassing" anybody. And so it is likewise a delusion to think that the dream-I with and on account of its mental reservation secretly surpasses his (alleged) surpasser, since there is no such surpasser here in the first place. Jung as the interpreter of the dream-I does not get in tune with that real sphere that this dream presents and wants to invite him into. He views the dream (as also the man-God relationship at large) completely from outside—unfeelingly, tough-mindedly from the point of view of the clear-cut hierarchical master-slave opposition so alien to this dream, from the point of view of that very opposition that in this dream is shown to have been overcome by its having gone under into itself and thus into the relation of Love. Will and power instead of Love.

Jung's main justification for the dream-I's defiance is "man's freedom." This concern of Jung's is certainly legitimate and, more than that, noble. But is his *notion* of freedom not that of an almost terrorist mind-set, when Jung conceives it as one that has to have the power to *threaten* Him who *threatens* it? Jung's notion of freedom remains merely semantic, abstract, logically positive; it has not become alchemically distilled into logical form (the *form* of freedom), not become syntactical, not absolute (itself *freed* ["absolved"] from the abstract opposition of itself and its opposite). It has and holds its own other (e.g., submission) outside of itself. No doubt, there is here a notion of freedom. But not being interiorized into itself, it itself retains the form of otherness and unfreedom (defiance!). The dream-father in his relation to "the highest presence," by contrast, shows true freedom, a freedom which precisely does not feel threatened by its inner need to whole-heartedly submit: the relation of Love.

* * *

Jung may have felt that his discussion of the dark, evil shadow-side of God is a revolutionary advance in the development of the God-image. But in reality it is a relapse (a relapse of course inalienably *on the ground of modernity* and *as* a thoroughly modern move) back before the logical state already in fact reached in the modern soul, as precisely witnessed by his own dream, back before the state of absolute negativity, interiority, or, alchemically expressed, the state of the *distillatio* and *evaporatio* of what formerly used to be a substantial prime *matter*. Jung's millimeter in the dream and his interpretation of this millimeter in *MDR* regressively throw us back into a decidedly pre-modern, perhaps medieval mentality (God as a kind of overwhelming feudal overlord). Even Jung's "Self" was substantiated. It retained the form of otherness, which means that it was not allowed to take the *form* of self. "Self" is just the label stuck on this decidedly *other* content.

The otherness of Jung's Self with respect to the subject is reflected in and solidified by the internal logic of the Self, namely by the fact that, defined as the God-image in the soul, the Self does not have its truth within *itself.* "... when I say as a psychologist that God is an archetype, I mean by that the 'type' in the psyche. The word 'type' is, as we know, derived from τύπος, 'blow' or 'imprint'; thus an archetype presupposes an imprinter. ... The competence of psychology ... only goes so far as to establish ... whether for instance the imprint in the psyche can or cannot reasonably be termed a 'God-image.' Nothing positive or negative has thereby been asserted about the possible existence of God ..." (*CW* 12 § 15). Oh yes, it has! The imprinter *is* presupposed. Even if this pre-sub-position—an *action* of the mind!—is tacit and on top of it bracketed and cast outside before ("pre-") the precincts of psychology's sphere of intellectual responsibility so that psychology can pretend to be innocent and to have merely *discovered* (in "direct experience") "archetypes" and "God-image" as simple "empirical facts"—as *objets trouvés*, as it were.

This relapse behind the status of distillation or logical form and "self" to "otherness" and "substantiation" was of course not a simple error on Jung's part, but the very purpose of the Jungian project, which in terms of cultural history is one of the many distinct exponents of what has been termed the "conservative revolution" of the first decades of the twentieth century. Nor is the impression it tries to give us of being a fundamental advance an error. Rather, this impression is the necessary means to achieve its unlikely goal of resurrecting something that has in the real history of the soul already been overcome: it needed to present itself as the necessary correction of and advance beyond the logical constitution of the modern soul (while actually being the refusal to enter psychological modernity) in order to be the perfect bulwark protecting us from it. *Perfect* as a bulwark because by giving us the impression that we have already surpassed that from which it is to shield us, in other words, that we are the cultural avant-garde, it makes its retrograde or bulwark character invisible and at the same time scotomizes the logical status reached by the soul in modernity.[17]

[17] We could express this thought also in the following way. The perfectness of the bulwark consists in that the notion of bulwark, other than Jung's notion of freedom, has become "absolute," fully interiorized into itself.

CHAPTER TWO

The "Patriarchal Neglect of the Feminine Principle": A Psychological Fallacy in Jungian Theory

Nemo contra Jungium nisi Jungius ipse, or:
Thinking the Jungian myth onwards

Psychoanalysis at large presently goes through a period of societal disregard, if not downright rejection ("Freud-bashing"). Jungian psychoanalysis in particular suffers an even worse fate. It is simply ignored by the scientific community, by the people in power, and by the major part of the general public. (One might think that this is more than compensated for by the enthusiastic attention it receives from the New Age movement and a segment of pop culture. But the embrace by the popular mind from without, as well as the undermining of the substance of Jungian thought by the popular mind working from within through many Jungians themselves, is rather a badge of infamy.) It may well be that the disrespect for Jungian psychology is not only due to the narrow-mindedness of an uninitiated public, but that it is in part deserved. Deserved, because its basic insights and tenets have not been convincingly worked out, not stringently thought through. Jung sometimes referred to his psychology as "my *critical* psychology,"[1] but there also seems to

[1] E.g., *CW* 10 § 350; *Letters 2*, p. 378, to Bernhard Lang, June 1957.

be some conceptual confusion in certain crucial areas of his psychology that cannot withstand criticism.

One of the oft-repeated ideas going around in many circles of popular thought is that it is the patriarchal neglect of the feminine principle that is to blame for much of what is thought to be wrong in our culture: one-sided rationalism, the ecological crisis, ruthless capitalism, the loss of meaning, the coldness of our modern world at large, the alienation from our emotions, our senses, our drives, and our body. This modern ideology is in my opinion *unpsychological.* But the trouble with it is that it is rooted in Jung's thought, indeed in an element of his thought very dear to him. This is the problem that will have to be explored in the following reflections as an example for the intellectual confusion mentioned.

In his *Memories, Dreams, Reflections*, in the beginning part of the chapter entitled "The Work," there is a passage in which Jung tries to establish a connection between Gnosticism and Freud (with respect to "the classical Gnostic motifs of sexuality and the wicked paternal authority"). Then Jung continues,

> But the development towards materialism which had already been prefigured in the alchemists' preoccupation with the mystery of matter had had the effect of blocking for Freud the outlook upon another essential aspect of Gnosticism: the primordial image of the spirit as another, higher god. According to Gnostic tradition it was this higher god who had sent the *krater* (mixing vessel), the vessel of spiritual transformation, to mankind's aid. The *krater* is a feminine principle which did not find a place in Freud's patriarchal world. Of course, Freud is by no means alone in this bias. In the realm of Catholic thought the Mother of God and Bride of Christ has been received into the divine thalamus (bridal chamber) only recently, after centuries of hesitancy, and thus at least been accorded approximative recognition. In the Protestant and Jewish spheres the father continues to dominate as much as ever. In the hermetic philosophy of alchemy, by contrast, the feminine principle played an eminent role, and one equal to that of the masculine. One of the most important feminine symbols in alchemy was the vessel in which the transformation of the substances was to

> take place. A process of inner transformation is yet again central to my psychological discoveries: individuation. (pp. 201f., transl. modif.)

(What Jung here briefly alludes to, the Catholic dogma of the *Assumptio Mariae* declared in 1950, he discussed more extensively in the last chapters of his *Answer to Job, CW* 11 §§ 743ff. We will have to refer to that text at times to elucidate the statements of the present quotation. In the following, all references to paragraphs without indication of a volume are to that text.)

Right away one is struck by a number of intellectual confusions. 1. Can one say that alchemy is a precursor of materialism, if what it sought was the *mystery* of matter, the spirit Mercurius? By the same token one might charge the Catholic Church of having prepared the way for materialism because of its focus, in the eucharist, was on the bread and the wine as Christ's flesh and blood. 2. If Freud's thought is dominated by "the Father," how can one call his frame of mind informed by materialism, which, after all, refers to the "mater" (if taken symbolically) and focuses on matter, body, substances (mythologically assigned to Mother Earth in contrast to Father Heaven)? And how can one accuse Freud of having no place for the feminine principle if one claims that he stands in the tradition of materialism? The problem Jung finds with Freud's frame of mind would have to be called more accurately his positivism.[2] It is this positivism (a *logical* category referring to the denial that the Universal could be inherent in the Particular, rather than a mythological category) that leaves no room for "the spirit as another, higher god." 3. How could alchemy have prefigured the modern mind's inability to take "spirit" seriously, if, as we know, alchemy was spiritual through and through?—These contradictions are not central to this paper. I mention them only to show that from the outset they tend to create an atmosphere of conceptual fuzziness that is not exactly conducive to making the reader approach the substance of Jung's actual specific argument with a certain amount of confidence. What is central to this paper is what

---

[2] In his 23 October 1906 letter to Freud, Jung actually states as much: "... one feels alarmed by the positivism of your presentation."– The Freud/Jung Letters, p. 7. I am grateful to Greg Mogenson for this reference.

Jung has to say about the feminine principle as *kratêr* or vessel, as the Mother of God and Bride of Christ; and about the exclusive dominance of the Father in the Protestant and Jewish mind. I will state my case bluntly in the form of a series of theses.

1. Up the Down Staircase. When Jung gives highest praise to Mary's reception into the divine thalamus as Mother of God and Bride of Christ in Catholic thought—in *Answer to Job* he goes as far as to designate the dogma of the Assumption of the Virgin Mary as "the most important religious event since the Reformation" (*CW* 11 § 752)—this move of his counteracts the very move on the part of the soul that Jung himself started out from in our passage and described as the Gnostic higher god's sending the feminine principle (the *kratêr*) down from heaven to mankind's aid. By approving of this recent (1950) Catholic dogma as a religious peak far beyond the Protestant, as well as Freudian, position, Jung unwittingly refuses, as it were, to accept this Gnostic god's gift to us humans, sort of writing "return to sender" on it, sending it back up into the heavenly, transcendental, or metaphysical sphere. Jung contradicts himself. He does not "stick" to the original image he himself introduced. This image has two aspects: the first is that of a content, the feminine principle in the form of a vessel, the other is this vessel's downwards movement. In his desire to give full appreciation to the *content*, he *elevates* the feminine principle again (Assumption!), insisting, e.g., that "the equality of women" (a this-worldly social development) "requires to be metaphysically anchored in the figure of a 'divine' woman, the bride of Christ" (§ 753)—not realizing that thereby he undoes (a psychoanalytic defense mechanism!) the *down-movement* of his own Gnostic image again and thus *malgré lui* even hurts the feminine principle as the content that he wants to give highest honor to: because according to the image in question this feminine principle is not supposed to be up there, but down here.

2. Psychological Materialism. But Jung also directly acts against the first (content) aspect of the image. He ignores the specific form in which the feminine principle is introduced: the *kratêr*, the vessel. Even though he points out that in medieval alchemy "one of the most important feminine symbols" was the (alchemical) vessel, thereby acknowledging a continuity from the particular Gnostic image to the alchemical one, he indiscriminately treats the image of the Mother of God and Bride of Christ in the modern dogma as an expression of the same feminine principle, totally ignoring the opposition of the two types of images. The Gnostic *kratêr* and the alchemical *vas* are empty, hollow containers, pure receptivity. Their essence is in the nothingness that they enclose, and the surrounding substantiality or materiality is, so to speak, no more than a necessary evil whose sole function it is to give that nothingness a determinate presence. *Kratêr* and *vas* are not supposed to be a "something" in their own right, but mere receptacles *for* things or substances. Thus they are images for *(logical) negativity* (even if still natural, concretistic images of such negativity).

Moreover, the alchemical vessel was supposed to be made out of glass, transparent. This transparent nature of the containing *vas* can be interpreted as an attempted negation of the opaqueness and impenetrable substantiality of its material nature and, by extension, of matter as such. What is actually intended (although of course not fully realized in practical reality) by the transparency and hollowness of the vessel is the negation altogether of the material reality of the vessel. Ideally the vessel is supposed to be immaterial, absolutely inconspicuous, totally disappearing from our vision as a thing in its own right, in order to give exclusively room for, and allow one's attention to go all the more to, the substantial contents it may contain. Ultimately, it is in itself the image *of* absence or a self-sublating, self-negating image, a non-image. This negativity does not mean that the vessel should not *exist* as a container. It only means that it should not do its containing *in a material, natural way*. While the Gnostic *kratêr* as a kind of baptismal vessel was merely *filled* with spirit, the alchemical vessel, at least in the last analysis, is supposed to be, in itself, a *spiritual* container, a *vas* that, *contra naturam*, contains in a nonphysical, nonliteral, that is in a "spiritual" way.

The Mother of God, by contrast, is a person, an imaginal figure, a "substantial" content and thus logically positive. By saying (§ 753), "The feminine, like the masculine, demands an equally personal representation," Jung demonstrates to what extent he thinks here in terms of positivity. He substantializes again what the soul had already dematerialized and spiritualized centuries ago. According to him, the feminine principle is supposed to be fully present, present as an imaginal person and body. In our text from *MDR* Jung states that through the new dogma the feminine principle was accorded only an "approximative recognition." As we learn from § 754, in his view the recognition would have been total only if Mary had been given "the status of a goddess" (which the dogma did not quite grant her). Psychologically, any god or goddess is the image of a highest and most intensive, most real, most (logically) positive soul *substance*, and the particular image of the *Magna Mater* emerging behind Mary as Mother of God is the primordial image of matter, nature, body—in short: positivity. By simply deserting the obvious negativity of the *kratêr* and the *vas* in favor of the positivity and (psychological) materiality of the idea of a goddess as imaginal bodily shape, Jung is guilty of *(psychological) materialism.*

3. The Incomplete Arrival of the **Kratêr.** It is not arbitrary and indifferent in what form the feminine principle appears. In the account Jung gives of the prehistory of his psychology, it primordially appears as a mixing vessel sent by the higher god. The Gnostic *kratêr* found its continuation in the medieval alchemical *vas*. For many centuries the psyche of Western man, through the eyes of all the individual alchemists, stared at the alchemical vessel and what it contained. What happens when you stare long enough and soulfully at an object before your eyes? You become assimilated to it in your consciousness. To put the same thing another way, the object is (as we are wont to say in psychology) "integrated" into consciousness. Consciousness itself is, as it were, "infected" by its own content: what as long as you look at the thing in front of you exists as a *content of*, or *image in*, consciousness slowly turns into your attitude, your mindset, into the very *form* or logical constitution of consciousness itself. The object comes home to you, comes home to the subject. It loses the form of object and takes on the form of a subjective style of thinking and experiencing, and thus the form *of form*. The original "object" of consciousness is dematerialized, spiritualized—sublated. This alchemical process of *distillatio, sublimatio, evaporatio* is what in the history of the Western soul happened with the alchemical vessel itself. The alchemical vessel slowly ceased to be an object or content of consciousness and a literal instrument for its operations in the laboratory and was "interiorized" so as to become the logical form of consciousness. This transition has, as we have seen, two distinct aspects. First, it is the transition from "out there" (*in* external reality, *in* nature) or "in front of consciousness" to "in here," "in ourselves" as subjectivity in the sense of "inherent in the *structure* of human consciousness itself"; secondly, it is ipso facto the transformation from "substance" or "content" to "form," from imaginal shape to attitude, category, perspective, spirit, or thought (in the sense of the *act* of thinking, comprehending).

Now, what was it that the consciousness of the alchemists was looking at, when they looked at the vessel (and its contents)? Consciousness was looking at the symbol, the (concretized) idea, *of form* as such, at *the (still literal) image or existing metaphor of (human) consciousness* itself. Consciousness can indeed be *imagined* as a kind of "empty or hollow container" for whatever content or image or experience it happens to be conscious of. But it is not, like a *kratêr*, a literal vessel, a substantial thing that merely happens to be shaped in such a way that it can serve as a hollow receptacle. Consciousness *is* the *sublated*, logically *negative*, "vessel." It has no solid containing walls anymore, as the *kratêr* still did. The spirit that the *kratêr* was filled with seems to have retroactively affected the container itself and decomposed its material nature, thereby turning it into an in itself *spiritual* container: into that *logical* mode of containing that we call thinking in the widest sense of the word, or grasping, comprehending.

As long as consciousness was informed by myth, there was no consciousness *of* consciousness, only a consciousness of things, beings, events, qualities (i.e., phenomena). At the time of myth, consciousness was totally given over to its contents. It was completely oblivious of itself, oblivious to such a degree that it seemed to be non-existent. It lived *in* or *via* its contents and *in* the natural world it experienced, and because it *absolutely* abandoned itself to the objects of experience, it was able to behold the world *absolutely*: in its divine depth, as gods and daimones. In the world defined by myth there was exclusively "objectivity" of experience; what from our modern perspective was subjectively experienced was, just like it was, absolute unquestionable truth, simply by virtue of its having indeed been experienced so. And the mythic gods were the mark by which both the nonexistence of "subjectivity" and "objectivity" in our modern sense and the nonexistence of a fundamental division between them can be seen. For in the gods subjectivity as such is itself absolutely objectified and ontologized, appearing to consciousness as objects from outside as it were, as consciousness' contents: as imaginal beings. (This is why my speaking of an exclusive "objectivity" of experience is an inaccurate, modernistic *façon de parler*; strictly speaking, the mythological mode of experiencing the world was neither subjective nor objective: it was *absolute*—absolved of (i.e., freed from, not subject to) the opposition of subject and object). "Man's intervention" and the "collaboration of the psyche—an indispensable factor" (*CW* 10 § 498) in what was experienced or observed remained invisible.

So now we can understand what the Gnostic higher god's gift to mankind was all about: its inherent telos was to offer to human consciousness the chance of becoming aware of consciousness as such, that is, the opportunity to become aware of *itself* and for the first time to acquire a sense and notion of subjectivity. The image of the *kratêr* as object or content is the first immediacy, the first inkling, the explicit symbol, of the idea of consciousness, but, because as *kratêr* (the image of a literal vessel) it is still no more than the first immediacy of this idea; it is consciousness still imagined, still reified and (as we put it psychologistically) projected out (although in reality this idea had of course never been "in" consciousness before and thus could not possibly be projected out). The nature of the higher god's gift was not that of a thing, but of a task, a *prima materia* to be *worked*. It was not a static vessel. As long as the god's gift stays the *kratêr* as which it was originally given, in other words, stays an imaginal *content* of consciousness, it has not really arrived yet. To really accept this gift meant to comprehend it as unfinished, as having an inherent teleology. It has fully arrived only when the telos of the hollow vessel as absolutely self-renouncing receptivity has been completed; when the hollowness of the vessel has hollowed out even the very substantiality of the vessel's containing walls so that nothing positive, no materiality remains. Then and only then has the femininity of the feminine principle been accomplished: fulfilled, redeemed, sublimated. This is the case when, as absolute negativity, it has come home to the soul from its original alienation as an object imagined "out there"; when the vessel has been absolute-negatively interiorized into consciousness and the soul has thus reached the point of a *self-reflective* awareness of itself *as* "inner," "subjective," "psychological."

4. The Metamorphosis of the Feminine Principle. It is, of course, significant that in the Gnostic tradition the higher god did not send a goddess or a (be it semi-divine or human) heroine to the rescue of us humans, in other words, not a personified figure, but the *kratêr*, a *kratêr* filled with spirit. Undoubtedly, Jung was aware of the, in part, parallel Christian motif of the Holy Ghost being sent down by Christ as the Paraclete, a helper and consoler. Often, the Holy Ghost is symbolized by a dove, the bird of the Ancient Near Eastern goddesses of love. What emerges here is the suspicion that around the beginning of the Christian era the feminine principle had undergone a fundamental transformation. It had left behind its historical positive and substantial ("mater-ialistic") form as Magna Mater, Earth Mother, goddess of love, as Mother of God and divine bride, and now appeared negatively, in its sublated form, as the image of a vessel, container, as the idea of The Spirit and, in the case of the Holy Ghost, also as the idea of nonsexual, non-erotic, non-emotional love. Through the further development of this symbol in the history of the Western soul, also through the alchemist's concentration upon the retort, the vessel became absolute-negatively interiorized. This is to say it ceased being an ontic, existing container and now has to be performative, the act of containing, of comprehending. The ontic vessel contains in a physical manner, it is a hollow *thing*. The absolute-negatively interiorized "vessel" contains immaterially, "spiritually," that is, *logically*. That which performs such containing is what we call thought, comprehending thinking, the concept. The vessel can now be known as the human psyche, man's conscious mind, our subjectivity.

This interiorization or sublation amounts to what Jung called the death of a symbol. The moment the previously imagined symbol of the *kratêr* or *vas* can be seen through as human consciousness and subjectivity, the symbol of the vessel is no longer "pregnant with meaning"; "its meaning has been born out of it," that "expression is found which formulates the thing sought, expected, or divined even better than the hitherto accepted symbol," and this is why "the symbol is *dead*, i.e., it possesses only an historical significance" (*CW* 6 § 816). By focussing on the vessel with all its soul passion for so long, alchemy inevitably interiorized the symbol of the vessel into consciousness and ipso facto rendered itself (alchemy) superfluous, obsolete—and *eodem actu* it provided the condition for the possibility a priori of the emergence of psychology. The moment of the birth of psychology is the moment of consciousness having become conscious of *itself*. That this change has the world-shattering consequence of removing the "place where the [not political or technical, but 'metaphysical'] action is" away from nature, from the *kosmos* (*in* which we humans once upon a time used to live) and into human subjectivity, and that it thus inevitably amounts to an irretrievable loss of myth, of symbols, of gods, and of an ultimately divine nature, goes without saying. Gods or God are *positive contents* of the imagination, and even negative theology cannot really undo their ultimate positivity, as much as it may try. Once the absolute has to appear under the conditions of a conscious awareness of consciousness, it cannot be imagined anymore. It just does not work. Psychology *is* the Fall from the innocence of a belief in God/gods and from "imagining things." If "present" at all, the absolute today must be *thought*.

Just as it was the telos or fate of the *kratêr* to disappear as the imagined vessel (symbol) that it had been and to turn into the notion (as well as experience) of consciousness, we may suspect that much earlier it had been the telos or fate of the various images of the *"personified"* and uncurtailedly *positive* form of the feminine principle as goddess (as Mother, Bride, Consort in diverse constellations) to be sublated into the image of the Gnostic *kratêr* and the alchemical *vas* as the first emergence of the explicit negativity of the feminine principle. Jung in 1912 wrote a book entitled, *Transformations and Symbols of the Libido*. Today it may be time to write an essay, *Transformations and Symbols of the Feminine Principle*. Or perhaps not "... *and Symbols*," inasmuch as within this transformation process it is the very fate of "symbols" to render themselves obsolete and give way to the absolute negativity of the corresponding *logical form*.

The metamorphosis of the feminine principle has fundamentally three historical stages:

Mother-Goddess → vessel → consciousness.

The same sequence could also be expressed in the following ways:

substance, embodiment → empty receptacle for a substance → logical form
simple positivity → (positive) negation → absolute negativity.

"Metamorphosis" implies that it is always "the same" that takes on a different guise or logical form. The goddess is already "vessel" inasmuch as she is also conceiving womb; the vessel is already a prefiguration of consciousness, and consciousness is still a (however sublated) vessel, and still somehow the (sublated) "spouse" in a divine drama. That the vessel is midway between the positivity of the goddess as archetypal person and the absolute-negative logical form of consciousness is more than a historical fact. This is also obvious from the nature of this symbol as the still *positive* symbol *of* absolute negativity or receptivity.

Admittedly it will be an imposition for the unpsychological, naturalistic mind to have to acknowledge the logical form of consciousness as the *successor gestalt* of "the feminine," just as the Holy Ghost is the successor gestalt of the ancient goddess of love as well as of Sophia. But this is what needs to be seen.

So it is not true at all, as Jung diagnosed, that the feminine principle "did not find a place in Freud's patriarchal world." Of course it did, just as it did in Protestantism. It is not gone at all. It merely did not manifest anymore in the gestalt in which Jung regressively expected it to appear: as a content, as the symbol or idea of a vessel, or, even more regressively, as a literal feminine archetypal figure. How did it appear? In Freud's talking about the *psychology* of people, in Protestantism's *subjectivized* religion, especially so precisely in the *personalistic* bias of Freudian analysis and in the *humanism* of Protestant religious attitude. Although I admit that psychological personalism and humanism are seriously wanting as to the truly appropriate forms of the feminine principle today (wanting since they are still *positivized* forms *of* logical negativity), they nevertheless are both an (imperfect) version of the feminine principle and a mode (somehow) expressive of the "consciousness" or "logical form" stage of the feminine principle.

Above I said that the *kratêr* is an image *of absence.* With "consciousness" or the "logical form," absence is no longer merely the special content of the symbol in which the feminine principle manifests, but also the form of the former image or symbol. "Consciousness" is not a thing like the literal *kratêr*, not a vessel as an imaginable symbol (*Dingsymbol*) either. It is a notion, a concept and thus does not have any positive existence; it is an intangible event in the mind. Once the logical level (psychology) is reached, there is, in all central and absolute (transpersonal, "metaphysical") regards, no room for symbols, images, archetypal figures, gods anymore. As a matter of course they now are all "absent," have to be "absent," inasmuch as they have been totally fermented, corrupted, distilled, evaporated, so that nothing positive remains. Now, in the age of psychology, logical negativity rules.

*5. **The False Bride.*** In § 743 of *Answer to Job* Jung summarizes the message of the *Assumptio Mariae* dogma saying, "Mary as the bride is united with the son in the heavenly bridal-chamber, and, as Sophia, with the Godhead." A few sentences before we read, "Therefore the Apocalypse closes, like the classical individuation process, with the symbol of the *hieros gamos*, the marriage of the son with the mother-bride. But the marriage takes place in heaven, where 'nothing unclean' enters, high above the devastated world. Light consorts with light. That is the programme for the Christian aeon which must be fulfilled before God can incarnate in the creaturely man." No doubt, Jung's line of thinking is backed up by a few religious documents, notably the Apocalypse and the dogma of 1950. But it absolutely contradicts the dominant dynamics and inherent telos of religious experience in the Judaeo-Christian world.

The major idea in this sphere of religious thought has been that the bride is to be seen somewhere else than where Jung looks for her. The feminine principle is by no means absent, it is not repressed by an exclusive Father-dominance; the bride, and the coniunctio of the Godhead with the bride, have not been altogether abolished. But there has been a truly revolutionary change with respect to the question *who* the Godhead's bride has to be: no longer (as it was during the times of myth) an equally divine goddess with a bridal-chamber in heaven, i.e., in the archetypal sphere, in the realm of transcendence. God, the Old Testament tells us, initiated a *covenant* between Himself and His chosen people. From then on not "light consorts with light," not a god with a goddess, both of equal standing and both equally personified figures, the perfect symmetrical couple up there in the beyond, but God unambiguously wants to marry *beneath Him*. God crosses the fundamental boundary separating the divine, archetypal, or "metaphysical" realm from the empirical and human, all-too-human one, which is inalienably located in this, our "devastated world." God's longing, a violent longing characterized by express jealousy, has long crossed over from "where 'nothing unclean' enters" to the side where there is certainly enough that is "unclean."

Christianity developed these ideas further. St. Augustine, for example, described the new "marital situation" expressly as: "Verbum enim sponsus, et sponsa caro humana" (*In Joh. Ev.* viii, 4). And as is well known, the imagery of bride and bridegroom is central in Christian thought. Christ is the bridegroom, and the *ekklêsia* (the congregation, the *Gemeinde*, the Church) is the bride. Jung, too, was of course aware of this,[3] and commenting on the Protestant rejection of the *Assumptio Mariae* he even referred to the fact that Protestant "hymnology is full of references to the 'heavenly bridegroom,'" but he ridicules those references by adding, "who is now suddenly supposed not to have a bride with equal rights. Or has, perchance, the 'bridegroom,' in true psychologistic manner, been understood as a mere metaphor?" (§ 752). This is of course absolutely off the mark. Jung sees that the Protestant standpoint is outraged, and from a psychological standpoint I would say rightly so, by "the boundless approximation of the Deipara to the Godhead" (ibid.). He concludes

[3] "The third and decisive stage of the myth, however, is the self-realization of God in human form, in fulfillment of the Old Testament idea of the divine marriage [*Gottesehe*] and its consequences" (*MDR* p. 328). But Jung draws the wrong conclusions from his insight. He says (*ibid.*): "Thus the unconscious wholeness penetrated into the psychic realm of inner experience," which is a psychologistic view and contradicts Jung's own opposite and equally implausible view that "the Christian concept of the trinity" "result[ed] from the efforts of the old theologians to push God out of the sphere of psychic experience into the status of absolute existence [*in ein absolutes Dasein*]" (*Letters 1*, p. 90f., to A. Vetter, 8 April 1932, transl. modif.). The idea of the Trinity and of Incarnation opened up the dimension of the *internal logic of the human mind* (in contrast to be it psychic "inner experience" or "the status of absolute existence").

from this that the idea of the bridegroom must have no more than a merely metaphorical meaning for Protestant thought, because in Jung's interpretation without *such* a bride there would be no real bride for the Godhead at all. He does not even consider the opposite possibility, namely that *he* deprives the *real* bride of her reality simply because he idiosyncratically wants to marry the Godhead off to the false bride, taking it for granted that only a bride of equal standing is a real bride and that only a *coniunctio* between *two archetypal or divine personages* and in the *heavenly* thalamus is a real *coniunctio*. He totally ignores the fact that God or the Son already has a real bride here in this real world, the Christian community, the Church, or he denies that it is a real bride. He says: "Just as the person of Christ cannot be replaced by an organization, so the bride cannot be replaced by the Church" (§ 753), which clearly shows his naturalistic and utterly personalistic prejudice.

Of course, when we hear "the Church" we tend to think mindlessly of the rather pitiful empirical (positive-factual) institutions that carry that name. But the *ekklêsia* as the bride is obviously not the church as an institution or (Jung's word) organization. Psychologically speaking, *ekklêsia* is the traditional Christian word for what we Jungians might call the depth of the "collective" psyche. Not the individual as ego, as empirical personality, but also not the empirical mass of believing individual ego's organized in a Church as institution and gathered in a church as a building, can be the Son's bride, but "the congregation" understood as the (transpersonal, universal) human mind, as what Kant called "*die Menschheit in der Person*," as the archetypal *anthropos*, as alchemy's *homo totus*, as Heidegger's *Menschentum*, as the Jungian Self (as long as the latter is not reduced to a personalistic understanding [*my* self], as it often is).

6. Regression, Procrastination, Extrajection. By construing things the way he does, in these matters Jung shows himself to be a psychological reactionary. He obstinately wants to hold on to the "materialistic" (substantializing, personifying) psychological mode of being-in-the-world as it was constituted during archaic times, the times of myth and ritual. He wants to push what is already in the stage of "Aquarius, the water bearer, the alchemist able to pour the waters instead of the fish swimming around in them" (Monika

Wikman) back into the stage of those fish (Pisces). He wants a female figure who at least as "mistress of heaven" is "functionally on a par with Christ" (§ 754), if she cannot be what he would actually prefer, a full-fledged goddess. He is not satisfied with a God that "humbled himself" to unite with a "bride" residing, not in heaven, but in St. Augustine's "human flesh," on this earth, and as human consciousness.

This regression is compensated for by what one might call procrastination or deferral. Jung "procrastinates" in that he pushes the event of God's "continuing incarnation" "in the creaturely man" (§ 746) off into the future, although it has already happened long ago and is continuing to happen. It may not have been completed, but it is already a reality. Jung imagines himself out of the accomplished incarnation by translating the already real incarnation into an event of the *future.* The appearance of a psychological consciousness, the rise of an awareness of human subjectivity, the absolute "secularization" of modern life, on the one hand, and the immense and continuously increasing power of creation and destruction given into human hands, on the other hand, are the tell-tale signs that, as Jung himself put it (without, however, drawing the inevitable *psychological* conclusions), "*Everything now depends on man*" (§ 745). It remains incomprehensible that despite this insight of his, he thought that we could and do still depend on a semi-divinization of the Virgin Mary and that the "Incarnation in creaturely man" (§ 744) depends on the prior accomplishment of a *coniunctio* of the Son with the mother-bride, and of the Godhead with Sophia up in heaven (this *hieros gamos* being, according to him, only the "*first step towards* incarnation."[4] In reality, I claim, the ongoing incarnation happens *as* an ongoing coniunctio with *human subjectivity.* Our psychological problem is certainly not that the intended and imminent incarnation in creaturely man cannot happen because the feminine principle has not found a "personal" "metaphysical representation" and is not "metaphysically anchored in the figure of a 'divine' woman" (§ 753). Our problem is very different. It is that we, as *realized* subjectivity having *psychologically*

[4] Jung supports the idea of the "continued Incarnation in creaturely man," but in one breath wants to deprive Mary of her creatureliness and instead raise her to the status of a goddess. A self-contradiction. It also prevents the occurrence of the Incarnation for us: for it confirms the stance of upward-looking, of worship, which would prevent us from realizing that "we are Gods" (see section 12 below).

become approximately equal to the Godhead and having unwittingly been subject to the influx of the Holy Ghost, are psychologically (and probably also literally) not at all up to this elevation in status and the enormous intellectual-conceptual challenge, emotional burden, and moral responsibility it brings.

Jung has to mystify the Spirit. He cannot see it in *our* actual way of life and in outer reality.

He can also not see that the move from literal person (personified figure) or, alternatively, literal and positivistic organization (Church) to *absolute-negative* "congregation" ("where two or three are gathered together *in my name*" (Matt. 18:20), i.e., *neither* in a physical building *nor* in an organization!) is precisely (an example of) the move made by Christianity to a fundamentally higher (or deeper) level, the advance from the primitive naturalism of mythic imagination to Spirit.

The "boundless approximation" to the Godhead that the Catholic Church bestowed upon the Virgin Mary is a projection or rather extrajection away from ourselves, to whom in fact this uncanny approximation has long happened. We have suffered this uncomfortable fate and have to bear it. In addition to the extrajection, there is also the problem of a misinterpretation: Jung naively took the dogma of 1950 as indeed speaking about the Virgin Mary (as theological or archetypal content), as providing "a symbolical fulfilment of John's vision [of the sun-woman]" (§ 744), and as a promising "dreaming the Christian myth onwards." He did not see that by what it said about Mary, the dogma actually spoke (not about something archetypal at all, but) *about us* today, the *real*, empirical, situation of man *in this century*,[5] only that this speaking happened indirectly, via a projection onto a mythical or metaphysical plane (much as, e.g., Heidegger and Derrida, when they criticize classical metaphysics, actually speak about 19th and 20th century conditions and not about classical metaphysics at all). Thereby, even while *expressing* it, the dogma nevertheless *obscured* the implicit insight and rendered it harmless. The insight is harmless if it appears to be about mythological figures or a theological dogma, because we know that *in our modern psychological status*, mythology and theology are no more than interesting pastimes and that the real place "where the action is" is

[5] This paper was written in 1998.

the consciousness of creaturely man. No divine or heavenly thalamus anymore. The thalamus today is here in this world, on this earth; it is human subjectivity, it is "we." "We," our consciousness, the mind of mortal man have to *be* the "thalamus," the *kratêr*, the alchemical vessel. ("We," that is, of course, not we as empirical, private, only-subjective ego-personalities, but as our innermost Other, the universal *anthropos* in us, the *Menschheit in der Person.*)

The extrajection of the thalamus away from us and into heaven and the positivizing of the feminine principle as a—posthumously—archetypalized feminine figure serve the purpose of distraction, of lulling us into sleep: of relieving us of our frightening psychological burden. What needs to happen appears as something out there, on the level of the *objects* or *contents* of consciousness, on the level of our dreams or unconscious visions, namely with the objectified "feminine principle," the Mother of God. It does not have to happen in, nay, *as* our subjectivity, as *its* logical constitution. We now can pretend as if nothing had happened and we were still living in the *status quo ante.* We can stay unconscious, innocent. Now "we" do not have to *be* the feminine principle, to *be* the bride of the Son, to *be* the approximation to the Godhead, to *be* God's real incarnation in the creaturely man. No, now it seems that just as in olden times we can *have* again a semi-divine "mediatrix" (§ 754) who will carry *our real* "metaphysical" (psychological) burden in our stead and thus allow us to feel and imagine ourselves as mere ego-personalities. The *coniunctio* happens safely in the beyond, "light" (psycho-politically correct) coequally "consorting with light" up there, far away from us, and so *we* are spared. No indecorous transgression from the transcendental, archetypal or imaginal to the human, from the ideal to the real. The coming of the Holy Ghost, God's incarnation in creaturely man, can now comfortably be *awaited* as events in the future. We can sit back and merely *imagine* or *dream* about the future individuation and incarnation. We become mere observers of, and perhaps believers in, a transcendental *coniunctio* drama, whereas in reality we are psychologically the stage and the co-actor and antagonist in this very drama, a drama that is already on and has been going on for some time.

The precondition for the incarnation as a *psychological* reality is that Mary has to stay the image of the human flesh. The conception of her as heavenly bride undoes the incarnation.

*7. **Derealization.*** One of Jung's pet ideas was that the Trinity had to be expanded into a quaternity, whereby the quaternity had the structure of 3 + 1. The Fourth was a distinct element, set off from the other three in its nature. But it was the Fourth that had to give *reality* to the Three, which were essentially of a merely *ideal* nature. "Becoming real" was one of Jung's main concerns, and it went in his theory (keyword individuation) above all under the titles "wholeness" or "completeness," which in turn implied the realization of the quaternity for him.

If the Fourth is needed for the ideal to become real, what or who is the Fourth? For Jung it was above all either The Feminine or Evil, as opposed to the exclusively male, light, and good Trinity. And he passionately sought to give to the Feminine and to Evil a metaphysical status, an archetypal rank. As we have seen with respect to his ideas about the Assumption dogma, he saw it as psychologically indispensable to have the feminine principle *elevated* to the rank of a (semi-) goddess. Mary had to be raised into heaven and be granted equal status with the Godhead, in order to be the proper bride for the Son of God and in order for the *coniunctio* to have a chance. Only if the feminine were *integrated* into the group of metaphysical or divine principles as their fourth, was, in his view, the quaternity perfect. Likewise, Evil had to be the light God's antagonist of *equal standing*, imaginally speaking, Satan. This is why he had to fight the *privatio boni* idea of evil so passionately.

In other words, according to his interpretation the Fourth could only perform its function of "making real" if it was itself real in the sense of having been granted the status of an "archetypal," "metaphysical," "transcendental" principle on a par with the Three. Jung placed all four elements, the quaternity as a whole, in the beyond. The Fourth had to be on the same side as the Trinity.

I claim that this is (a) a misinterpretation of the archetypal idea and phenomenology of the quaternity and (b) self-defeating with respect to Jung's own project.

(a) The moment all four elements are on the same side and of equal standing, the radical difference, indeed opposition, that is at least implied by the 3+1 structure is obliterated. *The difference is no longer syntactical and structural, but merely semantic*: male versus female, light versus dark, good versus evil. But if, e.g., the quaternity manifests phenomenologically as the image of three animals and one human figure, this obviously is a structural difference. There is no equality of status: the three and their fourth belong to different classes or orders of the real. Jung's whole effort expressly goes into leveling the structural difference; the feminine principle must have its "metaphysical representation," the bride must be of equal standing. The difference between the Three and the One as Fourth is by Jung reduced to an imaginal one, one with regard to content or shape. Considering the image of the quaternity in the form of three animals plus a human form, what is more obvious than that the quaternity has to be understood as the (otherworldly, divine, archetypal, ideal) trinity plus creaturely man? The Fourth is us.

It is our consciousness, our coming onto the scene of the archetypal drama, our entering it with the intensive realness of our presence that alone provides the missing reality to the transcendental Three. Through and in us humans can what formerly was merely the *idea* of the trinitarian Godhead come down to this earth, into empirical reality.

(b) By sending the Fourth into heaven, Jung renders it just as ideal and unreal as the other three. It is just as much only an idea, a fantasy image, as they are. Obviously, the *fantasy* or *idea of* something whose function it is to provide reality does not itself possess the power to *actually* provide reality. By apotheosizing the feminine principle, Jung, as it were, kicks the principle of reality upstairs. The reality principle is immunized, checkmated, frustrated. Its realizing function can never do its job. It can not really cross over into reality, but has to run idle yonder, on the other side of reality, because it has been systematically separated from the real. The Virgin Mary is safely shelved in the heavenly thalamus. The quaternity and wholeness as completely heavenly and only "semantic" are themselves derealized, only ideal or imaginal, although they admittedly still are the idea or image *of* full reality. In this context, what an idea is semantically about is of lesser importance than what its status is. Only a quaternity that within itself, *within its own structure or syntax*, i.e., logically, crosses the line between the ideal and the real, the metaphysical and the physical, the imaginal and the literal and "unclean" and that encompasses both is a *real* quaternity, *real* wholeness—in contrast to imagined or dreamed-about wholeness.

In those times when myth and ritual were the real and sufficient expression of the *whole man (homo totus)* and of the total reality of his lived life, the ideal (or archetypal) quaternity was also truly sufficient, because it was all-comprehensive. But as Jung himself stated, modern man exists *extra ecclesiam*, divorced from myth, he now has a more or less independent consciousness somehow "outside" and vis-à-vis the so-called "unconscious." It is obvious that under these circumstances the *archetype, the idea, or a symbol*, of wholeness does not suffice anymore. It does not overarch that dimension of modern human existence that has emancipated from myth, from the Church, from "the unconscious," from the imaginal. And thus it simply has no handle on it. Today, the *archetype* of wholeness is itself only a partial reality, and the idea *of* a partial reality. It does not express the very wholeness that it is supposed to represent. At least one whole half of our psychological reality, and not the least important, is simply left out of this version of supposed wholeness; this quaternity has absolutely no relevance for, no bearing on, such extremely important areas of modern existence as industry, technology, capitalism, globalization, shareholder value, cyberspace, the scientific mind, genetic engineering, television, entertainment, advertising, etc. Times have changed. Today real wholeness would require *much more* and something *radically else* than the bodily reception of Virgin Mary into heaven, which is old hat, the wholeness of archaic, pre-Christian times imitated and warmed over in a Christian, if not post-Christian, context. It would require more than *dreaming* of wholeness, *having* dream images of wholeness. By buying Jung's quaternity, we have the splendid chance of indulging, at no cost to ourselves, in the idea of wholeness, of "watching" (like on TV) symbols of wholeness yonder, in our dreams, in "the unconscious"—while ourselves stoutly upholding the neurotic dissociation informing and permeating modern existence.

8. The Avoidance of Dialectics. Real wholeness or the real quaternity is a logical structure that *within itself* both *establishes* the opposition of the ideal and the real, drawing a line or boundary between them, *and* that crosses this boundary, bridging the opposite realms. Such a structure is obviously self-contradictory, a *complexio oppositorum*, a unity of the *difference and* unity of the opposites.[6] The moment we become conscious of a contradiction (a contradiction not due to faulty thinking but inherent in the structure of an idea), the imagining and pictorially thinking mind comes to the end of its wits. It is the moment where *thought*, dialectical thinking, has to take over. The moment when the soul has moved from semantics to syntax, from the fish swimming in the waters to the waters themselves, from content to logical form, there is no way around thought. Jung's insistence that the feminine principle needs a personal and metaphysical representation can now be seen as an attempt to rescue the innocence of the *imagining*, dreaming, or pictorially "thinking," mind. By shoving the Virgin Mary into the heavenly sphere, the *image* of the feminine principle, the anima, and thus image as such, the mode of imagining, is eternalized as well as "divinized": it is established as *the* principle, the *non plus ultra*. Thought (or the animus) cannot threaten the imagination (or the anima) anymore, it is expelled from the sphere of what is psychologically significant, being reduced to a mere ego-function that has its only legitimate use in pragmatic "outer"-reality coping. It is the imaginal that now, by having the real-making factor in itself, is declared to be the ultimate reality. The moment the feminine enters the ranks of the three persons of the Godhead, the feminine, the body, the earth, reality are psychologically swallowed up by the ideal world. Rather than bringing the ideal into reality, reality and matter are idealized. This is what accounts for the blown-up and hollowed-out talk about wholeness and gods in much of analytical psychology after Jung. Mystifications. The opposite of what was explicitly intended.

But Jung himself sowed the seed for this inflation (in the monetary sense of the word). It was he who refused to enter thought. He wanted to be the "empiricist," the innocent observer of images, the mere "visionary" (voyeur) with respect to "the unconscious." The essential psychological development was supposed to happen in the unconscious, on the (semantic or "fish") level of the symbols it produced, in our dreams, so that, I claim, *our* reality (we as subjectivity and consciousness) might continue to stay untouched. We were of course

---

[6] Myth has two *separate* myths for this: Heaven-Earth separation and *hieros gamos* of Heaven and Earth.

supposed to interpret and feel the dream messages, and apply them to our reality, but this was only our own ego-activity. Our reality was not supposed to be *immediately* and *integrally* involved in the divine drama. To *think* such an immediate involvement would have required the loss of innocence and a Fall into dialectical thought. No, the ego as neutral observer was supposed to remain intact, untouched. For this purpose, the feminine principle, the principle of realization, had to be projected into the heavenly sphere and shelved there.

9. Fraternizing With Popular Demand. The psychological authority on which Jung, as the empiricist he wanted to be, felt he could base his theory about the Assumption dogma was "the popular movement," i.e., the "visions of Mary which have been increasing in number," the "fact, especially, that it was largely children who had the visions," the "deep longing in the masses for an intercessor and mediatrix who would at last take her place alongside the Holy Trinity ...," and "the longing for the exaltation of the Mother of God" that "passes through the people" (§ 748). This is the same authority that Jung sees in part at least also behind Pope Pius XII's move: "The papal declaration has given comforting expression to this yearning" (§ 754); "... the popular movement which contributed to the Pope's decision solemnly to declare the new dogma" (§ 749). Incredible. Jung fraternizes with the nostalgic and thus egoic longing of the masses—much like Aaron in the story of the Golden Calf sympathized with the longing of the people, who, during the times of hard-to-bear revolutionary religious changes, just as we are experiencing in our days, said to him, "Up, make us gods ..." (Exod. 32:1). Jung applauds the Pope for his complying with the masses' exactly analogous urging him, as it were, "Up, make us a goddess, exalt the Mother of God."

What Jung calls a popular movement is only a movement in a very limited section of the population. It is by no means representative of society at large. But even if it were a majority movement: it is nevertheless not supported by the objective spirit of the age. Does a truly popular movement outweigh the logic of the soul's real development? Can one put what the masses or, for that matter, what the Pope says on the same or even a higher level than what Schopenhauer, Feuerbach, Marx, Nietzsche—to mention only these four modern examples of *great minds*—said? In what the latter stated, we have so to speak "documents of the soul"—because the soul or logos of the age expressed itself through them as its mouthpieces. These great minds were in contact with the truth of the age. What Jung's "popular movement" longs for and what the Pope condoned is expressive of a reactionary medieval kind of piety. The New Testament's admonition (1 John 4:1): "Beloved, believe not every spirit, but try the spirits whether they are of God: because many false prophets are gone out into the world," translated into the language of the psychologist, would read: try the spirits whether they are expressive of the objective soul or of human, all-too-human feelings of lack, of subjective longings and opinions. We are no longer in the Age of the Church Fathers. What they said was at the forefront of cultural development and the voice of truth. But the Pope during our age is only the spokesman of one of the many ideologies and interest groups competing on the meaning market.

During an age of revolutionary social, economic, psychological, and religious changes, when the loss of meaning, the death of God, the collapse of almost all traditional values is painfully felt, it is *not astonishing* that popular nostalgic demands come up in personal psyches, demands for a mother goddess, for a "personal metaphysical representative of the feminine principle," and thus for the perfect archetypal consort to be conjoined with the heavenly Father or the Son, so that, just as in the good old days of paganism, we might have again what Erich Neumann called World Parents and could be again their children embedded in the fold of an intact *metaphysical* "family." But it *is* amazing that such popular longings would be taken as psychologically authoritative by the *depth* (!) psychologist, who thereby anticipates what we now know as pop psychology. Does he not know "the people, that they are set on mischief" (Exod. 32:22)? No discrimination of what is psychologically authentic and what is a mere reaction formation and thus a defense.

The mere fact that those visions are, in an external, formalistic regard, of archetypal *content* suffices for Jung to take them as psychologically expressing the state of the art level of the (as he terms it) "collective" psyche and as being of truly archetypal depth. Jung is blind to the psychological or logical *status* in which such seemingly archetypal content stands and which is by no means one of archetypal significance (just as the Nazi movement, that Jung credited with an archetypal depth, namely as an expression of the Wotan archetype, was psychologically phony from the beginning, being merely the result of *complexes* on the personalistic, subjective level of the mass psyche, the result of *ressentiments*, defenses, ideologies, emotionalism, etc., and did not at all have the dignity of a manifestation of what Jung meant by "the objective psyche").

Jung here, on a *psychological* level, does exactly the same thing that the consumer goods industry, the advertizing and entertainment industries, and drug dealers do on a *literal* level: he appeals to, satisfies, and awakens the base regressive (nostalgic) cravings of the personal psyches of the masses. Jung does not stay faithful to the *objective* dynamics and inherent telos of the Christian substance. He falls prey to the ambiguity of his own misnomer: "the collective unconscious," whose literal meaning can just as well refer to the unconscious *personal* psychology of the masses (that is, the personal psychology not of the members of the masses each individually and personally, but that of "the collective" as a whole) as its intended meaning is supposed to refer to the depth of the *transpersonal objective* psyche.

10. The Signs of the Times. In *Answer to Job* Jung declares concerning the *Assumptio Mariae* that "This dogma is in every respect timely" (§ 744). By contrast, "the Protestant standpoint has lost ground by not understanding the signs of the times ..." (§ 749). In particular, "Protestantism has obviously not given sufficient attention to the signs of the times which point to the equality of women" (§ 753). My theme here is not Protestantism, but the "signs of the times." I flatly deny that Jung's position as to what is "timely" or not is tenable. I think it is unpsychological.

At first glance, Jung seems to have an unbeatable point when he refers to the development pointing to the equality of women. One of the predominant features of this century has been this development. This is an all too obvious and undeniable fact. So Jung seems to be right when he considers this movement to be one of the significant signs of the times. But the question we have to raise is: *what* is this significant *for*? Here the difference between various standpoints comes into play. Only from a social-history or natural-consciousness point of view, only in terms of empirical social reality, does this change imply a greater importance of woman. Psychologically, however, it has the opposite meaning. It is a sign that *psychologically* woman has become unimportant, that the whole question of the sexes, of gender, of sexuality has become absolutely indifferent. These are no psychological issues anymore. The whole women's and the sexual liberation movements are movements towards *emancipation*, emancipation, that is, *from the soul*, from a higher meaning, from those obliging archetypal or mythic images and roles that women and men from early on had to embody and had been unquestionably identical with. The soul has released the entire area of sex from its "sphere of interests" or "jurisdiction," as it were, and released it into our personal freedom, our ego arbitrariness. It is a similar change as with agriculture centuries ago. In the beginning of agriculture, ploughing, sowing, harvesting were in themselves religiously significant acts (rituals). In modern times they have become totally secularized, devoid of any meaning other than what they mean pragmatically. The soul has withdrawn from this area of life and left it at the free disposal of the ego. Likewise, today one can live in sexual regards just as one likes. One can live faithfully in a marriage, promiscuously, gay or lesbian, bisexually, in celibacy, without any sex-life at all—it is up to the individual. The clear border between male and female is blurring. One can even have one's sex changed. Anything goes. The soul has no stake in, no claim on, those concerns. Our love life and our personal relationships, as important as they still (or even increasingly) are for the ego, in other words, subjectively, are *psychologically*, as it were, "trivial pursuits," devoid of any mythical, religious or metaphysical dignity, and thus also devoid of any (non-personal) psychological restraints. There is nothing in them for the soul anymore. They are part of the human, all-too-human, and *only* this. The *numen* has emigrated from them.

The emancipation of women is part of the long general emancipation on the part of Western man from the divine, the metaphysical—from the soul's archetypes. Apart from the dictates of external necessity, how we live is today determined by how we individually feel, what our subjective preferences or collective fads and trends are or how we have been biologically or sociologically conditioned. We live in the time of breaking all taboos. It is, under these circumstances, absurd to want to supply any metaphysical anchorage (§ 753) to woman. This is precisely what is against "the signs of the times." Woman cannot be patterned anymore by an archetypal role model, such as the Virgin-Mother-Bride. We are not in the age of psychological childhood anymore. We do not have a Heavenly Father and a Heavenly Mother. Today we have to live *Man for Himself* (Erich Fromm) and woman for herself. We are archetypally naked, *extra ecclesiam* also with respect to sex and gender. Here, too, we each have to "sew our garment ourselves" (*CW* § 9/i § 27), i.e., to invent our sexual identity individually all on our own, with no divine prototype to lean on.

It is psychologically absurd to consider the dogmatization of the assumption of the Virgin-Mother-Bride "timely" *at the very time* when the words "virgin" and "bride" have become meaningless sounds (especially so "virgin"). Apart from hearsay knowledge, we do not have an inkling anymore of what "virgin" psychologically, i.e. archetypally, means (to be precise: once *meant*).[7]

It is absurd today to put one's hopes on a *hieros gamos* of the Son and his Bride in a heavenly thalamus *at a time* when the very concept of marriage in an archetypal sense is factually deconstructed by millions and millions of people in real life. Many men and women live together these days without marriage, showing that marriage is felt to be superfluous, and where marriages still do occur they are *empirical*, pragmatic connections of a strictly private nature. The frequency and regularity with which divorces happen underlines the loss of conviction inherent in the idea of a *coniunctio* today. Quite obviously, human marriage is no longer a re-enactment of an archetype.

It is unworthy of a psychologist to say with explicit reference to the women's movement, "The feminine, like the masculine, demands an equally personal representation" (§753), when (a) the psychological reality of our age is that even the masculine does not have any metaphysical personal representation anymore ever since "God is dead," but above all (b) since men and women are no subject of psychology to begin with. Psychology is about the soul, about the soul's logical life. It does not know about "men" and "women," much as chemistry does not know about the Son of God and Virgin Mary, or theology about H_2O, Jupiter's moon, and viruses. Men and women are possible subjects of sociology, biology, and anthropology, but not

[7] I discussed the psychology of the virgin in Part 3, ch. 2, of my *Neurosis. The Logic of a Metaphysical Illness*, New Orleans (Spring Journal Books) 2013.

of psychology. "The feminine" and "the masculine" are, in psychology, possible *symbols* or *metaphors* for the psychic opposites which in themselves are totally *unanschaulich* (irrepresentable, invisible, unimaginable). They do not refer to men and women and to what in a literal sense might be considered masculine and feminine. To talk about gender issues in psychology is psychological baby talk.

Jung full well knew that psychology presupposes the obsolescence of mythology (cf. *CW* 9/i § 50). They are mutually exclusive. It is the special character of the mythological mode of being-in-the-world that natural phenomena, and thus also real men and women, just like that can represent what we call archetypal aspects. Thus for millennia, woman was a priori cloaked in *archetypal* garments; she had to play out archetypal roles. Young, unmarried women *had* to be virgins. On her wedding day the bride *was* the Goddess of life. After her wedding day she *had* to be Wife and Mother. This is the sphere in which woman needs (but also has) a metaphysical personal representation in the guise of divine feminine figures. Today these archetypal garments have fallen off from woman and from sexuality (as they had long ago from most other realities), now leaving woman, too, metaphysically naked. Psychology is only possible and necessary when the situation of a mutual reflection of the empirical and the archetypal in each other, the whole system of symbolic representation and re-enactments, is over, when, in other words, man has emancipated from myth, so that whatever he does has no immediate archetypal significance anymore. It is a situation which has the positive reverse that under these circumstances finally "man's intervention" and the "collaboration of the psyche" in what he does, what he feels, and believes can possibly become *conscious*: the age of psychology.

Jung knows that modern woman does *not* have a personal metaphysical representation in the pleroma anymore. But he refuses to be taught by this actual psychological situation. Instead, he wants to correct it. This is why, on the one hand, he grabs at this spurious, psychologically bizarre, event of the declaration of the *Assumptio Mariae* dogma and attributes highest psychological significance to it and, on the other hand, clings to the obvious literal (surface or *naturalistic*) meaning of a modern fact (the *social* development towards the equality of women) as support for his meant-to-be-psychological claims about "the feminine." What Jung does here, in trying to provide a metaphysical anchor and personal representation in heaven for literal women, is unpsychological, even antipsychological: it is his *opus contra animam*.

Whereas psychology has to be an *opus contra naturam*, what Jung is trying to do is—on the surface—a restitution of long obsolete (*psychological*) Nature (= mythological mode of being-in-the-world): a restitution both of mythical representation as such (the mode of *having* representations in the pleroma) and of the representation of the particular idea *of* the *natural* (the Mother archetype). But at bottom it is something else. It is a last desperate attempt to archetypally legitimize, and thus rescue, *natural consciousness* even for psychology! To rescue the old status of consciousness, our modern everyday consciousness, the status of "semantics," of the sole awareness of the "fish," the "contents," and to rescue it *from* the threatening fall into psychological, or *thinking*, consciousness in the spirit of the alchemist as water-bearer. This ordinary or natural consciousness, not modern woman, is what "*needs*" a metaphysical representation in the form of a mother goddess to prop it up. But the fact that Jung feels, and responds to, a *need* (to something that is felt to be lacking, something that *is* not) betrays his thoughts about the Assumption of Mary as ideological, as a mystification and ego stuff. All this is his *doing*, *his* correction attempt, and not a simple perception of, and attending to, the self-display of phenomena. Much as Heidegger's talk of a "coming God" (to mention only one of many examples), Jung's ideas about the *Deipara* find their place within what has been called the "conservative revolution" of the first half of this century so rich in ideologies.

11. "Archetypal Positivism." One should think that archetypalism and positivism are strict opposites. But what we witness here in Jung's assessment of the psychological phenomena (dreams, visions) backing up the Assumption dogma forces us to entertain the surprising idea of a positivism within the very center of archetypalist thinking. The question whether the manifestation of an archetype did or did not occur is decided exclusively upon on the basis of positive facts, of positivizable properties of psychic phenomena. The fact that (a) the increasing number of Virgin Mary visions came "from the unconscious" (dreams, visions) and (b) had, considered formalistically, a "mythological" content is thought to be sufficient to assign archetypal dignity to them, the dignity of an event in the transpersonal psyche and of ultimate importance for the objective psyche. The simple equation here is: dream + "mythological character" = epiphany of an archetype. This is obviously positivistic, because it solely relies on positive factuality, which, as Jung hoped, any person could objectively verify. This secret positivism is also reflected in Jung's adamant, almost obsessive, insistence that "Analytical psychology is fundamentally a natural science" (*MDR*, p. 200) and that he is presenting nothing but *facts*. Positive facts, objectively given and intersubjectively verifiable properties, are to relieve us of the task to *discern the spirits* (cf. 1 Cor. 12:10) on our own responsibility, the task not to believe every spirit indiscriminately, but, as already quoted, to try the spirits whether they are "of God" (cf. 1 John 4:1) or, as we would say today, whether they possess psychological "*truth*": the living truth in which and out of which a people *psychologically* in fact lives.

Whether something is a psychological truth and "of God" or not cannot be established on the basis of positive facts, of "objectively" ("intersubjectively") discernable characteristics. It is not such that it could be empirically observed. "Truth" or "God" have their place in absolute negativity. And thus they require *our* coming forward with a personal judgment, our taking a stand, hopefully on the basis of a certain psychological sophistication, a refined sensitivity, a well-developed feeling-function in things psychological, an *intelligence du coeur* and above all a differentiated mind—a mind that has the distinction between the truly archetypal and the phony (the nostalgic, the sentimental, imitations, simulation, etc.) as categories at its disposal. Only a mind that has suffered the falling apart of experience as a whole into this distinction and is thus in itself structured by it can discriminate psychological phenomena accordingly.

But analytical psychology teaches us to indiscriminately take as truly archetypal whatever is characterized by analytical psychology's positivistic trinity: (a) material from "the unconscious," (b) in formal regards parallel to mythological motifs or archaic symbolism, (c) accompanied by a heightened emotional state (which, just like that, is interpreted as a sign of "numinosity"). Under these conditions one can of course not discriminate anymore between, on the one hand, the raves of teenagers in the presence of their favorite pop star, the mass hysterics caused by the destruction of the New York's World Trade

Center Towers, the longings for a divinization of Mary, the enthusiasm of the more fervent members of the Nazi movement, the (formalistically) "archetypal" motifs used in advertising, and, on the other hand, what is truly expressive of the psychological truth and depth of our time. "The unconscious has spoken," "my dream said ...," "I had a numinous experience," "I feel"—this is supposed to be enough. This *idolatry of "the unconscious," of dreams and visions*, is unpsychological because the *literal* products of the unconscious represent only the positivistic, naturalistic, personalistic depth, not (at least not *ipso facto*) the real depth of the soul, which is logically negative depth.

The emphasis on the unconscious is only justified within individual, personal psychology, which, centering on *my* problems and conflicts, *my* development, is inevitably positivistic to a large extent. But with respect to what is really going on in the depth of the cultural psyche, the distinction between the literal unconscious and literal consciousness is irrelevant. What Jung meant by "the objective psyche" and what I called the psychological truth of the age cannot be identified with either. Being absolute-negative (incapable of being positivized), it stands, as it were, at right angles to the distinction between conscious and unconscious. There are *no a priori privileged phenomena* which so to speak *ex officio* would express the real needs of the transpersonal soul. As a depth-psychologist I therefore cannot give so much credit to dreams and visions of Virgin Mary in our age: there are so many dreams and visions about all sorts of things!

We do not live anymore in the age of the Pharaoh when what concerns the public soul often came in the form of dreams, like the one about the seven well favored, fatfleshed and the seven ill favored and leanfleshed kine (Genesis 41). In those good old days the gods indeed manifested directly through dreams, through visions, oracles, signs in nature—because this was the anima stage of consciousness, a consciousness still unwounded by the animus and its reflection. But in our psychological situation, dreams and visions as well as the entire so-called unconscious are no longer the place "where the (psychological) action is." Dreams and visions today are phenomena of the *private* psyche. They are the stirrings of the sublated, historical past we carry in ourselves.

Why can the products from the unconscious today no longer be the epiphany of psychological truth? Because we are no longer that *innocent* that we could pose as passive recipients of what we need to know, in the sense of the Biblical motto, "It is useless to work so hard ... For the Lord provides for those he loves, while they are asleep" (Psalm 127:2, *The Bible in Today's English Version*). Those days are bygone. What is psychologically really important to us is no longer served, as on a silver platter, to the *sleeping* mind, to the *blind* seer, the *entranced* Pythia or shaman, to the merely *observing* augur. Today, when it is a necessity for us to *be* as the feminine principle and ipso facto no longer to *have* and *watch* it as an image in the imaginal realm, the place of the action has to be the quaternitarian wholeness, which, as we have seen, is what (in addition to the "transcendental," the imaginal, the "unconscious") a priori also actively involves ourselves, our conscious, wakeful mind in the very *production* of the "symbols" valid for us. In other words the place of the decisive soul events today is *thought* (of course not positive, literal thought in the superficial sense of abstract ego activities, but that true thought that occurs in the absolute negativity of the soul and expresses itself not only, but predominantly in great works of art, philosophy, poetry, etc.). I placed the word "symbols" in quotations marks because the moment when the quaternitarian wholeness has become the place of creativity, the logical form of what is produced cannot be that of symbols and images anymore. It now has the form of the Concept (concept not in the sense of Aristotelian, but of Hegelian logic).

12. Incarnation. Jung expects God's incarnation in empirical man as an event in the future. He preaches "the continuing incarnation," the fact "that God has eternally wanted to become man, and for that purpose continually incarnates through the Holy Ghost in the temporal sphere" (§ 749). But what he is preaching he cannot recognize when it is right before his eyes. He fails to see that what he is still expectantly looking out for has long been an accomplished fact. He fails to see that this process, which *began* with Christ (as well as, e.g., with the Gnostic higher god's sending the *kratêr*), has (certainly not come to its end, but at least) come so far that the hope for the future birth of the divine child amounts to a terrible regression. What is worse, his deferral of the incarnation into the future amounts to a *rejection* of the incarnation which already *is* (to the extent that it is). We *are, have long been* in the age of the Holy Ghost. The latter does not need a future coming. He has already arrived and, to an incredibly high degree, permeated our existence. What in Gen. 3:5 ("For He [God] doth know that ... ye shall be as gods") is still an anticipation has come true. Psychologically we *are* gods in the sense of the Biblical "Ye are gods" (John 10:34, following Psalm 82:6; often quoted by Jung himself). This is why we cannot *have, possess* anymore; why we have lost all myth and symbols; why God is dead; why we do not have a heavenly Father or Mother anymore. We have to *be* in the logic of our existence what formerly could be had and looked up to as an objective image or content. The name for this our *having to be* is *thinking*. Jung, as it were, promises a learned man as a great future hope the primer with which he learned to read and write as a child.

Incarnation means that God wants to *become* man, which means more and something else than our "becoming conscious of" the God-image. How can He *become* man if not by relentlessly disappearing as a vis-à-vis, an object of worship, as a God-image that we *relate* to? God's "becoming (man)" and then "being (man)" implies the sublation and absolute-negative inwardization of the subject-object relation, which underlies the mode of having. It is just as in our personal biographies: how else can we *become* and then *be* adults, fathers, mothers, unless we have left our own parents, not only literally, but also psychologically, by negating, dethroning, sublating them as parents that we *have*? As long as you *have* parents in a psychological sense, you are still a psychological child, even if biologically you are a grandfather. The incarnation of God in man presupposes the absolute loss of God, His total *kenôsis* (emptying, Philippians 2:6, cf. *MDR* p. 337), and our absolute "spiritual poverty" (*CW* 9i § 29).

Jung shirks away from this total *kenôsis* and our total poverty. He says, "If this God wishes to become man, an incredible *kenôsis* (emptying) is required of Him, in order to reduce His totality to the infinitesimal human scale" (*MDR* p. 337). Jung uses the word *kenôsis*, but obviously he does not have a real notion of it. What he is talking about is something different; it is more a shrinking, much like the "incredible" shrinking performed by the demon in the story of the Spirit in the Bottle. Jung imagines "infinitesimally small," whereas what is required is "empty," i.e., *nothing*. He substitutes a reduction in degree for a logical revolution. The reduction is the way in which you can achieve two mutually exclusive ends simultaneously: you pay a tribute to the psychological necessity of today while retaining, and *so that* you can retain, the old status of consciousness.

His shirking away from the absolute emptying means the inability or refusal to recognize in our present reality the fulfilled age of the Holy Ghost and the realization of the incarnation that he seeks and preaches. For Jung our reality is obviously too meager, too empty. He naively imagines incarnation as something more spectacular, more mysterious, more *literally mythical*, namely as something to be expressed in images of a heavenly Mother-Bride, a *hieros gamos*, the birth of a divine child. But the incarnation or the birth of psychological man is nothing spectacular and grandiose. It is precisely not a literal and miraculous influx of divinity or holiness or higher spirituality into man. "Incarnation" is just the (still mythological, imaginal) *word* for a change in the logical constitution of consciousness. The change is *only* psychological, *only* logical, syntactical. It is beneath the surface. Seen from outside nothing much happens. Despite the incarnation of God in creaturely man this creaturely man remains just as creaturely and human, all-too-human as before. He merely has *to be* in his subjectivity what before he was able *to have* as object of worship and content of his consciousness. He has become psychological. This is all. Jung relegates to a beyond, into the unconscious, what is already here. Jung thus mystifies. This in turn means that due to these naive splendid expectations concerning the incarnation he has to read *unpsychologically* the reality that *is*: from an external, everyday consciousness point of view. He cannot see through our mythological poverty to its "archetypal" or soul depth, cannot see it as the *sine qua non* of psychological man.

13. Trinity and quaternity. Jung's retention of the mode of possessing culminates in Jung's idea of the "incomplete Christian God-image" (e.g., *MDR* p. 318) and of the need to correct this incompleteness. For him the Christian Godhead as Trinity is only light. Therefore a Fourth, the "missing" Fourth, has to be integrated into the Trinitarian structure so as to arrive at a quaternity or wholeness. Again one sees how Jung wants to cure the problem not in the very subjectivity, but out there, in the object of consciousness, in the image.

By making the object (the God-image) complete, he at once cements consciousness's mode of object-relation and possessing as such. The new quaternitarian God-image has become an unassailable bulwark of the mythologizing mind. The Trinity has lost its native openness, its intrinsic *dynamic* nature. It is now fixated, since through the quaternity it has, as it were, been satiated: closed.

Here it is necessary to have a brief look at the psychology of circle, square, and triangle. The circle has always been experienced as the symbol of perfection. It belongs to the sphere of the Divine, to Heaven. An oft-cited Hermetic dictum from the *Liber XXIV philosophorum* reads, "God is an infinite sphere whose center is everywhere and the circumference nowhere" (the beginning is also frequently quoted as, "God is an intellectual" or "an intelligible sphere" or "is a circle ..."). In most ancient cosmologies, heaven was round, a dome or a round disk. In ancient China in particular, Heaven was such a round disk or a kind of umbrella overarching the Earth, which, by contrast, was square (the surface of a cube) and carried Heaven on four pillars. Because the vault of Heaven was somewhat smaller than the Earth, the latter's four corners were not covered by Heaven and thus eluded the shine of its stars. In accordance with this cosmology, Lü Pu-wei (Lü Buwei) says: "Heaven's ways are round, earth's ways are square" (cf. *CW* 11 § 247, note). I mention this because the idea of a correspondence of circle with heaven and of the square with the earth has a continuation or extension. This we find expressed in the third of Hegel's *Habilitation Theses* of 1801. It reads (in translation from Latin), "The square is the law of nature, the triangle that of the mind." The first half of his thesis is equivalent to the second half of the one by Lü Pu-wei. Hegel's second statement provides the new addition for us. St. Augustine (*De trinitate*) had already exposed in detail the trinitarian structure of the human mind.[8]

We now have the following sequence of correspondences:

Heaven, God	—	circle
earth, nature	—	square, quaternity
mind	—	triangle, trinity.

[8] On Augustine and *De trinitate* see at the beginning and end of part II of Chapter Three below.

This is convincing. The circle implies perfection, the square reality (the created world), the triangle interiority. If one accepts this view, it becomes apparent that Jung, by moving from the Three to the Four, in truth regressed to "nature," to an external-reality standpoint. And the Christian Godhead being a Trinity was not, as Jung claimed, an incomplete God-image in need of a Fourth. Inasmuch as this Godhead was divine, it was just as perfect and circular as any other deity, if not more so. What needs to be understood is that there is no conflict between the three persons of the Christian God, on the one hand, and the circular perfection of the Godhead, on the other hand. The Trinity has, psychologically, a totally different meaning or "function." It does not touch the question of imperfection or incompleteness, nor the question of ideal versus real at all. It reveals the *internal* logic and dynamic of the Godhead, its inner nature or constitution. The fact that the Godhead was all of a sudden conceived as a Trinity is expressive of a revolution in the history of the soul, a transformation of the status of consciousness. Consciousness had *conquered* new "territory," a new "category" of psychological existence for itself. It had entered the new realm of the mind, of thought, of interiority, subjectivity, of consciousness itself.

Before, during the "age of myth" and "the age of metaphysics," consciousness had been more or less totally enveloped by "nature," it had been in the "nature" status of consciousness and had accordingly imagined the world and human existence in terms of natural imagery (of thing-like objects or beings and their behavior) that only metaphorically implied mind. It had not had any explicit access to the mind as such, no consciousness *of* consciousness itself. But with Christianity the conception of God had left the status of nature gods and had instead entered a new status where God had to be comprehended *as* spirit or subjectivity as such (not as a divine figure or being as "substance" who merely possessed subjectivity). Now it was no longer possible to imagine God as one who could be located in specific places or aspects of nature or be identified with certain natural phenomena ("... the hour cometh, when ye shall neither in this mountain, nor yet at Jerusalem, worship the Father. ... the true worshippers shall worship the Father in spirit and in truth," John 4:21+23). The fact that God was all of a sudden comprehended as a Trinity is the sign that something in some distant way corresponding to the Gnostic higher god's sending the mixing vessel had happened. The feminine principle had come down and been received by mankind, activated in man himself as his own mind. The mind had become the new "thalamus," the new locus of ultimate experience. The feminine principle's having come down made a difference also for the corresponding male principle. *Everything* was transformed. The Gnostic *kratêr* was filled with spirit pure, with *literal*, overt spirit (not with spirit cloaked in natural things as *symbols* or *metaphors*), and human consciousness had similarly to conceive of God directly as Spirit or as the Trinity (which notably is no longer an *image* [three separate beings]—as, e.g., the very ancient feminine "trinities" of girl, mature woman, old woman were—but a *concept* and as such a priori the inalienable and undisguised property of the mind).

Jung got it all wrong. He confounds two distinct aspects or categories. The *first aspect* concerns the difference between two historical stages of consciousness, the "mythological," "metaphysical," or "natural" one, on the one hand, and the modern "psychological" one, on the other. The mythological stage is determined by, and operates within, the Heaven-Earth-Distinction (in the spirit of Lü Pu-wei's dictum). This distinction does not play any role anymore in the modern psychological stage of consciousness. It is replaced by the distinction between the mind (the "inner," the sphere of intelligibility), on the one hand, and external reality, on the other hand. The *other aspect* is that of the "definition" of the "content" of the Trinity, how its nature, quality, or essential character is conceived. At this point the confusion comes in. It is the confusion between the *unsatiatedness* of the Trinitarian content, its internal dynamic and unrest (in contrast to the completeness and stillness of a quaternity), on the one hand, and an alleged *lack of reality* of this (in itself unsatiated, i.e., dynamic, moving) structure as a whole (and the corresponding status of consciousness), on the other hand. Because the Trinity was the expression of the *dimension of* the mental and intellectual, Jung felt it was also *itself*, as a psychological structure of consciousness, merely "ideal" (abstract thought) and lacked realness. But obviously, a dimension or structure can be very real, even if it is the dimension *of* something "ideal" (mental): consciousness, for example, can be very real although it is the reality *of* something only "ideal" (intelligible, mental).

The idea of the *structural* deficiency of the Trinity denounced the latter as being in itself unreal—i.e., not merely unreal because of an insufficient seriousness about the Spirit *on our part* and therefore of too feeble a presence of this stage of consciousness in our world. Jung understood by "realization" (in this context) the restoration of the quaternitarian structure of "natural" consciousness, of the mythologizing mind, when as psychologist he should have promoted the deepening of the reality of the mind stage of consciousness, the stage when the mind is knowingly informed by a Trinitarian (strictly speaking, we should not say "structure," but) logic.

We don't need more natural images of a *hieros gamos*, of a divine Mother and Bride, of the birth of a new divine child, images that draw consciousness away from its awareness of *itself* and instead direct its attention to *objects* of the imagination in the sense of a regressive restoration of object-relations. Today we need an intensification and expansion of the soul's capacity to comprehend itself as logical life pure and simple. The logical movement *immersed* in "earth" and *cloaked* in natural phenomena as images, as during the age of myth, will no longer do. In other words, we need more "Trinity," not less; a more *real*, stronger, better "Trinity." *This* is where the realization effort should go.

What Jung interpreted as incompleteness is actually only the mark of distinction of the mind stage of the mind. As of old, and as also Jung said, the number Three was understood as expressing movement, dynamics, change, unrest. Whereas Jung interpreted this as a longing for the Fourth and thus for wholeness, the Christian Trinity is to my mind the indication that in all *essential* (not merely pragmatic or scientific) matters a thinking in terms of things, objects, solids, figures, beings has become obsolete and that the soul instead has advanced to a status where it is conscious of itself *as* fluidity: a thinking in terms of pure relations (in contrast to relations between "objects") and a dispersed field of differences, a thinking on the level of the syntactical, the level of language.

To sum up this part of the discussion, Jung thought he was giving reality to the God-image by working toward a quaternity. What, by doing so, he in actuality did was, however, something else. After the fact, he tried to translate the God-image from our modern, the psychological, level of consciousness back into that of the age of myth, the total horizon of which is described by the dictum, "Heaven's ways are round, earth's ways are square." For this level, the *mind* has not surfaced yet as a reality of its own. "Striving towards wholeness," towards quaternity, is the futile attempt at a restoration of the innocence of this prepsychological situation *on the ground of, and within*, our *real* already modern, already psychological situation. (The contradiction between the attempted restoration and the logical status of reality within whose horizon the restoration is to be achieved is the reason why his attempt inevitably has the status of a mere simulation.) But wholeness is the one thing that nobody has to strive for, since wholeness is always there. It is inescapable. We live on, and partake of, the earth whose ways are square.

CHAPTER THREE

Materialistic Psychology: Jung's Essay on the Trinity[1]

If we proceed from our knowledge that Jung time and again insisted on being seen as an empiricist, the following statement of his does not come as a surprise. "I must call your attention to the fact that I have no theory that God is a quaternity. The whole question of quaternity is not a theory at all, it is a Phenomenon. ... I would not commit such a crime against epistemology. ... I am in no way responsible for the fact that there are quaternity formulas" (*Letters 2*, p. 584, to Witcutt, 24 Aug. 1960). Jung pleads innocent. *He* does not have a theory. He is merely presenting facts or phenomena. Now we are certainly willing to concede that *there are* such things as quaternity formulas. But obviously *there are* also trinity or triadic formulas as well as dyadic and, of course, monistic ones, not to mention all the other numeric schemes with seven, twelve, twenty, sixty elements. However, in the case of Trinity and quaternity, Jung is not merely interested in the existence of corresponding formulas and their psychological description and analysis. He also claims that the Trinity

[1] This essay is based on an unpublished long manuscript written in German in 1993 ("Zur Psychologik des Trinitätsdogmas. Analyse von C.G. Jung's Argumentation in seiner Schrift zum Thema"). *Part I* of the present English version (which dates from January 2011) is pretty much a translation of the corresponding sections of the original German text, whereas *Part II* is, on the basis of new insights, a rethought and newly written version of one part of the older manuscript. Two concluding parts contained in the German text, one on the Trinity and Evil and one on the problem of "the Self" and Jung's psychologism (both as discussed in or emerging from Jung's essay on the Trinity) have been omitted altogether from this English version.

is fundamentally wanting, deficient, that it needs to be transcended in the direction of a quaternity. And particularly as far as God is concerned, he thinks that psychologically it is a vital necessity that the trinitarian conception be expanded by the inclusion of a Fourth, either evil (Satan) or matter, the feminine (the Virgin Mary). Does the idea that something is a necessity in the sense of an "ought" qualify as a statement of fact, or is it not much rather a theory (or thesis), if not a program, after all?

Of course, there is also another type of necessity, namely in the sense of a law of nature, such as the law of gravity. Under the conditions specified by this law all falling objects with mass accelerate at the same rate regardless of their weight. In *Memories, Dreams, Reflections* (*MDR*), Jung reports that while in Africa near Mt. Elgon, the governor of Uganda requested that Jung and his party take under their protection an English lady who was on her way back to Egypt via the Sudan and thus followed the same itinerary as they had. Then Jung makes the following comment:

> I mention this episode to suggest the subtle modes by which an archetype influences our actions. We were three men; that was a matter of pure chance. I had asked another friend of mine to join us, which would have made a fourth. But circumstances had prevented him from accepting. That sufficed to constellate the unconscious or fate. It emerged as the archetype of the triad, which calls for the fourth to complete it, as it has been the case again and again in the history of this archetype (*MDR* p. 260f., transl. modif.).

"The triad, which calls for the fourth to complete it"! It is inherent in the triad, so Jung suggests, to feel incomplete and to call for the fourth. This Jung conceives as a kind of general psychological law, which can be seen from the fact that, as he claims, it has happened all the time in history. So in this *MDR* passage Jung implicitly operates *mutatis mutandis* with a similar type of necessity as the one suggested by the laws of physics. If this were the dominant sense of the relation between the Trinity and the quaternity, Jung could have leaned back and relaxed, because the historical development would inevitably and of its own accord convert the Trinity into a quaternity. The whole sense of urgency and passionate argumentation against the Trinity as insufficient and in favor of the quaternity that we find in many of his later writings and in *MDR* would be unnecessary. The deep emotionality with which Jung speaks about these matters betrays that he has a personal stake in the issue.

But let us first consider the particular episode that occasioned Jung's comment about the triad that calls for the fourth. There are several problems with it. Why was the fact that they were three men merely "a matter of pure chance," whereas that they were asked to accept a lady into their party was the work of fate in the form of a constellated archetype? Why is this latter event not also a matter of pure chance, an ordinary-life happening without any deeper meaning? What justification is there to claim that an archetype was at work? Many times Jung himself insisted that "Occam's razor" had to be respected, the admonition that one should not make use of additional explanatory principles if the simpler ones are perfectly sufficient. Jung does not give any reason why there had to be this lady as a fourth and why there could not just as likely have been, e.g., two ladies, or a married couple, who wanted to join them, or, conversely, not anybody at all. If Jung's third friend had been able to go with them, could this lady not also have wanted to be taken under their protection during her trip to Egypt (which would have made her a fifth)? The introduction of the idea of "the subtle modes of the workings of an archetype" seems in this case farfetched, if not superstitious.

A second problem is that Jung does not give any support for his claim that in the history of this archetype it happened "again and again" that Three were completed by a Fourth. This thesis would need to be corroborated by numerous examples. But as far as I see, Jung did not provide any evidence anywhere in his work for the alleged fact that there is an archetype of the triad which calls for the fourth to complete it. As it stands, it is more likely that it is the human subject C.G. Jung who is the one who calls for the fourth.

In addition, does one archetype from within itself *call for* the other? Are not both the Trinity (or the triad) and the quaternity, just as all archetypes, independent archetypal structures, complete and sufficient unto themselves? Does the Trinity not have its dignity, truth, and completeness all within itself? Does it need, as Jung claims, to obtain its completion outside itself in an other? This does not make sense. We are, when we speak of trinity and quaternity, not in the sphere of the numbers of the counting mind, for whom one, two, three sort of *calls for* four, but then of course also for five and six. When speaking about archetypes and the Trinity we are in the sphere of archetypal number symbolism, the sphere of the soul. And for the soul, all numbers have equal status as independent particular soul truths.

It is of course true that archetypes are not to be seen abstractly in isolation, but involve other archetypes, which in mythology is frequently expressed in the images of marriage, love-affair, family relationship, strife or hate, and so on. The senex may appear as the father of the puer, Venus is shown to be in love with Mars. But all this is no more than, let us say, the "foreign relations" of in themselves "sovereign" archetypal structures. Venus is not in herself fundamentally incomplete and therefore "calling for" Mars to "complete her." This, however, is exactly how Jung sets up the relation between the triad and the quaternity.

Furthermore, the historical phenomenology of ternary thinking does not support Jung's view. There is strong evidence for the self-display of "three" as complete. Aristotle, for example, wrote in *De caelo*, 268a 1-13,

> We may say that the science of nature is for the most part plainly concerned with bodies and magnitudes and with their changing properties and motions, as also with the principles which belong to that class of substance; for the sum of physically constituted entities consists of bodies and magnitudes, beings possessed of body and magnitude, the principles or causes of these beings. The continuous may be defined as that which is divisible into parts which are themselves divisible to infinity, body as that which is divisible in all ways. Magnitude divisible in one direction is a line, in two directions a surface, in three directions a body. There is no magnitude included in these; for **three are all**, and **"in three ways" is the same as "in all ways."** It is just as the Pythagoreans say, **the whole world and all things in it are summed up in the number three**; for **end, middle and beginning give the number of the whole**, and their number is the **triad**. (My emphases) [2]

This text provides a strong case for the all-comprehensive completeness of the triad (which of course is not to be taken as an

[2] Transl. by W.K.C. Guthrie in the Loeb edition of Aristotle's *On the Heavens.*

argument against the quaternity as *another* self-sufficient and in-itself complete archetypal structure with a very different psychological function). And it does not merely claim the triadic structure for the physical world of bodies, which the initial part of the quote might suggest. By including "end, middle and beginning," Aristotle indicates that the triad prevails also in a temporal sense and even in the very logic of Judgment or Syllogism. For the middle (*meson*) is, since Plato, the copula or the *terminus medius*: subject — copula — predicate.

It is also noteworthy that in this quotation we do not only get the relatively late view of the classical philosophers Plato and Aristotle. In this passage the latter refers back to the Pythagoreans,[3] who in turn continued the much older religious tradition of the Orphics. For Anaximander, who, clearly influenced by the Orphics, developed the first "scientific" cosmology, the all-pervasive significance of the triad is obvious: the diameter of the Earth is three times its depth, that of the solar wheel three times three times three, that of the lunar wheel three times three times two, and that of the fixed star wheels three times three times one.[4]

In the political sphere, we find in Roman history the phenomenon of triumvirates. Did in their case the triad call for the fourth to complete them?

For another historically important case of self-sufficient triads let me point to Neoplatonism. According to Plotinus and Porphyry there are three substances (*hypostaseis*), the One, the Divine Mind, and the Soul. And in Plotinus as well as Proclus, we find the strong triadic thinking above all also in the *dynamic*, dialectical triad of *monê* (remaining, indwelling), *prohodos* (proceeding forth, emanation), and *epistrophê* (reversion, returning into itself). In all

[3] In *CW* 11 §§ 179f. Jung shows that he is aware of the significance of the number three for the Pythagoreans and later Greek thought. By quoting a passage from Zeller he even mentions the very idea, which was contained in our quote from Aristotle above, that three is the first number "that is uneven and perfect, because in it we first find beginning, middle, and end" (§ 179).

[4] With the description of triadic structures in the thought of antiquity I follow Claus-Artur Scheier, "Die versammelte Klugheit der Zeit – philosophiegeschichtliche Bemerkungen zum Modellcharakter von Innovation," in: Antje Gimmler, Harkus Holzinger, Lothar Knopp (eds.), *Vernunft und Innovation. Über das alte Vorurteil für das Neue*. Festschrift für Walther Ch. Zimmerli zum 65. Geburtstag, München (Fink) 2010, pp. 19–28.

cases, these triads are complete structures. There is nothing that would be missing or could be imagined to be added. During the 6th century A.D., Pseudo-Dionysius Areopagita, another thinker in the neoplatonic tradition and the inventor of the term "hierarchy," structured the other world, in particular the hierarchical sphere of the angels, according to a strictly triadic principle.

And by way of two last examples, from more recent times, I mention Johann Gottlieb Fichte for whom there was a triad of *Grundsätze* (fundamental principles) and who showed that with the third *Grundsatz* the number of fundamental principles is exhausted, and Hegel's dictum from his *Habilitation Theses* of 1801 that "The square is the law of nature, the triangle that of the mind."

As I pointed out, there can be no doubt that quaternity formulas exist, also those of the particular 3+1 structure. But as far as this structure is concerned, 3+1 is from the outset a type of *quaternity* and the, as it were, secondary articulation of the internal logical form *of this quaternity*. It is not first a trinity, especially not the Christian Trinity, complemented by a fourth. One must not confuse the *quaternity-internal* three of the 3+1 structure with the wholly different and self-sufficient three of the Trinity. And one must not literalize this "+" as if it pointed to addition, complementation, completion of the triad. It is much rather the sign of an internal qualitative difference of or distinction within the Four.

The question that needs to be answered is how Jung supports his claim that the Trinity is incomplete and requires completion through addition of a fourth. The work in which Jung presented the evidence that is supposed to make his thesis plausible is his essay, "A Psychological Approach to the Dogma of the Trinity" in *CW* 12. I will now turn to it to examine Jung's argument and the material presented by him in support of the necessity of the Fourth.

Part I

Realization through the "recalcitrant Fourth"

Jung writes towards the end of his essay, summing up one essential point of his examination, "the number three represents a mental schema only [*ein Gedachtes*, something thought]," and "Without the fourth there is for the three no reality[5] as we know it ...." This is "the fact that we found in our analysis of the *Timaeus* [Plato's dialogue]" (*CW* 11 § 280, transl. modif.). We will have to see how Jung arrived at this "find" and how convincing his understanding of the supporting texts is. But what we can already state here in advance is that Jung, applying himself to the conflict between mere contents of the mind and reality (that which has in fact become real), shows his eminent stature as a psychologist. Jung saw "becoming real" as a vital problem of psychological life, a problem that needed to be faced and shouldered as a psychological task. Today we see all the time how easy it is for psychology to cocoon itself in beautiful ideas and images devoid of reality, in the bubbles of belief-systems, wishful thinking, and an emotional consumerism, so that the question how and under which conditions reality, realness, can be achieved is a pressing one. But of course, when we call to mind that right from the very beginning, with Parmenides, and throughout the age of metaphysics down to the time of Hegel our Western tradition had been based on the conviction that *Thought* and *Being* coincide (*to gar auto noein estin te kai einai*), we immediately see that Jung's basis and starting point is the thoroughly modern situation, the modern fundamental dissociation of mind and being, subject and object. This dissociation is the cause of Jung's struggle with the problem of realization, and his deep hope and passionate belief was that the dissociation could be overcome through the addition of the "recalcitrant fourth" to the merely *mental* trinitarian structure. This is why he developed his "quaternity schema" of which he said that it "puts trinitarian thinking in chains, the *chains of the reality of this world.* The Platonic freedom of spirit does not allow for a *Ganzheitsurteil* [a judgment expressing and doing justice to the whole], but wrenches the light half of the divine picture away from the dark half. ... Part of the picture of the whole is the dark weight of the earth" (§ 264, transl. modif.). "The unspeakable conflict posited by duality [the duality of light and darkness, good and evil] resolves itself in a fourth principle ..." (§ 258).

But before Jung discusses the relevant passages from the *Timaeus*, in which he believed to discern the "recalcitrant fourth," he briefly

[5] Jung's term *Wirklichkeit* can mean reality, but in some contexts, such as here, it might be better translated as actuality.

comments on (the Babylonian and) the Egyptian trinity. In Egypt the theme of trinity is part of the theology of kingship. "Egyptian theology asserts, first and foremost, the essential *unity* (homoousia) of God as father and as son (represented by the king). The third person appears in the form of Ka-mutef ("the bull of his mother"), who is none other than the *ka*, the procreative power of the deity. In it and through it father and son are combined not in a triad but in a triunity. ... The divine procreation of Pharaoh takes place through Ka-mutef in the human mother of the king. But, like Mary, she remains outside the Trinity" (*CW* 11 § 177, transl. modif.).

I only mention this Egyptian trinity because here we get an idea of a trinity about which it would not make any sense to say that the light half of the divine picture has been wrenched away from the dark half. The Pharaoh and his divine Father were not cut off from the dark weight of the earth. That the queen mother "remains outside" the trinity obviously does not indicate that the Egyptian triunity belongs to a sphere of the "freedom of spirit" and merely represents a mental content of the mind. The Pharaoh was an integral part of the reality of life on earth in all its sensuality and (light-as-well-as-darkness-containing) wholeness.

But if this is an example of a triadic structure which does not represent merely a mental schema that lacks reality, then the lack of the dark weight of the earth that Jung diagnosed both in Plato and in the Christian Trinity cannot be inherent in the triadic structure as such. If that were the case, the quality of realness would also have to be missing from the Egyptian trinity. The fault that Jung ascribes to the Trinity and wants to repair through a quaternity has nothing to do with the triadic or trinitarian thinking per se. If, as Jung claims, it exists in the Greek context and in Christianity, then it must be due to other factors. The number Three can appear as a one that is satiated with reality or as one that is only a mental schema. By the same token, it is to be assumed that a quaternian scheme must not ipso facto guarantee a presence of the dark weight of the earth.

Timaeus 31b–32a and the tetrad of the physical elements

In *Timaeus* 31b–32a Plato explains how the Demiurge assembled the body of the universe out of fire and water. This unification of two required some bond, and this bond is, according to Plato, (progressive geometrical) proportion. "Now if it had been required that the body of the universe should be a plane surface with no depth, a single mean would have been enough to connect its companions and itself; but in fact the world was to be solid in form, and solids are always conjoined, not by one mean, but by two" (§ 182, a quote from *Timaeus*). For this reason air and water were placed as connecting links between the opposites fire and earth. Jung comments: "The union of one pair of opposites only produces a two-dimensional triad: $p^2 + pq + q^2$. This, being a plane figure, is not a reality but only a thought. By contrast, it needs two pairs of opposites, that is, a quaternio ($p^3 + p^2q + pq^2 + q^3$), to represent physical reality" (§ 183, transl. modif.).

In *Timaeus* the composition of the universe as a whole out of the four elements and their cohesion is explained by means of geometric progressions and proportions, which can best be represented in algebraic formulae (as they occur in Jung's quote). What necessitates the transition from the triad to the quaternio is the difference between plane and solid or body. Jung claims this difference between plane surface and solid, or two-dimensionality and three-dimensionality, for *his* issue of "the *dilemma of mere thought versus reality*, or rather, *realization*" (§ 184, transl. modif., Jung's italics). And he alludes to Plato's pitifully failed attempts to realize his political concepts on Sicily under Dionysius the Younger in order to give us an idea of the dimension of the psychological problem of "realization," that, according to Jung, Plato wrestled with here. In addition, Jung wanted to make plausible the idea that Plato's awareness of the problem of the gap between what is only thought, on the one hand, and reality, on the other, must have grown considerably on account of this deep disillusionment and the dangerous collision with reality (Plato only narrowly escaped the fate of being sold into slavery). There are a number of problems inherent in Jung's exposition.

1. Mathematical formulas do not transcend the sphere of "mere thought"

We do not need to get involved in Plato's (for us somewhat strange) argumentation in his discussion of the four elements as there is no need in our context to understand it in detail. What we, by contrast, need to pay attention to is that Plato, here all Pythagorean, argues *mathematically* from the outset. However, in believing to be able to interpret this argumentation as a contribution to the topic of realization, Jung succumbs to a momentous mistake. The transition from two-dimensional plane to three-dimensional solid, from $p^2 + pq + q^2$ to $p^3 + p^2q + pq^2 + q^3$ has nothing whatsoever to do with the "realization" of something that is merely thought. The solid and the four-term formula are just as much "mere mental objects" as is the plane. They all have in the same way their place in the sphere of mathematics, geometry and algebra, which by definition are concerned only with mental, ideal objects, with abstractions, and are systematically divorced from the sphere of concrete reality. Mathematics is not physics. The sphere of pure, timeless forms is not left behind. Both the psychological and the political problem of realization (as Plato, for example, attempted it in Syracuse) is not touched on. Plato thinks here only the transition from the *mathematical* two-dimensionality to a likewise *mathematical* three-dimensionality. What Jung believed to find here and what he thought Plato established here drops out of this discussion altogether. A fourth that indeed might possibly have brought the issue of reality into play, if it had been included, is the dimension of time: transitoriness, coming-to-be and passing away imply materiality.

Jung, to be sure, states a little later, that "the missing element he [Plato] so much desired was the concrete realization of ideas. He had to content himself with the harmony of a painting of airy thoughts that lacked weight, and with a paper surface that lacked depth" (§ 185, transl. modif.). Jung even refers to the perfect creation produced in *Timaeus* by the god's mentioned procedure as being such a painting of airy thoughts (a "two-dimensional world of thought," § 184), because in reality "[e]ven God's fairest creation is corrupted..." and "laziness, stupidity, malice, discontent, sickness, old age and death fill the glorious body of the 'blessed god' [i.e., the world]" (§ 185, transl. modif.). And nevertheless, despite Jung's verdict, he claims that the procedure that according to Plato leads to this (in Jung's eyes unrealistically glorified) creation, namely the step from the Three to the Four in the context of a thinking in terms of mathematical proportions, expresses the solution for his own (in no way mathematical) topic of "realization" of "what is merely thought-out"! *Timaeus*, which after all is seen by Jung himself as a two-dimensional world of thought, becomes his chief witness for quaternity as "realization in [the world of] three-dimensionality" (§ 184, transl. modif.). As if a solid in geometry did not also lack weight. But Jung's conclusion concerning the weightless character of the result of the step from the Three to the Four is conversely precisely evidence that even the Four as such, as belonging to the mathematical sphere, has its place in the unreality of what is merely thought.

When we previously had to realize that the problem that Jung saw as given with the triad has nothing to do with the triad or Trinity, so we now have to say conversely that the power that Jung ascribes to the Four, namely the power to provide realization, is not confirmed by the very example he uses to develop his notion of quaternity and from which he derives it. Speculation about the Fourth as that which would finally add reality to the triadic structure of mental ideas cannot serve as a real support for Jung's quaternity theory, because this speculation remains itself unreal inasmuch as it belongs to the "mere thought" sphere of the mathematical.

In general, it is all the more surprising that Jung is willing here to attribute such enormous significance to Plato's algebraic formulae when we recall his report in *Memories, Dreams, Reflections* (pp. 27 ff.) about the "outrage" he felt about algebra and his "*moral* doubts concerning mathematics." It was Jung's outrage against thought as such, pure thought in contrast to imaginings, his (as he saw it) "moral" rejection of the abstraction from "concrete" (*anschaulich*) things. "Why should numbers be expressed by sounds [what Jung actually refers to is of course letters, not sounds]? One might just as well express *a* by apple tree, *b* by box, and *x* by a question mark. ... / Equations I could comprehend only by inserting specific numerical values in place of the letters ...."

2. That Plato had a deep longing for concrete realization is merely an insinuation

"Plato certainly did not lack spirit; the missing element he so much desired was the concrete realization of ideas" (§ 185). That Plato desired concrete realization and felt Ideas to be deficient amounts to an entirely unplatonic assertion. It contradicts everything that Plato wanted to achieve with his doctrine of Ideas and what he stated about them. Ideas are precisely the *ontôs on*, the really real, that which possesses true being. What we ordinarily call the real has with respect to Ideas precisely only a secondary, weak degree of reality or being, as is, for example, illustrated in Plato's image of the shades. How could Plato possibly have longed for a concrete realization concerning that which was already in itself the highest, the full reality? (It must be clear that in this context we speak only about Plato as the author of his dialogues, about the philosopher Plato, not about the "inner," "personal" feelings and desires of the man Plato.) And how could he have desired for it *that* kind of "reality" which for him was no more than one of shades? With his doctrine of Ideas, Plato is already from the outset in possession of the key to the question of reality, and the real and highest reality at that. A "*dilemma of mere thought versus reality*" (§ 184, transl. modif., Jung's italics) does not exist for him. Indeed, this very wording is inadequate because it sets up thought and reality as alternatives and thus, from Plato's point of view, starts out from a false, modernistic, positivistic concept of reality. At the same time this means that Plato's concept of Idea is misconstrued. Jung tacitly treats the platonic Idea here as if it were "idea" in the modern sense, namely a mere (subjective) representation in consciousness.

The implicit model that is behind Jung's thinking here is that of a craftsman or architect. A human craftsman has at first only an idea (conception, blueprint) in his mind and thereafter begins to realize this idea. The example of an architect is even more appropriate because here the transition from two-dimensionality to three-dimensionality comes most impressively into play. The architect first draws a weightless blueprint of the house that he wants to build on two-dimensional paper, and then he has masons and carpenters realize this plan so that a three-dimensional house comes into being.

This is worlds apart from Plato's Ideas and from his concept of reality. It is true, when Plato became politically active in Syracuse, he succumbed to the temptation to "realize," like an architect of the body politic, his *conceptions*, *not* the (Platonic) Ideas! And he failed pitifully. But in this case he was precisely not thinker, philosopher, but politician, and a poor one at that (just as philosophers, and, we might add:

psychotherapists, will generally make poor politicians). The politician, as a practitioner, has a program that is something "merely thought-out" in Jung's sense and is therefore still in need of becoming realized. However, to interpret the doctrine of Ideas according to this model of an ego agenda is a mistake. The thinker Plato does not design blueprints for realization; he simply *thinks* the real (which is always already, and also without him, real).

The reason for Jung's strange view seems to be that he does not take Plato seriously as a *thinker*, does not approach him thinkingly, but views his philosophy from the worm's eye view of everyday experience, just as if Plato had wanted to proclaim a world view. It is two fundamentally different things whether, in addition to its given and unquestionable existence, one also *thinks* the real, that is, tries to comprehend the real-per-se in concepts—or whether one develops *one's own* "ideas" or conceptions *about* the real. For him who proceeds from the idea of a world view, ideology, or theories as the standpoint from which to apperceive the world, the question naturally arises how to in fact get out of containment in subjectivity and reach reality. "*What a spectacle! But alas, only a spectacle! How can I get in touch with you, infinite Nature?*"[6] For a thinker, this problem does not exist because he is with the real all along and dwells with it. He does precisely not pictorially imagine or represent the world in his mind this way or that way, but he thinks it, in other words, all he does is to provide the logic or the concept of the real.

3. *Timaeus* is not concerned with "realization" but with "beautiful" order

In the previous section I rejected the view that Plato had longed for realization. Now we have to show that realization is not the topic and concern of the *Timaeus* at all.

The demiurge did not create the world in the manner of the Christian Creator. He is not a creator in the first place. On the contrary, he took over precosmic, chaotic reality and then brought *order* into it. Gadamer put it most clearly: "The demiurge of the 'Timaios' stands at any rate for nothing more than for the transportation of a condition

[6] J.W. von Goethe, *Faust, Part I,* lines 454 f. (my transl.).

of disordered movement into a condition of order."[7] And in a note to this passage Gadamer adds, "... Precisely the making of the world order—or the 'world creation'—is equally far removed from popular belief as it is from the mystery religions. Cosmogony is at bottom the most extreme opposite to 'creation' or demiurgy." The theme that Timaios in Plato's dialogue is here concerned with, is thus the transition from chaos to cosmos, from wild muddle to harmonious order and to a firm and organic state in which the parts fit into each other. Order is the mark of the good, and as already stated in *Phaidon*, "the good" is what holds all things together. The demiurge found the four elements, too, as given. He merely imprinted mathematical order on them (53a-b) and established, through the proportional mixture, the wholeness and unity of the cosmos (32d-33a). The cosmos is, to be sure, not perfect, but it is the best and to the highest degree long-lasting living organism. Timaios emphasizes repeatedly that it is καλῶς ἁρμοσθέν and εὖ ἔχει (beautifully joined together and well constituted). Its parts are joined together in bonds of "friendship" (φιλία, 32c) in such a way that they are certainly not altogether indissoluble (everything combined is dissoluble, 41a), but can be dissolved only by the demiurge himself. And the latter, as the passage 41b informs us, since he is good, will not dissolve what is *well* joined together.

If that is the case, the question to which Plato's dialogue provides an answer can by no means be the one that Jung assumed, namely how to get from mere thought to reality or how "to represent physical reality" (§ 183). If "representation" at all, then the issue is to "represent" the beautiful order. Physical, bodily reality is presupposed from the outset. And it is presupposed within the cosmological thought picture that is shown to us in *Timaeus*, but it is also presupposed for Plato himself. Just as the demiurge does not fabricate the concrete material reality of the world, but imprints its order upon it, so that it might receive a share of νοῦς (spirit, mind), so Plato on his part, too, as a thinker starts out from reality as a given and attempts to *think* it, to grasp it in concepts, that is, to reconstruct it in the mind. From that point of view there is an analogy between the demiurge and the

[7] Hans-Georg Gadamer, "Idee und Wirklichkeit in Platos Timaios," in: *Sitzungsberichte der Heidelberger Akademie der Wissenschaften*, Philosophisch-historische Klasse, Jg. 1974, 2. Abh., p. 11.

thinker. Material reality in its givenness is not a question at all, as it has in all likelihood not ever been a question for any Western thinker.

The four elements in particular were also a given for Plato, both in reality and in the history of philosophy (Empedocles). Plato did not have a choice whether he wanted to start out from two, three or four elements. The number and the kind of elements had already been settled from the start (just as, by the way, according to 32c *all of* the fire, water, air, and earth was used by the demiurge, that is to say that the whole of what had been given was included in the shaping of the cosmos. The demiurge thus did not merely cherry-pick the best parts and ignore what did not fit: nothing of the real was left some place outside of the cosmos, neither by the architect of the world in his work (32c), nor by the thinker himself).

Correspondingly, at no time in the *Timaeus* was it a question of a choice between a two-dimensional and a three-dimensional approach. The three-dimensionality (of the pre-cosmic "world," as also of the individual elements) was a given fact to begin with. The question that Timaios answers is how the fact that there are four elements can be deduced and how their relation can be thought as the relation of ones that are not merely *noted* to exist (in the mode of perception), but *conceptually comprehended*. Another issue was to explain philosophically the fact that the world and the processes within it can be "scientifically" understood and follow determinate laws. The intention or intellectual movement that Jung takes for granted and those of Plato are thus reversed. Plato as well as his demiurge start out from what is given as something all along real and move on to the *noys* or to thought. Jung starts out from something that is merely thought, in other words, representations (in the modern sense) in consciousness, and aims for a realization that the representations lack.

Accordingly, the step from the triad to a quaternity does not occur in Plato. The fourth by no means grants "reality," for the first time, as Jung assumed. "It is probably revealing that Plato first represents the union of opposites as an intellectual problem (two-dimensionally), but then comes to realize that in this way reality cannot be attained. In the former case we have to do with a self-contained triad, in the latter with a quaternity" (§ 183, transl. modif.). First of all, the four-term formula also remains in the realm of pure thought. And secondly, what for Plato is attained with the quaternity is not reality but the aspired order! As Guthrie states,[8] "Plato does not say that two elements by themselves cannot mix: the emphasis is on *kalôs*" (beautiful); the point for him was a rational bond, the *most beautiful* (the harmonious and most lasting) of bonds (δεσμῶν κάλλιστος, 31c). And A. E. Taylor points out[9] that *one* geometric mean between two cubic numbers a^3 and b^3 can certainly be determined, namely the one that is the square root of a^3b^3. For example, the mean between 2^3 (= 8) and 3^3 (= 27) is the root of (8 x 27) (= 6 x the root of 6). But this is an *irrational* number, whereas what was aimed at was precisely rationality. Not because *one* mean by itself (allegedly) implies incorporeality and unreality or because between two cubic numbers a mean would not be possible, does Plato introduce two means, but because he needed *whole rational* numbers as intermediates. *His* quaternity thus has to provide nothing else but the rationality and proportionality of the union of the elements.

The phrase "bodily world" is equivocal. It can be used in the sense of geometric three-dimensionality (solid, cube), and it can be used in the sense of a realization of "mere thought" within the realm of earthly weight.[10] The fact that, merely on the basis of this equivocation, Jung imposes here onto the text a concern of his own, which, however, is far removed from Plato's interest, becomes once more obvious in Jung's conception of the four elements (in this dialogue) as two pairs of opposites in the shape of a quaternio (§ 183), which cannot really be reconciled with Plato's representation. As the four-term algebraic formula shows, and as Plato's aim to present the relation of the elements as one of a geometric proportion makes evident, Plato did not at all conceive the elements in the form of two *crossing* pairs of opposites. Fire and earth are, to be sure, opposites. But air and water do not, as a second pair of opposites, stand at right angles to the former. If that were the case the whole project of this *Timaeus* passage would be destroyed. Plato introduces air and water as mediating connecting links *between* the extremes and thus positions

---

[8] W.K.C. Guthrie, *A History of Greek Philosophy. Vol. V, The later Plato and the Academy*, Cambridge (Cambridge University Press) 1978, p. 277.

[9] A.E. Taylor, *A Commentary on Plato's Timaeus*, Oxford (Clarendon Press) 1928, ad 31c 4 - 32a 7, p. 97.

[10] Jung should have been alerted to this equivocal meaning through his Kant studies. Kant's prime example for the difference between analytic and synthetic judgments are the sentences: "all bodies are extended" versus "all bodies are heavy."

them into a gradational, but linear series (one could almost say: as in a scale). The gradation from fire to earth via air and water has the character of gradual cooling, becoming darker and more solidified. Air and water are no longer comprehended as completely independent elements in their own right, as would have to be the case if, along with Jung, one conceived of them as a quaternio. They are not (in addition to fire as p^3 and earth as q^3) two additional elements r^3 and s^3! They now much rather appear as (so to speak mirror-imaged) derivatives of and products out of the two other ones, as p^2q and pq^2 (it is absolutely astounding how Jung could perceive in $p^3 + p^2q + pq^2 + q^3$ a quaternio). This again shows that there is neither an increase from dyad or triad to quaternity, nor an increase in realness over and beyond what is "merely thought." What there is is a mathematical mediation between the extremes, fire and earth, that is, an increase in proportionality, in internal integration and thus precisely in clarity *of thought*. *That* is all, but it is also that which Plato wanted to achieve.

4. Derealization of the form of being-in-the-world through mathematization

Jung does not seem to realize what the implications of his interpretative move, of his using Plato's argument for an (alleged) step from Three to Four for his idea of "realization," are. What he unwittingly does is promote a fundamental derealization via the mathematization of the human relation to the world. Plato starts out from the two elements fire and earth. Originally they are both concrete, physical realities. The earth is the firm ground on which we stand, the soil that the farmer tills by the sweat of his brow, the stones that the sculpturer forcibly shapes, the impenetrability, resistance and workable corporeality of matter as such. And fire, although "spiritual," burns as flame in three-dimensional space. It is utmost reality, be it consuming fire in the realm of sensibility, or be it αἰθήρ (fiery heaven),[11]

[11] The *aithêr* is, of course, not mentioned in *Timaeus*. According to Xenocrates, Plato is supposed to have later added to the four the ether as a separate fifth element. For Aristotle the doctrine of five elements is important. It permits him to introduce a separation (untypical for Plato's cosmology and for the earlier philosophers of the Greeks) of two cosmic realms each with very different laws of motion: the supralunar, heavenly world with its perfect circular motion and with the *aithêr* as the fifth element and the sublunar world of the four elements. By contrast, it had previously been assumed that in the *entire* universe the same laws of motion are in effect.

the place of the stars and the gods who determine our fate. It is easy to understand that fiery heaven and earth require mediation. Without mediating connecting links fire might either consume the earth or, conversely, earth might smother fire if they are brought into contact. Otherwise, heaven and earth could not come together at all, but would exist as extremes vis-à-vis each other without any connection.

A serious, difficult problem lies here, a problem which during the age of ritual cultures was solved, e.g., through blood sacrifices, on the one hand, and through the institutions of initiation, on the other hand, that is, through actions and experiences of *humans*, as well as through the gods' manifest appearance and their engendering acts here upon the earth. But this was something entirely different from what Plato is concerned with here and what we consequently have to concern ourselves with.

We must raise the question of what it means that Plato conceives of the elements in the way he does. It can only mean that Plato has already left the level of *natural* elements and has translated the formerly *physical-material* elements into something abstractly mathematical. In other words, the very operation in which, according to Jung, the step from the Three to the Four (claimed to be absolutely indispensable for realization) is achieved actually and on the contrary performed a first-time disembodiment of the previously natural, concrete, and all-too-real elements, inasmuch as they were, in contrast to the natural-mythic experience of the preceding millennia, pushed down into the status of mere principles (or should we rather say: elevated, sublimated, evaporated?). They are pulled into the abstractness of mathematics and in this way reduced to merely mental objects. Even more than that. The immanent purpose of the operation performed by Plato is the derealization and disembodiment (dematerialization) of the *concept* of physical reality itself! According to Jung it seemed as if the physical corporeality of the elements needed to be supplied in the first place; but because Plato construes their (as a matter of course presupposed) corporeality as something abstractly mathematical, the elements are not only dispossessed of the natural materiality and physical corporeality that was their native property. What Plato demonstrates is in the service of the negation (sublation) of the elements as elements of concrete natural reality, so that they might be regained as abstract *principles* within the completely new realm of pure thought. The said dematerialization must therefore not be held against Plato as if he had neglected, or had wished to eliminate, an essential aspect of reality. He merely fulfilled the task of the thinker, a task that, generally speaking, consists in the translation or transportation of human being-in-the-world as a whole from one status or medium into another one, namely from that of "natural" experience into the reflected, sublated one of thought.

The transformation of material reality into what has its place only on the level of principles does not only become apparent through the passage about the elements to which Jung refers and which we have discussed so far. In the further development of the *Timaeus* it is brought out even more explicitly. The passage that we looked at was presented by Plato as no more than a rough preliminary outline. Later (48b) Plato takes back the (at first simply taken-for-granted) status of fire, air, water, and earth as primordially given elements in order to show in what follows that they can in turn be put down to something more fundamental (namely empty space, χώρα [chôra]). The dynamic at work in this train of thought, or its intention, is to translate the whole world from (mythically experienced and thus actual, i.e., sacramental) nature in its concrete materiality into the status of reflectedness, into the form of pure thought: into the status of "two-dimensional plane." This is a status in which even the very idea *of* corporeality or reality is itself necessarily "two-dimensional," "merely thought-out," inasmuch as now it is reduced to geometric three-dimensionality and a mathematical formula. Matter, the pre-cosmic ὕλη (*hylê*), is after all now no longer the counterpart of the Ideas. They now have as their real opposite nothing more than the abstract extendedness of space. Everything substantial in its materiality has thus sublated itself into the Ideas as pure form determinateness, on the one hand, and into space as a purely passive receptacle, on the other hand.

Ernst Hoffmann gave perhaps the clearest expression of the mathematization of reality in Plato's cosmology. "But what makes things to be things, bodies to be bodies, what produces reality, that is the geometric boundary of all things of the cosmos. Just as mathematics was the model for all dianoetics, for all knowing that mediates between purely intellectual and sensory-perception-based cognition, so is the mathematical, geometrical determinateness of the bodies their peculiar nature that lets them participate in the Ideas and in space. This is the reason for the proportionality and the strictly geometric structure of the platonic elements. It is not primal matters that give rise to the composition of the elements, but primal faces; 'the geometry' of the spatial arrangement informs us about the composition of the substance. The smallest modification in quality is nothing else but a change in the geometric dimension and the concomitant change and movement in the configuration of the bodies in question. Movement and modification are at bottom the same."[12]

This whole intellectual dissolution of the primal matters into mathematical proportionality and geometric structure is evidently in diametrical opposition to what Jung's thesis aims for. What Jung imputes to Christian Trinity, namely that it remains within the two-dimensionality of pure thought, and what he wants to correct through his going over to quaternity, is the very thing which is for the first time to be *gained* through Plato's discussion of the four elements (in which Jung believes to be entitled to see a step from the Three to the Four). But Jung interprets this as something that supports his interest in the realization of something merely thought-out. That the question of realization is no topic for Plato in this context is also underlined by Gadamer, who says about the second discussion of the elements: "Timaios is not interested in the way how the real elements come about out of the stereometric solids. ... The 'transition' into the reality of the visible natural world is as such not at all described ..."[13]

Above I spoke of a momentous mistake. What is confounded is ultimately

(1) the (unspoken) attempt by Plato in this passage to regain in the realm of thought the concept of corporeality by proceeding from the mathematical two-dimensionality to mathematical three-dimensionality of the universe, this in order to wrest it away from ordinary reality or nature and to completely replace the natural concept through an "artificial" one (for us in the Jungian tradition this could

---

[12] Ernst Hoffmann, "Methexis und Metaxy bei Platon," in: *idem*, *Drei Schriften zur griechischen Philosophie*, Heidelberg (Carl Winter) 1964, pp. 29-51, notes pp. 73-77. [This paper was first published in: *Sokrates. Zs. f. d. Gymnasialwesen. Abteilung: Jahresberichte des Philologischen Vereins Berlin*, 45, 1919, pp. 48-70.] Here p. 50. My translation.

[13] Gadamer, "Idee und Wirklichkeit in Platos Timaios," *op. cit.*, pp. 25f.

mean the overcoming of the anima stage and the recreation of the world within the [still abstract] animus stage)

with

(2) the totally different concern common to both Jung and Plato to establish a connection between heaven and earth for the purpose of ensuring the cohesion of the whole world and the participation (*methexis*) of the earthly in the heavenly, the communion of the *mundus intelligibilis* and the *mundus sensibilis*, which alone could give rise to actuality in the full sense of the word.

This, however, is a problem that cannot even be conceived with mathematical means, let alone solved. For mathematics passively dwells with the intuition of "objective" relations "out there in front of us," and abstract thought has likewise its object vis-à-vis itself. Man keeps out of it. But that sought-after actuality/reality depends on an entering (*inire*, initiation) on the part of man, on his self-exposure and active-productive involvement. Initiation, sacrifices, rituals, incest (for instance, the siring of the new Pharaoh through the *ka* of the father god in queen mother according to the Egyptian trinity) were, *on the anima stage* of consciousness, the preferred modes of a binding participation of man in nature or his entanglement in it—modes of the creation or maintaining a connection between here and yonder. What today could take their place, long after this stage has become obsolete in the subsequent animus stage that is now nearing its fulfillment and end, is an open question. It will probably have to be sought in the sphere of *educated, intellectually refined feeling* and feeling-based commitment.

If Jung's interpretation of the four elements as quaternio in Plato's account and his claiming them as support for his view of the Fourth as that which provides actuality are not corroborated by Plato's text, it is conversely astonishing that Jung feels justified in pointing to "laziness, stupidity, malice, discontent, sickness, old age and death" as objections to Plato's description of "God's fairest creation" "as Plato's inner eye envisaged it" (§185). Just as if Plato presented a one-sided picture of the world, indeed one painted in rosy colors. It is also astonishing that Jung does not point out that Plato from the outset presented his account about the cosmos as a schematic, and somewhat artificial, sketch. Furthermore it is surprising that Jung does not mention that the described excellence and rationality of the world is qualified by Plato through the fact that it is characterized as only the *one* side of the whole picture of the world, which in a second part of the same work is contrasted by another, additional and more radical description.

In his representation Plato elaborates the different, but logically simultaneous aspects of the cosmos one after the other, so that something discussed at the beginning must not out of hand be taken as the authoritative and complete view. Plotinus already stated, "Only the exposition forces him [Plato] to treat what exists in the very nature of the All as being produced through generation and creation, because it must present in sequence what in truth is a permanent simultaneity of being and becoming."[14] This is said, to be sure, with special reference to the question whether the world creation in *Timaeus* is to be understood literally as a temporal process, or whether (as Plotinus and many other ancient and modern interpreters think) an analysis of the (atemporal) structure of the world has been given a temporal sequence merely in its narrative form.[15] But quite apart from this question of whether temporal origin or not, the more general idea of the necessity to represent the individual features or "layers" of a complex picture each by itself one after the other also applies to our question about the different (rational or chaotic) aspects of the world.

In quite this sense we read at a certain point in the line of thought of the *Timaeus*:

> The foregoing part of our discourse ... has been an exposition of the operations of Reason; but we must also furnish an account of what comes into existence through Necessity. For, in truth, this Cosmos in its origin was generated as a compound, from the combination of Necessity and Reason. ... Wherefore if one is to declare how it actually came into being in this wise, he must include also the form of the Errant Cause, in the way it really acts. To this point, therefore, we must return, and taking once again a fresh starting-point suitable to the matter, we must make a fresh start in dealing therewith, just as we did with our previous subjects. (47e-48c, R.G. Bury in the Loeb edition)

---

[14] Plotinus, *Enneads* IV.8.4. My translation.

[15] On this question see M. Baltes, *Die Weltentstehung des platonischen Timaios nach den antiken Kommentatoren*, 2 vols., Leiden (Brill) 1976–79.

The solely good, rational demiurge has as a counterpart and opposite another, *equally eternal* principle which produces the irrational, chaotic share of the course of events and makes up the "nuisance-value" of reality, as Robinson[16] puts it.[17] The picture as represented so far therefore has only preliminary validity. It now has to be corrected and supplemented in what follows, taking account of the irrational principle that newly has come to our attention. This occurs with respect to the four elements in 53c. The principle of the aimlessly roaming-around Cause ruled in the precosmic Chaos, and despite the work of the demiurge it is still active even in the formed cosmos, because it is, after all, eternal. But the demiurge tamed it ("persuaded it": ὑπὸ πειθοῦ) through his creation of the cosmic order at least to such an extent, but no further, that it now appears as the (of course not rational, but at least) mechanistic causality which in everyday life as well as in science allows us to make fairly reliable statements and assumptions about the course of events.[18]

By paying attention to this principle, Plato in his own way gave due credit to the earthly weight of reality and the dark aspect, which Jung missed. Nothing is in principle lacking, especially not if, like certain interpreters (already Plutarch,[19] U. von Wilamowitz-Moellendorff,[20] and E.R. Dodds[21]), one is willing to connect the blind Necessity of *Timaeus* with Plato's doctrine from *Nomoi* (X, 896–897) about the "*two* souls," the rational, good, "best soul" (τὴν ἀρίστην ψυχήν) and the chaotic "evil soul" (τὴν κακήν) and to interpret

[16] T.M. Robinson, *Plato's Psychology*, p. 161.

[17] A psychological interpretation of this "Necessity" occurring in Plato's *Timaeus* was presented by James Hillman in his paper, "On the Necessity of Abnormal Psychology: Ananke and Athene," in *idem* (ed.), *Facing the Gods*, Irving TX (Spring Publications) 1980, pp. 1–38, here pp. 13 ff. with note 38 on p. 35.

[18] Gadamer, "Idee und Wirklichkeit in Platos Timaios," *op. cit.*, to be sure shows that already in the realm of Necessity an understandable and as such "rational" pre-ordering takes place (even if without insight into the use intended for the cosmic order), a pre-ordering on which the demiurge later can fall back. Necessity "acts as if it wanted 'beauty' on its own account," p. 31. But concerning *Timaeus, Philebos* as well as *Republic* he also stresses that the "function of 'utopia' that Plato turns into, his overall frame story by no means claims to deny the real conditions and necessities even for the political-societal task of mankind" (p. 36, my translations).

[19] In his treatise *De animae procreatione in Timaeo.*

[20] U. v. Wilamowitz-Moellendorff, *Platon*, Berlin ²1920, p. 321.

[21] E.R. Dodds, "Plato and the Irrational," in: *Journal of Hellenic Studies* XLV (1945), pp. 18-25, here p. 21.

this doctrine as an almost gnostic-manichean one of an evil principle, an evil world soul, which is the origin and source of evil in the world.

The picture of the cosmos in *Timaeus*—if seen in its totality (wholeness!), that is, if a first-presented partial aspect is not split off from its later-introduced correlating complement and an expressly preliminary description is not taken as the final one—by no means, as Jung has it, "wrenches the light half of the picture away from the dark half" (§ 264). So the lacking "wholeness" here may be a problem of the perspective and of the viewing subject rather than of the picture that is viewed. In other words, it is arguably Jung who wrenches here the light part of the painted picture from its more earthly aspect (presented by Plato later in the same dialogue, from 48a onwards) and to then put the blame for this one-sidedness on Plato as the latter's one-sidedness of an exclusively light depiction.

Timaeus 35a and the Alleged Quaternity of the World Soul

By means of the doctrine of the elements in the platonic dialogue Jung acquired for himself an initial concept of the two-dimensional triad as mere thought and of the Fourth as that which supplies three-dimensional bodily reality, although on the basis of a misinterpretation. All of Jung's further exposition is based on this concept. At first, however, the latter is deepened and supplemented by means of a second passage from Plato's *Timaeus*, namely the description of the creation of the world soul (35a). I agree with Jung: "The passage as a whole, however, is far from simple. It also has been translated in different ways and interpreted in even more different ways" (§ 189, transl. modif.). Nearly all commentators and interpreters (e.g., A.E. Taylor,[22] Cornford,[23] Gadamer[24], Guthrie,[25] T.M. Robinson[26] ...) seem

[22] A.E. Taylor, *A Commentary on Plato's Timaeus*, Oxford (Clarendon Press) 1928, Sp 106: "We now come to the most perplexing and difficult passage of the whole dialogue ..."

[23] F. Macdonald Cornford, *Plato's Cosmology. The Timaeus of Plato*, London 1937, p. 59: "one of the most obscure in the whole dialogue."

[24] Hans-Georg Gadamer, "Idee und Wirklichkeit in Platos Timaios," *op. cit.*, p. 13: "gilt seit dem Altertum als die rätselhafteste und schwierigste Partie des ganzen Werkes."

[25] W.K.C. Guthrie, *A History of Greek Philosophy*, vol. V, Cambridge et al. (Cambridge Univ. Press) 1978, p. 293.

[26] T.M. Robinson, *Plato's Psychology*, Toronto (Univ. of Toronto Press) 1970, p. 70.

to agree that this is the most difficult and darkest passage in the whole dialogue. Already during antiquity there were controversial interpretations of it (e.g., by Xenokrates and his disciple Krantor).

Jung also briefly touches on Cornford's (not insignificant) exposition which deviates from Jung's own view, a view which mainly relies on Apelt's translation. And already through his choice of words he tries to weaken the validity of Cornford's interpretation: according to Jung Cornford "constructs" (the word "*konstruiert*" could also imply "fabricates") an opposition ... "by means of the conjecture that ...," and Jung does "not know whether the text permits of such an operation" § 191, fn. 27 [fn. 60 in *GW*]).[27] In this way he makes Cornford's interpretation appear as a rather capricious commentary which is due to artificial speculations and imposed upon the text. But to me the relation seems to be the other way around. It is Cornford's interpretation which is most closely corroborated by the wording of the text passage and by the context and the spirit of Plato's philosophy as a whole; and most Plato scholars since then have supported it, at least as far as the conception of the sentence in question here is concerned, if one may not even consider it the presently accepted one. Robinson, who in 1970 presented a new exposition of Platonic cosmology as a whole and who in a number of other individual points even disagrees with Cornford's opinion, thus showing that he is not a blind follower of Cornford's interpretation, states (after having pointed out that in view of the extremely abstract nature of its content he does not find the obscurity of this passage astonishing):

> Solutions have been many and various, but the one which seems to me to do most justice to the text as we have it and to make some sort of philosophical sense is that of Proclus, championed in recent times by Grube and Cornford.[28]

And Mohr (1985), who, to be sure, considers the report about the composition of the world soul (35a) to be precisely rather unfathomable, nevertheless on his part again refers to Robinson's interpretation as "a reasonable attempt at an interpretation."[29]

---

[27] The translator of the English *CW* got rid of the sideswipe by taming the text of the footnote down.

[28] T.M. Robinson, *Plato's Psychology*, Toronto (Univ. of Toronto Press) 1970, p. 70.

[29] Richard D. Mohr, *The Platonic Cosmology*, Leiden (E.J. Brill) 1985, p. 171 footnote.

When Gadamer writes, "Nor is there—especially after Cornford's precise commentary—any need for a new examination of the description about how the construction of the 'world soul' is carried out in detail,"[30] then this shows what power of conviction he ascribes to Cornford's analysis.

Jung's interpretation, by contrast, is altogether idiosyncratic. Far and wide it is completely isolated. Of course, this would not have to mean that it is untenable. It could just as well mean that Jung all alone had a deeper insight than all the experts; that on the basis of his psychological knowledge he had access to a level of understanding that remained closed to the other interpreters. In that case his view would need to be corroborated by cogent arguments to be made really plausible; it would have to prove convincingly that it is not only in accordance with the literal text philologically and with the philosophical meaning of the present passage as well as the entire dialogue (and perhaps Plato's philosophy at large), but also that it is capable of disclosing the meaning to our understanding in an extraordinary way—in other words, that it would simply prove to be the stronger interpretation in comparison with others.

If Jung had not been aware of Cornford's commentary it would have been easier to understand that he could interpret the passage that we are concerned with the way he did. But it is absolutely astounding that Jung continued to stick to his idiosyncratic interpretation even after perusing the extremely careful and convincing commentary by Cornford and to feel that he could brush aside with a few casual remarks Cornford's view as a pretty dubious interpretation.

Jung's view, very briefly summarized, is that Plato started out from two separate pairs of opposites arranged in a quaternio (1. the Indivisible and the Divisible, 2. the Same and the Different) and that the soul was created at the point of the intersection of the two axes as the common Intermediate, namely out of the Intermediate formed between the Indivisible and the Divisible *and* out of the Intermediate formed between the Same and the Different. This is why Jung speaks of "the fundamentally *fourfold nature* of the world soul" (§ 186, fn. 18, Jung's italics). In this scheme, the one triad (the Indivisible and the Divisible with its Intermediate)

[30] Hans-Georg Gadamer, "Idee und Wirklichkeit in Platos Timaios," *op. cit.*, pp. 12f.

represents what belongs to mere thought and still is devoid of actuality. For this reason a second mixing was required through which the "Different" was by force, as Plato says, united with the Same. The Different is, according to Jung, the Fourth which as adversary of the harmony resists the other three. With it, however, the desired "*being*" is intimately connected. Here Jung reminds us again of the impatience the philosopher must have felt when reality proved so recalcitrant to his ideas (§ 188).

On the basis of Apelt's version of the passage (quoted in English translation in *CW* § 186), Jung's interpretation can be justified to some extent. But now I simply present to begin with another translation of this text passage by way of comparison and contrast, my English translation of the German version by Hieronymus Müller as revised by Klaus Widdra (1972).[31]

> Between the indivisible and always changeless Being and the divisible Being subject to change in the realm of bodies he mixed a third form of Being out of the two. But as regards the nature of the "same" and that of the different, he again prepared in those accordingly a third Kind each between the Indivisible of them and that which is divisible in the bodies. And he took these three and united them all into *one* figure, by making by force a harmonious combination of the difficult-to-mix nature of the different with that of the "same" and mixed them with the Being.

Expressly following Cornford, Widdra, too, puts a comma after βίᾳ, and a period after οὐσίας.[32]

The understanding expressed in this translation is not only in agreement with the reading by Cornford and Robinson, but also with that of commentators from antiquity. That Cornford, following Grube, cited Proclus as support was already mentioned. Instead of the Proclus passage, easily available in Cornford's work, I quote this passage in the version of a less known ancient author, a version which, not being a literal quotation of Plato's passage, is all the more revealing. Aristeides Quintilianus (probably late 3rd century A.D., i.e., earlier than Proclus) writes in his work *On Music* (Περὶ μουσικῆς):

[31] Platon, *Werke in acht Bänden (griech. und dt.)*, vol. VII, Darmstadt (Wiss. Buchges.) 1972.

[32] *Ibid.*, note on 35a8f., p. 49.

> The divine Plato, too, says in the *Timaeus* approximately the following: after having taken a mean between the indivisible Being and the divisible Being and having, in the realm of the "same" and the different, added the intermediates between the divisible and the indivisible natures to the intermediate between the forms of Being and having made a blend of these three, the demiurge divided the entire blend again according to these numbers ...[33]

What we have here is first an opposition between the indivisible, unchangeable (i.e., the Intelligible, the realm of Ideas), on the one hand, and the divisible, the physical, that which is subject to change (i.e., the Sensible, the realm of empirical phenomena), on the other hand. In these two we can recognize, within the sphere of abstract thought, the successor configuration of what in the sphere of the mythic experience of the world used to be Heaven and Earth, Uranos and Gaia, in other words, gods. "Successor configurations" does not mean anything like a new avatar (a new incorporation), in which the character would be preserved, but it means the logical sublation of the old concrete figures of gods and a new engendering of them under completely new conditions or on a completely new level, namely now as abstract concepts. A fundamental metamorphosis and semantic change has taken place, a change in which a new creation of the whole world upon the animus stage is reflected.

What happens for the purpose of creating the world soul is that an intermediate is mixed three times between these two opposites, namely

(1) the intermediate (between the Intelligible and the Sensible) as regards *Being* (οὐσία [*oysia*]),

(2) the intermediate (between the Intelligible and the Sensible) as regards *Identity* (the "same": ταὐτόν [*tayton*]),

(3) the intermediate (between the Intelligible and the Sensible) as regards *Difference* (ἕτερον [*heteron*]).

---

[33] Aristidis Quintiliani *De Musica* libri 3, ed. R.P. Winnington-Ingram, Lipsiae (Teubner) 1963, book III, ch. 24, pp. 125f. (my transl.). Here the Greek text: λέγει γάρ πως καὶ ὁ θεῖος Πλάτων ἐν Τιμαίῳ τάδε ὡς τῆς ἀμερίστου καὶ μεριστῆς οὐσίαν λαβὼν καὶ ἐπὶ τῆς ταὐτοῦ καὶ θατέρου μεριστῆς τε καὶ ἀμερίστου φύσεως τὰς μεσότητας τῇ τῶν οὐσιῶν μεσότητι συνθεὶς καὶ τούτων τῶν τριῶν κρᾶσιν ποιησαμένος ὁ ψυχῆς δημιουργὸς πάλιν κατ᾽ ἀριθμοὺς τούσδε τὸ σύμπαν κρᾶμα διεῖλεν κ.τ.λ.. I became aware of this text through Guthrie, *op. cit.* (p. 293, fn. 4).

These three intermediates (which are each the result of a mixing on a first level) are combined once more on a second level of mixing. Widdra expresses it most succinctly: "The blend consists of mixed Being, mixed 'same,' mixed 'different.'"[34] Similarly, Gadamer speaks of a "mixture, occurring in two phases, of sameness, difference, and Being."[35] Thus there are originally three ingredients, each of which occurs in two forms.

This interpretation is not only in line with the cited translation of the Plato passage by Hieronymus Müller/Widdra and the rendering of the passage by Aristeides Quintilianus, but is also in agreement with those by Cornford and other modern scholars. Bröcker, for example, says by way of elucidation: "What Plato wants to say is this: in the realm of the sensible, it is, in contrast to the intelligible, not only Being that is divided (there is only one Idea of man, but there are many people), but identity and difference are also divided. An old man, for instance, is the same person as the one that he was as a child, and yet he is not the same, he is an other and not an other. This is inherent in the nature of Becoming. The soul is defined as something that in each regard, as regards Being, identity, and difference, is an intermediate between the intelligible determined by indivisibility and the sensible determined by divisibility."[36] To be sure, at first this text is only concerned with the "world soul," not by a long shot with the human soul. And the world soul is actually, as it turns out, nothing else but the paths of the motion of the starry heaven,[37] on which sameness can be observed in the fact that during the turning of the fixed star heaven the heavenly constellations remain unchanged, and difference can be observed as the change of position of the sun, the moon, and the planets during their journey in their orbits.

But it is especially the continuation of the text which suggests that this interpretation is necessary, indeed makes it necessary. The next sentence (35b) reads: "And when he had made out of three One, he divided this whole again in so many parts as was appropriate, each of which was mixed out of the 'same,' the

[34] Platon, *Werke in acht Bänden*, *op. cit.*, note on 35a8f., p. 49.
[35] Gadamer, "Idee und Wirklichkeit in Platos Timaios," *op. cit.*, p. 13.
[36] Walter Bröcker, *Platos Gespräche*, Frankfurt a.M. (Klostermann) ²1967, p. 511.
[37] Gadamer, "Idee und Wirklichkeit in Platos Timaios," *op. cit.*, p. 13.

different, and Being." According to this sentence a "fundamental fourfold nature of the world soul" is out of the question. The world soul consists of three components, or, if you wish, of six (insofar as each of the three occurs in turn in the two forms of the divisible and indivisible), namely of three parallel pairs of opposites.

This triad, however, is a different one from the one Jung posited as the "platonic" triad. Jung says (§ 188): "Indivisible and divisible, together with their mean, form a simple triad ...," and he considers the "different" as the recalcitrant Fourth which is added to this triad. This is odd, inasmuch as one would have to assume, according to the quaternio diagram presented by Jung himself in the same paragraph, that the triad has to be the "Same," the Indivisible, and the Divisible, to which the Different would be joined as the Fourth, whereas, again according to Jung's diagram, the mean would actually be a Fifth in addition to the tetrad, the *quinta essentia*, as it were. But the "same" (identity) seems to be simply passed over by Jung.

In viewing the indivisible and the divisible, on the one hand, and the "same" and the different on the other, as two crossing pairs of opposites, Jung does not make the mistake of earlier interpreters (Gomperz,[38] Taylor,[39] Friedländer[40]) for whom the second opposition is merely another synonymous naming of the first (the indivisible = the "same"; the divisible = the different). Such interpreters were therefore forced to assume that first the indivisible and the divisible were blended into a mean and thereafter this mean, formed out of the two, was once more blended with the same indivisible and the same divisible which were, after all, its parent components. Guthrie rightly states about this view: "It is strange to speak of three ingredients in a mixture if the so-called third is a blend of the first two."[41] And to my mind the text does not allow for this reading. Even Robinson, a carefully

[38] Th. Gomperz, *Griechische Denker* II (1912), p. 487. Jung cites Gomperz in § 186, fn. 18.

[39] A.E. Taylor, *A Commentary on Plato's Timaeus*, Oxford (Clarendon Press) 1928, p. 109. About Taylor's interpretation as a whole in this quite useful work it must be said that it proceeds from the strange prejudice (today probably not thought to be acceptable by anyone) that Plato in his dialogue had the intention of reporting with historical faithfulness, quite apart from his own philosophical tenets, a conversation having actually taken place and thus the views of the real Pythagorean Timaios at the level of knowledge of around 420 B.C.

[40] Paul Friedländer, *Plato*, Berlin, New York (de Gruyter) ^{3}1975 (^{1}1930). pp. 339f.

[41] W.K.C. Guthrie, *A History of Greek Philosophy*, vol. V, Cambridge et al. (Cambridge Univ. Press) 1978, p. 293, fn. 4.

weighing author who is not prone to daring hypotheses, speaks with respect to Taylor's similar view of a "basic misinterpretation" and states quite bluntly: "His defence of his position is neat and succinct, but it cannot make up for the fact that he misreads the text and upholds a position which Plato never affirmed."[42] Ernst Hoffmann, who does not precisely identify the divisible and the indivisible as a and b with the different and the "same," but nevertheless lets them, as α and β, be akin and set off from them only by a difference in rank, is able to bestow a certain plausibility on this idea by, not unintelligently and not without some philosophical sense, comparing the one blend to a chemical, the other one to a physical one (concerning the latter case just think of the phrase "by force"!) and attempting to demonstrate the different capacities of these blends for the different cognitive faculties of the soul.[43] Nevertheless, compared with the form of the text that has come down to us, this interpretation is not really satisfactory.

Jung for his part (§ 189) thinks[44] that the "for an understanding critical point" is the phrase, συνέστησεν ἐν μέσῳ τοῦ τε ἀμεροῦς, which literally translated would be "he compounded (a form of the nature of the 'same' and the different) *in the middle of* [= between] the indivisible ...", whereas Jung renders it as: "*in the intermediate of* the indivisible (and divisible),"[45] meaning in a substantiating way the result of the first mixing and deriving from this reading the view that the two intermediates coincide. But interestingly enough, he breaks off the quote in the middle of the sentence after the word ἀμεροῦς; he not only leaves out the counterpart concerning the divisible (which, however, he adds in parentheses in his *translation*), but he above all omits right after ἀμεροῦς the indispensable word αὐτῶν ("of them"), which does not appear in his translation either. If, however, we take this word into consideration then it is a question of a compounding in the middle of (or between) the indivisible *of them* and the divisible [of them], with the "them" in "of them" referring to the "same" and the different. But then it is also clear that the "same" and the different

[42] Robinson, *op. cit.*, p. 72.

[43] Ernst Hoffmann, "Platons Lehre von der Weltseele," in: *Sokrates*. Zs. f. d. Gymnasialwesen, Abt.: Jahresberichte d. Philol. Vereins zu Berlin, 41, 1915, pp. 187–211., reprinted in: idem., *Drei Schriften zur griechischen Philosophie*, Heidelberg (Carl Winter) 1964, pp. 9–28, here pp. 13f.

[44] He may have been misled by Apelt's false translation.

[45] The *CW* translation deviates from Jung's wording.

each have their own indivisible and divisible and cannot be a completely independent pair of opposites crossing the other opposition of the indivisible and the divisible. Thus Jung's arranging the four concepts in a quincunx has become impossible (but Hoffmann's interpretation, too, should thereby be defeated).

With his interpretation Jung is, it seems to me, completely isolated. Only in Zeller (1889) can be found a suggestion that could possibly have served as a stimulus for his idea of the two crossing pairs of opposites and the tetrad. There we read that the "same" is more closely akin to the undivided, the different to the divided, but that they by no means coincide; "both pairs of concepts have much rather a different meaning and in their combination make two crossing divisions."[46] However, Zeller's further interpretation in the continuation of this footnote no longer converges with Jung's view.

Especially important for Jung is that into the second mixing (according to his count) the different (or the "other") is driven in by force. "The Other is therefore that *Fourth that reveals itself as 'adversary'* and resists harmony" (§188, transl. modif., Jung's italics). Jung's next sentence is: "But with it, as the text says, is connected the so much yearned-for *Being*" (transl. modif.). I already showed that it is not Plato's text that says this, but only Apelt's translation, and that in the first place a "so much yearned-for" Being is out of the question in Plato, because he starts out from Being all along. The difference that can only by force be mixed together with Identity is for that reason not that eminent Fourth of Jung's that resists harmony and is thus the bringer of Being. It is one of three (besides Identity and Being), and it is "recalcitrant" not for the whole, but only with respect to its being combined with the one intermediate, that of Identity, whereas both Difference and Identity seem to go together with Being without force.

As Taylor has pointed out, Plato, in his talk of the mixings and the consecutive divisions of the soul, alluded to the everyday Greek custom at banquets to mix water and wine in a mixing vessel (*kratêr*) and then to distribute it to the guests.[47] With this in mind one could say that just as water and wine can easily be mixed, so also Identity

[46] Eduard Zeller, *Die Philosophie der Griechen* II.1, Leipzig 1889, p. 770 note.
[47] A.E. Taylor, *Commentary*, p. 106.

and Being as well as Difference and Being can go together without difficulty, whereas Difference relates to Identity more like oil that one wants to mix with water. This is the light in which the phrase "by force" needs to be understood. Difference is thus not at all fundamentally recalcitrant, not "the adversary." It just cannot easily be made to go along with the one of the two other mixtures, that of Identity, for obvious reasons: they are opposites.

This allows us a glimpse into the paradigm at work behind and in Jung's conception. Although "the Fourth" is a totally abstract term, Jung conceives it in childlike concretistic, anthropomorphic terms—in terms of the ego, of personalistic or people's psychology. The Fourth is represented as "adversary," which is also a name for the devil. And it is described as recalcitrant. In other words, the categories that inform Jung's thinking here are the subjective will, subjective love or hate, and ultimately good and evil. The 3+1 structure is seen as if it were a family with three well-behaved and agreeable children and one child that is negative, ill-willed, and on principle against anything that comes from the others. Neither Difference nor oil are ill-willed. And it is also not clear whether the difficulty in one's mixing of oil and water is the oil's fault, or not perhaps the water's fault. Does the oil not "want" to go with the water, or is it rather that water "refuses" to let the oil in or, conversely, to blend with the oil? That Difference and Identity cannot easily be mixed is simply due to their definition. It is a logical incompatibility that has nothing to do with ill will. There is a simple objective difficulty that the demiurge has to overcome by force, not an adversary. Plato, as a thinker, takes into consideration what the inherent implications of a wish for blending two substances is, if the one substance happens to be Identity and the other Difference. He thinks. For Jung, by contrast, the reason force is necessary does not follow from the *particular properties* of the ingredients, their incompatibility, but because "the Fourth" *qua "the Fourth"* is defined from the outset as recalcitrant. To be recalcitrant is the job of the Fourth, its true nature. It *is* "adversary" and nothing else. This is why Jung is so fascinated by this one minor phrase "by force" in Plato and gives it a totally exaggerated significance, blowing it up to almost mythic relevance beyond the really only pragmatic, almost technical meaning it has in the doings of the demiurge. "The problem of the fourth, for instance," Jung says about Plato

(§ 192), "... can hardly have fully reached his consciousness. If it had, the forcefulness of the solution within a harmonious system would have been much too offensive." We see here how Jung thinks that Plato's *solution* was not organic, but forced and artificial, in other words, that it is a flaw of the philosophical system. But in reality it is not that his philosophical solution is violent, but that the elements that he is talking about require this force. No sign of unconsciousness. The force used is perfectly above board. The violence is as consistent with his system as is the inclusion of the concept of volcanic eruptions in a perfectly harmonious or consistent theory of nature. No ground for Plato as a thinker to become embarrassed.

The abstract-formal relational pattern of three harmonious elements plus one "adversary" is the absolute dogmatic presupposition with which Jung approaches the Plato text. *What* the three ingredients and *what* the one (the fourth) ingredient might be in their own right, i.e., what properties or character each of them has and what their "name" (their substantial nature) is, is for Jung rather irrelevant. Jung is only interested in the formal constellation, the abstract "family romance," the "object relations," as we could say, between the 3 and the 1 as between harmony and adversary or between good and evil.[48] Plato, by contrast, is concerned with concrete ingredients, contents: Being, Identity, and Difference.

Jung's assumption that the indivisible, the mean, and the divisible form the "platonic" triad is also untenable because for Plato there are according to our version three of these triads, three times a divisible and an indivisible each and three times a mean between them. Likewise, from the outset the second blending (nor the adding of a Fourth) is not needed *for the purpose* of achieving realization in the sense of "worldly materiality" (§ 251) because this materiality is precisely all along given through the fact that Plato (in addition to the Indivisible) *starts out from* "the divisible Being subject to change *in the realm of bodies*" and because realization and materialization of what is merely thought is not the issue, as Jung

[48] Good and Evil are psychologically categories of the childish mind. Good guys, bad guys, the evil empire, etc. The mature mind takes even the "bad guys," the IRA, the Hisbollah, terrorists, communists, totalitarian regimes as realities which one may at times even have to accept as partners at eye-level in open-ended negotiations. In such negotiations the issue is one of substances: *what* do they want and *what* do we want. Good and evil have become irrelevant.

seems to believe, indeed cannot be the issue. The aim is much rather the mediation between the Intelligible and the Material-Sensible through the fabrication of the world soul as an intermediate that participates in both sides, the eternal and the earthly. Although the world soul is a blend that also contains the material element, it is nevertheless nonsensible and invisible. It is the living substance that animates (i.e., 1. moves, 2. *thinks*) the matter of the cosmos.

If one accepts our reading, it disposes of Jung's entire conception. Not one of the three tenets of Jung's theory so dear to his heart are to be found in those *Timaeus* passages that he presented as evidence for and the foundation of this very theory, neither that of

- an eminent Fourth, nor that of
- a yearning for reality/actuality and a Fourth that brings the yearned-for reality, nor that of
- an "adversary" or a recalcitrance.

What to me is especially astounding to see and painful is the fact that Jung, when given the chance to be put on the right track through Cornford's very careful and well-arguing commentary, proved immune to the better argument and brushed it aside without himself being able to refute Cornford's discussion in any way. The only answer that I can find to the question why he was unable to open-mindedly weigh the evidence, to listen to reason, and to stand corrected, is that subjective emotional-ideological needs must have blinded him—and made *him*, as it were, recalcitrant! (It must have been the same ideological need that made it impossible for him to see that the move from a three-term to a four-term algebraic formula or from geometric two-dimensionality to geometric three-dimensionality does not take one from "mere thought" to physical reality.) The dogma of the recalcitrant Fourth and of the yearning for actuality must have been so precious to him and so powerful; so much, it seems, must have been personally at stake for him with this doctrine that it simply could not be neutrally up for discussion, let alone be possibly wrong. Its status was for Jung not "hypothetical" but "categorical." Of course, consciously it was a hypothesis for him for which he precisely tried to provide "empirical" proof, evidential support: from the work of Plato. But unconsciously its truth was already, as it were, "a priori" certain for him so that it had to be conversely Cornford who "fails to catch the subtlety contained in Plato's allusion to the recalcitrance of the fourth" (§ 191, transl. modif.). But this subtlety is obviously so extreme that it cannot be found in the evidence, in Plato's text. It is solely the property of Jung's mind as reader of the text.

Also disposed of, with the reading given above, is Jung's attempt to invalidate Cornford's view that the "hint of three intermedia" (§ 191, transl. modif.), namely "Intermediate Existence," "Intermediate Sameness," "Intermediate Difference," are the essential point. Actually, however, the threeness of the three intermedia are not merely a "hint," as Jung discreditingly puts it, but a statement in Plato's text ("καὶ τρία λαβὼν" κτλ.). Now, how does Jung try to invalidate Cornford's cited view? He says that "He [Cornford] insists mainly on the threefold procedure and not on the four substances of the latter" (§ 191, transl. modif.), and in order to substantiate his comment Jung refers to the medieval idea of the *quattuor elementa* (A, B, C, D) and the *tria regimina* (three procedures) through which the former are united (A-B, B-C, and C-D). But this is in no way a parallel. Rather, it is a distinction that comes from a very different sphere and has no correspondence in the Plato passage. In that passage there are not, as we have seen, four substances.[49] We have much rather five (2 + 3) principles or kinds (Indivisible vs. Divisible, on the one hand, and, sort of at right angles to these,[50] Being, Identity, Difference, on the other hand, whereby the latter three each occur in the forms of the former two). If we wanted to relate this to Jung's medieval reference, we would have to say: we have three "substances" and two procedures (mixings), of which the first procedure is carried out three times, one time *within* each of the "substances," namely between the Indivisible and Divisible of each.

---

[49] With these "four substances" Jung probably refers to the Indivisible, the Divisible, the Same, and the Different (as we can conclude from his diagrams, the quaternio of § 188 and the quincunx of § 189)—although this is in conflict with the conception of the "simple triad" which is formed by the first two substances (Indivisible and Divisible) together with their Intermediate and which is complemented by the Different so as to form a tetrad. This latter is a conception in which, as we have seen, the Same would fall by the wayside.

[50] This means that in accordance with Cornford's view (rejected by Jung as a "conjecture") "Indivisible and Divisible are attributes of each of the three principles" (§ 191, fn. 27, transl. modif.).

As to these five principles or Kinds Bröcker says: "The five Greatest Kinds of the *Sophistes* return here, with the only change that the difference between the sensible and the intelligible is not determined as that of motion and rest, but rather as that of divisibility and indivisibility."[51] And R.G. Bury remarks in his edition (Loeb Classical Library no. 234, p. 66) concerning this passage: "The choice of these three as constituents of the Soul is explained by the use of the same terms in the *Sophist* (244-245) to denote certain 'Greatest Kinds' or main categories." And then he quotes Prof. Paul Shorey with the comment:[52] "It is necessary that the Soul should recognize everywhere ... the *same*, the *other* and *essence*, those three μέγιστα γένη [*megista genê*] of the ... *Sophist*. Hence, on the Greek principle that like is known by like, Plato makes real substances out of these three abstractions and puts them as plastic material into the hands of the Demiurgus for the formation of the Soul."

Because the *Timaeus* passage appears to be interlocked with the corresponding discussions in the *Sophistes* and the passage which at first seemed obscure has now become truly translucent even in its wording, the interpretation presented here acquires, over against Jung's view, a persuasiveness that can hardly be doubted. However, I do not want to withhold the fact that the reference, already propagated by Cornford, to the Greatest Kinds of the *Sophistes* has been called into question by a few scholars because according to their opinion the *Timaeus* has to be dated much earlier and is thought to still present the classical doctrine of Ideas that in the *Sophistes* is left behind.[53] The parallel seems to me, however, too conspicuous to ignore, especially since (even if one were to adopt the view that *Timaeus* is earlier) it might also be possible to see in its five Kinds an early foreshadowing of the later concept. But for our purposes of an examination of Jung's quaternity theory there is no need to decide this question. For whether the reference to the *Sophistes* is justified or not does not really make any difference one way or another concerning the question at issue here and the translation of 35a (the blending of three ingredients, each of which is in itself already a mixture of the divisible and the indivisible).

---

[51] Bröcker, *op. cit.*, p. 511, my transl.
[52] *Amer. Journ. Philol.* IX, p. 298.
[53] See on this question Robinson, *op. cit.*, pp. 72 ff. with references.

THE MISSING FOURTH IN THE OPENING SENTENCE OF THE *TIMAEUS*

We had to realize that Jung's belief in the "Platonic formula for the triad" (§ 196) and in "the subtlety contained in Plato's allusion to the recalcitrance of the fourth" (which allegedly escaped Cornford) (§ 191) is built on sand. A factual fourfold nature of the world soul and of the world body exists in the *Timaeus*, to be sure, through the fact that the demiurge divides the whole product of his fabrication and combines it in the Form of an X (*Chi*). But Jung based his argument precisely not on this passage and does not use it as his prime evidence. He merely mentions it briefly (§ 190). Rightly so, for what is discussed in that passage is only a secondary *ordering scheme* imposed on the finished composition of the substances making up the world soul, but has nothing to do with a composition out of "four substances" nor with the complementation of a triad by a recalcitrant Fourth. In each of the two cases we have entirely different phenomena of fourfoldness. That viewpoint which is decisive for the entire further discussion in Jung's work on the Trinity and which Jung believed to have evolved out of Plato's text is not contained in the latter. Even if Apelt's translation may indeed have given him a certain, limited support for his theses, we must nevertheless say, as our overall result, that the standard that Jung in the later chapters of his work will apply to Christian Trinity does not stem from the *Timaeus* (not even from Apelt's translation of it), but has been read into the text.

The only support that might possibly remain for Jung's thesis in the *Timaeus* is the opening words of this dialogue about the fourth (host) who could not come: "One, two, three,—but where, my dear Timaeus, is the fourth ...?" These words are, for an initial assessment, merely part of the foreground of a frame story for the following real philosophical discussion. But when Jung states that with them Plato "is alluding to something of deeper import" (§ 184, transl. modif.), that their being mentioned in the text is not "attributable either to the jocosity of the author or to pure chance" (§ 185), when we further take into consideration that, as Jung puts it, "we are certainly entitled to ascribe to this thinker an extraordinary degree of genius" (§ 192, transl. modif.), then it could possibly make sense to see in them a deeper, substantial meaning. According to Jung's interpretation Plato (or rather not Plato, but a force unconsciously at work in him, the "*spiritus rector*" in him, § 192) made it clear that the Fourth is an indispensable part of wholeness, but that it was lacking in Plato himself, or rather in his philosophy (precisely also in the theory as a whole described in *Timaeus*). Or we could say that the quaternity or wholeness, simply because it is a psychological (archetypal) reality, at certain points of least resistance pushed its way through what on the whole was "merely thought-out" so that even against the philosopher's conscious intellectual intention it received some form of explicit expression—not despite the fact that we have to ascribe to this thinker an extraordinary degree of genius, but precisely because of it. The greater the mind, the more it is in contact with the living matrix of psychic reality and the more it is open for its necessities and "influences," quite independently of his conscious thoughts. With this idea the discrepancy has been explained between the two-dimensionality, diagnosed by Jung, of the platonic dialogue as a whole as a "painting of airy thoughts that lacked weight," on the one hand, and the opposite fact that there are two passages in this dialogue (four elements; creation of the world soul) in which Jung sees expressed the insight into the connection of the Fourth with "realization."

I must admit that Jung's interpretation of the indeed a bit mysterious-sounding opening words has something impressive about it (which is even increased by the interesting reference to Goethe's lines about the fourth Cabir in *Faust II* who did not want to come). What impairs the interpretation that these words received from Jung is, however, that the "conscious reference to the underlying problem of the recalcitrant fourth" (§ 192), which alone would give to the opening words the asserted hidden profundity and brisance, does not exist inasmuch as this issue ("the dilemma of three and four" § 183) does not come up in the following text. If this topic is not at least touched on in the dialogue itself, then the allusion contained in the opening words of the frame story is too much up in the air to be considered a profound allusion. It has nothing *to which* it would allude.

Maybe "more banal" interpretations make a little more sense, even if they are not completely satisfying, like those of Constantin Ritter or of Friedländer, that with the opening words Plato alluded to his project of a trilogy or rather tetralogy of dialogues. The *Timaues* announces itself as the first of a series of dialogues. The fictitious situation which is presupposed is that Socrates the day before gave a report to four persons (Timaios, Kritias, Hermokrates, and an unnamed fourth, who just now cannot come because of illness) about the discussion that was written down in the *Republic* and that now it is the others' turn to present something to Socrates. The three friends agreed that today Timaios should speak about the creation of the world and tomorrow Kritias about Athen's prehistoric daring fight against the attacks from Atlantis. We do not expressly hear what (and if) Hermokrates was to present on the third day. Plato completed the *Timaeus* and part of *Kritias*. It seems, however, that a *Hermokrates* dialogue has not been written. Ritter's theory is that with the unnamed fourth Plato wanted to keep open the possibility of expanding the projected trilogy into a tetralogy, whereas Friedländer interprets the missing fourth as indicating that a *Hermokrates* dialogue was to be expected, but not in addition a fourth dialogue, a new *Republic*.[54]

As to the Goethe passage, we have to say that it, too, is as isolated within *Faust* as are the opening words in *Timaeus*. Two short lines out of a work of more than 12,000 lines and a tiny element within a host of scenes with numerous figures. A problem with Jung's use of these lines is also that he does not view them in the context from which they come nor in the context of Goethe's thinking at large. He takes them as if they expressed a stand-alone monolithic archetypal idea, whereas they are a (tiny) *functional* element within a large-scale poetic whole, and as if their only real reference was, apart from the depth of the soul, directly to the Platonic cryptic statement ("Goethe's intuition grasped accurately the significance of this [Plato's] allusion ..." § 183, transl. modif.). But we know that Goethe got his material for the scene of the Cabiri directly from Creuzer's *Symbolik und Mythologie der alten Völker*, vol. 2 (1811) and above all from Schelling's highly speculative, syncretistic *Über die Gottheiten von Samothrace* (1815): book-learning, not intuitive archetypal revelation. And he made very ironical, indeed jocose (!) use of the mythological material. He also distanced himself from Creuzer's *Symbolik* with very derogatory words, calling it something like "a dark-poetic-philosophical-

---

[54] Constantin Ritter, *Neue Untersuchungen über Plato*, München 1910, p. 181. Friedländer, *op. cit.*, vol. 3, p. 331.

sanctimonious wandering-around like a lost soul," and also from Schelling's speculations. Nevertheless he felt that the material he found in these works came in very handy for particular artistic purposes he had in this act of his drama and for expressing some point he wanted to make. And so he utilized the mythological material very consciously and deliberately as *poetic* signs to express conceptions of his own.

This is not the place to discuss this Goethe passage in its own right. But what becomes apparent right away is that it does not support Jung's topic of the recalcitrant Fourth that bestows reality to "mere thought." For in Goethe, the Cabiri came from the sea, from the world of water.[55] Water is the element from which all life originates. It is highly significant that the Cabiri are the only figures in this whole sea scene who remain mute. They lack speech and any knowledge of who they are. The fact that the not-present fourth Cabir is "the one who thinks for them all" means that in him they would have their consciousness, their awareness that they themselves precisely lack.[56] Goethe represented in this scene a divine cosmic dynamic that is at work in the stuff of water, a force that, unconsciously stirring from within the physical element, hungers for life and spirit and, ultimately, divine figures, as the highest form of life. In the Cabiri, Goethe represented this deeply unconscious urge and longing inherent in the formless element of water for form and shape, for living figures. So instead of a movement from "mere thought" down into physical reality and "worldly materiality" we have here an upwards move precisely from within the concretely real material world (Goethe's central motif of *Steigerung*, heightening, of a "chain" of life from its lowest forms to its highest, divine forms).

---

[55] Goethe's Cabiri as poetic signs are thus by no means identical with Jung's Cabiri, which "are, in fact, the mysterious creative powers, the gnomes who work under the earth..." (§ 244).

[56] Jung's personalistic interpretation of the fourth (§ 244 with fn. 1, as also in *CW* 12 § 203 ff.) in terms of his "psychological types" scheme (thinking vs. feeling) is embarrassing and silly. Goethe is dealing with serious *issues*, not displaying his personality traits.

* * *

"Ever since the *Timaeus* the 'fourth' has signified 'realization,' i.e., entry into an essentially different condition, that of worldly materiality ..." (§ 251). A bold statement. Has it really? Both "ever" and "since" are questionable. As to "since": Jung's crown witness changed his testimony under cross-examination; the *Timaeus* support for his thesis has crumbled away before our eyes. And as to "ever": where are the examples from the 2,000 years between *Timaeus* and Goethe that substantiate this continuous signification? And why did it need Goethe's "intuition" if, after all, ever since the *Timaeus* the 'fourth' has signified what Jung said it signifies? Why then was it at Goethe's time not all along explicit knowledge in the more insightful minds?

Whenever Jung in various places in his diverse works comes to speak of the problem of the Fourth, his only supporting references time and again seem to be those same ones to *Timaeus* and to Goethe's Cabiri lines. Never anything else, as far as I can see. The alchemical so-called *Axiom of Maria* (Prophetissa, § 184), although frequently cited by Jung, does not seem to qualify as support inasmuch as it is not concerned with the 3+1 idea and the recalcitrant Fourth, not with the development from triad to quaternity, but consists of a cryptic and obscure (Jung himself once called it "enigmatic" and another time "muffled and alembicated") rune about a development from one to four: "One becomes two, two becomes three, and out of the third comes the one as the fourth" (*CW* 12 § 26). One can read what one wants into such a context-less piece of (probably Gnostic) number speculation. "The one as the fourth" does not even produce a quaternity, a square, a quaternio. Rather, it is expressly stated to be the oneness of the *three*,[57] much like, it seems, the fifth as the "quintessence" is the oneness of the four (quincunx) rather than a pentagon. For the topic of the Trinity and for Jung's recalcitrant Fourth nothing is gained with this formula.

Now, Jung's "A Psychological Approach to the Trinity" would have been his chance to supply the evidence that really substantiates his unusual thesis. As long as the Platonic text could be considered to have provided sound proof for it, we might perhaps not need to bother about

[57] The dictum does precisely not say, "... and out of the third comes the fourth," not even "... and out of the third comes the fourth as the one."

detailed discussions of other examples during the time after Plato that would underpin his view about the Fourth. A short listing of other instances from different centuries that manifest the established signification of the Fourth as realization might have been sufficient. But without the foundation in Plato? And without any other hints to other existing historical evidence?

All that really remains after our examination are the (with respect to the Jungian sense of the Fourth highly dubious) opening words of *Timaeus* and the Goethe passage with a likewise questionable relevance for Jung's thesis. These two isolated, context-less sentences are the two thin twigs up in the air which have to carry, as its *foundation in empirical reality*, the whole weight of the heavy edifice of Jung's personal quaternity theory and, as a consequence of this theory, both his radical attack on two thousand years of trinitarian Christianity and his own salvational doctrine.

Jung has of course presented ample evidence of the 3+1 structure as well as of "square" and "circle" as symbols of wholeness. But this (symbols of wholeness, the existence and occurrence of the formal 3+1 structure in the history of the phenomenology of the soul) is not the issue here. I have also not questioned it. Jung's claim is that the triad and the Trinity are psychologically deficient and that the 3+1 quaternity is the correction of this deficiency. This he was unable to show. And I think it is anyway a serious psychological mistake to see the Trinity as a deficient quaternity and thus to view this one archetypal structure in terms of, or as an incomplete sub-set of, another archetypal structure rather than each as a distinct and independent psychological truth in its own right, with its own dignity and its own specific psychological function, purpose, and meaning. A nomad herdsman is not a deficient agriculturalist. What a mindless blunder to identify the Trinity with the Three in the quaternian 3+1 structure! It shows that nothing has been understood of the peculiar psychological meaning of the Christian Trinity. And as far as the history of the soul is concerned, it seems to me highly questionable to see the quaternity as the future, the coming answer to and final fulfillment of the Trinity. Whereas both quaternity and triadic symbols existed from time immemorial and on the earliest, most primitive levels of civilization (as well as of child development), the *Christian Trinity* is a completely new and unique phenomenon in the history of the soul, a very late acquisition and an absolute peak in the *objective soul's* psychological differentiation, to which, however, not many individuals were and are *personally* able to rise.

PART II
REJECTION OF SPIRIT

TWO GENERAL OBSERVATIONS

Jung's essay on the Trinity has six main chapters, I–VI, (if we count his lengthy "*Schlußbetrachtung*" ["Concluding Reflections," *CW*: "Conclusion"] as one). So far I have only applied myself to chapter I ("Pre-Christian Parallels to the Idea of the Trinity"). After chapter I, Jung, now fully relying on the views he developed through reading Plato's *Timaeus* passages as well-established truths, turns to the Christian Trinity and discusses it with all the various facets that he sees in it and gives his detailed psychological commentary. Before we delve into the details of his presentation, I want to confront his discussion of the Christian Trinity as a whole in his essay with two observations coming from outside. Two observations from very different, completely unrelated areas, that nevertheless, as we will see, will turn out ultimately to provide more or less the same insight. The first observation concerns a question of scholarship standards, namely the fact that in his essay on the Trinity Jung does not discuss, not take note of, indeed not even once mention, Augustine's *De trinitate*. The second observation refers to Jung's personal biography and notes with astonishment the discrepancy, indeed, incompatibility between Jung's reaction to the Trinity as an adult and his original question about the Trinity when as a boy he received his Confirmation instruction. Certainly, both the adult's and the boy's involvement in the topic of the Trinity were passionate. But the discrepancy between the two passions, i.e., the directions into which the interest of the boy and that of the man go apropos one and the same topic is such that one starts wondering whether the boy Jung and the man Jung are not really two totally different persons who merely happen to have the same name and body.

I begin with the first observation. How is it possible that a responsible psychological scholar, in writing a major essay on the Trinity, refers to Plato, Pythagoras, Clement, Irenaeus, Epiphanius, Ambrosius, and a host of others, to the Gnostics and to medieval alchemy—but completely ignores the most essential, profound, and authoritative work on the subject that Christianity has produced in its history, Augustine's *De trinitate*? Absolutely incredible. Jung mentions Ambrosius, who was a teacher of Augustine, but not the latter, who was much more important and a much greater mind. Curiously, Jung's essay opens with a frequently quoted motto taken from another work of Augustine's.

Jung's textual basis for the discussion of the Christian Trinity is mainly the various *symbola* of the early Church. But the symbola relate to a work like *De trinitate* as in scientific journals abstracts relate to the main text of the articles. The symbola are dogmatic declarations, and as such condensations, abbreviated formulas. They can be mindlessly memorized and reeled off. It is inherent in the form of symbola that they do not of themselves require one's living understanding. And since they do not explain but just declare something, they don't offer any help for understanding either. Just as an abstract, at least in the humanities, can only be really understood after one has read the text of the article, so the symbola give not much more than somewhat longer headings. Without a detailed exposition of what in them is condensed to a symbolon, one is really dealing with not much more than words, words, words.

Maybe the *word* "symbolon" that is given to the various articulations of the Christian Creed can throw a light on Jung's focus on them rather than on an extensive highly speculative-thinking work as *De trinitate*. Jung likes to work with symbols as self-contained, stand-alone elements and "psychic facts." Just as he used Goethe's lines from the Cabiri scene of *Faust II* and the *axiom of Maria* each as an isolated self-sufficient unit, so here he takes the compact symbola as thing-like entities, without feeling the need to occupy himself with a lengthy discussion of the complex thinking behind the condensed formulas and what is meant by them.

At this point it may already be helpful to introduce my second observation concerning an episode from Jung's youth. Jung tells us (*MDR* p. 52f., transl. modif.) that his father, the minister,

> gave me my instruction for confirmation. It bored me to death. One day I was leafing through the catechism, hoping to find something besides the sentimental sounding and usually incomprehensible as well as uninteresting expatiations on Lord Jesus. Then I came across the paragraph on the Trinity. Here was something that challenged my interest: a One which was simultaneously a Three. This was a problem that fascinated me because of its inner contradiction. I waited longingly for the moment when we would reach this question. But when we got that far, my father said, "We now come to the Trinity, but we will skip that, for I really understand nothing of it myself." On the one hand I admired my father's honesty, but on the other hand I was profoundly disappointed and said to myself, There we have it; they know nothing about it and also do not think."

When we look at Jung's essay on the Trinity we discover that the problem which, because of its inner contradiction, had fascinated him during his boyhood is not discussed, not even mentioned as a *challenging* problem for the author of the essay, although it is clearly expressed in the last of the symbola quoted and acknowledged as such by Jung (§§ 218f.). The Trinity is, just like that, taken for granted, as a given, and viewed as if it were a simple triad, Father, Son, and Holy Ghost. The author of the essay on the Trinity is only concerned with the triad, what it means and how it is to be judged. The Trinity itself, the One which was simultaneously a Three, this puzzling and fascinating contradiction, does not hold any interest anymore for Jung. But this was the same contradiction that Augustine set out to explore and account for in his work on the Trinity. Jung's ignoring Augustine's text and his having lost his youthful interest about the inner logic of the Trinity fit together.

Showing himself as a faithful son, mature Jung follows in his father's footsteps. Like his father, the minister, he *as* the adult psychologist, so to speak says to himself *as* one who is deeply fascinated by the contradictory question of the One that is Three and the Three that are One: "... but we will skip that." However, other than in the case of his father we cannot admire his honesty, because he did not *openly* skip it, not expressly admit that he did not understand it or was not willing to understand it. He did not, like his father, simply go over to "the next paragraph in the catechism," i.e., to other topics. Rather, he *pretended* (before himself and before us) to be devoting himself with full energy to the full topic of the Trinity and to do justice to it, even providing an answer to the question raised by the Trinity—whereas in reality he had, while retaining the *label,* unwittingly and tacitly exchanged for a totally other one the original question and topic to which the label in truth referred. He had even condemned the Trinity as faulty, and in need to be overcome in favor of the quaternity. Clearly, Jung had betrayed his own original question, his own spontaneous living interest.

The boy Jung had wanted to get *into* the inner logic of the Trinity, its contradictory logical life, or rather he had already been captivated by, and thus transported into, this idea so that he looked at it *from within.* We could also say *his soul* had intuitively been "initiated" into it. By contrast, finding himself thus in it, having his standpoint within it, he *as subjective mind* found himself confronted with its internal contradiction (which had of course also been that very thing that had captivated his soul in the first place) and was naturally totally puzzled. But, being open to the soul, he was also deeply intrigued and fascinated. He was hooked: the One that is Three and the Three that are One. That this contradiction was profoundly important, that it was, as we today could say, a psychic reality and psychological truth, the boy (or the soul in him) had instinctively grasped. Otherwise, if he had only looked at it from outside, it would have been no more than an absurdity or, at best, a curiosity from former times, if, which is the most likely possibility, it would not merely have been one of those things that the adults say needs to be memorized and that one memorizes mechanically without wasting a thought on it.

The boy Jung had *wanted* to think. His was an intellectual interest, a wish to understand. The philosophical question of a logical contradiction had spontaneously and profoundly captured his imagination and was experienced by him as a personal challenge. That the boy Jung felt, was able to feel, this challenge means that implicitly he had already understood what the contradiction inherent in the Trinity means (he was, I said, "initiated" into it); only his conscious mind still needed, but was not yet able, to follow suit. The implicit understanding needed to become an explicit one. Millions of boys in the past had had to read the paragraph about the Trinity in their respective catechisms. But I think it must have been an extremely rare occurrence that one of them felt personally challenged by the contradiction it contained, challenged so much that he could hardly await the moment when it would be explained in Confirmation class. That Jung as a young boy did feel challenged shows that there was a philosophical potential in him, the potential of a thinker.

Adult Jung did not accept this challenge. Indeed, he in all likelihood no longer felt it. He had closed the door on the internal logical issue raised by the Trinity altogether, namely the problem of the contradiction of the One that is Three and the Three that are One. The psychologist Jung was no longer captivated by the Trinity. He therefore did not want to *think* the Trinity, did not *need* to think it either, for the purpose of getting into its inner complexity, its internal life, which is logical life. He had his standpoint outside as a mere psychological observer of "facts." He had left the Trinity-internal issue behind so that the Trinity itself had become for him an object, a wholesale *package* with three different items, figures, entities in it.

And so he could pass judgments *about* it, saying: it is deficient, fundamentally one-sided, does not express wholeness, belongs to the sphere of mere thought, it lacks the weight of the earth. Passing judgments about it means viewing it from the standpoint of externality ("from outside"), and ipso facto unpsychologically (provided that psychology means viewing phenomena *from within*). His replacing the Trinity with the quaternity sealed his external "uninitiated" approach to it. Like the boy Jung about his father, so we, too, are "profoundly disappointed" and can say: "There we have it; he does not know anything about it and also does not think."

Above I compared the symbola to journal abstracts and Augustine's work on the Trinity to the journal articles themselves, their full text, in which the ideas are fully unfolded and explored. We can also use a different comparison. Only taking the symbola into account is as if a psychotherapist only relied on the behavior of the patient visible from outside, while neglecting to listen to the patient's story, to his own explanations, his feelings, perceptions, and ideas, his self-expression. *De trinitate* is so to speak the self-expression, self-elaboration and unfolding of the whole thinking behind and enveloped in the neo-Nicaean symbolon (in the Western, *Latin* theological tradition) of which this symbolon only presents the briefest condensation, in the form of mere assertions, declarations without explanation or argumentation. And *De trinitate* is the profoundest penetration of the Trinitarian idea.

Any critique of whatever theological or philosophical idea must be based on a real understanding of this idea where it is at its best and where its arguments are especially strong, an understanding of its highest and profoundest potential. It is clear that a criticism of an idea on the basis of a merely external apperception of it and a knowledge of poor representations of it does not really criticize that idea but its own limited, superficial version of it and thus falls back on the critic himself.

It is not clear to me whether Jung was simply not aware of Augustine's work on the Trinity or whether he deliberately ignored it. On the one hand, it seems unlikely that he had not come across it in both his studies of the Church Fathers and in the secondary literature he consulted on the Trinity. In numerous works Jung cites passages or ideas from other works of Augustine, and, as already pointed out, he opens his essay with a quote from Augustine's *De veritate*. Jung knew Latin well enough to be able to read *De trinitate*, but, a German translation by Michael Schmaus with notes had been published in 1935–36 as well, which would have allowed Jung to get an easy preliminary access to this work.

On the other hand, in § 221 Jung refers to the *Liber de Spiritu et Anima* from the High Middle Ages (12th century), saying that "already"[58] in it "an attempt of a psychological interpretation of the Trinity was made," and then adding that the train of thought in it starts out from the assumption that by self-knowledge one could attain to a knowledge of God. The *mens rationalis*, that is, the thinking intellect, is said to be what is most similar to God. If it recognizes its own likeness to God it will the more easily recognize its creator. The first (rather external) interesting thing in our context is that Jung quotes this book from Augustine's *Opera omnia* VI edition of 1836 (because it had erroneously been ascribed

[58] In the *CW*, the "already" has been dropped.

to St. Augustine, as Jung notes). So if he came across this minor pseudo-Augustinian work in the printed version of Augustine's *Opera*, why did he not go directly to Augustine's own treatise on the Trinity? One is led to think that he simply must not have been aware of *De trinitate*. And yet, if he found the edition of the rather obscure *Liber de Spiritu et Anima* in the 1836 edition of the *Opera omnia*, one wonders how he could not have come across the more central work.

The second (and more intrinsic) interesting thing is that what Jung finds in this book as "*already*" having been stated in the High Middle Ages, he could precisely have found discussed on a fundamentally higher, subtler level and with much greater speculative strength in Augustine's *De trinitate*, written more than seven centuries earlier. It had been Augustine who discovered that the ability to understand the concept of "Trinity" could not be acquired through one's reading the relevant Biblical passages because in order to understand those passages one already needed this capability to understand it; that therefore another, namely a *natural* approach was necessary, an approach via our human, earthly self-knowledge. In addition to being necessary, this approach was also possible because man was *imago dei*. In his analysis of the internal structure of consciousness, the structure of the human mind, Augustine discovered its trinitarian structure. Here Jung could have found an entry into a truly psychological understanding of the Trinity—"psychological" not according to the modern personalistic (and also the medieval) sense of psychology, but really in the sense of a "psychology" as the discipline of interiority. But Jung mentions this pseudo-Augustinian treatise instead of Augustine's own work, and on top of it mentions it only as a kind of subscript to his chapter on the symbola, where it appears as an isolated curiosity that is not integrated into Jung's overall argument and has no bearing on the three following chapters of his essay.

THE WORM'S EYE VIEW OF THE TRINITY

The first chapter in Jung's essay after his discussion of the pre-Christian parallels to the Christian Trinity, above all in Plato, opens the discussion of the Christian Trinity to which the series of all the remaining chapters is devoted. It is entitled, "Father, Son, and Spirit" and thus turns directly to the main "components" of the Christian Trinity, but introduces right away a distinction between the *logical idea* and the *psychological reality of the Trinity* (§ 196), which "bring us back to the ... ancient Egyptian ideas and hence to the archetype, which provides the authentic and eternal justification for the existence of any trinitarian idea at all." With this in mind, he discusses "The psychological datum" which consists of Father, Son, and Holy Ghost. Pointing out that if there is a father, the idea of a son does not propose any difficulties for us, whereas the idea of the Holy Ghost does not logically follow from those of father and son. It is something special.

For Jung *the Father* refers to a specific psychological condition of the world, a condition of original oneness. In the "world of the father" (which at the same time corresponds to that of man in his childhood state) "man, world, and God form primordially a whole, a unity unclouded by criticism" (§ 201), nor by doubt or moral conflict. The question about the origin of imperfection and evil in the world is here of no concern. But the One cannot be the sole principle of the cosmos. The One has to be supplemented by the Other. And so there is a time when the world of the Father and primordial oneness is superseded by the *world of the Son*. This is a radically new status, characterized by the intrusion of reflection and doubt and thus by the split of the original unity. Earlier Jung had expressed the same psychological progression from the original oneness of the world of the Father to that of the world of the Son or from the One to the Other in terms of number psychology. He said, "one is not a number at all; the first number is two. Two is the first number because, with it, separation and increase begin, which alone make counting possible." "Two implies a 'one' [*eine Eins*] which is different from the uncountable One [*das Eine*]. For when the Two appears, a unit is produced out of the original unity [*tritt aus dem Einen die* Eins *hervor*], and this unit [*Eins*] is none other than that same unity reduced by the splitting and turned into the 'number one' [*das durch die Spaltung geminderte und zur Zahl gewordene Eine*]" (§ 180, transl. modif.).

Being thrown, through the soul's historical development, into the "world of the Son," man "looked longingly *back* to the world of the Father, but it was lost forever, because an irreversible increase in man's consciousness had taken place in the meantime and made it independent." The rupture from the One to the Two is radical. A real cut. Irreversibility. With the emergence of the Two, the original (absolute) One was irretrievably lost. No way back. But on this new level of consciousness things were revealed "that could not possibly have been known in the Father as the One" (§ 203, transl. modif.), just as, conversely, what is revealed, or prevails, in the Father, the (absolute) One, cannot possibly be known in the Son.

When he discussed the transition from One to Two he had said, "With the appearance of the 'Two,' an *Other* appears alongside the one, a happening which is so striking that in many languages 'the other' and 'the second' are expressed by the same word. Associated with it is frequently also the idea of right and left and remarkably enough, of favourable and unfavourable, even of good and bad" (§ 180, transl. modif.). The stage of the Son, as that of the Two, "is therefore a conflict situation *par excellence*" (§ 272), "the world of moral discord" (§ 259), and a "conflict to the last" at that, an "unspeakable conflict posited by duality" (§ 258).

With the Holy Ghost another stage is reached. Like the Egyptian Ka-mutef, "the Holy Ghost is hypostatized procreative power and life-force. Hence, in the Christian Trinity, we are confronted with an actually archaic idea, which, however, possesses such an extraordinary value because it is a hypostatized, supreme representation of *thought-as-such* [*des Gedachtseins*] (two-dimensional triad!)." "A third and connecting element is interposed between 'Father' and 'Son,' an element that is spirit and not a human figure" (§ 197, transl. modif.). "(I)t is precisely not a question of a natural factor [*Naturbedingung*], but of a human reflection that is added on to the natural sequence of father and son" § 235, transl. modif.). "It is precisely of paramount importance that the idea of the Holy Ghost is *not a natural image*, but a recognition, an abstract concept of the living quality of Father and Son as the Third between the One and the Other" (§ 236, transl. modif.). As an idea it "can only be comprehended as resulting from the *interposition of a human process of reflection*" (§ 237 transl. modif.). "... the Holy Ghost represents the completion of the godhead and of the divine drama. For the Trinity is undoubtedly a higher form of God-concept than mere unity since it corresponds to a more reflected, i.e., more conscious condition of mankind" (§ 205, transl. modif.). "Nobody can doubt the manifold superiority of the Christian revelation over its pagan ancestors ..." (§ 206, transl. modif.). Through the Christian "message," "Western man was psychically revolutionized" (§ 222, transl. modif.).

Jung's description of "the world of the Father" and "the world of the Son" represents extremely important and valid insights into the *psychology* of early stages and logical statuses of the development of consciousness. However, why in Heaven's name does he tell us all that in a work about the Christian Trinity? What have the archaic "Father" as original oneness and the "Son" as the Other and as the state of discord got to do with *that* Father and *that* Son that are part of the Trinity? Jung conceives the Trinity as a representation of the development of consciousness, as the image of its own prehistory that led to it, as if it wanted within itself to depict how it came about through historical evolution from an archaic soul condition through an intermediate condition to a higher condition. He historicizes and temporalizes the intra-trinitarian relations.

It is all very well to write about the long prehistory of the Christian idea of the Trinity, certainly an interesting and important topic. But to confuse the prehistory not only with a discussion of the Christian Trinity itself, but also with what this Trinity represents is like confusing modern science with the history of science. Time and again Jung confirms his historicist or developmental interpretation of the Trinity. "The trinitarian conception of a life-process within the Deity ..." (§ 206). "The Trinity and the intra-trinitarian life appear as a self-enclosed circle of a divine drama ..." (§ 226, transl. modif.). "As a psychological symbol the Trinity denotes, first, the homoousia or essential unity of a three-part process, to be thought of as a process of unconscious maturation ..." (§ 287). "... regarded as a psychological symbol, the Trinity represents the progressive transformation of one and the same substance, namely the psyche as a whole" (§ 289). But the Trinity, as an idea that appeared in history, is, to be sure, the *result* or *product* of a long historical process, a progressive transformation of the psyche as a whole, but it is not in itself a process and the depiction of this process. There are not different developmental stages within it; rather, it is what appears when a historical development has arrived at a certain stage, and it expresses the truth of this stage, the God-idea of that consciousness that has reached this stage or logical status. The three persons of the Trinity are not, as Jung presents them, in a diachronic relation, but in a "synchronic" one. Altogether they represent the inner complexity of one and the same new *structure*, sort of the internal constitution, the self-definition of the inner essence of the Christian God as a strictly monotheistic God, or the *logic* of this new God conception, not an historical process.

Jung had expressed his precious insight that the moment when the "world of the Son" was reached, the "world of the Father" and its original oneness was "lost forever." A negation and sublation had happened. The same radical cut and irretrievable loss happens of course also between the "world of the Son" and the stage of the third person in the Trinity, the Spirit, with the result that for it, both the "world of Father" and that of the Son are bygone. The Father of the Trinity and the Son of the Trinity are entirely new psychic ideas or realities. The sameness of the names must not mislead one into confounding them with what "world of the Father" and "world of the Son" means in Jung's psycho-historical description. They are the Holy Ghost's, the Spirit's version of Father and Son. A true new birth: the birth of the Father from the spirit of Spirit. "Everything old has passed away; behold, everything has become new!" The name Father and the name Son are still the same, but they receive a totally new definition. And so the Bible teaches clearly that "God is spirit" and "God is love." Similarly, Christ is "the way, the truth, and the life" (and of course "life" precisely not in the sense of natural life). But for Jung the Father within the Trinity is still the archaic God of the Old Testament and, psychologically, the symbol of archaic oneness. Indeed, the psychological reality of the Trinity "brings us back directly to the—many centuries older—Egyptian conceptions ..." (§ 196, transl. modif.). By the same token we could say that the psychological reality of the atom bomb brings us back directly to the axes of the Stone Age.

Jung has an insight into the irretrievable loss of the old status ("Father") that occurs in a new status ("Son"). But he applies it only on the *content* level and to ancient situations. He does not apply it to his own interpretation, his own thinking and style of consciousness. *His* consciousness while discussing the Trinity is "directly brought back" to the history that lies behind the "world of the Trinity," that is, behind the Holy Ghost stage of consciousness. In other words, he does not himself perform the cut that he talks about. No negation, no sublation; Jung clings to "everything old" despite the fact that according to the new status reached with the Christian Trinity everything old has precisely passed away. If he had applied his insight to his own way of thinking, to the syntax of his own consciousness, then in devoting himself to the theme of the Trinity he could have completely forgotten about all the comments about the prehistory of the Christian Trinity (as interesting and worthwhile they may be as a topic in their own right to be discussed another time).

The Trinity needs to be understood solely in its own terms, on the high level that has been reached with it. The Egyptian and other precursors are of psycho-historical interest, but do not illumine but rather obfuscate the Christian Trinity. Jung, so we must say, practices a *reductio in primam figuram*. Against Freud's psychoanalysis (and with respect to the area of *personal* psychology and neurotic problems) Jung said, "So often its main endeavour seems to lie in trying to explain everything backwards and downwards" (*CW* 10 § 355), whereas Jung opted for trying "to experience what it [a neurosis] means, what it has to teach, what its purpose is" (*ibid.* § 361). But here we see that in his own field, in the area of the objective soul's religious ideas and symbols, Jung falls prey to the same style of backwards and downwards explanation.

This is underlined by several other aspects. Jung emphasizes that there is an internal incommensurability within the Trinity between Father and Son on the one hand and the Holy Ghost on the other hand. "Hence, as the 'third,' the Holy Ghost is bound to be incommensurable, indeed paradoxical" (§ 236). We already heard that "It is precisely of paramount importance that the idea of the Holy Ghost is *not a natural image*, but a cognition, an abstract concept of the living quality of Father and Son as the Third between the One and the Other" (§ 236, transl. modif., Jung's italics). The Holy Ghost "is *psychologically heterogeneous* ..." (§ 237, Jung's italics). Jung asks: "Why, in the name of all that's wonderful, wasn't it 'Father, Mother, and Son?' That would be more 'reasonable' and 'natural' than 'Father, Son, and Holy Ghost.' To this we must answer: it is precisely not a question of a mere natural factor [*eine bloße Naturbedingung*], but of a human reflection that is added on to the natural sequence of father and son. This reflection is the life and characteristic soul abstracted from the natural entities [*vom Natürlichen*]" (§ 235, transl. modif.). In other words, in addition to the temporal difference within the Trinity there is also an ontological division going through the Trinity, separating Father as the One and Son as the Other as natural images or as *Natürliches* from the Holy Ghost as the Third, which is "an artificial construction of the mind" (§ 237). Through the Third, which is thought-as-such, "the masculine relation (father-son) is lifted out of the natural order, which includes mothers and daughters, and translated into a sphere from which the feminine element is excluded .... this special sphere ... is the sphere of primitive mysteries and masculine initiations. ... Through the initiations the young men are systematically alienated from their mothers and are reborn as spirits" (§ 197, transl. modif.). "There can be no doubt that the doctrine of the Trinity originally corresponded with a *patriarchal order of society*" (§ 223, Jung's italics).

Here we see the thoroughly *naturalistic* form of Jung's thinking. To be sure, he goes to great pains to show that the Holy Ghost is precisely nothing natural. But *his own* frame of reference is and remains the natural family. The mother is excluded from this family, in her stead something heterogeneous, a spiritual element is added as an overarching reflective superstructure. The Holy Ghost is *derived* from the natural father-son relation: abstracted from them, a kind of extract, their "life and characteristic soul." Despite Jung's emphasizing the heterogeneity of the Spirit, he still portrays it, or its origin, in naturalistic terms: its procession from the Father and the Son is a *spiration* (§ 197). The Father together with the Son *breathe* the Holy Ghost, and the Holy Ghost *breathes* in man, it is the hypostatized "*breathing* (spirare) and *Hauchen*[59] of the Godhead" (§ 235, transl. modif., Jung's italics).[60]

And above all, the Father and the Son of the Trinity remain to be envisioned by Jung in the context of the human family—a (psychologically) *barbaric* interpretation, just as later, in *Answer to Job*,

[59] "*Hauchen*" is usually also translated with breathing. But it is a soft kind of blowing, different from ordinary blowing in that it comes directly from the lungs.

[60] To be sure, this description is not Jung's invention. He relies on traditional views. But the question is: why does he choose from out of the wealth of conceptions that have come down to us just these naturalistic descriptions rather than the highest forms of understanding the Trinity?

his question, "What kind of father is it who would rather his son were slaughtered than forgive his ill-advised creatures who have been corrupted by his precious Satan? What is supposed to be demonstrated by this gruesome and archaic sacrifice of the son? God's love, perhaps?" (*CW* 11§ 661), portrays a *literally* barbaric interpretation. Of course, if one wishes one can wonder, "What would the Rabbi Jesus have taught if he had had to support a wife and children? If he had had to till the soil in which the bread he broke had grown, and weed the vineyard in which the wine he dispensed had ripened?" (§ 264). But what has the Rabbi Jesus to do with our wish to understand the Christian Trinity? What a barbaric, philistine objection and what an *abaissement du niveau mental*! The sphere of soul has been left, and all of a sudden we are in positivistic practical reality, the sphere of the human, all-too-human, in people's psychology. "The Son" of the Trinity as Joe Blow.

Here may be the place to comment on another of Jung's statements. "'Creation,' i.e., 'matter' is not included in the Trinity formula, at any rate not explicitly. In these circumstances there are only two possibilities for the material world: either it is real, in which case it is an intrinsic part of the divine 'actus purus,' or it is unreal, a mere illusion, because outside the divine reality" (§ 290, transl. modif.). With this idea Jung follows the logic of "either – or": *tertium non datur*. All—or none, and acceptable is of course only "all." No gradation. A similar mediationless "either – or" underlies the statement, "If evil has no substance, good must remain shadowy ..." (§ 247). But the neoplatonic notion of "prohodos," the medieval concept of an *analogia entis* and of evil as a *privatio boni*, the Biblical idea of an *imago dei* (in contrast to God as prototype), Hegel's distinction between *Realität* and *Wirklichkeit*, in general the difference between finite and infinite, Leibniz' idea of monads and the different degrees to which they are capable of reflecting God, etc., are all concepts that have been readily available for many centuries and that allow one to think of a fundamental distinction between God and the material world AND at the same time of the world's being included in God. Jung is unable or unwilling to think that the *factual reality* (Hegel's *Realität*) of evil in the world consists precisely in its *not* verily being real (*wirklich*, actual in Hegel's sense): this, i.e., the situation of something not being in accord with its concept, is what makes it "evil."

All this betrays that Jung makes absolutist demands. *(Logical) negation* and *mediation* as essential aspects of reality are excluded from his thinking and, as his crusade against the *privatio boni* shows, are even supposed to be altogether eliminated. But Jung, of course, does not succeed in getting rid of negation and *privatio*: he merely reifies, hypostatizes them as the "recalcitrant Fourth," evil, Satan. They, as it were, are the return of the repressed. What ought to be psychological, namely a logical form of thinking, part of the syntax of consciousness, is externalized, namely ontologized and reified as a "reality," i.e., a semantic content and part of a world view (a scheme of the divine depth of the world, Jung's *Ganzheitsformel*).

By insisting that the material world can only be real if it is an intrinsic part of the divine 'actus purus' (nothing less!), Jung actually betrays, *malgré lui*, his (unconscious) contempt for the material world in its deficiency (privation) and finiteness. He cannot forgive the world that it is deficient. But he cannot deny its deficiency either. As a way out of this dilemma, he simply *immediately and absolutely divinizes the deficiency per se*: he performs its *assumptio* into the "actus purus"! The moment "evil" and the imperfection of the world are thus "kicked upstairs," the deficiency no longer hurts. It is now no longer truly deficient. It is, after all, divine, transfigured! Psychologically this is the rage-inspired move of a child[61] that simply refuses to accept disillusionment or disenchantment and to wake up from the dream of perfection and sympathetic oneness. Rather absorb evil into the pleroma itself than own up to the loss of the dream of the pleroma as a present reality altogether. Rather allow, on the semantic level, the harmony, beauty, and innocence of the pleroma to be wrecked by the direct presence of evil within it, than admit that the syntax of "pleroma" has been lost. One's *logical status* of "pleromatic existence" must be rescued at all cost, even if the price is that the truly *pleromatic nature* of the pleroma has to be given up. But, this we must add, a *rescued* logical status or syntax is ipso facto phony.

If Jung had not avoided Augustine's *De trinitate*, he could have read there that the human family is not suitable as a model for understanding the Christian Trinity. How can one insist on a heterogeneity of Father+Son, on the one hand, and the Holy Ghost,

---

[61] "Child" like "puer" and "senex" as a psychological stance and not as a literal age.

on the other hand, if what is called by the old name "Father" is (on the new level of consciousness reached with the idea of the Trinity) comprehended to be Spirit just like the Holy Ghost? Father and Holy Ghost are of equal rank and on the same level. The same insight that Jung had about the Holy Ghost as fundamentally removed from "the natural order," from "the masculine relation (father-son)," and *vom Natürlichen*, applies just the same to the Father and the Son of the Trinity. They are just as much *thought-as-such* and products of reflection as the Holy Ghost is, or else there is no real Trinity. Jung does not allow the Father to rise to the new level of consciousness, the Holy Ghost stage. He weighs him down with the weights of the natural and the weights of the past, of what he formerly used to be in archaic or Old-Testament times. The cut, the negation, the sublation is prevented. And here it is precisely Jung's historicist, developmental conception of the "divine drama" or "process" which helps him to hold the Father (and also the Son) down: instead of letting *him* "develop" and fundamentally outgrow, overcome, leave behind, the naturalistic "definition" of him, the Father (or Jung's "the world of the father") is conceived as having this development *outside of him* in *others*, in consecutive stages, that of the Son and of the Holy Ghost, so that the Father and the original condition can remain what they had been before (although now within the Trinity). The development is not allowed to come home to that from which it started and to "revolutionize" it in the sense of giving it a completely new definition (Jung had conceded a revolutionizing effect on Western man only to the Holy Ghost element of Trinity). This is a psychology as a discipline of externality.

It is ridiculous to see the Trinity as a reflection of the patriarchal order of society and to speak with respect to Father and Son (insofar as they are "persons" within the Trinity) of a masculine relation and say that the mother has been excluded. This is precisely proof of Jung's clinging to the natural human family as his interpretative paradigm and to the literal, everyday meaning of the word-symbols used ("father," "son"). But the Father has become Spirit in the sense of the Holy Ghost. Is this Spirit masculine? Can one apply to it the difference between the sexes, male-female, the preferred categories of primitive thinking and of psychological naturalism (nowadays hardly disguised as gender studies)? It does not make any sense to say that the mother has been excluded unless one really wants to push the Trinity back down to the level of "primitive mysteries and masculine initiations." Together with "literal father," the term mother has become obsolete on the Trinity level of consciousness.

In a paper about "The Freud-Jung Antithesis"[62] Jung criticized what he thought was the "vicious circle" in which Freudian psychology is caught. "There is nothing in it," he wrote about the latter,

> that would offer a possibility for escaping the inexorable straightjacket of the biological. In despair we would have to cry out with St. Paul: "Wretched man that I am, who will deliver me from the body of this death?" And the spiritual man in us comes forward, shaking his head, and says in Faust's words: "Thou art conscious only of the single urge," namely of the fleshly bond leading back to father and mother or forward to the children that have sprung from our flesh—"incest" with the past and "incest" with the future, the original sin of perpetuation of the "family romance." There is nothing that can free us from this bond except that opposite urge of life, the spirit. ... In Ernst Barlach's play *The Dead Day*, the mother-daemon says apropos the tragic ending of the family romance: "The strange thing is that man will not learn that God is his father." That is what Freud would never learn, ... We moderns are faced with the necessity of experiencing the spirit again, that is, to have primordial experience [*Urerfahrung*]. This is the only possible way to break through the magic circle of the biological (*CW* 4 § 780, transl. modif.).

From his whole psychology it is obvious that Jung had successfully broken through the magic circle of the biological, overcome the fleshly bond leading back to father and mother, and that in contrast to Freud he had learned the lesson pronounced by Barlach's mother-daemon "that God is man's father." But the utterly astounding thing is that in his theology or theosophy, that is to say, precisely in that very domain that is explicitly beyond the straightjacket of the biological and that is the expression of "the spiritual man in him," it comes out that Jung himself commits that "original sin of perpetuation of the 'family romance'" that he accuses Freud of. The syntax or logical form of his thinking makes him perceive and judge the Christian Trinity in terms

[62] *CW* 4 renders the title as "Freud and Jung: Contrasts."

of father and mother. In the innermost structure of his mentality the magic circle of the biological still rules. It informs the style of thinking with which he approaches the not-biological, the Spirit and God. "That opposite urge of life, the spirit," has unwittingly become infiltrated, or rather been taken prisoner, by "the single urge." In his theosophy, on the higher level of the spiritual, Jung *malgré lui* proves, as it were, to be a dyed-in-the-wool Freudian. So we see that his having overcome the inexorable straightjacket of the biological is reserved for the semantics of his psychology. It takes place only on the literal level, in the personalistic (psychic) sphere, but not logically, not psychologically: not "in spirit and in truth."[63]

It should actually go without saying that for a truly psychological understanding of any new psychic configuration such as the Trinity, i.e., for a *thinking* approach to it, the peak insight, or the highest point of the development of consciousness reached with this configuration, has to be the standard and measure for every internal detail of the whole configuration. Jung himself considers the Holy Ghost to be the "culmination of the trinitarian process" (§ 236, transl. modif.). One's conception of the Father and the Son must not fall short of the highest category and of the most advanced and differentiated cognition achieved, here the Holy Ghost. In the telos, the fulfillment and pinnacle of the whole development of consciousness (up to that point), *not* in their beginnings or past history, do they too have their truth. That many Christian authors both in the early Church and later had not really attained to the highest level of comprehension that had already been reached by the deepest Christian insight itself, and that they thus often tried to interpret the Trinity in outdated naturalistic terms, must not be used as an excuse for the modern psychologist.

The ultimately *ontological* character of the incommensurability postulated by Jung comes out most clearly in his view that the Holy Ghost is "the hypostatizing of a quality" (or "property," § 239), a

[63] How inadequate his notion of the spirit is comes also out in the above quotation. Nothing else but the spirit can free us from the fleshly bond, he had said, but in the last two sentences we hear what his notion of the spirit is: it is *Urerfahrung*, primordial experience—as if spirit were something semantic, an event, an object of our experience, and not much rather truly *spirit*, the spirit *in which* we live and *through which* we apperceive the world and what happens, the spirit that permeates and informs our thinking, but as the Spirit in the Christian sense is also at work in the depth of the life of the world.

"hypostatization of an attribute" (§ 235, cf. also the whole discussion in § 197), namely the natural beings' abstracted life that has been "endowed with a separate existence" (§ 235). So only Father and Son are substances, substantial realities, while the Holy Ghost has the nature of a mere attribute, and as "an hypostatized noumenon tacked on to the natural family-picture of father and son" (§ 236) it *ipso facto* lacks the reality of a substance. It is, after all, only "an artificial construction."

Here we again see how Jung falls short of a congenial understanding of the Trinity (and of an understanding of psychology[64]). From the Trinity's own point of view the Holy Ghost is by no means an attribute, but a full, substantial reality, indeed the highest and innermost truth of reality. It is not an abstraction from the natural. It is precisely the other way around. The natural images are the abstract attributes abstracted from the actual "substance," from the Holy Ghost.

In archaic times the human mind was merely not yet able to free itself from the *unio naturalis*. The Spirit[65] that had been the truth of reality and a substantial reality all along and even then, could under these conditions of the mind not yet be apperceived as such. It had, for the consciousness of those times and peoples, still been far too much imprisoned in the matter, in the physical of the material, which for that reason clung and stuck to it the way it was represented in the concepts of people. Therefore the abstraction process described by Jung does not tell us anything about the origin of the Holy Ghost, but only about the long-lasting attempts of *the human mind* finally

---

[64] For psychology all ideas, even the most primitive and natural sounding ones, are not natural, but "artificial constructions." Soul-making! Free inventions and fabrications by the soul for its own purposes, merely often cloaked in natural images. Reality of the soul.

[65] The understanding of the use of the word "spirit" in Jungian psychology is hampered by Hillman's setting spirit and soul radically apart as mutually exclusive opposites: "spirit" belongs to the peaks, "soul" to the vale, etc. As insightful and valuable as this distinction is as a description of one possible, very specific distinction on the *semantic, phenomenological* level (for particular contexts), it must not go to the head of the psychologist and be used as the syntactical criterion for deciding what psychology itself is and what not. Originally, soul and *Geist*, ghost, spirit were synonymous. And the soul as such in its innermost nature IS *Geist*, now as ever (what else could it be?), even if *within itself* soul at times differentiates between itself as soul and itself as spirit ("spirit" now in a narrower sense) or between anima and animus. The soul as the subject-matter of psychology with its infinite phenomenology must not be reduced to and identified with one particular manifestation of itself, e.g., the anima.

to come home to itself, to free itself from its initial inevitable naturalism. The appearance of the idea of the Holy Ghost is the moment in the (Western) history of the mind when, as the culmination of a long development that had started with the Greek shift from *mythos* to *logos*, the mind had at long last become capable of realizing that the Spirit is, and has always been, its own true reality and truth. Here the Spirit had *for human consciousness* come home to itself, that is to say, here the mind or soul or consciousness has conceived its true origin. In history, for a true psychology at least, the origin does not lie in the past and in the beginnings, but in the telos, the culmination. It has to be born.

In his view of personal psychology and of neurotic pathology, Jung had from early on opted for a final-constructive ("what it means," what it is heading for; the symptom as the first immediacy of a new personality that wants to emerge) in contrast to a causal-reductive approach. Similarly, in his alchemical studies he would never have taught that the prime matter in its initial and miserable state as *massa confusa* is the real thing. He knew that the whole point of the *opus* was to bring out for the first time the truth of the matter. And he knew full well that all the torturous processes of the alchemical work, *mortificatio*, *putrefactio*, *calcinatio*, *corruptio*, *divisio*, etc., did not aim to abstract a mere noumenon from the natural matter and hypostatize it, but, on the contrary, to ruthlessly and pitilessly strip off the physical of the matter in order to free the spirit Mercurius who was "the beginning, the middle, and the end of the procedure." Two very different instances in Jung's own work of basically the same figure of thought.

But when it came to the Trinity, Jung reversed this order. He regressively insisted on the natural as the real substance and denied the Holy Ghost true reality. He refused to get an adequate understanding of the Holy Ghost (and I say "refused" because we know from his deep involvement in the question of the Trinity during his Confirmation time that he had all it needed to become initiated into the Spirit and had already from within himself been set on its track). The Spirit stayed ultimately a hypostatized noumenon for him (which is mirrored by the fact that the other two "persons" within the Trinity, above all the Father, retained their pre-Christian natures).

Jung's thesis of the heterogeneity between Father-Son and Holy Ghost amounts psychologically to a dissociation. Whereas in truth the Trinity idea is all of one piece, one uniform whole, Jung (who certainly did not think himself to be merely a hypostatized noumenon) placed himself firmly on the positivistic earth with the natural images of Father and Son and kept the Holy Ghost high above himself in the sky, like a balloon, as a mere abstraction and noumenon, although he knew full well that man is (and should know himself to be) an "arbor inversa," a tree that has its roots in the sky and its treetops in the earth (*CW* 13 § 410 ff.). He kept his roots in the naturalism of the imagination, in a picture thinking in terms of visible things or the human family.

But *psychologically* this naturalism means—perhaps for some paradoxically—that his was a fundamentally *abstract* thinking, a thinking located up in the clouds: because the *psychological* Tree has its ground in Heaven and its top in the earth. In the syntax of his own thought, Jung avoids the inversion. The idea of the Father and the Son as substantially real, that is, the naturalistic interpretation, is precisely that very abstraction and that noumenon that Jung wishes to ascribe to the Spirit in the Trinity. The same applies to his ideas of the Fourth (the "Mother of God," matter, evil as ontologically real). As ideas or images they are bubbles. And by trying to improve the Trinity through his adding the Fourth, Jung in fact pursues a derealization of the Trinity (in contrast to a supercession of it, as *he* thinks). The mere fact that something is an idea *of* matter and substantiality does of course not turn that idea itself into a substantial reality. To come *psychologically* down to earth from cloud-cuckoo-land requires precisely that that which for the naturalistic, uninverted view is a mere noumenon and an abstraction from nature has become one's standpoint: the ground on which one stands, and the true reality and substance. Only then has one entered the sphere of psychology.

Jung had caught sight of the idea of the Holy Ghost, but he refused to let it come home to him. For him it was and remained no more than a semantic content of his consciousness. It did not "infiltrate," "infect," subvert and thus restructure the logical form of his consciousness. No "behold, *everything* has become new!" No redefinition of the trinity as a whole (let alone of the world). Jung did not *think* the Holy Ghost, but only "dreamed" and talked about it. He did not let it become real in his thinking, a substantial reality in the *psychological* sense. He did not do his homework.

And this is also why for him the Holy Ghost "points ... into the future, to a continuing realization of the 'spirit' ..." (§ 272). Even two thousand years after its appearance, it has for Jung not yet become a present reality. Jung defers it constantly into the future. "The further development of the [Christian] myth," he tells us in *Memories, Dreams, Reflections* (p. 333, transl. modif.) concerning his hope and program for the *future*, "should probably begin with the outpouring of the Holy Spirit upon the apostles ...." As if this further development had not begun precisely at that moment back then and as if it had not already long since step by step taken place in reality, in the real history of the West (of which Jung himself, after all, once admitted that it was revolutionized by the Trinity idea, § 222)! What he envisions for the future, the realization of the 'spirit,' had already been accomplished fact for two centuries at least (although ordinary consciousness, because it refuses to place itself firmly on the standpoint of the Spirit, is as a matter of course not aware of it).

The lack of reality of the Spirit in Jung's understanding is the one explanation for his obsession with the topic of "realization." It is not "the archetype of the triad, which calls for the fourth to complete it." What calls for the Fourth is, unbeknownst to Jung, his own feeling of lack. Because *he* has not made the Spirit real for and in himself, that is, because *he* has not irrevocably *made it the standpoint and principle* of his perspective, he experiences a fundamental lack and thus also the need for a—future—realization of what *through his own act (or rather neglect)* is set up as a *mere* thought-thing, a *mere* noumenon. The reality that he misses is the result of *his* refusal to make the semantic content of his consciousness real by letting it come home to himself and turning it into his ground and foundation. Reality in a psychological sense is not a given. Reality has to be *made* by us, although not in an ego or technical sense, but through our self-exposure to what wants to become real.

But this is what Jung, at least as far as the Trinity idea and the Holy Ghost are concerned, did not allow to happen. Instead, he strove for an *external* solution, a kind of mechanical, technical solution: through the addition of "the Fourth." Because *he* did not rise to the level of the Third, did not allow the Third to become real in and for him, to become his own binding reality and the real standpoint of his thinking, he wants to add "reality" to it as if reality (actuality) were an *ingredient* that could be added to a noumenon to make it real. Add a pinch of shadow, of Evil, of the Feminine, of Mother to the Three and it will cease being a mere noumenon and become a reality. The Fourth is supposed to do the job for him that Jung himself did not do. Psychologically, "reality" in the sense of this context is something fundamentally intrinsic, a subjective event and logical act in me, in the syntax of my soul, not something that could be added as the fourth to a triadic structure on the level of semantic contents. And here it makes no difference whatsoever whether the addition is thought of as an ego addition or as one coming from and happening in the unconscious: the externality and schematic nature of such a realization project via an addition of an ingredient is the same in both cases. "The Fourth" is an excuse and scapegoat so that the subject (the I) might escape unscathed.

The second and complementary explanation for Jung's obsession with the topic of "realization" is that against appearances his real standpoint, his naturalism, is (*psychologically*) without ground. It is up in the air, purely "theoretical" (in the pejorative sense). This lack of reality of his own position created (or immediately manifested itself as) a powerful unconscious desire informing his consciousness, a desire for something that might provide the missing reality. Jung's conscious mind tried to turn this desire into a rational theory. But the strong affect and the defensiveness that accompany this theory show that it is not simply rational. At any rate, psychological reality cannot be obtained by a stop-gap, by the Fourth, through the addition of some other element. What it needs is (in our context) that precisely the Third, this airy nothing and no-thing (David Miller), is turned into one's real starting-point and the true substance.

Adding "Evil" or "the Feminine" to the Trinity does not provide *any more* (psychological) reality to it than the algebraic fourth did to the three-part algebraic formula. A formula stays a formula, a noumenon, no matter how many or what kind of elements you add. Something is psychologically real only to the extent that it is the truth out of which I live, the real conviction that in fact determines my behavior and informs my thinking. And this applies to all types of contents or beliefs, to polytheism, to monadic monotheism, to trinitarian monotheism, to Marxism-Leninism, Maoism, pacifism, or what have you. Any noumenon, be it the greatest illusion or delusion, that takes possession of me and has really formed my *character* is *ipso facto* psychologically real. Psychological realness is a question of character and one's real attitude. It is not a *numeric* issue. The whole topic of the Fourth as the bringer of reality is psychologically pointless, when the topic is the Trinity.

Just as is Jung's obsession with the Fourth in general,[66] so is also his obsession with the reality of evil in particular fired by something in his own stance, in this case: by his own defection from his very own original question about the Trinity and from his chosen subject, the Trinity itself. The ideas of the "counter-will" and the "adversary" are objectified theoretical reflections of his own attitude towards his own soul and truth. The adversary attitude in him (him as mind, as psychological thinker, not him as civil man) insists on receiving an expression, and since it is expelled from the syntax of his own thinking style, it necessarily has to insist on manifesting as a content, an objective reality in the very scheme of the world, so as not to appear as a subjective problem of his. This is what gives to the "counter-will," the "recalcitrant fourth," and the "adversary" their enormous importance in Jung's passionate fight against the privatio boni theory of evil.

In reality, Jung's topic was not reality and realization, but "wholeness," but he oddly identified the striving for wholeness with a striving for realization. Something that is incomplete is just as real as something that is whole. Through becoming aware of my shadow, for example, I do not become more real, but only more conscious and differentiated.

The interest in "wholeness" expresses a completely abstract, schematic thinking. Jung speaks time and again of *Ganzheitsurteil* ("judgement expressing wholeness," e.g., §§ 246, 247, 264. *CW* says "whole judgement"), *Ganzheitsformel* (§ 242, *CW* says "formula of wholeness"), and *Ordnungsschema* (§ 246, "ordering schema," *CW* translates "coefficient of order"; and § 281, *CW*: "organizing schema"), and in §§ 256 and 258 we get schematic diagrams. These concepts

---

[66] Here one might ask with Greg Mogenson (personal communication): Was "the Fourth" real for Jung?

are incompatible with the concern of the Trinity, no matter whether one applies "formula of wholeness" directly to the Trinity (as in § 242) or, conversely, criticizes the Trinity for not being an adequate *Ganzheitsurteil* (as usually)—as if the Trinity claimed and wished to be a formula expressing wholeness. Its concern is with *Geist*, with living spirit, with the distillation, sublimation of the traditional naturalistic God-concept, with the latter's intellectual-spiritual redefinition, and *ipso facto* with raising consciousness as a whole and as such to a corresponding new plane. This has nothing whatsoever to do with "wholeness." Jung misses the point of the Trinity and confronts it instead with an incommensurable, purely idiosyncratic interest of his own. Polemicizing against certain rationalistic and intellectualistic interpretations of the Trinity, Jung states that "it never occurs to these critics that their way of approach is incommensurable with their object" (§ 228). Obviously this applies not only to *these* critics.

Formulas of wholeness and ordering schemata are sterile, pedantic, rigid structures, really mindless (spiritless). They are appropriate for the ego that wants to finds its bearings in the world (Jung's scheme of the four orientation functions in his typology) and gain control over reality (reality as created by the ego for its needs of control). And they betray the presence of a mind-frame that in its theorizing looks for a "mechanical" or technical solution and is still in the status of a representational or object-consciousness. The ego as viewing subject has the quaternity diagrams vis-à-vis and in front of itself. "Wholeness" is supposed to happen out there sort of mechanically in the formula or schema, in the object or semantic content of consciousness, or in the image "from the unconscious," with the I or consciousness itself as the fundamentally external and detached observer. But even where quaternity appears as a spontaneous symbol, it does not mean or bring wholeness, but rather the *idea* or *fantasy* of wholeness, that is to say, it tends to induce a psychological state of detachment from particularities of life, the state of a distanced overview over an abstract (alleged) whole (mandalas as schematic images of the whole world as seen from outer space, as it were!), and puts the soul at rest, into a meditative state, perhaps after (and at any rate in contrast to) a passionate involvement and entanglement of consciousness in particular concrete issues of life. In their own phenomenology there is no indication that mandalas, for example, have to be seen in terms of a developmental scheme and represent the idea of the final goal of a long individuation process. They are, just like all symbols, *particular* images for particular soul situations and soul concerns, images that can pop up, and have their place, at all sorts of moments within the changing flow of life and on very different levels of the history of consciousness.

To want to get reality in a "formula of wholeness," through the addition of a Fourth to the Trinity, implies that consciousness or the I wants to keep out of it (which in Jung's case is furthermore nicely illustrated by his deferring the Holy Ghost, a discovery of two millennia ago, to the future). But reality in a psychological sense comes exclusively about through *my* wholehearted entering that which is to become real, *my* committing myself and going all the way through with it. Reality depends on my "leap after the throw,"[67] my leaping in accordance with the *Hic Rhodus, hic salta* dictum. Jung tries to get away with a cheap "*judgment* of wholeness," in other words, a mere noumenon.

Jung's *negative* move of refusing to let himself in for the peak idea of his subject-matter, the Spirit within the Trinity, on the one hand, and his *positive* move of advocating the addition of the Fourth for the purpose of achieving "worldly materiality" (§ 251), on the other hand, together make up his psychological *materialism*. The latter amounts to his stabbing psychology in the back, to a regression behind the *opus contra naturam*. Of what possible concern can worldly materiality, the world of positive facts, external reality (*realitas vulgi*) be to psychology? Psychology is the discipline of interiority.

I had mentioned that whereas in archaic times the spirit had still been "imprisoned" in worldly materiality, the appearance of the idea of the Holy Ghost was the moment in Western history when the mind had come home to itself. "Mythology" is the name for the state of the imprisoned spirit. Psychology also speaks of a "projection" into the external world. In a way there is a grain of truth, but no more than a grain, in Jung's characterizing Plato's and the Christian Trinity's standpoint as paintings of airy thoughts. But the "mere thought" quality as which he denounces this standpoint is in truth only the

---

[67] This is a reference to my essay "The Leap After the Throw. On 'Catching Up With' Projections and on the Origin of Psychology," in: W. G., *The Neurosis of Psychology*, New Orleans, LA (Spring Journal Books) 2005, pp. 69–96.

external appearance of the fact that now the world has been seen through, has been reflected-into-itself, has become interiorized.

Jung's fundamental error is the confounding of two differences, (1) the positive-factual difference between "mere thought" in its abstractness or "representations" in the mind, on the one hand, and the real in the sense of worldly materiality, on the other hand, and (2) the logical difference between the intelligible and the sensible / natural / positive-factual. The intelligible is what cannot be known through external experience. Jung reductively identifies the first term of the second difference with the first term of the first difference, misreading the historical discovery of the intelligible and logically negative character of certain realities such as the Ideas and the soul or mind as "mere thought" without reality. That there has been a shift in the history of the soul from the mythologizing naturalism of object-consciousness to the self-consciousness of both the soul of man and the soul of the real as something not-natural, not-sensible, but intelligible, and that reflection has become the new standpoint of consciousness, is ignored by Jung.

Actually, however, this is not quite correct. Jung *had* realized that there has been a fundamental shift, "that there are peoples and epochs where it [the soul] is outside, peoples and epochs that are unpsychological, as, for example, all ancient cultures" (which is what I referred to as the time of "mythology," the time of the imprisonment of the spirit in the physical of the matter) and he *had*, by contrast, explained the emergence of psychology by the fact that modern man had *outgrown* the traditional form of religion and that only for this reason we today have a psychology (see *CW* 10 §§ 158–161). He had fully accepted *as a fact* (i.e., positivistically) that the time of myth and the gods and spirits out there in nature was over. He knew and stated that one could not go back behind *the modern level of spirit, reflection, and psychology.* He was fully aware of and had acknowledged the fact that "God is dead,"[68] as we can clearly see already in his *Red Book.*

But instead of also *logically* simply going along with this movement, so clearly seen and acknowledged by him, and taking his standpoint

[68] See also Wolfgang Giegerich, "God Must Not Die! C.G. Jung's Thesis of the One-Sidedness of Christianity," in: *Spring 2010,* Vol. 84 (God Must Not Die! Or Must He?), Fall 2010, pp. 11–71. Now Chapter Four in the present volume.

in its result (the absolute negativity of the soul or in the spirit), Jung in his thinking and theorizing counteracted this historical development by inventing, as it were, a new "physical in the matter," namely "the unconscious" as a new positivity, a stratum or organ in the human animal. And instead of conceiving this historical process in terms of his own alchemical categories as one of distillation, sublimation, vaporization (and its result merely for *this* reason as "airy" and "weightless": absolute-negative, intelligible), Jung imagined a "fall of the stars" from heaven into the unconscious (*CW* 9i § 50), and the spirit's descending from its fiery heights and its becoming *heavy* and turning into *water* (*CW* 9i § 32)—an unmistakable avowal of his fundamental naturalism.

The invention of "the unconscious" therefore really amounts to nothing else than a "naturalization" (positivization) *of the status of reflection as such*, a status that had unmistakingly already been reached by Jung, as we have seen: "the collective unconscious" IS the hypostatized and submerged (and only in this sense also repressed) *reflectedness, sublatedness,* and *obsolescence* of "the stars," i.e., of the old world of the gods and God. God *is* no more, but this "*no more*," the pastness of the past, is substantiated and literalized as "the unconscious" and through this substantiation turned into its opposite: a *present* reality, indeed the "ever-present maternal ground and primordial source" of all ideas, mythic images, gods. This is why "the unconscious"—as the dissimulated "no more"—is the only place where, according to Jung, today God can be found (as "the Self"). Reflection as a state of the mind, a purely mental, intelligible reality, was literally pressed down from the "fiery heights," the level of living thought, into the solid state of an ontic, empirically given (almost biological) part of the personality.

Small wonder that Jung had difficulties with the Holy Ghost and the Trinity.

His move was therefore not really atavistic, because, as I pointed out, he did not want to go back. No, *on* the fundamentally new level of the modern soul he wanted to add, as the Fourth, the simulation (or simulacrum) of the archaic worldly materiality to his scheme as the new psychologistic, introjected replica of the mythological world of old, thereby imprisoning the spirit in matter again (or rather entertaining the counterfactual fantasy of the imprisonment of the spirit). Too late, of course, since with the emergence of the idea of the Holy Ghost the spirit had already in fact escaped the bottle long ago and had become active as the transformative agent in the cultural history of the West.

Jung warns, "Anyone who does not understand the events that befall him is always in danger of getting stuck in the transitional stage of the Son" (§ 276), but without realizing that this is exactly what happened to him. Because he did not understand and rise up to the level of the Third, his mind-set remained stuck in "the world of the Two." The stage of the Son was defined by Jung as "a conflict situation *par excellence*" (§ 272), "the world of moral discord" (§ 259), and a "conflict to the last" at that, an "unspeakable conflict posited by duality" (§ 258). When we look at his diagrams we immediately see that absolute moral *opposition* is the guiding perspective that informs Jung's own thinking. Jung thinks in the terms of Good and Evil, Christ and the Devil/Lucifer/Satan as his main categories (in this area). His whole passion goes into this opposition as well as into his attack on Christianity for not doing justice to this oppositional structure. About the devil Jung states, "As the adversary of Christ, he would have to take up an equivalent counterposition [*Gegensatzposition*] and be, like him, a 'son of God'" (§ 247). Equivalent counterposition! This is precisely what is depicted in Jung's diagrams. (It is also well known that, quite apart from the present diagrams and the special topic of the Trinity, the opposites as a general thought structure play a significant role in Jung's entire psychological thinking.)

This is a point at which we also realize that the *quaternity* does by no means transcend and supersede the Trinity, but rather regresses behind it to "the world of the Son" and the oppositionalism determining it. The quaternity is simply two pairs of opposites at right angles to each other; it is, as it were, merely the duplication of "the world of the Two." Psychologically, however, 2 x 2 is not more than 3, namely 4, but less, namely again only 2. It is 2 because what counts psychologically is the prevailing oppositional thought-structure (syntax), the conflict thinking. By holding the two pairs of opposites neatly apart as well as holding the opposites within each pair as fixed, strictly self-identical opposites, Jung does not allow the Spirit to become active and effective so that it would permeate and revolutionize, indeed reinvent the whole rigid structure from within itself (much like the Biblical leaven or yeast or the alchemical "fermenting corruption"). The Third is immobilized, depotentiated, reduced to a numeric third. Jung allows himself to be misled by the mathematical (the *counting* mind's) number four into thinking that his scheme was an advance beyond the Trinity associated with the number three, whereas it is the (disguised) celebration of the refusal to rise to the level of the Trinity. Jung looks at the Trinity from the worms' eye perspective.

The radically oppositional structure of Jung's thinking also comes out in his well-known preference for thinking psychologically in terms of violence and the clash of opposite wills, of being compelled, being overwhelmed against one's own will. Jung's definition of God as "the name by which I designate all things which cross my wilful path violently and recklessly ...,"[69] his repeated reference to God as "counter-will" (§ 290, transl. modif.), to man's "ability to 'will otherwise,'" to his "disobedience and rebellion,"[70] Jung's assertion that individuation "always amounts to a collision of duties" (all § 291, transl. modif.), his idea of empirical man's having to suffer "from the violence done to him by the self"[71] (§ 233, *Vergewaltigung durch das Selbst*: the first word is also the usual German term for "rape")—these are some of the formulations that betray the general fantasy informing Jung's consciousness in these matters, a fantasy that clearly reflects the violent character of his own time, the age of Industrial Modernity with its heavy industry, its steel works, its colonialism and imperialism, its class struggles, world wars, its totalitarian systems and accompanying resistance movements. God, defined as violently and recklessly overpowering force, is conceived in the image and likeness of Stalin, Hitler and all the other totally abstract, ruthless dictators of the first half of the 20th century.

[69] *Letters 2*, p. 525, to M. Leonard, 5 December 1959. Cf. "[...] 'God' is the overwhelming experience κατ' ἐξοχήν" *ibid.* p. 275, to Hilty, 25 October 1955.

[70] The *CW* translate "*Empörung*" erroneously with "self-disgust" instead of "revolt or rebellion."

[71] In a footnote Jung backs this up with the reference to his probably favorite Biblical story of Jacob's struggle with the angel at the ford.

This is an idiosyncratic definition of God. Of course, Jung believes that this had been the meaning of the term "God" at all times ("I use this term because it has been used for this kind of experience since time immemorial. From this point of view any gods, Zeus, Wotan, Allah, Yahweh, the *Summum Bonum* etc. have their intrinsic truth."[72]). But are Zeus, Wotan, Allah, the *Summum Bonum* indeed defined as this kind of *personal experience*, as powers "which cross my wilful path violently and recklessly"? Are they not first and foremost cosmic realities? For the Old Testament God one can of course adduce the experiences of the prophets and to some extent perhaps Jung's own example of Jacob's struggle with the angel. Here there can indeed be found an "unbearably exaggerated I-Thou relationship"[73] in the sense of a clash between two wills, a human will and the overwhelming power of a personal God as a true Thou. Jung might also have thought of how Saul was violently thrown off his horse and turned into Paul. But precisely this story would not support his definition of God, because St. Paul's God is not defined as a ruthless overwhelming one. God is the God of justice and love, whose *peace* surpasses all comprehension. It is St. Paul's God who in Jesus Christ underwent the *kenôsis*. St. Paul's *personal* conversion *experience* did precisely not enter the *definition* of his *God*. It was merely his *particular way to* the Christian God, and with its violent character it symbolizes the transitionless abruptness that *logically* separates the Old Testament God from the New Testament one, the switch from the

[72] *Letters 2*, p. 276f., to Hilty, 25 October 1955.

[73] I take this phrase from *CW* 9i § 11 where Jung speaks of Europeans who "landed themselves in a Kierkegaardian neurosis, or whose relation to God, owing to the progressive impoverishment of symbolism, developed into an unbearably exaggerated [*zugespitzt*] I-You relationship [...]" (transl. modif.). By reducing God in his definition of Him to the clash with an overpowering will, Jung himself exemplifies the "progressive impoverishment of symbolism" bemoaned by him. God is reduced to sheer power, to the abstract, utterly formal aspect of being the counter-will. The richness of material predicates, of substantial contents, of imaginal qualities, in the definition of God is lost. From here it becomes immediately apparent why Jung also insisted on comprehending God as the *coniunctio* of Good and Evil. "Good and Evil" is the *conceptualization* and *reification* of the *experiential* clash of wills; it is this clash sublimated into an abstract thought, a universal principle. (Good and Evil are the zero form of the mythic or imaginal, and historically the transition point from image to abstract concept.) And conversely, in the human experience of being overwhelmed by God, the inner nature as which—according to this definition—God as supreme principle *is*, is enforced and enacted *between* God and man.

mythically imagined and ritualistically worshiped God to the radically post-natural, post-imaginal Christian God. Paul's personal experience is *his* radical conversion *from Saul to Paul*, and at the same time it concretely illustrates a revolutionary psycho-historical change *in the notion* of God and not, as Jung would have it, a clash of wills *between* man and God.[74]

From here, from the discussion of Jung's fascination with the idea of a violent ruthless overpowering counter-will,[75] we can see once more that the Trinity's "Son" and the son of Jung's "stage of the Son" are worlds apart. The Son's message, "Love your enemies, bless them that curse you, do good to them that hate you, and pray for them which despitefully use you, and persecute you" (to mention only this) shows an entirely different, unoppositional mentality.

This is also why Jung's interpretation of "the central Christian symbolism, the Cross" is incommensurable with the Christian spirit. According to him, the Cross "symbolizes God's suffering in his immediate collision with the world" (§ 250, transl. modif.). But in Christian terms, there is no *collision* with the world here, inasmuch as the Crucifixion is the culmination of Christ's *kenôsis*, his voluntarily emptying himself of his original divine status and humbling himself by taking on the status of a man and even slave and being "obedient to the point of death, indeed, death on a cross" (Phil. 2:5–8). Sure enough, from an unpsychological, external

[74] The validity and authenticity of Jung's definition of God as overwhelming counter-will is further undermined by the fact that his own root experience of this overwhelming power was apparently not a spontaneous experience of his, but the result of his own machinations. I refer to his Basel cathedral visionary thought and my analysis of it in my papers "Psychology as Anti-Philosophy: C.G. Jung" and "The Disenchantment Complex. C.G. Jung and the Modern World," chapters 2 and 3 in vol. 5 of my Collected English Papers (*The Flight Into The Unconscious. An Analysis of C.G. Jung's Psychology Project*, New Orleans, LA [Spring Journal Books] 2013).

[75] There has been the facetious attempt, condoned by Jung, to see—*nomen est omen*—the essence of each of the psychologies of Freud, Adler, and Jung prefigured in their names: Freud ("joy") had to focus on the pleasure principle, Adler ("eagle") on the striving for power, and Jung ("young") on rejuvenation, rebirth (the fountain of youth). But the present discussion shows that maybe even deeper than his focus on spiritual rebirth and his dedication to concrete symbols and images was Jung's commitment to abstract Power, the abstract Will, not, as in Adler's case, his will to power, but conversely the submission to an *absolute* power (and through this submission the establishment of The Absolute, God). Already his whole innocent-looking, seemingly empirical-scientific conception of "the unconscious" is *ultimately* in the service of the logic of submission and thus in the service of the rescue of God under the adverse conditions of modernity.

point of view, this violent death was done to Christ, it was a result of a clash with the authorities, and he was an innocent victim. But seen psychologically, in terms of the meaning of the symbol of Crucifixion, this was part of Christ's own going under. Nothing was done to him, indeed, nothing could possibly be done to him: because he did not show "disobedience and rebellion," was not filled by a "counter-will." The whole oppositional structure that Jung projects onto the Crucifixion is not there. On the level of consciousness reached with Christianity, it does not make any sense to view it in terms of a logic of "conflict to the last." The Crucifixion, insofar as it is seen as the highest symbol of *kenotic logic* (and not as a substitutionary atonement), is in itself already a manifestation of Spirit and Love in the sense of the *third* "person" of the Trinity.

Of course, Jung says, "the central Christian symbol, the *Cross*, is unmistakably a quaternity" (*ibid.*). But is it really? I think it is that only for the external, naturalistic stance that clings to the sensible appearance of the Cross. If you abstract from everything else and focus only on the Cross as a visible thing consisting of two beams at right angles to each other, you are of course entitled to see in it a depiction of quaternity, reminiscent of Jung's own various quaternio schemas. But for a psychological understanding, the visible cross is not a symbol at all (in the context of Christianity), but only a *sign* for the actual symbol, namely for the Crucifixion as the culmination of the *kenôsis*. The *kenôsis* is the name for a revolutionary move into a new logic, a new spirit, into a general form of consciousness and a corresponding real way of thinking and way of life.

Jung's quaternity ideas and diagrams suggest, one might say, a thinking about the Godhead in terms of "object relations" (this psychologically disastrous concept). The two crossing lines each keep two opposites nicely apart and make them appear to be strictly self-identical, separate entities, components, or aspects. It locates these "entities" in space, like *res extensae*, which is again a sign of the externality and the naturalism informing this thinking.

Far from being able to summarize Augustine's work on the Trinity, I will now only present, by way of no more than a hint, some of the crucial figures of thought at work in his interpretation that make his view commensurable with the peak idea of the Trinity, the Holy Ghost, the Spirit, because they leave all naturalistic, spatial thinking and all object-consciousness clearly behind.[76]

According to Augustine, if the logic of finite man could not in any way be mediated with the logic of God, then a God having become man could not be a full-fledged God. And, conversely, man being *imago dei* must have some of God's own nature within himself, even if only in finite form. And this, the *imago dei*, is his soul, the *mens humana*. Because the divine Trinity is beyond our finite human understanding, Augustine instead sets out to uncover the trinitarian structure of something that is immediately accessible to us, the soul of man, the human mind, as an analogy to the nature of the divine Trinity. This approach is necessary because he insists that the Trinity can precisely not be understood simply from the Biblical texts (nor, I add, from the *symbola*, from dogma). In order for the mind to be able to understand the Biblical passages about the Trinity in the first place some kind of intrinsic knowledge about the nature of "trinity" must already be there, an always already present, though to begin with only implicit, knowledge that the mind can only find *within itself* (self-consciousness). As Augustine states, thinking precedes believing (*prius esse cogitare quam credere*).[77] It can precede believing because the human mind is in itself from the outset the (of course finite) image and likeness of the divine Trinity as the prototype.

Three thought figures in Augustine's understanding the trinitarian structure stand out:

1. The substantiality of the *mens humana* consists in its self-reflection and self-referentiality and not the other way around (there is not an entity, a substance, that reflects and relates, but self-reflection and self-referentiality *are* the very substance).

---

[76] Of the huge secondary literature on *De trinitate* I mention only two recent outstanding and most helpful works: Johannes Brachtendorf, *Die Struktur des menschlichen Geistes nach Augustinus. Selbstreflexion und Erkenntnis Gottes in "De Trinitate,"* Paradeigmata 19, Hamburg (Meiner) 2000, and Roland Kany, *Augustins Trinitätsdenken. Bilanz, Kritik und Weiterführung der modernen Forschung zu "De trinitate,"* Studien und Texte zu Antike und Christentum 22, Tübingen (Mohr Siebeck) 2007.

[77] Augustine, *De praedestinatione sanctorum* II.5. Compare with this thesis of the priority of thought Jung's statement: "For belief has anticipated the summit which thinking tries to win by toilsome climbing" (§ 170, transl. modif.). The idea of toilsome climbing applies only to *se cogitare*, explicit thinking, not to *se nosse*, implicit thinking or primordial self-knowledge.

2. The human mind (*mens humana*) does not relate to its self-knowledge (*notitia sui*) and to its self-love (*amor sui*) the way a substance relates to its attribute/accident or the way the whole relates to its parts. It represents together with them a true trinitarian structure: every individual component (Augustine explores them under the terms *memoria sui, intelligentia sui, voluntas sui*) represents within itself the whole; every individual act of one component permeates all three components, and each of them wholly.

3. All three components together are not larger than any one single component. They cannot be added together. (E.g., in the divine Trinity, the Son does not add anything to the Father.)

In addition Augustine made the great discovery that the mind's self-knowledge (*se nosse*) must not be confused with the mind's actual ("literal") self-reflection or thinking about itself (*se cogitare*). One's explicit self-reflection (*se cogitare*) is always already grounded in an implicit, a priori self-knowledge. The mind IS self-knowledge (and not an existing "organ" that in addition to its existence also thinks about itself and thus gains knowledge about itself).

These indications, meager as they are, nevertheless suffice already to make it obvious that here the Trinity is in fact approached from the standpoint of true interiority and in the spirit or logic of Spirit. Here the idea of the Trinity has come home to itself. There is no chance of attempting to depict this living relational "structure" according to the naturalistic paradigm of the human family or in the form of a simple schematic diagram and within a spatial imagination. It needs to be thought. It has fully left behind the naturalistic everyday logic of self-identical things or beings in space relating to each other, and along with it the standpoint of externality. The three remain distinct and yet are one in the fluidity of thought. And this complex relation actually exists as the reality of the human soul. Here the boy Jung would have found the answers to his burning question about "a One which was simultaneously a Three" and its fascinating "inner contradiction" that he had so longingly been waiting for and that his father could not provide. And the only answer lies in the revolutionary move from the standpoint of naturalism and externality to the standpoint of interiority.

For a psychologist it is both moving and revealing to see that in his attempt to understand the Trinity Augustine saw himself forced to study the human soul or mind and thereby discovered its innermost nature and structure, its internal logical life. This is one more indication that the appearance of the idea of the Holy Ghost in history is indeed the spirit's home-coming to itself. Quite apart from any religious faith or any commitment to a particular belief system, the thought of the Trinity reveals itself to be the entrance to the very heart of psychology (namely the nature of the human soul as an *intelligible*, not a sensible reality), provided that psychology is conceived as the discipline of interiority.

I will close with a comment on the Augustinian motto that Jung placed at the beginning of his work. *Noli foras ire, in teipsum redi; / in interiore homine habitat veritas*[78] does not, especially in our context, the context of *De trinitate* and its concept of self-knowledge (*se nosse*), refer to modern psychologistic introspective self-exploration that aims at discovering one's contingent subjective, strictly private, particular inner images and impulses in one's unconscious, which are accessible exclusively to each individual "me,"[79] but to the recognition through self-reflection of the (we could say: objective, universal) "truth" of the mind, a truth that is the same in every individual and also, in principle, accessible to every (intelligent) individual.

---

[78] "Do not go outside, return into yourself; truth dwells in the interiority of man" (*De vera relig.* 39, 72).

[79] *Mutatis mutandis* the same is true concerning the famous inscription on the temple of Apollo at Delphi, *Gnôthi seauton*, Know Thyself, which was translated by Cicero as *Nosce te [ipsum]* (*Tusculanae disputationes* I, 22, 52).

CHAPTER FOUR

God Must Not Die![1]
C.G. Jung's Thesis of the One-Sidedness of Christianity

"As far as the Christian nations are concerned," Jung tells us, "their Christianity has fallen asleep and has neglected to develop its myth further in the course of the centuries. ... People do not even realize that a myth is dead if it no longer lives and is not developed further any more" (*MDR* pp. 331f., transl. modif.). The last statement is a gross generalization. Genuine *myths* and similar folk tales are precisely characterized by their impressive conservatism; even in historically progressive Europe, fairytales that probably date back to the Stone Age were kept alive in the traditions of the uneducated population way into the 18th century without having undergone *essential* changes. The Christian "myth" is of course not really a myth in the strict sense. It is a religious story, something that originated long after the radical shift from *mythos* to *logos* and philosophical reflection and has much of highly developed Greek thought as one of its fundamental ingredients. And, conversely, as the example of Islam (another religion that arose *after* that fundamental shift) shows, a religion, too, can stay vitally alive even if its doctrine has not been further developed for centuries. But in the case of Christianity we need to include the idea of its further-development

[1] Cf. "The irrational cannot and must not be extirpated. The gods cannot and must not die." (*CW* 7 § 111). I am indebted to Greg Mogenson for bringing this quote to my attention.

in its definition, although not in the same sense as here implied by Jung. In a letter Jung wrote something that is closer to what I have in mind. "The thought of evolution is Christian and—as I think—in a way a better truth to express the dynamic aspect of the Deity, although the eternal immovability also forms an important aspect of the Deity... The religious spirit of the West is characterized by a change of God's image in the course of ages" (*Letters 2*, p. 315, to Kotschnig, 30 June 1956). "What is remarkable about Christianity is that in its system of dogma it anticipates a process of change in the Deity, that is, a historical transformation on the 'other side'" (*MDR* p. 327, transl. modif.). This idea is closer to what is needed for a truly psychological discussion of this topic, but it is still too theological, rather than solely phenomenological (Jung expresses an opinion about the nature of the *Deity*, capitalized!).

The inner motive force of the Christian ideas

What I am driving at is only a phenomenological observation. I do not speak about the deity, but simply about the logical character of the historical phenomenon of Christianity. My thesis is that Christianity did not begin as a finished doctrine. Its central message had much more the character of a seed or intuition that needed to be unfolded over the course of time. What it was really about could not be fully grasped right at the beginning. It needed centuries for it to come home to itself. Everything was already there at the beginning (there is for me precisely no need, as there is for Jung, of a further development of the myth through the *addition* of new doctrinal contents), but it was there only implicitly, enveloped, and it needed to germinate, incubate, be "alchemically distilled," in order at long last to become explicit and explicated and thus fully conscious and fully real. Christianity needed and wanted to be interiorized into itself (whereas what Jung had in mind, when he spoke of its further development, was obviously its *extrapolation beyond* itself).

This inherent dynamic nature, which is the logical or syntactical character of Christianity, at one point even comes out in the semantic message of Christianity itself, namely when Jesus says, "But the Comforter, which is the Holy Ghost, whom the Father will send in my name, he shall teach you all things, and bring all things to your remembrance, whatsoever I have said unto you" (John 14:26). The full realization of what is meant by the original teachings was considered as only becoming possible at some time in the future and needing a new teacher, and not one in the three-dimensional world, but in the spirit (*pneuma*). The Christian message required a *spiritual* understanding ("... not of the letter, but of the spirit: for the letter killeth, but the spirit giveth life" 2 Cor. 3:6). That we have and can read or hear the biblical text with its stories and its dogmatic statements is one thing. But then the real question arises, "Understandest thou what thou readest?" (Acts 8:30). That the teacher will only come in the future points to the fact that the achievement of a full understanding is not a matter of a few years of study or even the study of a lifetime, but a historical task, a task for centuries, if not millennia. Christianity has thus the character of an impulse or a project.

And the coming of the spirit should itself be spiritually understood: not as a mysterious apparition or sudden spectacular event, a literal arrival of a new teacher from outside, but rather as the slow coming alive of the inner spirit of the message from within itself. From the outset the Christian truth had everything it needed within itself. The Holy Ghost who *literally* was announced by it as being sent only at a later date was, for a spiritual understanding, already there from the beginning, and stirred and agitated from within. The spirit contained in Christianity's "letter" worked on its own releasement. All that Christian truth needed was in the course of time to be unfolded, to slowly come home to consciousness.

Complexity

The inherent need of the Christian message itself to be driven beyond its immediate literal meaning to its deeper and more subtle pneumatic meaning through an interiorization of the ideas into themselves makes the Christian material on which to base our interpretation complex. There are always several levels of understanding for the same thing. But in addition to the complexity due to the implicit-explicit difference, there is another one which is due to the fact that after the decline of the Roman Empire, Christianity, which was a product of the deep and long-evolved Jewish religious and the highly sophisticated Greek philosophical thinking, was in the West taken over by intellectually and psychologically still primitive nations who had had no written culture and came from a pagan nature-based religious tradition. Their reception of the Christian message was naturally quite naive at first, restricted to the easily accessible biblical *stories* and rather literal. It mostly had to rely on Gospel harmonies, because coping with four different gospel versions (let alone with the theology of St. Paul and the Church Fathers) was already overtaxing.

It also stands to reason that the new religious contents and ideas were received by a consciousness that was still pretty much thinking and apperceiving the new message in pagan and concretistic, naturalistic terms. Also, some of the pagan traditions and rituals were even absorbed by the Church and merely "rechristened." But over the centuries, the Western mind was then slowly *trained* to acquire a higher-level, more philosophically *theological* understanding of its own Christianity (Scholasticism). The result of this complicated history is that we get versions of the same Christian ideas that belong to very different historical layers of understanding and different degrees of differentiation, as well as Christian phenomena that *de facto* are part of the actual historical tradition of Christianity, but in spirit are not truly Christian at all. And even one major present form of Christianity, Roman Catholicism, is *syntactically* (as far as its logical form is concerned) still a pagan religion merely with Christian contents (a Christian semantics). Its pagan spirit shows, for example, in the fact that it has priests, a sacrificial ritual, holy places and sacred objects and an only dimly disguised polytheistic cultic practice (with Saints and the Mother of God in addition to the Trinity), and that in general it appeals to the senses (splendid gowns and cathedrals, impressive public ceremonies, incense and holy water)—all of which is incompatible with the specific inner logic of the Christian idea. Christianity in its deepest essence is fundamentally beyond the naturalistic *worldliness* of sacred acts, things, persons and visible shows, because it finds itself *only* "in spirit and in truth" (John 4:23).

Because of this *embarras de richesses* to choose from, anybody can put together his own Christianity. When we now want to examine Jung's thesis of the fundamental one-sidedness of Christianity we need a criterion for what to consider as relevant. This criterion follows from what I discussed so far. We have to be guided by the inherent dynamic and inner momentum of the heart of the Christian message itself to let become explicit what had been implicit and to do justice to its need to come home to itself. The heart of the Christian message is what is absolutely new, special about, and vital to it in contrast to other religions or other ways of thinking. "The heart" is also the essential Christian impulse or thrust over against all the peripheral, marginal, sometimes serendipitous details found in the rich material that attached itself to this nucleus.

Our questions must be, does Jung and do we get stuck in the letter, the literal, the image, the narrative story, or was he and are we able to negate and push off from the letter so as to understand the teachings "in spirit and in truth"? Does the syntax of Jung's and of our thinking fully correspond to the semantics of the message, so that the semantic message is *released* into its truth? Does Jung and do we allow ourselves to be bound by the inner logic of the Christian teachings as having everything they need within themselves, or does he, do we approach them with external categories and expectations and bring in other stray elements from outside?

And, when coming from the other side, from the actual course of Western history, and looking at it with the question to what extent the workings of the Christian impulse can be discerned therein (or, the other way around, to what extent this history can be interpreted as the realization of the Christian impulse), does Jung and do we focus on the major transformations of *the general logical form of consciousness* or does he, do we cling to the semantic level, only having eyes for selected individual ideas, visions, dreams, images, opinions that, to be sure, actually happened to occur in history, but that are capriciously privileged by us as the psychologically significant ones?

The charge of one-sidedness

Jung's views of Christianity are well known. "... the Christ-symbol lacks wholeness in the modern psychological sense, since it does not include the dark side of things but specifically excludes it in the form of a Luciferian opponent" (*CW* 9ii § 74). Christ "is one side of the self and the devil the other" (*Letters 2*, p. 133, to White, 24 Nov. 1953)

"... one of the things they [the Gnostics] taught was that Christ 'cast off his shadow from himself.' ... we can easily recognize the cut-off counterpart in the figure of the Antichrist" (*CW* 9ii § 75). "Christ is without spot, but right at the beginning of his career there occurs the encounter with Satan, the Adversary, who represents the counterpole of that tremendous tension in the world of the psyche which Christ's advent signified" (*CW* 9ii § 78). "... the first thing Christ must do is to sever himself from his shadow and call him devil" (*Letters 2*, pp. 134f., to White, 24 Nov. 1953). Christ "has chosen the light and denied the darkness" (*Letters 2*, p. 473, to Kelsey, 12 Dec. 1958).

"In the Christian concept ... the archetype is hopelessly split into two irreconcilable halves, leading ultimately to a metaphysical dualism—the final separation of the kingdom of heaven from the fiery world of damnation" (*CW* 9ii § 74, transl. modif.). "The myth [= the Christian myth] must at long last go through with its monotheism and give up its (officially denied) dualism" (*MDR* p. 338, transl. modif.).

"We stand face to face with the terrible question of evil, and one is not even aware of it, let alone of how to answer it" (*MDR* p. 331, transl. modif.). "The old question posed by the Gnostics, 'Whence comes evil?' has been given no answer by the Christian world ..." (*MDR* p. 332).

"I do not doubt that the alchemical figure of Mercurius is a medieval attempt at a compensation for the Christ figure" (*Letters 2*, p. 619, to A. Jung, 21 Dec. 1960, transl. modif.). "Alchemy was well aware of the great shadow which Christianity was obviously unable to get under control, and it therefore felt impelled to create a savior from the womb of the earth as an analogy and complement of God's son who came down from above" (*CW* 14 § 704, transl. modif.).

Christ's initial meeting with the Tempter

First I would like to take a closer look at Christ's encounter with the devil at the beginning of his career (Matth. 4:1ff.). Jesus had fasted in the desert for forty days and was hungry. In this situation the devil appears and tempts him, first by asking him to use his power as the Son of God to turn stones into bread, secondly by asking him to throw himself down from the pinnacle of the temple and allowing himself to be safely supported by angels, and finally by taking him to an extremely high mountain from which all the kingdoms of the world could be seen and offering them to him.

The first thing to be noticed is that obviously this devil is not Luciferian, satanic, absolutely evil. He does not represent the dark side. He does not want to seduce Christ to commit a crime, to gratify evil lusts (as, for example, sexual child molestation). Instead he merely represents the *natural*, concretistic perspective versus a non-literal one. The first temptation is ultimately about social welfare, providing enough to eat for everyone. The second temptation is about performing a spectacular miracle that would make him credible to the masses as someone to put their hopes on. And the last one is about becoming a political world leader, who would by no means have to be a cruel despot, but could just as well be a wise and just ruler, a benefactor of the world, maybe like Emperor Augustus bringing a long-lasting period of peace and the flowering of culture. These are the devil's offers. The issue here is not the choice between good and evil. It is by no means as Jung represents it: "Both sides appear here: the light side and the dark" (*Letters 1*, p. 268, to Zarine, 3 May 1939). In fact we see that as far as the semantic substance of the goals is concerned, the devil and Jesus are not at all apart. Both were thinking in the same direction. Jesus showed the same concern for people being fed and he would later teach his followers to pray, "Give us this day our daily bread," he performed numerous miracles, and he also conceived himself as the ruler of the world. The only difference is that Jesus gives to the goal shared by both a fundamentally other meaning: "My kingdom is NOT of *this* world" (John 18:36), "Blessed are they who have NOT seen, and yet have believed" (John 20:29), and "Man shall NOT live by *bread* alone, but by every word that proceedeth out of the mouth of God." What is at stake in the dispute between the devil and Jesus was beautifully highlighted by Dostoevsky in his parable, "The Grand Inquisitor."

There is no trace here of an "unspeakable conflict posited by duality" (*CW* 11 § 258) and, as a matter of fact, not a real *duality* either, not a thesis and an antithesis. Jesus and the devil are by no means divided by the strict opposition between good and evil, which is a horizontal opposition much like that between right and left. No, both aim for the good, namely "bread" and "kingdom." There is no dispute between them about the goal itself. Theirs is the vertical difference within one and the same semantic content or concept (e.g., "kingdom") between "of this world" and "*not* of this world." Jesus negates and *er-innert* (inwardizes) the notion of "kingdom" into itself. The crude moralistic opposition between two totally different desires or goals imagined by Jung thus gives way for us to the sophisticated difference between two different modes or styles of understanding of the same desire, between a naturalistic, external sense of "bread" or "kingdom" and an inner, logical sense, between the literal and the spiritual, between positivity here and logical negativity over there. Rather than rejecting "kingdom" altogether and opting for something totally different, Jesus pushes off from and sublates, sublimates, distills, evaporates the concept of "kingdom." What a kingdom that is not of this world is he cannot show. It does not exist as a positive fact. It is logically negative and exists only for (i.e., if there is) a soulful understanding. Much like the alchemists said, "*aurum nostrum non est aurum vulgi*," Jesus says, "My kingdom is not of this world." He overcomes the worldly naturalism of the meaning of the words used and opens up a new dimension and inner depth of meaning of the same words that did not exist before. What *their* gold was, the alchemists, too, were unable to demonstrate because it exists only in and for the absolute-negative interiority of the mind or soul.

Jung does not see that what happens in the temptation scene is an act of logical negation and sublation. Instead, he says, "then, thanks to the function that results from every conflict, a symbol appears: it is the idea of the Kingdom of Heaven, a spiritual kingdom rather than a material one. Two things are united in this symbol, the spiritual attitude of Christ and the devilish desire for power. Thus the encounter of Christ with the devil is a classic example of the transcendent function" (*Letters 1*, p. 268, to Zarine, 3 May 1939). Maybe one can call the Kingdom of Heaven a symbol, although it lacks the sensory element so essential to symbols. But it certainly does not mysteriously "appear," and not appear from out of a conflict. No, it is produced by Jesus's consciously, deliberately pushing off from an initial superficial version of his idea of what he wants to a deeper one. If one wishes to think personalistically of a desire for power on his part (but why should that be a priori "devilish"? Do we not also need rulers in the world?), one could speak of his self-overcoming.

The mistake of thinking that the Kingdom of Heaven is a unification of two conflicting tendencies is that it overlooks the fact that "the spiritual attitude" must not be naturalistically presupposed as a personality trait that existed in Jesus from the beginning. It is not a question of a subjective attitude at all. A "spiritual attitude" could not exist because "spirit" in *this* sense had been unknown, it was not available; it was only the *result* of the revolutionary Christian move, a radically new creation. So what we witness here in this scene is the first-time conquest or birth of this new objective soul dimension, the dimension of spirit as logical negativity, through the process of negating the natural desire or the naturalistic understanding of the desire. Jesus, we might say, sees through the superficiality of the literal (political) kingdom. He gets a clearer, deeper self-understanding about his actual desire. He for the first time becomes aware that he is indeed striving for "kingdom," but also comes to realize that he would only fool himself if he gave in to this wish for "kingdom" in the external sense of literal, political power as offered by the devil, and that that sense of kingdom would not at all give him what his soul in truth needs. No *transcendent* function, no "symbol" as the resolution on a higher level of an insoluble conflict (and no conflict either). On the contrary, an absolute-negative *interiorization*. Instead of the clash of two opposite theses we find the logical movement from a preliminary thesis to a deeper, more sophisticated one.

Should we call the devil in this story Jesus's shadow? Maybe the possibility of misunderstanding his mission in the sense of positivity and acting it out is indeed a possible shadow aspect of what Jesus was striving for, but if so, then certainly not in Jung's sense of shadow here, as the "counterpole of that tremendous tension in the world of the psyche which Christ's advent signified."

The second point to be noted is that according to this story, Christ did by no means "sever himself from his shadow" at the beginning of his career. No cutting-off. If we accept for the moment Jung's view of the devil as his shadow, Jesus's behavior is an absolutely exemplary mode of how to deal with the shadow. He allows him to surface, he lets him state his case and show what he has to offer, he calmly and, I suppose, open-mindedly listens to him and even lets himself be guided by him to that high mountain. He lets "the shadow" become fully conscious and faces him directly. And rather than splitting the shadow off, suppressing him, fighting him, he merely *answers* him, openly contradicts him, says "no" to him. The encounter happens as a true dialogue, on the level of *speaking*. Both put their cards on the table and so *know* now where they stand with respect to each other.

Jesus's knowledge gained about "his shadow" (at least the one that appeared here) is neither repressed nor gets lost for Jesus in the times to come. Because inasmuch as his own goal is the determinate negation of what the devil offered him and is the result of Jesus's pushing off from it, he always carries with him what he pushed off from, the same way the alchemist who aims for "*his*" gold always stays aware of the gold in the ordinary literal sense. One might even surmise that the devil's spelling out his offers was indispensable for Jesus to clearly become aware of and define the totally other dimension of logical negativity ("spirit") that was to be his own specialty. Without getting the literal option clearly spelled out he could not have clearly pushed off to the figurative sense of kingdom that was his own goal. A negation presupposes the position. So the devil, rather than being his shadow in the usual sense of the word, was, as a literal devil's advocate, his maieutic psychopomp. He helped Jesus to find himself, to find into his own.

For a psychological understanding, this story is not really about two separate figures, the devil and Jesus, at all. Rather, what is actually one single process of self-reflection and self-clarification (acquiring a clearer, deeper understanding of himself and his project) in the loneliness of the wilderness is merely *narratively* played out as the interaction (or rather dialogue) between two figures. As psychologists we should not take literally this substantiating or personifying, which is only due to the needs of the narrative genre. But this means that the whole talk about Christ's shadow is misplaced as far as this story is concerned.

I said that a negation presupposes the position. However, in the sphere of the soul's logic the "position" is not an ontic fact, entity, or situation, nothing naturally existing. It has more the character of a presupposition than a literal *pre*-existing starting-point. And thus it is that the negation *posits within itself* the presupposition from which it "then" pushes off. This underlines our insight that the devil in this story must not be seen as an externally existing being, nor as a projection or split-off and denied part of the whole personality. He is precisely internal to the whole operation, namely as the soul's or mind's instrument for taking a radical step forward to a new status of itself.

It is amazing that Jung read the undialectical horizontal good-evil split and a "tremendous tension" between a thesis and an antithesis into this story and did not become aware of the very different vertical sublimation-inwardization process described in this story. Its topic or issue is very, very different from what Jung saw in it. Since Jung was a very intelligent and psychologically extraordinarily insightful man I can only assume that he could not see this because he was in the grip of an agenda of his own.

Incarnation

With the topic of incarnation, we come to the very heart of the Christian doctrine and what distinguishes it from probably all other religions. Jung, too, considered it "the essence of the Christian message" (*MDR* p. 338). The theologically most significant passage is Phil. 2:5–8. There we are told that Jesus Christ,

> although he originally existed in the form of God,
> did not cling to his being-equal-to-God as his inalienable privilege,
> but emptied himself [of it] (*ekenôsen*, from which we get the key term *kenôsis*),
> took the form of a slave,
> having been born like a man
> and living like a man,
> he humbled himself
> and was obedient to the point of death,
> indeed, [a criminal's] death on a cross.

The *kenôsis* means that Christ relentlessly gave up his divinity. It is a voluntary renunciation, his own doing. The incarnation is one consistent downward movement from the height of divinity to the lowest possible form of human existence, that of a slave, and further to the most contemptible form of death. Christ went all the way to the utmost end. The passage makes it very clear that there is no reserve. Christ does not leave himself a way out. The descent is total.

His is not a *journey* from heaven down to earth, a change of location, nor merely a *metamorphosis* such as we know it from many mythological gods who appeared on earth in human or even animal shape. A metamorphosis is a form change. Those gods of mythology, when having taken on human shape, never ceased being gods. Their transformation concerned only their *physical* form, their bodily *appearance*, and was only temporary, reserved for a particular purpose. Christ, however, became man for good and in earnest. Instead of a journey or metamorphosis, his incarnation was therefore in addition to a loss of status or prestige ("he humbled himself") much more radically a *logical or ontological form change*, a change in his very essence, substance, or innermost nature, in his definition or identity, so that we could also think of it as an "alchemical" (mercurial) change, e.g., of a *putrefactio* and *mortificatio*. It was a *category* change (Christ switched from the category God to that of mortal man).

Our passage tells of one powerful dynamic, one vigorous movement of going under. The incarnation is not only about Christ's being *born* as man ("Christmas") in the sense of a one-time event, as it appears to the merely imagining mind. It is continued beyond his birth and goes through his life on earth as a whole right into his death. The incarnation is a complete going under and is only fulfilled with his crucifixion. And not even with this crucifixion as such alone, but only with its culminating in his absolute loss of God ("My God, my God, why hast thou forsaken me?"), which is not mentioned in our passage. Only with this experience or insight had the *kenôsis* become absolute. Only then was the last trace of divinity truly emptied out. As long as there was trust in God Father and the faith or hope that he, Jesus Christ, was God's son, his child, did he indirectly still possess his divinity, even if he did not possess it immediately in himself (who had in fact already become nothing but human), but in his other, God, and in his faith in Him. The complete *kenôsis* includes the death of God, the loss of "having" a God altogether. Without the loss of God it would only be a partial or token "emptying." And only if he has lost his God has he really, unreservedly, become human, nothing but human, and emptied his cup fully.

This radical dynamic movement of *kenôsis* is the thought and intuition that was the assignment given by early Christianity to all future generations to be thought through, to be slowly more and more comprehended and integrated into consciousness.

Christ's death on the Cross together with the absolute loss of God brought by it was, by the way, also the mode—and the only mode—

how the dictum, "My kingdom is not of this world" could be in fact redeemed, made true and real. It is easy to talk big about a kingdom that is not of this world. But that it is more than an ideal representation in the mind, namely a reality, and what it actually means and involves, comes out only in Christ's *dying into* this kingdom of his, the imaginal sign of which is his crown of thorns. Before his death, it had been no more than an idea, an intuition.

Jung resists the logic of this movement. He is immune to the unambiguously vertical thrust of the *kenôsis* and immediately substitutes for it the horizontality of the good-evil opposition. "With the *incarnation* the picture changes completely, as it means that God becomes manifest in the form of Man who is conscious and therefore cannot avoid judgment. He simply has to call the one good and the other evil. It is a historical fact that the real devil only came into existence together with Christ. ... But becoming Man, he [God] becomes at the same time a definite being, which is this and not that" (*Letters 2*, p. 134, to White, 24 Nov. 1953[2]). And in the same spirit, Christ's crucifixion means for Jung his suspension *between* the opposites.

We see that Jung does not stay within the specific conception of the incarnation as offered by the biblical text. He brings to bear upon it an extraneous and irrelevant point of view. Jung approaches the incarnation with his own program. Good and evil are simply no topic and of no interest in the logic of *kenôsis*. They have no place in this thought. If you think practically, it is, to be sure, true that becoming Man means becoming a determinate being "which is this and not that" and which probably needs to "call the one good and the other evil." But why mention this? This is not at all the point made by the incarnation idea. Wrong categories. Of sole interest is the going-under movement and the dynamic of total self-depletion of the divine nature.

It is no doubt true that the idea of the devil as "the Adversary" appears in the New Testament, but it is a leftover from widespread conventions of contemporary Jewish thought (Qumran, *pseudepigrapha*, etc.) and precisely not on a level with the incarnation/*kenôsis* idea, so to speak not state-of-the-art. In interpreting, one always

[2] This passage is also a clear sign that Jung understood the incarnation as the one-time event of a God's taking on a human shape at the beginning of his life on earth, whereas what happens in his life as man was seen as wholly another story.

has to start with the *apex theoriae* and the heart of it, with where it is at its best, and judge all the individual more peripheral or incidental elements it also contains from there. They have to justify their existence within the doctrine up for discussion (and their existence in that particular *form*) in the light of its highest point and deepest principle. Noteworthy in our context is also that in contrast to those contemporary Jewish thought patterns, the New Testament teaches that the might of Satan has been broken by Jesus, whereby this deprivation of Satan's power is subject to the "already / not yet" tension characteristic of Christian thinking. It is the tension between the logical and the positive-factual or empirical or between the implicit and the explicit.

It is also true that throughout the Middle Ages and even later the threat of the devil and the fear of eternal damnation in hell were (often extremely) powerful factors in the actual religious life and beliefs of Christians. Although these ideas and fears are part of the belief system of Christianity *as it historically existed* and developed, they are not elements of the authentically Christian message, Christianity as it is "in spirit and in truth." They had merely a *propaedeutic*, educational function: in a slow, centuries-long process they had to get collective consciousness psychically ready for the logical subtleties of the actual Christian idea. The terrible fear of damnation was no more than an instrument used by the soul to brutally, painfully dislodge and evict the mind from its *natural* state, its being bound by *imaginal* conceptions and expectations, to catapult the soul out of its *unio naturalis* and to thrust consciousness into the fundamentally post-natural constitution necessary for doing justice to the Christian idea (as it is expressed, e.g., in "My kingdom is NOT of this world," which is not an imaginal reality but a logical or intelligible one, one of absolute negativity). The damnation was eternal, that is, absolute, which shows that despite of its imaginal form it is actually an abstract thought, the thought of a total *determinate* negation (not a total annihilation!). The terrifying fear of eternal damnation was the *psychic* (emotional and still somehow imaginal) way how was made real what is actually a radical *(psycho-)logical* negation and sublation of the (to begin with pagan-mythological, imaginal) logical form of consciousness. As a total negation of all natural hope it had to once and for all block the way back to the imaginal mode of conception and initiate into the level of the Concept.

As psychologists we must not take at face value and for real what is purposely produced by the soul as a means to an end, to do something to itself. But Jung falls for the idea of the devil. And despite his long and thorough study of alchemy, he does not develop a mercurial understanding of the incarnation. He comes to the notion of incarnation with his dissociative moralistic mindset. And thus, despite his own methodological insight that the fantasy-image has everything it needs within itself and that we must not let anything from outside, that does not belong, get into it, he burdens the idea of the incarnation with what is external and detrimental to it.

The opposition of good and evil is also not a concern of Christ's preaching. On the contrary, he radically overcomes this harsh opposition. He himself stays with the "publicans and sinners"; against the Mosaic law, he saves the adulterous woman from being stoned; in his Sermon on the Mount he reduces to absurdity the idea of goodness, righteousness. In the same spirit, St. Paul teaches that "all have sinned, and come short of the glory of God" (Romans 3:23). If all have sinned, the "absolute opposition" (Jung) between good and evil is fundamentally relativized. Already *here* "the time or turning-point is reached where good and evil begin to relativize themselves, to doubt themselves, and the cry is raised for a morality 'beyond good and evil'" (*CW* 11 § 258), a time or turning-point that Jung wants to postpone to a late future past Nietzsche's 19th century. Clearly, it does not make sense to say that "The world of the Son is the world of moral discord" (*CW* 11 § 259), at least as long as one stays *within* the central thrust of the Christian message and does not, like Jung, bring in all kinds of external material or take as authoritative what *people* commonly made the Christian message to mean. *Christianitas nostra non est christianitas vulgi.* Christ precisely overcomes this discord, he frees, absolves people from this "unspeakable conflict posited by duality." "Son, be of good cheer; thy sins be forgiven thee" (Matth. 9:2). Christ has come to save the sinners, not the righteous. There will be more joy in heaven about one sinner who repents than about ninety-nine righteous ones. Man is *simul iustus et peccator* (Luther). We are also told the parable of the Prodigal Son who is unconditionally forgiven by his father. At the same time, we see that the shadow is also not denied or projected out into a separate figure, the Antichrist. Christ has no illusions about the *reality* of "evil," sin. In the authentic Christian stance—I mean of course in its objective logic, not necessarily in the actual practice and attitudes of those who call themselves Christians—the shadow has a priori been integrated: it is conscious and acknowledged.

There are above all five fundamental methodological lapses in Jung's approach to Christianity, that I will discuss under the following headings: (1) *Reductio in primam figuram*, (2) regression to naturalistic thinking, (3) theosophy, not psychology, (4) positivism, and (5) the disregard of the phenomenological evidence.

Reductio in primam figuram

Jung's insistence in practical psychotherapy on understanding psychic phenomena from within themselves instead of viewing them in terms of the past history that preceded them is well known. The fantasy image, he said, has everything it needs within itself, and in contrast to the Freudian method to understand neurosis from what happened in early childhood he made it very clear that for him, "The true cause for a neurosis lies in the Now, for the neurosis exists in the present. It is by no means a hangover from the past, a *caput mortuum*, but it is daily maintained, indeed even generated anew, as it were. And it is only in the today, not in our yesterdays, that a neurosis can be 'cured.' Because the neurotic conflict faces us today, any historical deviation is a detour, if not actually a wrong turning." (*CW* 10 § 363, transl. modif.). Instead of a causal-reductive and (in a narrower sense) analytical interpretation of psychic material, Jung opted for a final-prospective, constructive, or synthetic approach. What was the material heading for? That was generally his question.

What we find, however, in Jung's interpretation of Christianity is precisely a "historical deviation," his reading, e.g., the Christian incarnation in terms of the historical past, of what preceded it, of the "*caput mortuum.*" He looks backwards. His question is: *Whence* evil? He comes to the Christian message with all the fixed ideas about the old angry Yahweh in his mind that he had developed in his (certainly interesting) study laid down in the earlier parts of his *Answer to Job.* He relies on the Old Testament and other pre-Christian texts (e.g.,

Enoch). He works extensively with the idea of prefiguration. What the idea of the Christian incarnation was aiming for, what it tries to achieve as its telos, is of course not totally disregarded by Jung, but he does not really give it a chance. He always keeps the old emotional powerful Father God in the background as the inescapable perspective. The New Testament, sort of "the child" of the Old Testament, cannot really come of age and be seen as a "person" in its own right, much as in many 20th century novels about a father-son conflict. Jung does his best to hold his interpretation of the incarnation in the old rut. Christianity is reduced by Jung to one moment in a long historical *program*.

Because of his Old Testament bias, Christianity's having *overcome* the Old-Testament Jahweh and moved to Spirit and Love cannot be accepted as true by Jung. He meets this essential constituent of the Christian doctrine with a hermeneutic of suspicion. For him the Christian idea of God as Love is no more than, let us say, wishful thinking or a pious claim; as far as Christianity's truth is concerned, Jung precisely insists on "nothing but" the angry vindictive God: "The more desirable a real relationship of trust between man and God is, the more astonishing becomes Yahweh's vindictiveness and irreconcilability towards his creatures. From a God who is a loving father, who is actually Love itself, one would expect understanding and forgiveness. The fact that the supremely good God demands for the purchase of such an act of grace the price of a human sacrifice, and, what is worse, the killing of his own son, comes as an unexpected shock. ... One has to stop and think about it: the God of goodness is so unforgiving that he can only be appeased by a human sacrifice! This is an insufferable imposition, which in our days one can no longer swallow ..." (*CW* 11 § 689, transl. modif.). The vindictive God is precisely *not* overcome. According to Jung's view, he even acts out his vindictiveness once more in the central event of Christianity, Christ's dying on the Cross.

This backwards interpretation of Jung's is also expressed in the very title of his work, *Answer to Job*, which is programmatic. The Christian truths are nothing in their own right. They do not have everything they need within themselves but refer fundamentally backwards outside themselves, to Yahweh's terrible injustice towards Job. Concerning the deepest point of the incarnation, Christ's "despairing cry from the Cross: 'My God, my God, why hast thou forsaken me?,'" Jung says, "Here is given the answer to Job ..." (*CW* 11 § 647).[3]

There is no doubt a very old tradition of reading Old Testament stories or motifs as prefigurations of New Testament themes. But this hallowed prefiguration concept starts out from the Christian truth as its base and reads the old texts precisely in the light of the new Christian spirit. Jung's procedure, I submit, reverses this direction. For him the prefigurations that he sees are in a historical and more or less causal sense precedents that lay the determining conditions—the rut—for everything that comes later.

Regression to naturalistic thinking

Jung can only put through his own program concerning Christianity because he does not really go along with the Christian move and impulse and thus does not view it from within itself, from

[3] Another question is whether there is any need for an *answer* to Job in the first place. Is the book of *Job* not itself the very answer to the question that according to Jung it raises, namely the question of the justice or injustice of God? It would seem to me that the very point of this book is to radically destroy the naive (Old Testament and Near Eastern) belief that ideas of morality and justice can be applied to God and that there could be a contractual relationship between man and God as if between equal partners or between feudal lord and vassal that would bind God in any way. Jung's thesis, however, is precisely that in contrast to Jesus Christ "Job ... was an ordinary human being, and therefore the wrong done to him, and through him to mankind, can according to divine justice, only be repaired by an incarnation of God in an empirical human being. This act of expiation is performed by the Paraclete; for, just as man must suffer from God, so God must suffer from man. Otherwise there can be no reconciliation between the two" (*CW* 11 § 657). What kind of consciousness is it that thinks about human misfortunes and terrible suffering as a "*wrong* done to him" (by God/Fate/Life) and as obviously requiring the repairing of an injustice? Do we have a vested right to be well-treated by life and to fairness? A category mistake. Behind it all is the innocent childlike belief in and demand for an ideal world and a good and just God. "We [modern man] have experienced things so unheard of and so staggering that the question of whether such things are in any way reconcilable with the idea of a good God has become burningly topical" (*CW* 11 § 736): the kindergarten idea of a good God! This consciousness was, to be sure, shocked to have to *semantically* admit that there is "unjust" suffering and terrible evil, but it is able to *logically* or *syntactically* defend its innocence by putting the cause for this suffering down to God's unconsciousness, his unconscious shadow, so that the *category* of God's justice remains unchallenged despite the forced acknowledgment of the *empirical* experience of what seems to contradict it. At the same time, consciousness can entertain the dream that there of course will have to be a full-fledged "reconciliation between the two." Jung's insistence that the gospel of love needs to be supplemented by a "gospel of fear" (*CW* 11 § 732) is a reflection of the innocence that still prevails in his consciousness. A psychologically mature consciousness knows that we live, so to speak, in the jungle, where a question like "Whence comes evil?" simply does not make any sense. But Jung insists on living in the innocence and "boundlessness of 'God's world.'"

its inner logical dynamic, but holds on to a fundamentally pre-Christian and extra-Christian stance from which he approaches Christian ideas. It is true, Jung cites the *kenôsis*, but at the same time he resists the logical movement it performs. He does not *think* God's becoming Man, but merely pictorially imagines it.

He states, "... God wants to become man, but not quite" (*CW* 11 § 740). But part of the Christian message is that God *had become* man. This is part of the Christian "dream text." Psychologically a *fait accompli*. Jung taught us that, "What the dream, which is not manufactured by us, says is *just so*. Say it again as well as you can" (*Letters 2* p. 591, to Herbert Read 2 September 1960). When it comes to Christianity, Jung does not follow his own maxim. Instead of "saying it again," i.e., thinking it, letting it fully come home to himself, Jung evades the text and falls back on psychologistic speculative explanations of his own about the subjective intentions of a subject called God. Whether God "wants" to become man or not is not the topic at all. We are told that he did become man. That is the only point. Whereas the Christian thought of the incarnation demands of us to see it as absolutely relentless and total (and this also means to think it through to its utmost consequence), Jung does not allow it to go all the way. Yes, there is incarnation for him, but something reserves itself. God does not really get beyond his inner wishing to incarnate, for ultimately in Jesus Christ he stays God after all.

"If this God wishes to become man, then indeed an incredible *kenosis* (emptying) is required, in order to reduce His totality to the infinitesimal human scale. Even then it is hard to see why the human frame is not shattered by the incarnation. ... Above all he [Jesus] lacks the *macula peccati* (stain of original sin). For that reason, if for no other, he is at least a god-man or a demigod. The Christian God-image cannot become incarnate in empirical man without contradictions—quite apart from the fact that man with all his external characteristics seems little suited to representing a god" (*MDR* p. 337, transl. modif.). The incarnation, so we must gather, was not a full-fledged incarnation at all inasmuch as Jesus stayed a god-man or demigod. Therefore, in flagrant contradiction to the Phil. 2 passage, the *kenôsis* was for Jung only a token one; it did not *really* empty Christ of his divinity all the way. For Jung the incarnation is merely "the birth and tragic fate *of a God* in time" (*CW* 11 § 647, my emphasis). "Both mother and son are not real human beings at all, but gods" (*CW* 11 § 626, the whole sentence was italicized by Jung).

Jung reverses the meaning of the incarnation almost into the opposite. It precisely does no longer mean that the divinity is renounced, up to the utmost point of the loss of the trust in God Father. It now means the representation of *God* in human shape. This is how the incarnation is understood if one merely imagines it; the predicate brings only an external change to an immune subject: the very *concept* or *definition* of God as a supreme being is not decomposed, but He stays God even when incarnated, which is sort of the reverse of our sending human beings in their spacesuits and space capsules into outer space where they also stay what they had been on earth. The incarnation does not really touch or reach God, God in his essence.

Only this can explain why Jung thinks that one would actually have to expect the human frame to be shattered by the incarnation. This worry is absolutely unfounded in the Christian idea of the incarnation, because there the *kenôsis* is total; there is nothing left that could be "shattering." But Jung clings to the notion and nature of God. He does not allow God to become man and to die as God. The divinity of God is to be rescued *against* the Christian decomposition of it in the *kenôsis,* which Jung reduces to mean a mere reduction of his all-encompassing totality to a more limited proportion: God squeezes himself into the tight human frame. For the Christian idea, by contrast, the *kenôsis* was not a question of *totality* (being the All) versus limited *finite nature,* but of the supreme *divine status* versus a *human, even slave status.* Not limitation of the all-encompassing extent of God to human proportions, not forcing divine infinity into the tight vessel of a finite being so that it threatens to explode the latter, but humbling and going under—logical decomposition—was the topic. If one *thinks* the sentence "God became man," the predicate dissolves the subject; the subject relentlessly dies into the process predicated of it.

The difference between merely imagining the incarnation and thinking it is like that between viewing things in terms of physics (my space travel example) versus in terms of chemistry/alchemy ("decomposition") or that between myth and logos. While the *kenôsis* idea describes a logical (or mercurial, alchemical) process, a process of a transformation of the inner constitution of the *concept* of God, Jung stays stuck in a naturalistic, literalistic ("physical") thinking in terms of a concrete, almost materially existing being, substance, or subject and its behavior, its (hi)story, the various changes (in the sense of external events) that happen to it.[4] He speaks of the "life-process within the Deity" (*CW* 11 § 206), the process of the "divine self-realization" (*Letters 2*, p. 316, to Kotschnig, 20 June 1956). Jung sort-of writes the biography of God, the events in His life. It is a substantiating thinking, mythologizing and personifying, not one of psychological analysis or interpretation.

This becomes especially obvious in his evaluation of the crucifixion. When he wrote the sentence quoted, "... God wants to become man, but not quite," he continued, "The conflict in his nature is so great that the incarnation can only be bought by an expiatory self-sacrifice offered up to the wrath of God's dark side" (*CW* 11 § 740). The same view is expressed in stronger terms some pages earlier in the same work in a passage (partly) already quoted above: Christ himself "offers himself as an expiatory sacrifice that shall effect the reconciliation with God. The more desirable a real relationship of trust between man and God is, the more astonishing becomes Yahweh's vindictiveness and irreconcilability towards his creatures. From a God who is a loving father, who is actually Love itself, one would expect understanding and forgiveness. The fact that the supremely good God demands for the purchase of such an act of grace the price of a human sacrifice, and, what is worse, of the killing of his own son, comes as an unexpected shock. ... One has to stop and think about it: the God of goodness is so unforgiving that he can only be appeased by a human sacrifice! This is an insufferable imposition, which in our days one can no longer swallow..." (*CW* 11 § 689, transl. modif.). About Christ's helplessness at the Cross, when he "confessed that God had forsaken him," we hear in a letter to Victor White: "The Deus Pater would leave him to his fate as he always 'strafes' those whom he has filled before

---

[4] Jung's fear that the human shape might be shattered by the incarnation indicates that he views the incarnation in analogy to the physical model of compressing, for example, a gas into a breakable vessel, and when he says that through the incarnation God became a definite being, which is this and not that, what is in the back of his mind is a social model like that of an absolute ruler who is, through some political change, reduced to an ordinary citizen. Jung treats God and his incarnation in ontic terms, as if he were an innerworldly, empirical being and the incarnation an innerworldly, empirical process. He does not see that the incarnation is not at all something that happens "out there" *in the universe* and to a *being* named God, but is a change in the *logic of the soul.*

with this abundance by breaking his promise" (*Letters 2*, p. 134, 24 Nov. 1953). God is disloyal, in fact a betrayer.

Jung treats God and the Son personalistically, anthropomorphically, as if they were people, separate, independent beings, who have their subjective passions and character faults and whose behavior needs to be explained in terms of them. Jung dwells on character traits and emotions: irascibility, vindictiveness, wrath, cruelty, irreconcilability, appeasement, expiation, and so it is not surprising that Jung also enters into this story with his own subjective emotions, *vide* his predicates "insufferable," "not to be swallowed," which is unprofessional. In Jung's hands, the act or event of redemption turns into a kind of Freudian family romance, a terrible, perhaps Kafka-like, human *drama* (if not soap opera) of an almighty, but vindictive, cruel father and an obedient son as his victim. "What kind of father is it who would rather his son were slaughtered than forgive his ill-advised creatures who have been corrupted by his precious Satan? What is supposed to be demonstrated by this gruesome and archaic sacrifice of the son? God's love, perhaps?" (*CW* 11§ 661). But this is the naive kindergarten version of the Christian idea, a simple story with a clear difference between a subject and a victim in an intimate family constellation perceived in categories of good and evil. Concerning the psychology brand to which Jung's thinking here belongs, we have to say that it is a personalistic object-relations psychology. All this is totally inadequate to do justice to what the incarnation and the crucifixion are actually about, if they are understood in their own terms, namely, as I indicated, "in spirit and in truth," or: if they are understood *psychologically*.

Here we see most clearly to what extent Jung falls short of the intellectual level on which the Christian message (at least in its highest form) is situated. In his writings about Christianity, we have a case of a true *abaissement du niveau mental*, but in a logical, not the usual psychic sense as a mere lowering of the *degree* of being conscious: Jung regresses to a much more primitive *level* of thinking, one that has precisely long been superseded by the degree of sophistication attained in Christian thinking (although not in the thinking of the popular believers). He is not up to the logical form of the Christian truths. It is preposterous to speak with respect to them of a "gruesome and archaic sacrifice of the son." Jung mythologizes, imagines in naturalistic terms. He himself cultivates an archaic thinking, whereas the Christian message ought to be understood in a highly advanced way, namely "in spirit and in truth" or "*in Mercurio*," as a so to speak alchemical process that is performed upon the 'substance' called God, and performed upon it not from without, but from within itself.

A truly psychological view would say that the Christian message with all its different moments (*kenôsis*, birth, crucifixion, etc.) has to be seen as one single soul truth, as the self-display of the inner dynamic logic of a particular soul situation at a particular historical locus. We must not construe the different figures that appear in the narrative form of the Christian message (here above all the Father and the Son) as independent and separately existing agents as if they were people in ordinary reality; they do not themselves *have* a psychology, but they are conversely—and only *together*—the imaginal portrayal of a specific psychology. They are especially not our patients to be psychoanalyzed by us for the purpose of revealing their true hidden motivations, their unconscious vindictiveness, resentments, doubts[5] and of speculating about what might have gone on in their minds. And in what passes between those figures in the narrative in which the Christian message articulates itself, we must (a) not see so many different events, but integral moments of the inner dynamic of this one soul truth, and we must (b) not view it as *empirical behavior* and personal *interaction* between those alleged separate people, but as the portrayal of the soul's *self-relation* and *self-unfolding*. We are psychologists, not behaviorists. The psychologist knows that we are dealing with images, symbols, and narratives that give pictorial expression to soul events or soul truths that in themselves are fundamentally irrepresentable (*unanschaulich*). This is generally true, even when interpreting ancient myths or archaic rituals, but doubly so when the theme is Christianity, whose specific purpose is to overcome the naturalistic level of understanding and to advance to *logos*, to the spirit ("in spirit and in truth"). The imaginal and narrative garb that a soul truth receives is, as I say with Jung, only a "thin veil" behind which—"behind the scenes"—"another picture looms up."[6]

---

[5] As to "doubts" cf., e.g., "... Christ nevertheless seems to have had certain misgivings in this respect" (*CW* 11 § 691).

[6] C.G. Jung, *The Visions Seminars*, From the Complete Notes of Mary Foote, Book One, Zürich (Spring Publications) 1976, Part One (Lectures October 30 – November 5, 1930), pp. 7f.

Jung himself at one point insisted: "It is precisely of paramount importance that the idea of the Holy Ghost [*Geist*, Spirit] is *not a natural image* [*kein Naturbild*], but a recognition, an abstract concept ..." (*CW* 11 § 236, transl. modified, italics by Jung).[7] In other words, it is the free property of logos. Especially when turning to Christianity, but not only to it, this insight is the standard and measure for our interpretation (the aforementioned apex theoriae) behind which we must not fall. Why then in his discussion of the incarnation and crucifixion does Jung revert to the naturalistic level of a family romance?

In other contexts Jung knew: "In myths and fairytales, as in dreams, the soul speaks about itself, and the archetypes reveal themselves in their natural interplay, as 'formation, transformation / the eternal Mind's eternal recreation'" (*CW* 9i § 400, transl. modified). Exactly the same applies to the Christian story. "God Father" and "the Son" have no separate existence *outside* the Christian "dream," but are posited, invented, generated within and by this "dream thought" as its own productions, its own ("dream-internal") "dream" images. And these images represent moments of this ONE dream thought, moments into which the inner complexity of this one thought unfolds itself.

The thought that is narratively portrayed in a given dream or myth or fairytale and therefore also in the Christian message must be *thought by us*. A dream talks about *itself*, displays the one particular thought or soul truth that it is about. It spells out the inner logical movement or dynamic that is the essence of this soul truth. But Jung refused to *think* the Christian message. He did not approach it psychologically and he resisted the pull of its inner logic, its pull towards the death of God as a substance and his (God's) transformation into Spirit and Love. Instead, he stubbornly mythologized, i.e., took the story with its figures and happenings literally, personalistically, at face value, as if it

---

[7] Cf. "... it is just the Trinity dogma, as it stands, that is the classical example of an artificial structure and an intellectual product ..." (*Letters 2*, p. 423). But when Jung continues: "... It is by no means an original Christian experience ...," we see that he operates with the binary opposition of "original experience" (which allegedly is not an intellectual product, but purely "natural") versus "artificial structures." He does not realize that even "original experiences" are as a matter of course intellectual products and "artificial," although more *implicitly* and *subliminally* so. The notion of "the unconscious" as pure nature is a mystification.

were a *news report* about historical or empirical-factual acts of an existing God, acts occurring outside this narrative in reality (which they may do for the naive believer, but certainly not for a psychologist). Only because Jung construes Christ's death on the Cross *unthinkingly* as a terrible melodrama ("the God of goodness is so unforgiving that he can only be appeased by a human sacrifice!") does it for him become "an insufferable imposition," and under that condition naturally so. But the insufferable imposition is due to this melodramatic, personalistic construal and the childlike imagination of God as a being. For a consciousness used to motifs of dismemberment in myth, of pulverization, flaying, mortification in alchemy and ready to see the crucifixion *psychologically*, it is by no means anything insufferable.

We must not substantiate and literalize elements in a dream (or other soul story), that is, to set them up as existing outside the story. Because this would be like giving the sounds or letters of a word an independent existence outside the word, instead of grasping, and exclusively concentrating on, *the meaning* conveyed by the word and letting the individual sounds go under in the very meaning produced, a meaning that could only emerge in the first place through *their* (the sounds') relentless *dying into* this meaning.

THEOSOPHY, NOT PSYCHOLOGY

The problem I found in Jung's discussion of the Christian message, his setting up "imaginal" figures from within a soul story as existing outside this story and thus literalizing them applies not only to individual episodes in the Christian story, but to his whole treatment of the Judaeo-Christian God image and thus to his whole discourse on religion in the Western tradition. His is not a psychological discourse, but a theosophic one. God is posited as existing outside *all* the different and separate stories from Old Testament times onwards. Jung reads all these stories as records of the development of *God* "in reality" from the creation onwards up to our time and beyond. The history of Biblical religious ideas or images is interpreted directly as a historical process of *God himself*. Jung's was "not the approach to 'Christianity' but to God himself and this seems to be the ultimate question" (*Letters 2*, p. 611, to Rolfe, 19 Nov 1960). Immediacy. The at first basically unconscious God, Jung suggests, slowly becomes more conscious and *he* later desires to become man, a desire which, for Jung, is not fulfilled once and for all with the birth and death of Christ, but—here Jung leaves history and extrapolates way into the future—requires "further incarnations" "in the empirical man" (*CW* 11 § 693) in the future. "God's Incarnation in Christ requires continuation and completion inasmuch as Christ, owing to his virgin birth and his sinlessness, was not an empirical human being at all" (*CW* 11 § 657 transl. modif.).

Both for a historian of religion and for a psychological point of view things would be different. The difference from the standpoint of the history of religion is twofold. First, all the different texts relevant to religion would be viewed as documents showing human conceptions, human views, what at certain times people imagined, namely that they imagined *that* there are in reality "gods" and *how* specifically they imagined them. Secondly, it would have to be seen how, in which sense, and to what extent the sequence of different religious documents in each case makes up one consistent historical development. Is, for example, a god in a later text truly identical with a same-named god in an earlier text? Each text would have to be understood in terms of its own time. In each new time, the notion god could possibly express something new and have a different function in the structure of consciousness as well as in the makeup of the society of the time. The difference could of course be the result of a further development of the same, but it could just as well be that a truly new function is merely called by an old name. It could be the opposite of what Freud called screen-memory: the name of the old phenomenon is retained, but what is now actually meant by it is something new.

For psychologists it would again be different. They would not view religious ideas as human fantasies, but as the self-expression, self-articulation of aspects of the soul. The different gods are garments in which the soul dresses itself (or aspects of itself) at certain concrete historical loci, and the sequence of god images in history would show the transformation of the soul, that is, of the *syntax* or *logical constitution* of consciousness. And to what extent new images or ideas have to be seen as a continuous further development or as a fresh start would remain to be seen in each case.

But for Jung it is really God himself who is the true subject of all history from the beginning to the present and into the future. He is for Jung the creator of the world; Jung speaks of his almightiness, omniscience, and his justice, but also of his unconsciousness, and it is, for Jung, *God's* wish or need to become man (not the soul's need to transform its own self-representation). This is also why Jung frequently capitalizes the personal and possessive pronouns referring to God (He, Him, His), which in German is only done in the particularly pious diction of believers. *God*, he thinks, needs to become conscious. Jung does not view all the changes in the image of God as a self-portrayal of the transformations of the logic of consciousness and God not as one garb of the soul itself. He always stays with "God" in "His" interaction with man.

Jung is of course *aware* of the fact that he is speaking from within the Christian *myth*. He insists time and again that he is by no means making metaphysical assertions. "I do not imagine that in my reflections on the meaning of man and his myth I have uttered a final truth ..." (*MDR* p. 339). "The psyche cannot leap beyond itself. It cannot set up any absolute truths ..." (*MDR* p. 350). He also explicitly declares that "the image and the statement are psychic processes which are different from their transcendental object; they do not posit it, they merely point to it" (*CW* 11 § 558). Even if the image and the statement may not posit the transcendental object, here: God, Jung obviously does. He asserts that outside the image and statement there is in fact a transcendental object that they point to. Which is a metaphysical hypostasis, a setting up of the object talked about as existing outside the soul's images or statements. For a psychologist this alleged difference between the image and the so-called transcendental object does precisely not exist,[8] because the image has everything it needs within itself. It does not point to anything outside of itself. It only points to itself.

[8] To be more exact and to avoid the impression of my making a metaphysical statement on my part, I should correct myself and say: for *methodological* reasons psychology has to *view* this difference as not existing. Psychological statements are only psychological if for them it does not exist. Psychology is the discipline of interiority: *absolute* interiority, that is to say, for it the difference between inside and outside is canceled. Everything that belongs has been absolute-negatively interiorized into the image or statement in question.

Again Jung says: "When I do use such mythic language, it happens in the full awareness that 'mana,' 'daimon,' and 'God' are synonyms for the unconscious, inasmuch as we know just as much or just as little about the former as about the latter" (*MDR* p. 337, transl. modif.). But the first problem with this statement is that he does not merely make use of a *mythological manner of speaking* for rhetorical purposes, but rather himself mythologizes or theologizes. He insists on our having to dream the [Christian] myth onwards, on the further development of the myth (cf. *MDR* pp. 331–334), which amounts to his insistence on speaking about these matters as a *homo religiosus*, a theologian or better: theosophist,[9] and not as a psychologist. Instead of merely observing the actual development of "myth" and interpreting it, he spins his own yarn. He is here in the myth-*making* business and thus himself takes over the job of the soul as anima.[10] He knows better than

[9] Whereas originally *theologos* simply meant "him who says the gods" and above all referred to the poets, nowadays theology is the name for the scholarly, rational unfolding and systematic explanation of Christian self-understanding (Christianity is the only religion that developed a theology in the strict sense). There is no room in it for what Jung means by "developing the myth further." But because this further development is Jung's concern, the term theosophist, "he who knows about God," seems more appropriate. However, we have to be clear about the fact that Jung does not claim to have *revelatory* knowledge of his own about God, like prophets do. Much like the theologians, he devoted himself to a careful interpretation of already given religious documents and ideas. But he drew forth from them a very different "myth" than the Christian self-understanding, a "myth" all of his own. It bases itself more or less exclusively on the Jewish and Christian corpus (except for the strong Gnostic slant), but makes something very different out of it. Because of this superimposed "overlay" character, his is an already reflected, one might almost say: meta-level, religion, the product of a modern intellect. This is an intellect which, as intellect and modern, nevertheless longs for a *religion* (although it calls it "myth"); it will not make do with a scientific worldview. What Jung did not see is that this religion is a compensation for long lost real religion and precisely *not* a further development of the Christian "myth" itself from within itself. Most revealing in this context is the term *Weiterbau* or *weiterbauen* that Jung sometimes uses for "further development" (e.g., several times in the German equivalent to *MDR* pp. 331-334). In contrast to a self-movement of the myth, *Weiterbau* means "further construction," an active doing. And so it is not surprising that Jung blames the ego: "The fault lies not in it [the myth] as it is set down in the Scriptures, but solely in us, who have not developed it further ...," he says explicitly (*ibid.* p. 332). The *Weiterbau* of the myth is an ego obligation and ego work. Jung would of course protest (his explicit general theory is the opposite: "It is not we who invent myth, rather it speaks to us as a Word of God," *MDR* p. 340), but this is nevertheless what his own text here betrays.

[10] Already the charge that Christianity is one-sided shows that Jung took on the role of arbiter over the soul's real development. Who are WE to meddle in the soul's process with our value judgments? Do we not have to allow the soul to do its thing, whatever it may be? For a psychologist the real history of the soul is not one-sided or wrong; it simply is the way it is and needs to be described, interpreted and appreciated for what it is, but in any case as a full-fledged expression of soul. Only the soul itself would have the right to find situations produced by it one-sided and possibly in need of correction.

Christianity itself what ought to happen with or in the Christian myth. "The myth must ultimately take monotheism seriously and put aside its dualism ..." (*MDR* p. 338): Jung argues myth-internally (or rather, since "myth" here means the Christian religion, religion-internally). "That [what "That" refers to is not relevant here] is the goal, or one goal, which fits man meaningfully into the scheme of creation, and at the same time confers meaning upon it. It is an explanatory myth which has slowly taken shape within me in the course of the decades" (*MDR* p. 338). Jung not only posits God and the Creator, but also the creation! To the extent that he does, he has left the precincts of the root metaphor of psychology, soul. By conferring meaning upon "the creation" and by coming up with an "*explanatory* myth,"[11] he established a quasi-religious belief system or ideology.

This is why he also vehemently rejects *demythologization*, which, after all, is inherent in the psychological approach to mythological phenomena. He says, for example, "How, then, can one possibly 'demythologize' the figure of Christ? A rationalistic attempt of that sort would soak all the mystery out of his personality, and what remained would no longer be the birth and tragic fate of a God in time, but, historically speaking, a badly authenticated religious teacher, a Jewish reformer ..." (*CW* 11 § 647). This quote (together with the rest of the paragraph from which it is taken) is very revealing. In Jung's thinking there are (at least here) only these two abstract extremes: either mythologizing or becoming personalistic, reductive, banal. The third possibility—doing psychology, psychologizing—has no place in his thinking *when* it comes to the question of God and meaning.

The psychologist demythologizes because he does not take gods as gods. But he does not either reduce gods or mythic heros to no more than human ideas or, euhemeristically, to important but ordinary people who were later glorified and divinized. Rather, the psychologist sees them as products of the soul, as ways of the soul's speaking to itself about itself, as its displaying its highest values and the inner hidden logic of man's being-in-the-world *at concrete historical loci*. Of course they are not *gods* for the psychologist. For him, the soul merely gave one particular truth of itself the *form* of "god," because in the

[11] A contradiction in terms. *Genuine* myths are the soul's speaking about itself, its self-representation in a particular one of its many possible logical "moments," not attempts at explaining anything.

status in which the soul was when it felt the need to do so, it was part of the truth of this content that it had to be venerated and looked up to as infinitely superior. The logic of the soul at that time was such that the soul at its one pole (itself as the *really existing* consciousness) was not yet up to itself as its other pole, its own deepest, innermost truth, its logic. Consciousness could only be aware of the latter *as* projected out far away, high above itself, into heaven.

Mythologizing and demythologizing are characterized by reversed dialectics. With the former, you enter the myth and *ipso facto* take its figures and events at face value, adopting them as your own thinking or belief (at least for the duration of your mythologizing), so that you are completely within the myth, enwrapped by it. The dialectic of one's being inside it is that the figures and events become positivized for oneself, extrajected from the mythic or imaginal story as having an independent existence as real beings, rather than as mere fiction, forms given by the soul to its truths. Because of this, Jung's assurance and awareness that he is merely expressing himself in a mythic style of language does not undo the metaphysical hypostasis character of his statements in this area. The hypostatizing is inherent in the *objective* logical form of his myth-making. All the epistemological assurances to the effect that his statements are not metaphysical statements are external reflections and subjective declarations after the fact that do not reach the myth told and thus remain essentially helpless. We have to go by what is in fact said and done in Jung's statements, not by the ego's stuck-on external warnings about how they are not to be understood.

The psychologist with his demythologization, by contrast, does not adopt the standpoint of the mythic tale. Although it is true that he, too, needs to see a mythic image *from within*, this "from within" comes about through a totally different methodological move. Rather than interiorizing *himself* as human subject into the myth so that the latter becomes his own meaning-bestowing myth, the psychologist tries to absolute-negatively interiorize *the mythic image* itself into itself, into its concept, its truth, its soul. And the dialectic of this is that thereby, through this very inwardization, he succeeds in having the mythic tale vis-à-vis himself, distinguishing himself from it, seeing it from outside as an objective soul phenomenon, without adopting it as his own view.

That Jung did not really distinguish himself from the Judaeo-Christian God comes out most clearly in his style and his explicit profession about that style, namely that he was passionately wrestling with this God, his injustice and vindictiveness. "I cannot, therefore, write in a coolly objective manner, but must allow my emotional subjectivity to speak if I want to describe what I feel when I read certain books of the Bible, or when I remember the impressions I have received from the doctrines of our faith" (*CW* 11 § 559).[12] "How can a man hold aloof from this drama? He would then be a philosopher,[13] talking *about* God but not *with* him" (*Letters 2*, p. 34, to Erich Neumann, 5 Jan 1952). A favorite paradigm for Jung was "the story of Jacob who wrestled with the angel and came away with a dislocated hip ..." (*MDR* p. 344).

So much about the first problem that is inherent in his awareness that with terms like mana, daimon, God he uses a mythic language. The second problem lies in the idea "that 'mana,' 'daimon,' and 'God' are synonyms for the unconscious, inasmuch as we know just as much or just as little about the former as about the latter." Here Jung succumbs to a self-deception. The problem with the first three terms is not that we do not know anything about them. About the gods and the Christian God we know a lot, we have volumes of books on them. No, the problem is that this knowledge has no empirical referent.

---

[12] Cf. Jung's letter to Hans Schär, 16 November 1951, *Letters 2*, pp. 28f., where he discusses why he could not "avoid sarcasm and mockery" in writing *Answer to Job*. "Sarcasm is the means by which we hide our hurt feelings from ourselves, and from this you can see how very much the knowledge of God has wounded me ..." From this statement one would have to conclude that the true author of *Answer to Job* was not C.G. Jung, the psychologist, but one of his unresolved complexes. In the preface to this book Jung writes that "Since I shall be dealing with numinous factors, my feeling is challenged quite as much as my intellect" (*CW* 11 § 559). Why does he write a book about a topic when he is still personally gripped by its "numinosity"? Why did he not see it as his obligation as a psychologist to work off (to have long ago worked off for himself) this "numinous" affect and overcome his feeling "wounded" by it? Why has there not long been a scar, but is there still a wound? (The answer would probably have to be that "God must not die!" and that certain emotions [being gripped by something "numinous," a counter-will] and feeling wounded is Jung's form of a proof of the existence of God.) Conversely, we also have to see that his feeling wounded by God is not due to an objective fact (something that literally was done to him by God), but the result of his own machinations. See my discussion of the boy Jung's manipulative processing his "Basel cathedral" experience ("Psychology as Anti-Philosophy: C.G. Jung" and "The Disenchantment Complex. C.G. Jung and the Modern World," Chapters 2 and 3 in: W.G., *The Flight Into the Unconscious*, Collected English Papers, vol. V, New Orleans, LA (Spring Journal Books) 2013.

[13] I have to add here: or a psychologist.

Daimon and God are noumena. Jung thinks that "the unconscious" is different because it is a "neutral and rational" term, "coined for scientific purposes, and is far better suited to dispassionate observation which makes no metaphysical claims than are the transcendental concepts ..." (*MDR* p. 336). But "the unconscious" is just as transcendental a concept as the other ones. It is a metaphysical hypostasis, a noumenon, an *ens rationis*. It is precisely not a scientific concept, not an empirical concept. It does not refer to an empirical referent. By contrast, the "nature" that the natural sciences study is truly different. It has empirical referents: trees and animals, rocks, volcanos, cells, radiation, stars, etc. But "the unconscious" is just a word. It does not point to anything. It exists only in the *theories* or *fantasies* of certain psychologists. Its transcendental nature is only dimly disguised. It merely *sounds* scientific.

And if it were not a metaphysical concept, how could it be a synonym for "mana," "daimon," and "God"? The difference that does indeed exist between "mana," "daimon," and "God" and "the unconscious" boils down to that between honest positive names (the first three) and a name that within itself refrains from naming, pretending to say nothing and claim nothing. "The unconscious" is a name that semantically purposely leaves a blank, an empty slot, but nevertheless logically substantiates this empty slot just the same. "The unconscious" in Jung's parlance is a "theological" term. It has no place in a true psychology. The same applies to Jung's term "the self." It, too, is a metaphysical noumenon. Jung repeatedly stresses that the "symbols of the self cannot be distinguished empirically from a God-image" (*CW* 11 § 289, cf. §§ 231, 282, 757 and elsewhere). Of course not. Because the only empirically real thing are images or symbols, and "the self" and "God," to which they are *said* to refer, are empirically nonexistent metaphysical concepts which are *defined* as being mirror-images of each other. That, for example, the mandala symbol signifies "the wholeness of the psychic ground" may easily be conceded, if one views it psychologically (other equally valid traditional interpretations are: an image, statically, of the world in its wholeness, or an image of cyclical Time in its circular movement). But how Jung arrives from this comprehensible interpretation at the unrelated, ultimately *personalistic* ideas that *as such* it also expresses "the *wholeness of the self*" or, "in mythic terms, the divinity incarnate in man" (*MDR* p. 335) remains his secret. It is his ideology. Neither "self" nor "incarnation in man" are part of the "text" (phenomenological appearance) of the mandala symbol, nor is the notion of the deity.

There is, however, a real difference that Jung does not mention. It is the difference between a God that is part of a living religion, that is in fact worshiped by the people of a whole society because he expresses the deeper inner truth or logic of the mode of being-in-the-world at the historical locus in question, a God who makes a noticeable difference in the practical way how people live their lives and how social life is organized, on the one hand, and the already *psychologized* God—mere subjective inner experiences, God-*images*, as they might come up, e.g., in the dreams of modern people—on the other hand.

That Jung's interpretations are myth-making shows in the fact that (1) he writes about one figure that is only known from the myths and only exists in and by virtue of the myths, God himself, but he writes about him as if he existed outside the myths, and (2) he presupposes that there is an *identity* and *continuity* of this God across all the separate mythic stories that originated at different historical times and are maybe expressive of very different concrete situations and different social climates. All the individual stories become interconnected moments of one single consistent story for him. Through this presupposition, Jung construes, as it were, a super-myth, a myth of his own about the slow maturation of God that extends from Creation to the psychological needs of our days. God is not only one and the same, he also remembers and learns from one episode to the next. Jung writes a *Bildungsroman* (novel of character development) about God.

It is one thing if one concludes from the changes in the God-image in different myths from successive periods that a certain development of *consciousness* in the history of the soul must have taken place. It is wholly another thing to suggest that across all of them the fate and development of God himself is displayed. Again it is one thing to say there is or was a tendency in the soul at a certain point in its history to bring its content "God" down from heaven by letting it become incarnate in man, and it is wholly another thing to say that God wants, or wanted, to incarnate in man. It is the difference between psychology and theosophy or myth-making.

* * *

I will now cite as examples a number of individual instances from Jung's descriptions that show his myth-making at work.

"... in omniscience there had existed from all eternity a knowledge of the human nature of God or of the divine nature of man. That is why, long before Genesis was written, we find corresponding testimonies in the ancient Egyptian records. These intimations and prefigurations of the Incarnation must strike one as either completely incomprehensible or superfluous, since all creation, which occurred *ex nihilo*, is God's and consists of nothing but God, with the result that man, like the rest of creation, is simply God become concrete" (*CW* 11 § 631, transl. modif.). Jung does not simply report what the myth says or draw conclusions from the mythic ideas. No, on his own he constructs a text-external background to it. He brings in from other sources God's omniscience, taking it as a fact, and finds corroborations for it in other myth-external *historical* facts (Egyptian records). Similarly, the following passage also shows that this mythic attribute, God's omniscience, as well as Satan are taken for real. Concerning the remarkable "unusual precautions which surround the making of Mary: immaculate conception, extirpation of the taint of sin, everlasting virginity" (all this is only part of a late 19th century new Church dogma), Jung comments: "The Mother of God is obviously being protected against Satan's tricks. From this we can conclude that Yahweh has consulted his own omniscience ..." (*CW* 11 § 626).

The first incarnation that happened in Christ was according to Jung necessitated by what happened with Job: "Job stands morally higher than Yahweh. In this respect the creature has surpassed the creator. ... Job's superiority cannot be made away with. Hence a situation arises in which real reflection is needed. That is why Sophia steps in. She reinforces Yahweh's much needed self-reflection and thus makes possible Yahweh's decision to become man. ... he indirectly (acknowledges) that the man Job is morally superior to him and that therefore he has to catch up and become human himself" (*CW* 11 § 640, transl. modif.). This is not only Jung's addition, but also shows how he takes Sophia for real, who also does not come from the "text" of the myth, but belongs to

Jung's own super-myth. The myth does not say anything about Yahweh reflecting nor of Sophia stepping in.

According to Jung the moment when Christ on the Cross feels forsaken by God is "the moment when God experiences what it means to be a mortal man and drinks to the dregs what he made his faithful servant Job suffer" (*CW* 11 § 647, transl. modif.). Similarly, the "passion of Christ signifies God's suffering on account of the injustice of the world and the darkness of man" (*CW* 11 § 233). Other than in the "text" of the myth, it is God who is the real subject that suffers in Christ's suffering through the loss of God. So the loss of God is only a suffering, but not a true loss at all, inasmuch as it is God who suffers. He stays.

"The new son, Christ, shall on the one hand be a chthonic man like Adam, mortal and capable of suffering, but on the other hand he shall not be, like Adam, a mere copy, but God himself ..." (*CW* 11 § 628). Jung sees God as a real being that plans and needs to make several attempts at realizing his plans until he arrives at a satisfactory result.

"We cannot and ought not to renounce making use of reason, nor should we give up the hope that instinct will hasten to our aid, in which case a God is supporting us against God, as already Job understood" (*MDR* p. 341, transl. modif.). God is here not a mythological idea, a form of the soul's self-portrayal. God is a real being.

"For it is not that 'God' is a myth, but that myth is the revelation of a divine life in man. It is not we who invent myth, rather it speaks to us as a Word of God" (*MDR* p. 340). In this statement an essential psychological insight is tainted with a theosophist dogma. The theosophist bias lies in the fact that the *form* of "God," of "Word of God," of "a divine life," and of "myth" is *absolutized* and *eternalized.* For a truly psychological view, "God" and "myth" are particular ways or forms that the soul uses at certain historical stages of its own development to speak about itself.

Spirit and Love

Paradigmatic for Jung is the image of Christ on the Cross suspended between the opposites. This is an image that parallels the situation of individuating modern man whose individuation comes precisely about by being not merely suspended between, but almost torn apart by the opposites in what Jung calls a *collision of duties.*[14] The same fundamentally undialectical structure of thought comes out when he speaks of thesis and antithesis and asserts that "between the two is generated a third factor as lysis ..." (*MDR* p. 351, transl. modif.).[15] It is a thinking about the opposites in terms of horizontality. I already pointed out that for the Christian thought of "the incarnation" the horizontal opposition of good and evil or of Christ and Satan is totally inappropriate. The Christian thought of "incarnation" is vertical, the dynamic move of a consistent going under all the way to the bitter end.

This applies even to the good-evil opposition. In John 1:29 we get the following image, "Behold the Lamb of God, which taketh away the sin of the world," which is probably modeled after Isaiah 53:4: "Surely he hath borne our griefs, and carried our sorrows: yet we did esteem him stricken, smitten of God, and afflicted," and has to be seen in the light of the fact that Christ dies the death of a criminal. Christ humbles himself, we heard before. He bowed down so low that he was beneath the evil of the world and could shoulder it. This is clearly a vertical relation. The lamb is of course the image of absolute innocence, sinlessness. But this sinlessness precisely does not shirk away from evil, projecting it out so that it receives a separate existence as Satan or the Antichrist. No, it gets involved with it, burdens itself with it, bears it. And the (criminal's) death on the Cross is the mode in which this idea of bowing beneath evil and shouldering it is "practically" performed, that is, how it becomes a reality.

To do justice to what these images are driving at, we must keep away all naturalistic thinking, all imagining of the described events as the actions or sufferings of persons or figures. Nothing must be substantiated and imaginally literalized. The terribly naive conceptions of Jung's about a deal necessary to bring about a reconciliation between

---

[14] *MDR* (as likewise the *CW*) translates this violent expression meekly as "conflict of duties." "Conflict of duties" suggests an abstract and passive incompatibility, whereas "collision" evokes the idea of a crashing of the two duties into each other. Instead of "torn apart" Jung also uses the idea of being "caught between hammer and anvil" (*MDR* p. 345), another metaphor of action and violence.

[15] The thesis, antithesis, synthesis formula is commonly assumed to describe Hegel's dialectic. But this tripartite scheme and its mechanical application amount to a complete mischaracterization of Hegel's thought. I briefly discussed this mistaken view in W.G., David Miller, Greg Mogenson, *Dialectics & Analytical Psychology. The El Capitan Canyon Seminar*, New Orleans, LA (Spring Journal Books) 2005, pp. 3-4.

man and an angry God, about the vindictive Father God himself who demands an expiatory sacrifice, the killing of his son, in order to become placated, is totally out of place. A retrograde interpretation. Indeed, childish. *Psychologically* understood, these images portray a certain logic, the dialectical logic of how to relate to and overcome evil as well as the evils in the plural, the injustices and wrongs of the world: not by powerful conquest and subjugation, not by rejection and condemnation, but conversely by, with resistanceless sufferance, allowing them to *be*, indeed, even embracing them, and *ipso facto* unrelentingly exposing oneself to them, letting them permeate oneself. Again, this must not be understood naturalistically as precepts for practical behavior or political practice. It is first of all a concept, an insight, a truth on a very deep and remote soul level. It is a *logic* to be comprehended, not a maxim to be acted out. It is the logic of Love.

The idea of a one-sidedness of the Christian message does not make sense here at all. This new revolutionary logic does not have any "sides" in the first place, it cannot take sides. Good and evil are here in a vertical relation. And this logic is comprehensive, the logic of integration and digestion in a quasi alchemical style, the logic of absolute-negative inwardization. Jung's logic of a "mediation between" the opposites, his image of being caught between hammer and anvil, is something completely different. It remains naturalistic, an "ontological" thinking in terms of thing-like substances and spatial relations. Since I just now mentioned the word "alchemical," I am again reminded of my earlier statement that Jung thinks the incarnation in the style of "physics" and does not penetrate to the (al)chemistry of the matter.

We see the same problem in his treatment of the topic of the Trinity. In his hands it becomes, very externally and crudely, a numeric problem, three figures, just as his solution is a numeric one, the addition of the Fourth. Precisely the *logical* issue, the contradictory nature of the Trinity, that originally fascinated him so much as a boy in confirmation class ("Here was something that challenged my interest: a oneness which was simultaneously a threeness. This was a problem that fascinated me because of its inner contradiction. I waited longingly for the moment when we would reach this question" [*MDR* p. 52f.]) was in his later research on the Trinity just as much ignored by him as this entire topic was, to the boy Jung's profound disappointment, skipped by his father, the minister and confirmation class teacher.

The Trinity is itself the imaginally expressed idea of a logical *movement* away from mythic or natural image, substance, person and the absolute-negative inwardization of God into his concept, his truth (rather than an adding of more, a tripling). As such it is at the same time the integration of what used to be mythically imagined as God, a semantic content of consciousness, into the syntax of consciousness. Jung was aware that the "religious spirit of the West is characterized by a change of God's image in the course of the ages" (*Letters 2*, p. 315, to Kotschnig, 30 June 1956), that "As history draws nearer to the beginning of our era, the gods become more and more abstract and spiritualized" (*CW* 11 § 193), that with trinitarian thinking there is a "'change from father to son,' from unity to duality, from non-reflection to criticism" (*CW* 11 § 242), and that "the 'Son' represents a transition stage, an intermediate state ... He is a transitory phenomenon" (*CW* 11 § 272). Jung even warns of the "danger of getting stuck in the transitional stage of the Son" (*CW* 11 § 276).

Yet despite all this and despite his thorough familiarity with alchemical thinking, with the processes of *distillatio, evaporatio, sublimatio*, he does not see the Trinity as one great dynamic, namely the dynamic of a logical distillation-evaporation process of the idea of God, of its going under into itself in the sense of its self-sublation into Spirit, which is of course tantamount to its coming home to consciousness, because by evaporating as a semantic content it enters the syntax of consciousness. The Trinity means, mythologically expressed, God's *dying*, *as* the Son (as the transitional form), on the Cross *into* his truth as Spirit and Love; his dying as a God of *this* world into a "God" who is NOT of this world[16] and *ipso facto* God *sensu strictiori* no longer. The mythical or imaginal God, the God as a substantial being or person as he exists for and in *our* standard naturalistic thinking, is dissolved. From here we can see that Jung's demand that "The myth must ultimately take monotheism seriously

---

[16] It is not transcendence that makes God be a God who is NOT of this world. To be transcendent is the most natural thing for a god. It is precisely part of our ordinary, this-worldly idea about God.

and put aside its dualism..." (*MDR* p. 338) bypasses the Christian truth, not only because the alleged moral opposition (God versus the devil) that Jung refers to with the word dualism is not a serious issue for Christianity, but much more radically because, seen from its telos, Christianity is the overcoming of *theism* as such.

Jung actually himself gets stuck in the transitional stage of the Son, of which he says that it is the stage of moral conflict *par excellence.* This is not only why he is fixated on the Adversary as Christ's other and why he thinks that today "We stand face to face with the terrible question of evil" (*MDR* p. 331), but also why he has to insist that Christ lacks the stain of original sin which means that he had not really become man but was a demigod. This indicates that he imagines the incarnation naturalistically, positivistically, as if it were (or ought to be) an empirical fact. But it is, I think as a matter of course, a psychological event, an event *in the logic of the soul* or in the logic of the world. It is a change of the concept of God, not the literal process of a literal God. It is the emergence of a new insight, of a new way to think, a new status of consciousness unheard of before. This is why we have to insist that in Christ God became man without curtailment, notwithstanding his sinlessness.

This sinlessness, psychologically understood, is not the sign of a divine or semi-divine status since it is not empirical-factual sinlessness, the sinlessness of an empirical being. It is an ingredient in, and follows from, the *concept* and *logic* of Love; it is a logical aspect of Christ. Jung, by contrast, imagines it mythologically (naturalistically) as if it were a *natural inborn* characteristic of Christ (with today's concepts we could almost say "part of his genetics"), a leftover of Christ's divine origin, and proof of the *kenôsis* having been left incomplete. Similarly, he takes the virgin birth for granted. That is to say, Jung deserts the level of thought, logos, and *pneuma* reached by Christianity and regresses to the wholly incommensurate sphere of myth and naturalism. No, the *kenôsis* was complete (but complete only with his crucifixion and God-forsakenness), and the stainlessness of Christ does not come from his past (a "hangover from the past, a *caput mortuum*"), as something natural and an inheritance of his divine origin, but is the fresh final result and *newly generated product* of what he achieved in his life.

It is, first and preliminarily, the product of his logical act of negation of the devil's splendid offers and his realizing that "My kingdom is NOT of this world." Christ's purity and his being free of darkness is logically generated by his pushing off from "this world," by his refusal to fall for the tempting idea of success in the world. Christ chose the path of logical negativity. And his sinlessness is, secondly and above all, the product, imaginally speaking, of his counter-natural obedience to the point of death "here in real life on the earth," his humbling himself and going under all the way, that is to say, his exemplifying the dialectical logic of Love (through which, as I pointed out, the said dictum, "My kingdom is NOT of this world" was first made *real*). Only by bowing under and bearing the sin of the world with resistanceless sufferance does he *become* the sinless Lamb of God. Not the other way around: an a priori sinless being shoulders the sin of the world. How can one, as a psychologist used to a final-prospective approach, think in such a simplistic fashion? "Do good to them that hate you" (Matth. 5:44). "For my strength is made perfect in weakness" (2 Cor. 12:9). *Contra spem sperare.* "If any man come to me, and hate not his father, and mother, and wife, and children, and brethren, and sisters, yea, and his own life also, he cannot be my disciple" (Luke 14:26). The *negation* of the natural way is so obvious in Christianity.

The generation of sinlessness through placing oneself under what is NOT of this world is to some extent structurally analogous to how for Kant a human being that is naturally subject to empirical causal conditions and constrictions can nevertheless become positively free by placing his will under intelligible, supersensory ethical law. Sinlessness is the result of Love (Love as logical negativity) and exists only within it, within its dialectical logic, as a logical moment of it, not as an empirical flawlessness. By the same token, Christ's virgin birth is not his literal (biological or biographical) beginning, but the result of his obedience to the point of death, because only through it does he *make* God's Spirit his true father.[17] The end is the beginning. Myths and soul tales follow a uroboric logic.

Does it make sense, when one has understood this, to say that Christ "has chosen the light and denied the darkness"? Or that Christ "is one side of the self and the devil the other"?

---

[17] Soul and soul truths are *made*, not discovered as already existing facts, as if one could stumble upon them.

And is it reasonable to think that today "We stand face to face with the terrible question of evil," in fact, that evil is a real *question* for us, and a terrible one at that? There are for us terrible evils and terrible evil-doing, but this fact does not pose a psychologically essential question for us. The soul in modernity is psychologically hard-boiled. It has accepted that imperfection is part of the world. For the soul in modernity, there is not such a thing as the act of Creation by an exclusively good God. The world originated in a Big Bang and developed through Darwinian evolution (these are not only scientific theories, they express our psychology). There is therefore absolutely no reason for making a fuss about "Whence comes evil?" The soul no longer naively believes in or is interested in the Good anyway, and so it cannot be psychologically or "metaphysically" shocked by the existing evil anymore, despite the fact that empirical man (as ego-personality) is still likely to be emotionally shocked when confronted with concrete empirical events of evil. Hannah Arendt was psychologically right when she spoke of the banality of evil. We do not think in terms of Evil, a numinous idea, but soberly of crimes, e.g., crimes against humanity. And today we explain human evil-doing rationally as coming from cruel parents or other bad social conditions in early childhood, from a lack of character education, from genetic causes, from political and economic misery, etc. Evil is human, all-too-human and an attribute for us, not a substance (as Jung wanted it to be with his violent fight against the *privatio boni* idea). And the devil has simply gone up into thin air. He is only a memory image from the past.[18]

We also ought to remember that the radical good versus evil, light versus darkness antinomy is a historical phenomenon and not an anthropological constant. It is relative to a certain stage in the development of consciousness and seems to have come up in those cultures that changed from a "shame culture" to a "guilt culture" at some time during the first millennium B.C., especially (in a religious-metaphysical sense) in ancient Iran (Zarathustra), spreading from there to other cultures, but also (in an ethical sense) with the Greek turn from *mythos* to *logos* in pre-Socratic philosophy (around 400 B.C.). As

[18] On the devil see Gustav Roskoff, *Geschichte des Teufels. Eine kulturhistorische Satanologie von den Anfängen bis ins 18. Jahrhundert*, Köln (Parkland) 2004, originally Leipzig 1869.

already Nietzsche showed, there is a *genealogy* of morals, an original social distinction between "noble, aristocratic" versus "ill-born, worthless" or a practical distinction between "brave, good, capable" versus "bad, cowardly" slowly having become transformed into the absolute moral or religious opposition of good versus evil. As everything historical, the absolute good-evil distinction, just as it began in time, so it also has an end in time. Today it has had its time: because it has done the job it had in the history of the soul, namely to raise consciousness to a higher level of itself by producing an extremely pronounced sense of "I" and "person." For modern consciousness it *ipso facto* has become psychologically obsolete.

I spoke of the logic of Love. Christian Love is nothing "natural," not an emotion, a feeling, a liking, a preference. But Jung refuses to enter the logic of Christian Love and into the concept of Love *as* a logic. When it comes to the topic of Love, his thinking stays completely naturalistic and naive. We see this most clearly when he insists that we today "can no longer swallow" that "a God who is a loving father, who is actually Love itself," demands the sacrificial killing of his own son in order to be appeased. First of all, this is again the naive kindergarten idea of Love and of God, God as a kind, good-hearted, loving father. But it is not only childish, it is also absurd: Jung construes a *conflict* between Love and the crucifixion (this absolute conflict is what makes the Christian idea impossible to swallow for him).

For his external concretistic thinking there are four separate items. (1) There is a God as an existing being, of whom (2) it is said that he happens to be loving and a "God of goodness." (3) In open contradiction to his being Love, he demands, however, the crucifixion of his son, because (4) only then can he forgive man. But for Christianity there is only one single reality here, the logic of Love, and everything else is *moments* of or within the dynamic of this logic. Love and the crucifixion of the Son are identical. The dying on the Cross IS the absolute *kenôsis*, the going under, the resistanceless bowing down under evil, and this IS nothing else but a spelling out of what Love is. And it is *in itself* and *as such* absolute forgiveness or redemption. No purchase of a desired salvation by paying a price for it.

This Love is nothing harmless and nice. It is a logic not in the spirit of the kingly, majestic logos of the Platonic tradition. And the fact that it is a logic does not mean that it is something abstract, a merely mental idea, cut off from life. No, it is—provided that it *is*—the actual *kenôsis* and "dying on the Cross" in real life. It *is* only if and to the extent that it is an existing logic, the logic of actually lived life. But conversely, the fact that it is lived life does not make it empirical-factual behavior or experience. It *is* something logical, intelligible, a thought, but a *real* thought.

To show how God fits into this one dynamic we can refer back to insights gained in our discussion of the Trinity above. The first point to make is that we must not situate and keep God outside and prior to the incarnation, as the Father who wants his Son to undergo this process. No, in "the Son" God himself became man. For the second point I can turn to the culmination of the incarnation, Christ's despairing cry from the Cross: "My God, my God, why hast thou forsaken me?" The incarnation or *kenôsis* completes and fulfills itself in the irrevocable death of the ontologized, substantiated God, which, however, is *ipso facto* the birth of God *as* Spirit and Love. Just as Christ's untaintedness by original sin is the *result* and *product* of his relentless humbling himself, so is God not the originator of the incarnation behind the scenes, but its outcome and product. Christianity is a New Beginning. Psychologically, it is a grave mistake to see its God as a continuation of the Old Testament Jahweh, as "*answer* to Job." "Old things are passed away; behold, all things are become new" (2 Cor. 5:17). The Christian God is a new God, a new creation. And he is the (holy) *ghost* of the old imagined God: the result of his death, of his absolute *kenôsis*; the product of the distillation and evaporation of God as a being or figure. That is to say: God as Spirit, logos, pneuma and as the logic of Love.

By the same token, Christ's resurrection is not the undoing of his absolutely emptying himself of his divine nature, not a return to the *status quo ante*. His resurrection is nothing but his going under into the logic of Love.[19] Kerényi showed that the ancient Greek concept of god, *theos*, was a predicate, not a subject (in Greek grammar the vocative, the case of address or invocation, did not exist for *theos*):

[19] Similarly, "hell" is not naturalistically a place for burning people after death, and "damnation" not a future fate. "He that believeth on him is not condemned: but he that believeth not is condemned already, because he hath not believed in the name of the only begotten Son of God" (John 3:18). The damnation that Christianity speaks about is inherent in, and no more than one's not finding one's way into, the logic of Love.

originally nothing was predicated of *theos*, but *theos* was predicated of other things. Helena, in the tragedy by Euripides of the same name, exclaims for example: "Oh gods, for it is god when one recognizes the loved ones." The event of recognizing those one loves is god. Another example: *deus est mortali iuvare mortalem* ("it is god for man, if one helps another person"). Linguistically, according to the form of the word, the original content of the name Zeus seems to have referred to the event or phenomenon lighting up or shining out and only later did it take on the meaning of the originator of this lighting up.[20] In the same spirit we could say that the resurrection as well as the new Christian God are nothing else but the happening of the logic of Love.

"God *is* Spirit" (John 4:24) and "God *is* love; and he that dwelleth in love dwelleth in God, and God in him" (1 John 4:16). The subject goes under into the predicate. These sentences do not speak of a being who happens to have the nature or quality of being spirit and love. When these sentences are spoken and ended, heard completely and comprehended, then what is left is Spirit and Love.

The *New* Gospel according to St. Jung

I admit, referring to Jung as "St. Jung" is a bit malicious. But all the authors of a gospel are automatically canonized (St. Matthew, St. Mark, St. Luke, St. John), and Jung with his super-myth is not writing as a psychologist, but is the author of a new gospel, new not in the sense of just another one parallel to the four existing gospels, but of a radically revised version, a "corrected" and "improved" one. What is the *gód spel*, the "good tidings," the *eyangelion*, the "Good News," brought by Jung?

The point of the "Good News" is to bring hope into a seemingly hopeless situation. It shows that there is a way out of being lost in "sinfulness" and alienation from God. It asserts that, completely unexpectedly, the way to heaven and redemption is open, after all. So we have to begin with the hopeless situation into which and against which Jung proclaims his new gospel.

---

[20] Karl Kerényi, "*Theós*: 'Gott' auf Griechisch." In: *Idem*, *Antike Religion*, München (Albert Langen) 1971, pp. 207-217, here pp. 210–214.

The truth of modernity into which Jung was born, a truth personally keenly felt by him already at the early age of eleven years[21] and later in his mature years repeatedly expressed, was that God is dead and that "Our myth has become mute, and gives no answers" (*MDR* p. 332). "No, evidently we no longer have any myth" (*MDR* p. 171). Today "we stand empty-handed, bewildered, and perplexed [...]" (ibid.). "There are no longer any gods whom we could invoke [...]" (*CW* 18 § 598).

Nietzsche said, "Dead are all gods: now we want the overman to live."[22] Analogously, Jung said in the same situation—not in these very words, but in what he did—"there are no longer any gods; our myth is mute: now we want God to come alive in the future." Jung's project is one of rescuing the core of the old religion by kicking it upstairs into the future and kicking the old version of it down into the irreality of one-sidedness.

The message of Jung's gospel is that God is by no means dead. The myth has become mute only because we did not develop ("construct") it further. The incarnation in the historical Jesus Christ was not at all the real thing. The real thing, the real truth, lies in the future. It is still coming. "*God wanted to become man, and still wants to*" (*CW* 11 § 739). The real incarnation and the true revelation of God still lie ahead of us.

A future promise and a roping modern man in for a great task, the task of individuation *as* God's incarnation, is the best way to make the dead God appear to be alive again. Life means future. And the feeling of having a great task, agenda, or mission in the world gives *psychically* reality to this idea of a future, because it means active involvement, "*striving* towards wholeness."

There is a reciprocity, indeed, identity of empirical man's individuation and God's incarnation. It is one and the same process, seen from two sides. "Just as man was once revealed out of God, so, when the circle closes, God may be revealed out of man" (*CW* 11 § 267). "The human and the divine suffering set up a relationship of

---

[21] See my "Psychology as Anti-Philosophy: C. G. Jung," and "The Disenchantment Complex. C.G. Jung and the Modern World," Chapters 2 and 3 in: W.G., *The Flight Into the Unconscious*, Collected English Papers, vol. V, New Orleans, LA (Spring Journal Books) 2013.

[22] Friedrich Nietzsche, *Thus Spoke Zarathustra*, at the very end of Part One.

complementarity with compensating effects. ... The cause of the suffering is in both cases the same, namely 'incarnation,' which on the human level appears as 'individuation'" (*CW* 11 § 233). "The dogmatization of the *Assumptio Mariae* points to the hieros gamos in the pleroma, and this in turn implies ... the future birth of the divine child, who, in accordance with the divine trend towards incarnation, will choose as his birthplace empirical man. This metaphysical process is known to the psychology of the unconscious as the *individuation process*" (*CW* 11 § 755, transl. modif.). "The future indwelling of the Holy Ghost in man amounts to a continuing incarnation of God. Christ, as the begotten son of God and pre-existing mediator, is a first-born and a divine paradigm which will be followed by further incarnations of the Holy Ghost in the empirical man" (*CW* 11 § 693). "That is the meaning of divine service [*Gottesdienst*], of the service which man can render to God, that light may emerge from the darkness, that the Creator may become conscious of His creation, and man conscious of himself" (*MDR* p. 338).

This is Jung's Good News. It is, of course, a utopia. However, be that as it may: "That is the goal, or one goal, which fits man meaningfully into the scheme of creation, and at the same time confers meaning upon it. It is an explanatory myth which has slowly taken shape within me in the course of the decades" (*MDR* p. 338).

But in order to give a future to God and his incarnation and revelation in empirical man, after Christianity had taught for 2,000 years that the incarnation and the true revelation of God had already happened in Jesus Christ, this existing Christian message has to be rendered ineffective and defunct. Christ's incarnation was not a real incarnation at all, according to Jung. "... Christ on the contrary lives in the Platonic realm of pure ideas whither only man's thought can reach, but not he himself in his totality" (*CW* 11 § 263).[23] "In the Christian symbol the tree however is dead and man upon the Cross is going to die, i.e., the solution of the problem takes place after death. That is so as far as Christian truth goes" (*Letters 2*, p. 167, to Victor White, 10 April 1954).

[23] This statement is obviously in conflict with Jung's other one that through the incarnation God became "a definite being, which is this and not that."

Positivism

But in Jung's scheme the Good News must not come as a new religion, the incarnation must not be through the birth of a new Messiah, and Jung not be a prophet. No, it has to be a Good News in the spirit of scientific, empirical psychology. Jung wants to appear as no more than an observer and interpreter of the historical phenomenology of religious symbolism *and* the phenomenology of the modern inner experience of people. And the Spirit or Holy Ghost is for him not really spirit and teacher at all, not the event of a deeper understanding of the logic of Love and its becoming more real. No, "He is the spirit of physical and spiritual procreation who from now on shall make his abode in creaturely man" (*CW* 11 § 692). Physical and in creaturely (i.e., natural) man, man as animal! The statements about the development of the Trinity "can—and for scientific reasons, must—be reduced to man and his psychology, since they are mental products which cannot be presumed to have any metaphysical validity. They are, in the first place, projections of psychic processes, and nobody really knows what they are 'in themselves,' i.e., when they exist in an unconscious sphere inaccessible to man" (*CW* 11 § 268). "If such a process exists at all, then it must be something that can be experienced" (*CW* 11 § 447 transl. modif.). Following the Gnostics Jung thinks that Christ ought to be *real* "as a psychic centre in all too perilous proximity to a human ego," "as an inner, psychic fact," as "Christ within" (*CW* 11 § 446). Before I said that Jung's project is one of rescuing the core of the old religion by kicking it upstairs into the future and rendering the real Christian message defunct. Now I have to add that it is at the same time one of kicking the incarnation down into the positivity and literalism of a personalistic development and private experience in the empirical man as factual individual—as the individuation process.

Whereas psychology would locate the incarnation, if I may say so, *in Mercurio*, in the coldness and remoteness of the logic or syntax of the *soul*, and comprehend it as the appearance and continued deepening of a real dawning of the objective *insight* into the logic of Love in the culture of our Western world, Jung psychologistically and concretistically stuffs it into the *psyche* as the appearance, in *people's* private dreams or visions, of certain symbols (symbols of "the self").

Psychology is reduced to anthropology (a "psychology" of people, cf. Jung's "must be reduced to man"), and what is a soul *truth* is either reduced to an experience or to an image. What actually is a question of the syntactical form of consciousness or of the logic of man's being-in-the-world becomes something semantic. Jung operates with the binary opposition of "metaphysical validity" versus "can be experienced." But the Trinity, being a soul truth, is neither a metaphysical claim nor can it be experienced. The emergence of the idea of the Trinity is the manifestation of a transformation of consciousness, from the mythological and naturalistic Father stage to the fundamentally post-natural stage of Spirit and Love. The change from one stage or logical status of consciousness to a succeeding one is something very real (nothing speculative, not an assertion of metaphysical entities), but it cannot be an experience, inasmuch as it is something syntactical and not something semantic, something psychological and not something psychic.

The correlate of experiences (even of so-called "numinous" experiences!) as well as of images is the modern ego. "Images" have their logical home in our modern world of television, advertising, slogans, labels, clichés, graphic arts, illustrations, pictures, and "experiences" belong to our modern world of entertainment, emotionality, excitement, thrillers, sensationalism. Whether images and experiences appear out there or inside people does not change their logical status. The *soul* has no stake in images, nor in private experiences. The soul is about truths, it exists in concrete universals, in logical *forms*.

Christianity's answer to Jung's Gnostic "Christ within, as an inner, psychic fact" is Matth. 18:20: "For where two or three have gathered together in My name, I am there in their midst." This does not mean that—naturalistically—Christ miraculously shows up among them. No epiphany, no literal appearance. Christ's *reality* is not the crude positivistic or naturalistic presence in literal experiences. It is a "subtle" reality, purely *logical*, intelligible: the logic of an interpersonal (communal) being-together *if* it is truly one "*in My name.*"

With his concept of "the self" Jung tried to translocate the *objective-soul* character of the soul from its being all around us as the generality of a soul *truth* or as the general logical form of consciousness into each private individual and imprison it there, into "the empirical man," who, as Jung well knew, is synonymous with the ego ("the ego—that is, the empirical man" *MDR* p. 346, cf. "man—that is, his ego" *MDR* p. 337, "the ego, i.e., the empirical, ordinary man as he has been up to now" *CW* 11 § 233, transl. modif.).

Soul truths are logically negative. But they have everything they need within themselves, including their realness. To the extent that Jung operates with the disjunction or dissociation of two abstractions, Christ living in "the Platonic realm of pure ideas whither only man's thought can reach" here and "incarnation in creaturely man" there, he shows that he has left the realm of soul, which—as truths or general logical form—is neither, but comprises both.

Jung's psychologistic positivism goes hand in hand with a metaphysical hypostatizing. Although he denies the possibility of assigning "metaphysical validity" to the psychic processes that he has in mind and says that they are no more than projections, he nevertheless toys with the idea of an *Ansich* ("what they are 'in themselves'") and of their existence independent of or outside human consciousness. This is the same mystification as whether there is a difference between the allegedly empirical images of the self and god-images and whether behind the god-images in the soul there might or might not be an existing God. Soul truths are neither positivistic nor metaphysical. They neither need our emphatically exercising an artificial restraint concerning their "validity" in the deliberate style of the empirical scientist, nor any mystifying speculation concerning what they might be "in themselves." They *are* what they are and suffice themselves. They are existing concepts, existing logical form. They within themselves encompass or permeate the mind just as well as the real.

The disregard of the historical, phenomenological evidence

Jung's positivism is the result of his retrograde clinging to the logical *form* of *myth* (substantiated figures, semantic contents) *at a time* that had long left the form of myth behind and was well advanced on its way into Spirit, i.e., syntax, logical form. He was already on the level of logical form, so that by trying to rejuvenate myth what he came up with was of course not myth in its authentic sense, but positivism, *semanticized* modernity, modern so-called "myth," i.e., ideology.

I said, "Spirit, i.e., syntax, logical form." I take this opportunity to expressly point out that "spirit" must by no means be understood in terms of the popular idea of and widespread craving for so-called "*spirituality.*" The latter is a mystification and inflated abstraction. But psychology has to stay down to earth and feel committed to concrete phenomena. It has to be able to account for what it is talking about. Much like the *Zeitgeist* is the inner form or soul of a real age, so our concept of spirit refers to the inner logical form of real phenomena. And just as the syntax of a given language can be analyzed, so the logical or syntactical form of real soul phenomena is (and must be) analyzable, demonstratable, communicable, not only an inner experience beyond speech. Spirituality is, as it were, one of our consumer goods; it is for people's subjective indulgence and gratification. Psychology has to be committed to the objective soul and its truths. Also, spirituality is the *remythologizing* understanding and *naturalistic* conception of the very thing that, as spirit, is precisely the overcoming of mythological image and naturalistic, substantiating thinking. Psychology must conceive of spirit "in spirit and in truth," rather than reifying it as "spirituality."

When one looks at "the case" that Jung presented for his utopia, one is struck by the fact that he spun his yarn mostly from very old material (Old Testament, New Testament, especially the Apocalypse, certain immediately pre-Christian Jewish texts, Gnostic texts, Church Fathers) plus one single isolated event from modernity, indeed from his own lifetime, the declaration of the Dogma of the *Assumptio Mariae* by Pope Pius XII in 1950. It is really a stray and rather obscure event, at the periphery of our real world, a piece of the Middle Ages belatedly emerging completely out of context in modernity and of no noticeable further consequence or impact, although Jung considered it "The only ray of light" (*MDR* p. 332) in our benighted days, which, however, only confirms how isolated it is.

This is a very thin phenomenological basis for a grand theory about soul history and what is historically needed today. Jung prided himself upon his empiricism. But except for a few passing references to Joachim of Flora, Meister Eckhart, Jakob Böhme, in other words, references merely to individual *semantic* phenomena, *the whole real development* of Western culture over the centuries, the rich phenomenology of the *real history of the soul* in the West, is ignored, that powerful history in which a consistent series of tremendous *form changes* concerning the syntactical constitution of consciousness took place. It is amazing that an empirical researcher passes the major mass of evidence by. What we think ought to have happened or ought to happen is psychologically neither here nor there. Psychologically relevant is only what in fact comes out in the "documents of the soul," the actual phenomenology of the real. Psychology has the task of studying the soul in the Real. It has to go by what actually happened in order to find out what the soul's *opus* is. Not archaic myth and not the texts of 2,000 years ago (which are only relevant for historical psychology), but the development that led to where we or rather where the soul is now have to be the basis for our conclusions.

Western culture underwent a historical development in which, as Jung correctly noted, among other things "The otherworldliness, the transcendence of the Christian myth was lost" (*MDR* p. 328). And this probably provides the answer why Jung did not deign this historical material worthy of his *psychological* attention. The soul, this was his bias, (a) simply had to be about transcendence, it had to be a soul *with* a God, and (b) only what had the form of mythic or archetypal image and of natural, personified figure, only what was substantiated—semantic—could be considered as psychologically relevant. Jung was unable (or unwilling) to see that the mentioned consistent evolutionary progress in the direction of a *transformation* of consciousness—which is precisely what Western history is about and what is its absolutely unique achievement—is exactly that *real* "further development" of the Christian "myth," that *real* "further development" of the incarnation that he demanded (although of course as a very different one from his idea of it). It is the consistent deepening of the *kenôsis* and a movement from myth to logos, from substance to Spirit (logical form, syntax, function). God had become man. How could Jung expect him to still be transcendent and otherworldly? God himself had died on the Cross. "My God, my God, why hast thou forsaken me?"—was this to be no more than an isolated one-time cry by one particular individual, without any consequences and without any *truth*, that is, without *general* validity? Just a subjective experience, literal personal suffering? Of course not. The process of the integration and realization of the *kenôsis* was the Western soul's *opus magnum*.

"The further development of the myth should probably begin at the point where the Holy Ghost was poured out upon the apostles and made them into sons of God ..." (*MDR* p. 333, transl. modif.). Jung sees that the point of this further development is the spirit. But he refuses to see that the historical *form change* hinted at by me *was* the work of the spirit and the only way how the workings of the spirit could manifest themselves. Jung wants to begin with the spirit alright, but he has no relation to spirit and therefore does not see the spirit where it has already long in fact realized itself. For him the spirit is not spirit at all, but simply another event belonging to *mythological* and *ritualistic* cultures: a status change of the *human persons*, namely their divinization ("that they were more than autochthonous *animalia* sprung from the earth, but as twice-born ones had their roots in the deity itself," *ibid.*, transl. modif.). This is something for which the Christian Holy Ghost is certainly not needed, since this was what in the initiations performed by the pre-Christian cultures of the mythological and ritualistic age had been perfectly achieved all along.

With Christianity the "Holy Ghost" *stage* of consciousness had been entered. This is something totally different from the task of turning people into sons of God. It is about a new syntax and as such beyond people's psychology and their inner experience and individuation process. In the Bible, the story of the outpouring of the Holy Ghost upon the apostles is not presented as turning the latter as individual persons into sons of God at all. It has nothing to do with their own inner process, their self-actualization. Rather, this outpouring leads to a *linguistic miracle*, the speaking "with other tongues," a speaking that is understood by all "in our own tongue, wherein we were born." Psychologically and symbolically understood this points to the fact that the spirit expresses itself in something general or universal, communal, in language, in logos, in something that is interpersonal (or transpersonal) and public (just as Christ's presence requires communality, the congegration, *ecclesia*: "For where two or three have gathered together in My name, I am there in their midst"). Not individuation, nothing private and personalistic. Rather, other *tongues*, new general *logical forms* of consciousness, *within which* individual persons may have their place.

Although with Christianity the "Holy Ghost" *stage* of consciousness had been entered, it nevertheless took about fourteen centuries until man's implicitly already being in this new stage was really caught up with and the new truth had been integrated into the very structure of consciousness, its syntax or logical form. The very further development of the "myth" that Jung demanded and projected into the future had already happened in real history. But because it had happened in the objective soul, in the general logic of man's being-in-the-world during the early modern period (starting early with Dante, Meister Eckhart, Nicholas of Cusa, the Renaissance and the Reformation and continuing up to Kant and Hegel) rather than in creaturely man as positive-factual individual, and because it as a matter of course amounted to the loss of "the otherworldliness, the transcendence of the Christian myth" and to the death of God as a semantic content, as a mythic god, a being or figure, Jung had to reject, condemn, and ignore it. God as a mythic figure and the archaic phenomenon of man's "*filatio*—the sonship of God" (*MDR* p. 333) had to be preserved at all cost, or rather atavistically reinstituted, which at the same time amounted to the scotomization of the whole level of syntax or logical form and to psychological consciousness's being restricted to focusing on semantic phenomena. And so Jung came up with a compromise formation. The very thing responsible for the actual historical dissolution of the transcendence of God, namely the Holy Ghost, was rightly supposed to be the point of departure for the further development of the Christian myth, but, as Jung's "further *construction*," it was supposed to be a matter of the future, of future incarnations of God in empirical man as the latter's private individuation or self-actualization.

THE CAMPAIGN FOR THE REALITY OF EVIL

Summarizing the moves necessary for Jung's theosophy to come about we can say:

Both the Incarnation and the "further development" were long accomplished facts in the real history of the soul. This their reality character had to be denied, they had to be rendered ineffectual and negligible (1) through the one-sidedness thesis concerning the Christian message and (2) through the psychological-irrelevancy thesis concerning the actual development of Western culture. The latter was denounced as merely expressive of ego-consciousness and abstract rationality, whereas the soul was declared to be active only in niches, in subcultures like Gnosticism, alchemy, heretic movements, the modern Roman Catholic Church, and of course inside of man in the famous "the unconscious." What had already happened and become real in the past had (3) to be unhinged and projected into the future as a new program, whereby a *retrograde* move donned itself as its opposite, a *utopia.* What was and would have to have the form of a soul truth had (4) to be newly construed as a positive-factual event and experience in empirical man; a concrete universal had to be reduced to a private occurrence. And (5) the God who had already distilled over and vaporized into Spirit and Love had to be repaganized, remythologized, resubstantiated as a figure; this was tantamount to the view that the core of the Christian message, the logic of Love or, as Jung put it, the "gospel of love," was "one-sided" and needed to be "supplemented ... with the gospel of fear" (*CW* 11 § 732). Jung's message that God is not dead falls, inevitably has to fall, behind the logic of Love and brings the "Good (?) News" that "*God can be loved but must be feared*"[24] (*ibid.*, Jung's italics).

The lever to perform this feat was the idea of the reality of evil and that *the* important psychological question that we are confronted with today is evil. Evil is the cornerstone in Jung's theosophic edifice. The topic of evil in Jung's thinking has its origin (efficient cause) not in phenomenology, in an empirical observation that evil is a central soul topic, which it clearly is not today (except for some fundamentalists who speak for example of an "evil empire" or an "axis of evil"), but needs to be understood in terms of its *causa finalis*, the functionality it has for the edifice of Jung's thinking about religion and God. Evil was an absolute necessity for his project of exposing Christianity as one-sided.

By declaring evil as *the* terrible question that modern man is faced with and by passionately rejecting the *privatio boni* idea of evil, the devil as a personified embodiment of evil could be resurrected and, far beyond the question of the devil, the renewed

---

[24] In other words, *love*: maybe, at times, optionally; but *fear*: indispensably, inevitably. From the point of view of the Christian truth God cannot be loved because God has transformed into Love itself so that he ceased to exist as a possible object of our love. The only way to still speak of God is in the style of what Kerényi taught us about the Greek word *theos*, as a predicate, not a subject. "It is god for man if one has in fact one's place in the logic of Love." And the moment you are in fear you are no longer (or not yet) up to the Christian truth, up to the logic of Love. For in this Love, fear cannot hold out.

pagan, mythological mode of thinking in terms of personified figures could be solidified. Of course, historically the devil had long been obsolete, even more than God. But other than God, who has no practical anchor in real life for modern man, evil behavior and tendencies, what we call the shadow, are still a concrete experience and very real. With this experience of the reality of evil acts or motivations Jung could catch the psyche of modern man, touch him at his weakness, his unconscious guilty conscience due to his subliminal awareness of his personal shadow aspect and inferiority feelings. "Evil" emotionalizes. The absolute moral opposition and the hopeless "collision of duties" bring man into a terrible, but indispensable fix ("between hammer and anvil") and *ipso facto* corner him, nail him down, forge him into a positivity.

On the one hand, this could be used to boost evil up to become a quasi metaphysical substance, the devil as a reality. On the other hand, this alchemical solidification and congealing of man in his positivity *is* the individuation in Jung's sense. Individuation means that the *psychological* is translated into something *psychic*, something literal (a process aiming at the ontic individual), that the soul is brought down and reduced from logical negativity to positivity. The soul (as the self) was not allowed to be only "underworldly" and to have its place only "*post mortem*" in "'*eternal'* life" "yonder." It had to be an immediacy here in this life as a psychic event.[25]

But this individuation as positivization was at the same time God's incarnation in empirical man, in creaturely man, man as literal individual. The one only happens *as* the other. God, too, had to become a positive experience, literal. It was not enough for him to be something in or for the soul, in faith and in a beyond.

---

[25] Repeatedly Jung sees critically cases where a solution does not happen in this life. Cf. above his statement, "In the Christian symbol the tree however is dead and man upon the Cross is going to die, i.e., the solution of the problem takes place after death. That is so as far as Christian truth goes" (*Letters 2*, p. 167, to Victor White, 10 Apr 1954). Or concerning Goethe's *Faust*: "... the conclusion of *Faust* contains no conclusion" (*MDR* p. 318). "... Faust's final rejuvenation takes place only in the post-mortal state, i.e., is projected into the future" (*CW* 12 § 558). "It is an unconscious reality which in Faust's case was felt as being beyond his reach at the time, and for this reason it is separated from his real existence by death" (*Letters I*, p. 265 to Anonymous, 22 March 1939). A psychological view would not interpret the solution's happening in a post-mortal state as a sign for its being projected into the future, but for its taking place *psychologically*, i.e., in the logic of the soul and "in spirit and in truth," rather than in the sphere of empirical *psychic* experience.

"I do not believe, I know." Jung obviously had fully understood that *for the soul* God was dead. In the logic of the soul God was obsolete. For this reason God could only be rescued or resurrected if he took his abode in empirical *man* (rather than in the soul), in other words, as something positive, as our *knowing* (no longer as faith, Love, and hope), as the immediate factual experience (*Urerfahrung*) of literal man. This is why psychology—actually psychologism (psychology anthropologized, personalistic)—was indispensable. "I cannot help believing that the real problem will be from now on until a dim future a psychological one."[26] God had to become incarnated (in Jung's new sense) *through* man's individuation (positivization), just as individuation could only occur through God's incarnation in the empirical man.

Jung could not want a new religion. It was clear to him that the time of religion, of Church, faith was over. Or rather, he could not want religion *in the logical form* of religion. He needed to preserve it in the form of "modern psychology," the "psychology of the unconscious." The place where it was to happen, the place where the real action was to be, was the empirical man's inner, his unconscious, "in all too perilous proximity to a human ego," "as an inner, psychic fact" (*CW* 11 § 446). The notion "God" had to be hid and stored away in "the unconscious" and given asylum in the absolute privacy of the inner experience of the literal individual, because it could no longer have a place in public "official" consciousness and in the *general* logic of modernity. Only in "the unconscious" and in the privacy of inner experience was God put out of reach of and immunized against consciousness and the critical mind, and had the notion God become absolutely unaccountable and unassailable, because it was merely subjective: "God is an immediate experience of a very primordial nature, one of the most natural products of our mental life, as the birds sing, as the wind whistles, like the thunder of the surf. ... You can just be glad to have such a conviction, like a man who is in a happy frame of mind, even if nobody else, not even himself, knows why, but certainly nobody could prove to him that he is unhappy or that his feeling happy is an illusion" (*Letters 2*, p. 253, to Snowdon, 7 May 1955). The incarnation had to become a positive fact in creaturely

[26] *Letters 2*, p. 498, 12 April 1959, to Werner Bruecher.

man. It was not allowed to be truly psychological: a mercurial reality, strictly intelligible, the logic of Love, and, above all, a *truth*. The singing of birds is not a moment of truth. It is only a natural event, and feeling happy is a subjective state.

Jung, as we have seen, operated with the abstract binary opposition between pure idea and positivity. For the soul's mercurial logic, which is neither merely intellectual nor a positivity, but nevertheless a reality, namely the reality of absolute negativity, there was no room in his thinking, at least his thinking about God.

"*The guilty man is eminently suitable and is therefore chosen* to become the birthplace for the continuing incarnation" (*CW* 11 § 746, transl. modif., Jung's italics). More than that: God is downright dependent on creaturely man and on the latter's superior awareness to become conscious of his, God's, own full reality, including his shadow. It is "evil," the "shadow," that gives—this is Jung's thesis—three-dimensional concreteness, earthly weight, and positivity to what otherwise would only be abstract thought, and forces God down into the empirical man.

Since the idea of God as an only good and loving Father had for the modern soul long degenerated into a sentimental cliché without the least power of conviction, merely an empty word, and had made "God" utterly boring, Jung's shocking ideas of the reality of evil and of the necessity of the "gospel of fear" had the function of making the topic God psychically exciting and lively once more. And Jung's harnessing the psychological mind for the task of "lodg(ing) the antinomy [between good and evil] in Deity itself" (*CW* 11 § 739) drew all attention to this great problem and so helped to divert the mind from the fact that this being, God, in whom the antinomy was to be lodged, was no longer real for it. If the devil or evil was a reality once more and if, furthermore, evil was to be internal to God, the faded idea of God received a seeming reality, too.

Only by integrating evil as substance (or as its personified and mythologized form, the devil) into the very nature of God as one of the latter's inherent aspects, could the God idea psychologically be reanimated and given again a seeming reality of its own, the God idea which by Jung's time had become a mere airy reminiscence of what former ages believed in.

Here we may want to remember that despite his frequent insistence on a *gnôsis theou*, God was apperceived by Jung primarily not at all as a truth and in terms of knowing, insight, revelation, but in terms of power: as an "opposing will" (*CW* 11 § 290), "a powerful *vis-à-vis*" (*MDR* p. 335), a "numinosity and the overwhelming force of that numinosity" (*MDR* p. 336), as something "which sets us at odds with ourselves" (*Letters 2*, p. 28, to Schär, 16 Nov 1951). As what crosses our own human will it is obviously in itself already "the Adversary"! The prototypical construction of this God-concept seems to have happened during Jung's twelfth year, when the thought about the beautiful Basel cathedral being smashed by a huge excrement dropped by God came to the boy Jung, and he reacted with the questions, "Who wants to force me to think something I don't know and don't want to know? Where does this terrible will come from? ... *I* haven't done this or wanted this, it has come on me like a bad dream. ... This has happened to me without my doing" (*MDR* p. 37). As can be shown,[27] at least in this one instance the whole idea of the "terrible will" that forced him to think something that *he* does not want is an artifact of the boy Jung's making. This "overwhelming force" was by no means a spontaneous experience, a "phainomenon" (something that showed itself of its own accord). Rather, God as this "opposing will" was nothing else than the projection and hypostasis of his resistance, his refusal (i.e., *his own* opposing will) to think his own thought, a thought necessitated by his inner maturation process and aiming for his becoming undeceived about his cherished existence in childhood paradise and in childlike innocence. But if "God as terrible opposing will" was at this early time the result of Jung's own machinations, it is likely that these machinations were also the prefiguration for and *logical origin* of his mature ideas about God.[28] And then we see immediately why the integration of evil in the nature of God was indispensable for

---

[27] See my "Psychology as Anti-Philosophy: C. G. Jung," and "The Disenchantment Complex. C.G. Jung and the Modern World," Chapters 2 and 3 in: W.G., *The Flight Into the Unconscious*, Collected English Papers, vol. V, New Orleans, LA (Spring Journal Books) 2013.

[28] Thus my view is also corroborated by another event in Jung's life, his Uriah dream and the discussion of it in *MDR* pp. 217 ff. See my "Jung's Millimeter. Feigned Submission – Clandestine Defiance: Jung's Religious Psychology," Chapter One above.

him. The reality of this God, born out of Jung's own powerful resistance, hinged upon God's "Adversary"-character.[29]

Through his "incarnation," Jung had said, this God would come into "all too perilous proximity to [the] human ego." The ensuing peril was inflation (that the empirical man identified himself with God). Jung was only able to structurally, logically evade the danger of inflation by taking recourse to a dissociation. He had to split the identity of the I into the ego and the self. Contrary to the actual meaning of "self," which as reflexive pronoun refers back to the subject (the I), the self had to be a full-fledged other to the ego, a not-I. By the same token, consciousness had to be artificially split into two, consciousness itself and its other, "the unconscious." Although, for Jung, God incarnated in the empirical, creaturely, guilty man, he did not incarnate in him as conscious personality, but only in his unconscious and as the symbol of the self. By having shelved the incarnated God in the unconscious, Jung had, to be sure, to live with a fundamental dissociation, but in return gained the advantage of not having to make any metaphysical claims of his own or stand up as a religious teacher. All he did, so he at least thought, was to innocently describe facts, his empirical observations of the self or the God-images in the unconscious, "Christ within." He was only a scientist presenting his facts-based theory.

The dissociation is the telltale sign that Jung's project of individuation as God's incarnation in the empirical man does not work. As a content of "the unconscious," the self or the incarnated God is

---

[29] Jung's Gnostic leanings and especially the Gnostic coloring of his peculiar God image (as above all displayed in his *Answer to Job* and characterized by the ideas of the dark Shadow of God, of God as terrible opposing will, of God's fundamental unconsciousness and his need of redemption by man, etc.) cannot, it seems to me, be explained as being due to mature Jung's having been influenced by his learned studies of Gnostic texts. It is much rather based on his early, deeply personal needs, namely on the boy Jung's decision to escape his initiation experience (the initiation *into the modern situation*) by refusing to resistancelessly think the thought that had powerfully forced itself upon him in the Basel cathedral incident. The boy Jung's own resistance was projected out and thus appeared to him as the alien terrible will of God who, as a tempting God, forced him to think an absolutely sinful thought. By attributing the authorship of the evil thought to God, the boy Jung rescued his own innocence (together with the innocence of the "childhood paradise," of he world as "God's world," in contrast to the godlessness of modernity). This stance, acquired at such an early age and never revoked by Jung throughout his long life, was the *psychological* fertile soil (in him) ready to receive whatever later *intellectual* stimulation (and corroboration) by Gnostic conceptions the scholar Jung may have received.

just as "only ideal" and just as out of reach for the ego as the Church God was for the traditional believer prior to the integration of the devil into God. The incarnation cannot be one in the empirical man, unless it were really to happen to the I, which, however, must not happen because it would be tantamount to inflation and psychosis. The dissociation cancels the "empirical-factual" aspect of the incarnation in Jung's sense. And it is how the soul's logical negativity appears when it becomes positivized (the *un*-conscious, the self as *not*-I).

We have seen that Jung's ideas about evil are not only, and maybe not predominantly, theoretical ideas or insights. What is at least as important is the psychological function they perform for Jung's psychology and for him personally. Jung's whole thinking about God, the incarnation, the Trinity, had the character of a utopian program. It was up in the air. The ideas of evil and the shadow had an anchor in the concrete personal experience of each individual. As such they had the psychological function to (psychically, for our human feeling) ground Jung's utopian views in empirical reality. This was Jung's deepest longing: to give *reality* and *conviction* to what he (unconsciously) felt was utopian or a mere ideology, a *counter-factual* agenda of his own (the rescue of God in modernity) against his already knowing better.[30]

This makes comprehensible the obsession with which Jung fought against the *privatio boni* idea about evil. It is very interesting to see how Jung tries with all his might to *rationalistically argue* against and disprove this idea as if it were nothing but an intellectual concoction, rather than a psychological idea. He needed to show that it was a *wrong* idea. But this is unpsychological, just as unpsychological as would be the insistence that, for example, the "virgin birth" is a wrong idea. Right and wrong are false categories for psychology. Jung himself once warned of an "artificial sundering of true and false wisdom," of one's succumbing "to the saving delusion that *this* wisdom was good and *that* was bad" (*CW* 9i § 31, transl. modif.). "As psychologists we are not concerned with the question of truth, ..., but with living forces,

[30] Because evil was *the bridge* necessary for God to be able to come down and incarnate in "the guilty man" and because this incarnation means that each of us becomes a son of God (even if only "in the unconscious"), evil had, in the last analysis, also the function of rescuing for Jung personally the grandiosity of the psychological ("metaphysical") child-status, the *filiatio*. "Ye are gods"—precisely by "metaphysically" staying children.

living opinions which determine human behaviour. Whether these opinions are right or wrong is another matter altogether" (*Letters 2*, p. 417, to von der Heydt, 13 Feb 1958). When he expressed these views, he spoke as a psychologist. But when it comes to evil and to God, Jung ceases to be a psychologist, even if his intellectual argument against the *privatio boni* is that it is *psychologically* false, bad for the psyche. The *privatio boni* may be a metaphysical assertion, but is it not precisely as such also "a psychic fact which cannot be contested and needs no proof" (*CW* 11 § 554, adjusted)? It has first of all been a psychological phenomenon, the soul truth of many centuries of the history of the soul in the West. It is absolutely pointless to argue for or against a phenomenon. But precisely because it is first of all a phenomenon and only secondarily a rational philosophical justification of this phenomenon, Jung needed so passionately and obsessively to attack it and prove it wrong as if it were *only* an intellectual theory. He needed the deified "opposing will," or else his resistance against his own insight into the truth of modernity would lose its seeming justification. His program was, after all, a counter-factual one.

But that evil is a *privatio boni* makes perfect sense within the logic of Love. For this logic, evil is not a substance, not, for example, the body, particular desires, drives, or passions. It is not anything ontic, a natural 'entity' like "the shadow." Nature is neither good nor evil. No, evil is something logical and, as such, negative (a *privatio*): namely one's NOT *negating* one's natural impulses and naturalistic imaginal perspectives, one's NOT placing oneself under supersensory ethical laws, one's NOT humbling oneself all the way and NOT (logically) bowing under the evil and evils in the world. It is the *omission*, or rather *refusal*, to overcome, time and again, one's "original sin"[31] by rising to the sphere of logos and the concept.

---

[31] "Original sin," in a psychological sense, means the discrepancy between man's implicitly having become human and thus having logically sublated his animal nature, on the one hand, and his explicitly staying a priori conditioned by his emotions and desires, on the other hand, emotions and desires which of course are the *human*, and thus post-natural, already fantasy-guided equivalent to the animal's animal nature, its instincts. "Natural" means something different depending on whether it refers to humans or to animals (or even to inanimate nature, for that matter). Our impulses are "natural" for us humans, mere events, but as impulses of *humans* they are *in themselves* beyond the merely natural. They are already, although of course only implicitly, ideas or concepts (in contrast to mere triggered "release mechanisms").

POSTSCRIPT 2013
THE "DEATH OF GOD" AND THE ASCENSION OF CHRIST

In aphorism 125 of his *The Gay Science* Nietzsche made a madman pronounce that "God is dead!" This statement reverberates the one of late Antiquity reported by Plutarch: "Great Pan is dead!"[32] We are well advised to go back to the Greek god Pan and reflect the "death of God" problematic in the light of a *psychological* view of his fate (in contrast to a view in terms of the history of religion, the history of ideas, or philology). In my essay "The Flight Into the Unconscious" (Chapter Six in my book with the same title[33]) I discussed one essential aspect of the god Pan, namely, that aspect that shows best in his relation to the nymph Echo.

There I developed the nature and fate of Pan in three stages.

(1) The goat-legged Pan chases the nymph Echo in order to rape her, but she escapes from him in an absolute sense by transforming into echo, that is to say, by altogether leaving the dimension to which Pan and his lust belong, the dimension of body, physical desire and literal behavior, and entering a totally different dimension that is absolutely out of reach for Pan-consciousness, the (alchemically speaking) evaporated dimension of resounding sound, i.e., (a) vibration of the air rather than anything like a substance and (b) "mere" reflection. Psychologically speaking this is the imaginal or symbolic portrayal of the dimension of absolute negativity. And by becoming echo, Echo did not primarily *escape*. Rather she came home to herself, entered into her own true (no longer "natural," i.e., bodily) nature.

(2) The fact that Pan despite his crude naturalism or "positivism" was attracted by Echo in the first place, a nymph whose inner essence was insubstantial, "vaporous," means, however, that it was from the outset Pan's very own vocation to head for the dimension of absolute negativity. Whereas according to the first stage it was Pan who initiated the course of events and forced Echo into her metamorphosis (which would be a personalistic reading of the myth), from the point of view of the second stage we can see that it was conversely Echo who initiated this whole episode. Psychologically expressed: The

[32] *De defectu oraculorum* 17.

[33] Vol. V of my Collected English Papers, New Orleans, LA (Spring Journal Books) 2013.

soul made *herself* as Echo appear to *herself* as utterly physical Pan in order to entice Pan (herself in her initial status of Pan-consciousness) to follow Echo—not for the purpose of sexually uniting with *her* in the flesh, but in order to make him follow her into her *dimension*. However, so I suggested, Pan's love was not potent enough to give him wings to be able to follow her. Instead of a flight on Echo's part from Pan we now realize that this story shows much rather Pan's abandoning Echo. Pan-consciousness is psychologically impotent. It is driven by a desire for a type of reality that for structural reasons it is incapable of attaining or comprehending.

(3) With the interpretations on the first two levels, we stayed within the *myth* of Pan (or one particular myth about him). When we now turn to Plutarch's story about the call that was heard resounding in late Antiquity, the call that "Great Pan is dead!," we have left this mythic tale and, more than that, along with it the entire sphere or level of myth proper. We have already entered the sphere of speculative thought and "literary production," that sphere to which Nietzsche's text also belongs. And as historians of religion will (rightly) insist, the Pan of Plutarch's story is not simply identical with the one who in mythology chased Echo. Ultimately, because the name Pan was homonymous with the word *pan* meaning "all, everything," Pan turned into the All-god of Greek speculative thought, so that the call reported by Plutarch could be interpreted in late Antiquity and by Christian Church Fathers as well as in later times as announcing the death of the nature gods as such, of the Greek polytheistic *pantheon*. However, what in Plutarch and according to the interpretation just mentioned still appears in imaginal style as a quantitative statement (*all* the nature gods, *pantheon*) and a statement about substantial beings and particulars (all the nature *gods*) must psychologically much rather be comprehended as an attempted statement about the whole *stage* or *logical level* of nature (the natural world) as the locus of the manifestation (or the "medium" for symbolic expression) of the soul's *essential* life. In other words, we ourselves in our conception of the call reported by Plutarch must perform the move from Echo (substance, person) to echo (logical form).

Psychologically, it is more than the fortuity of homonymy that allowed this idea of the All-god to attach itself to the *mythological* Pan. Despite the real difference between Great Pan and Echo's Pan, I claim that the call reported by Plutarch is also relevant for the latter. The point is that the resolution of mythological Pan's disaster, the problem of his being fundamentally incapable of attaining that dimension that he was unwittingly driven to desire, could not happen within myth, on the soul's nature level. It could only be realized outside the level of myth and imagination. And it could only become possible through Pan's own Echo-like transmutation in the sense of a distillation or evaporation of his crude physicalness and substantiality, so to speak only "over his dead body," i.e., through his "death" as the old bodily Pan. The All-god of speculative thought was already a bit on the way to the goat-legged Pan's sublimation.

Considered in this light, the death of Great Pan in late Antiquity is for the adherents of the old polytheistic religion (i.e., for that consciousness that remained informed by the soul's nature stage of mythical imagination) much the same as what *within* myth itself had been the disappearance of Echo for Pan, an irrevocable loss, only now one on a more fundamental level. Just as Echo did not really escape, but on the contrary came truly home to herself through what for Pan-consciousness was her disappearance, so Great Pan's death does not mean that he (and along with him mythological Pan) is simply gone. Only *for the old Pan-consciousness itself* is Pan dead. But for a psychological understanding, Pan finally managed, through what seems to be his and Great Pan's *death*, to ascend into the dimension of absolute negativity and thus, as we might figuratively say, be united with Echo. The goal the soul had set for Pan, for itself as Pan-consciousness, within myth by enticing Pan to follow itself as Echo has been *reached.* But it could only be reached *outside of* myth and through the "death" of Pan himself, that is, when the very stage of the imaginal style and polytheistic imagination had been overcome: when the naturalistic, "positivistic," polytheistic consciousness of the mythological imagination as a whole had been left behind altogether.[34]

[34] It is important to realize that overcoming the logical stage of myth and nature does not mean that thereafter the practice of the mythological imagination would have become impossible. Individual events of mythological fantasy and particular imaginal contents are still possible, but they then occur on and within a new level of consciousness, as sublated moments. It is similar to how we can still today practice archery or use spinning wheels, but only as a hobby within a world whose style of warfare or yarn production happens on fundamentally higher technical levels. Logically obsolete does not mean having factually totally disappeared.

But this means that Great Pan is dead and bygone only for that consciousness that despite Pan's death and sublation in late Antiquity *persists* to be Pan-consciousness—thoroughly naturalistic or imaginal, and takes this call literally. Then the call, "Great Pan is dead!" is heard from Pan-consciousness's worm's eye view. By contrast, for an understanding that in itself was able to truly follow Echo's move and has itself undergone the same "death" or negation that happened to Great Pan, Pan has merely been "alchemically" sublimated, distilled, evaporated: sublated into logical or syntactical form—the *form* or *style* of consciousness.

If we keep this in mind and aim for a psychological view, that is, for an understanding that views such stories and other psychic material as artless expressions, self-articulations, of the soul's logical life (rather than historically and philologically in terms of influences, of the historical development or migration of literary, religious, or ideological motifs, and their explicit meaning and intended function at their own time), then we can begin to realize the surprising fact that Plutarch's story about the death of Great Pan, on the one hand, and the Biblical story of Christ's Ascension, on the other hand, describe "the same" *psychological* event—"the same," however, from opposite standpoints (and in this sense also not the same), namely, once from naturalistic, "positivistic," and imaginal Pan-consciousness and its worm's eye view and once from the standpoint of a consciousness that has been reached by an at least implicit awareness[35] of the status of absolute negativity. This psychological event described in these two different ways is nothing else but the negation and overcoming of the whole level of Pan-consciousness itself (of the nature standpoint of myth and polytheistic

[35] The awareness is only implicit inasmuch as the Ascension is still described from the worm's eye viewpoint of those who stay behind and initially experience it as an external event, and this event as one of a loss, a disappearance. This feeling of loss is then *compensated* by the expectation of a Second Coming, by the Christian virtue of hope, and needs a Comforter, the Holy Ghost. The idea of the Holy Ghost *as a mere Comforter* betrays an insufficient understanding of the Holy Ghost. For in truth, "the Holy Ghost" *is* the very goal and not merely a consolation for a loss. Pentecost *is* in itself already the so-called Second Coming, even if only implicitly. Nothing more is to be expected. But because the believing Christians were not able to comprehend this, their understanding was still only implicit, although by comparison with the Plutarch story, the way we interpreted it, it was a true step from not understanding to understanding. The true Second Coming would therefore consist in nothing but the change from the implicit to an explicit *understanding* of the Holy Ghost.

imagination, alchemically speaking of "the physical in the matter") in favor of that level that the New Testament, for example, refers to by the phrase "in spirit and in truth" and for which in psychology we are wont to use such a designation as "absolute negativity."

The fact that this "same" event is seen from opposite standpoints also explains the fundamental differences between the two stories themselves, e.g., that the one talks about Pan as protagonist, the other about Christ, the Son of God, God having become man—crucial differences that seem to obscure their "sameness," their common topic. If you *begin* the story with a Pan, you cannot really overcome and transcend Pan and his naturalism. All you can possibly get to is "the *death* of Pan," his mysterious disappearance, to a loss. The *prôtê archê* (first beginning, starting point, principle) determines the scope within which the outcome has to happen, the boundaries that cannot be overstepped. An Ascension, in the sense of a metamorphosis from physical substance to an absolute-negative status, is precluded if it is a story about someone like Pan. If, by contrast, a story aims for the veritable sublation of the natural level as such and wants to *reach* the level of absolute negativity, then it *has to* start out with a protagonist that *a priori* has his true origin outside the natural world, like the ("merely") *incarnated* Son of God, just as, on the still mythological or imaginal and thus "naturalistic" level, the nymph Echo could only turn into echo because she had been Echo all along. *De nihilo nihil fit.* In the land of soul you have to already *be* there if you want to get there. You have to have arrived before you set out on the journey that is to take you to where you want to arrive. Only he who has shall be given.

This paradox is resolved the moment we realize that psychological stories can only describe the movement from "implicit" to "explicit." Their end is the coming to light of what was already inherent in the beginning. No new events. No external influences. Nothing new happens. The point of soul images and narratives is to present and portray one single particular moment or soul truth. And what appears as their narrative action (plot) is merely the self-unfolding of the inner logic of this self-enclosed[36] moment or truth, that is to say, its full releasement into its truth.

---

[36] Cf. "The image has everything it needs within itself."

Within myth, there could not have been a "Great Pan is dead!" The pronouncement of Great Pan's death presupposed that the boundaries of myth had syntactically already been transcended. But by nevertheless semantically still being about Pan, Plutarch's report could nevertheless *not show* that his death was his Ascension to the sphere of absolute negativity, the sublation of semantics into syntax. This can only be expressed and realized if the stories about Pan himself are completely transcended (forsaken) in favor of, for example, a story about the fundamentally *transcendent* Christ, his birth, death, and ascension, and thus with a semantic content that within itself *from the outset* expresses the sublation into syntax. The call "Great Pan is dead!" contradicts itself. Semantically it pronounces Pan's death, but syntactically it celebrates him and keeps him alive. The physical weight of the image of Pan evoked through the sentence subject is so great that in the sentence his death can only be semantically proclaimed, but cannot become syntactically real. The message of the predicate is merely externally stuck on the sentence subject (Pan), but does not permeated it. This dictum becomes released into its truth only when the thought about Pan has been left behind altogether. The Great Pan can only be *really* dead when his place has been taken by a successor-figure as the protagonist of the story, a completely new, no-longer natural figure.[37]

On the basis of these reflections about Pan's fate and destiny we can return to Nietzsche's "God is dead!" and how it has generally been understood by modern consciousness and say that it, too, is pronounced and conceived from the worm's eye view of the (thoroughly modern, not only post-mythological, but now also post-Christian and post-metaphysical) equivalent of the (much more innocent) ancient Pan-consciousness.

"God is dead! ... And we have killed him!" Really? Not at all. The whole idea and experience of loss bears witness to a superficial apperception. And we understand also why the one who pronounces this insight of the death of God in Nietzsche's piece has to be a

[37] The sublation, e.g., of semantics into syntax or of the positive into absolute negativity cannot be witnessed and not be described in present-tense (or past-tense) sentences. It can only be described in the perfect tense. It must always already have happened. The only thing that *can* be witnessed and narrated is the move from "implicit" to "explicit," vide Echo turning into echo.

madman.[38] Foolish he is not only from the perspective of the ordinary, commonsensical people who have become utterly irreligious and, with much amusement, ridicule the madman's search for God. No, he is also foolish from a higher perspective because he searches for something with a lantern that cannot, and never could, be found like a lost key-chain or like the virus that causes a particular illness. The commonsensical people's laughter is perfectly justified. A search for God is silly, a misunderstanding.

Why? Nietzsche's madman himself unwittingly gives us a clue when at one point he says, "Do we not smell anything of the divine decay [*Verwesung*]?" For us the word "decay" evokes two associations. The first is the alchemical notions of putrefaction and fermenting corruption, the decomposition of the thing or image form of a matter. The reference to smell points to the transformation from a solid state and thus visible or imaginal form to a gaseous one (*evaporatio*). But of course, just like in the case of Echo's transmutation into echo, echo was still a merely physical, sensual symbol of what was actually meant (absolute negativity), so here smell is likewise the still sensual symbol of the actually intended evaporation product.

Secondly, since the German "*Verwesung*" can, according to its literal and contrary to its dictionary meaning, also be understood as suggesting a process of transformation into one's essence (*Wesen*), "essentification," we can also think of a form change from imaginal or semantic content of consciousness into the logical form or syntactical structure of consciousness itself, or from object to subject. "God is dead!" thus does not mean dead, bygone, over, in the naturalistic or positive-factual sense. It means *verwest* in the non-dictionary sense of this word, his having come home into his *Wesen* (essence), into his true home or true form as "spirit and truth," his having been absolute-negatively interiorized into consciousness. Not: "*we* have killed him." Rather, the soul, once it had reached the level and gestalt of the Christian God, has subjected this its own highest value to a *Verwesungs-* and thus *digestion* process of integration into itself as consciousness. Integration into consciousness is an alchemical process, the psychological analogue to the physical digestion of food. In both cases it is a form of catabolism and, finally, absorption. Both

---

[38] "*Der tolle Mensch*" is not really a madman, but a mad (foolish) *man*.

alchemy and biological digestion first mechanically break down the intact shape (thing form, imaginal form) of the foreign matter/food into small particles (pulverization, mastication, etc.) and then proceed to a "chemical" decomposition, which in digestion breaks larger molecules down into smaller ones that can be absorbed into the organism's own blood stream. Psychological integration also ultimately absorbs the broken-down object of consciousness as an other, as something foreign, into the soul's "blood," that is, into the liquidity of its own logical or syntactical life.

But Nietzsche's madman stays stuck, if I may *anachronistically* say so, in Pan-consciousness, and this is why *Verwesung* only means literal decay for him, whereas "essentification," distillation, sublimation, integration remain fundamentally outside the naturalistic scope of his mind. He construes God as an entity, a positivity (something, by the way, god/God had never been, even when he was still alive).[39] To treat God like a factual object and to search "out there" for him, for something that by the 19th century has long been interiorized from object of consciousness into the constitution of consciousness, of the very consciousness searching for him, and that already literally "informs" it (permeates its form), is mad. But it is also a sign of radical unconsciousness. Unconsciousness is consciousness's ignorance of itself or possibly, on a higher level, its misconception (illusion) about itself.

This madman is of course not a particular individual, but the image of the inner depth of modern man at large, the man of the 19th and 20th centuries, just as likewise the ordinary people who laugh at the sight of the madman do not represent individual people, but modern man's superficial ego-consciousness cut-off from his depth, what Heidegger called "the They" ("*das Man*") in contrast to "authenticity."

I said that my ascribing a Pan-consciousness to the madman of Nietzsche's text was clearly anachronistic. Pan-consciousness had not been so primitive as to confuse the divine with positivities, with things to be found in broad daylight or searched for with a lantern. This is already obvious from Pan's interest in such logically "negative" nymphs

---

[39] This is what is thoroughly modern (a tribute to 19th century positivism) about Nietzsche's dictum. The Pan of the ancient myths had not positivistically been apperceived as an entity or positive fact.

as Syrinx and Echo. No, as I pointed out above, the madman's consciousness is thoroughly modern, post-mythological, post-Christian, and post-metaphysical. It is on a fundamentally higher, more sophisticated logical and psychological level than ancient Greek Antiquity or Christian consciousness had been. However, *on (and within) this its own higher level*, the modern mind regresses beneath itself and even far beneath the much more naive former levels of consciousness.[40] Only a highly advanced modern consciousness can be so primitive and reductive as to cling to a positivistic stance.

In Nietzsche's story this stance comes out in the motif of "the lantern in broad daylight." Despite the fact that it clearly harks back to the story of Diogenes going through Athens searching during daytime with a lantern for "a man," or, as some less likely reports have it, for "an honest man," the motif in Nietzsche's text must be understood in terms of the modern situation and in particular of its fundamental positivism. For a psychological understanding the use of the lantern symbolizes first of all the scientific approach to the ultimate secrets of the universe by means of technical devices, starting, for example, with Galileo's telescope and van Leeuwenhoek's microscope and ending, for the time being, with such extreme apparatuses as the "Large Hadron Collider" at CERN, etc. These are "lanterns" inasmuch as they are meant to enhance the power of the unarmed eye, which is considered to be insufficient.

And *these* lanterns are, sort of by definition, *always* used in "broad daylight," because they focus exclusively on the world of positive facts, on what is accessible to empirical observation. In this sense they restrict experience, systematically narrowing it down ever more to the technical-functional aspect of reality. Empirical observation can never get "behind the impressions of the daily life," "behind the scenes," to that "other picture that looms up, covered by a thin veil of facts,"[41] and that provides *for us* the soul picture of the respective aspect of the world. No doubt, the sciences do manage to penetrate far "behind" what for the everyday understanding would be of the impressions of daily life, precisely because they equip the natural eye with extremely

[40] Regression can never return to a previous status of consciousness. It can only within its own level of consciousness fall short of the latter's standard, sometimes terribly short, and usually to a more primitive, more brutal form than that of the previous level of consciousness. The higher the logical sophistication of the level of consciousness, the deeper it can fall, far deeper than would have been possible at earlier stages.

[41] C.G. Jung, *The Visions Seminar*, vol. 1, Zürich (Spring Publications) 1976, p. 8.

powerful technical "seeing aids." But psychologically, rather than getting *behind* the eye's impressions they merely enormously expand the range and scope and detail of the "thin veil of facts" by providing a much closer look at it. The most blown-up close-ups of the *veil* do not show "that other picture" and do not take us into the depth or to truth. From here, coming back to the madman we can say that his lantern on principle fixates him in front of the veil. And when Hegel said, in another context, "It is manifest that behind that so-called curtain which is supposed to conceal the inner world, there is nothing to be seen unless *we* go behind it ourselves [...],"[42] we understand in our context that *if* we are interested in depth and truth, we have to throw away all lanterns. *If* we want to do psychology, we have to give up empirical observation (the impressions gained by the eyes and the ever more sophisticated armament of the eyes, today, for example, in neuroscience through magnetic resonance imaging) and begin with speculative thought. The correlate of empirical observation is the positivity of facts.

Apart from the sciences, "lantern" can, however, also refer to what at first glance might seem totally opposite, namely to something that seems precisely to come close to *our own* going behind the veil or curtain that Hegel had spoken about. But this is an illusionary appearance. I am referring to psychological introspection. The latter is just as much a "lantern," a technical "apparatus," as are the scientific instruments, even if in a more figurative sense. As a *method* it is technical, and it also equips the unarmed eye, i.e., natural experience, with a new seeing aid. Introspection, too, searches "in broad daylight," namely for the *facts* of the inner life, of "the unconscious."[43] The facts of

[42] G.W.F. Hegel, *Phenomenology of Spirit*, translated by A.V. Miller (Oxford University Press, 1977), p. 103.

[43] "The unconscious" must not be compared to the mythological Night. As something systematically investigated and studied by the modern positivistic mind and with *the latter's* method of introspection, it is just as much part of what psychologically we call the world of facts as are the farthest nebulae in the universe, the big bang at its beginning, the tiniest subatomic particles, or the strange phenomena of quantum physics. All these things can only be detected by means of "a lantern in broad daylight." "Detected" is the right word. Science has from Bacon's days onwards been seen as kind of a criminal investigation, as "putting nature to the torture." Modern science has similarly, but differently, been interpreted as a kind of "industrial espionage" (Claus-Artur Scheier): man's spying directed towards discovering the secrets of nature for the purpose of exploiting them in human industrial production. In extensive investigations, Greg Mogenson has shown how the courtroom metaphor permeates the self-understanding of depth psychology.

the inner life thereby made accessible also merely expand the scope of the "impressions of the daily life" and the "thin veil of facts." That is to say, the focus on the facts of the inner life, too, is sold on empirical observation. Psychology begins only once *we* have stepped behind this veil.

Furthermore, outside of Nietzsche's story we find the fundamentally *regressive* and *primitive* status of the fundamentally *higher* consciousness in modern man's (and Nietzsche's own) *existentially suffering* from "the death of God," from nihilism, from the loss of meaning, as well as in the corresponding compensatory nostalgic yearnings. This existential suffering is very different from the use of "lanterns in broad daylight," be it ones of the sciences or of psychological introspection. But it is the *existential-emotional* equivalent of the *theoretical* search with the lantern. Its regressiveness shows in the fact that, abstractly, formalistically viewed, it falls way behind the position reached with Christ's Ascension to the Plutarchian level of "Great Pan is dead!" But we know already that it is not a return to what I called "Pan-consciousness." It is both much more advanced than the latter, decidedly modern, and at the same time much more primitive.

At the end of Antiquity, the experience of the death of Pan was the first immediacy of post-polytheistic, post-imaginal thinking, which is a style of thinking or a level of consciousness that came home to itself in the experience of Christ's Ascension. *Implicitly*, the death of Great Pan meant Ascension, the fundamental sublation of the naturalistic and imaginal standpoint as a whole. It meant the mind's being reached by the idea of absolute negativity. What the death of Great Pan implicitly heralded, but what it had as yet been incapable of expressing, or capable of expressing only in a negative way, became thus explicit in the Christian idea of Christ's Ascension.

Logically, psychologically, in the image or notion of the Apostles' seeing Christ rise and slowly disappear from sight in the infinite distance of the height of heaven, a fundamental distancing is taking place. It is a distancing, or *différance*,[44] between the world

---

[44] I use Derrida's term, but not for what it refers to in his thought. His thought has its locus in modernity. I use *différance* precisely for an aspect of the premodern world. In a way, what Derrida has in mind when he talks of *différance* could be interpreted as the modern secularized and "positivized" (operationalized) version, after the end of

down here and infinity, not, however, as an abrupt opposition between, and harsh juxtaposition of, the finite and the infinite, separated by an unbridgeable gulf, but as a continuous, seamless transition and extending from the one to the other. In and through this image the dynamic of this distancing inscribed itself emotionally into the soul in the course of history via the deeply felt experience of Christ's disappearing. Centuries later, by the time of the Renaissance, the dynamic of this disappearing in infinity, which at first had merely been the external image of the Ascension, had fully interiorized itself into the soul. This becomes visible and finds its objective representation in the invention of central perspective in painting with its vanishing lines and vanishing points, and, again a little later, also expressed itself theoretically in the emergence of infinitesimal calculus. In both cases, what once had been, qua Christ's Ascension, merely a single seen or envisioned object or content now had developed into a general principle, the mind's own way of seeing and method of thinking. The Ascension had come home to itself.

Among the many central motifs or symbols of the story of Christ, the Ascension is that one that has the function to represent the opening up, *within* the unity of human world experience, of a radical difference between this world and "other world" in the sense of the described continuous transition, the establishment of this difference through the world's gradual "disappearing," in this absolute-negative mode, in its own inner depth and infinity.[45] This pull towards infinity is one of the several crucial, essential aspects of Christian being-in-the-world and of metaphysics. What emerged here is the entirely new sphere of otherworldly *transcendence* and *infinity*.

"Transcendence" had, prior to modernity, been the soul's home and dimension in the Christian West for nearly eighteen centuries.

metaphysics, of the fundamental distancing at work in the Christian soul's move into transcendence as explicitly described in the motif of Ascension. "Positivized": "grammatology" instead of metaphysics; not Ascension (verticality), not infinity and absolute negativity, but the horizontal, endless *operation* of deferral.

[45] It is, however, clear that the popular and conscious (explicit and enacted) understanding of Christianity did not always match the latter's inner absolute negativity. Very frequently a crude understanding in terms of an irreconcilable opposition of this world and the other world prevailed. But this literalism belongs only to the sphere of people's psychology. The soul in the Christian West, under the surface, went pregnant with the inner truth of the Christian images. The soul does not get misled by the noise on the surface.

Now, when at the end of the epoch of metaphysics, the end of the era of Christianity, that is, roughly speaking the time of the turn from the 18th to the 19th century, the experience of the death of God made itself felt, this was by no means a repetition of the psychological problem and experience of late Antiquity. The death of God could not at all have found its resolution and fulfillment in the idea or image of Ascension, the way "Great Pan is dead!" did. The "death of God" did not need a move *to* the dimension of transcendence. At the time when the death of God was experienced this dimension of transcendence had been old hat, if I may express myself so casually. For after all, the Christian soul had lived in the logical status of transcendence for hundreds of years. No, "God is dead!" is precisely the first immediacy of an entirely new status beyond "the Ascension of Christ" and the transcendence it had initiated. This is so because the experience of the death of God once and for all has the psychology of Christ's Ascension behind itself (and, of course, along with it the entire answer of Christianity to the foregoing psychology of pagan Antiquity). But on the other hand, the idea of the death or loss of God is still a first immediacy and the merely implicit and merely negative form of what is actually intended. What is this that is actually intended and in fact, even if only in a negative way, heralded by "God is dead!"?

As pointed out, the Ascension was still sensually *imagined*, which means (1) seen as an external event, something happening to an Other (the Lord Christ), and (2) described in sensual terms as a movement in space up to heaven. Therefore, although it was already the event of the soul's being reached by the notion of its home country (absolute negativity), it was still no more than the pictorial imagination of it and thus its merely *implicit* truth. As the movement into *transcendence* it is only the *imagined*, somehow concretized and substantiated form of absolute negativity, its first immediacy, absolute negativity still in the form of otherness, as a yonder. Now, what had happened with the entrance of the soul into modernity was that this whole level of transcendence, which as the first immediacy of absolute negativity had first been explicitly entered through the notion of Christ's Ascension, had been sublated, overcome by the soul. This is why we speak of the end of the age of metaphysics. And this is also what "God is dead!" actually means. Just like "Great Pan is dead!" did not merely announce the psychological obsolescence of a particular deity but that of the entire *level* of such a thing as nature gods and, more than that, even of the corresponding form of imagination and status of consciousness, so also "God is dead!" does not so much speak merely about the fate of God, but, by means of the image of God and thus implicitly, about the death of the soul's transcendence stage at large.

Inasmuch as the experience of the death of God is still the implicit form and first immediacy of the overcoming of the soul's transcendence stage it is at the same time the first immediacy of a becoming *explicit* of what the Ascension in its turn once was *implicitly* actually about. The notion of Christ's Ascension, this is crucial to realize, was not already in itself complete. It was fundamentally preliminary. It is the conception of a rise and disappearance by a consciousness which, however, itself stays behind. It only talks about a movement as an *observed* or *envisioned* event, but an event that does precisely not take that consciousness that envisions it along on its journey of ascension, transporting it to a new dimension. In this sense, as something that is merely envisioned from a worm's eye view, it has the form of a hope or promise whose possible fulfillment lies on principle in the future, similarly to how Moses was, to be sure, reached by the idea of the Promised Land and could dream about the latter, but himself had to stay behind, not being able to ever enter it.

The notion of Christ's Ascension is deficient also for a second, namely formal reason. It is inherent in its imaginal, pictorial form that it presents itself as a movement in space, a literally upwards movement to heaven as a region above us which inevitably is thus confused with the sky. But by a truly modern psychological consciousness, which is fundamentally beyond the imaginal, the image of the Ascension can of course not, and must not, be *imagined* anymore. It is clear that it aims for something that the imaginal form in which it appears is not capable of expressing in its truthful way, but can merely hint at.

The deficiency of the image of Ascension and the promise character of the envisioning of it gave it a dynamic, a teleological thrust. The Ascension wanted to come home to itself, home from its alienation in the imagination and the form of otherness, from the form of an external movement in (imaginal) space and from a movement by some other. Its inner telos was to become the soul's, consciousness's, own movement and thus attain its own actual arrival in that dimension to which the *envisioned* Ascension had only transported Christ as a *content* or *object* of consciousness. Only then, only through the absolute-negative interiorization into itself of the notion of Ascension, only through the homecoming of the Ascension from semantic content to syntactical form of consciousness, we could also say, only with the logical move from "object" to "subject" ("subjectivity"), from (imaginal) otherness to (psychological) self,[46] would the idea of the Ascension have completed itself—but *ipso facto* also rendered itself superfluous, its work having been done.[47]

And again, the fulfillment of the promise and the realization (actual reaching) of its inherent goal cannot happen on the level of consciousness to which the idea of the Ascension itself belongs. It can only occur outside its own historical stage of consciousness, i.e., after the end of the Christian eon, on an entirely new stage of consciousness.

The modern experience epitomized in Nietzsche's dictum "God is dead!" is the sign that the event of the emergence of this new stage of consciousness has in fact and irrevocably happened. This death of God marks both the obsolescence of the transcendence level of consciousness as represented in history as Christian theology and as metaphysics, and at the same time—for many probably paradoxically—(the first immediacy of) the final fulfillment of the notion of Christ's Ascension, its absolute-negative interiorization into itself. But at the same time, "God is dead!" is also the sign that this fulfillment, although it is already real, is still misconstrued by a consciousness that remains stuck in the former, metaphysical way of thinking, in the transcendence mode of the soul. This is why the death of God is viewed only as something negative, a loss, death, disappearance, which, positivized, appears as nihilism.[48] As always in the soul, *factual* arrival at a new stage is not enough. The fact of arrival[49]

---

[46] I am talking here of the logical *form* of self, not about the Jungian Self.

[47] Here the reader can see that for the psychologist such a motif as Christ's Ascension is not a dogmatic assertion within a belief system, an assertion about something *as* a timeless truth that would give rise to the critical question of whether it is in fact true or not perhaps false. For psychology it is an indisputable psychological phenomenon in which (1) the soul gave expression to itself at one point in the historical development of its logical life and which (2) had a particular psycho-historical *task*, that is, was an active substance, an agent.

[48] Following Mogenson (personal communication) we can say in response to this: "Of course, 'God is dead' is a speculative sentence. He is not a being who in addition to being also dies; 'death' is rather an essential predicate, the subject a second time, i.e., the Holy Ghost, logical negativity."

[49] In the present context: the fact of what arrived with Nietzsche, with Hegel, and also, in a resistant way, with Jung.

has to be duplicated and catch up with itself, come home to itself, become psychological. Consciousness needs to become initiated into its already prevailing truth in order for this truth to become released into its truth.

If we wanted to summerize the described movements in schematic form, we could present them thus:

1a. Myth, polytheism — 1b. philosophical speculative thought
2a. Pan is dead! — 2b. Christ's Ascension
3a. God is dead! — 3b. Ascension absolute-negatively interiorized into itself

In this scheme

1a and 1b represent the nature stage of the soul,
2a and 2b the transcendence stage of the soul, and
3a and 3b the logical form stage of the soul.

Here "nature," as a status of soul, is the *form* of "literal other," sensual object or phenomenon; modern psychology often thinks of it in terms of projection.[50] "Transcendence" is sublated, distilled, or spiritualized other*ness*; this means it is a "projection" changed from literal object or thing, or entity, into conceptual form. As such it is also the fulfillment of ancient philosophical speculative thought, its having come home to itself. And "logical form" is sublated transcendence—or homecoming of the "projection" to self. In each stage, the a-version represents, first, the experience of the death or loss of the entire previous stage and, secondly, it is already implicitly what b is explicitly. Thirdly, it is at the same time the first immediacy of what the new stage is as a whole, whereas b in each case is, first, the releasement of the a-version from its preliminary and ununderstood form into its truth and thus, secondly, the fulfillment of the entire new stage. However, in addition it is, thirdly, also the first immediacy of the next "higher" a-version.

Now that we have come to the end of my exposition about "The 'death of God' and the Ascension of Christ" we can see that any "God must not die!" would not only be counterfactual, but also prevent the movement inherent in the notion of Christ's Ascension from finding

[50] "Projection" as an attempted explanation for the fact that natural phenomena were seen as the epiphany or direct presence of nature gods.

its fulfillment and thus also prevent the soul from achieving its ends. It would hold us in (a modern version of) the worm's eye view.

In conclusion, let me add two notes. (1) By working with the notions of "myth," mythological Pan, "Great Pan is dead!," Christ's Ascension, and Nietzsche's "God is dead!," I have availed myself of religious or "theological" material in order to discuss the soul's movement. Despite the fact that religious ideas are most precious to the soul and usually present the highest soul values, I do not wish to suggest that these ideas are the only authentic or at least the foremost way to account for the soul's historical development. The same development could have been described by focusing on any one of a variety of other, nonreligious topics. The religious material here merely functions as one possible exemplification, one that in the present context was, of course, determined by the topic of the present paper. (2) Although especially Christ's Ascension, but also "God is dead!" are theological motifs and seem to belong to the sphere of religious faith or disbelief, I did not apperceive them as such and treat them theologically, or as matters of faith. The soul has no stake in gods, in religious ideas, religious faith *per se*. Nor do I. Psychologically, such ideas are "symbols," means of the soul's speaking about itself, its artless self-articulation for its otherwise irrepresentable issues, and relative to the respective particular stages of the historical development of the soul's logical life. It is in this spirit that I worked with them in this Postscript.

CHAPTER FIVE

The Reality of Evil?
An analysis of Jung's argument

1.

"Psychology does not know what good and evil are in themselves; it knows them only as judgments about relations: 'good' is what seems suitable, acceptable, or valuable from a certain standpoint; evil is the corresponding opposite. If what we call good is 'really' good for us, then there must also be a 'bad' and 'evil' that is 'real' for us. So one sees that psychology is concerned with a more or less subjective judgment, that is, with a psychic opposition that is indispensable for designating value relations .... There are things which from a certain standpoint are extremely evil, that is to say dangerous" (*CW* 9ii § 97, transl. modif.). "For how can you speak of 'high' if there is no 'low,' of 'right' if there is no 'left,' of 'good' if there is no 'evil,' and the one is as real as the other?" (*ibid.* § 113). It is an "evident [*natürliche*] fact that with the predicate 'high' you immediately postulate 'low'...." Good and evil "are a logically equivalent pair of opposites ..." They are, from the empirical standpoint, "coexistent halves of a moral judgment" (*ibid.* § 84).

Here Jung moves on a strictly logical level and comprehends good and evil as *Relationsbegriffe* (concepts of a relation), as a pair of opposites, where the one immediately implies the other because they are correlates so that you cannot have the one without also having the other. "The reality of 'evil'" means in this context no more than *logical* coexistence with "good." The terms or concepts coexist. It does not in any way imply an *ontological* sense of "real." This is all the more emphasized by Jung's insistence on the merely subjective quality of these terms. They are, as human judgments, categories by means of which the human mind evaluates its relation to things and events in reality (or rather the other way around, what things and events mean to us). These predicates exist only in the human subject, not in objective reality, only *in mente* and not *in re*, as we might say with a medieval philosophical distinction. We *call* something good or bad. It is good or bad *for us*. "Evil" therefore means (at times) simply "dangerous." Furthermore, the specific meaning of good and bad, that is, the question *when* we call something good and *when* bad, is not a fixed one. It depends entirely on our standpoint. This idea becomes especially evident if we think of the one other pair of opposites alluded to by Jung as formally equivalent to the moral one, namely left and right. If I turn around at the place where I stand, what was left of me before is now right of me. Nothing has changed "out there." The things referred to as being to the left or right are the same and at the same objective location. Only my point of view has changed. By the same token, what is "good" from the standpoint of one person may be "bad" from that of another. If you sell your house and prices happen to be up, it, the same transaction and at the same time, is good for the seller, but bad for the buyer.

So far, nobody can have any reservation concerning Jung's thesis of the reality of evil, since it means here no more than the real existence of this notion as a logical category in the mind. We also cannot doubt, on the present level of Jung's argument, that evil is just as 'real' as good, because they are indeed inseparable correlates. The problem with Jung's comments is of course that tacitly, by implication, he uses the idea that evil coexists with good within the moral judgment to support his thesis of a very different reality of evil. This is the reason for the strange introduction of the surprising term "real" into his discussion of logical categories, where it does not belong. On the level of the mind's moral categories, evil is not really just as *real* as good (because the notion of "reality" does not belong here at all; moral categories are nothing but subjective forms, means for *evaluating* the real), but simply the logical counterpart to "good." The word "real" is surreptitiously smuggled into the logical discourse to help strengthen by implication the very different ontological thesis of the reality of evil.

But if Jung clearly understands that good and evil are subjective value judgments, why does he nevertheless attack the idea of evil as a *privatio boni*, and so, e.g., Basil the Great's (330–379) idea that "evil does not have a subsistence of its own" (*CW* 9ii § 82, transl. modif.)? And why does he instead insist that "One must, however, take evil rather more *substantially* when one meets it on the plane of empirical psychology" (§ 75, my ital.)? If, "from the empirical standpoint," good and evil are "coexistent halves of a moral judgment," evaluations by the subjective human mind, how then can they all of a sudden "on the plane of empirical psychology" have an ontological reality? How can Jung wish to ontologize and *hypostatize*[1] evil, that is to say, turn what is actually only an attribute or predicate (a value judgment) *applied* to real events or deeds into a noun, a substance, a real in its own right? Jung asserts point-blank: "Evil is a reality."[2] "This classic formula [of the *privatio boni*] robs evil of absolute existence .... If evil has no substance, good must remain shadowy ...." (*CW* 11 § 247). *This* evil is no longer the logical category or concept that Jung had said it was for empirical psychology, no longer a subjective moral judgment from a certain standpoint. Now it is an independent subsisting reality, an objective existence, a fact out there. Evil per se.

This hypostatizing of (i.e., this granting substantiality to) a human *judgment* must be judged by us as a logical blunder, and it of course amounts to a metaphysical assertion, a dogmatic prejudice. Here Jung is *malgré lui* not an empirical psychologist who "shrinks from metaphysical assertions" (*CW* 9ii § 85, cf. § 112, also its footnote ["What I do is not metaphysics," transl. modif.]). He—unwittingly—*starts out* from a metaphysical position.

In supporting his rejection of the *privatio boni* concept, Jung makes statements like these: "One must be positively blind not to see the

---

[1] By rejecting Basil's thesis that "evil does not have a subsistence of its own" Jung opts for the opposite thesis that it does have a subsistence of its own. The Greek word for "subsistence" in the quote from Basil is *hypostasis*!

[2] C.G. Jung, *Über Gefühle und den Schatten*. Winterthurer Fragestunden. Textbuch, Zürich and Düsseldorf 1999, p. 60. My translation.

colossal role that evil plays in the world" (§ 114). "One cannot claim that only 'good' exists and 'evil' does not exist. It *exists*! Every father confessor knows that if a person has confessed his sins ... then he goes around the next corner and sins again. Nobody can live without sin!"[3] There are two serious problems with these arguments. The first one is that they do not speak of "evil" per se, nor about "evil" as a category of the human mind used in moral judgments, but rather of deeds and conditions, actual incidents that may merely be *judged* to be evil by the human mind, positively existing things or occurring events in empirical reality. On account of such a judgment these deeds or conditions might then be called "evils." But the reality of such concrete "evils" in the plural is a totally different topic from the question of a possible reality of evil per se. With his reference to what a father confessor hears, Jung is thinking of people's factual wrong-doings in the world. In other words, we are all of a sudden in a third distinct sphere. With these statements Jung has moved away from (a) the arena of the human mind and the categories the latter needs for its cognition and judgments; he has also left (b) the plane of philosophical assertions on which he had wished to grant to evil per se an ontological dignity and thus to establish it as a subsisting reality in its own right; rather he now (c) is moving all of a sudden within the—psychologically—banal sphere of events to be observed in empirical, everyday reality and practical life. One does not need psychology (in Jung's high sense of the word) at all to become aware of the colossal role that evil in this plain sense plays in the world or of the ubiquity of "sins." It is very strange to see Jung use such trite observations to try to underpin his wholly other metaphysical thesis of the realness of evil as such in the sense of its having "a subsistence of its own."

The second problem with Jung's pointing to the all-too obvious evils in the world is that he thinks that the upholders of the theory of evil as *privatio boni* are ignorant about evil in sense (c) and that he believes that in this way their theory could be refuted. But those thinkers who supported the *privatio boni* definition of evil never doubted that there are evil deeds and events in the world. That "Human nature is capable of an infinite amount of evil, and the evil deeds are as real as the good ones" has never been questioned,

[3] C.G. Jung, *Über Gefühle und den Schatten*, op. cit. p. 60, my transl.

let alone denied. The Christian West, whose main tradition was to uphold the idea of the *privatio boni*, had been convinced throughout of the fundamental sinfulness of human nature. The Bible already states: "They are corrupt, they have done abominable works, there is none that doeth good" (Psalm 14:1), which was upheld by all major theologians throughout the ages. Even the very Basil, whose refutation of the substantiality of evil Jung rejected, is quoted by Jung himself as saying: "That evil exists no one living in the world will deny" (§ 83). In philosophy, as late as during the second half of the 18th century Kant for one spoke of "the radical evil in human nature" and of a "predisposition" of every human being for evil. This was the prevailing self-understanding of man during the Christian eon. Very practically, a dominant theme of the constant preaching of the Church was the sinfulness of man and the admonishments to struggle to avoid sins. In addition, the idea that human existence was a life in the valley of tears was continually present and corroborated by the actual experience people constantly had of illnesses, numerous deaths in one's family, wars, the plague, poverty, crimes, injustice, torture, executions. There was no room "for a too optimistic conception" (§ 113) of human existence and behavior in the world. No, the *privatio boni* theory did not serve the purpose of "gloss[ing] over this evil" for "lull[ing] one into a sense of false security" (§ 97, modif.). It was not "a euphemistic *petitio principii*" (§ 94). I cannot agree when Jung declares that "It is difficult to avoid the impression that apotropaic tendencies have had a hand in creating this notion, with the understandable intention of settling the painful problem of evil as optimistically as possible" (*CW* 11 § 247). On the contrary, it was developed on the very basis of an intimate familiarity with and acceptance of the real evil in the world.

Privatio boni and a very sober, realistic view of human nature and the world went together. What we see precisely from Basil is that the *privatio boni* view does not in any way get in the way of the awareness of the empirical reality of evil deeds and events in human life (nor of course, we could add, of the notion of the so-called "reality" of evil as one half of a pair of opposites used by the mind to evaluate real deeds and events in empirical life). They are all three perfectly compatible. Why? Because they address different questions, have their place on different levels or in different discourses. They cannot interfere with each other, but also not corroborate each other.

The second blunder Jung commits in his discussion of evil is that of a hidden, but systematic equivocation. At one moment his "empirical psychology" focuses on evil as a human value judgment, at another one on evil as events or deeds in the real world, and his overall purpose is to prove the reality of evil as such, without spelling out that these three are heterogeneous issues. Correspondingly, we also get three different senses of "reality" or "existence" of evil that need to be kept apart. The one is that of the *logical* coexistence of evil with "good" in the moral judgment, the other one is that of the *empirical* reality of factual doings that can be morally judged to be evil, and the third is *ontological* realness in the sense of subsistence (*hypostasis*). Jung confounds the logical with the empirical and with the ontological sphere, thereby unintentionally covering the issues with a smokescreen.

He believes that with his clear and justified comments in the one area, namely about good and evil as being no more than elements of the moral judgment, he has done enough to prove once and for all that he is an empirical psychologist and not a metaphysician *also in the other area*, namely when he is rejecting the *privatio boni* thesis, so that in that other area he is relieved of any cares about not becoming metaphysical in his argumentation. At the same time, he seems to hope that the use of "real" in his discussion of the logical issue and the use of the same word in his references to empirical reality could support his main thesis, which is an ontological one, even if it is *declared* to be one "on the plane of empirical psychology." But it is not, as we will see more clearly in section 2.

The smokescreen I spoke of must by no means be interpreted as a deliberate strategic move on the part of Jung. (If it is a strategy at all, then it is one by the unconscious force that drove him to establish the idea of the reality of evil as such and in whose grip he was.) Rather, this smokescreen is a sign that, while tackling the *privatio boni* idea, Jung was himself not aware of the entirely different level on which the discussion of *this* idea takes place and had not reached this level. Jung missed the point of it because his interpretation of it is fundamentally underdetermined, not up to it. We will have to come back to this later.

2.

Jung views the *privatio boni* theory as historically necessitated by Christianity's being threatened by Manichaean dualism (*CW* 9ii § 85). Discussing a particular vision from "the (Jewish-Christian?) apocalypse, the 'Ascension of Isaiah,'" he says:

> This paints a picture of complementary opposites balancing one another like right and left hands. Significantly enough, this vision, like the Clementine Homilies, belong to the pre-Manichaean period (second century), when there was as yet no need for Christianity to fight against its Manichaean competitors. It was still possible to give a description of a genuine yang-yin relationship, a picture that comes closer to actual truth than the *privatio boni* (§ 104).

The last part of this quotation, the phrase "a picture that comes closer to actual truth than the *privatio boni*," is most revealing. It is a rare moment in which Jung unintentionally lays bare the logical underground under his argumentation. What betrays itself here is the fact that Jung approaches the theme of the *privatio boni* from the standpoint of one who is in possession of the knowledge of "actual truth" (*tatsächliche Wahrheit*). And so, in *Answer to Job*, Jung can even speak of "the nonsensical doctrine [*der Unsinn*] of the *privatio boni*" (*CW* 11 § 600 note) and thereby simply throw it away. He knows that the *privatio boni* is nonsense. Concerning the issue of good and evil, he does not come to his topic as empirical psychologist. For the empirical psychologist all that exists is the psychological phenomena, in our case for example the 2nd century complementary opposition of good and evil as the two hands of God, on the one hand, and, on the other hand, the later view of Being as good (Thomas Aquinas would much later state, *ens et bonum convertuntur*) while evil is no more than a privation of goodness. Psychologically, one view, provided that it is a real phenomenon in the history of the soul, is as good as the other. The psychologist can only observe, impartially observe, which views, which phenomena, exist and which changes in the prevailing views occur, but he does not have an a priori or externally given standard by which he could measure which one is closer to "the truth" than the other. Because for the psychological standpoint each phenomenon *is* itself a psychological *truth*. By the same token, when Jung states

"Clement's theology was in a position to bridge [a certain] contradiction in a way that fits the psychological facts" (*CW* 9ii § 99), we have to remind him that Clement's theology is itself only one of the psychological facts and cannot be compared to alleged "*the* psychological facts." "The idea," Jung himself had taught us, "is psychologically true inasmuch as it exists. ... But we are so used to the idea that psychic events are wilful and arbitrary products, or even the inventions of a human creator, that we can hardly rid ourselves of the prejudiced view that the soul and its contents are nothing but ... the more or less illusory product of supposition and judgment" (*CW* 11 § 4f.). The psychological "standpoint is exclusively phenomenological, that is, it is concerned with occurrences, events, experiences—in a word, with facts. Its truth is a fact and not a judgment" (*ibid.* § 4). Judgments, theories, hypotheses can be true or false. Not so psychological phenomena. They *are* what they are and have to be taken as such. One cannot, as psychologist, side with one phenomenon and against the other one. As psychologist, one cannot polemicize against certain psychic phenomena. It would be comparable to a biologist who, as biologist, is in favor of one animal species and wants to eliminate another one.

The point here is not whether something *is* a supposition and judgment by humans, on the one hand, or an occurrence or event, on the other. This is not a fixed, quasi-ontological distinction; they are not givens. No, psychology is constituted by the *methodological decision to conceive* even of suppositions and judgments, of theories and ideas that people came up with, *as* phenomena, *as* psychological truths, *as* "facts" (that is, in this context, as in fact having occurred in, and belonging to, the historical phenomenology of the soul, as parts of the *soul's* self-display), and *not* as *people's* suppositions and hypotheses. This methodological viewpoint is what distinguishes the psychologist from the historian of ideas.

But Jung in the passage cited clearly prioritizes one view and rejects the other view, and he does so in the name of "the actual truth," of a third above the phenomenological level. This means nothing less than that in this instance Jung has left the psychological standpoint, for which the phenomenologically-existing ideas are themselves true and represent the only truths the psychologist knows about, and now views the phenomena from an external dogmatic position, a presupposition. For psychology, the phenomena have their truth within themselves, "in their existence." Jung's own idea of psychological truth discussed in *CW* 11 § 4 could even be expressed with the Scholastic "*ens et verum convertuntur.*" The only meaning that the phrase "the actual truth" could have for the psychological standpoint is that it is the phenomenology of the soul as a whole, as "formation, transformation, Eternal Mind's eternal recreation." And the shift from the dualistic view of good and evil as the two hands of God to the view for which God is *summum bonum* and evil a *privatio boni* could, from a psychological position, not be judged as a right or wrong move. How could the psychologist possibly know what is a right and what is a wrong move for the soul? He would have to have an Archimedian point. He has only the phenomenology itself to go by. The actual phenomenology together with its self-movement is the only kind of truth that exists for him.

Rather, from the psychological point of view that move from the "two hands of God" to the *privatio boni* would express a fundamental change in the depth of the soul, in its self-definition and self-constitution. The questions arising for the psychologist would be of the following type: What does it mean psychologically that the soul shifted, for example, from polytheism to monotheism or from the pre-Manichaean view of a complimentary opposition of good and evil to the post-Manichaean *privatio boni* view? What does the soul do to itself by moving from the one to the other, what does it want to achieve for itself? For Jung here, however, the phenomena, the views about good and evil, have their measure of truth outside of themselves. At the same time, this means that he does not treat them as psychological phenomena, as products of the soul and as its self-sufficient self-representation, but as people's "suppositions and judgments" *about* reality, which of course has the immediate consequence that the question arises whether they are adequate or not.

The time-honored *privatio boni* idea determined the thinking of the Western mind for more than one and a half millennia. The greatest minds have engaged themselves for it. It is a *phenomenon*; and it truly *exists.* It has in the course of centuries shaped consciousness as well as our world, and as such has soul dignity, the dignity of a soul truth. But Jung tries to wriggle out of the psychological standpoint by boldly asserting, "The *privatio boni* cannot be compared to the quaternity, because it is not a revelation. On the contrary, it has all the earmarks of a 'doctrine,' a philosophical invention" (*CW* 18 § 1613). As if the major philosophical doctrines were not just as much "revelations"! As if the soul were not also speaking through great philosophy and art. Are we not enwrapped by soul on all sides? Jung had no difficulty attributing soul dignity and revelatory value to Goethe's *Faust.* But was *Faust* not an invention, produced by a very conscious, alert mind and calculating artist? Did it have the truth of a "revelation" for Jung only because it seemed to support his own views? Are "revelations" not also the product of human thought? (Or are we supposed to believe in *literal* "revelations," in verbal inspiration, from out of a mysterious source, be it directly from God or from a *literal* "unconscious"?)

The psychologist must not be selective. He must not rage against the *privatio boni,* even if it is a *doctrine,* and dismiss it as "nothing but." It is not a flimsy concoction by the ego. The psychologist can only wait and see how the self-unfolding of the soul's truths continues and where the soul's self-movement may next lead to. Leave the soul to its own devices. Psychology comes after the fact and does not have a project for the future of its own, in fact is not oriented towards the future at all. At any rate, it is not for us to try to interfere in the soul's process with our own schemes and wishes. The fact that Jung does rage against the *privatio boni* concept is psychologically out of order. It shows that he has his own agenda, his own program.

3.

Jung's thesis is: "We can no longer simply claim that it [evil] is a 'μὴ ὄν,' something non-existent."[4] But he gives a weak, poor *reading* to the *mê on* and the corresponding *privatio boni* idea. There are mainly two serious shortcomings in his understanding. The one concerns the horizon into which Jung places them. The other concerns Jung's own logical form of consciousness with which he approaches them.

a) Jung interprets the notion of evil as something non-existent as if it were a statement about human behavior, about events and deeds in empirical reality, and a thesis about moral philosophy. Through this reading, the *privatio boni* theory of evil becomes for him "a too optimistic conception of evil in human nature" (*CW* 9ii § 113). It is

[4] C.G. Jung, *Über Gefühle und den Schatten*, op. cit. p. 60, my transl.

"a euphemistic *petitio principii*" and a "fallacy" (§ 94, transl. modif.). The *privatio boni* has an "apotropaic" function (*CW* 18 § 1537, *CW* 11 § 247) and amounts to "a welcome sedative" (*CW* 11 § 457). It is "such a horrible syllogism" (*CW* 18 § 1593), "a regular *tour de force* of sophistry" (*CW* 11 § 470) for the purpose of appeasing an uneasy conscience. "Evil deeds simply do not *exist* [that is, according to it]. The identification of good with *ousia* is a fallacy, because a man who is thoroughly evil does not disappear at all when he has lost his last good. ..." This theory "is a desperate attempt to save the Christian faith from dualism" (*CW* 18 § 1593).

There is one place where Jung informs us about the origin of his interest in this theory.

> I should never have dreamt that I would come up against such an apparently out-of-the-way problem as that of the *privatio boni* in my practical work. Fate would have it, however, that I was called upon to treat a patient, a scholarly man with an academic training, who had got involved in all manner of dubious and morally reprehensible practices. He turned out to be a fervent adherent of the *privatio boni*, because it fitted in admirably with his scheme: evil in itself is nothing .... It was this case that originally induced me to come to grips with the *privatio boni* in its psychological aspect" (*CW* 11 § 457).

Here Jung tells us the starting point of his studying the topic of the *privatio boni* and at the same time also reveals the horizon within which he pursued it. This starting point is thus an abuse by his patient of this doctrine for the man's egoic-neurotic purpose of "deceiving himself," for "self-deceptions," for "glossing over an immoral act by optimistically regarding it as a slight diminuation of good, which alone is real, or as an 'accidental lack of perfection'" (*CW* 11 § 457). The question for us is: why did Jung not merely criticize the abuse, but instead lay the blame for this silly defense at the door of the doctrine of the *privatio boni* itself, as if the abuse were indeed inherent in it? Is the latter really concerned with the question of "evil *in human nature*" at all, with whitewashing "*people* who are thoroughly evil"? Does it really have an apotropaic function, is it really a *desperate defense* and a euphemistic glossing over? These are all absurd insinuations or suppositions. The mere suggestion that the argumentation of this patient of his, on the one hand, and the theological-philosophical concept of the *privatio boni*, on the other hand, were intrinsically related is ludicrous.

If it is only a question of in therapy combating such obvious, primitive self-deceptions Jung would not have had to go into the theological, philosophical topic of the *privatio boni* at all. Tackling the latter for getting a handle on the former, namely on the wish by certain modern neurotic persons to utilize it for glossing over their dark shadow, is like using a steamroller to crack a nut. It has nothing whatsoever to do with it. I already showed that the existence of evil-doings was by no means denied by the adherents of this doctrine, nor was a euphemistic belittling of evil behavior their purpose, nor did they have a far too optimistic view of human nature. It had an entirely different focus. It was not a theory about the moral question (the moral evaluation and justification of human deeds or character traits [shadow aspects]) at all. But Jung seems to have fallen for his patient's abuse and gotten stuck in this his patient's view that the *privatio boni* idea is an attempt to present evil as non-existent in the real world, the world of practical behavior. The fact that Jung considers it necessary to point out the triviality that "a man who is thoroughly evil does not disappear at all when he has lost his last good" clearly shows that his horizon in this matter is ultimately that of a concretistic thinking in terms of literal empirical reality and of personalistic psychology, people's psychology—and thus not of a true psychology informed by the psychological difference. Concerning the theory of *privatio boni* Jung obviously misses the point. He fails to see what this concept is about (and thus also what it is psychologically about).

By the same token, if, as Jung says in order to a priori immunize his views against possible objections, "my criticism is valid *only within the empirical realm.* In the metaphysical realm, on the other hand, good may be a substance and evil a μὴ ὄν. I know of no factual experience which approximates to such an assertion, so at this point the empiricist must remain silent" (*CW* 11 § 459), then why does he nevertheless attack the *privatio boni* doctrine so emphatically and continuously, a doctrine which, after all, has its place *only* in what Jung calls the metaphysical realm? Why *does* he not remain silent? Why does he, as he admits, "encroach upon the territory of the other [realm]," despite the fact that he acknowledges that "Here the theologian has a certain right to fear an intrusion on the part of the empiricist" (*CW* 11 § 456)? The answer to this question is a bit complicated as it requires a number of differentiations.

The fact that Jung radically contrasts the empirical and the metaphysical (or theological) realms as *toto coelo* separate and restricts himself (or at least claims that he restricts himself) to the former means that at this point he does not think psychologically but positivistically and that thus neither the empirical events nor the theological concepts can be seen in terms of soul, as the soul speaking about itself. Now, all of a sudden, psychology is treated as if it had a "delimited field" (cf. *CW* 9i § 112), and theology seems to lie outside of it, which is the only reason why Jung feels he has to speak of "encroaching." The very point of a true psychology is that it does not, cannot possibly, compete with other sciences nor encroach upon their fields because it has its place on a fundamentally different level. It is the *sublation* of all possible fields, in some way comparable to how in linguistics one distinguishes languages as first-degree languages from a metalanguage (the purpose of which is to describe and analyze the first-order languages). Psychology, if it *is* psychology, is open to the phenomenology of empirical experience just as well as to that of theology, physics, literature, etc. It cannot encroach upon theology at all because the two fields (psychology and theology) do not lie side by side on one and the same plane, with a fence between them. It can perfectly legitimately turn to theological ideas because it does so on a fundamentally "higher" level ("higher" in a logical sense, I could also say "deeper") and from an entirely different viewpoint.

In the fact that Jung sets psychology and theology up as two separate realms vis-à-vis each other, a second fact betrays itself, namely that Jung indeed encroaches on the other realm. The questions arising within the empirical realm would have to be resolved within this realm. One cannot expect any help from theology or whatever other field. On that count it is completely superfluous to study the Church Fathers and their *privatio boni* idea in order to deal with moral problems coming up in the consulting room and in the psyche of modern people. But it was absolutely essential for Jung to take up and criticize the theological idea. And now I can answer the above question, why he did not remain silent. In the *logical form of his consciousness* he wanted to hold on to the pre-psychological mindset that construed psychic reality after the model of things and persons and their interactions, while *semantically* he felt the need to transcend the limited human, all-too-human and personalistic horizon and conceive of psychology as the study concerned with the soul's self-sufficient *transcendent universal truths* (which he usually called archetypal ideas or images and what Hillman would later term "the imaginal"). They are transcendent in the sense that they do not express what people think, feel, or imagine, but conversely what shapes their thinking and feeling, and in the sense that they do not exist for our sake, but conversely are realities that human existence revolves around. Jung's encroaching is in the last analysis more than an external trespassing from one field into another, as which it appears to a superficial view. It is really the intrapsychic, psychological misdemeanor of ignoring a discrepancy and incompatibility which exists between the semantics and the syntax of his consciousness: that Jung feels justified to approach semantic contents (here, the *privatio boni* and *summum bonum* ideas) that actually are already truly psychological contents, because they are the result of a sublation of both the sphere of empirical reality and the sphere of literal theology, *with a consciousness* that in its logical constitution or syntax has not gone through this sublation, but stays on the level of the old logic and is informed by the logic of empirical reality. Conversely, it means that he inflates the rather banal, human-all-too-human moral issues of good and evil in modern life (or ego-psychology) with excessive mythological, archetypal importance.

b) With the last ideas we have already entered the second topic of the logical form of consciousness with which Jung approaches the *privatio boni* doctrine and that determines his interpretation of it. That his consciousness in its logical form is not up to the logical form of the material to be studied shows itself above all in two features. The first one circles around the monotheism-dualism question. Jung blames Christianity for its unacknowledged dualism and demands that, "The myth [i.e., the Christian myth] must finally go through with monotheism and give up its (officially denied) dualism, which up to now allowed an eternal dark Adversary to coexist alongside the omnipotent Good" (*MDR* p. 338, transl. modif.). The next sentence points to how Jung imagines a solution: "Room must be made within the system for the philosophical *complexio oppositorum* of Nicholas of Cusa and the moral ambivalence of Jacob Boehme; only thus can the One God be granted the wholeness and the synthesis of opposites which should be His .... the myth of the necessary incarnation of God—the essence of the Christian message—can then be understood as man's creative engagement with the opposites and their synthesis in the self ..."

We have to add a few more quotations to get a fuller picture of the structural determinants of Jung's view. "Psychological experience shows that whatever we call 'good' is balanced by an equally substantial 'bad' or 'evil.'" (*CW* 11 p. 357). "Accordingly the realization of the self ... leads to a fundamental conflict, to a real suspensions between opposites (reminiscent of the crucified Christ hanging between two thieves) ..." (*CW* 9ii § 123). "This great symbol [i.e., the image of the Saviour crucified between two thieves] tells us that the progressive development and differentiation of consciousness leads to an ever more menacing awareness of the conflict and involves nothing less than a crucifixion of the ego, its agonizing suspension between irreconcilable opposites" (*CW* 9ii § 79). "... good and evil represent equivalent halves of an opposition" (*ibid.* § 79 note). With approval Jung (repeatedly) refers to Clement of Rome's "conception of Christ as the right hand and the devil as the left hand of God, not to speak of the Judaeo-Christian view which recognized two sons of God, Satan the elder and Christ the younger" (*CW* 11 § 470).

What appears from all these views of Jung's, quite apart from their semantic content, is that his thinking is *structured* by horizontality, duality, and opposition. Two hands of God, two sons of God, suspension between the irreconcilable opposites, conflict, equivalent halves, evil coexisting *alongside* the good. It is a thinking in terms of space, which comes out most blatantly in the ideas of left and right (hands) and (Christ) hanging between (two thieves). That is to say, it is a pictorial thinking. We can now also understand why good and evil both have to be substances for Jung because his thinking is informed by the *model* of *things* in the ordinary visible world or of *people* ("father" and "two sons"). His is not a *thinking* in the strict sense at all. It is mythologizing. And his passionate standing up for good and evil as substantial opposites is not only concerned, on the semantic level, with the moral question, but also driven by the deep powerful need to *defend this logical form of consciousness*. His allergy against the *privatio boni* is in part to be explained as his sensing the threat that it poses for this style of consciousness. It also follows from this that he had to misconstrue the *privatio boni* and *summum bonum* theory: that theory is the product of a fundamentally different consciousness that has left the mythologizing mode behind, so that, in Jung, what it comes up with has to be translated into the more primitive pictorial thinking of the mythologizing consciousness and thereby misconceived.

Quite obviously, the *privatio boni* idea has the form of verticality in contrast to Jung's passionately defended horizontal thinking. This vertical thinking is in the tradition of Greek philosophical thought which distinguished the temporal from the timeless or eternal, the finite from the infinite, the principles from what is principiated by them, the phenomenal or real from the Ideas, and it conceived of their relation to each other as negation or privation.[5] Already Anaximander taught that the temporal distanced itself from the timeless through ἀδικία (wrongdoing, injustice). For Plato the sensory world can be understood as the effect of a deficiency or lack of Being, a privatio (στέρησις). And later, Plotinus thinks the world as a whole in terms of *emanation*, the emanation from the One (which is perfect and the primordial Good) in several descending stages, whereby matter, as the lowest grade, is μὴ ὄν and evil, the absolute negation of the primordial One. But it is not only Greek philosophy that paved the way to the *privatio boni* conception. According to the Bible, too, the empirical world as it really is is viewed as deficient, the result of the Fall. It is not as it was created, not in its paradisiacal innocence and perfection.

Behind all these forms of thinking, there is, as the primordial (i.e., pre-philosophical, pre-reflection) mythological paradigm of verticality, the conception of the universe as consisting of two (or three) levels, those of Father Heaven and Mother Earth (plus the Underworld, the realm of Death and the dead), which are held apart by the World Tree, the very image of verticality itself. We can be sure that the vertical relation of the temporal or finite to the eternal or infinite in philosophy is the same old mythological, imaginal Heaven-Earth difference *translated* and *inwardized* from its sensibly imagined form as cosmic entities into the very different medium of reflected thought. This

---

[5] Jung was aware of the pre-Christian Greek background of the *privatio boni*: "Although the *privatio boni* is not the invention of the Church Fathers, the syllogism was most welcome to them ..." (*CW* 18 § 1639).

translation did not merely change the two opposites from the sensible, imaginal form of Heaven and Earth into the abstractness of the *thoughts* of "the eternal" and "the temporal" (or the various specific versions of this thought that the opposites received in the different philosophies in the course of time). It also altered the two other elements of the mythological scheme. In the latter, the World Tree (as the one other element to be discussed) was an (imaginal) object, a concrete thing, which both held apart and at the same time connected the opposites. The literalness of such a metaphorical separating-connecting *thing* transformed itself, within the medium of thought, into the living, fluid form of *mediation* as a logical separating-and-connecting. And the third world-level of the mythological world conception, the Underworld (as the second other element to be discussed), being the concretistic *imaginal version* of logical negation—negation pictured as an existing realm at some place in the cosmos—returned in the philosophical medium as the negativity of this mediation: "injustice," "privation." It is obvious that "privation" and "emanation" and, in religion, "Fall" simultaneously express the separation and the connection of the opposites.

This then is the time-honored ancestry of the *privatio boni* concept, which makes it from the outset altogether unlikely that it was nothing but sophistry and an apotropaic euphemism.

When Jung speaks of good and evil, he has the *substantiated* human *judgments* in mind, good and evil per se as substances, as realities in their own right. Starting out from this conception, he measures what the Church Fathers said about good and evil against the standard of his own scheme, being blind to the fact that when they spoke of the *summum bonum* they were not primarily interested in "*the* Good" per se, but that they rather the other way around described the essence of *God* as absolutely good. Not: the Good is real, the Good is God, but: God *is* pure Goodness. The *summum ens* IS *summum bonum*. And with their idea of the *privatio boni* they also were not interested in disposing of the "pressing question" of evil. Their fundamental topic was not the moral difference per se at all. Their interest was much rather to describe and comprehend the difference between God and world, between the Creator and the fallen creation, *to which* "good" and "evil" were applied. It is true, they responded to the challenge of the Manichaean heresy and its dualism. But, in contrast to how Jung seems to think, they did not take the Manichaean dualism *tel quel* and merely deprived *it* of its one pole by belittling it and taking its reality and substantiality away from it. Rather they rejected the whole *dualistic horizontal* view and countered it with their entirely different paradigm in keeping with the Western philosophical tradition. We could also say that they defended a more advanced way of thinking or higher status of consciousness against the intrusion of a regressive restoration of a more primitive thinking.

4.

For us this means that we now first have to look into the structure of consciousness expressing itself in the Manichaean dualistic view of good and evil, secondly determine Jung's position in comparison with it, and thirdly investigate what the function and merit of the *privatio boni* type of thinking is, that is, why it can be considered to be expressive of a more advanced form of consciousness.

In Manichaeism, Good and Evil, or Light and Darkness, are totally independent principles, there being no possibility whatsoever of seeing them as derived from a third as their common source. In other words, they are the thought (or rather the semantic idea) of the abstract, absolutely irreconcilable opposition as such. Historically, this idea of the absolutely unmediated vis-à-vis of the naked opposites goes back to the early dualism of Zoroastrianism, which was also the absolute opposition (imagined as a cosmic battle) of two irreducible forces, personified as the Good Spirit (Senta Mainyu) and the Bad Spirit (Angra Mainyu), Ahura Mazda (or Ormazd) and Ahriman, Truth and Lie, Light and Darkness. We see that in Manichaeism as well as Zoroastrianism we have a decidedly horizontal thinking. Zarathustra, the founder of Zoroastrianism, developed this religion or philosophy in contrast to the Persian polytheism of his time. This is essential for our comprehending what it amounts to. On the level of polytheism or the mythological world experience, there is no dualism. There are numerous gods and demons or spirits, and they each have ambivalent natures, even if certain ones may be predominantly benevolent and productive while others may be predominantly dangerous and destructive. That is to say, on the level of myth, thought has not risen to the concept of abstract opposition. A purity of *principles* and abstract concepts does not exist yet. What happened with Zarathustra is something extraordinary. Consciousness rises to the level of the abstract opposition of Good and Evil as *principles.*

Now we must not think that Zarathustra came up with the notions of Good and Evil because he was a particularly moral person and primarily concerned with morality. It is the other way around. In Zarathustra we witness *within* a mythological, imaginal consciousness the first emergence of the idea of the possibility of what is fundamentally *beyond* the imaginal mind. We witness the first immediacy of the medium of thought, thought proper, Logos. And the first appearance of the possibility of thought as such has the *form* of the *moral* opposition. Good and Evil, Truth and Lie, Light and Darkness are the first veritable concepts, and the first concept of contradiction and logical negation. They are exclusively the property of the mind. Good and evil do not derive from sensible experience and do not have a referent in nature. They are no longer mythic powers who merely happen to be antagonistic and at war with each other. They are not natural opposites, like Day and Night. As the first veritable concepts they *are* (even if only *in nuce*) the negation of the entire stage of mythic consciousness.

And Good and Evil are not each something that exists in its own right and happens to have this or that character, not entities equipped with their own complex natures. No, they are what they are only together. They have their truth only in their togetherness, because in the last analysis they are the thought of abstract contradiction as such, of $A \neq$ not-A. "Good" is what it is only as the simple negation of "bad" or "evil" and nothing more; "good" is what "evil" is not, just as "evil" is nothing but the negation of "good." (This is also why Jung had insisted so tenaciously on the coexistence of the "judgments"—we could also say: the concepts—of good and evil. With the one, the other is also immediately and inevitably posited; and conversely, if the one is taken away, the other is also gone. They "represent equivalent halves of an opposition," as he had rightly said.)

In the fact that good and evil each are nothing but the negation of each other lies the singleness and poverty of their meaning. Both real phenomena in empirical reality and mythic gods have complex natures with many different qualities. Good and evil have only one single meaning. Furthermore, they are not really *two* distinct realities, but together they are the *one* thought of *contradiction*, much perhaps as in nature the one reality of electricity appears as the unity of + and -.

Zarathustra can perhaps be considered the discoverer *avant la lettre* of the logical principle of contradiction. It is logical that the first thought that thought proper comes up with, and, furthermore, that the first concept with which the level or medium of thought makes its appearance in the history of consciousness, is the thought of contradiction. Historically it represents the breakthrough through the whole horizon of mythology and imaginal thinking, and logically it is the principle constitutive for thought as *logos* in contrast to *mythos*. Contradiction is the entrance to the form of thought because as contradiction and logical negation it (a) contradicts the whole *form* of mythology; it amounts to the negation of and the pushing off from the form of mythic thinking. And (b) it is, as it were, the acid that cleanses ideas from their contamination with remnants of sensible perception, imagination, and emotions and so creates the purity of the *concepts* that thought proper entertains. "Abstraction" is the name we usually give to this cleansing.

So Zarathustra's doctrine is the event of the soul's initial rising to the new level of reflecting consciousness, the level of conceptual thought. However, it is the emergence of this new status of consciousness merely as a first inkling or intuition still within a mythologically imagining consciousness. This is why the strictly abstract concepts of Good and Evil nevertheless appear mythologized (or ontologized) as cosmic powers, personified as Good Spirit and Evil Spirit, and why their abstract relation of contradiction is depicted as the idea of an actual battle, and the whole scheme as a dualistic religious one. It is also why what is actually *one* single concept, namely contradiction, appears *narratively* or *dramatized* as the opposition between *two* ontic absolute opposites, Good and Evil. So in Zarathustra's *semantics* he had advanced to the level of Logos, but in his logical form or syntax of consciousness, he stayed on the old imaginal level. The utterly new semantic idea makes its appearance on the ground of and within the old syntax, though it is implicitly in excess of this as the first immediacy of the new syntax.

It was up to the Greeks to transport the semantic vision of conceptual thought to the new level of reflecting consciousness and into the logical form of conceptual thought, by interiorizing it into itself and thereby bringing it home to itself, releasing it from its "imprisonment" in the emotionality of people on the imaginal level, and releasing it into its truth, that is, upon its own territory, the territory of Logos. Heraclitus of Ephesus, the philosopher who bestowed upon us the philosophical term *logos*, logic, who was a subject of the Persian King Darius and was traditionally believed to have been his friend, is sometimes thought to have been influenced by Zoroastrianism, although there is no sure evidence for it.

I compared good and evil to positive and negative electricity. Maybe we even have to say that the terms good and evil, like + and - or A and not-A, have no meaning of their own at all. The opposition or contradiction itself is here the real concept, the only conceptual reality, and "good" and "evil" are merely how this actual concept articulates itself, merely its two internal moments *when* it is still semanticized or mythologized. In other words, the whole "moral opposition" is in truth perhaps no more than the abstract, strictly formal-logical contradiction, however this contradiction only *the way it appears when* it is *submerged* in the concrete medium of human emotionality, as a passionate "for and against," and *imagined* as two subsisting, substantial metaphysical realities, *the* Good and *the* Evil. The revolutionary transition from the level of myth to the level of thought was highly unlikely on account of the soul's enormous natural inertia, the strong reluctance it shows against its own inner need to transcend itself. This unlikeliness can explain why the first immediacy of the thought of contradiction had to have the form of the *moral* opposites and not of some other abstract opposition: it needed the tremendous suggestive, mobilizing, and emotionalizing power of "good" vs. "evil" to harness the whole strength of the soul for its project of overcoming its own inertia and catapulting itself into the new status of thought.

It follows that the moral question of good and evil in general and at any time must not be taken literally. We must not fall for it as if it were *in itself* truly a moral concern and as if what it semantically *says* were of utmost importance. Rather it is a compromise formation between the first entrance into thought proper through the principle that constitutes it, the principle of contradiction, on the one hand, and the mythological stuff in which this new medium makes its appearance. *Psychologically* viewed, whenever the notions good and evil become central and pressing topics for a consciousness, this is an indication that the entrance gate to thought has been reached, that the soul is struggling to acquire for itself *a consciousness* in the status of thought, but still remains only at its threshold without passing across it; it is an indication that the *authentic* mythological and imaginal style has, to be sure, clearly been left, its innocence and naiveté has been lost, but its logical form is still retained. Consciousness has become one that already has abstract concepts (but only *has* them, has them only in the hybrid form of emotionalized and imagined concepts: metaphysical powers). Again we see: "Good and evil" and a moral consciousness are in this sense the first emergence of the *medium* of thought proper reduced to a *semantic content* in the old medium of an imagining consciousness or, in other words, the first primitive immediacy of the logos stage of consciousness that, however, is not able, or not willing, to go through with itself. A soul interest that misunderstands itself. It takes its semantic, emotional content (good and evil) as what it is actually about, whereas its real, but unrealized content is nothing but the strictly formal thought of pure opposition, contradiction, negation (without anything that would be negated). If *this* content were realized, it would no longer be merely a content, but would have revolutionized the form of consciousness.

The Manichaean opposites are opposed to each other point-blank, absolutely unmediatedly. Because they are substantiated we get a dualism. Jung with his praise for the idea of good and evil as the right and left hands of God and of Satan and Christ as the two sons of God lays himself open to the same charge of dualism. He was aware of it and thus tried to refute it. About the right/left hands idea Jung states, "Clement finds this altogether compatible with the idea of God's unity. ... At all events this view ... proves that the reality of evil does not necessarily lead to Manichaean dualism and so does not endanger the unity of the God-image" (*CW* 9ii § 99). "Clement's view is clearly *monotheistic*, as it unites the opposites in one God. / ... Later Christianity, however, is dualistic, inasmuch as it splits off one half of the opposites, personified in Satan .... If Christianity claims to be a monotheism, it becomes unavoidable to assume the opposites as being contained in God" (*CW* 11 p. 358). But for Jung even this comprehension of God as a *complexio oppositorum* is not sufficient. There will have to be a further step now or in the future: "Through his further incarnation God becomes a fearful task for man, who must now find ways and means to unite the divine opposites in himself" (*CW* 18 § 1661).

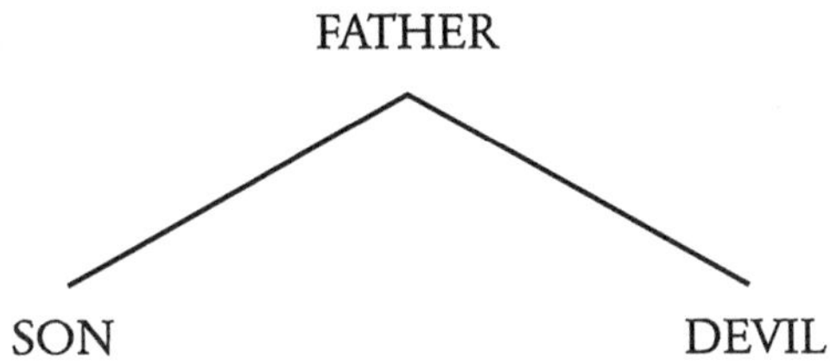

Figure 1: Jung's diagram in *CW* 11 § 256.

But in contrast to Jung it seems to me that the dualism that comes with the moral opposites is not overcome simply through the fact that it is One God who has those two hands or those two sons, Satan and Christ. Or at least it is only a superficial, merely external unification, a very abstract one. In effect, the duality remains, and that God Father is the ultimate, superior principle does not mean much for the alleged "monotheistic" quality if, as we know, the really determining factors in what happens and counts in the world are after all the two sons in their absolute opposition and not the father in whom they are united. Even if they are one in a Third, they nevertheless *themselves* remain absolutely unmediated, as is evident in Jung's diagram. What has happened is merely that the absolute opposition and thus the dualism has *as a package* been subsumed under the Third or, in Jung's *complexio oppositorum* idea, been internalized into it as its container. Therefore, the dualism itself that has been subsumed or internalized remains intact and thus also the irreconcilability of the opposites. The opposites remain absolutely unrelated, oppositional, *dissociated* from each other. The dualism may have been semantically or imaginably absorbed into and contained in God (or, later, in Jung's individuation psychology, become interiorized into man) and thus into some larger unifying whole, but the *dualistic structure* itself remains unchanged. Even the interiorization is here a merely external one of subsuming or swallowing. This lasting *structural* dualism, that is, the dualistic or oppositional thought structure of Jung's thinking, comes out most clearly in Jung's favorite already quoted idea of the "ever more menacing awareness of the conflict," "the crucifixion of the ego, its agonizing suspension between irreconcilable opposites" (*CW* 9ii

§ 79). Also, Jung's frequent *quaternio* diagrams of two crossing lines, each of which keeps one pair of opposites apart, underlines the externality in which the opposites are imagined.

Jung's is a thinking in terms of space (the sense of externality), on the one hand, and in terms of substantiation, of static objects like in physics (in contrast to any (al)chemical interacting of the opposites), on the other hand. It is a picture thinking that views the opposites from an observer standpoint vis-à-vis itself like things in space. This is what accounts for the incontrovertible duality of opposites. Because it is this dualistic logic that structures Jung's thinking, the desired solution of "the unspeakable conflict" (*CW* 11 § 258) must inevitably be deferred, temporally into the future as a utopian hope or task and logically into the unconscious, which is, hopefully, supposed to produce new reconciling symbols (without, however, there being the least evidence that this is the case. All that has been produced as alleged evidence is *images* from dreams and personal visions, or mandala *pictures* as a result of a so-called "painting from out of the unconscious," but never a *symbol* that would deserve this name because it in fact *functions* like one). The *archê*, the principle and structural presupposition of one's thinking, which in Jung's case, at least in the area of the moral and the God questions, is *dissociation*, determines what is possible under its rule and what not.

A structure of duality, an abstract, absolutely unmediated opposition, and the horizontal juxtaposition of substantiated opposites seem to have been an irrenunciable *need* of Jung's. He clings to this ultimately dualistic scheme and, through it, to that *primitive* form of a consciousness that seems to have made its first appearance in Zoroastrianism and reappeared in Gnosticism and Manichaeism, a consciousness which, although it is clearly no longer a mythological, but already a conceptually thinking one, as we have seen, is nevertheless only the primitive form of this consciousness because it represents only the first immediacy of it and because its new achievement, its *thinking*, remains only its semantic content, without attaining to the form of thinking. It operates with substantiated concepts as if they were objects in space and that therefore lack the potential of a mediation between them. In other words, it is an in itself still *unthinking* form of *thought*. Jung's need of the opposites and his obsession with good and evil as well as his fight against the *summum bonum* and *privatio boni* ideas can *psychologically* be comprehended as his celebration of and passionate defense of this primitive form of consciousness (primitive form of an already reflecting consciousness).

What was to be defended? It is precisely the *first immediacy* character of the ancient new post-mythological consciousness, or this consciousness *in its first immediacy*. And what was to be warded off? Its inherent necessity and drive for its further-development and self-unfolding beyond its first immediacy stage, through an inwardization into itself and a dynamicization of the static opposition of the rigid opposites of this consciousness so that it would come home to itself and come alive, become living thought. Jung's enemy was exactly this: the fluidity of living thought. He wanted substantial objects as semantic contents of consciousness or an object-consciousness drilled to observe facts, in other words, *he insisted on the logical form of externality* (which is the "transitional" form between the externalized interiority of mythic imagination and the interiority inwardized into itself of philosophical thought).

But this movement from the abstract dualism to the fluidity of living thought is exactly what the *privatio boni* theory achieved. In order to see this we must push completely aside Jung's powerfully presented view about good and evil with its great suggestive power, because it leads inevitably to the idea that with the *privatio boni* concept something essential was unreasonably and irresponsibly eliminated or euphemistically belittled. We have to push Jung's view aside to become free to approach the *privatio boni* theory with a fresh, unprejudiced gaze and to try to see it in its own terms. We will especially have to focus on what it psychologically achieves.

(1) Good and evil in the Zoroastrian-Manichaean as well as in Jung's version are absolute others to each other, absolutely unrelated, like two things in space.[6] The *privatio boni* concept removes them from their separateness and establishes an intrinsic relation, connection between the opposites. Evil is the privation of Good. It is not wholly other like two different entities, two hands, two sons. The one opposite can be expressed in terms of the other. This takes me to the next point.

---

[6] I am speaking here about the logic of the terms good and evil. A very different question is the empirical-practical use that is made of these terms by people, and with respect to this latter question Jung always insisted on the relativity of good and evil.

(2) The one opposite (evil) has, to be sure, not been subsumed under the other (good), like a species under its genus, but it has indeed been removed from its horizontal juxtaposition (abstract vis-à-vis) and logically internalized into ONE thought that contains the former rigid, static opposites in dynamic, fluid form. This is reflected in the "vertical" nature (referred to above) of the new scheme. The dualism inherent in Jung's version is now truly overcome. His claim that with the Clementine view of the two hands or the two sons of God monotheism was rescued relies on a very external notion of monotheism, and the very mediation between the opposites offered by his view is also a fundamentally external one, namely a mediation in an additional Other, a *third* entity or being (God Father). The mediation between the two hands or two sons or good and evil is not internal to them, their very own mediation. The *privatio boni*, by contrast, mediates between the opposites in thought itself, in the *thinking* of good and evil (in how *they* are thought). It is their own relation that mediates between them. No external third is needed.

(3) As long as the opposites are totally abstract negations of each other in horizontal opposition, their names are actually exchangeable, which is all Jung means when he speaks in other contexts of the relativity of good and evil. Relativity in this thinking has the character of exchangeablity, not of mediation. Why the one is called "good" and the other "evil" and not the other way around remains an open question. This indeterminateness is even more obvious if we use the two sons or two hands ideas. One hand is intrinsically as good as the other. That "right" is good and "left" bad is arbitrary. There is nothing that would within itself define the evil pole of the opposites as evil. The value judgments are assigned from our human value system external to them. *We* prefer Light to Darkness; in our culture "right" is privileged as "good, correct" and associated with Right and Law.

But the view of evil as a *privatio boni* is capable of defining the bad or evil in its own terms as *intrinsically* bad or evil. It provides us with a new insight. Now we *know* and can say *what* evil is. Evil or bad has become a comprehended concept and ceased being the mystification of a metaphysical hypostasis, a mere power-word, an unthought label, or the mystification of a mythic-numinous person, Satan. The bad or evil understood as a privation of the good is bad or evil because it *differs from itself* (we could also say "sins" against itself, rather than merely, as "evil" in the abstract dualistic scheme, being totally different from the *other* opposite), and this is what makes it bad or evil. It differs from *its own* good, its own true nature, its own Being, its own determination—not merely from *the* Good outside of itself as the other pole of the opposition. Bad or evil has here been comprehended as a specific self-relation: an ontological self-contradiction. Something bad or evil deviates from, or maybe even violates, what it is meant to be. It wrongs *its* own concept. It is deficient or *false* being (which shows once more that the *privatio boni* idea does not, as alleged by Jung, pose in any way the danger of a denial of the existence of evil in the world at all; all it does is to clarify what precisely evil *is*. "Being" in this ontological sense is not = "empirical existence." Heidegger spoke of the ontological difference as the difference between the ontic and the ontological, between an entity and its being. What Jung does not get is that the *privatio boni* is at right angles to his "moral question."[7] Jung sees it as a curtailment or amputation of his own naive view, which treats good and evil, to use Heidegger's distinction, as ontic factors). A knife with a dull or broken blade is a bad knife; a man who murders is evil because he violates his own conscience, his own inner moral law, the concept of Man that he himself is. Crimes against humanity violate the perpetrator's own humanity. *This* is the privation of the good.

On all three counts, the *privatio boni* vision has the decided advantage that it has advanced from a purely external account of good and evil to an inwardized one. They are not quasi-"metaphysical" or numinous powers, as in Jung's view owing to his penchant to a pictorial thinking, but have been interiorized (not into our inner, but) into themselves and thus into the objective soul. They have been returned to the soul's logical life as its living thought. This is what should make the *privatio boni* notion attractive

[7] The standpoint of the moral question in Jung's sense amounts to an *acting out*, in consciousness (not in behavior), of the opposition, a looking up to the mystified-hypostatized opposites like to two stuffed mummies and feeling speechlessly ("the unspeakable conflict") suspended between them. By contrast, the standpoint of the *privatio boni* "remembers," *thinks*, what the other standpoint acts out and projects out. Thought cuts into and cuts through the thoughtlessness of reified opposition. If it is a curtailment, then the only thing that it cuts away is the mystification and dumbfoundedness surrounding the hypostatized good and evil, not the reality of evil.

to psychology, at least much more attractive than Jung's insistence on "the unspeakable conflict" and the inflated idea of a suspension between the opposites. Logical contradiction, whose first immediacy had been the abstract opposition of Good and Evil, has come home to itself as the opposition of "absolute identity with itself" (*summum bonum*) and ontological self-contradiction.

5.

In calling Christianity dualistic Jung is of course right *to the extent that* Christianity did entertain the ideas of Satan whose existence antedates that of man, of the Antichrist, and of eternal damnation. But first of all, this rather primitive quasi-mythological narrative has already been superseded by the *privatio boni* theory, which is intrinsically in accord with monotheism, and secondly, why did Jung select these ideas and harp upon them *at a time* (the 20th century), and as relevant for that time, when they had long pretty much disappeared from Christian thought and feeling, and had been rendered obsolete in the history of the soul? Why does he need to dig out and dust off these notions? Why does he, at the end of the *Christian* eon, zoom in on the ambivalence of the *Old Testament* YHWH—as if this to some extent archaic[8] God were the same as the New Testament God as well as the God of Christianity, as it later developed on the soil of Greek thought? Why did Jung make use of these historical relics not merely for the purposes of a psycho-historical study, but *for our, or the soul's, present concerns*, for what he termed the "individuation process"?

No doubt, the ideas Jung focused on in this regard were indeed elements of the entire phenomenology of the Christian religion. But Christianity, as all high religions with a long history, is a very complex reality. When confronted with it, it is essential for a psychological, not merely positivistic-historical, investigation to make use of two criteria for deciding what is to be emphasized. The first principle can be expressed as the insight into the "simultaneity of the nonsimultaneous" (Ernst Bloch). The second principle circles around the commitment to a study, in each case, of what the soul in

[8] This is a descriptive, not a judgmental term. It is especially Jung who highlights YHWH's archaic characteristics.

the Real happens to be in contrast to a commitment to a presupposed knowledge of archetypal truths.

As to the first principle, Jung himself pointed out,

> I tend to impress it upon my pupils not to treat their patients as if they were all cut to the same measure: the population consists of different historical layers. There are people who, psychologically, could have lived just as well in the year 5000 B.C., i.e., who can still successfully solve their conflicts as people did seven thousand years ago. There are numerous barbarians and people psychologically belonging to the Ancient World living in Europe and in all civilized countries, as well as a very large number of medieval Christians. There are, by contrast, relatively few who have reached the level of consciousness possible today. We must also reckon with the fact that a few of our generation belong to the third or fourth millennium A.D. and are consequently anachronistic. So it is psychologically quite "legitimate" when a medieval man solves his conflict today on a thirteenth-century level and treats his shadow as the devil incarnate. For such a man any other procedure would be unnatural and wrong, for he is devout like a thirteenth-century Christian. But, for the man who belongs by temperament, i.e., psychologically, to the twentieth century, certain considerations come into play which would not enter the head of a medieval representative of the species at all (*CW* 11 § 463, transl. modif.).

Jung was here speaking about the *people* living today. But we can apply what he said also to the historical body of the basic Christian *ideas* and *texts*. The books of the New Testament, to mention only them, contain ideas that correspond to quite different psychological frames of consciousness of different "historical layers." Some are more advanced, others may even be regressive. Some are immediately accessible to a still mythological way of imagining, some are the first intuitions of very subtle ideas requiring a developed consciousness that still needed to be developed in the course of time. From this consideration we can get our first criterion: as psychologists we should be oriented towards the most advanced ideas of early Christianity, where it is at its peak and at its best, and not stay stuck in such ones that also de facto occur in it, but have clearly already been superseded by its other much more advanced ones. And conversely, if, e.g., during the 20th century there was, as Jung insists, a popular "longing for the exaltation of the Mother of God" (*CW* 11 § 748) and if the dogma of the *Assumptio Mariae* has been declared in response to it, we must of course also take the consideration into account that this is possibly a case of an anachronistic development in the reverse sense of the above quote, a being "devout like a thirteenth-century Christian," and not take it as evidence of what the soul wants. "There are," Jung himself had said, "relatively few who have reached the level of consciousness possible today." And in fact is not the Roman Catholic Church as a whole a *medieval* historical monument jutting into the modern world? Not everything new in an abstract temporal sense is up to where the soul is today. The psychologist should at least aim at looking at things from that level of consciousness that is "possible today."

This criterion we have to especially apply to the primitive archaic conception that Jung imputes to the Christian God. Repeatedly Jung describes the Christian story of salvation as follows (or in similar terms): "Our sins consist in a disobedience. The Creator of the World is each time terribly annoyed, that is, annoyed to such an extent that he can only be reconciled by his son's being slaughtered. Just imagine such a gory story!"[9] Such a description is beneath criticism. How can Jung dare to give such a childish, primitive interpretation to Christ's Crucifixion? Here Jung goes to the lowest possible level of a primitive consciousness in order to imagine what Christ's death is about. This is absolutely inappropriate for the religious content Jung is dealing with. What the actual story is about is reductively and concretistically interpreted in terms appropriate for a Freudian personalistic family romance. God is pulled down to the level of a human, all-too-human person with merely subjective emotions in the context of empirical-practical reality. Kindergarten stuff. And an insult to our intelligence. Jung *deliberately* ignores that the Christian God idea has its place on an entirely different level, an already reflected, theological, intelligible level, far beyond anything like the irascibility that (maybe) some mythic gods might have betrayed. That in Christianity God has become *Spirit* and *Love* (not to be confused with a *being* that merely *shows* spirit and love!) and thus is far beyond anything like an immature, irascible being is of course known to Jung but not taken as

[9] C.G. Jung, *Über Gefühle und den Schatten.* Winterthurer Fragestunden. Textbuch, Zürich and Düsseldorf 1999, p. 26 f. My translation.

the basis of his concept of God. Jung goes *with* consciousness *beneath* the level of consciousness already achieved. He is obviously in the grip of some personal emotion and/or some resulting ideological need.

The childishness, and the origin in childhood, of Jung's emotion as well as of his conception comes out rather clearly in this quote: "It was only psychology that helped me to overcome the fatal impressions of my youth that everything untrue, even immoral, in our empirical world *must* be believed to be the eternal truth in religion. Above all, the killing of a human victim to placate the senseless wrath of a God who had created imperfect beings unable to fulfil his expectations poisoned my whole religion" (*CW* 18 § 1643). "The *fatal* impressions of my youth ..." and "... *poisoned* my whole religion"! Here we can still sense the resonance in 82-year-old Jung of the terrible shock of disappointment that he as innocent little child must have experienced, the destruction of the child's God believed to be a benign, fatherly old man with a long white beard sitting on a cloud, a God who all of a sudden turned out—for the childish mind—to be in truth a blood-thirsty killer of His own child. It was a disappointment and shock that in *his* (Jung's) case, however, did not catapult Jung to a more advanced, more mature level of consciousness as it normally would do, but merely *poisoned* the old innocent, childish consciousness[10] that was nevertheless stubbornly held onto: simple negation instead of determinate negation and sublation. One cannot help seeing in Jung's story of the wrath of God the story of Jung's wrath against this God (as He had been idiosyncratically pictured by the boy Jung); that Jung was not able to advance, at least as a mature man, beyond the child's silly personalistic and literalistic construal of the Christian story of redemption and the accompanying vehement emotions of resentment, and that instead he seems to have retained them unchanged, taking them with him into his grave, is astounding.

Jung took it all personally, as if it concerned him as ego *and not the soul*, and as if Christianity was not an objective symbolic formation—a soul truth—but a private interaction between people

[10] Concerning the effect of this poisoning one cannot help thinking of Nietzsche's adage (*Beyond Good and Evil* # 168): "Christianity gave Eros poison to drink—it did, no doubt, not die from it, but it degenerated: into a vice." In Jung's case: not the death of Christianity (i.e., something like atheism), but its degeneration (a corrupted view of Christianity)!

on earth. When he begins his *Answer to Job* with the motto, "I am distressed for thee ..." (2 Samuel 1:26), and states at the end of his preface, "I cannot, therefore, write in a cooly objective manner, but must allow my emotional subjectivity to speak if I want to describe what I feel when I read certain books of the Bible, or when I remember the impressions I have received from the doctrines of our faith" (*CW* 11 § 559), he tells us indirectly that he is not so much engaging Christianity as a religion, a psychological phenomenon, that is to say, a self-articulation of the objective soul, and *from* the standpoint of professional psychology, but rather that he elaborates his own subjective complex. Why does Jung deign what *he* as private individual *feels* worthy of being communicated to the public (in a not-autobiographical work and a work not addressed to his fan club), indeed, not only being communicated but directly displayed (acted out)? Of what business and interest are his subjective feelings to us when we want to learn something about the psychology of Christianity?

Jung's justification is of course that "Since I shall be dealing with numinous factors, my feeling is challenged quite as much as my intellect" (*ibid.*). But this is all wrong.[11] First of all, if he were indeed dealing with numinous factors, writing an argumentative book about them would be an inappropriate response. But secondly and above all, what he will be dealing with in his book *is* not at all numinous factors but the kind of symbolic material that in other cases he would have termed psychic "facts" and discussed in just that "cooly objective manner." (We see this cooly objective manner for example in his essay on "Transformation Symbolism in the Mass," the Mass which on the basis of its particular content certainly could be just as much said to be dealing with "numinous factors"). There is no reason why the Biblical material, which has been known collectively for millennia and personally by Jung since the early days of his childhood, should be experienced as particularly numinous. Jung has been used to them all his life. They are well-worn. The alleged "numinosity" (numinosity: *'s klingt so wunderlich!*[12]) is in this case an ennobling euphemism for a "feeling-toned complex" of *his*

[11] I will not go into the problem of the dissociation of feeling and intellect expressed in this statement.

[12] Goethe, *Faust II*, Act 1, "Finstere Galerie," line 6217.

subjective psyche dating back to his childhood, a complex that has not been seen through and overcome. It is the complex's heightened feeling-tone or emotion that, while in reality stemming from his "personal unconscious," is projected onto an "archetypal" story of the "collective unconscious" (or the objective soul) as *its* objective quality of "numinosity." "You see," Jung himself told us at some other occasion, "whenever you make an emotional statement, there is a fair suspicion that you are talking of your own case; in other words, that there is a projection because of your emotion. ... If you are adapted you need no emotion; an emotion is only an instinctive explosion which denotes that you have not been up to your task."[13]

At any rate, this is why Jung shows a predilection for the traces of archaic features at some points still shining through the depiction of God in the Old Testament as well as a predilection for such views of his like the one that "Later Christianity, however, is dualistic, inasmuch as it splits off one half of the opposites, personified in Satan, and he is *eternal* in his state of damnation. This crucial question of πόθεν τὸ κακόν (whence evil?) forms the point of departure for the Christian theory of Redemption" (*CW* 11 p. 358). With this idea Jung points to something that certainly played a role in the actual history of Christianity for a still naive consciousness not yet up to height of "the level of consciousness possible" on the basis of the Christian teachings. Our first criterion demands of us to apperceive Christianity from the highest level of consciousness possible within it.

Now I come to the second criterion. I will exemplify it by means of Jung's thesis expressed numerous times that "the terrible problem of evil" (*MDR* p. 331) has become virulent in our time. "In our present time the problem has simply come alive again. And quite clearly through what happened historically. There are only few centuries during which such terrible obscenities have occurred as in ours. It is simply dreadful! And that is what has ripped open the problem of evil." "It is as a matter of course that we are these days again confronted with this historical question, which lay dormant for two-thousand years, namely: What about the dark side?"[14] I think that this view of

[13] C.G. Jung, *Nietzsche's Zarathustra. Notes of the Seminar Given in 1934–1939*, ed. by James L. Jarrett, vol. 2, Princeton University Press 1988, p. 1497.

[14] C.G. Jung, *Über Gefühle und den Schatten.* Winterthurer Fragestunden. Textbuch, Zürich and Düsseldorf 1999, p. 60 and 62. My translation.

Jung's is idiosyncratic. True, incredible atrocities have been committed and evil abounds, terrible crimes, sexual abuse and murder of small children, killing sprees, genocide, torture, mass murder, all sorts of brutality and injustice. This we can concede to Jung. But all this did not, does not lead to "the *question* of evil." It does not disturb the soul. It does not stir the religious feelings and imagination. Rather, all this is quite pragmatically and empirically, if not banally, a matter for courts (ordinary courts, Nuremberg trials, the International Criminal Court), for international law, for human rights activist groups like Amnesty International, for historians and sociologists, for the psychological study of the psyche and the ego development of offenders, for social workers and trauma psychologists, for peace studies, and so on. There are in the modern world no virulent ideas and serious emotions concerning the Antichrist, Satan, or Evil as a substantial reality. Evil events and deeds are seen as human, all-too-human happenings. They result from bad socialization and maladaptation, from complexes acquired through defects in early mother-child bonding or traumatic experiences in childhood (all of which show, in a way, the *privatio boni* in action[15]), which is why the modern penal system operates much less with the idea of punishment than with the concept of resocialization. Even where the genes or hormones of a compulsive sexual offender may be seen as the cause of crime, modern man does not hold God as Creator

[15] Jung's view was that the *privatio boni* leads to the notion that "man is the author of evil" (*CW* 9ii § 84)—in the sense of the adage, quoted and rejected so frequently by Jung, "Omne bonum a Deo, omne malum ab homine" (e.g., *CW* 9ii § 95). Here now we see that this view is not borne out. In the modern situation neither God nor man are seen as authors of evil. Rather, for it, as already for Basil the Great, evil simply "arises from a 'mutilation of the soul'" (§ 85). Contrary to Jung who says at the same place "If the soul was originally created good, then it has really been corrupted and by something that is real," and contrary again to his suggestion that the eternal devil's falling away from God "proves firstly that evil was in the world before man, and therefore that man cannot be the sole author of it, and secondly that the devil already had a 'mutilated' soul for which we must hold a real cause responsible" (*ibid.*), the notion of the mutilation of the soul does not support the idea of the reality of evil in Jung's heightened sense, but only that in the banal empirical sense. We see clearly how Jung here confounds the question of the empirically real evils in the world and the empirical mutilations of the soul with the totally different metaphysical or theological question about who the metaphysical cause of *Evil per se* is, god, man, or the devil, and thus also where the devil's "mutilated soul" came from. In the last analysis Jung is unable or unwilling to explain empirical "mutilations of the soul" simply in terms of empirical innerworldly causes (the way the modern mind does). He inevitably leaps out of the empirical level and goes back to the transcendent metaphysical level of (the devil and) God (who made the devil and thus ultimately also evil), the *metaphysical* question "Whence evil?"

responsible but thinks in terms of biology. It may of course happen now and then that someone asks how God can allow that such horrors happen. But if this happens it is more a curious occurrence within our modern world, if it is not merely a rhetorical return to an outdated formula. The type of highly emotional "metaphysical" struggle with the question of evil as we find it in Jung's psychology, a struggle that involves the very nature of God, cannot be detected in the collective soul. The soul in modernity does not reckon anymore with God as the cause of the world and of what happens in the world. God is *really* dead and bygone for it.

It is impossible for the soul in modernity to entertain the idea of Good and Evil as realities in their own right. The soul has come down to earth, down from the clouds as its previous psychological place of existence, and now really and irrevocably dwells on the earth, without toying any longer with the notions of eminent origins, with the ideas of mythological otherworldly agents behind the scene or prior to the beginning of the world.

(Here I might add in passing that rather than seeing in the *privatio boni* a euphemistic diminishment of evil, it amounts, in its ultimate consequences, much more to the diminishment of the *summum bonum* as an existing God because it tends to dissolve all metaphysical entities into the fluidity of thought, into the mind's own concepts. Ultimately, that formula is the overcoming of the *positivity* of the moral opposition as such and thus, by distilling it into an absolute-negative opposition, our introduction into a consciousness beyond good and evil [in the usual positivized sense of good and evil]. It *is already* "the turning-point" "where good and evil begin to relativize themselves, to doubt themselves,[16] and the cry is raised for a morality 'beyond good and evil,'" a development that Jung, however, found absolutely "out of the question" "[i]n the age of Christianity and in the domain of trinitarian thinking" [*CW* 11 § 258]. Ultimately, it is the insight that the world "is *only* that!" The question, "Whence evil?" is psychologically obsolete: meaningless, based on untenable presuppositions of a more primitive consciousness than the one already "possible" [and real] today.)

[16] Instead of "relativize" and "to doubt themselves" I would of course prefer something like "become logically negative."

So the second principle requires that psychology is attuned to and abides by what is really going on in the depth of soul at the time in question. The *actual* phenomenology of the soul is what counts for the psychologist. We must not apodictically declare something to be the soul's timeless archetypal truth as the unchanging standard by which the present reality has to be judged, i.e., prejudged. Concerning the soul's truths and concerns, we have to look and see afresh into the *depth* of what is actually going on and not look *back* or *up* to presupposed archetypes or other values or models as a priori givens. We have to be taught by the real course of events what the soul in the Real (not merely the empirical surface reality of it) in fact happens to be. What does in fact show itself in our time of its own accord? That is the question. And, of course, for determining what is indeed truly an objective-soul phenomenon, a phenomenon in the depth of the soul, and what is perhaps nothing but a subjective excitement or mass fad or complex reaction on the ego level, a differentiated feeling function is indispensable, an affinity to and sensibility for *soul.*

If Jung states that "The world of the Son is the world of moral discord, without which human consciousness could hardly have progressed so far as it has towards mental and spiritual differentiation" (*CW* 11 § 259), then he is absolutely right about the indispensability of the moral discord during the Middle Ages for this further development of consciousness. The idea of the μὴ ὄν ("something non-existent") "together with that of original sin formed the foundation of a moral consciousness which was a novelty in the history of humankind" (*CW* 14 § 86, transl. modif.). Agreed. But two problems remain. First, consciousness has, in the history of the soul, advanced beyond the medieval "world of the Son" to the early-modern "world of the Spirit," the metaphysic of *representation* and *subjectivity*, best exemplified or symbolized, perhaps, by infinitesimal calculus and central perspective in painting, for which a thinking in terms of building-block-like entities and the crude point-blank juxtaposition/opposition of the opposites is even more passé than for the much older privato boni thinking.[17] And secondly, even the interpretation of the

[17] The modern world (beginning with the closure of metaphysics at the time of Hegel, economically with the Industrial Revolution, politically with the post-French-Revolution, post-Napoleonic time) is of course already beyond this stage of "the world of the Spirit."

world of the Son as a world of "conflict to the last extremity [i.e., the conflict between Christ and the 'adversary,' the devil]" and of the "*absolute* opposition" between them (*CW* 11 § 258, transl. modif.) was a weak interpretation of the Christian religion to begin with, appropriate, to be sure, for a rather primitive mind still informed by mythological thought-structures, but not really adequate to the level of consciousness already achieved in Christianity. In its depth Christianity had already overcome any dualism and opposition or conflict from the outset. Indeed, the overcoming (the having been overcome) of the opposites—salvation, redemption—was not only its message,[18] but above all also its inner logic (the logical *movement* of Christ's *kenôsis*; God comprehended as Spirit and Love, rather than as a Being who *has* spirit and is *loving*).

If for Jung the question "Whence evil?" has in our time psychologically become once more *the* pressing problem, and if he suggests that "The *complexio oppositorum* of the God-image[19] thus enters into man, and not as unity, but as conflict .... It is this process that is taking place in our times, albeit scarcely comprehended by the official teachers of humanity, although it would be their task to recognize these things" (*MDR* p. 334, transl. modif.), the question for us arises what was motivating him. It seems to me that the only explanation we can get on the basis of the insights gained in the foregoing investigation is that he wanted to regressively restore the logical form of substantiated

[18] And as message not only a promise for the future, for life after death or for the end of the world, but also as already *in fact having happened*. With this idea, consciousness had risen to a complex thought structure, one for which something can be already *implicitly* and in fact true, even when *explicitly* it is not visible, indeed, when it seems to be even contradicted by what one sees in the world. It is true within an advanced status of consciousness, true within a consciousness that has the power of thought, the power, we might say, of being able to *think through*, rather than merely "seeing through or imagining things."

[19] Frequently Jung refers with the *complexio oppositorum* idea to Nicholas of Cusa and his *coincidentia oppositorum*, but generally he withholds from the reader the fact that Cusanus makes it explicitly clear (*De docta ignorantia* II, 2. h 65, 17–66, 6, also *De ludo globi* II, h n. 81) that this *coincidentia* does precisely not apply to Good and Evil! Transitoriness and sinning are contingent deficiencies that belong to the individual beings in this empirical world. They are not ontologically constitutive opposites united in the *coincidentia*. There is one passage in Jung that indicates that he was aware of this exclusion: "Nicholas of Cusa calls God a *complexio oppositorum* (naturally under the apotropaic condition of the *privatio boni*!)" (*CW* 18 § 1537), but he does not state in plain terms that he appropriates the phrase of Nicholas of Cusa for that very aspect and only for it, namely the moral opposites, that according to Cusanus is on principle grounds excluded from the coincidence.

contents, specifically of a consciousness that *has* a God. He tried to defend against a modern consciousness that has relentlessly come down to earth and *ipso facto* has left the stance of upward-looking and for which the world is now "*only* that!" He refused to give himself unreservedly over to the soul of the contents of consciousness so as to go under into it, into the fluidity of thought. He felt he needed mystified objects and images "out there" vis-à-vis himself, thereby holding himself in the observer standpoint ("felt experience"; numinous experiences), even if this vis-à-vis could—this he realized—at his time no longer be made plausible as a transcendent cosmic one the way it had been in the olden times of myth and metaphysics, but nowadays could only have some chance if it were psychologized and retreated from the real world into our personal inner and our personal experience. *This* interiority is the literalized and itself externalized (positivized) form of inwardness: the interiorization into empirical man instead of into the respective content's own concept, its soul. Jung desperately needed the mystification of evil. Because it was the key or cornerstone to mystification as such. Jung's ultimate image is that of Man speechlessly and utterly helplessly suspended between the opposites of Good and Evil and through this suspension becoming conscious of the moral opposites that God could not become conscious of by himself: "That is the meaning of divine service [*Gottesdienst*], of the service which man can render to God, that light may emerge from the darkness, that the Creator may become conscious of His creation [*nota bene*: only in and through man!], and man conscious of himself" (*MDR* p. 338). And by in this way helping God to become conscious, Man, so the idea goes, redeems God who is helplessly entangled in his unconsciousness—but, so we can say, Man also (counter-factually) once more *rescues* the substantiated idea of God as an Other[20] *for himself*, and along with it, albeit for the price of having to regress, the for Jung so precious *form* of EXTERNALITY, ABSOLUTE OPPOSITION (*dissociated* duality), and SUBSTANTIATION as such, which belong to the *primitive* level of the (post-mythological, reflecting) consciousness.[21]

---

[20] Interestingly enough, Jung uses the term "Self" for what has the form of otherness for him. The Self is to be experienced, and it is the God-image or the image of transcendent wholeness.

[21] As the *primitive* form of (already *reflecting*) consciousness it cannot enter the logical form of thought and give itself over to the fluidity of thinking, but is characterized by substantiating and externalizing, projecting and hypostatizing.

"Just as man was once revealed out of God, so, when the circle closes, God may be revealed out of man" (*CW* 11 § 267).

What an inflated, pompous image![22] What absolutely "numinous" self-importance! What a mystification of human existence! Religion! Quasi-recuperated religion. Not psychology.

The form of externality and substantiation comes out most clearly in how Jung conceives the very idea, taken over from Nicholas of Cusa and so precious to him, of the *complexio oppositorum.* Jung merely *imagines* this *complexio.* He stays stuck in a picturing thinking that either subsumes the opposites (in Jung's case, contrary to Nicholas, the opposites of good and evil) as His two sons under "God" or lets them be contained in Him as His two attributes (like His two hands), thus always retaining their dissociated duality. He never advances to the thought of the *coincidentia*; he seems to be unable, or unwilling, to really *think* this *coincidentia.* If the thought that Good and Evil really coincide (in God) were *really* thought, they would—at least in man's highest thought, God—despite being distinct, indeed, opposites, nevertheless have to be *indistinguishable, just as beginning and end are in a circle.*[23] No terrible conflict. Each point of a circle is both—and simultaneously—beginning *and* end. Picture thinking can, to be sure, imagine the uroboros, but it cannot go through with what the image of the uroboros implies and what it therefore demands of us. If *quod natura relinquit imperfectum ars perficit*, then the *image* of the tail-eater (with its distinct mouth and tail) demands of us as adepts of the *ars* to complete and perfect it: by sublating this (naturalistic) image in the thought of a circle or, even better, of the internal circulating and self-contradictory movement (pulsating logical life) within one single stationary point.[24]

---

[22] Cf. also: "I am guarding my light and my treasure .... It is most precious not only to me, but above all to the darkness of the creator, who needs man to illuminate His creation" (*Letters 2*, p. 597, to Serrano, 14 September 1960).

[23] But Nicholas of Cusa rightly rejected the idea of a *coincidentia* of good and evil.

[24] Jung's theory is of course that the absolute conflict of the opposites in (or for) us humans is indispensable for God (in whom the opposites are united) to become conscious. But this only shows once more the dissociated duality: man – God. Jung takes God literally and substantially, as a real Other. Just as he does not see that the moral opposition in the literal Zoroastrian or Manichaean style has in the soul's history long been overcome and sublated, he does not realize that consciousness (and thus, for example, the human imagination and thinking about God) is psychologically all there is. There is not a God as an external referent who would need to become conscious. For psychology, it is in human "theology," as in myths and fairytales and as in dreams, that

Another function that the paradigm of the individual suspended like Christ between the opposites of Good and Evil has for Jung's scheme, in addition to cementing the form of externality, is that it helps to underpin the extraordinary importance that Jung assigns to the individual as the "the makeweight that tips the scales?" (*CW* 10 § 586), as the one important factor on whom the rescue of the world depends (*ibid.* § 536). The "individual human being" has to be "in the centre as the measure of all things" (*ibid.* § 523). Whereas this overestimation of the individual again presents, as a hope for the future, something that has already been historically fully realized in the early-modern soul and, in our age, is clearly nearing its end—the high time of the individual seems to be definitely over—there is one aspect of Jung's idea of the individual's suspension between the opposites that I can fully appreciate and find significant. This has to do with the fact that it views the ethical problem (as I prefer to say instead of moral problem) as one that cannot rely on an already existing set of clear-cut answers to the question what is right and what wrong in each concrete situation of a conflict between values. The norms of society, which are always abstract and *external* judgments, are not always the ultimate measure. There may be situations in which the morally right decision may be one that violates the prevailing collective ideas of what would be the right behavior. In a painful and very personal process the individual has to allow *his* subjective and fundamentally *unforeseeable* answer to this question to mature in himself, and this answer will accordingly also be valid only for himself. No claim for the generality can be connected with it, for how others would have to decide in this situation. Here Jung interiorizes the "moral question" (not only and not so much into the individual, but much more) into the eachness of each concrete situation that requires a moral decision.

the soul speaks about *itself* (and *not* about God, for example), and that the archetypes reveal themselves in their natural interplay, as "formation, transformation / the eternal Mind's eternal recreation" (cf. *CW* 9i § 400). The human imagination and thinking about God IS (part of) the *self-display* of the logical status reached by consciousness, it IS (part of) consciousness's becoming conscious. The actual thinking of the idea of the *coincidentia oppositorum* more than 500 years ago IS already that having become conscious (in the area of the theme of the opposites) on the part of consciousness that Jung is still hoping for as a necessary future development to be achieved. And by hoping for something that is already real, it is the regression to the place before the threshold that in the history of the soul has long ago been crossed. Jung's utopianism (i.e., the deferral into the future) and his wanting *God* to become conscious are structurally one and the same externalization.

But that Jung puts his hope, concerning such situations, on the unconscious as that which produces "reconciling symbols" seems less convincing to me. There is a difference between one's waiting for a symbol from the unconscious, on the one hand, and one's letting oneself slowly come to one's own decision after carefully weighing all aspects, considerations, and values that come into play in the given situation, on the other hand. Only the second option is truly ethical because here the individual shoulders the responsibility for his decision (it will be truly and exclusively *his*, despite the fact that it is not a rationalistic ego decision, but a decision of the "whole man"), whereas with one's waiting for a symbol to appear one ultimately delegates the decision to another agency, the unconscious, and retains a logical innocence. And above all, this subtle, interiorized view of the ethical problem that moves away from the idea of a fixed moral code to the necessity of one's having to (as it were, "creatively") *find* one's own answer in an inner struggle—does it in any way involve the thesis of the "reality of Evil," or require the question "Whence evil?" which according to Jung, after having lain dormant for two thousand years has today been ripped open again?

Psychologically, both the historically first emergence of the question "Whence evil?" and Jung's renewed passionate interest in, indeed, insistence on it seem to presuppose a consciousness possessed by the grandiose demand for a perfect world and an infinite Creator whose creation *ipso facto* also ought to be infinite and absolutely perfect. This question is reflective of a consciousness unwilling to get over its disappointment about its own already real discovery that the world is essentially finite after all. The narcissistic blow that comes with this discovery is answered by a refusal to come down to earth and to grow up, that is, the refusal to integrate, as its very own constitutive insight, the knowledge gained of the fundamental finiteness of the world and human existence as their necessary character, as simply inherent in the concept of a "created world." This refusal results in a deep resentment, if not anger. The world's finiteness is resentfully seen as a fault, a wrong. In other words, consciousness's own fault of not integrating its own experience is projected onto the world as *its* congenital defect.

"Whence evil?" amounts to the question "whose fault is it?" or "Whodunit?" and thus to a psychology of blame. It is a compromise formation. By displaying a fixation on or obsession with "evil" it is a clear reflection of the fact that the disappointment, the loss of the (solely) Good Father in Heaven, has indeed irrevocably happened to this consciousness. But by means of the "whence?," that is, the question about the originator or perpetrator, it nevertheless manages to preserve for itself the *position* of the child's naive God-Imagine (God as a substantiated being, person, and acting subject with human characteristics) and, thus, the father-imago and the guarantor of a higher meaning, even if it had to give up the Father's pure goodness.[25] At the same time, precisely through this insistence on the metaphysical reality of evil and this dwelling on "evil" the experienced imperfection of the world is, paradoxically, *logically* stored away (and thus defused), partly in this metaphysical Other as the one of His two hands or two sons,[26] and partly, after man's individuation, in the human *unconscious*. Ultimately, God and the unconscious are the ones who are responsible for the existence of evil and of the imperfections of life on earth. *We* are relieved of the necessity of having *on the logical level* to acknowledge our own ultimate finiteness and imperfection as our very own responsibility by integrating this loss of grandiosity into the very definition of ourselves—and this precisely not in the sense of the dictum, *omne bonum a deo, omne malum ab homine*, which would only be the storing away of the disappointment in the opposite place (in empirical self instead of metaphysical Other), i.e., the reversed psychology of blame, this time along the lines of the defense mechanism of the "identification with the aggressor."[27] No, it is not our personal

[25] In a way, at least by implication, what has been discussed here provides a counterpart—the process in the area of the Father imago—of what I demonstrated having happened in Jung's thinking with respect to the Mother topic in my "Irrelevantification. Or: On the Death of Nature, the Construction of 'the Archetype,' and the Birth of Man," in: Wolfgang Giegerich, *The Soul Always Thinks*, Collected English Papers vol. 4, New Orleans, LA (Spring Journal Books) 2010, pp. 387–442.

[26] Jung's insistence that the two hands or two sons of God are completely compatible with monotheism is significant in this context: in his scheme, the disharmony belongs to a logically lower level. It is subsumed under the fundamental and (logically, not in the sense of a value judgment) superior idea of the One God, in the idea of whom *consciousness* rescues for itself its irrenunciable idea of the ultimate harmony and intactness of the world order and thus its own innocence (unwoundedness, harmlessness). The disappointment does not have to truly dis-appoint (*ent-täuschen*: undeceive, disillusion) consciousness.

[27] Maybe Jung's railing against the idea *omne bonum a deo, omne malum ab homine*, which, I agree, is unacceptable, has the added and particular motivation behind itself of freeing man from having to define himself (and the world as such) as finite and rather wanting some metaphysical Other to be blamed. Jung of course wanted us to integrate what he called our shadow, but this move remained one on the merely psychic and

fault, our guilt, nor our shadow[28]: the imperfection is simply the general objective and *all*-permeating character of the world and existence in the world at large.[29]

empirical level. Logically, psychologically, however, we were to stay grandiose children of God, or some god(dess). Jung about himself: "At Bollingen I am in my truest essence, I am most deeply myself. Here I am, as it were, the 'age-old son of the mother' ..." (*MDR* p. 225, transl. modif.). I have the impression (as far as I can see from outside and from what has become known about him) that *psychically*, on the *empirical-personal* level, Jung was by no means inflated. But on the psychological or logical level he cultivated inflation. Jung, we could say with the title of a comedy by Oliver Goldsmith, stoops, but stoops only in order to conquer. The stooping occurs on the psychic level, the level of the empirical man (shadow integration), or in "Küsnacht," but the conquering takes place on the psychological level, in the logic of his self-definition (the grandiose Self), or at "Bollingen." To do justice to him, it is important to see both aspects, but to see also that any belief that by one's shadow-integration on the personal, empirical-practical level, as indispensable as it is, the psychological grandiosity would have been overcome is an illusion and self-deception. The soul does not accept pinch-beck as currency. It does not even accept genuine empirical gold, *aurum vulgi*. It demands payment in *aurum nostrum*: logical gold (the concept, the definition), and, of course, only payment in full. One cannot really get away with fooling or cheating it.

[28] Shadow integration pursues an immunization strategy and is thus fundamentally opposed to *omne malum ab homine*. The latter idea amounts to the relentless admission of the imperfection or sinfulness of the whole man. "[M]an is the author evil" (*CW* 9ii § 84), each man hook, line, and sinker, each me of his own. But the idea of the shadow operates with the distinction (logical dissociation) between me and the shadow that I *have*. The integration of the shadow merely means that consciousness becomes conscious of the fact that I *have* a shadow and what precisely my specific shadow is. It must under no circumstances mean that I identify myself with the shadow (which for Jung, for whom the shadow is, ultimately, an archetype, would amount to an inflation). I still only *have* a shadow, but I *am not* the author of whatever specific evil. The shadow concept allows Jung to *subsume* our personal concrete evils and imperfections *under* the concept of ourselves as the whole man in just the same way as he *subsumed* the retained dualism of Good and Evil under the monotheistic God as his two sons or two hands.

[29] I have to unmitigatedly end with the idea of finiteness and imperfection because here we are concerned with issues in the sphere of positivity ("the reality of evil," the metaphysical God, the empirical man, the real world). But this insistence on the irrevocable finiteness by no means precludes the importance and legitimacy of the notion of infinity in the sphere of *absolute negativity*, the sphere of meanings and the soul's depth.

Part II. Hegel

CHAPTER SIX

Jung's Betrayal of His Truth
The Adoption of a Kant-Based Empiricism and the Rejection of Hegel's Speculative Thought

If one goes by the paucity of Jung's references to Hegel in his published works and letters and by the marginal nature of the comments that he did make about Hegel, one is likely to conclude that "Jung and Hegel" is simply a nonissue. But I want to show that the position Jung took in the case "Kant versus Hegel" had far-reaching consequences for Jung's conception of psychology as a whole. A close look at what Jung thought about Hegel is capable of revealing a fundamental structural deficit in Jung's psychology project, a deficit that amounts to a systematic, even though unintended, "betrayal" of his own cause. "Betrayal" here does not necessarily imply a deliberate ego intention. It expresses an objective relation.

To have a foil against which to set off and evaluate Jung's response to Hegel, I will first turn to a very different topic.

I. Jung's self-set life-task: Expiation for Faust's crime.

When Jung built his Tower at Bollingen, he placed an inscription over its gate: "*Philemonis Sacrum—Fausti Poenitentia*" (Shrine of Philemon—Repentance of Faust). In his *Memories* Jung tells us what the background for this inscription was. It had to do with his assessment of and reaction to a particular scene in the fifth act of Goethe's *Faust II*. "... and when Faust, in his hubris and self-inflation, caused the murder of Philemon and Baucis, I felt guilty, quite as if I myself in the past had helped commit the murder of the two old people. This strange idea alarmed me, and I regarded it as my responsibility to atone for this crime, or to prevent its repetition."[1]

The murder of Philemon and Baucis is more than just any murder of two innocent old people. Philemon and Baucis were that mythical couple who, themselves poor, nevertheless were the only ones during an ungodly age to hospitably house and host the Gods wandering on earth in the guise of homeless humans. So when Faust in Goethe's drama caused the murder of this couple, this implies the irrevocable end of that mode of being-in-the-world where man understands himself in terms of the Gods and knows that he is free *only to the extent that* he is on the leading strings of God. Instead, it inaugurates an age in which the human self-definition is "Man For Himself" (Erich Fromm).

By placing that inscription over the gate of his Tower, the literal inner sanctum of his life, Jung indicated that it was a kind of motto under which he had put his whole existence and its inner meaning. Even more distinctly than in the above quotation from *Memories*, Jung made this clear in a letter of 5 January 1942 to Paul Schmitt. "... all of a sudden and with terror it became clear to me that I have taken over *Faust as my heritage*, and moreover as the advocate and avenger of Philemon and Baucis... ... it seems to me unavoidable to give an *answer* to Faust..."[2] We must assume that not only this one thing, his Tower at Bollingen, but also his entire psychology (the spirit and structure of its theory) was supposed to be a "shrine of Philemon."

Shrine of Philemon—what does this mean? It involves two things. First, preparing the ground for a new housing and hosting of the God(s), but this, secondly, not by way of an inflated enthusiasm, but conversely through a "dis-identification with the God" (Jung),[3] in other

[1] C.G. Jung, *Memories, Dreams, Reflections*, ed. A. Jaffé, New York (Vintage Books) 1989, p. 234. In other contexts I have discussed the theme of Jung, Faust and Philemon in my "Buße für Philemon: Vertiefung in das verdorbene Gast-Spiel der Götter," in: *Eranos 51-1982*, Frankfurt (Insel) 1983, pp. 189–242, and in my "Hospitality Toward the Gods in an Ungodly Age. Philemon – Faust – Jung," in: *Spring 1984*, pp. 61–75, now Chapter Ten in my *The Neurosis of Psychology*, vol. I of my Collected English Papers, New Orleans, LA (Spring Journal Books) 2005.

[2] C.G. Jung, *Letters II*, Princeton University Press, pp. 309f.

[3] Cf. his letter to Count Keyserling of 2 January 1928, *Letters I*, p. 49.

words by returning to the earthiness, modesty and humanness that the mythological old couple displayed. For as Jung realized, the "Man For Himself" attitude of Faust as well as Nietzsche amounts to an unwitting identification with the God.

To sum up, Jung saw his life's task to be the advocate and avenger of Philemon, to expiate Faust's crime, and to prevent its repetition. And the fact that he erected his Tower at Bollingen and placed this inscription over its gate must be seen as a kind of concrete symbol of what he meant to achieve with his work and life.

Now we are ready to turn to our actual topic.

II. Jung's emphatic rejection of Hegel and his adoption of the Kantian position.

In 1935 Jung wrote:

> Kant in particular erected a barrier across the mental world which condemned to futility even the boldest leap of speculation into the object. Romanticism was the logical counter-move, expressed most forcefully, and most cunningly disguised, in Hegel, that great psychologist in philosopher's garb. (*CW* 18 § 1734, transl. modif.)

"Hegel, that great psychologist"—in the mouth of the psychologist Jung this sounds like a handsome compliment. But it is a downright insult.

Why? Because the full phrase is, "that great psychologist in philosopher's garb." Jung denies that Hegel was a philosopher proper. In a letter from the same year 1935 (31 July, to Friedrich Seifert, who had contributed an article on Hegel and Jung to Jung's Festschrift), Jung wrote,

> It was always my view that Hegel was a psychologist *manqué*, in much the same way as I am a philosopher *manqué*. As to what is "authentic," that seems to be decided by the spirit of the age. ... Hegel seems to me a romantic thinker in contrast to Kant and hence a typical child of his time; and as a romantic he is already on the way to psychology. The thinking form is not authentic any more but is a vehicle. (*Letters I*, p. 194, to Friedrich Seifert, 31 July 1935.)

("A psychologist *manqué*" is the translation of *ein uneigentlicher Psychologe*, which means: a psychologist, to be sure, but not a psychologist in the literal sense of the word, not formally or properly so, and in the phrase "as to what is 'authentic,'" "authentic" is the translation for *eigentlich*, the opposite of *uneigentlicher* [*Psychologe*].)

The two quotations elucidate one another most beautifully.

A third and a fourth quotation from later years are even more outspoken and complete our understanding of Jung's view of Hegel.

> I think it is obvious that all philosophical statements which transgress the bounds of reason are anthropomorphic and have no validity beyond that which falls to psychically conditioned statements. A philosophy like Hegel's is a self-revelation of the psychic background and, philosophically, a presumption. Psychologically, it amounts to an invasion by the unconscious. The peculiar high-flown language Hegel uses bears out this view: it is reminiscent of the megalomanic language of schizophrenics, who use terrific spellbinding words to reduce the transcendent to subjective form, to give banalities the charm of novelty, or pass off commonplaces as searching wisdom. So bombastic a terminology is a symptom of weakness, ineptitude, and lack of substance. But that does not prevent the latest German philosophy [this is in all likelihood aimed at Heidegger, cf. the passage quoted next, where Hegel's and Heidegger's language are lumped together] from using the same crackpot power-words and pretending it is not unintentional psychology. (*CW* 8 § 360).

It is worth noting that this emotion-laden quotation comes from the probably most important and definitive work of a strictly theoretical nature which Jung has ever written, not from more casual comments in letters originally not intended for public access. As belonging to a published essay, the statement must be considered as well-conceived.

The last passage I want to quote here reads,

> Aristotle's point of view had never particularly appealed to me; nor Hegel, who in my very incompetent opinion is not even a proper philosopher but a misfired psychologist. His impossible language, which he shares with his blood-brother Heidegger, denotes that his philosophy is a highly rationalized and lavishly

> decorated confession of his unconscious. (Letter to Joseph F. Rychlak of 27 April 1959, *Letters II*, p. 501.)

Far from being ambivalent, wavering between praise and contempt, Jung's Hegel-image in all his sparse utterances on this topic over the years is absolutely consistent. It is always one identical view that is expressed in slightly different formulations. And this view is absolutely devastating for Hegel, but, inasmuch as it is uninformed and "incompetent" (as Jung himself said in the last quotation, even if probably without meaning it literally[4]), it falls back on Jung himself and is devastating for him, too.

In Jung's eyes, Hegel is "the great psychologist" because his so-called philosophy is the mere "rationalization" of "psychically conditioned statements," a "confession of his unconscious." He suffered an "invasion by the unconscious." This is why his personal psychology can be seen more or less directly from both his language and what he says. "*Great* psychologist" means nothing more than that we get the opportunity to see an immediate "self-revelation of the psychic background," inasmuch as "in Hegel identification and inflation" (*CW* 8 § 359) rule. His questionable 'greatness' as psychologist thus consisted in no more than that his work expresses the contents from the unconscious "most forcefully" and in that he "gave ideas a chance to prove their unknown power of autonomy" (ibid.). But he was not a great psychologist in the true and positive sense, in the sense of how Jung wanted to be a psychologist. He was only an "*uneigentlicher Psychologe*," a "psychologist *manqué*," "a misfired psychologist." And why? Because his was an "unintentional psychology," a kind of accident, his actual intention, of course, being to appear as a philosopher. But, so goes Jung's claim, he was not a philosopher at all. The philosophical character of his work is a pretense ("pretended"), a "presumption," a "disguise," a "lavish decoration," a "garb." The "thinking form" (*denkerische Form*, the philosophical form, the form of thought) is *uneigentlich*, a sham, a mere "vehicle."

This is why Hegel is a romantic for Jung: "as a romantic he is already on the way to psychology," that is to say, to a soul condition

[4] But in the letter to Rychlak (ibid.) he states explicitly, "I have never studied Hegel properly, that means his original works."

in which the soul's autonomous ideas (which as eternal truths are banal, even though highly numinous, commonplaces) force their way into consciousness without having to pass through a critical, rational filter and thus cause consciousness, on account of their numinosity, to use a "peculiar high-flown language" and "spellbinding," "crackpot power-words" for actually very ordinary truisms. Hegel is completely subject to the "spirit of the age," "a typical child of his time," which implies that his thought is not guided, not necessitated by the inherent logic of the problems he tackles, but by what the spirit of his age (and thus the unconscious constellated during this age) demands.

Above all Hegel is a romantic in Jung's eyes because he practices "speculation," which for Jung apparently meant performing that "boldest leap of speculation into the object" across the Kantian barrier erected by Kant through the mental world, a leap that on account of this barrier is once and for all condemned to futility and therefore unworthy of a proper philosopher. Jung decided that philosophy proper is defined as the respect for this barrier as an unsurmountable one.

With this verdict, Jung commits a *petitio principii*. By speaking (with Hegel in mind) of the "boldest leap of speculation," he shows that he has already decided beforehand (prior to his examining Hegel's arguments against the validity and reasonability of Kant's barrier) that Kant's barrier is an indisputable truth. Only for him for whom that unsurpassable barrier is an undeniable fact to begin with does the attempt to actually get to, and be with, the object (in the form of true knowing) require the boldness of a daredevil who would nevertheless try the impossible, the gigantic leap over that barrier. It is not surprising that under these circumstances this leap is in Jung's view a priori condemned to futility and that thus the word "speculation" takes on the *derogatory* meaning that it obviously has for Jung here. Jung had the dogmatic idea that Kant's barrier in fact defines the limits of reason as such. But this would have to be demonstrated. What Hegel did was uncritically interpreted by Jung as "transgressing the bounds of reason" and "having no validity beyond that which falls to psychically conditioned statements." This is Hegel's fault as an alleged romantic. Much like a puer aeternus, we could say, Hegel did not want to be bound by reason and, in a "counter-move" to the "senex" Kant's admonitions, directly and illegitimately transgressed into the object, into infinity.

Jung simply dismissed Hegel's thorough philosophical critique of Kant as not worthy of an intellectual response. Instead, he argued against Hegel by means of psychological labels, but such an application of psychological diagnoses for defaming the *opponent* qua person ("symptom of weakness," "lack of substance") instead of refuting what he *says* is bad style. An opponent has a right to be met on the level of his arguments.

The same begging of the question appears in the third quotation. Who would want to disagree with Jung's statement that "it is obvious that all philosophical statements which transgress the bounds of reason are anthropomorphic"? But the question, which Jung did not discuss, is whether Hegel's statements in fact transgress the bounds of reason or not. He takes it simply for granted. This is an obvious prejudgment, which shows Jung to be himself guilty of the very fault that he imputes to Hegel, namely that his statement about Hegel is "anthropomorphic" and no more than the self-revelation of *his* psychic background.

It could of course be possible that Hegel is not to be taken seriously as a philosopher because he is no more than a clinical case. Then Jung's dismissal would present no problem. But such a daring and, considering Hegel's reputation and his place in the history of thought, rather unlikely diagnosis would require a detailed refutation of Hegel's thought. As long as this refutation has not been provided, it is a presumption on the part of Jung to defame a philosopher of Hegel's stature as "not even a proper philosopher." It is more likely that such verdicts as "transgressing the bounds of reason," "spellbinding power-words" and "symptom of weakness, ineptitude, and lack of substance" are a reflection of Jung's own philosophical ineptitude and lack of understanding. If *you* cannot make sense of something, you tend to think that *it* is beyond all reason. If *you* are not up to the language of a philosopher (which in the case of Hegel, I venture to say, is truly simple: unpretentious, economical and sober[5]), it is easy to think that *it* is high-flown and inflated. *Jung's* (subjective) refusal to seriously, and that means *thinkingly*, let himself in for the subject-matter of Hegel's thought appears in objectified form *in front of* Jung's consciousness as *Hegel's* philosophical unauthenticity.

---

[5] It is only his *subject matter* and *thoughts* that are of an uncommonly high degree of complexity and sophistication. This is why his texts are hard to understand.

III. JUNG'S "FAUSTIAN CRIME."

We have seen how Jung felt about the Faust-Philemon theme and where he positioned himself with respect to Kant and Hegel. Are these two very different complexes in any way connected? Indeed. By erecting a fundamental, untranscendable barrier across the mental world, Kant—according to Jung's interpretation—did exactly the same thing that Faust did, when he committed the murder of the two old people who represented man's hospitality toward the Gods. The only difference is that Faust's crime is portrayed as a symbolic act, occurring in a poetic, imaginal sphere, while Kant operates explicitly on an intellectual, conceptual level on which under the conditions of modernity the real psychological decisions occur. What Kant did was to state that the object, the transcendent, the thing-in-itself is absolutely inaccessible so that you have to once and for all confine yourself to the empirical world, to the finite, to what Kant termed the appearance. Whether you in that world in which man has essentially turned 'physicist' or 'technician' follow Kant, *or* whether under the conditions of a mythological and ritualistic mode of being-in-the-word you "kill" in Philemon and Baucis the very symbol, or archetype, of the "condition of the a priori possibility of" man's hospitality toward the Gods amounts *psychologically* to the same thing. Both cases (erecting that barrier / barring out the homeless Gods) are variations of saying "Man For Himself." The "thing-in-itself" (and what all goes along with it) is simply one modern guise in which what formerly was seen as the transcendent is either hospitably received or turned away.

It is by no means necessary to go into the arguments with which Kant established that we have to restrict ourselves to the world the way it appears to us (the way it is fundamentally pre-shaped by our mind), and have to give up any hope of ever being able to achieve true knowing, part of which would of course also be the *gnôsis tou theou* (the knowing of God) and true knowledge of the soul. We do not have to know whether his reasoning is sound, his results valid and his whole position irrefutable or not. All that we have to be concerned with here is that *if* Jung felt that what Faust did was a terrible crime, one that he, Jung, had personally to atone for, *then* he could not possibly condone what he understood Kant to do, but instead would have had to "atone" for *it*, too.

But he did condone it. He adopted, as his own unshakeable theoretical foundation for psychology, the restriction to the Kantian phenomenal and Kant's closing the door on the noumenon, i.e., the 18th century version of that door that Philemon and Baucis, in their obedience to the cult-practice of hospitality, kept open. This is why he time and again proudly insisted on his being "an empiricist first and foremost."

Jung did more than adopt Kant's halving of the world. He also vehemently rejected Hegel and, by denying the philosophical status of his work and by practically going as far as to use clinical diagnoses on him ("inflation," "reminiscent of the language of schizophrenics"), he did him in as a philosopher. Now we have to remember that Hegel is the philosopher who taught, bluntly speaking, the *parousia of the absolute*, in other words, exactly what Philemon and Baucis stand for. So if Jung without sufficient *rational* refutation vehemently rejected Hegel, which he did, this was the symbolic way in which Jung committed *his* murder of "Philemon." Intellectually and psychologically, Jung burdened himself with grave guilt when he dressed Hegel down frivolously.

As in the case of Kant we do not have to prove or disprove here the rational substance of Hegel's claim that it is precisely a requirement of *reason* to hold that the absolute is with us to begin with and that we are with it. Our interest is only in how Jung worked out, within and for himself, the conflict between the two philosophers. In the context of this question it suffices to know that Jung has provided no valid argumentation to prove his case against Hegel, had no thorough first-hand knowledge of what he was passing judgement on, and that he confines himself to not only sweeping, but also highly emotional statements concerning Hegel. Although I hate to argue *ad personam* by explaining the statements someone makes from his personal psychology, I think the affect to be sensed in Jung's verdict against Hegel and his lack of substantial argumentation force one to conclude that this verdict is a complex-reaction on the part of Jung. His allergic reaction to Hegel and his obsession about his empiricism are two sides of the same coin. And both indicate an unacknowledged inner discomfort with his own position.

But what we should do is to see what the truly *psychological* response to the emergence of the fantasy of a "barrier across the mental world which condemned to futility even the boldest leap of speculation into the object" would have been.[6] Here I will merely give a hint by referring the reader to my paper on "The Leap Into the Solid Stone" in vol. 4 of my Collected English Papers[7] and suggest that one's running up against an impenetrable wall or barrier is *psychologically* always the invitation to leap *into* it, into the barrier itself (*not* across it to the *imaginary* object on the other side of it)! For Jung, by contrast, the barrier that he saw erected by Kant became a "wall at which human inquisitiveness *turns back*" (*CW* 18 § 1734, transl. modif.).

Psychology is the discipline of interiority. All phenomena represent for the psychologist at first such a wall, because our seeing always begins from outside. Our task as psychologists is to interiorize ourselves into the phenomenon at hand, whatever it may be. Turning around, turning one's back to the wall in order to direct one's attention to things in front of the barrier: this is the sin against the spirit of psychology. (Interestingly enough, as far as Hegel is concerned anyone studying him will notice that he did precisely not at all perform that boldest leap of speculation into the object beyond the barrier. He moved patiently, one step at a time, and not forward, but *deeper* into the notion at hand.)

Jung, by the way, does not realize that precisely by prohibiting the *empirical* leap of speculation across the barrier into the object *logically* commits this very leap, because how else would he know that on the other side of this barrier there is an object at all? Jung's fantasy of a leap across the barrier is that very leap beyond the wall. Psychology's leap is a leap *contra naturam* into the impenetrability of the object or phenomenon, which is itself what at first appears as a wall. Whether turning back or leaping beyond, in either case the psychological task is missed.[8]

IV. Mock atonement.

What we have seen so far results in the contradictory insight that Jung felt the need to personally expiate for a crime that had not been

---

[6] This and the next paragraph are additions made in 2010.

[7] Chapter 7 in Wolfgang Giegerich, *The Soul Always Thinks*, New Orleans, LA (Spring Journal Books) 2010.

[8] Let me also simply quote here, out of its own context and without further comment, a relevant passage from another paper of mine ("'The Unassimilable Remnant': What

his and to prevent its repetition, while all the while himself committing the very equivalent of this crime, only on a different level. One is reminded of the familiar phenomenon that people of any time tend to persecute the contemporary prophets in the name of the meanwhile venerated prophets of former times, who at their own time had similarly been persecuted by their contemporaries. Or one is reminded of the members of the nobility in France immediately prior to the French Revolution who formed committees to do some good for the slaves in America while never wasting a thought on the slaving peasants at home. Jung meant to build a shrine of Philemon and to atone for Faust's murder. This was, as it were, the meaning and purpose of his life. But now it turns out that precisely by building his Tower as a literal *Philemonis sacrum* he missed out on building a real shrine of Philemon and on really atoning for the murder of the ancient couple, because that mythological and imaginal Philemon was more or less irrelevant in Jung's time. Philemon had become one of our psychological antiques. *Jung*'s "Philemon," his *real* "Philemon," would not have been the literal Philemon, a mythological and literary figure; and the real crime to be atoned for was not Faust's. Jung acted out and solved other people's, other ages', problems while remaining unconscious about where the Faust-Philemon problem was really constellated for *him*. What would have been demanded of Jung, *if* he wanted to build a "shrine of Philemon," would have been to *philosophically* come to terms with the absolute, the transcendent, *for example* by learning to comprehend

is at Stake? A Dispute with Stanton Marlan") from the same volume (Chapter 17, p. 467): "If, as Heraclitus claimed, you can never come to a boundary of soul, no matter which road you take and how far you travel, how then did Jung get to his barrier and Marlan, with all the philosophers he cites behind him, to the unsurmountable 'not'? Did they disprove Heraclitus and show that there *is* a limit, after all—or is what they found perhaps something very different from a boundary of soul and its deep logos? Or is it their own putting a stop to the movement suggested by Heraclitus, that is, to the unreserved movement into this movement's own self-negation, into its further and further going under into itself? The barrier and the remainder are ultimately the *reified* 'not.' And whereas this reified 'not' allowed Jung to turn his back on it, when it has the form of the unassimilable remainder it allows one to always keep it at the same safe distance in front of oneself while one is moving, instead of oneself moving deeper and deeper into, and exposing oneself to the work of, the *living* negation (where 'oneself' does of course not refer to the person, but to the logic of consciousness). Could it be that both Jung's empiricist observer and his 'the unconscious' are located outside the sphere of soul, in the land of positivity? The soul all right, but displaced from its native state and translated into the foreign language of positivity and naturalism?"

Hegel's thought and to see through his Kantian bias as devastating for psychology, because this is the level and sphere where the Faust-Philemon conflict really came to a head for Jung.

What I mean becomes perhaps clearer when we analyse what Jung's Bollingen Tower, as a concrete symbolization of his intended life's work, psychologically was. I am not interested in the Tower itself, as a literal fact. I want to look at it merely as a *visual aid* which helps to bring out the logic of his psychology project. The Tower can be considered as a condensation and concrete materialization of what Jung' wanted to achieve with his psychology of the collective unconscious. It symbolizes the substance of what was most dear to the psychologist C.G. Jung also in his psychological theory. What is the status of Jung's Tower, what was it psychologically? It was *his private Disneyland*, his kind of "Neuschwanstein" (that imitation fairy-tale castle built by Ludwig II. of Bavaria during the second half of the nineteenth century, a castle which is as much a tourist attraction for the general public as Jung's Tower is for Jung enthusiasts). The real Disneylands cover a wide range of spectacular things that are primarily meant as what they literally are (medieval castle, jungle, Wild West saloon, etc.). Jung's Bollingen Tower, by contrast, was not so much important as the pseudo-medieval house that it literally was; its primary significance was that it was Jung's *psycho*-Disneyland, a Disneyland making accessible the "psyche's hinterland." And real Disneylands, as commercial undertakings, are by necessity open to the masses. Jung, by contrast, was able to afford the luxury of having his "Neuschwanstein" or "Disneyland" all for himself as his *buen retiro*. But whether private Tower or public Disneyland, in both cases there is a kind of park with (often miniaturized) remakes of buildings or landscapes that are to provide the inhabitant or visitor temporarily with the opportunity to romantically experience how life must have been in former times or in exotic places, at any rate in times and places that are *not* those of his own present-day reality. In his *Memories, Dreams, Reflections* Jung tells us about his Tower at Bollingen,

> There is very little about it to suggest the present. If a man of the sixteenth century were to move into the house, only the kerosene lamp and the matches would be new to him. There is nothing to disturb the dead, neither electric light nor telephone. (p. 237, Vintage Books ed., New York 1989)

His Tower allowed Jung, one might say, to play sixteenth century. It even allowed him, a man of the technological twentieth century, to play "sympathetic, or mythological, mode of being-in-the-world" or "anima country" as the following passage shows.

> At times I feel as if I am spread out over the landscape and inside things, and am myself living in every tree, in the plashing of the waves, in the clouds and the animals that come and go, in the procession of the seasons. ... here is space for the spaceless kingdom of the world's and the psyche's hinterland. (*ibid.*, p. 225f.)

It is a fine thing that Jung was able to have such a place and such experiences. But this is not the point. Is Jung's having such a Tower (and, during those periods when he was there on *vacation* from his *real* life in Küsnacht, having such experiences there) what legitimately could be considered atoning for Faust's crime? Is Jung's "Tower" (of course, not it literally, but what it stands for, the attitude it represents, the psychological project it symbolizes and epitomizes) a convincing contribution to the psychology of our age? Does it really address, and actually meet, the soul problem raised by the *Faust* drama, to which, after all, Jung himself felt compelled to *answer*? Does it make a difference, a difference in the spirit of Philemon, i.e., with respect to the godlessness of our time—*or* is it not much rather no more than a curiosity of strictly personal significance, indeed, a mere ego-trip (no different from other people's more conventional ego-trips, such as in mass tourism or private hobbies)? For we must not be misled: the wish to experience the anima sphere or the *Self*,[9] or, to put it in a slightly different way, the (by all means authentic) experience *of* the Self, can certainly *be* an *ego*-trip (have the status of an ego-trip)! It can be soul-tourism, in no way fundamentally different from other kinds of tourism except for having a more noble, more inward content. In general, the great longing for meaning on the part of modern man, for religious or even mystical experience, for soulfulness and a feeling of man's oneness with nature, even the striving to overcome the ego, are, of course, typically modern *ego* concerns. Their connection with the Self consists in no more than equivocation via the term *self*-indulgence.

---

[9] Cf. "Here I am, as it were, the 'age-old son of the mother.' That is how alchemy puts it, very wisely, for the 'old man,' the 'ancient,' whom I had already experienced as a child, is personality No. 2, who has always been and always will be." *Memories*, p. 225.

To avoid a misunderstanding, I am not expecting that Jung, one single man, could or should have factually changed the way of modern life. I am concerned only with the question whether the logical *status* of what he considered to be his advocacy, and avenging, of Philemon in itself indeed qualifies as such. The factual effect on society at large and the extent of this effect are a wholly different matter.

Also, I am not suggesting that there is anything wrong with trying to have such experiences and, e.g., to build a Tower such as Jung did, just as there is nothing wrong with enjoying a campfire or a candlelight dinner (during which we try to be temporarily relieved from the brightness, sterility and predictability of our modern electrified world). But just as campfires and candlelight dinners are absolutely non-committal and inconsequential and thus, in the terrible sense of the word, completely harmless, mere pastimes that do not truly *respond* to the pressures of modern life but on the contrary support them by providing safety-valves, being themselves part of the very system that they are to provide relief from, so Jung's periodical and voluntary regression to the sixteenth century is an absolutely harmless undertaking, self-contained and without any pang. It does not touch the psychological situation of our modern existence.

This cannot be what "expiation for Faust's crime" means. It is too easy, too literal, too positive to establish such a self-contained and self-serving asylum and carve some inscriptions into stone, too easy to look for ways to feel close to the ancestors and to experience how people of by-gone ages might have felt. Jung took Faust and Philemon literally and "solved" *their* conflict on *that* literal level. He did not ask *what* the shape is that that conflict takes today, where *our* psychological battlefield is on which our fate is decided. What's Hecuba to us, or we to Hecuba, that is to say: what are Philemon and Baucis, that ancient couple, to us? Of what concern is it to us what their myth *literally stands for*, namely feeling as if "spread out over the landscape and into things," i.e., an *animated* nature and the experience of all the Gods that go along with this mode of being-in-the world, more generally all the fantasy images of an innocent mythological imagination? All that has been psychologically obsolete since the end of antiquity, at the latest. Where it still occurs, it has the status of "entertainment." "Nature" (*animated* nature), myth and images were the form in which truth showed itself under earlier psychological conditions. We have to address our own problem, or the new *form* in which the same problem poses itself to us, not solve a problem that has long been settled one way or another by history because it was the problem of the past, or the problem in that form in which it was raised for former ages. *Hic Rhodus, hic salta.*

Our "Faust" is the positivistic *logic* underlying the modern sciences and technology. It is the logic that was cemented by Kant's philosophy. This "Faust," this logic remains absolutely undisturbed and unanswered by Jung's "shrine of Philemon," and "he" would remain unanswered even if all the people in the world would each build their own Bollingen Towers. A literal shrine, a literal return to the ancestors, to the Gods and the sympathetic mode of being-in-the-world leaves the so-called hubris of our real "Faust" intact.

If that barrier that Kant erected across the mental world is not refuted, in other words, *if* Jung thinks it to be logically and epistemologically legitimate, then he has no right to find fault with what happened in *Faust*. The murder of Philemon and Baucis, as humanly deplorable as it certainly is (and, for that matter, was for Faust himself), is then not only inevitable but also unimpeachable. It is justified.

One can't have it both ways. On the level of our psychic antiques, the literal mythic images of old, one bemoans the disruption of the bond between the humans and the Gods as a terrible crime that one wants to undo, while at the same time one bases one's psychology on a logic that absolutely precludes a connection between the humans and the Gods, the phenomenal and the noumenal worlds. I say: Not empiricism first and foremost. No, first and foremost one has to tackle the problem that was raised by the erection of the Kantian barrier, a barrier that inevitably also cuts through psychology itself (Kant's dissociation of the "determinable self," which is accessible to empirical study, from the "determining self," the subject as the transcendental unity of apperception, which remains absolutely inaccessible to our knowing).

Ordinarily we call this a neurotic dissociation. The right hand (the "Kantian" empiricist in Jung residing in Küsnacht) must not *know* (in the full sense of the word) what the left hand (the experiencing, feeling, envisioning Self in the same Jung in Bollingen, who indulges in the kind of imaginings that would be forbidden to a true Kantian as speculative) is experiencing. The scientific theorizing of the psychologist and thus the logical constitution of psychology follow one set of laws that are completely immunized against the other set of laws governing the life of the soul that the same psychologist studies. In Jung's *commuting between* "Küsnacht" and "Bollingen" the officially rejected "boldest leap of speculation" beyond the Kantian barrier returns. It *is* this direct leap "into the object" yonder ("At Bollingen I am in my truest essence, I am most deeply myself. Here I am, as it were, the 'age-old son of the mother' ..." *MDR* p. 225, transl. modif.), the way this "leap" appears in the empirical-practical sphere of human behavior, namely as ordinary commuting between two places, places, however, that logically, psychologically, belong to two fundamentally different orders of reality. The fact that Jung in his theory of knowledge as well as in his practical execution of his science prohibited[10] himself from performing that leap does not mean that he escaped its horizon!

Building a literal shrine of Philemon and commuting between "Küsnacht" and "Bollingen" is no more than mock atonement. Psychologically it does not cost anything, because it avoids the real issue. It merely tries to replay a historical battle, wanting to give it a different outcome after the fact, but ignores, and *diverts* form, the actual battleground, the frontline where the opposites clash today. The battleground is in our days the *logical status* of consciousness, the logic of modern life and modern society.

This is also why the return to pagan polytheism in archetypal psychology is no real response to our psychological situation. It also is nothing else but the attempt to build a *literal* shrine of Philemon, though not with actual stones, but with sublimated ones: images. Structurally there is no difference. The place "where the real action is" is by-passed just the same (*vide* Hillman's express rejection of involving psychology in philosophical issues). But as long as these issues are bracketed, the old logical form of consciousness, as it is expressed, e.g., in the philosophy of Kant, is left intact, and the return to the ancient Gods or the imaginal at large is then no more than the equivalent in psychology to what, in the outer world, restoring old

[10] We might also ask: what does it mean for psychology to have to live with an emphatic *prohibition*, a *barrier*?

buildings classified as historical monuments is. Very nice. But also very harmless; with no bearing on where the soul is today, in our technological and information civilization that is more and more spreading over the whole global village. Just a beautiful, and certainly very cultured, compensation and consolation within an affluent society that can afford such luxuries. And changing the *special faculty* that consciousness uses, from intellect and will to the imagination, amounts only to a rearranging of the furniture in the house of consciousness, not to a transformation of the structure of the house itself.

Above I came to the conclusion that Jung's irrational dismissal of Hegel was indicative of a complex-reaction on his part. I wonder whether his allergic reaction has to do with his having vaguely sensed that it is on Hegel's territory that he would have found the place for building a real, up-to-date "shrine of Philemon" and for *really* expiating for "Faust's" crime. Perhaps subconsciously Jung could not forgive Hegel that his thought tended to remind him that he had cut corners, and to reveal to him his mode of expiating as a harmless substitute for the actually intended and required atonement, from which he, Jung, shirked away because he did not want to enter that territory, which entering would have required subjecting himself to the slow and patient *labor* of the concept. The theme of "labor" takes me to the next section.

V. THE NEUROSIS OF PSYCHOLOGY.

One might think that whether Jung actually succeeded in his project of atoning for Faust's crime or not is only a question of biographical significance. But more is at stake: the whole "definition" and constitution of psychology.

In his *Memories* (pp. 30ff.) Jung relates how he fell into a brief episode of a childhood neurosis and how he overcame it. In his twelfth year, another boy had knocked him off his feet so that he fell with his head against the curbstone, almost losing consciousness. At the moment when he felt the blow the thought flashed through his mind: "Now you won't have to go to school any more." From then on he began to have fainting spells whenever he had to return to school or was told to do homework. For more than six months he stayed away from school, which was for him like paradise. "I was free, could dream for hours, be anywhere I liked, in the woods or by the water, or draw. ... Above all, I was able to plunge into the world of the mysterious. To that realm belonged trees, a pool, the swamp, stones and animals, and my father's library." His parents were very worried, took him to various doctors, but no one could help. One doctor thought he had epilepsy. One day he overheard his father express his fear that his son might be incurable and thus not able to earn his own living. Jung states that when he heard this, he was thunderstruck. "This was the collision with reality. 'Oh, I see, here you have to work!'"[11] he thought. He realized that "the whole affair was a diabolical plot on my part." From then on he forcefully overcame his fainting fits and went on to study hard. "Those days saw the beginnings of my conscientiousness ..."

It is marvelous to see how Jung overcame his personal neurosis all by himself and how thoroughly he really did overcome it. From what Jung did in his life, and said in his work, one gets the impression of a remarkably unneurotic *personality.*

But in his *psychology* (on the level of its theoretical setup) the same situation as in his childhood neurosis seems to recur. Concerning his childhood neurosis Jung gave the following self-interpretation.

> What had led me astray during the crisis was my passion for being alone, my delight in solitude. Nature seemed to me full of wonders, and I wanted to steep myself in them. Every stone, every plant, every single thing seemed alive and indescribably marvelous. I immersed myself in nature, crawled, as it were, into the very essence of nature and away from the whole human world. (*Memories*, p. 32.)

The purpose of his childhood neurosis had been to hold on to the strongly felt oneness with nature, the "sympathetic mode of being-in-the-world," and to defend this childhood mode of existence against the needs of entering the adult conditions of life. His fainting fits enabled him to successfully escape those needs and instead "*to plunge into the world of the mysterious.*" The end of his neurosis was accordingly brought about by his sudden realization, "*Oh, I see, here you have to*

[11] My translation of "*Aha, da muß man arbeiten!*" instead of "Why, then, I must get to work!" in *Memories*. Jung had a general insight into the conditions of life: here, that is in life, on earth, one has to work in order to get through life.

work!," which Jung considered to be his collision with reality. He understood that he had to, as it were, cut into his own flesh and turn away from his beloved "world of the mysterious"—not (as we can say in retrospect) to give it up forever, but in order, through a long period of serious studies, to put himself into a position where he would be able to re-establish access to that same world of the mysterious, but on a fundamentally new level and in the "objective" and communicable form of a formal *discipline* (psychology). Whereas his plunging into the marvels of nature in his childhood was a strictly personal, subjective pleasure, his work as a psychologist could not only be communicated to others (like most personal experiences, too), but was also from the outset in the *status* of something that as a discipline and an oeuvre belonged to the collective, to mankind, or better: to the world of the mind. His insight about "having to work" at least implicitly, or in hindsight, entailed the more general insight that you have to leave "paradise," as it were, and enter this world, if you want to really *find* "paradise." The way proceeds via a negation. The shortest road to the goal is via a detour, as Jung himself once declared to a youthful interlocutor.

On the theoretical plane, in his psychology, this inevitable negation did not happen. *As a person*, Jung had indeed given up his self-indulgence and learned to work extremely hard and conscientiously; it is incredible what all he was able to achieve, to wit his extensive studies on the myths of all nations, on typology, on parapsychology, his laborious pioneering study of alchemy, to mention just a few of the areas thoroughly covered by Jung during years of self-renunciation. But *Jung's analytical psychology itself* was allowed to stay in the state of logical innocence corresponding to that in which the eleven year old Jung had been prior to his revolutionizing insight. What for the *person* was strenuous work, for *psychology* was sheer pleasure. *It* was allowed *to plunge into the world of the mysterious*, to be led astray by its passion for the world of dreams, images, myths, rituals, synchronistic phenomena, and so on. It was allowed, as it were, to "feel free, to dream for hours," that is to say to "steep itself in" the marvels of the inner world and to "crawl into the very essence" of the life of the soul. Here, on the level of the structure of psychology itself, the "collision with reality" that the pupil Jung had experienced did not occur, although the encounter with Hegel could easily have brought it about. Hegel could have been "overheard" by Jung as he had overheard his father. But his encounter with Hegel did not lead to a similar spontaneous insight, one that could be formulated here as: "*Oh, I see, psychology has to get to work!*" that is to say, it cannot simply go on to *directly* and self-indulgently plunge into fascinating psychological phenomenology; it has to first turn against its own innermost passion; it has to, as it were, go back to its "study" (as the pupil Jung had gone into his father's study to cram for school) and, constantly overcoming its "fainting fits," do its *homework* first; it has to lose its logical innocence and submit to a long *labor* of the concept—to achieve, via this detour, a fundamentally new logical level of consciousness, one which could at long last qualify as a truly psychological consciousness.

Why would having had such an insight amount to a collision with reality? Because it would have shocked psychology out of its self-containment, self-indulgence. Without this insight, psychology is in its own bubble, unreal. This insight, on the other hand, makes psychology see itself from outside. Psychology becomes conscious of its own thinking form, and this in turn entails the promise that its eyes to the world, to reality, are opened.

Jungian psychology, let alone all the other brands of psychology, only takes responsibility for the *contents* it studies, not for its own mind set, its own logical *form* of consciousness, or, to use Jung's words, the "thinking form" that prevails in it *when* it delves into the phenomenology of the soul. Once Jung said so explicitly: "... the empiricist must also foreswear an intellectual clarification of his concepts [*Klärung seiner Begriffe in denkerischer Hinsicht*] such as is absolutely imperative for the philosopher. His thinking has to mold itself to the facts ..." (*CW* 18 § 1731). This is, by the way, a terribly naive statement implying that a) the philosopher would not have to mold his thinking to "the facts" and b) that there were such things as bare facts not already permeated by thought! It was not Hegel for whom the "thinking form" had become "unauthentic"; *it is the mind of the field of psychology that has this problem*. In fact, Jung, when he said about Hegel that "as a romantic he is already on the way to psychology. The thinking form is not authentic any more but is a vehicle," indicated that for him psychology is defined by the absence of an authentic thinking form; psychology is, as it were, a philosophy minus "thinking form," the psychologist a "philosopher *manqué*," just as philosophy seems to be defined for Jung by the absence of thought's molding itself to the facts. To be sure, Jung repeatedly indicated that psychology was that strange science whose object was the *subject* of all sciences. "There is a psychology that always has another person or thing for an object ... But besides this there is a psychology which is a knowing of the knower and an experiencing of the experiencer."[12] But this remained only another *idea* or *content* in psychological consciousness. It did not really make any difference to the structure of consciousness itself. It was a helpless attempt to express the right insight without psychology having to be *affected* by this insight. Psychology now only studied a "subjective factor" or the "knower" (e.g., the Self) as its *new* object, in other words, as far as its logical form was concerned the "subject" was objectified and turned into a content.

This is not what was meant and would be needed for psychology to be psychological. The point is not *what* your *object* is (whether something external or internal, a literal object "out there" or "the subjective factor" *in* ourselves, another person or the knowing of the knower); the point is whether psychology has overcome the logical form of "object" and thus stops objectifying (studying objects or contents) altogether. The question is whether it takes responsibility for the thinking form in which it operates. Psychology *has to come home.* It wants to come home; it does not want to stay exiled into the form of contents and thus remain alienated from itself. It has to be *er-innert* (remembered, recalled: interiorized) into itself, be internal to itself: this is (or would be) the interiority that defines it. Psychology cannot be the field of the *content* called "interiority." It has to be the field that is characterized by the interiority in the logical form of its thinking, whatever it may be that it is thinking about. Psychology needs the *absolut negative Er-innerung* (absolute-negative interiorization, inwardization) of itself (and all its contents) into itself.

But psychology abounds in objectified contents: *the* psyche, even the *autonomous* psyche, *the* unconscious, *the* Self, psychic *reality*... Or in other schools even literally: object-relations. Or in archetypal

---

[12] *CW* 18 § 1733. I corrected the false translation "an experiencing of the experiment" (for: "*ein Erleben des Erlebenden*") into the above.

psychology: *the* imaginal, the archetypal perspectives, the Gods. Often these contents are even hypostatized (reified, ontologized, made into entities). But even where this is not the case, the logical form of these ideas is that of objects or contents of consciousness. Psychology projects out and acts out, thereby keeping itself, as subject, out and preserving its untouchedness and innocence, much as the eleven year old Jung had preserved his childhood ego. No doubt, psychology defines the soul as interiority. But it nevertheless extraverts by always wanting to be immediately with the psychological facts or phenomena "out there." It *imagines* (*vorstellen*) its own ideas and *ipso facto* turns them, as far as their logical status is concerned, into imagined (inner) "*things*" that consciousness has *in front of* itself and that thus are, psychologically speaking, "out there" (even if it may explicitly deny this). In other words, it operates within, exemplifies, and is driven by, the *difference of consciousness*, i.e., the difference between itself as subject and what it is conscious of as object, always, to be sure, unconsciously *being* the first, but totally forgetting *itself* over all the interesting objects and contents and images that it is concerned *with* and over all the ideas it *has*. *As* psychology it should be the living consciousness of the difference or interplay as a whole, in other words, the *sublation* of this difference.

This is why Kant (the way he understood him) was so important to Jung. By basing psychology on a *Kant*-based empiricism, psychology was once and for all relieved of the concern and responsibility for its thinking form or for the logical status of its own consciousness. Empiricism (in Jung's case it had better be called phenomenology) means that all you have to take note of is what appears to you in front of yourself, before your consciousness. Psychology had a licence to onesidedly delve into psychic phenomenology just like that, without further ado, and this means also a licence to forget, or remain absolutely unconscious about, itself. Empiricism is the licence to *act out* (i.e., act out on the level or in the sphere of *theory*) and to stay unconscious. This in turn meant that you could do psychology with the habitual everyday consciousness or the same consciousness that also prevailed in the sciences. You could begin to do psychology as you came off the street. No doubt, you had to undergo *personal* analysis and examine your own inner life, its complexes, your shadow and the images in your unconscious process. But the *thinking form* was no question. It had been taken care of once and for all, for example by Kant. This means in familiar psychological terminology that it was the habitual ego, Jung's personality No. 1, that was allowed to do psychology (and thus also, among other things, allowed to preach individuation: becoming Self).

Small wonder that Jung reacted allergically to Hegel, particularly finding his language "laborious." For "Hegel" would have implied: having to undergo a laborious process of working through the mind, in order to in the first place raise its form to the status of "science" (in Hegel's sense). The consciousness that could do psychology is not finished. Psychology has not "arrived." It does not exist yet. It is still on the way to itself and has a long way to go. Psychology is not simply a continuation of science (in the ordinary sense), the scientific mind's turning to a new subject matter, the interiority of man. No, psychology (if it existed) would owe its existence to a revolution, a reversal of consciousness, and would *be* as *sublated* science. It cannot simply be the science *of* the internal, but has to be the *inward* "science," the "science" that has become itself internal in its logical form.

Hegel's philosophy provides first of all an "alchemical" transformation of the mind (not the transformation of the person, of personal consciousness!), through many stages of putrefaction, mortification, vaporization, distillation, sublimation. Jung studied alchemy all right. But again only as a literal object and content of consciousness. Where alchemy had become a nonliteral, not objectified reality in action, namely in Hegel, Jung refused to see it.[13] Instead, he in a sense acted it out; he projected a task that would have been that of a radical processing and reconstitution of the *form* of consciousness into the *personality*, burdening *it* with the job of becoming Self. All the while the thinking form would remain untouched. The insistence on the empiricist stance of psychology psychologically served the unconscious purpose of protecting the old ego, that very ego that by the explicit theory of the same psychology had to be overcome. The idea of overcoming the ego was only a content or conviction, and as a practical task it was relegated to the personality. Each person was

---

[13] I have given my interpretation of alchemy as an implicit logic at some length in my book, *The Soul's Logical Life: Towards a Rigorous Notion of Psychology*, Frankfurt/Main, Berlin, Bern, New York, Paris, Wien (Peter Lang) 1998. Earlier I presented this view more briefly in my *Animus-Psychologie*, Frankfurt/M. et. al. (Peter Lang) 1994.

supposed "to work," and to work on his overcoming *his* personal ego (on the level of contents, of psychological complexes or attitudes), so that psychology's (and the public mind's, in other words, the *universal*) ego-*form* of consciousness (as a logical problem and as the *knower* of the knowing) might escape unnoticed.

VI. Psychology's bubble.

It was a psychologically fatal mistake of Jung's to split psychology off from philosophy, i.e., from its *intrinsic* speculative nature, and to base his psychological approach on an empiricism for which he relied on the findings in some *other* field, the philosophy of Kant (the way he understood him), and for which psychology therefore was not, and could not possibly be, itself accountable. Jung's decision for "empiricism first and foremost" was made outside psychology. Prior to his entering the field of psychology he had "Kant's barrier" in his baggage, and he burdened psychology with this a priori handicap. For psychology, the field of interiority, it is absolutely intolerable to be based on a base *external* to itself, be it the Freudian bedrock of biology or Jung's methodological stance of a Kant-based empiricism. It is intolerable to bring in Kant's unsurmountable "barrier across the mental world" from outside (from philosophy, which has been explicitly excluded) into psychology to rule there, as an almighty and unquestionable god, over the psychic phenomena. Actually, one would think that a person with such profoundly religious experiences as Jung had, and a psychologist who dealt with the deepest myths and rituals in the soul, and with the Self as God image, would have been either very critical of Kant's "barrier" or deeply disturbed by it. Instead, Jung was grateful for it and vehemently defended his empiricist bias. Jung, it seems, *needed* this barrier. The question is why.

I think it was because this barrier, the way Jung interpreted and used it, gave psychology licence to "plunge into the world of the mysterious" *without* having to be *intellectually responsible* for these experiences and without having to do its logical homework first, through which alone it would acquire the *entitlement to having such experiences* in the first place. This barrier gave psychology licence to conceive of itself as what Jung had blamed Hegel for: a logically unfettered "romanticism" for whom the thinking form was a mere vehicle. The only restriction that Jung accepted (and even required in order for psychology to be a science and not a *literal* romanticism) was the restriction through what is "outside," *vis-à-vis*: "the empirical facts" of psychic phenomenology. It is obvious that what is most central to Jung's opus is actually, if viewed with respect to its logical form, of a *speculative* nature: wholeness, the Self, Mercurius, the *lapis*, the soul child, *mysterium coniunctionis*, trinity, to mention only a few subjects. The Kantian barrier immunized psychology as a field against its own contents, against their speculative character, so that it could self-indulgently and innocently observe and imagine them (like we watch television), without itself having to undergo that alchemical decomposition-sublimation process that it liked to observe and talk about and that would have put psychology (if it had entered it) into a position where it could, and would have to, itself *think* speculatively, dialectically.

Speculation, one could say, is that kind of thought where the "thinker of the thought" (or the form of consciousness) is itself *in* the same alchemical vessel as the thoughts (or the "contents" of consciousness); speculative comprehension of reality is the opposite of the *abstract* view of things. Psychology, in its theoretical stance, was allowed to remain in the status of sensory intuition (*Anschauung*), perception, imagination and that means safely outside the vessel, as an observer. It did not have to advance to the logical status of thought (thinking). The modes of intuition and imagination inevitably reaffirm and blindly act out the difference of consciousness (subject–object); thought, by contrast, is that mode in which this difference is sublated (*aufgehoben*), remembered, interiorized within itself, so that the soul is truly at home with *itself.*

And, what is the same thing or the other side of the same coin, that barrier helped to encapsulate the experienced *speculative themes* by giving them the status of "empirical facts," "nothing but a God-*image* in the soul," "only psychological phenomena," "imaginal fantasies." You now could have it both ways: psychology could get the benefit of the experience of the mysterious or speculative, it could indulge in myths and talk about the Gods in the spirit of a "polytheistic psychology" and yet hold on to the soundness of the old ego's common sense. The magic word that made this miracle possible was "psychology." You were safely protected from "metaphysics," that is to say from the speculative, religious, and metaphysical character inherent in all the ideas, images, and phenomena that you were involved with, because what you did was "only psychology." It was expressly not metaphysics, not philosophy, it did not imply an ultimate truth. It was only "*psychologically* true." In other words, psychology invented a new species of truth just for itself—as if truth was something that occurred in a variety of species. And having this additional private, self-contained "truth" is what defines psychology as we have known it.

Hillman's archetypal psychology went a step further and tried to circumvent this problem by simply bracketing the whole question of truth, expelling it from psychology altogether. In whichever way psychology proceeded, *what* you experienced did not have to revolutionize the frame of mind of psychology, psychology which after all claimed to be the knowledge of such experiences. On a personal and literal level, this duplicity in the field of psychology is mirrored in the duplicity of Jung's commuting between Küsnacht (= psychology as a discipline) and Bollingen (= the soul). Both are neatly immunized against one another, neither one challenging, seducing, infecting, decomposing, the other. No *coniunctio oppositorum*, no *mysterium coniunctionis*, no "psychology of transference" *in* the logical structure of psychology *itself*, namely between the knower and the known, logos and psyche, theory and phenomenon, but rather a right hand that does not have to know what the left hand is doing.

The idea of a special "psychological truth" is the compromise formation that (a) provided the mediation, or rather allowed for the commuting, between the two while at the same time (b) keeping them absolutely separate. It was this concept of psychology's own species of truth that made the impossible possible for Jung: to maintain that he was an empirical scientist and yet to do his psychological work without having to close his eyes to the full phenomenology of the soul, including its mysteries and speculative thoughts. The splitting of truth into two was the trick that allowed Jung to hold on to Kant's "barrier" and yet to indulge, as it were, in his kind of "Dreams of a Spirit-Seer." "(Only) *psychological* truth": this guaranteed that the conflict with the public truth, the truth of science, philosophy and religion, was avoided. Psychology did not challenge the common sense. "Psychological *truth*," on the other hand, allowed for the attribution of the highest emotional value to the images of the soul.

Another way for saying "psychologically true" is "esse in anima." Jung believed that with this idea "the whole ontological argument" and the "division between *esse in intellectu* and *esse in re*" could be made "superfluous" (*CW* 6 § 66). He hoped that through this idea psychology would be "a mediatory science," "capable of uniting the idea and the thing without doing violence to either" (*CW* 6 § 72). No doubt, it does no violence to either, but not because it mediated between them (which a positive and static third never does), but because it evades the whole issue, unadmittedly *being* the *commuting* between the two extremes, *esse in intellectu* and *esse in re* (like Jung's commuting between Küsnacht and Bollingen). As such, it IS their dissociation: not a *mixtum compositum* of both or their integration in each other, but either the one or the other, and therefore neither truly the one nor the other. It is the convenient shift between the two. When psychology is accused of metaphysical mystification on account of its speaking, e.g., about mythic images and Gods, it quickly produces the "*in anima*" from within its *esse in anima,* insisting that it is only talking about images, ideas, or metaphors, which corresponds to the nominalistic (or in modern terms: idealistic) *esse in intellectu* position. When, however, it is charged with reducing God to nothing but "psychology," it suddenly is all "*esse*" (the other element of *esse in anima*), insisting on psychic *reality* (in other words, on the *in re* standpoint). The either-or of the *in intellectu* and the *in re* is not overcome at all. It is acted out, but this acting out is "cunningly disguised." The *esse in anima* IS this conflict *contracted* into one *seemingly* conflict-free phrase. It is the reified *sacrificium intellectus,* the unthoughtness of a mediation between the idea and the thing, an unthoughtness that is imagined (*vorgestellt*) positively as a third thing in between, which, however, is not a thing, but merely a subjective claim (it is *supposed* to be the mediation). Much as the concept of a "first cause" is the thoughtless attempt to arbitrarily end the infinite regression, within the sphere of causation, by collapsing the unending series of causes into one imaginable primal cause, so the *esse in anima* is the violent ending of all further reflection on the problem of *esse in intellectu* and *esse in re* by simply replacing the whole dilemma with a mystifying phrase. This phrase is such that it speaks to, and thus satisfies, the *imagination* and thereby diverts the *mind* from the still unsettled problem—as a pacifier put into the mouth of a small child helps to take its mind off some other discomfort or desire. The original conflict, the whole ontological problem, is still there, as unresolved as ever. Psychology's *esse in anima* is a nihilistic phrase, notwithstanding the fact that it is honestly *meant* to be the opposite of nihilism.

As little as I can accept Jung's solution, it does him credit that he struggled with this problem of truth and with the conflict between the phenomenology of the soul and the demands of reason, trying to give both their due *without reducing* the one to the other. This is in contrast to many Jungians today, who don't even see any problem here because they either are mere pragmatic administrators of psychic disorders or myth-mongers.

VII. Psychology's betrayal of the soul.

In *CW* 13 § 55, after having said in the preceding paragraph that "We are still as much possessed by autonomous psychic contents as if they were Olympians. Today they are called phobias, obsessions, and so forth; in a word, neurotic symptoms," Jung expressed the following opinion concerning the names we use for these phenomena.

> It is not a matter of indifference whether one calls something a "mania" or a "god." To serve a mania is detestable and undignified, but to serve a god is full of meaning and promise because it is an act of submission to a higher, invisible and spiritual being. ... When the god is not acknowledged, egomania develops, and out of this mania comes sickness.

"When the god is not acknowledged"—I ask: is it a real acknowledgment if the Self is said to be only the God-*image* in the soul and not God Himself? Immediately preceding this quote, Jung quoted the Biblical dictum, "Verily I say unto thee, thou shalt by no means come out thence, until thou hast paid the uttermost farthing." Is this talk of the God-image in the soul the payment of the uttermost farthing? Is "God as a postulate of practical reason resulting from the *a priori* recognition of 'respect for moral law necessarily directed towards the highest good, and the consequent supposition of its objective reality'" (*CW* 6 § 66), payment of the uttermost farthing? (This is a reference to Kant's *Critique of Practical Reason,* which Jung cites as "an attempt on a grand scale to evaluate the *esse in anima* in philosophical terms.") God a mere *postulate* and *supposition—this* is supposed to be a full-fledged acknowledgment? Ridiculous. God-image, to be sure, is not as "detestable and undignified" as "mania." But nevertheless, what Jung said about "mania" and "god" applies here too: it is not a matter of indifference whether one calls the Self "*only* a God-image in the soul" or "God," *when* it is a question of acknowledgment. Jung did not eat his own medicine. He evaded the logical consequences that his own findings or conceptions were pressing for. The "God-image in the soul," which is expressly not to be God Himself, is an attempt to encapsulate and thereby depotentiate the metaphysical dynamite that the idea "God" actually—and inevitably, provided you are honest—represents. God is castrated. "God as autonomous psychic content": this *is* the castrated notion of God. It is the *avoided* "act of *submission* to a higher, invisible and spiritual being,"[14] more than this, the reversed submission, namely the submission of God to our human (or ego) postulates and suppositions. Here we see Jung's adaptation of the Kantian barrier to psychology in action. This whole artificial distinction (or should we say dissociation?) between image (God as he appears, as a Kantian appearance) and God Himself (God as the thing-in-itself) is a subterfuge, invented *to rescue the ego-form of the mind,* i.e., we might say, to allow it to stay safely *vis-à-vis* and *before* (outside) the alchemical vessel. In order that one not see and acknowledge that the ego is a logical *form* (constitution) of consciousness, the ego is reified as "the center of consciousness," a "complex," a kind of psychic "organ."

Just as his atonement for Faust's crime proved to be a mock atonement, so *this* acknowledgment is a mock acknowledgment. As a practicing analyst Jung refused to hide behind a scientific theory. He knew that in one's work with patients one had to come forward as oneself.[15] But *on the level of theory* Jung hid behind the "science" character of his psychology the moment when metaphysical issues became unavoidable and when he would have had to come forward

---

[14] Cf. "Feigned Submission – Clandestine Defiance: Jung's Religious Psychology," Chapter One above.

[15] Cf., e.g., *Memories,* pp. 152f.

and show his true colours as a theorist, gladly using Kant's unsurmountable epistemological barrier as a *deus ex machina* to cut off all further reflection.

Now there can be no doubt that it would have required no small feat to be able to truly acknowledge what the experience demanded. It would, of course, not have been merely a "matter of words," of saying the *word*, "God," the way in "polytheistic psychology" the words God and Gods are used freely, noncommittingly. Archetypal psychology certainly does not declare itself a follower of empiricism, like Jung. It does not *need* a declared empiricism as a literal method anymore, because it has the empiricist relation to the object and the Kantian barrier *interiorized* into its own structure to such an extent that it no longer needs to act it out. Its consciousness thus has as its object the self-contained, free-floating "imaginal." A true acknowledgment would also not have been as simple as uttering a *confessional* statement. A simple relapse into a naive metaphysical or believer's stance was out of the question and, above all, not sufficient, being merely subjective. It would have had to be a theoretically legitimate statement that could stand up before reason. Thus there is a *real* logical difficulty here! And so it is easy to understand that Jung was happy to find a seemingly elegant way out of this dilemma. For he did not have the logical means for a true acknowledgment of God, or, more generally speaking, for his coming forward on the level of theory and resolving the conflict between the demands of "the ego" (which in this instance represents reason) and the demands of the soul ("Küsnacht" vs. "Bollingen"). This dilemma could not be solved on the level of contents (phenomenology: experienced dream images, etc.). It would have required an awareness of the problem of the "thinking form," or, as we could also say, an entering the alchemical vessel. And this, in turn, would have required of psychology to do its logical, alchemical homework instead of directly plunging into the *phenomenology* of the soul, just like that. Psychology would have had to be first of all put into the position of a thoroughly worked through, decomposed-and-distilled form of consciousness that alone would be entitled to say, e.g., "the Self is God."

I have been talking about the Self as God-image versus God Himself for the sole reason that it is the probably most blatant example for the general and structural betrayal that psychology performs with respect to its subject matter at large, the soul. Despite many literal statements attempting to produce a different conception, Jung's psychology *ultimately* shared with all other kinds of psychology the problem that it remained psychologistic and reductive. The soul and the individual expressions of the soul were not allowed to be free, not let loose. They were a priori imprisoned in the straightjacket of the concept of "autonomous complexes in the psyche" as well as the concepts of people's representations, ideas, images, impulses, emotions. They were mere contents, and as such, they were logically and "metaphysically" harmless, manageable. Psychology, as it was defined, *is* the reduction and depotentiation of the soul and its manifestations. The latter are nothing but "factual occurrences," like nature events or things are, nothing but facts or phenomena which psychology could, and had to, record, understand, meditate upon, work through, experience and "feel," perhaps even put into practice, but which it was *logically* immune to. The ego-form of consciousness was not threatened. *Not* being immune to these "events" would have meant comprehending them as truth, which in turn would have meant having fallen into dialectics and speculative thought. But psychology, as it historically developed, was invented for the sole purpose of preventing the experiences' or images' assaulting it (and thus the form of our mind) with a claim for their truth. This is why psychology needed its own private species of truth, cut off from truth as such.

But it is not enough for the soul and each of its expressions to be observed, experienced, deeply felt, understood, beautifully expressed. It is not enough for them to be said to be *psychologically* true. This is only a token acknowledgment, a consolation prize. In general, what a disaster for a discipline if it claims for itself its own variety of truth! Thereby it has logically disconnected itself from "public truth" (a black raven: truth *is* public by definition), and no talk after the fact about a "*collective* unconscious" and a "*trans*personal psyche" and about the "*autonomy*" and "*numinosity*" of the psychic contents can make up for this structural deficit. With the idea of "psychological truth" psychology has unwittingly but objectively (namely logically) shelved the manifestations of the soul in a special fenced-in asylum, a protected and insular space like a museum or nature reserve, or, for that matter, like a nursery, ipso facto, but unwittingly and unadmittedly, turning soul phenomena into something that does not really count and to which the laws that generally are in effect are not applied. What a humiliation and disparagement for the soul! "Psychologically true": Present-day psychology is no more than mock psychology. *Logically* it does not take the soul seriously, *as much value and importance it may indeed attribute to it* emotionally and in its subjective meaning. Psychology does not own up to what it is about. It does not have the logical means to own up to it. This is what exonerates psychology (it cannot be expected to do what it does not have the means to do), but in the very fact that it *has* this excuse lies its guilt.

The soul wants to come home from its exile, it wants to be inherent in the logical form of consciousness instead of being reduced to a content of consciousness, a content serving as a mere *occasion* for consciousness to feel soulful or to *have* the experience of a meaning of life, just like beggars are occasions for us to feel like benefactors. *Ars requirit totum hominem.* "The whole man" includes reason, the organ of truth. The soul also wants to be declared logically, intellectually, rationally legitimate. It does not want to remain held down in the disowning status of "images" or "contents."

Because Jung's psychology was logically split in itself and operated with a duplicity of truths, it landed itself in all sorts of unnecessary problems. To mention only one: the eternal conflict in analytical psychology between the 'clinical' and the 'symbolic' persuasions. I believe that a discipline that has not really come home, that logically is not simply resting in its truth, is what explains the fact that analytical psychology has attracted so few minds. It has become popular instead, which is one of the worst fates that can befall a body of thought. And as to professional Jungians, many of them, it seems, have turned to analytical psychology *as amateurs, for subjective gratification*: out of a personal longing for meaning, out of a personal drive to help others, out of the personal need to find warmth in a group of like-minded others or to be in a profession that qua profession, through the institution of analysis, provides intimate relationships of sorts (transference). Even though Jung's work would have deserved better, one can understand that it had to be so. It was its own internal contradictions that paved the way for the reception it received from its followers as well as from the public. A discipline that provides a private species of truth of its own to its subject-matter has placed itself offside. A work that logically stays contained in its own bubble is bound not to be taken seriously by the thinking public, and conversely attracts those who turn to it with strictly subjective agendas (which is probably also the reason for the ill-advised but widespread desire today to construe psychology as "objective science" and to establish formalized codes of professional ethics: by way of compensating for, and covering up, the fundamental subjectivism in psychology's logical status and in one's personal motivation).

We do not have to be or become Hegelians. No new fan club. No new -ism. But Hegel is at least one place in the history of the mind where psychology could learn what the kind of alchemical mind-processing might be like that could enable it to do justice to the soul. Jung had said that Hegel was a (misfired) psychologist precisely because he was not a proper philosopher. This shows the reductive conception of psychology prevailing here: psychology *excludes* philosophy, excludes the "thinking form." We have to realize that to the contrary Hegel was a "psychologist" in a new and radical (and no longer derogatory) sense precisely where he was at his best as a rigorous philosopher.

VIII. Finis.

It might appear to the one or the other reader that my purpose in this paper has been an inimical attack on Jung, perhaps an attempt to pull him down from his throne, as it were. But Jung has not been my target at all. The target is our psychology, is *we*. Jung is too great a thinker, and I feel personally too indebted to him for a wealth of insights, to think an unsparing exposition of the weaknesses of his conception could do him any harm. Quite the opposite, if we felt that we have to spare him radical criticism, we would not respect him. For me at least, Jung will, despite my radical critique here, remain a lasting source of inspiration. In a certain way, this paper has, of course, also been unfair to Jung. He probably *had to* vehemently reject Hegel, he *had to* close his eyes to the problem of the logical form because otherwise he could not have done his pioneering work in the "archaeology" of the soul. This was what his daimon demanded and what needed his total concentration. We might even have to say he had to betray his truth in order to undisturbedly unearth it in the first place. Furthermore, I did not give Jung any credit for going as far as he did in acknowledging the mythical, metaphysical depth of the soul, astoundingly far if measured against the positivistic spirit of his age. I also did not point out that Jung, under the cover of his explicit empiricism, allowed himself to have a lot of *intuitive* thoughts with which he in fact came very close to Hegelian views.

Nevertheless, the one-sided criticism of Jung's psychology is necessary to pull *us* out of the contented assumption that *basically* Jung had done it all; that what he bequeathed to us was already accomplished psychology, psychology proper, only needing to be applied to ever new cases and themes, to be modified in a few details, and to be completed where Jung left areas unworked. The relentless exposition of the structural faults in the theoretical foundation of Jung's psychology has the purpose of showing us what job remains for us to do. It is for us to build psychology into a *real* "shrine of Philemon," *truly* expiating for "Faust's" crime, and, along the lines of Jung's experience of a "collision with reality," to introduce the insight into the theoretical structure of psychology itself: "Oh, I see, here you have to work!"

CHAPTER SEVEN

"Jung and Hegel" Revisited[1] Or: The *Seelenproblem* of Modern Man and the "Doubt-that-has-killed-it"

Twelve years after the publication of a paper about Jung's adoption of a Kant-based empiricism and the rejection of Hegel's speculative thought[2] it is possible to strike new sparks from the topic of Jung and Hegel.

I will begin with the same quotes. In 1935 Jung wrote:

> Kant in particular erected a barrier across the mental world which condemned to futility even the boldest leap of speculation into the object. Romanticism was the logical counter-move expressed most forcefully, and most cunningly disguised, in Hegel, that great psychologist in philosopher's garb. (*CW* 18 § 1734, transl. modif.)

In a letter also from the same year 1935 (31 July, to Friedrich Seifert, who had contributed an article on Hegel and Jung to Jung's Festschrift), Jung wrote,

> It was always my view that Hegel was a psychologist *manqué*, in much the same way as I am a philosopher *manqué*. As to what is "authentic," that seems to be decided by the spirit of the age. ... Hegel seems to me a romantic thinker in contrast to

[1] Written in 2010.

[2] Now Chapter Six in this volume.

> Kant and hence a typical child of his time; and as a romantic he is already on the way to psychology. The thinking form is not authentic any more but is a vehicle. (*Letters I*, p. 194, to Friedrich Seifert, 31 July 1935)

("A psychologist *manqué*" is the translation of *ein uneigentlicher Psychologe*, which means: a psychologist, to be sure, but not a psychologist in the true sense of the word, not formally or properly so; and in the phrase "as to what is 'authentic,'" "authentic" is the translation for *eigentlich*, the opposite of *uneigentlicher* [*Psychologe*].)

The next, highly emotion-laden quotation comes from the probably most important and definitive work of a strictly theoretical nature which JUNG has ever written, not from more casual comments in letters originally not intended for public access. As belonging to a published essay and appearing in an absolutely serious theoretical context, the statement must be considered as well-conceived.

> I think it is obvious that all philosophical statements which transgress the bounds of reason are anthropomorphic and have no validity beyond that which falls to psychically conditioned statements. A philosophy like Hegel's is a self-revelation of the psychic background and, philosophically, a presumption. Psychologically, it amounts to an invasion by the unconscious. The peculiar high-flown language Hegel uses bears out this view: it is reminiscent of the imperious language of schizophrenics, who use terrific spellbinding words to reduce the transcendent to subjective form, to give banalities the charm of novelty, or pass off commonplaces as searching wisdom. So bombastic a terminology is a symptom of weakness, ineptitude, and lack of substance. But that does not prevent the latest German philosophy [this is in all likelihood aimed at Heidegger, cf. the passage quoted next, where Hegel's and Heidegger's language are lumped together] from using the same crackpot power-words and pretending it is not unintentional psychology. (*CW* 8 § 360, transl. modif.)

The last passage concerning Hegel that I want to quote at this point reads,

> Aristotle's point of view had never particularly appealed to me; nor Hegel, who in my very incompetent opinion is not even a proper philosopher but a misfired psychologist. His impossible

> language, which he shares with his blood-brother Heidegger, denotes that his philosophy is a highly rationalized and lavishly decorated confession of his unconscious. (Letter to Joseph F. Rychlak of 27 April 1959, *Letters II*, p. 501.)

Hegel, one of the greatest philosophers of all times, is boldly charged with the worst accusation imaginable for a philosopher, namely that he was not really a philosopher at all, that he merely pretended to be one and even cunningly disguised his (philosophical) weakness, ineptitude, and lack of substance by hiding them behind a front of crackpot power-words. Philosophically, his work is a "presumption," a "lavishly decorated" "garb." In other words, Hegel is a charlatan, a fraud. Jung high-handedly throws Hegel away.

As unlikely as this lump-sum dismissal of Hegel is, there could of course theoretically be the possibility that Jung indeed saw something, saw through to something, something that others were not able to see. Maybe the thousands of scholars who hold Hegel in high repute precisely as a philosopher, as a true thinker, simply fell for Hegel's "cunning disguise." So to begin with we will have to examine two questions. (1) Do "the facts," does the phenomenological appearance of the body of Hegel's philosophy in any way support Jung's charges as far as his specific accusations are concerned? Is there any evidence in Hegel's work as a whole for Jung's view of it? (2) To what extent was Jung competent and qualified to pass judgment on Hegel? What was his knowledge-base about him, his familiarity with his work? And furthermore, to what extent did Jung have an authentic access to philosophical thought, to "the thinking form," in general?

1. Projection

Jung's first point is that Hegel's philosophy is the mere "rationalization" of "psychically conditioned statements," a "confession of his unconscious." In it we get a "self-revelation of the psychic background" (*CW* 8 § 359). His work expresses the contents from the unconscious "most forcefully" (*ibid.*). "The thinking form [*denkerische Form*, the specifically philosophical form, the form of thought] is not authentic any more but is a vehicle."

A contemporary of Hegel's who was actually critical of him because he felt that in Hegel's thinking "the dry fire of intelligence" "sucks out the whole moist life of nature," and who personally preferred "the fresh, life-warm springtime breeze that breathes everywhere in Schelling's *Naturphilosophie*" nevertheless acknowledged: "A greater strength in holding fast a pure thought and compelling it to explicate all immanent moments of the concept I have not found anywhere ...."[3] This is of course only an opinion, one person's opinion, and as such does not prove anything. But it at least shows that there can be the view that Hegel deserves the absolutely highest marks precisely concerning "the thinking form" and the "dry fire of intelligence." The "dry fire of intelligence," if it were a correct assessment, would preclude any possibility that Hegel's work was nothing but the subjective "confession of his unconscious" and its philosophical form merely a garb or vehicle, because "confession of his unconscious" and "self-revelation of the psychic background" mean that the true source and material substance of his philosophy was what spontaneously emerged (Jung even speaks of "an invasion"!) in the way of his imaginings and ideas *autistically*[4] from within his own personality. No "object-relation." What Jung's interpretation totally excludes is the possibility that Hegel's philosophy is precisely the reflection of the subject's (Hegel's) *cognitive relation to* an object, of an interaction between subject and object, in other words, that his thought derived from the wakeful world-experience of Hegel as a thinking mind, from his thinkingly perceiving and absorbing what was going on *in the world* (as well as in human existence in the world at large) and processing all this in the depths of his mind, giving a human and intelligent response to the questions and conflicts inherent in his time and in our being humans. "Confession of his unconscious" implies a lonely, isolated and self-enclosed individual and his fundamentally private experiences emerging exclusively from within, from *his* inner, from "the unconscious," as ones that are totally unrelated to the world around him, to the public experience of life, to the social and historical reality in which he lived and to what can only be known through serious study

[3] Ernst v. Lasaulx in a letter to Joseph v. Görres, 15 May 1831. Quoted from *Hegel in Berichten seiner Zeitgenossen*, ed. by Günther Nicolin, Hamburg (Meiner) 1970, # 666, p. 429.

[4] Jung repeatedly stressed from early on that he had a fundamental secret that he could not talk about with anyone and that this secret was his true treasure. "My entire youth can be understood in terms of this secret. It induced in me an almost unendurable loneliness" (*MDR* p. 41).

and learning, on the one hand, and through *empirical* experience of reality, on the other hand.

We find the paradigm underlying Jung's interpretation of Hegel in terms of an "invasion by the unconscious" in Jung's own self-interpretation, his fantasy about the origin of his own work. At the end of the chapter on his "Confrontation with the Unconscious" during the years of disorientation after his separation from Freud (1912–1917), summarizing the significance of this period for his life and work, Jung states:

> As a young man my goal had been to accomplish something in my science. But then, I hit upon this stream of lava, and the passion contained in the heat of its fire reshaped my life and put it under a new order. That was the primordial stuff [*Urstoff*] that compelled it, and my works are the more or less successful endeavor to incorporate this incandescent matter into the world view of my time. ... / ... My entire later activity consisted in elaborating what during those years had burst forth from the unconscious and at first swamped me. (*MDR* p. 199, transl. modif.)

We have in this fantasy a distinction between the mutually exclusive spheres of science (as well as of "the world view of his time"), on the one hand, and the stream of lava, on the other hand. Science is fundamentally a public project. It is (a) on principle intersubjective as well as (b) based on what by Brentano and in Husserl's phenomenology is called the *intentionality* of consciousness, consciousness's necessarily being directed to some object. Intentionality implies a fundamental difference or vis-à-vis between subject and object and thus an interrelation between "two." In the sphere of intentionality of this type, truth is the *adaequatio rei et intellectus*, the correspondence between what the human mind thinks (its judgments) *about* reality and reality itself. The experience of an inner stream of lava, by contrast, is the opposite on both counts. It is (a) completely "autistic" or "solipsistic," if I may say so, and (b) consciousness is invaded or swamped, which is to say that all input comes from the primordial stuff within the subject itself and precisely not through consciousness's having directed its attention, in the sense of intentionality, toward some object, some Other outside of itself. The stream of lava does not (and does not have to) correspond to anything outside of itself. It is sufficient unto itself, fundamentally monocentric, and even spills its "truth" all over the subject, swamping it with its "truth," subsuming it under itself, violently forcing a seamless identity and ego-syntony of the subject with what swamped it. Its "truth" does not have the character of "statement about ..." that would have to be justified in the sense of a *rationem reddere* or *logon didonai*. It IS nothing but its power, its being. It's powerful existence *is* its "justification," the only justification required for it. It reveals only *itself*, and thus, qua self-*revelation*, self-representation, it a priori comes as true. This is why Jung says about psychology: "Its truth is a fact and not a judgment. When psychology speaks, for instance, of the motif of the virgin birth, it is only concerned with the fact that there is such an idea, but it is not concerned with the question whether such an idea is true or false in any other sense. The idea is psychologically true inasmuch as it exists" (*CW* 11 § 4). "Fact" implies an originary selfsameness or identity, alchemically speaking the unbroken *unio naturalis*. "Judgment" (*Urteil*[5]), by contrast, presupposes a difference or duality, the diremption of the primordial oneness into subject and predicate and their conjunction through the copula.

Intentionality implies a distance, as the phenomenologists say, between the *noesis* and the *noema*, and an *act* (namely, the *noesis*) on the part of the subject, the mind. If consciousness is swamped, there is instead an absolutely *immediate* being-informed, an *immediate* knowing. No distance and difference to be bridged by an act of cognition. Consciousness does not have to *perform* any intentional act. On the contrary, all attempts on the part of the subject at becoming active and relating *to* any object are simply washed away by the onrush of the stream of lava, which is the only active subject and reduces consciousness to a passive recipient.[6] This

[5] Hölderlin, with a creative but false etymology, thought that *Urteil* as a logical term means "*Ur-Teilung*," "primordial ("*ur-*") division or diremption," an interpretation that was adopted by Schelling as well as Hegel.

[6] In this connection we can also remember Jung's understanding of religion. Reading as a youth Biedermann's *Christliche Dogmatik*, "I learned from him that religion was 'a mental act of man's self-relation to God.' I disagreed with that, for I understood religion as something that God did to me; it was an act on His part, to which I am simply exposed, for He was the stronger" (*MDR* p. 56 for., transl. modif.): the rejection of the idea of "mental act" and the insistence on the subject's total passivity or victim status. Jung is committed to the logic of absolute unidirectionality. This is also the logic that

is also why Jung, at the time when he experienced the onrush of these overwhelming fantasies, seriously feared to become insane and why he also does not have any compunctions about speaking about Hegel's language as being reminiscent of the "*schizophrene* (*'Machtsprache'*)" ("the [imperious language of] schizophrenics"), just as in an impromptu oral talk from the year 1959 he dared to say about Heidegger, whom, after all, he considered to be Hegel's blood-brother: "They [the insane persons] invent for example a special language. They have these neologisms, they express themselves hyperbolically, as for example Heidegger, ... and do not notice that they withdraw into 'power-words,' into the magic words of the primitives."[7]

In Jung's view Hegel was, as it were, completely autistic, in the sense of his being overwhelmed by the unconscious and having no real relation to the world around him whatsoever. In contrast to Kant, who "put certain bounds to human knowledge in general," and in contrast to "natural science and common sense," which "without difficulty came to terms" with those bounds, Hegel, according to Jung, "projected great truths out of the sphere of the subject into a cosmos he himself had created" (*CW* 8 § 358, transl. modif.). In other words, he did not even project them on the real world; Hegel's philosophy does not engage the world, reality, at all. He stayed enclosed in his *idios kosmos* (which is the conception from which we got our word "idiot") or, as Jung put it himself, he "seemed to me like a man who was caged in the edifice of his own

informs Jung's idea of the unconscious. — But whereas "unidirectionality" might still suggest a duality, we must realize that due to the absolutely overpowering quality of God (or "the Other") the human "subject" is really turned into an object. Ultimately, as the exclusively receiving pole of two, it is (logically) subsumed under or swallowed by the active one, so that the duality becomes (logically) reduced to a monocentric structure (the ego circling around the Self). Duality is seen as, and reserved for, the structure of neurosis ("dissociation" between ego and self). Jung tried to mend this flaw (the human subject being surreptitiously turned into an object) on the *semantic* level, by assigning to the human subject the powerful role of the redeemer of the unconscious dark God as well as by his thesis of the necessity of a certain defiance against God ("Man always has some mental reservation, even in the face of divine decrees. Otherwise, where would be his freedom? And what would be the use of that freedom if it could not threaten Him who threatens it?" *MDR* p. 220). But this is a fundamentally secondary and merely semantic or psychic (*behavioral*) modification which does not alter the underlying psychology, the logical structure.

[7] C.G. Jung, *Über Gefühle und den Schatten*. Winterthurer Fragestunden. Textbuch, Zürich and Düsseldorf 1999, p. 21 (my translation).

words and on top of it with a proud air strutted around in his prison" (*MDR* p. 69, transl. modif.),[8] his own private insane asylum.[9]

Now, comparing this view of Jung's with Hegel's philosophy, anyone who has some knowledge about it can only say that this is an absurd interpretation, one that on its own part does not in any way get in touch with reality, here: with the real Hegel. With this view Jung stays himself enclosed within a fantasy of his own making that he projects onto Hegel.

About Schelling, his friend and roommate from student days, Hegel later said: "He absolved his philosophical education before the public." This was stated in reference to the fact that Schelling, as the intellectual prodigy that he was, from age 18 onwards wrote and published in rapid succession one philosophical work after the other, time and again revising his conceptions and so slowly coming into his own. Hegel, by contrast, remained publicly silent for a long time, undertaking most extensive studies in various fields, acquiring for himself a solid knowledge-base, patiently excerpting all sorts of works from different fields, with the result that in this way he acquired an up-to-date encyclopedic familiarity with the knowledge of his time. And throughout his life he kept abreast of the new research going on. This fact alone shows that Hegel was anything but "autistic" or "solipsistic," his work anything but a subjective "confession." In the Preface to the *Phenomenology of Spirit* Hegel wrote, "For it is the nature of humanity to press onward to agreement with others; human nature only really exists in an achieved community of minds. The anti-human, the merely animal, consists in staying within the sphere of feeling, and being able to communicate only at that level." And he ridiculed the fact that "the man of common sense makes his appeal to feeling, to an oracle within his breast." The oracle within his breast! In other words, exactly that which Jung accused him of, while himself relying on it. For what is "what during those years had burst forth from the unconscious and at first swamped me" other than this oracle from within his breast?

[8] Considering what Jung had said about the unendurable loneliness due to "his secret" (see footnote 4 above), could we not say that he, Jung, was a man caged in the prison of his secret and also, no doubt, proudly so ("I had the feeling that I was either outlawed or elect, accursed or blessed" *MDR* p. 41)?

[9] Jung's fantasy is obviously influenced by the impressions he received during many years as psychiatrist in the Burghölzli clinic.

The material input, with which Hegel worked, came from outside, not from within. He was thus, to put it in modern phenomenological terms, definitely dominated by the "intentionality" of consciousness, or, to put it yet in other terms, the libido that expresses itself in his philosophy is, as it were, "extraverted," directed toward "the object," rather than "introverted." Its interest is not "revelations" from within, but real *knowledge* and *insight*, and knowledge and insight about what had been found out through empirical means as well as through the intellectual theorizing by his contemporaries and those who came before him. All this was to be thought through and comprehended. This is why his philosophical work is satiated with and soundly based on the learning of his time and shows his truly being in touch with the world. Certainly, there is not a trace of his being "caged in the edifice of his own words." In his entire work he is devoted to the comprehension of the Real, be it the natural world or the social, economic, and political worlds, or human consciousness and psychology, Law and ethical life, the arts, the religions of mankind, the history of thought, etc.

He was also an astute observer of the dramatic political and social revolutions and changes of his time. Such a biographical detail as the one that every year he opened a bottle of wine or champagne on the 14th of July and drank it in commemoration of the storming of the Bastille betrays his inner connection with the real world around him.[10]

That he called his work on logic *Science of Logic* is not a "cunning disguise" of something that in truth is of a projective nature, a philosophical kind of "active imagination." Quite apart from the question of whether one agrees or disagrees with his results, there can be no denying that in its form this work is really a "scientific"[11] study. Although the *Logic* examines the most abstract forms or determinations of thought itself, this subject matter is just like any other, more concrete topic one that is objectively given to the researcher,

[10] This, by the way, contrasts favorably with Jung's early fascination with the reactionary Nazi movement, which Jung did not even hesitate to credit with being a manifestation of an archetypal force, the god Wotan. – That Hegel's commemoration of the storming of the Bastille is not an expression of a naive enthusiasm and a blindness to the absolute terror of the French Revolution (the way many French Marxist intellectuals systematically closed their eyes to the Stalinist terrors) becomes clear from his chapter "Absolute Freedom and Terror" in his *Phenomenology of Spirit*.

[11] Of course "scientific" not in today's usual sense which refers to the positivistic natural sciences.

namely by the whole history of thought before him as well as the history of the specific thought about thought (logic), and thus it is of course not a subjective confession.

Again in the Preface to his *Phenomenology of Spirit* Hegel described what in his mind was the task of philosophy and had to be its form. "The true shape in which truth exists can only be the scientific system of such truth. To help bring philosophy closer to the form of Science, to the goal where it can lay aside the title '*love* of knowing' and be *actual* knowing—that is what I have set myself to do." The *form* of science vs. the stream of lava! Two opposite and mutually exclusive ideas. Jung puts down the rational character of Hegel's works as nothing but a secondary "rationalization" of what in truth are "psychically conditioned statements" (*CW* 8 § 360, transl. modif.). But for Hegel the rational character, the form of science, was the primary aim. It was for him what the whole business of philosophy is about.

And we can also state that Hegel's subjective declaration concerning what he *intended* to do is fully corroborated by the actual character and spirit of his work as a whole. His focus is always on *die Sache*, the issue or matter, his aim "the knowledge of what *is*." And conversely, his scorn is time and again directed at all expositions of philosophy that see the purpose of philosophy in "suppressing the differentiations of the Notion and restoring the *feeling* of essential being," in short in "providing edification rather than insight" and "the ferment of enthusiasm." "But philosophy must beware of the wish to be edifying."[12] The impulse driving his work is clearly counter to any type of self-expression or any offering himself as the passive mouthpiece of a "self-revelation of the psychic background." If Hegel despised anything then it would have been what Jung imputes him to be doing, namely to project "great truths out of the sphere of the subject into a cosmos he himself had created." Such "great truths," or as Hegel himself worded it, "the immediate knowledge of the Absolute," were precisely absolutely pointless in his view. "But it would be better by far to spare oneself the effort of bringing forth ultimate truths of that kind; for they have long since been available in catechisms or in popular sayings, etc."[13] Not "the

[12] G.W.F. Hegel, *Phenomenology of Spirit*, transl. by A.V. Miller, Oxford (Oxford University Press) 1977, p. 17.

[13] *Ibid.*, p. 42.

Absolute" but the *worked-out* Concept or Notion, i.e., the *conceptual knowledge* of what there is to be known, was to him the job of philosophy, the careful rational *account* of the real.

Most telling is of course also the role of scepticism in Hegel's thinking. He thought very highly of Greek scepticism, but in addition expressly conceived of the movement of thought, and thus also specifically the movement of his own philosophical project, as "this thoroughgoing scepticism"[14] (*dieser sich selbst vollbringende Skeptizismus*, i.e., a scepticism that accomplishes itself by going all the way to its very end), as a deepening of the Cartesian methodological doubt (*Zweifel*) into (likewise methodological) *Verzweiflung*, despair, in the sense of a hopeless abandonment of the position doubted. In view of such a stance, can one entertain with respect to Hegel the idea of a "lavishly decorated confession of his unconscious"? The methodological principle of his work is precisely, so we might say, the systematic determinate negation of any "lavish decoration" with which ideas originally come.

Hegel's (if I may use this Jungian jargon in order to highlight the difference to the image Jung paints of Hegel) "extraverted" commitment "to the facts" shows also quite blatantly in another and rather different characteristic feature of his proceeding. The works he produced were fundamentally conceived as "works in progress." He never thought of them as anything like the last word on whatever the subject matter happened to be or as "ultimate wisdom." Referring back to the story that Plato was supposed to have revised his books about the *Republic* seven times, he resignedly expressed, in the preface to the second edition of the first book of *Science of Logic*, the wish "that for a work which, as belonging to the modern world, is confronted by a deeper principle, a more difficult subject matter and a material richer in compass, leisure had been afforded to revise it seven and seventy times." He did not hesitate to change his earlier expositions and views. For example, the high estimation of the productive imagination (*produktive Einbildungskraft*) still expressed in his early work *Faith and Knowledge* (1802) gave way to the fundamentally different conception in his *Encyclopedia* (1830) that not the *Einbildungskraft*, but the *Gedächtnis* (memory), as "retentive," "reproductive," and "mechanical" memory,

---

[14] *Ibid.*, p. 50.

provides the transition to thought: "We *think* in names," that is, in fundamentally external signs (§§ 461 ff.)! And in his university lectures on one and the same topic, which over the years he gave several times, particularly in the ones on religion, one can see quite nicely how every new time he not only took into account new literature that had meanwhile appeared (such as first translations into European languages of classical texts of India, Persia, China) and worked them into his philosophy of religion, but he also continued to revise certain aspects of the basic *conception* in order to come closer to an adequate description. He kept wrestling with the issues, in the case of religions with the religions that had in fact appeared in the history of mankind and their objective phenomenology and historical development, not with his personal views of what religion should be and what one "should" believe.

And then there is also the style of his works, the style considered on a sentence to sentence basis. He is committed to the "labor of the concept," the "discipline of thought" and, scorning all impatience, follows step by step "the cold march of necessity in the thing itself [*der kalt fortschreitenden Notwendigkeit der Sache*]." A detailed explication of the content of each phenomenon or thought is provided. I already quoted v. Lasaulx as saying: "A greater strength in holding fast the pure thought and compelling it to explicate all immanent moments of the concept I have not found anywhere ...." Clearly not self-expression. Patient hard work. And yet, not work in the sense of manipulation.

As far as nature in particular is concerned, it was the unique achievement of Hegel's philosophy of nature (*Philosophie der Natur*, in clear contrast, e.g., to Schelling's *Naturphilosophie*) to unburden, in a critical way, the empirical study of nature from all the metaphysical categories that the mind, consciously or unconsciously, still carried along, thus freeing it to devote itself to the whole wealth of concrete *unanticipatable* experience. This was the result of the fact that for Hegel the Idea is, to be sure, in itself divine, but *as* Nature it appears in, released itself into, the form of its otherness and externality.

Jung taught us to begin an active imagination by keeping calmly and dispassionately looking, for example, at a figure from one's dream until it begins to move. We can use this image as a structural analogy, in the sphere of intuition and imagination, to what happens in Hegel in the sphere of thought. Hegel puts, as it were, an initial thesis, thought, or phenomenon as his prime matter into a retort, holding it fast therein, and by "gazing" at it intently, or closely listening to what precisely it actually states, becomes aware of its self-movement, a self-movement through which it both explicates one by one its immanent thought determinations, because each time it proves itself to in truth be in contradiction to what its claim was, so that it sublates itself, going over into its opposite. The sublation is not inflicted on the initial thought by the philosopher. *He* is only the "observer" of *its* self-sublation, self-sublation that is reenacted by him and becomes plausible to the reflecting mind. But in both cases, in active imagination and in Hegel's thought, the self-movement of the image or thought, respectively, can only come about if there is the devoted "gaze" of a conscious mind. This intent gaze on the part of the adept is, as it were, the indispensable drink of blood provided by a human visitor, like Odysseus, to the dead souls in the underworld that alone permits their (otherwise dormant) memory to return to the shades.

The fundamental difference to the self-movement in active imagination is that *what* will happen in the imagination is determined by numerous unknown extraneous factors (the personality of the person practicing it, his memories, the contingencies of the person's history and present life conditions, etc.), whereas the self-movement of the concept simply unfolds sort of analytically (in the Kantian sense) the immanent moments of the concept itself, its "memory," its internal life. This is why Hegel spoke of "the cold march of necessity...." And it is possible because the concept is, as it were, hermetically enclosed in the retort. The imagination may also follow laws, its own laws, but especially in the case of a modern ordinary person's deliberate active fantasizing—in contrast to great works of literature or art—it is highly contaminated by fortuitous subjective factors and in addition usually has a "synthetic" character, narratively and additively passing from one image to the next, a kind of gliding of the signifiers. Active imagination, as the imagination in general, usually has no containing vessel and no hermetic seal. It can go on and on, and the image's self-movement can go off and away in all sorts of different directions and to new images. Not so the concept. It cannot go off. Being firmly enclosed in the retort, its self-movement is forced to go into itself.

Jung, it has become clear, has no leg to stand on concerning his bold assertion that Hegel is not truly a philosopher at all and that the "thinking form" is inauthentic in his case. *His* "Hegel" is a figment of his imagination.

There is in addition another charge that Jung raised against Hegel, the one about his high-flown, bombastic, imperious language and his crackpot power-words. But we can turn to it only after we have discussed the question of Jung's competence and qualification as a critic of Hegel's philosophy and style.

2. Ignorance

In a letter of the year 1959, from which I quoted a portion before, Jung wrote in response to a question concerning the influence of Hegel's philosophy on Jung's work:

> In the intellectual world in which I grew up, Hegelian thought played no role at all; .... Hegel's dialectics, I can safely say, had no influence at all, as far as I know myself. ... / I have never studied Hegel properly, that means his original works. There is no possibility of inferring a direct dependence .... There is, of course, a remarkable coincidence between certain tenets of Hegelian philosophy and my findings concerning the collective unconscious (*Letters 2*, pp. 501 f., to Rychlak, 27 April 1959).

According to his own explicit statement, Jung had never studied Hegel's works and can exclude the possibility of a direct influence. All that he knew or believed about Hegel must thus have come from secondary sources.

Now it would of course be possible that Jung in his old age did not remember correctly, or that he had reasons to play down any familiarity with Hegel's work. But there is some evidence in Jung's work that speaks for the correctness of the information Jung gave about his knowledge of Hegel and of the possibility of a direct influence of Hegel on him.

The character of Jung's work as a whole speaks against such an influence. There is no structural affinity between his and Hegel's approaches. Even the alleged "remarkable coincidence between certain tenets of Hegelian philosophy and my findings concerning the collective unconscious" appear as such probably only to superficial observers who do not really understand either the one of the two authors or both. Instead of really *thinking* thoughts, Jung merely *has* thoughts, that is, *beholds ideas* as contents of consciousness, as objects in front of consciousness. He enjoys mysteries, paradoxes, enigmatic speculative ideas (such as "subtle body"), mythical images, statements of wisdom, but he as the subject stays vis-à-vis them, as onlooker or consumer. One only needs to see how he worked with the concepts of the *privatio boni*, the Trinity, Incarnation and *kenôsis*, the ontological proof of God, in order to realize that he does not approach them *thinkingly* and as *thoughts*, but as thing-like *ideas*, ideas *about* which he reasons (in external reflection), much like a child plays with building bricks. By the same token, the way he apperceived Kant's thinking one sees that he made for himself a simple world-view (something to be pictorially imagined) and epistemology out of it and did not enter the sphere of Kant's *thought*.

True, the term "dialectical" does occur in Jung as in Hegel, which might make people believe that there is some affinity, but it has a fundamentally different meaning, referring in Jung to the interaction in therapy between two "psychic systems." In general, Jung thinks in terms of entity-like opposites and not of dialectics. He does not enter the sphere of thought at all. The "transcendent function," sometimes thought to be a parallel to Hegel's dialectics, is incompatible with Hegelian dialectics, operating, as it does, with fixed opposites that exclude each other (cf. Jung's favorite idea of a "collision of duties") and with the idea of an unpredictable emergence of a reconciling third. For Hegel, by contrast, the *dialectical* moment "is the self-sublation of such finite determinations and their passing into their opposites" (*Encyclop.*, 3rd ed., § 81) ....

In *Psychological Types* in the chapter "Definitions," *sub voce* "IDEA" Jung briefly (in three sentences) discusses Hegel's "idea" and thereby quotes two statements or phrases from Hegel (*CW* 6 § 735 = *GW* 6 § 814). In two footnotes he provides the page numbers from two of Hegel's works as references. Here we have to turn to the German original, because the English edition of Jung's works obliterates the feature that I want to point to. The footnote to the first quote reads succinctly: "*Ästhetik.* I, 138." The other footnote accordingly: "*Logik.* III, p. 242 f." So far so good. These footnotes give us the impression that Jung quoted from those two works by Hegel. But when one now turns to the bibliography at the end of the book to get the full title and bibliographical data of the works, one discovers a note added to the entry in the bibliography stating, "Quoted in Eisler, R.: *Wörterbuch der philosophischen Begriffe (Dictionary of Philosophical Concepts)*. 3rd edition, Berlin 1910" (my transl.). And looking at Eisler's *Wörterbuch der philosophischen Begriffe*, one finds that even *what* Jung said in this short paragraph of his about the "idea" in Hegel is also more or less directly taken over from Eisler's brief and rather mindless discussion. Even the very external fact that in Jung's immediately consecutive footnotes the page number is inconsistently given one time without and the other time with a preceding "p." seems to indicate that the page references have directly been copied from Eisler, where we find the same inconsistency.[15]

I think this tiny example is rather conclusive support for Jung's own claim that he has "never studied Hegel properly, that means his original works." When wanting to say something about the central concept of Hegel's logic and his philosophy at large, the idea, he had to have recourse to a general philosophical dictionary and to copy statements from *its* text directly into his. And even *what* he said in this case seems to me to indicate that he did not have any direct access to Hegel's work, because the statement that "Hegel hypostatizes the idea completely" is, reported as it is out of context and without qualifications, simply silly. The fact that the specific content of the term "idea" in Hegel's thinking deviates from that of this term in all previous philosophical discourse and belongs to Hegel alone should have prohibited Jung's assertion, an assertion which tries to suggest that Hegel merely did something (something illegitimate at that) to the "same" traditionally known "idea," namely that he "hypostatized" it. We know what this meant in Jung's eyes. It meant the "deadly sin of making a metaphysical assertion, i.e., to hypostatize a mere noumenon, a thing-in-itself..." (*MDR* p. 70, transl. modif. Jung is here referring to Schopenhauer). But this is all nonsense. Nothing of the sort is happening in Hegel. If Jung had studied Hegel, he could hardly have made such a statement. But if he got his information about Hegel only from general philosophical dictionaries and other such secondary literature, one cannot be surprised.

---

[15] Although Eisler used the German "S." while Jung switched to the Latin "p."

Nor can one be surprised that Jung parrots in other cases popular prejudices based on ignorance of the facts, which again supports the idea that he relied only on secondary sources and hearsay. In an early lecture, also on "Psychological Types" (*CW* 6 § 865), Jung, talking about James's "tender-minded" individuals, makes the following comments: "They care little for facts, and the multiplicity of empirical phenomena hardly bothers or disconcerts them at all; they forcibly fit the data into their ideal constructions, and reduce everything to their *a priori* premises. This was the method of Hegel in settling beforehand the number of the planets." It cannot be our task here to go into the issue alluded to. All that needs to be pointed out in our context is that this is another example of Jung's picking up some assertion copied from one uninformed author to the next without any one having gone to Hegel's own text, in this case to his early *Dissertatio Philosophica de Orbitis Planetarum,* where he could have found that the opposite of what is asserted is the case. Walter Jaeschke, commenting on this widely prevailing misconception, says: "This criticism common up to the present time presents here, with a confused mixture of antipathy and ignorance, the example of an 'inverted world': Hegel, the supposed wildly speculating thinker and enemy of empirical knowledge, [in fact] argues precisely against drawing conclusions about empirical reality from abstract models...."[16] Anyone interested in the facts should consult the cited work of Hegel's and the careful commentary provided in a new edition of it.[17] At any rate we see that in this case at least it was Jung who "cared little for facts and forcibly fit Hegel into his ideal construction," precisely by accusing *the latter* of this very fault.

Similarly, at another time Jung states, "Hegel was the Prussian state philosopher, considered to be a famous wise one .... Hegel was a philosopher in a definite political system; one always finds such a fellow in every political system—that is, the ass harnessed by the powers of

[16] Walter Jaeschke, *Hegel-Handbuch*, Stuttgart, Weimar (J.B. Metzler) 2005, p. 108. My translation.

[17] Hegel, *Dissertatio Philosophica de Orbitis Planetarum. Philosophische Erörterungen über die Planetenbahnen*, transl. [into German] and with Introduction and Commentary by Wolfgang Neuser, Weinheim 1986. Especially pertinent: p. 56. In this context I would also like to refer back to what I briefly pointed out above about Hegel's philosophy of nature.

the earth to the political cart."[18] Again this is a popular prejudice mindlessly passed on from one author to the other without their acquiring a knowledge of their own about what they are making bold statements about. Von Franz by the way, repeats the same view about Hegel.[19] Judging from her reference, she also obtained her "knowledge" about Hegel only from secondary literature (apart, of course, from the fact that she had probably listened to Jung's lectures). How wrong this idea of Hegel as "the Prussian state philosopher" and as "the ass harnessed by the powers of the earth to the political cart" is cannot be expounded here. Enough has been written on the subject. I will only cite here one recent author writing in English. Terry Pinkard in his *Hegel. A Biography*, points to "Hegel's scathing references to K.L. von Haller, who was more or less the 'official' philosopher of the most reactionary elements of the Prussian court." "Hegel provides long citations from Haller's work to illustrate what he takes to be its idiocies, and he lambastes it with the kind of sarcastic polemic that always revealed Hegel's more aggressive side. It would have been difficult (especially in those times) to launch any more clear attack on the ruling ideology of the reactionary elements at court ...."[20] In a note (n. 97, on p. 726) Pinkard reminds the reader of the fact that "Allen Wood in G.W.F. Hegel, *Elements of the Philosophy of Right* demonstrates the clear affinity between Hegel's text and the aims of Prussian reformers such as Stein." And earlier, he had related that Hegel, as in every year (I had mentioned as much) also in 1820 drank a toast to the storming of the Bastille on July 14, even sort of publicly in the company of many students and friends and "at the height of the reaction and at a time when he himself might have been in danger" (p. 451).[21]

In *CW* 6 § 66, in the context of his discussion of the ontological proof of God, Jung writes, "Hegel cast the reproach at Kant that one could not compare the concept of God with an imaginary hundred thalers. But, as Kant rightly pointed out, logic strips away all content,

[18] C.G. Jung, *Nietzsche's Zarathustra. Notes of the Seminar given in 1934–1939*, ed. by James L. Jarrett, Princeton (Princeton University Press) 1988, vol. 2, p. 1121.

[19] Marie-Louise von Franz, *C.G. Jung. Sein Mythos in unserer Zeit*, Frauenfeld and Stuttgart (Huber) 1972, p. 57.

[20] Terry Pinkard, *Hegel. A Biography*, Cambridge (Cambridge University Press) 2000, p. 459 f.

[21] On the wider implications of this whole theme see Rebecca Comay, *Mourning Sickness. Hegel and the French Revolution*, Stanford (Stanford University Press) 2011.

for it would no longer be logic if a content were to prevail." A silly rejoinder, and another indication that Jung did not familiarize himself with Hegel's thought. It makes no sense at all to *simply repeat* the very argument that has been criticized by Hegel and think that this could serve as a refutation of the criticism. One does not need to agree with Hegel. However, if he wanted to find fault with Hegel's theses, Jung would have had to engage Hegel's argument. The latter was of course familiar with this one-sided, instrumental idea of logic, "formal logic" (the only one Jung knows), both with its merits and with its fundamental limitation. But he had also stated (and shown) that "if logic is supposed to lack a substantial content, then the fault does not lie with its subject matter but solely with the way in which this subject matter is grasped."[22] And as far as Jung's way of grasping this subject matter is concerned, it is certainly true that to it applies Hegel's critique[23] of the ordinary notion of thinking: "we immediately think that 'thinking' means our thinking, the way it is in consciousness. Here, however, [i.e., in Anaxagoras, about whom Hegel is speaking here] strictly objective thought is meant ...." In other words, when the topic was that of thought, the very psychologist who wanted us to advance to the standpoint of the objective psyche himself remained stuck in a decidedly *ego-psychological* notion of thinking. Jung unthinkingly takes it simply for granted that thought is "ego," not "soul." The implication of this would be: consciousness may think about soul, but the soul does not think (which is of course also why "soul" in Jung is basically defined as "the unconscious" and as "pure nature"). Jung merely asserts a dogmatic prejudice, absolutizing one particular commonsensical concept of "logic."[24] (But even Jung's authority in these matters, Kant, knew about a philosophy [and thus also a logic] according to its *Weltbegriff* in contradistinction to its *Schulbegriff*, which is why he was also able to introduce the concept of a "transcendental logic," which is certainly not identical with formal logic.)

---

[22] *Hegel's Science of Logic*, transl. by A.V. Miller, Atlantic Highlands, NJ (Humanities Press International) 1989, p. 48.

[23] In the section on Anaxagoras in Hegel's *Lectures on the History of Philosophy*.

[24] For a philosophical discussion of the different types of logic see Stefan Schick, *Contradictio est regula veri. Die Grundsätze des Denkens in der formalen, transzendentalen und spekulativen Logik*, Hegel-Studien Beiheft 53, Hamburg (Meiner) 2010.

What one might say in favor of Jung concerning his making such wrong statements about Hegel is that these were simply the conventional opinions about Hegel during the time of Jung. After Hegel's death, his thinking had quickly fallen into disrepute and was succeeded by the entirely different, much more positivistic-scientific spirit of the age of modernity as well as, in philosophy, by the outspokenly anti-Hegelian schemes of Schopenhauer, Feuerbach, Marx (at least partially). Then there were Nietzsche and, later, Neo-Kantianism. At the time when Jung grew up and studied, Hegel was "a dead dog."[25]

However, what at first might seem to be a possible excuse for Jung's misrepresentation of Hegel turns precisely against Jung. How can a man of Jung's scientific training, professional standing, and academic status contribute to the not only unfounded, but directly falsifying gossip about Hegel? How can he, with a certain passion, pass absolutely devastating judgments about a philosopher *as* philosopher if he had not read his work, let alone studied it? How could he reconcile such an irresponsible behavior with his own standards? He made it very clear what his standards were when it was a question of other people's passing judgments on his own work. Reacting to an American professor of psychology who had sent him the draft of a chapter about Jung, he made, among other severe criticisms, the following comment:

> Somebody tries to present Mr. Plato's philosophical work. We in Europe should expect that anybody trying to carry out such a plan would read *all of Plato's writings* and not barely half and chiefly the earlier part of them. Such a *procedere* would not qualify and could hardly be called responsible or reliable. One could not even advocate it with an author as insignificant as myself. (*Letters 2*, p. 185, to Hall, 6 Oct. 1954).

But obviously Jung had no compunctions about advocating, or rather practicing, it with a philosopher as significant as Hegel. The moment it was a matter of turning to the latter, Jung must have dissociated

[25] Cf. the title of a conference in Oldenburg, Germany in 2007: "Ist Hegel ein toter Hund? Über die Wirklichkeit der Vernunft in postmetaphysischer Zeit." The expression "a dead dog" had above all been used by Lessing for how Spinoza had been treated from after his death up to Lessing's time and was later repeatedly (be it affirmatively or negatively) also applied to other thinkers by other thinkers (e.g., by Stirner, Marx).

himself from the demands that, according to his own statement, "We in Europe" make on presentations of or judgments about an author. That psychology professor had obviously really read at least some of Jung's writings and gone to the effort of doing justice to them. And yet Jung charged him with incompetence and irresponsible scientific behavior. It is not to be imagined how incensed Jung would have been, and rightly so, if someone made bold assertions about him, Jung, merely on the basis of what is to be found in a superficial psychological dictionary, such as, for example, *A Critical Dictionary of Jungian Analysis* by A. Samuels, B. Shorter, and F. Plaut! By not reading Hegel, let alone laboriously penetrating into his thought, Jung reduces Hegel for himself to a Rorschach blot. Another time, when hearing about disputes among London Jungians about some issues of his psychology he wrote: "From such discussions we see what awaits me once I have become posthumous. Then everything that was once fire and wind will be bottled in spirit and reduced to dead nostrums. Thus are the gods interred in gold and marble and ordinary mortals like me in paper" (*Letters 2*, p. 469, to von der Heydt, 22 December 1958). But interment in paper is still better than what he did to Hegel: interment in downright untruth.

3. Hegel's language

Now we are ready to look at Jung's statements about Hegel's language. Let us review what Jung has to say about it. Hegel uses an "impossible language," a "peculiar high-flown language" "reminiscent of the imperious language of schizophrenics, who use terrific spellbinding words to reduce the transcendent to subjective form, to give banalities the charm of novelty, or pass off commonplaces as searching wisdom. So bombastic a terminology is a symptom of weakness, ineptitude, and lack of substance." His language was "as laborious as it was arrogant" (*MDR* p. 69, transl. modif.). "Crackpot power-words," which for Jung implies "the magic words of the primitives." Speaking specifically about Paracelsus, but, as the text shows, also including "certain modern philosophers" (which doubtlessly refers to Hegel and "his [alleged] blood-brother" Heidegger), Jung reveals the general basic fantasy underlying his assessment of Hegel's language.

> Generally certain symptoms appear, among them a peculiar use of language: one wants to speak forcefully in order to impress one's opponent, so one employs a special, "bombastic" style full of neologisms which might be described as "power-words." This symptom is observable not only in the psychiatric clinic but also among certain modern philosophers, and above all, whenever anything implausible has to be insisted on in the teeth of inner resistance: the language swells up, overreaches itself, sprouts grotesque words distinguished only by their needless complexity. The word is charged with the task of achieving what cannot be done by honest means. It is the old word magic, and sometimes it can turn into a veritable obsession (*CW* 13 § 155, transl. modif.).

The two questions that arise from Jung's verdict about Hegel's language are of course whether his charge can be substantiated, i.e., whether it corresponds "to the facts," and whether Jung was entitled to pass judgment on it in the first place. Beginning with the second aspect, it is obvious that it is pretty brazen of one who had not studied Hegel to make such devastating claims. Whether Hegel's language is (1) meaningful or rather consists of nothing but "crackpot power words" and (2) whether its "complexity" is adequate and appropriate or rather "needless" becomes accessible only to him who has penetrated into his work and acquired an understanding of *what* is being said in this language. Without understanding a foreign or strange language I cannot evaluate it. That Hegel's language is "laborious" is no argument. By the same standard I could also call the language of higher mathematics and quantum physics "bombastic" and "full of neologisms" and "a symptom of weakness, ineptitude, and lack of substance": simply because I don't understand it. But the fact that I have no inkling of what higher mathematics and quantum physics are talking about does not justify me in assuming that these fields use this language merely "to impress" others and "pass off commonplaces as searching wisdom."

But for Jung his own ignorance and lack of understanding is precisely his main, if not his only, argument, a fact that gives rise to the suspicion that the designation of Hegel's language as "impossible," "bombastic," etc., is not really what it is purported to be, namely a description of a facet of Hegel, but in truth nothing but the projection of Jung's own not understanding. In the imperiousness of Hegel's alleged "*schizophrene Machtsprache*," which is allegedly used by him to forcefully insist on "something implausible" "in the teeth of inner resistance," there appears as object *before* Jung's consciousness nothing else but the vehement resistance and antipathy prevailing in Jung's own consciousness, his refusal to let himself in for what Hegel is wrestling with in his philosophical works. This is a common phenomenon. One is annoyed that one does not understand something and accuses the author of writing in an impossible language or of saying nonsense: Kafka's works must be bad literature because it cannot be understood at first sight .... When Jung believes that Hegel's work is a "revelation of the unconscious," this belief of Jung's much rather reveals Jung's unconscious rejection. But it should be clear that one must not judge something that is above and beyond one's own horizon. What Jung himself once stated, namely that "he who is truly and hopelessly little will always drag the revelation of the greater down to the level of his littleness, and will never understand that the day of judgement for his littleness has dawned" (*CW* 9i § 217),[26] applies to his own stance toward Hegel (although I do not by any means want to suggest that Jung was *in toto* truly and hopelessly little. His littleness is a specific one. It refers to a certain topic and comes out particularly in his emotional reaction to Hegel and Heidegger).

Time and again in his works and letters Jung warned of the danger of getting caught in words. "May I give you some advice?" Jung wrote to correspondents, "Don't get caught by words, only by facts" (*Letters 2*, p. 474, to Tjoa and Janssen, 27 Dec 1958). But when Jung sees in Hegel (and Heidegger) nothing but "the old word magic," "the magic words of the primitives," he himself does precisely the opposite of what he suggested. Because Jung stares at the surface of Hegel's words and does not go beyond it and penetrate to *die Sache*, the subject-matter, the substance, the reality, that is debated by the words (the equivalent of Jung's "facts"), they become "terrific spellbinding words" for Jung. This reminds me of a mongoloid person who had sort-of learned to read and loved to read in order to be like the other people in his family, but did not understand much of what he read;

[26] I became aware of this quote from Greg Mogenson's "Jungian Analysis *Post Mortem Dei*," in: *Spring* vol. 84, 2010, p. 243.

when he asked for a new book from the library of his father, he would usually respond to the first suggestions that were made with comments of the following type: "No, this book is too red," "this one is too blue." He only saw the cover.

Not having crossed the threshold to what is meant, the words, in this way seen completely from outside and without Jung's having come in touch with their *meaning*, become overly impressive, indeed monstrous for Jung. *He* is primitively spellbound by the magic of Hegel's *words*[27] because, on the one hand, he refused to advance to what the words are about, to an understanding of the *meaning* of the words, and, on the other hand, because he could not either simply let go of Hegel, letting him do his thing, saying, as it were, "this is not my cup of tea," "I do not understand a word of what Hegel is trying to say." The spellbinding experienced by Jung (even if one only through projection) and the alleged "word magic" are the result of the combination of two things: Jung's refusal of, *and* his simultaneous fixation on, Hegel, his seeing an enemy in him to be attacked and disparaged.

Hegel scholarship—and with this I finally come to the first of the two questions I said were raised by Jung's verdict, namely whether Jung's judgment about Hegel's language can be substantiated—has sufficiently proven that the opposite is true: that what Hegel says always makes very much sense, provided one penetrates to an understanding. Speaking about Hegel's *Phenomenology of Spirit*, a 20th century philosopher, Ernst Bloch, stated: "Nowhere can it be seen more precisely what great thought in its emergence is, and nowhere is its course already more completely unfolded." Again I cannot demonstrate this here (it would involve a penetrating understanding of Hegel's thought and a comparison of his thought and the language used to articulate it). But I will put two more quotations here that address specifically Hegel's language, although they of course again amount to no more than *opinions* by two authors (albeit informed authors and well-founded opinions). The first comes from a renowned scholar of German literature from Jung's own city, a professor of the university of Zürich, Emil Staiger. He wrote, speaking about Heidegger's language, in 1936 in the main Zürich

[27] The magical use of words treats them as powerful entities, not as linguistic signs.

newspaper (that I assume was also read by Jung, especially since he occasionally published in it, for example, in 1934, so that it is quite possible that he had also seen Staiger's article),

> We admire this language, ..., precisely as a scientific language.... We call it originary [*ursprünglich*], just as Hegel's language—the only other example within all of German philosophy—is original, as today no other German-speaking person at all, including all poets, speaks in an originary way.... And with such originary masterliness, this language is sober, just as everything authentic, the philosophically authentic as much as the poetically authentic is always sober."[28]

Even 30 years later, but without explicitly including Hegel, Staiger upheld his assessment of Heidegger, speaking of "this much-reviled language which still today appears to me as one of the greatest achievements in the area of philosophical prose."[29]

The second author to be quoted is a renowned Hegel-scholar, Terry Pinkard, whom I cited before. Discussing Hölderlin's early impact on Hegel he writes,

> The interests binding the two young men, though, were deep. Hölderlin has been called, rightfully, the first great "modern" European poet, and Hegel's strong interest in modern life were echoed by his friend's interest in creating a "new sensibility" that would help to usher in the modern age. Hölderlin's conviction that it was the poet's responsibility to fashion a new language appropriate to the new age – and to create a responsibility on the part of his readers to participate in fashioning this 'new sensibility' – had a profound effect on Hegel; it was to lead him to make a decisive shift near the end of his stay in Frankfurt to abandon in his philosophical writings the more easygoing prose style of his earlier years and to adopt instead his own analogue of Hölderlin's notion of demanding that his readers actively participate in fashioning this new way of assuming responsibilities to the world and to each other. It was certainly Hölderlin's most

[28] Emil Staiger, "Noch einmal Heidegger," *Neue Zürcher Zeitung*, 23 January 1936. Now in: *Antwort. Martin Heidegger im Gespräch*, ed. G. Neske and E. Kettering, Pfullingen (Neske) 1988, p. 270.

[29] Emil Staiger, "Ein Rückblick," in: *Heidegger. Perspektiven zur Deutung seines Werkes*, Köln-Berlin 1969, p. 242.

> ambiguous legacy to his old friend that he convinced him to cast his philosophy in a form that demanded of his readers to take him on *his* terms.[30]

In a note (# 79) Pinkard quotes Hegel's aphorism from his "Wastebook": "While those [thoughts (*Gedanken*)] are to be made valid *through themselves*, as concepts they ought on the contrary be made comprehensible (*begreiflich*), so the kind of writing thereby undergoes a change, [acquiring] an appearance demanding a perhaps painful effort, just as with Plato, Aristotle." And Pinkard adds, "The kind of project he envisioned for himself clearly called for him to make his views 'comprehensible,' 'graspable' in a manner that *precluded people being able to appropriate them effortlessly*. It is, interestingly, similar to the kind of strategy adopted by much later modernists such as T.S. Eliot, Ezra Pound, and James Joyce, except that Hegel certainly never intended his difficult categories to be playful, even in the slightest. For him, it was a matter of modernist *Wissenschaft* that was at stake."[31] From this it might emerge for us that Jung's problem with Hegel's and Heidegger's language is mainly his own problem with modernity.

4. The gulf between "modern" and "pre-modern." The new form

The word "modernist" in the phrase "modernist *Wissenschaft*" may remind the reader of a passage quoted above in which Hegel referred to Plato's having revised his *Republic* seven times and expressed, concerning his *Science of Logic*, the wish "that for a work which, as belonging to the *modern* world, is confronted by a deeper principle, a more difficult subject matter and a material richer in compass, leisure had been afforded to revise it seven and seventy times." What Hegel implies is that in comparison with the world of Antiquity, the modern world makes fundamentally higher demands on the

[30] Terry Pinkard, *Hegel. A Biography*, Cambridge (Cambridge University Press) 2000, p. 82.

[31] *Ibid.* note 79, p. 676. Cf. in this connection also Jung, *Letters* I, p. 425, to Wilfrid Lay, 20 April 1946: "As a matter of fact it was my intention to write in such a way that fools get scared and only true scholars and seekers can enjoy its reading." But this was not Hegel's purpose. His was: an *appropriate* language for the logical form of the content and for the modern situation.

philosopher. Philosophy has to come to terms with "a *deeper principle*," "a *more difficult subject matter*," and "a *material richer in compass*." The complexity that Jung senses in Hegel's language thus has its foundation really in the higher complexity of the modern world, to comprehend which is what Hegel saw as his responsibility as a modern philosopher.

Interestingly enough, Jung had, in his own way, however with respect to symbolism, come to a similar conclusion about the difference between the ancient and the modern worlds. Jung is acutely aware of

> the unfortunate fact that far greater demands are made on present-day man than were ever made on people living in the apostolic era: for them [the people living then] there was no difficulty at all in believing in the virgin birth of the hero and demigod, and Justin Martyr was still able to use this argument in his apology. Nor was the idea of a redeeming God-man anything unheard of, since practically all Asiatic potentates together with the Roman Emperor were of divine nature. We, by contrast, do not even have an insight into the divine right of kings any more! The miraculous tales in the gospels, which easily convinced people in those days, would be a *petra scandali* in any modern biography and would evoke the very reverse of belief. The weird and wonderful nature of the gods was a self-evident fact when myth was still alive ... "Hermes ter unus" was not an intellectual absurdity but a philosophical truth. On these foundations the dogma of the Trinity could be built up convincingly. For modern man this dogma is either an inaccessible mystery or an historical curiosity, primarily the latter. For the man of antiquity the virtue of the consecrated water or the transmutation of substances was in no sense an enormity..." (*CW* 9ii § 274, transl. modif.).

A very similar diagnosis. Far greater demands are made on present-day man than were ever made on people before! What are the greater demands? If what once was a "philosophical truth," which here only means as much as "true wisdom" (in contrast to a truth of philosophy proper, a truth in the form of thought), has for modern consciousness become an intellectual absurdity; if for the people of the apostolic era the virgin birth presented no intellectual difficulty at all: then it becomes clear that the new difficulty for the modern mind and the greater demands made on it are ones in the area of the *thinking form* of the contents of dogma and not of the contents themselves. The shift from antiquity to modernity amounts to a move from a simpler to a much more complicated, sophisticated level of consciousness. For this consciousness, what once upon a time was *immediately* convincing (simply *qua semantic content or image*, regardless of how unrealistic or miraculous it was, if only it was "archetypally" authentic) has all of a sudden the status of no more than either "an inaccessible mystery" or "an historical curiosity," so that "The best that can happen, therefore, is that the effect remains stuck in the sphere of feeling,[32] though in most cases it does not get even that far." But at any rate they "are miles away from a modern man's conscious understanding" (*CW* 9ii § 275). The same old dogmatic ideas require today a fundamentally different form in order to become intellectually comprehensible and thus able to reach the whole man. The sphere of feeling, of the emotional, of

[32] Another time Jung states apropos the revealed knowledge of the world religions: "We [i.e., we today] can no more than feel our way into it and sense something of it [*es nur noch einfühlen und anempfinden*]" (*CW* 9i § 10, transl. modif.); *einfühlen*: often translated as "empathize with" literally indeed means something like to feel one's way into it; but *anempfinden* means actually to produce in oneself, through some effort, feelings, moods, etc., that one does not have oneself, i.e., their affectation. Both verbs indicate externality and some kind of artificiality (in contrast to feelings or convictions that spontaneously appear in oneself or that, as time-honored traditional convictions or cultural feelings and values, one has, as it were, imbibed with one's mother's milk). Both verbs belong to the sphere of reflectedness, not immediacy. This is the status of our modern feeling: *einfühlen* and *anempfinden*. – But "stuck in the sphere of feeling" in addition implies something else. Feeling something, having emotional, "numinous" experiences, if it is merely "the best that (under these circumstances) can (still) happen," is on principle not enough for a symbol or dogma to be a psychic reality or soul truth: justice needs to be done not only to the "emotional pole" "by virtue of its [the symbol's or dogma's] numinosity" (the impressiveness of *what* the *image* shows, the content), but also to the "conceptual pole" of the whole personality "by virtue of its [the symbol's or dogma's] form" (*CW* 9ii § 280, transl. modif.). Obviously, it is a psychological fallacy to concentrate and put one's hope on numinous experiences and the sphere of feeling, the emotional level. This is what would precisely reduce symbols and dogma to the status of "inaccessible mysteries," in other words, it would mean to cultivate mystification (and ipso facto self-stultification). But real symbols and dogmas also aim to, indeed, require to, be intelligible, intellectually "convincing," accessible to "a modern man's conscious understanding"; they want to be what makes possible the highest intellectual illumination. They want to be "philosophical truths" (§ 274; in this phrase of Jung's, "philosophical" should not be taken in the strict sense, as referring to the thinking form, but has more generally the meaning of "intellectually acceptable wisdom"). They want to be accessible to "every farthest range of thought" (*CW* 9i § 10, literally: *jeder denkerischen Ausschöpfung zugänglich*, accessible to every possible way how the full meaning contained in them can be exhausted through conceptual thought). Jung had used the word *denkerisch* (usually translated by "intellectual") also when speaking of what has been translated as "thinking form" (*denkerische Form*).

numinous experiences does usually not pose a problem for modern man. Modern man indeed craves for, and knows full well how to produce, feelings of "highs." But what Jung realizes is that such emotional experiences are neither here nor there. It is reductive, a getting stuck, "stuck in the sphere of feeling." Experiences on this level may of course highly impress the ego, *but do not give satisfaction to the soul.* The soul derives satisfaction only if the contents are, quite soberly, what Jung here called "philosophical truths" for it.

Jung once wrote that "the gods die from time to time ..." (*CW* 9i § 22). This could mean a historical change simply on the level of contents, such as from the traditional Greek religion to the Mithras cult or the other Hellenistic mystery religions based on the import of divinities from Near Eastern or Egyptian traditions. Such a change would leave the old form intact. It would not leave the horizon of consciousness as it was constituted in the world of Antiquity. But both Hegel's "deeper principle, more difficult subject matter, material richer in compass" and Jung's "far greater demands" point to a change of a fundamentally different order, a change from the *horizon* of the world of Antiquity (including the apostolic era) to the altogether *new horizon* of modern consciousness and thus the radical change of the *thinking form* or intellectual form itself. "Everything that one has not made accessible to thought and that has therefore been deprived of a meaningful connection with consciousness, which, after all, is a further-developing one, has been lost" (*CW* 9i § 28, transl. modif.) and will get lost and be obsolete. This is the new situation.

This is why Jung realized that "... we cannot go back to the symbolism that is gone. ... Doubt has killed it, has devoured it" (*CW* 18 § 632). And in this context Jung also made it very clear that the problem is not the content, but the form. By way of example he explained: "We cannot turn the wheel backwards; we cannot go back to a symbolism that is gone. [...] I cannot go back to the Catholic Church; I cannot experience the miracle of the Mass; I know too much about it. *I know it is the truth*, but it is the truth *in a form* in which I cannot accept it any more. I cannot say 'This is the sacrifice of Christ,' and see him any more. I cannot. It is no more true for[33] me; it does

[33] I changed "true to me" into "true for me" because this avoids the misunderstanding of what Jung meant as if it wanted to imply an issue of the Mass's loyalty or faithfulness to him.

not express my psychological condition. My psychological condition wants something else. I must have a situation in which that thing becomes true once more. I need *a new form*" (*CW* 18 § 632, my italics). "One cannot turn the clock back and force oneself to believe 'what one knows is not true'" (*CW* 11 § 293).

But what do we find when we examine Jung's response to his own insight that he needs a new *form*? Did he accept the challenge of the level of form, accept the challenge of the modern world, did he let himself in for the "greater demands" that the modern world made on us? Was the solution that he offered one in the mode of *denkerische Form*? The answer has to be a straightforward "No."

To be sure, Jung clearly saw and accepted the modern psychic reality that "God is dead." He saw and repeatedly expressed the modern predicament, more than that, he truly wrestled with it ("I asked myself time and again why there are no men in our epoch who could see at least what I was wrestling with. ... I see the suffering of mankind in the individual's predicament and vice versa" [*Letters 2*, to Herbert Read, 2 September 1960, pp. 586, 589]). But he saw it precisely only as a predicament, a pathological condition, as "our benighted present" (Letters 2, p. 396, to Trinick, 15 Oct. 1957). His basic stance was an anti-Enlightenment one, as much as he forced himself to keep the bust of Voltaire (and thus a prototypical image of the Enlightenment period) in front of himself on his desk. "It is the fateful misfortune of medical psychotherapy to have originated in an age of enlightenment, when the old cultural possessions became inaccessible through [man's] own fault [*durch Selbstverschulden*] ...." (*CW* 10 § 370, transl. modif.). Here it is to be noted, in order to bring out the anti-Enlightenment affect contained in it, that with the word *Selbstverschulden* Jung polemically alludes to, and turns into the opposite, Kant's well-known definition of the Enlightenment as "man's emergence from his self-imposed [or: self-incurred, *selbstverschuldet*] immaturity ...." Precisely that which for Kant was the *emergence from* a wrong state due to man's own fault, Jung now presents as the very sin [*Schuld* = guilt].

But all this shows and refers only to Jung's inner attitude. Much more weighty in our context is the objective quality of his answer to the modern predicament. Here we see that Jung did precisely not try to work on the level of form. The one of his two major moves in this area was clearly not one to a "new form" at all. By insisting on "*dreaming* the *myth* onwards" he showed that he precisely held onto the old *form* characteristic of the primitive and Ancient, in part also medieval and early-modern, worlds, namely the form of contents, images, narratives in their immediacy. And his major specific move concerning the myth dreamed onwards was the one from the Christian Trinity to quaternity, a move from Three to Four. Clearly, this is a move on the level of the content of "myth" and not on the level of form. Whether you have a strict monotheism as in Islam or a Trinitarian monotheism as in Christianity or a quaternity that includes within the Trinity, as a Fourth, the reality of evil or Mary as the Mother of God, makes no difference as far as the thinking form is concerned. They all three are different alternatives on one and the same logical level (the semantic level), and they share the same basic thinking form of traditional religious thinking, namely pictorial thinking. Instead of making a vertical move from the previous to the new level reached by "consciousness, which, after all, is a further-developing one," Jung tried to solve the modern problem on the old level and in the old mythic, imaginal form by adding on an annex. This is much the same as was in Hellenistic times, for example, the expansion of the Greek and Roman pantheon by the addition of the Egyptian goddess Isis.

The second major move of Jung's was the shift of the *locus* of truth away from the public communal knowledge to the privacy of the individual's immediate inner experience (*Urerfahrung*) and at the same time the stuffing of truth away from the status of illumined transparency into that logical status of self-enclosedness and occludedness ("facts of nature") that he called "the unconscious." Again, this is not a move from content to form but a shift *of* semantic content (whatever content) to a new location or department.

So Jung contradicts himself. His statement "I need a new form" had no consequences. Jung did not follow it up. What he instead really, with the whole passion of his heart, tried to bring about *and offer as a solution for the predicament of modern man* was, as we have seen, partly another *story*, another *myth*, and partly subjective (inner) experience. But obviously, Jung's quaternity is in no way more intellectually "convincing," more accessible to "a modern man's conscious understanding" than is, for example, the Trinity or the virgin birth. If Jung could not go back to the Catholic Church, could not experience the miracle of the Mass, because doubt has killed it and he knows too much, it is not to be understood why it should be any easier for him (or anybody) to embrace and experience the dogma of the *Assumptio Mariae* and the thesis of the Quaternity. Are they all of a sudden exempt from the "doubt that has killed it" and from Jung's knowing too much about them? The obsolescence that Jung rightly diagnosed is certainly not to be healed or overcome by staying on the image, myth, dogma, or content level and simply inserting an additional figure (Mary or the devil) into the Christian dogma or into the imagination of the Christian Godhead, nor by transporting what dogma said about God into the personal-psychological realm, into the inner of man as "the Self" and the "God-image in the soul" to be privately experienced in one's inner. It is a fundamental mistake to think that a new *archetypal structure* or pattern, a new image, on the one hand, or immediate experience of one's inner, on the other hand, could solve the modern predicament that Jung saw as his task to address himself to. Why? Because (a) "As to what is 'authentic,' that seems to be decided by the spirit of the age," as Jung himself had realized, and our age happens, as Jung also realized, to be the age of the "doubt that has killed it," and because (b) of the particular character of that "doubt" that we are here concerned with. What sort of doubt is it?

5. "Doubt" as the intrinsic form of truth in modernity

First of all, the doubt that Jung spoke about and had keenly become aware of is not a psychic event or condition in him as individual, the personal experience of his feeling attacked by gnawing doubts about something. Jung did not say: *we* doubt. He said that doubt has (objectively) *killed* the rituals and dogmas. If they have been "killed" then God IS dead, the contents of religion ARE obsolete. *They* have lost their validity. Not: *we* are not pious enough.

The doubt Jung spoke about is not either a methodical-epistemological doubt as in Socrates or Descartes, which, at least in Descartes' case, served the purpose of arriving at a *fundamentum inconcussum*. Nor is it Christian doubt in the sense of *vexationes* or *tentationes*, which accompany faith and are a tribulation through which faith has to prove itself. It is also not the explicit subjective mental act in individuals, such as Enlightenment philosophers, of discrediting dogmas, nor the general attitude of being skeptical, merely having a radically critical consciousness. Doubt here does not refer to scepticism, uncertainty, ambivalence. And secondly, *what* is "doubted" is not this or that particular content. No, it is "doubt" in a very different sense: *objective* "doubt," "doubt" as the underlying objective world-character of modernity as such. Jung's statement expresses the awareness of the fact that modernity as such is characterized by the fundamental intrusion of critical *thought* into the very domain of archetypal images and religious faith themselves, into what alchemically speaking is the prime matter itself, an intrusion that is *fundamental* because it is precisely not an *external* reflection *by* people *about* beliefs (as the object doubted). It is not a human doing or thinking, nor a human attitude. Rather, this "doubt" is the appearance of the "thinking form" as the now prevailing form of consciousness as such.[34] Thus it is now inherent in the very form of the contents of consciousness themselves as their own logical status (and inevitably so), much like the products of industrial production themselves have their "fetish character of commodities" (Marx) as their own objective character in themselves. It is, as it were, the contents' own internal "discrediting" themselves, nay, their now always already having "discredited" themselves, their coming as "discredited."

This is why Jung had to say: "I know it is the truth, but it is the truth in a form in which I cannot accept it any more. It is no more true for me." *The soul truths themselves* (regardless of which truths), the images and symbols, have on principle and once and for all lost their previously prevailing innocent and unquestionable convincingness and certitude. *Within themselves* they undermine, alchemically decompose themselves: become logically negative. Within themselves they present themselves as *always already* negated. They come as "killed by doubt," i.e., in the status of absolute negativity. It had not been Jung's doubting, his own skeptical reflections about the Catholic Mass, that had made it impossible for him to go back to it. "Doubt" or "the thinking form" is, in the modern soul condition, inherent in the very phenomenology of the psychic phenomena themselves.

[34] But of course, because it is only the first immediacy of this appearance, it occurs in the negative way of "doubt." This particular doubt, however, rather than implying uncertainty and vacillation, is a firm (negative!) *knowing* that what it refers to is no longer true ("One cannot ... force oneself to believe 'what one knows is not true,'" Jung had said).

The very derogative-sounding word "doubt" for the intrinsic form of truth in modernity thus turns out to mean in truth no more than that the traditional soul truths are no longer a *present reality* (this is expressed in: "it is no more true for me"), but exist only in *mnemosyne* for us, only as a historical presence (the *presence* of the pastness of the past: "I know it is the truth").

Whereas before, the thinking form belonged only to the side of the subject, was only the form of how subjective consciousness thinks *about* the object, now, with the emergence of the "doubt" that Jung identified, the thinking form has come fully home to itself so that it also appears in and determines the object itself, the matter, the truths, as their own intrinsic form or status. Before, the thinking form existed only in, and as the character of, a special compartment of cultural activities: the field of philosophy. Now it is the general objective and a priori character of experience as such, of any content that the mind can turn to. The soul truths themselves have thereby lost their logical status as *revelations*, a status that they had for psychologically naive, pre-modern consciousness. Revelations *come to* consciousness as indubitable truths.

That "doubt" that Jung spoke about and had keenly become aware of did therefore, according to what we just learned about it, not merely kill this or that particular idea of God or this or that dogma or symbol, for example, the Trinitarian notion of God, or the idea of the virgin birth, or the "miracle of the Mass." No, it "killed" (made psychologically impossible, turned, as Jung put it, into "intellectual absurdity") the very *form* of religion as such, the *logic* of the idea of gods or the Self, the innocent belief in "the imaginal." It "killed" the *capacity* of the form of image or content and the form of personal experience to express "the psychological condition" of modern man and to give, as "philosophical truths" (i.e., revelations, indubitable insights), satisfaction to the soul. The *logic* or *syntactical form* as such of religion, of such a thing as God or gods, of image, myth, or symbol, has become obsolete. Jung's "doubt has killed it" means that the general foundation has objectively been pulled out from under such a thing as religious experience and articles of faith (*whatever* they may be) as well as from under an *imagistic* eachness. Consciousness has moved to a new foundation. And this fundamental objective "doubt" (in contrast to our contingent personal doubting in the sense of an external reflection) *is* the new foundation.

Hillman's innocent sense of imagistic eachness[35] is the result of a dissociation. The modern phenomenon's own internal "doubt," "self-negation," or "thinking form" is split off and exiled, so that only the abstract semantics and "face" of the phenomenon is left. The exiled negation then returns as the repressed outside of the phenomena themselves in a likewise abstract experience of the modern world at large, namely of modernity as a Fallen, soulless world, as totally literal, rationalistic, and Saturnian. This cleansing the phenomena of their inherent syntax, this abstraction from their own innate modernity, is what makes the innocent imagistic eachness of phenomena possible. Hillman thinks that what I (W.G.) do is to literalize time and history, whereas he (allegedly) follows Plotinus for whom "time is in the soul (it is a psychological phenomenon)." But he is unable to see that this view (whether Plotinian or not) is precisely my position. Yes, indeed, the soul is itself time, is historical. Historical time is inherent in phenomena, in the actual images, intrinsic to their particular phenomenology. Psychic phenomena are inevitably the expression or articulation of *their* time, just as we all, together with our ways of thinking, are inescapably children of our time. Time, and thus also the possible obsolescence or negatedness of images, is not external to the phenomena.

For Hillman, however, phenomena obviously have their time outside of themselves—or no time at all. He seems to think that it is our choice to place phenomena in a historical time-frame, or not. But modern phenomena themselves within themselves distinguish themselves from their pre-modern namesakes. Time is not an external agent or factor that inflicts obsolescence on the phenomena (regardless of whether one thinks that this agent is a literalized historical time or we who—unnecessarily—choose to lock the phenomena into a time scheme). Time is the soul's self-movement in its phenomenology. And conversely, the phenomena's eachness (in the imagistic sense) resides only in their methodically produced timelessness, their deliberate insulation, or being logically cleansed from, their own time.

---

[35] I mention only his "Cosmology For Soul. From Universe to Cosmos," in: *Sphinx 2*, 1989, pp. 17–33, and his "Image-Sense," in: *Spring 1979*, pp. 130–143.

These reflections allow us to give yet another description to "the doubt-that-has-killed-it." It is also the objective manifestation of the soul's dawning awareness of itself as being Time. The character of soul as time, as historical movement, and as the *process* of its self-production, self-representation has come home to the soul itself; it has been inwardized and integrated into its form of manifestation. Before, the soul had of course also been time, but it had not been conscious of it, had not explicitly been what it implicitly always is. It had much rather presented itself in "ontological" terms, as (as if it were) eternal substantial beings (gods, demons, spirits, etc.) or truths.

What we are concerned with when we comprehend modern "objective" doubt as the new foundation is thus the fundamental character of the mode of being-in-the-world of modern man *as "born man,"* man whose knowing is all of a sudden *released* from the shelter of metaphysics in the sense of a *prima philosophia*, which was what before had guaranteed the soulfulness or absolute negativity even of the positively held, substantiated beliefs and truths as well as of the real things and events in the world. As long as metaphysics prevailed, man could, with an easy mind, concentrate on the semantic contents and trust to find his meaning of existence in them, because the general Ground that was provided by metaphysics, so to speak automatically and unspokenly, bestowed the logical status of absolute negativity upon them. This is what had turned them into "philosophical truths" for the soul and enabled them to give satisfaction to the soul. The semantic contents could simply speak for themselves, because *in* their speaking they were, under the conditions of a *prima philosophia*, immediately expressive of the metaphysical ground.

Without a *prima philosophia* the need arises for man to advance to an awareness of the *form of form* and to *explicitly himself produce* this negativity in the style of his apperception. For without a *prima philosophia* modern man can, to be sure, while staying on the level of semantic contents, gain positive (positivistic) knowledge about the facts accumulated by the sciences. But these facts, this factual knowledge about the world, cannot *speak* for themselves, cannot by themselves provide a meaning or soul depth. They are inevitably only positivities. Meaning can now, on the semantic level, only be secondarily *imposed* on the world in the form of ideologies, such as those of "scientific-technical progress," "preserving the creation," "eco-psychology," "healing our planet," "worldholism," if they are belief systems, *or* in the form of consumer goods, if they are emotional experiences, and in both cases as simulation. "Doubt" in this radical sense is the clear sense of a fundamental loss of all meaning as an objective existence on the content level, of truth as such in a semantic sense—and thus also the invitation to an initiation into "a new form," the "thinking form," the form of form, as that which alone could re-produce (or rather *be*) the form of logical negativity (and thus soul) for the modern world. For it is clear that the form of form is in itself logically absolute-negative because it has no content.

Logical negativity entails the awareness of the irrevocable subjectivity of the objective soul. Not a substance that thinks, but objectively ongoing thinking. The performative nature of the soul.

Biographically, as a youth and young man, Jung had on the existential level experienced a living example of this doubt in his own father (the way, at least, how he had perceived him). Jung realized "that my poor father ... was consumed by inward doubts. He was taking refuge from himself and therefore insisted on blind faith" (*MDR* p. 73). Being a protestant minister, his father, when his faith was undermined by such *fundamental* doubt, naturally found himself in a terrible fix. This inner conflict made him terribly irritable and moody, which, because of his frequent fits of temper, ruined the atmosphere in Jung's parental home, which in turn must have made a deep impression on Carl Gustav concerning the effective power and reality of this doubt. Jung's *immediate experience* in his own family had thus been the encounter with doubt as the logical status of modernity. Of course, in his father this all-pervasive logical character of modernity as such still appeared only in its first immediacy as a psychic state, on a merely existential personal level, his father's gnawing doubts in the plural. But this experience is nevertheless the prefiguration of Jung's own later diagnosis that "doubt has killed it"—killed it not merely subjectively, but objectively: "doubt" as the truth of his own psychological condition as well as of the collective condition of all of us: "*We* cannot go back ...." "... 'what one *knows is* not true.'"

How did Jung position himself vis-à-vis his father's doubt, then and later, i.e., at the time of writing his chapters on these years of his life in *MDR*? I begin with a general comment about how Jung saw the relation between his own life task and his parents. Commenting on a dream from much later years, he says that he had the feeling that in this dream his parents had been burdened with a problem that "in fact was really my task." "Something had remained unfinished and was still with my parents." It was "reserved for the future" (*MDR* p. 214).[36] Elsewhere we hear: "Indeed I have often thought: if only I could have opened my father's eyes! But he died before I had caught the fish whose liver contains the wonderworking medicine" (*Letters 1*, p. 194, to Erika Schlegel, 31 July 1935). Jung's theological reflections in late years were also explicitly conceived as serving the purpose of resolving the problem left unfinished by his father. But already as a young man Jung had wanted to redeem his father from his religious predicament.

However, rather than seeing the doubt as the symptom that *brings* the cure[37] and thus rather than recognizing in this doubt the *lapis in via ejectus* as the real thing to be redeemed, Jung fell into the personalistic trap by wanting to redeem (1) his *father* and (2) *from* his doubt. Confinement in the private chest of his father is the wrong place, the form of psychic suffering (personal symptom) the wrong state for this doubt. The mercurial spirit stirring in this suffering wants to be released from the bottle, freed from its imprisonment in the physicality of material existence; the doubt as a mere symptom needs to be released into its truth, the *form* of truth. In the experience and his memory of his father's suffering from the "Amfortas wound" (*MDR* p. 215) of this doubt, fate had given Jung ample opportunity to absorb and integrate "doubt" into his consciousness as its new structure. His historical locus had presented the psychologist in him with his *sujet*, with his psychological task, with his prime matter to be alchemically worked: to be distilled, sublimated, that is to say, transformed from a particular psychic condition into a universal psychological truth, from a personalistically, literalistically misunderstood existential suffering into an eye-opening insight into the prevailing logical status of modernity. The experience of his father's doubts had so to speak been a personal invitation to Jung to become initiated into

[36] See Chapter One above.

[37] "We do not cure it [the neurosis]—it cures us. ... what the neurotic flings away as absolutely worthless contains the true gold we should never have found elsewhere" (*CW* 10 § 361).

the soul of modernity,[38] at the same time also an invitation to consciousness to become initiated into the status of psychological absolute negativity. What is this doubt if not the first immediacy and thus the still concretized, congealed, and literalized appearance of the form of absolute negativity? In his early witnessing this suffering from doubt, fate had placed into Jung's lap the egg that needed to be hatched by him. Here lay Jung's *Hic Rhodus, hic salta.*

But instead of "leaping," instead of honoring the symptom as the first immediacy of the "new personality" that wants to emerge and as *the new form of soul* (as Jung would normally say about psychopathology[39]), he had disparaged it. He had hoped to be able to talk his father out of his doubts and instead to antidotally force his own panacea of an immediate experience of God on him: a clear case of once again throwing the lapis away *in viam* and *in stercus* (dung), the lapis which, when it appears in the form of doubt, is of course, as always, *exilis* (uncomely) and *vilissimus* (most contemptuous). It was Jung himself who "made approximately the same mistake as did the old school of medicine when it attacked the fever in the belief that this was the noxious agent" (*CW* 10 § 369). When he says that "I could not understand that he [his father] did not seize every opportunity offering itself to come pugnaciously to terms with his situation" (*MDR* p. 92, transl. modif.), we see that Jung approached the problem of his father's doubts in terms of ego willing[40] and not in an alchemical style, not with a fantasy of

[38] Initiated also, we might add, into becoming able to embrace the spirit of Hegel's "this thoroughgoing scepticism."

[39] "In reality neurosis [i.e., in our case: doubt] contains the patient's soul..." (*CW* 10 § 355, transl. modif.). "Doubt" is the new logically negative form of soul.

[40] Jung criticized that his father "insisted on blind faith, which he had to win by struggle and wished to force to come with contorted efforts. Therefore he could not receive it as a grace" (*MDR* p. 73, transl. modif.). But at the same time he blamed him for not pugnaciously trying to come to terms with his situation. That in the modern situation there would and could still be this grace is a "metaphysical" prejudgment and the expression of Jung's egoic wish or demand. For were the years of the 19th century (and are our years) still truly "years of grace" (the way one was *justified* during the Middle Ages and early-modern times to say, e.g., "in the year of grace 1250"), so that the expectation of grace would have been authenticated? Furthermore, obviously the grace Jung had in mind could only come about through pugnacious struggle, which betrays that it is the opposite of itself. Jung also does not realize that what he felt was his own experience of "grace" (through the Basel cathedral incident) was the result of his contorted efforts, his twisted mental manipulations, and by no means what one normally would understand by "an experience of grace." Jung's father may have been too honest to exchange, with respect

fermenting corruption, distillation, and releasement into its truth, a releasement which would be tantamount to its integration into the form of consciousness. Instead of embracing his father's suffering, he rejected it as false, thereby betraying him (and of course himself, too, his own experience of the power and reality of this doubt). Jung's rejection of Hegel is really a repetition of his rejection of the truth inherent of his own experience of his father's doubts. Throughout his life the commitment to the will remained Jung's style of thinking (at least in this area of faith and God), expressing itself most powerfully in his late work, *Answer to Job*.

To sum up this discussion about his father's doubts we can say that Jung knew quite well, and from continued deeply painful personal experience, about the "doubt" that has killed the old form of the soul's truths. But on the whole he swept this his own knowledge aside, pretending that what came from "the unconscious" were still *revelations*, immediate truths, semantic truths.[41] And accordingly Jung also wrote throughout his life in what Terry Pinkard in his discussion of Hegel's youthful language had called "a more easygoing prose style," in a style that was immediately and effortlessly accessible to ordinary conventional consciousness. Due to his exclusive emphasis on "immediate experience" (we will get to this topic later), Jung did not demand of his readers *to actively participate in producing a new sensibility, in a new way of assuming responsibilities to the world and to each other.* All that was maybe strange and new for a new reader coming to his work was the particular ideas. The form of prose in Jung's writings is, however, that of the *conventional* everyday language, and the form of thought likewise that of the ordinary level of consciousness, the consciousness of "the man on the street." Jung did not waste any

to his conflict between the demands of his faith and the reality of his doubts, the level of truth for the level of pugnacious willing. In the sphere of these topics Jung's own thinking, however, remains firmly held fast within the category of willing and power and is he incapable of allowing (or unwilling to allow) the truth of his historical locus to show itself of its own accord the way it happens to need to show itself. Even God himself is, in typically 19th century manner (Schopenhauer, Nietzsche, physics, heavy industry), conceived by Jung in strictly egoic power terms, as an overwhelming, terrible will (*der Gotteswille*).

[41] Cf., for example: "Freud would say [to a particular delusional idea of an insane patient]: 'An incestuous wish-fantasy,' because he would like to save the poor patient from a bit of obnoxious nonsense. But I would say to the patient: 'What a pity you are too stupid to understand this *revelation* properly.'" (*Letters 1*, p. 266, to Anonymous, 22 March 1939. My emphasis.)

thought on the form of consciousness, but only on contents and on their being based on personal experience.

Interestingly enough, in contrast to his railing against Hegel's "impossible" language, Jung did not really have any objection to the difficulty and darkness of the writings of the alchemists, because *their* impossible mode of expression was not one of language or thinking style (which were straightforward), but merely one of confusing, enigmatic, paradoxical *ideas* and statements. For years Jung undertook the labor of deciphering what the meaning of their cryptic expressions was, in other words, the labor of learning their language, but he shunned the "labor of the concept" and the labor of learning Hegel's language. To express *ignotum per ignotius* was right down Jung's alley: because in this fashion one stayed stuck (of course this time not in the sphere of feeling, but) in the sphere of what he called (and at other times actually criticized as) intellectually "inaccessible mysteries." And this, although Jung knew full well that the form of inaccessible mystery was no solution, but rather an additional problem: "Moreover I seriously wonder whether it is not much more dangerous for the Christian symbols to be made inaccessible to conceptual thought and to be banished to a sphere of unreachable unintelligibility. ... man has the gift of thought that can apply itself to the highest things" (*CW* 11 § 170, transl. modif.). But he nevertheless evaded the necessity, *his own* necessity, of addressing the predicament of modern man *on the level of* the thinking or intellectual form and in a corresponding linguistic form of expression. By unpuzzling the language of the alchemists, one could stay with the contents of consciousness, whereas undergoing the effort of understanding Hegel through the labor of the concept would have meant an education and working-through of consciousness itself.

His clear insight concerning the "doubt-that-has-killed-it" would actually have demanded of Jung that his thought advance to the notion (and project) of something like Hegel's "this thoroughgoing scepticism (*dieser sich selbst vollbringende Skeptizismus*)." Hegel had, as it were, *embraced* the doubt (*Zweifel*), had gone all the way through with it by deepening it into *Verzweiflung*, despair, thus integrating the experienced doubt into the very form of his thinking. Jung had refused to embrace this doubt and on the whole even simply ignored it. His whole project was the opposite; it was to establish a bulwark against it through his two major moves already mentioned: by "*dreaming* the *myth* onwards," i.e., providing a new content, a new "theology," and secondly, more generally, by insisting on a new "primordial experience" (*Urerfahrung*, new *revelations* from "the unconscious") on the part of each individual and thus a new unquestionable conviction,[42] a new innocence or naiveté. He tried to counteract the inescapable scepticism, treating it like a mistake, a faulty development, the modern neurosis, in other words, an enemy to be fought. In absolute contrast to Hegel and, by the way, Hölderlin, he could not appreciate it as the special legitimate characteristic of modernity, modernity's own main *merit, talent, achievement, and its particular contribution* to the history of the soul. And he did not go all the way through with it. Instead Jung believed he could *take a shortcut* to an alleged immediacy, innocence, and unbroken naturalism of felt experience. Today's psychological experience was, in his scheme, not supposed to be one that always already and within itself has paid tribute to the logic of "doubt" and to modernity. "Doubt" and modernity at large were not allowed in as intrinsic and inalienable and honored ingredients of all modern experience. The reality of the soul was conceived by Jung in such a way that it on principle excluded modernity. And this is what usually in Jungianism is meant deep down when one praises Jung for his "return to soul." This fundamental anti-modernism is inherent in the stance of all varieties of "anima-only" psychology.

6. The resuscitation of the "soul" as the betrayal of the soul

Now it is certainly true that not everybody needs to let himself in for the form of thought, for the form of form, and for the form of

[42] "God is an immediate experience of a very primordial nature, one of the most natural products of our mental life, as the birds sing, as the wind whistles, like the thunder of the surf. ... You can just be glad to have such a conviction, like a man who is in a happy frame of mind, even if nobody else, not even himself, knows why, but certainly nobody could prove to him that he is unhappy or that his feeling happy is an illusion" (*Letters 2*, p. 252 f., to Snowdon, 7 May 1955). "[T]he certitude of inner experience" (*Letters 2*, p. 378, to Bernhard Lang, June 1957). "... the essential experience, that is to say the *primordial* religious experience. This alone forms the true and unshakable foundation of his inner life of belief" (*Letters 2*, p. 486, to Tanner, 12 February 1959). "The older I grow ... the more I take recourse to the simplicity of immediate experience so as not to lose contact with the essentials, namely the dominants which rule human existence throughout the milleniums" (*ibid.*, p. 580, to Earl of Sandwich, 10 August 1960).

absolute negativity, just as it cannot be demanded of everybody to understand higher mathematics and modern physics. There are enough respectable professions and walks of life in which one can do nicely without all this.

As long as Jung would have contented himself with being an academic experimental psychologist who did such things as word-association studies, intelligence testing, research on psychological types or learning theory, in other words, positivistic research about the "behavior" of the human animal; or, a second option, as long as he would have been satisfied with being a scholar of comparative mythology and symbolism; as long, furthermore, as the *personalistic* idea of practical psychotherapy would have been able to fulfill his demands, I mean psychotherapy the way it was, for example, conceived by Freud or Adler, as a project that has its true horizon in the consulting room, so long Jung could have done quite well without ever entering the sphere of thought. However, the moment that he instead conceived of a psychology that wants to apply itself to the *Seelenproblem des modernen Menschen* (translated as: "The Spiritual Problem of Modern Man," title of a paper contained in *CW* 10[43]) and to the objective psyche, the moment that he says, "I see the suffering of mankind in the individual's predicament and vice versa"[44]: at that very moment the fact became *a betrayal of his self-set task* that he radically refused to let himself in for the problem of form and that he immunized the stuff of psychological experience against the intrusion of modernity's native principle and foundation, the thinking form.[45] He performed this

[43] But I use the title phrase of this article apart from the article itself, as an apt overall formulation for what Jung had set for himself as a life-task as a psychologist to address himself to. *Seelenproblem* is probably best translated as the "predicament of the soul," of [modern man's] soul. Both "psychological problem" and "spiritual problem" are too specific, the one making one think in terms of people's psyche, the other in terms of what we now understand when we hear "spirituality." *Seelenproblem* certainly involves the spiritual or religious dimension, but has nothing to do with our spirituality in the New-Age sense and the spirituality section in bookstores. It refers to the problem of the *objective* soul in which we have our place, i.e., to the depth dimension of modern human being-in-the-world as such.

[44] *Letters 2*, p. 589, to Herbert Read, 2 September 1960.

[45] The *denkerische Form* is of course much older than modernity. It dates back to Antiquity. However, from Antiquity through the early-modern period of classical metaphysics the thinking form was only a subjective mode of apperception and tackling the *essential* questions. It had been part of an external reflection. What is special about modernity, with the "doubt-that-has-killed-it," is that the thinking form has become objective. It is the intrinsic objective character of the modern world as such, of the

immunization in actual deed by, for example, developing the theory of timeless, never-ageing archetypes, a theoretical construct which was later by other Jungians transformed into the likewise immunized or immunizing theory of "the imaginal."

The betrayal mentioned can be described by means of the title phrase just cited. Jung tried, so we could say, to heal the *Seelenproblem des modernen Menschen* by restoring the soul to him. *Modern Man in Search of a Soul*! "Jung's resuscitation of images," Stanton Marlan said (and might in all likelihood have found Jung's full approval for his view), "was a return to soul and began a reversal of the dominant historical process that had depotentiated images and reduced soul to rational intellectual spirit."[46] In other words, it was, so to speak, the project of the Restoration of the psychological *Ancien Régime* after the event of the psychological French Revolution. Jung focused and concentrated on the soul, on the archetypal images, on the religious conceptions: on the semantic, the content level. But this is precisely how he missed his own self-set task.[47] Because the real problem to be addressed does not at all lie in the first element of Jung's essay title (the *Seelenproblem des modernen Menschen*), but in the second element, in "modern man" (the *Seelenproblem des modernen Menschen*), or to be more precise: in the *modernity* of modern man, the modern *form* of consciousness or being-in-the-world. And the specific character of modernity is of course nothing else but the fact that "doubt has killed it." *This*, the fundamental "doubt"-status of the modern situation, is the psychological topic, and precisely *as such* it is also the real

truths themselves that need to be apperceived and attended to. As I pointed out above: within themselves the truths undermine themselves as innocent truths to be believed. Within themselves they demand to be *thought*. The "doubt" referred to by Jung is the negative reverse side of what from its positive other side is the form of thought having become objective, immanent to the *stuff* of essential experience. By saying that Jung betrayed his task and immunized the stuff of psychological experience against the thinking form I therefore do by no means want to indicate that his task would have been to *philosophize* in external reflection about our soul predicament. His task would have been to meet the *Seelenproblem* on its own level, that of "doubt" or *denkerische Form.*

[46] Stanton Marlan, "From the Black Sun to the Philosopher's Stone," in: *Spring 74 (Alchemy). A Journal of Archetype and Culture*, Spring 2006, pp. 1–30, here p. 9.

[47] The fact that Jung *after* having gained clear insight into the "doubt that has killed it" and the necessity of a new form nevertheless insisted on systematically staying on the semantic level could be interpreted with a psychological, not-religious version of the Biblical idea of the sin against the Spirit (Matth. 12: 31f., "the blasphemy against the Holy Ghost"). The most blatant example of this "sin against the Spirit" is Jung's handling as a boy his Basel cathedral experience, which is an obvious refusal of his initiation. See Chapters Two and Three of Vol. 5 of my *Collected English Papers*.

Seelenproblem des modernen Menschen, the real issue that needed *therapeia*: devoted attention and cultivating. But this was more or less totally avoided, indeed even systematically excluded from the conception of Jungian psychology.

What good is it for a blind man to be given the most colorful presents, and what good to *modern* man if soul is returned to him and images are resuscitated? It is absolutely pointless. Jung himself had in principle provided the right answer to this question (without, however, drawing the right consequences from it for himself). "Like greedy children we stretch out our hands and think that, if only we could grasp it, we would possess it too. But what we possess is no longer valid, and our hands grow weary from the grasping, for riches lie everywhere, as far as the eye can reach" (*CW* 9i § 31). In the same essay Jung said, "Heaven and hell are the fates meted out to the soul and not to civil man, who in his nakedness and dullness would have no idea of what to do with himself in a heavenly Jerusalem" (§ 56, transl. modif.). We could replace "civil man" by "modern man" and add to the one example given by Jung ("heavenly Jerusalem") the words "as well as all other mythic or archetypal places and ideas and numinous experiences." Despite the greedy consumption of mythic images and so-called numinous feelings so popular among numerous modern individuals, the latter in fact have *psychologically*, in their essential nakedness and dullness, no inkling of what to do *with themselves* in the sphere of myth, archetypal images, and numinous experiences, and of what to do *with those numinous experiences* and images themselves, that is to say, of how to authentically *integrate* them into modern consciousness and modern life. For to all these archetypal contents and numinous emotions, indeed, to the "return to soul" itself, there applies what Jung had stated about the Catholic Mass: "It is no more true for me; it does not express my psychological condition. My psychological condition wants something else." But "my psychological condition" is precisely the modern condition. So what good are all the mythic images and numinous experiences, what good is it "to return to soul," if they are no longer true for us, do no longer express our psychological condition and if they are ipso facto no longer capable of giving satisfaction to the soul? And conversely, what good are they if they meet in us with our "nakedness and dullness," our (let me say) "metaphysical" blindness?

This nakedness, dullness, blindness are not to be understood as personal shortcomings. They are merely the reflection in man of the objective *modern* condition of being-in-the-world, namely that it is a living under the condition of that "doubt that has killed it," or, as we could also say, the condition of *born man.*

Despite his insight, Jung ultimately and on the whole merely accommodated the craving of the greedy children (also his own craving as God-greedy or revelation-greedy child), instead of attending to modern man's psychological condition, to the inherent "blindness and dullness." His main work was precisely to spread out for us and make palatable still more and more of the archetypal riches that lie everywhere: myth mongering ("archetypal images") and "drug" dealing ("numinous experiences"), thereby ultimately making more unconscious, *cultivating* unconsciousness. The point is that it is not the soul that in our time is repressed, nor the imaginal or the image, let alone the emotions or "the body." Rather, what is repressed is *our special "psychological condition"* as modern persons, the particular distinction and gift of modernity itself, the *form and level of form*, whose first immediacy is the experience of the "doubt that has killed it." This is denounced as abstract intellectualism and rationalism, on the one hand, and as nihilism, on the other hand.

We have contents, images, archetypal ideas, emotions galore. No lack of all that. What is lacking is a condition which grants the possibility that a content (whatever content) is true for us, in fact expresses our psychological condition, has the "new form" in which it truly expresses our psychological condition.[48] By putting all his hope

[48] Jung was rightly unhappy about the modern use of drugs like LSD to induce visionary experiences, stressing that "you *merely fall into* such experiences without being able to *integrate* them. The result is a sort of theosophy, but it is not *a moral and mental acquisition.* It is the eternally *primitive* man having experience of his ghost-land, but it is not an *achievement of your cultural development.* ... It is to my mind a helpful method to a *barbarous* Peyotee, but a *regrettable regression* for a *cultivated* individual, a dangerously simple 'Ersatz' and substitute for a true religion" (*Letters 2*, p.382 f., my italics). How true! But also how close a parallel of the logic at work in these comments to that of my argument above! The semantic content of experiences is not enough, it may even lead to regression. We do not need more felt experience, more imaginal input, more Ersatz. What counts is the form, the cultural level (and the advancement of this level) of consciousness. Jung did, however, not take his own medicine when it was a question of his own psychological answer to the soul predicament of modern man. The mere source of experiences (drug-induced visions versus spontaneous visions or dreams, different though they are) should not make a *decisive* difference. Because in both cases alike it is "the eternally primitive

on new *Urerfahrung* and on the immediacy of it, it is precisely Jung himself who thinks that all we needed was to "grasp it" and that then "we would also possess it too." But, as he had himself seen, what we possess is—we might add: ipso facto—no longer valid. And this applies, contrary to Jung, precisely also to his solution: immediate individual experience. What is direct experience ("as the birds sing, as the wind whistles") other than this crude, uneducated, formless grasping, this mindless, ultimately positivistic wish to *possess*? "I need a new *form*," Jung had said, but this need is totally incompatible with *Urerfahrung*. The need of a new form is the need of an *education* of consciousness. On the whole, his psychology gives a damn about the psychological issue of form and opts for the regressive (and illusionary) restoration of the (long-lost) *unio naturalis* ("the most natural products of our mental life," of which, as we know, he himself had had to admit that doubt has killed them). He prefers the crude and the raw and the direct relation of consciousness to it. The new form would involve *absolute negativity*. No grasping, no possession, no immediacy. Our psychological condition is not the pre-modern one anymore for which (semantic) soul truths a priori came as ones being in the status of absolute logical negativity. For born man the soul has come home to itself. It can no longer be true in the external form of semantic contents, of ideas beheld or experienced. Owing to an alchemical process of distillation and evaporation in the history of the soul, truth has recursively progressed to the level of the syntactical, of logical form.

The insistence upon and devotion to the semantic, i.e., to personal experience, to images, metaphors, and fantasies, myths and symbols, is, under the conditions of modernity, an expression of psychological positivism. A focus on concrete *contents*. And it is perhaps no coincidence that Marlan, whom we have heard lauding Jung for his having resuscitated the images, wrote a book about *The Black Sun* and a darkness that refuses conscious assimilation. Having Schopenhauer in particular in mind, Nietzsche once said about Man, "and rather is he willing to want *the nought* than *not* to want" ("und eher will er noch *das Nichts* wollen als *nicht* wollen"). The nought is, syntactically, still

man having experience of his ghost-land," or, in imaginal psychology, entertaining myths and thereby indulging in Ersatz. By the way, "helpful method to a barbarous Peyotee, but a regrettable regression for a cultivated individual" also parallels Jung's statement about the Mass, "I know it is the truth, but it is no more true for me."

something, a substance, a positivity (even if semantically, in itself, it *means* nothingness), and this positivized nothingness is, apparently, far better than "not," than negativity itself. Whereas "the nought" is a noun, "not" is only syntactical, only form, the form of negation. By the same token we might say that Jungians prefer to possess the *positive image* of an imageless condition (of a void, a darkness in which absolutely nothing is to be seen) to *not* possessing. They prefer object or content to logical form. In the image of the black sun and its total, unassimilable darkness, positivity celebrates its ultimate triumph, the triumph of the *Ancien Régime* of semantic content, proving itself absolutely unassailable for any "not." For in this image, positivity has (literally) "done in," subsumed its own opposite, negativity, so that it, positivity, remains as the sole and unchallenged master. The only problem with it is that in reality doubt has long ago killed it.

The conventional view in Jungian psychology is that the modern world is neurotically dissociated. It is one-sidedly rational and intellectual and has lost soul, and it split off image, emotion, and body. Something about modernity is fundamentally wrong, sick, ill (just think of Marlan's "reversal of the dominant historical process" as one example). But what we have to realize is that this view IS itself the very dissociation that it projects upon the modern world. *It* is consciousness's turning its back on the Seelenproblem of *modern man*, on *his* psychological condition, on his need for a new *form*, and responds to all this by an attempt at "a reversal of the dominant historical process that [allegedly!] had depotentiated images and reduced soul to rational intellectual spirit," as Marlan had aptly put it, in other words, by an (attempted) repristination of the old form (which, of course, once "doubt has killed it" can in truth be no more than a *simulation* of the old form). So many Jungians think along these same lines, that it is our job as psychologists to mend history and to ensoul "once more" the world. But apart from the terrible inflatedness and illusionariness of the wish to mend history (who are we to wish to mend *history*?! We might just as well want to change the law of gravity. Who are we to think of being able to ensoul *the world*[49]),

[49] This wish also amounts to an ego program, i.e., the opposite of itself. Only the soul could ensoul the world! And what a megalomania to think that "the world" could be a possible object of our endeavors!

this is the anti-modern interpretation of modernity, the denouncement of the "rational intellectual spirit" as soulless and as the result of a faulty development.

But concerning the modern situation, the soul is not the innocent victim of a violence performed upon it, namely its reduction to rational intellectual spirit. The soul is much rather the driving force behind this "dominant historical process." And it is not either a question of reduction at all, but rather the soul's advancement to a new form of itself, to the form of form, to absolute negativity, and thus an attempt on the part of soul to come to its home territory, absolute-negative interiority, to come home to itself, after its primordial exile in the form of sensible imagination, that is, in the status of being projected out into the form of externality.

It is in this *denouncement* that the entire *Seelenproblem* of modern man lies and not, as this denouncement wants to present it, in the prevailing "rational intellectual spirit." The latter is merely the way how the *dissociating* and *defensive* mind perceives the modern psychological condition: that condition that needs "a new form," the thinking form, the form *of form*, and absolute negativity. And this denouncement *is* the Seelenproblem because it is of course the modern *soul* that needs the new form, that soul for which the images, rituals, and numinous felt experiences—even though it still "knows them to be the truth"—*are* no longer true because they are "the truth in a form in which the soul cannot accept them any more," the truth in a form that "no longer expresses the soul's present-day condition"—and ipso facto has become untrue.[50] About the use of "mind-expanding" drugs Jung had said, "It is to my mind a helpful method to a barbarous Peyotee, but a regrettable regression for a cultivated individual." Once one has understood this, how can one then nevertheless think that we

[50] Psychology must not operate, like, for example, atheism and religious dogmatism, with the undialectical, binary opposition of truth and untruth, truth and error or falsehood, with, as Jung put it, "the artificial sundering of true and false wisdom" (*CW* 9i § 31). Rather, it is committed to *absolute truth*: the notion of truth "absolved," freed, from that Either-Or type opposition. This is why for psychology, it is only *truths* (in the full sense of the word) that can become *untrue* and *obsolete* (cf. "I know it is the truth" – "it [this very truth] is no longer true for me"), just as it is only consciousness that can be unconscious. Neither does the fact that something is a truth contradict the other truth that it may now be untrue, passé, merely "an historical curiosity"; nor does its untruth mean that it needs to be totally rejected and thrown away as having intrinsically and from the outset been an illusion, a wrong belief. In contrast to any dogmatism, absolute truth is what *dieser sich selbst vollbringende Skeptizismus* arrives at.

could do justice to the *Seelenproblem* of modern man on *modern* consciousness's *own barbarous* level: on the level of images, semantic contents, of *aisthesis* and emotion, in other words, beneath the *cultivated*, *educated* level of modern consciousness reached during the history of the soul already two hundred years ago, beneath the level of the "thinking form" and "syntax"—beneath "Hegel"? It is like trying to approach a microchip with the tools and mindset appropriate for mechanical machines.

The "resuscitation of images" and "the return to soul" is really *Ersatz* in the literal sense. It construes the *Seelenproblem* of modern man as if it were something like a vitamin deficiency to be healed by dispensing vitamin pills, i.e., without having to go into and all the way through the *Seelenproblem* itself. The underlying presupposition about the soul that makes such a view possible is that soul is an additive, something optional; that it may or may not be there, that it can be missing or be restored. This view is reductive. It reduces soul to an embellishment. For this reason it also leads to dreams of psychologists about "Ensouling the world." This is, we could say, the "reforestation" idea of soul-work, planting new trees in the desert of modernity. Simple compensation (complementation) of a one-sidedness (cf. Jung's interpretation of medieval alchemy as a compensation of the alleged one-sidedness of Christianity).

A true psychology must reject this belittling of the notion of soul and insist that soul is not an alternative to the Real—not something like the luxurious growth of vegetation that is "missing" in a desert. The Real has everything it needs within itself, even if the Real happens to have the form of desert. We do not need to be "in search of a soul." We do not need to restore soul. Because the soul was never lost. It is always there. We are always in it. The soul is simply the inner truth and depth of the Real, regardless of whether the Real at a given time happens to be like a desert or like a tropical rainforest or like cultivated land. There is no Other. *This* is it! *Hic Rhodus, hic salta*!

What makes it difficult for consciousness today is only the fact that soul changed its form, that in modernity it all of a sudden appears in the form of absolute negativity. The widespread feeling and idea of a loss of soul must not be taken literally, as if soul (as a positive substance or ingredient) were in fact missing. No, we have to understand that this feeling is nothing else but the reflection of the fact that the soul in this its new form of absolute negativity is not acknowledged as soul, that accordingly the "not" of its absolute negativity is substantiated and positivized as a lack (a nought). The feeling of loss betrays that consciousness is not adapted. Used to the immense riches in semantic, substantial contents of meaning and expecting the same today, it "does not understand [we could add: or refuses to understand] how the world has changed for it, and how its attitude would have to be in order for it to be adapted again" (*CW* 9i § 61, transl. modif.). Consciousness did not have the experience that *something* was lost, that it was deprived of something. No, it is the other way around: it "lost" (cast away) its depth-connection to the world, refusing to own up to it as its very own world, its one and only world. Subjective failure, not objective loss. What is missing is not it, soul. The soul is still there, as always. What is truly missing is modern man's adaptation to his world and time, modern man's *leaping* at HIS *hic*, the only *hic* that exists for him.

About Jung we can say that he betrayed his own task and his own truth, because *he* had in fact arrived at the explicit insight that the problem was the missing new form that would be capable of really expressing the new soul condition. It goes without saying that by betraying this his own task he also betrayed the soul. Those who followed him on his way, however, merely continued to betray the soul, but not their own task, because they had for the most part never advanced to the insight of the form problem and also had never shouldered the task of the *Seelenproblem* of modern man. They simply fell for and greedily embraced the powerful impulse showing itself in Jung's attempt to solve, on the old semantic, image, object level, the modern soul problem by having recourse to images and to immediate experience. And they embraced it as a kind of doctrine or worldview: a ready-made.

7. The affect-driven rejection of the "thinking form"

One central question remains. In none of the contexts of Jung's writings was there any need for him whatsoever to express an opinion on Hegel or Heidegger. If he did not understand their language, if he had not studied Hegel (and probably Heidegger not either), why would Jung have felt the need to nevertheless make time and again such nasty little statements about them?

Ordinary prudence would normally suffice to prevent a person from risking to make an absolute fool of himself by passing sweeping and completely deviant judgments about a thinker that he knows nothing about. It must have been a powerful unconscious complex, a deep-seated resentment and aversion, that got the better of him and made him repeatedly slip in such highly affective and scathing comments about Hegel, even characterizing his language as "schizophrenic" and denying his status as philosopher precisely with respect to the aspect of the thinking form.

But where does this vehement antipathy (and the vehemence of it) come from? In *MDR* p. 68 f. we read about the time between Jung's sixteenth and nineteenth year,

> I read a brief introduction to the history of philosophy and in this way acquired a certain overview of what all had already been thought. .... Above all I liked the thoughts of Pythagoras, Heraclitus, Empedocles, and Plato, despite the long-windedness of Socratic argumentation. They were beautiful and academic like a picture gallery, but somewhat remote. Only in Meister Eckhart did I feel the breath of life, without having understood him completely. Christian Scholasticism left me cold, and the Aristotelean intellectualism of St. Thomas appeared to me more lifeless than a sand desert. I thought, "They all want to force something by tricks of logic, something that has not been granted to them and of which they do not really have any knowledge. They want to prove a belief to themselves [*sich einen Glauben anbeweisen*[51]], whereas it is, after all, a matter of experience!" They seemed to me like people who knew by hearsay that elephants existed, but had never seen one, and were now trying to prove by arguments that on logical grounds such animals must exist and that their nature must be such as it in fact is. The critical philosophy of the eighteenth century did for the time being not reach me for understandable reasons. Hegel put me off by his language, as laborious as it was arrogant, which I regarded with unreserved mistrust. He seemed to me like a man who was caged in the edifice of his own words and on top of it with a proud air strutted around in his prison. (Transl. modif.)

[51] Like *anempfinden* (see above), *anbeweisen* is hard to translate. It means to force a belief upon oneself by means of "logical" proofs, a belief that one does not really have of one's own accord, that is, as an authentic, natural belief. Rather the logical argumentation has the purpose of fighting down an actually prevailing disbelief or doubt.

We do not go wrong in the assumption that Jung here described the *temporal* origin of his antipathy to Hegel, his Hegel-complex. It dates back to Jung's youth and has, as far as Jung's knowledge about Hegel is concerned, as its foundation no more than "a brief introduction to the history of philosophy." It is probably not surprising that a youth rashly jumps to conclusions merely on the basis of subjective likings and personal emotions evoked by insufficient information. But it *is* astounding that Jung seems to have held on to his youthful prejudices about Hegel throughout his life. One would have expected one of two possible ways for Jung to proceed: that he, as a mature, scientifically trained man, would either have regarded it as necessary to review his early-acquired bias on the basis of a later serious study of Hegel's texts or, if he simply was not interested to undertake such an endeavor (which for him as a psychologist might, from a positivistic, compartmentalizing standpoint, have been perfectly legitimate[52]), that then he would have felt obliged to refrain altogether from any judgment about something he did not know anything about. The reason for his in public making completely unfounded venomous statements about Hegel must of course be that it was not merely a prejudice or dislike that *he* had, but a powerful "feeling-toned complex" that "had *him*."

The temporal origin therefore does not explain the psychological reason for the emergence of a complex, Jung's Hegel-complex. There can be no doubt that there was such a complex at work in Jung, but for the explanation for why it existed and why it compelled him to repeatedly raise absurd accusations against Hegel we have to come up with our own hypothesis. Complexes such as this one arise on the basis of deeply-felt threats (or the like) to one's self-definition *if* one's self-definition is already somehow *unconsciously* known to be untenable, but is nevertheless stubbornly defended at all cost.

My suspicion is that mature Jung *intuitively*, *instinctively* sensed that Hegel had precisely performed what was inherent in Jung's own

[52] From a truly psychological standpoint, however, it would not have been legitimate. A psychology *with soul* must not keep philosophy outside of itself. What a poor conception of psychology if it is construed as one that can be done by an uneducated—especially philosophically uneducated, ignorant—consciousness! And as far as the modern soul situation is concerned, Hegel in particular happens to be indispensable (which does in no way mean that we would have to become Hegelians and consider his philosophy *the* answer to our predicament; rather, it means that his work is indispensable for the training and education of the mind).

self-set task (to tackle the *Seelenproblem* of *modern* man), what therefore would actually have had to be performed by him (Jung), but what he not so much neglected as rather on principle rejected to do because of an irrevocable decision to hold onto the pre-modern form of semantic contents—as if the contents could still truly *speak* for themselves. If in Jung's fantasy Hegel becomes "that great psychologist in philosopher's garb" and he views him as "a psychologist *manqué*, in much the same way as I am a philosopher *manqué*," we see that Jung imagines a simultaneous near-identity and yet radical difference between himself and Hegel. They are, in his fantasy, inimical twins, each other's counterpart or reversal.

What divides them is obviously the *denkerische Form*. For this is what turns Hegel into a psychologist *manqué* because, the way Jung sees it, the thinking form ruins what in itself is (and for Jung ought to remain) "a self-revelation of the psychic background," which in turn is responsible for the alleged "remarkable coincidence between certain tenets of Hegelian philosophy and my findings concerning the collective unconscious." On the other hand, Hegel is "not even a proper philosopher but a misfired psychologist" because the thinking form is in Hegel's case no more than an external "decoration" and a "cunning disguise" of the psychological substance. And, conversely, the *denkerische Form* is also what turned Jung on his part into "a philosopher *manqué*" because the stuff from the unconscious that Jung dealt with was actually the raw material of a philosophy, but Jung was not able or willing to give it the necessary *denkerische Form* to truly raise it to the status of a veritable philosophy. So the thinking form must have been the crucial bone of contention for Jung. It was the sore spot. He must somehow, subconsciously, have feared that Hegel, both with his "laborious" language and the "thinking form" (which, as we know, culminates in "scepticism brought to its completion and fruition"), might have let himself in for the modernity of modern man and ipso facto also for modern man's real *Seelenproblem* in a more appropriate way than he, Jung, himself had. But this possibility was not allowed to be true. Jung's decision to escape the inner logic of modernity was absolutely unnegotiable. Therefore it had to be the decision to tackle that *Seelenproblem* precisely *only* in the mode of the old form, simplistically: merely on the semantic level and in his easygoing conventional language, by *directly* returning to soul, symbol, myth, and image as well as by swearing by the innocent immediacy of "immediate experience."

Yes, Hegel was indeed laborious, cumbersome, and this precisely and necessarily *because* he addressed the problem where it really was and because this problem of modernity was based on a "deeper principle," represented a "more difficult subject matter," a "material richer in compass" and thus was a problem that inevitably made "far greater demands" on the investigator. His language was laborious because he demanded of the reader—of *consciousness*—to undertake the personal effort to become adequate in its very constitution to this higher complexity, to feel responsible for the new sensibility required by the modern situation. He knew that what was needed was an *education* of *consciousness*. His language style aimed at the *form* of consciousness (instead of merely providing, like Jung, new edifying contents or experiences for it: archetypal, numinous images). This is, I claim, why Hegel was a thorn in Jung's flesh: Hegel was the really-existing reproach for his, Jung's, own taking a shortcut around the problem of the complexity of the modern soul; the reproach for his selling this his (absolutely and on principle) ignoring the real problem of modern man qua modern man nevertheless as the real cure of modern man's soul problem. This is why his Hegel-complex insists precisely on doing Hegel in, throwing him altogether away by characterizing him both as pathological and as an imposter. Jung's own cheating appears to him as Hegel's fraud (as to "fraud": compare Jung's accusation: "The word is charged with the task of achieving what cannot be done by honest means"[53]). And what was precisely Hegel' strength, the form of thought, had to be denounced as inauthentic.

Very early Jung had taken the decision I spoke of, on a deep, unconscious, existential level. Very early he had thrown his whole weight behind what later became his dogma of "the immediacy of overwhelming experience," "experience" in a mindless sense (nothing but "facts"! Pure nature!). It was during his twelfth year that the die

[53] But in truth, Jung means with this: what cannot be done simplistically, with the means of everyday language. In other words, *without* involving the constitution of consciousness itself. Consciousness was supposed to be a neutral vessel.

was cast, that Jung had set the course for himself for all his life by making his choice,[54] and clearly a choice in the sense of a dissociation: anti-philosophical, anti-intellectual, against the "thinking form."

We know this from Jung's own report from his late years in *MDR* about the "Basel cathedral" incident[55] (his spontaneous thought during his twelfth year that a huge turd coming from God's throne in heaven falls on the cathedral and smashes it). The boy Jung had managed to reverse the inherent meaning of this spontaneous fantasy, blinding himself about the very point that his fantasy made and instead, through artful contrivances of his own, repurposing and reconstruing this fantasy as one which "was forced on me and I was compelled, with the utmost cruelty, to think it." This was, in his interpretation, his collision with the absolutely overwhelming *will* of God and as such also an undoubtable spontaneous *Urerfahrung* of God Himself: "one of the most certain and immediate of experiences." He had arrived at "[his] certainty about God." God was "as obvious as when a brick falls on one's head" (*MDR* p. 62, transl. modif.). *This* experience became his great powerful[56] "secret," as he called it, a secret that was surrounded by an absolute taboo, so that he could not share it with anyone for many decades. And as this secret it was, on a deep existential level, the underlying foundation or unconscious guiding principle for his whole future outlook as psychologist (at least as far as he was not only concerned with merely genuinely *scientific* psychological questions, for example, word-association studies, but with the predicament of the modern soul).

We have also already heard above that Jung had hoped to be able to cure his father allopathically from his inner doubts and to win him over to the way of immediate experience. His discussion is most revealing. Realizing that his father, on account of his inner conflict

[54] It is essential to realize that his concept of "immediate experience" is not itself an immediate experience or based on one, but rather a product of the boy's intellectual reflections and manipulations! I discussed this in detail in Chapters Two and Three of *The Flight Into the Unconscious*, vol. V of my Coll. Engl. Papers, New Orleans (Spring Journal Books) 2013. It was the result of a decision of ultimate import on the part of the whole person (*homo totus*). And because it was a vital decision, a total commitment, it took on the character of an unshakeable absolute truth for him, the character of his *articulus stantis et cadentis*.

[55] See the reference given in the previous footnote.

[56] "Later my mother told me that in those days I was often depressed. It was not really that; rather, I was brooding on the secret" (*MDR* p. 42).

with his need to believe caused by his doubts, "had to quarrel with somebody, so he did it with his family and himself." To this Jung adds, "Why didn't he do it with God, the dark author of all created things, who alone was responsible for the sufferings of the world?" (*MDR* p. 92). A clear *petitio principii.* How could his father have quarreled with God if his inner doubts had pulled the floor out from under his belief in God? You cannot quarrel with someone you don't assume to be real. Jung's father stayed honest, faithful to his real situation. He did not, like Carl Gustav Jung did, trick himself into an immediate experience of a God whose reality had in fact already been decomposed for him ("who was," we could say, "no longer true for him").

8. Blind knowledge and thought-blindness

We see from Jung's description, especially from the image of the brick that falls on one's head, that his certainty and knowledge about God was an in-itself fundamentally *mindless, insightless* knowledge (if one can call such a blind certainty "knowledge" at all), and that "immediate experience" is ultimately nothing but the experience of being hit on the head by brute force. Consciousness as such was not involved (it merely had to *be there* [in the sense of *Dasein*] so that there would *be* something to be hit by the falling brick). Intelligibility was radically cut out, the subject's possible intrinsic inherence and involvement in an essential experience was excluded. Jung criticized his father's "blind faith" and wished that he (Carl Gustav) "could have opened (his) father's eyes." We have to criticize Jung's insistence on blind knowledge. His father's doubts *and blindness* could have become the entrance gate to *illumined* knowing. By turning against it, Jung, to be sure, moved from faith to "knowing," but he retained the *form* of blindness and missed the form of self-transparency, self-reflectedness of his "knowledge," which could only have been achieved by going all the way through with the blindness that he saw in his father.[57] (Any

[57] *Together* his father's blind faith and his doubts are two halves of one veritable truth. Each one has what is missing from it in the other. Faith has its own enlightenment in the doubts. The doubts have their content in the father's faith. Intuitions without concepts are blind, concepts without intuitions are empty, Kant had said. A similar relation prevails between blind faith and illuminating doubt. The dissociation between the two halves of one whole is, however, not a mistake. It is the soul's alchemical operation of *separatio* of the *unio naturalis* between semantics and syntax, a *separatio* which is indispensable for making, for the first time within the history of the soul, the level of

understanding, if at all, could in this scheme only happen after the fact, as external reflection, as we will see later.)

The fact that his experience of God had to remain an absolute secret enclosed in his chest also speaks for the mindlessness and internal blindness of this experience. "Brick" and "secret," although not alike, are nevertheless the Same. The mindlessness of being hit by the brick means that the "knowledge" thus gained could not come out into the open, could not confidently be exposed to discussion, i.e., was not allowed to *be* true (= *alêthes*, "unconcealed").

About secrets we learn from Jung himself: "As beneficial as a secret shared with several persons is, so destructive is a merely private secret. The latter works like a burden of guilt, cutting off the unfortunate possessor from the communion with his fellows" (*CW* 16 § 125, transl. modif.). Jung says this without thinking of the fact that this applies to his own absolutely private secret. "The possession of secrets acts like a psychic poison that alienates their possessor from the community" (§ 124).[58] But much worse than isolating the *possessor*

logical form or syntax conscious and explicit. But the condition of dissociation also means that faith without its own illumination and authorization from within itself, through its own intrinsic syntax, which now through the dissociation has been extracted, externalized, and objectified as those doubts, becomes blind semantics (usually known under the title of "ideology"), a semantics that on account of its missing *internal* authorization needs to be propped up from "outside" by ego willing. Conversely, "doubt" deprived of its own intrinsic semantic substance remains empty (which is usually experienced under the titles of "nihilism," "loss of meaning," or, as here, "doubts"). A *coniunctio* of the separated opposites remains a *mysterium*, by which I do not mean, like Jung did, a mysterious happening, a mystical experience as a positivity, but refer to the fact that it is something still completely unimaginable, let alone thinkable. It would require that a higher level above the opposites has been reached.

[58] Jung has of course also a very different, highly positive view of the function and importance of a secret, and I am indebted to Greg Mogenson for urging me to include this aspect here. Jung stated for example, "There is no better means of intensifying the treasured feeling of individuality than the possession of a secret which the individual is pledged to guard" (*MDR* p. 342), "Like the initiate of a secret society who has broken free from the undifferentiated collectivity, the individual on his lonely path needs a secret which for various reasons he may not or cannot reveal. Such a secret reinforces him in the isolation of his individual aims" (p. 343). There is something to be said in favor of such secrets. Secrets like those of secret societies belong to those of the soul's general "religious" strategies for creating something *absolutely* precious to which also taboos and the distinction between a *temenos* or *templum* or inner sanctum, on the one hand, and the profane, on the other hand, belong. Jung is probably right in stating, "The individual who is not grounded in God [here we might want to say instead: grounded in some absolute ground, and interpret this as referring to the content of "the secret"] can offer no resistance on his own resources to the physical and moral blandishments of the world" (*CW* 10 § 511). But it is well known that a real groundedness in God which can offer such resistances must by no means always have the form of a secret; it can also be professed. Just think of Dietrich Bonhoeffer. Or St. Paul. And even where it is a literal

of such a secret from the community,[59] i.e., from consciousness-as-such, is what the absolute concealment means for the secret (its subject matter) itself: it deprives it of its potential to be a truth and to become (logically, psychologically) conscious. Because truth as well as consciousness *require sharedness*, or, as Hegel had put it, "an achieved community of minds."[60] Just as there cannot be a private language (Wittgenstein), so there cannot be a private truth. *My* knowing of the content of my secret is by no means sufficient to make it conscious in

secret as in secret societies, it must not logically be an *isolating* secret. About the Pueblo Indians Jung said, "They make it a policy to keep their religious practices a secret .... [It is a] secret known to all the communicants .... This strange situation gave me an inkling of Eleusis whose secret was known to a whole nation and yet never betrayed" (*MDR* p. 249, transl. modif.). It is, in other words, a secret in the logical status of sharedness, communality! This is a wholly different type of secret from the one based on egoic fear and motivated by a defiant withdrawal into privacy and isolation, i.e., by a defensive attitude. The latter applies to Jung's own secret and makes it subject to his criticism cited above ("poison"), all the more so since its substance was not based on a veritable spontaneous revelation, but on a mental fabrication. Jung's secret produced an "almost unendurable loneliness" and cut him off from the community of minds! For Jung, the secret that he praises is already the absolutely private possession of the modern (fundamentally isolated, split-off) individual. We can, by contrast, think of Pascal's *Mémorial* as an example of a literal secret without any trace of a dissociating purpose. What Pascal kept strictly to himself was in itself, logically, nevertheless *not* cut off from the communal faith.

[59] It is conversely quite likely that Jung's having such a fundamental secret (I am referring to the *form* of secrecy as such, to the psychic *act* of dissociating something from the natural further-developing life of consciousness, of freezing it and insulating it, and to the character strength of keeping it secret, not to the content or "inner truth" of the secret) and his being *absolutely* committed to his secret as if it were *the* absolute truth was what gave him, or at least contributed to his having, the impressive magic power of personality experienced by so many of his analysands and disciples. The "psychic poison" of a secret can also act like a magic potion. At the same time it is likely that Jung's having this all-important and absolutely tabooed secret intrapsychically created an enormous tension that functioned as a source of *creative* energy for Jung. His feeling of being "either outlawed or elect, accursed or blessed" (*MDR* p. 41) on account of his secret is an excellent *psychological* precondition for creativeness. Creativity is not *only* based on inborn giftedness. – Jung was not totally unaware of the poison in his own case. He said that certain Christian ideas about God "poisoned my whole religion" (CW 18 § 1643). But here he confused cause and effect. The real poison was his secret, with which he immunized himself against the medicinal effects of what *he* considered to be the poison inherent in Christianity.

[60] Not necessarily empirical-factual (social) sharedness, but certainly *logical* sharedness: in consciousness-as-such. If a content is in my mind objectively construed as the property of consciousness-as-such, of the generality, it can still be a truth even if, under the prevailing social conditions, I conceal it from other people or merely entertain it in the solitude of my mind. – Jung was of course aware of the indispensability of "sharedness," but he had to logically "repress" it into the unconscious (as "the *collective* unconscious") and thus into the logical status of the past, of obsolescence. Where it would count, namely in consciousness and on the level of modernity, it was in Jung's scheme eliminated.

the full sense of the word. What I alone (*psychically*) know and what I feel needs to be kept absolutely secret is, in a *psychological* sense, unconscious. A merely private "knowing" does not count. It is not knowing, *conscious* knowing, at all (an often deeply felt insufficiency which is what drives some people to confession, some to psychotherapy, or certain undetected criminals occasionally years after their deed even to the police to disclose their crime).

To Jolande Jacobi Jung wrote on 25 August 1960:

> I was very impressed and pleased to hear that my autobiographical sketches have conveyed to you something of what my outer side has hitherto kept hidden. It had to remain hidden because it could not have survived the brutalities of the outside world. But now I am grown so old that I can let go my grip on the world, and its raucous cries fade in the distance (*Letters 2*, p. 585).

"Brutalities of the outside world" is here Jung's phrase for what in reality would be the asserted truths' *acid test*. Mystics generally had no qualms about making their inner experiences public. They did not fear any "brutalities of the outside world" (often even during the times of Inquisition). They trusted in the validity of their visions. But then they were pre-modern. Jung as a modern man is of course right, "it *had to* remain hidden," *had to* be insulated as an absolute secret, "because it could indeed not have survived" the acid test. And why not? Because in modernity such truths are *intrinsically* (in themselves) in the logical status of the "doubt-that-has-killed-it." But Jung *wanted* his secret to survive as a logically positive truth, as "his light and his treasure" that needed to be guarded.[61] He wanted to protect it from the alchemical process of fermenting corruption, distillation, evaporation, from having explicitly to enter the status of absolute negativity (into which that "doubt" had *implicitly* and *in fact*

---

[61] "I am guarding my light and my treasure, convinced that nobody would gain and I myself would be badly, even hopelessly injured, if I should lose it. It is most precious not only to me, but above all to the darkness of the creator, who needs man to illuminate His creation" (*Letters 2*, p. 597, to Serrano, 14 September 1960). His secret is of cosmological and soteriological significance. And it needs to be kept a secret. Precisely *as* a guarded secret it is nevertheless supposed to illuminate God's creation. Compare and contrast this with: "No man, when he hath lighted a candle, putteth it in a secret place, neither under a bushel, but on a candlestick, that they which come in may see the light" (Luke 11:33).

transported it all along), from "this thoroughgoing scepticism." Jung's choice of the word "brutality" reveals above all his own *Zärtlichkeit* (his having too much of a soft spot), his insistence on retaining his own logical childhood innocence and virginal unwoundedness.

Going back to Jung's description of his reaction to the various philosophers, as they were represented in the brief introduction to the history of philosophy which he had read between his sixteenth and nineteenth year, we can say, after our having become aware of the mindlessness and fundamental unconsciousness (blindness) of Jung's secret "knowledge" of God and his need to defend his logical innocence, that it does not come as a surprise that Jung shows that he simply has no access to philosophical thought, in particular to what is specific to it: the *denkerische Form*, on the one hand, and its fundamental communality (its being a priori addressed to consciousness-as-such), on the other. He suffers, as it were, from a "thought-blindness" (the way some people suffer from color-blindness). For him the thoughts of the philosophers are not really *thoughts* at all. He apperceives them with a substantiating, picturing mentality merely as ideas, opinions, semantic contents, i.e., as (mental) objects in front of consciousness—things, to be sure, in the mental sphere but otherwise nevertheless like the things in nature. I already compared them to the building bricks children play with. And this is also why he approaches them with aesthetic categories: To the extent that he liked the thoughts, "[t]hey were beautiful and academic like a picture gallery": mere *ideas*, something *to look at* with a passive consumer attitude, but not anything to be *thought*. His mind had to be an immune consciousness, as immune vis-à-vis the contents as a mirror or a glass vessel are. Thinking, by contrast, involves and even affects the subject's very form of consciousness. In thinking the subject takes responsibility for what it thinks. The "object" it thinks "about" is its own product or thinking process: a thought, not an external entity *given* to it like paintings in a museum.

In those cases where this kind of aesthetic "looking-at" (and deriving pleasure from it) clearly did not work, as in the cases of the long-winded Socratic argumentation or of the Christian Scholasticism of St. Thomas, Jung rejected it as "more lifeless than a sand desert," contrasting it with Meister Eckhart as the only one in whom he felt "a breath of life" (which reminds us of Ernst v. Lasaulx's comment about "the fresh, life-warm springtime breeze that breathes everywhere in Schelling's *Naturphilosophie*"). Concerning these feeling reactions we must keep in mind that this report, coming from old-man Jung, does not merely inform us about what the youngster Jung felt. Rather, it also reflects Jung's stance towards philosophy and thought *at the time of his talking about* his youth. There is not a trace in his report of a critical distancing himself from these early reactions.

The problem here is by no means that Jung prefers the "breath of life." Anybody would. No, the problem is his incapability to perceive this very "breath of life" in the instances of true philosophy, of thoughts in the authentic "thinking form"![62] This is what reveals his "thought-blindness." It is his own philosophical sterility, his own keeping his mind as a mere onlooker out and vis-à-vis (i.e., his refusal to *think* the thoughts, instead of merely to entertain them as "ideas"), that turns the Aristotelean intellectualism of St. Thomas for him into a sand desert. He does not get *into* the inwardness of the adventuresome process of thinking.

In late letters Jung wrote, "If there is one thing that put me off, it was dead conceptualism" (*Letters 2*, p. 543, to Karl Schmid, 9 February 1960, transl. modif.). "Abstract thinking can lead us no further than to intellectual sophistries" (*ibid.* p. 620, to Albert Jung, 21 December 1960). No doubt, "dead conceptualism" and "intellectual sophistries" would put everybody off, also the major Scholastic philosophers. This goes without saying. The question is, however: is Jung with his clear anti-philosophical bias at all in a position to judge where living thought ends and dead conceptualism begins? Did he have an inkling of what the "thinking form" is? It is as if Hegel had already one and a half century before Jung anticipated and answered the latter's reproach of sophistry, when he said: "For 'sophistry' is a slogan used by ordinary common sense against educated reason, just as the expression 'visionary dreaming' [we remember Jung's phrase, 'lavishly decorated confession of his unconscious'] sums up, once and for all, what philosophy means to those who are ignorant of it."[63]

[62] While this is forgivable in a youth, it is not in a mature psychologist of Jung's caliber. But there is nothing to indicate that mature Jung's assessment was any different from his youthful one.

[63] G.W.F. Hegel, *Phenomenology of Spirit*, *op. cit.*, p. 43.

A peasant, during the early 19th century, had something to talk over with the local pastor. As he approached the parsonage, another peasant was just leaving it. The newcomer, wanting to know if he would disturb the pastor in some important work, asked: "What is the minister doing?" The answer given was, "Oh, nothing at all, he is just sitting at his desk writing."

From the peasant's perspective only manual labor qualifies as working. Writing and thinking is not working at all. Similarly, for Jung only "beautiful ideas" like those in "a picture gallery" count as having life in them; only immediately accessible[64] cosmological or *weltanschauliche* ideas *in their positivity* as he presented them in his *Red Book*, or emotional *Ergriffenheit* (being gripped), which he offered as the only good alternative to the "abstract thinking" rejected in the last quote from his letter to Albert Jung. By contrast, genuinely philosophical thought (as, by the way, we also find it in many of Meister Eckhart's texts, who was not merely a "mystic," but a true thinker of highly abstract, but living thought![65]) is dead—but, we have to realize, it is dead only because it fundamentally disappoints the naive expectation that it should reveal its life *immediately* to the passive consumer and because Jung does not go to the trouble of himself *entering* the thoughts, of giving himself seriously over to them. He stays committed to externality. He remains the innocent spectator, who judges on the basis of the outside appearance and subjectively felt attractiveness of the contents of thought.

Jung's mistake is that he interprets his subjective antipathy ("left me cold," "put me off," "unreserved mistrust") as the objective fault of philosophy. Instead of saying: "I am not the right person for philosophical thought, I am not willing or capable of thinking (in the full, philosophical sense of the word)" he said that philosophical thought is more lifeless than a sand desert.

If for this view thought proper has—allegedly—the soul outside of and vis-à-vis itself and if this psychological scheme thus works with a dissociation (the either-or of image vs. rational intellect), it becomes understandable that what was felt to be needed was a "*resuscitation* of images," and "a *return* to soul" and "a *reversal* of the dominant historical

---

[64] "Immediately accessible": without involving consciousness. Consciousness could stay the immune observer of "facts."

[65] Just see, for one example, his *First Paris Quaestio* of 1302.

process that had depotentiated images and reduced soul to rational intellectual spirit." But all these moves are the reflection of the fundamental split between image (and, likewise, immediate experience) as what is exclusively soulful, on the one hand, and the work of living thought that involves the subject as itself having to take responsibility for the thoughts, on the other. Here the soul's life is not all-comprehensive, surrounding us on *all* sides. It is present only in a particular part of the whole real phenomenology (e.g., mythic images), while the other part of it has to be scorned.

The dissociation is clearly expressed in our passage by the opposition between "forcing something by the tricks of logic" vs. "a matter of experience." As if St. Thomas (or any of the other greater Scholastics) had needed to *sich anbeweisen* a belief! Ridiculous. As if they had not been always already firmly standing in their belief and as if the Christian belief had not been the completely natural, self-evident, and all-pervasive principle, the ground *and* horizon for medieval man! Even much later, for as long as metaphysics in the sense of a *prima philosophia* prevailed, the belief in God was the generally prevailing objective truth *within which* people lived, the same way that the biological human organism lives within the earth's atmosphere. Jung talks as if for the Scholastics Christian belief had been in desperate need of being secondarily supported against a gnawing doubt, indeed of even being "forced" on consciousness, which ipso facto would have had to be a disbelieving and resisting consciousness. Jung retrojects here the situation of modern man into the Middle Ages. It is to be assumed that what was predominantly in the back of his mind was the image of his own father's struggles to combat his inward doubts (he "insisted on blind faith, which he had to win by struggle and wished to force to come with contorted efforts" *MDR* p. 73, transl. modif.).

Jung could have known the altogether different soul need that inspired the "Aristotelean intellectualism" of the Scholastics: namely the soul's need for the belief which it *has*, and out of which it *lives* anyway, to also become perfectly illumined and intellectually transparent to itself; the need for acquiring a true knowing about *what all* this belief involved. A belief which was precisely not only "immediate," a natural event, a brute fact, fundamentally irrational and simply taken for granted (the way we take the air that we breath for granted). And also not merely a certainty comparable to the instinctual certainty of beasts, or one resulting from an "immediate experience" as overwhelming and irrational as one's being struck on one's head by a falling brick. But rather a belief worthy of human beings in whom there is a mind, a mind that in turn was a spark from the Divine Intelligence. *Fides quaerens intellectum,* as Anselm—Jung knew this of course well enough—in the spirit of St. Augustine put it. *Quae de Deo sive de eius creatura necessario credimus* (what we necessarily believe about God or his creation) must *sola ratione* (through reason alone) become expounded. For the soul, "having experiences" is, in itself, nothing, or at most only a meager beginning.

Concerning Jung's dictum, "I do not believe, I know," we can recall what we already had to realize above: being hit on one's head by a brick is precisely *not* knowing. This "knowledge" is, as his subjective experience, logically inevitably his private secret, a fact that deprives this "knowledge" of its truth (in the full sense of the word), its unconcealedness and sharedness. But the *intellectum* that made the common faith of the Scholastics translucent to itself was a priori, by definition, a public, shared intellect and understanding, even if empirically it may in a concrete situation have been used only by one individual in his loneliness. Thought (in the thinking form), even the thought of an empirically solitary mind, necessarily, namely logically, takes place in the sphere of generality (because it appeals to reasons, justifies itself [*logon didonai*] before the higher [transpersonal] court of consciousness-as-such). So what the Scholastics did was actually a full-fledged *veri-fication, Wahrmachung,* of that which as long as it was in the form of *fides* was the truth in a form still unconscious and implicit to itself. To conceive knowing, the way Jung did, as being overwhelmed by an immediate experience (in his sense) would amount to a perversion of the very concept of knowing, indeed to a veritable *sacrificium intellectus*! And it would never take the stigma of a (logically) absolutely private secret, and thus of its irrationality, away from what is "known," even if psychically, empirically, it would be divulged.

It is true, Jung certainly did not literally *sich anbeweisen* a belief, let alone through logical arguments. However, his thinking about God follows precisely the same *logic* of something being unnaturally foisted on consciousness. It was he himself who did what he unjustly charged the Christian Scholastics with, he who operated with a proof, a killing argument—the only difference being that what in the case of the Scholastics—at least according to *his* fantasy of them—had been a consciousness-internal process, a self-relation (*their* forcing a belief on *themselves* through their own logical argumentation) in his case was construed as an external relation. The killing proof came over consciousness from outside, over consciousness as the absolutely innocent, passive and also dumb "victim" of the overwhelming force of an "immediate experience."[66] But whether the killing proof is produced by consciousness itself or whether, with the logic of externality and dissociation, it is seen as an autonomous Other—the structure of "*anbeweisen*" is in both cases the same.

9. Immediate experience: the crushing of "doubt" and the subordination of the subject as dumb subject

The need for this insistence on being overwhelmed, for this moment of violence, is a sign that there was something that needed to be overcome, some resistance or doubt. It was of course not merely a subjective, personal doubt concerning God, doubt as a psychic act or event, but much rather "doubt" the way Jung had meant it in his passage about the Catholic Mass and the way I described it above: as the general objective situation of modern man, as the prevailing logical character of modernity (its having entered the status of logical negativity), in other words, a "doubt" *in which* Jung as a modern man inevitably lived, and not only one that he personally had within himself and that gnawed on him.

Jung's answer to the situation of absolute doubt was this: this fundamental doubt had simply to be steamrollered, overthrown by coup, and a priori so, namely *through the overwhelmingness of immediate inner experience.*

---

[66] Cf. the "Basel cathedral" experience from which Jung originally derived his certainty about God: "*I* haven't done this or wanted this, it has come on me like a bad dream. ... This has happened to me without my doing." "*Why* should I think something I do not know? I do not want to, by God, that's sure. But *who* wants me to? Who wants to force me to think something I don't know and don't want to know? Where does this terrible will come from?" (*MDR* p. 37)

What he said about the Scholastics, that they are like people who only knew by hearsay that elephants existed, but had never seen one,[67] and were now trying to prove by arguments that on logical grounds such animals must exist, applies *mutatis mutandis* to him too. It is of course true, he did not prove anything *on logical grounds*. No, but "immediate experience" served as *his* proof. The point here is that immediate experience was by no means, to stay within Jung's image, a direct encounter with an elephant (his actually seeing one), but merely an event within the isolated subjectivity of his private psyche, which did not get him any closer to real elephants "out there" than any "logical grounds" did. Whether emotional event (in Jung's case) or rational grounds (in the case of Jung's fantasy of the Scholastics) makes no difference: they are both used as knockout arguments to compensate for the lack of ever having really seen elephants. Philosophy, by contrast, does not have this problem. In *thinking* a thought (in contrast to merely entertaining, imagining it like an idea), consciousness is really and directly seeing "the elephant," that is to say, what that thought is about.

Jung's whole emphasis in general on direct experience, on being an empiricist, and on "facts, nothing but facts" has ultimately to be seen as being fired by his deep psychological need to construe the subject as fundamentally dumb[68] (mindless) and as absolutely

---

[67] Jung could express the same idea also in a less figurative way, in the context of comments about the general fundamental blindness of men: "I was equally sure that none of the theologians I knew had ever seen 'the light that shineth in the darkness' with his own eyes ..." (*MDR* p. 93).

[68] I already mentioned (note 6) that Jung tried to somehow mend the reduction of the duality of human "subject" and overpowering *true* subject (God or immediate experience in general) to a monocentric structure (e.g., the ego revolving around the Self) on the semantic or behavioral level. In a certain dream (*MDR* p. 219 f., see Chapter One above), in which it would have been his task to completely submit, like his father, to the "highest presence," he pretended to touch his forehead to the floor, but did not really go all the way down. And his comment to this is: "Something in me was defiant and determined not to be the dumb fish .... Man always has some mental reservation, even in the face of divine decrees. Otherwise, where would be his freedom?" So we see that here Jung has become explicitly aware of the problem that exists if the human subject is construed as "dumb fish," or, as I had said, dumb victim. However, he did not tackle this problem on the level on which it was created, namely the level of *psychology*; he did not revise the underlying logic of his thinking. Rather, he addressed this problem only outside psychology itself, on the level of literal (merely *psychic*) behavior: by means of an empirical act of defiance (resistance) or mental reservation after the fact. What would really have been needed was a fundamental retraction of this psychological dogma of immediate experience, the structure of "anbeweisen." What Jung did not see is that *the*

innocently receiving victim, a victim being *overwhelmed* by an autonomous Other.[69] Not insight. Not illumination, comprehension.[70] No *intrinsic* and *originary* involvement of the subject as thinking form, of the conscious mind, that is to say, no cognition (no cognitive relation *to* reality, no need for an *adaequatio rei et intellectus*). Thus also no primary responsibility on the part of the subject itself, no account-giving.[71] We must remember here Jung's foundational metaphor of the stream of lava that bursts forth from the unconscious and ruthlessly swamps consciousness. Immediacy, directness. "Revelation." "Pure nature."

What this means in truth is that it was Jung's deepest need to let the subject's modern psychological condition, the "doubt" or logical negativity *as which* it exists (usually called the modern ego), be simply crushed—so that man might once more be able to say with conviction: I do not believe, I know. The absolute dissociation was needed if it was a question of rescuing the idea of the divine under the conditions of the modern world, of born man. The only choice Jung seems to have seen in the modern situation was that between modern "doubt" OR "being overwhelmed." Only "brute force," so we must analyze Jung's unconscious inference, could still bestow *irrefutable* credibility

defiant fish remains as dumb as before. The "dumb fish" problem cannot be resolved on the level of ego willing and a power game. This is a category mistake, a *metabasis eis allo genos*: acting-out instead of remembering/inwardizing. As a matter of course, the "dumb fish" problem needs to be addressed on that level on which it exists, the level of mind, of truth and insight. Willful defiance does not undo dumbness; resistance does not make the fundamentally blind (cf.: men "are born dumb and blind as puppies") see "the light that shineth in the darkness" (cf. *MDR* p. 93). What alone could have taken away this dumbness is precisely the "doubt that has killed it." Defiance is Jung's substitute for letting himself in for that "doubt" that is the underlying *logical status* of modernity, his substitute also for the true freedom that *he* erroneously fancies to be able to defend with a *reservatio mentalis.*

69 Jung also used his empiricism thesis quite literally (i.e., on the behavioral, no longer logical level) as a *knockout argument* against some of his critics (for example, Martin Buber) stating that they did not have clinical experience and thereby implying that they were simply not competent to criticize his work. No need, therefore, to take their criticism seriously. Objections raised by the intellect, by intelligent minds, could simply be wiped away in this fashion.

70 Jung himself, as individual, had, however, many rich deeply psychological *insights* into concrete matters and situations. Again and again one is astounded by his deep understanding. But these were sort of happenings and did not induce him to alter his basic theoretical outlook and actual stance.

71 "... the experience of God, the most evident of all experiences. I knew enough about epistemology to realize that knowledge of this sort could not be proved, but it was equally clear to me that *it stood in no more need of proof* than the beauty of a sunset or the terrors of the night" (*MDR* p. 92, my emphasis).

onto the idea of an (of course *psychologized*) *ontological* reality of God(s) or of archetypal powers. Without irrefutability the reality of God(s) would immediately be subject again to the very "doubt" to crush which was, after all, the prime motif and motor of Jung's project.

Here, however, I must hasten to add that this crushing of the modern mind (and the radical elimination of intrinsic intelligibility from experiences, as mentioned before) was not a *psychic* overpowering—which would have resulted in inflation or psychosis. It was exclusively a logical, psychological being crushed, an achievement by a logical brute force. It happened in the background sphere of how things were *defined* and *construed* (not in the immediate experiential sphere, the sphere of events that happened to and were noticed by the ego). Jung's is a *logical* irrationalism, just as the fundamental dissociation in his scheme between the subject and its experience is a logical one. Psychically (empirically, practically, experientially), by contrast, or, as we could also say, as civil man, he retained the full control over his intellectual powers and always insisted precisely that we should *emotionally feel* what the experienced images contained, that we should *intellectually understand* them, and that we should take *ethical responsibility* for our experiences from the unconscious.

But the feeling, understanding, and ethical response that he had in mind were to be ones that (1) could only come *after the fact* as an external reflection or reaction and by the same token (2) *occurred* on this side of the unsurpassable logical barrier between "the ego and the unconscious," namely on the consciousness or ego side, whereas *what* the consciousness had to understand was logically irrevocably situated yonder, on the other side, namely in what is a priori *defined* as the irrevocably *un*-conscious "archetypes or archetypal images of the collective unconscious." The intellectual understanding and ethical involvement, coming essentially after the fact and being supposed to be psychic acts, cannot possibly reach that level on which the psychological problem is located. They cannot possibly undo or heal that dissociation that the very theory of psychology had set up as its premise or axiom. But they also *had to* stay external to the "matter" of the experience on the side of the unconscious because only in this way could it be guaranteed that they would be protected from the possibility of being infected by the modern condition, its "doubt," the logical status of absolute negativity.

(Archetypal Psychology inherited the same need to hold itself in the sphere of the positivity of semantic contents untouched by "doubt," i.e., by logical negativity. But it did not have to go through the logical moves that Jung had needed to take [his developing his "secret" and his insisting on the logical violence of the knockout argument of overwhelming primordial experience and empiricism in general]. It could simply rest on the logic of the *result* that Jung had struggled to achieve through his moves, on the logical ground prepared by Jung, and move from there to its now much more light-weight, free-floating, aestheticizing scheme of "the imaginal." A sublimation, no doubt, but by no means an alchemical one. Archetypal psychology much rather likewise protects its images from becoming subject to an alchemical process of fermenting corruption. Their timelessness is one clear index of "the imaginal's" fundamental shieldedness. That imaginal psychology is a much more light-weight undertaking than Jung's is mainly due to the fact that it has given up the criterion of truth altogether, which for Jung was still essential,[72] and exchanged it for the aesthetic self-sufficiency of images, their shine of "beauty." Jung had, after all, been concerned with "actually seeing a real elephant out there." Truth remained indispensable. We remember his statement: "I must have a situation in which that thing becomes true once more.")

The large-scale paradigmatic example of this radical dissociation between primordial experience *first* and secondary intellectual processing *thereafter* is of course Jung's own self-interpretation: first there was, completely irrationally, the "stream of lava," and only later on did he produce his scientific works, which "are the more or less successful endeavor to incorporate this incandescent matter into the world view of my time." "My entire later activity consisted in elaborating what during those years had burst forth from the unconscious and at first swamped me" (*MDR* p. 199, transl. modif.). This temporal split is the precondition for (or, if you wish, conversely: the result of the need for) the timelessness of the archetypes and of "the imaginal" and their immediate presence and relevance for humans of all epochs ("The archetype is ageless and everpresent," *Letters 2*, p. 394, to Trinick, 15 October 1957). And it

[72] Although for Jung truth (in the form of unshakeable certainty) had, with a *contradictio in se*, become privatized as each person's individual truth.

is the reflection in time and in real process of the theoretical-structural split in the psyche or personality between "the unconscious" and consciousness (or "the ego").

And this dissociative logic prevailing in Jung's scheme is the reason why the individual's feeling, understanding, and ethical response to experiences from the unconscious are in Jung's thinking (as we can say with Jung's own words directed against others) "*charged with the task of achieving what cannot be done by honest means.*" "Dishonesty" in this context, that is to say psychological dishonesty, means that the individual is given the task of performing what the logic of the objective stuff of experience itself as well as the logic of psychology at large a priori exclude. The individual has the task of getting himself, in the privacy of his inner, into the stance of *upward-looking* (this is the job of analysis and of the individuation process) when in truth modern man is logically already irrevocably in the status of *born man*. The individual person's feeling, understanding, and ethical response have to supply that life, meaning, and binding validity that the experienced image does not have of its own accord (because, as we know, "doubt has killed it"). "Dishonesty" means, more generally, that the semantics (as well as the empirical-practical goals and efforts in the therapeutic process) are contradicted, and thus logically undermined, by their own syntax or logic (which is a reflection of the logic generally prevailing at the time). It means that subjective psychic acts are supposed to achieve what is on principle denied by the objective psychological premises. It is a case of dissociation, where the one hand has a priori refuted, and keeps refuting, what the other hand tries to achieve.[73]

"By honest means" would, by contrast, imply that the semantic content of the experience would be able to self-sufficiently speak for itself, that it would merely in a concrete way exemplify, portray, and perform in actuality what is already, in a most general form and on principle, outlined in the prevailing "syntax."[74] The fundamental work

[73] A full-fledged dissociation in the psychological sense is not merely a difference between left and right hand, not harmlessly only the one's *not knowing* what the other is doing. Neurotic dissociation implies self-contradiction, or more precisely: a split that prevents the self-contradiction from becoming openly visible and thus from self-destructing or self-sublating.

[74] The difference between "semantic" and "syntactical" is the static, structural equivalent to that other pair of opposites denoting a performance or action, be it a spontaneous or methodical one: "acting out," on the one hand, and "'remembering,' interiorizing-into-itself," on the other hand.

of authentification would be done by the logic or syntax. The content would be the explicit manifestation of the *prevailing* truth. The empirical-practical behavior of individual consciousness would thus be relieved of the burden of itself having to establish the fundamental (structural[75]) validity and fulfilling meaning of the content. Consciousness would know itself to be a priori supported and fully backed up. Dishonesty reverses this relation and thus amounts to a psychological life on credit, with no hope of ever being able to pay back the debts amassed. But dishonesty is unavoidable if the truth of the modern condition is logical negativity while consciousness nevertheless insists (in the area of *essential* questions) on the positivity of meaning and knowledge.[76]

Likewise, the psychic, empirical individuation process was in Jung's scheme charged with the task of achieving the *coniunctio oppositorum* that was excluded from the logic of his psychological theory. *This* dissociation (unbridgeable difference) has the form of a deferral, or *différance*, into the future. It is the same kind of logic as prevails in the "intentionality" of consciousness in Husserlian phenomenology, where each *noesis* (intentional act) can never catch up with itself. Of course, the whole relation between this particular *noesis* and its *noema* can itself become the object or *noema* of a new intentional act, but this new meta-level *noesis* is then again on principle divorced from itself, and so on *ad infinitum*. The only difference (in this regard) between Husserl's phenomenology and Jung's idea of the individuation process is that in phenomenology the unbridgeable difference is explicitly disclosed and discussed, whereas Jung disguises the same difference prevailing in his scheme, sending us, as it were, on a wild-goose chase, as if the *coniunctio oppositorum* and "individuation" in his sense were a *real* option.[77]

---

[75] By "structural" I am hinting at something like the "secure statics" of the content.

[76] We can distinguish three aspects that together make up one structure. (1) The fundamental construal of the subject as "dumb fish" overwhelmed by immediate experience, which (2) is possible only through the radical dissociation on the syntactical level between immediate experience and the thinking subject (which as modern subject is irrevocably in the logical status of "doubt"), and (3) the illegitimate (psychologically "dishonest") secondary rescue of the "freedom" (Jung) of the subject through a kind of "acting-out" on the semantic or psychic level.

[77] Of course, by at one occasion saying, "The goal is important only as an idea; the essential thing is the *opus* which leads to the goal: *that* is the goal of a lifetime" (*CW* 16 § 400), Jung seems to admit, although only indirectly so, that the goal cannot ever be actually reached. By then, however, declaring the *opus* of striving for the goal to be the

If Jung's irrationalism, as I pointed out, is "only" a logical, not an empirical or semantic one, we see that his theory, which in itself, in its semantic appearance, is totally committed to semantic contents and rejects the level of syntactical form or *denkerische Form*, itself nevertheless operates on the level of logical form, and as *modern* theory of course inevitably so. Jung's stuffing the soul's life onto the semantic level of experienced images and into "the unconscious" is not itself an act on the semantic level, but a syntactical act. The psychology committed to "immediate experience" is not itself based on or expressive of "immediate experience." The Scholastics and all philosophers (including Hegel, of course) perform their logical operations out in the open. The psychology of the unconscious and of direct experience pushed its logical operations out of itself into its invisible background, keeping itself unconscious about them (which is why it is rightly termed "psychology of the unconscious" [*genitivus subjectivus*]!).

Sometimes, although pretty well camouflaged, Jung had recourse even in a more visible way to "logical grounds," to much-scorned "intellectual sophistry," namely by making equivocal use of the word "experience," giving his "immediate experience" (in the sense of an inner, subjective event, a "vision" or fantasy) out as (as if it were) the direct experience of real elephants. "Accordingly when I say as a psychologist that God is an archetype, I mean by that the 'type' in the soul, a word which, as we know, is derived from τύπος = 'blow' or 'imprint.' The mere word 'archetype' presupposes an imprinter" (*CW* 12 § 15, transl. modif.) We know of his mental contortions concerning the relation between the God-image in the psyche and the real God (e.g., in the same paragraph). Already the boy Jung had, through an (implicit) logical deduction, extracted from his "Basel cathedral" thought a "Who?," the mystification of a "real," but hidden agent as the external originator of and behind his thought ("But *who* wants me to? Who wants to force me to think something I don't know and don't want to know?" *MDR* p. 37).

In his categorical decision to respond to the modern situation and its fundamental "doubt" concerning the religious question with his

new real "goal of a lifetime," he pretends that there is a *real* goal after all and that what he somehow admitted to be a wild-goose chase *is* this real goal. At the same time, we see here clearly how the *empirical opus* is "charged with the task of achieving what" *theoretically* is set up as being categorically out of reach: as existing *only* "as an idea."

knockout argument of "immediate experience" we have the deepest root not only of his rejection of philosophical thought, but also of his Hegel-complex. Having embraced doubt and integrated it into his own thinking by making it the *spiritus rector* of his very method, Hegel had, on the one hand, done what, on the basis of how Jung construed his whole project, was absolutely forbidden, but, on the other hand and at the same time, "Hegel" threatened, if he were to be taken seriously, to hold the mirror up to Jung, reminding him of the trickery and violence underlying his (Jung's) solution. Deep down there must have been in Jung a profound discomfort and uncertainty, if not guilt-feeling, about the brick-like "certainty" that he had created in himself (and kept absolutely hidden as his "secret"[78]) through his having crushed the "doubt-that-has-killed-it" when it first wanted to appear to his consciousness in the Basel cathedral episode and thereafter when it was the impressive and lasting experience of his father's inner torment. There must have been a fundamental uneasiness because such a "doubt" does not *really* disappear by being crushed. And crushing the very character of modernity is of course not a real solution for the *Seelenproblem* of *modern* man. "Immediate experience" gets him nowhere in the area of *essential* questions, except to "beautiful images like in a picture gallery,"[79] to the phoniness of ideologies,[80] and to inflating emotions of "numinosity."[81]

But if Hegel was neither a true philosopher, nor a true psychologist,[82] and his language nothing but arrogant and pompous, then "Hegel," as the certainty-spoiling external reminder for Jung of Jung's act of having crushed the logical status of modernity, was once and for all crushed too. The threat posed by the "thinking form" to

[78] Jung had told us that such secrets as his "act[-] like a psychic poison that alienates their possessor from the community"!

[79] One can think here above all of the cult of the image and "the imaginal" in "imaginal psychology."

[80] Examples are the orthodox-Jungian striving for wholeness and individuation, the personal myth movement, "the myth of meaning," the new "eco-psychology," esoteric holistic worldviews, etc.

[81] *Vide* all the individuals and institutions that are in the business of selling the idea of "Portals to the Sacred," of promoting "numinous" experiences, and promising new religious feelings.

[82] Jung's thesis is that Hegel is really nothing, zero, because in him the psychologist and the philosopher simply cancel each other out. The cunning philosophical disguise ruined the psychological substance and the psychological origin from the unconscious invalidated the philosophical significance of his work.

Jung's project and, more closely, the threat posed by Hegel's dialectical thinking[83] to Jung's irrenunciable principle of a fundamental dissociation between (archetypal) experience and experiencing subject as well as between semantics and syntax were eliminated. The only thing that ultimately remained was Jung's secret, his absolutely incommunicable secret that was concealed, for example, behind his late verbal statement, "I do not believe, I know." At the same time, immediacy, logical innocence, externality, and the exclusiveness of the semantic realm, which together make up the simulation (not a return to!, not a *renaissance* or resuscitation!) *in modernity* of the logical *Ancien Régime*, were safeguarded.

10. Self-castration *ad majorem Dei gloriam*. Jung's *Habemus Papam*

With the last sentence we have already moved from our more causal-reductive analysis to the truly psychological final-prospective aspect of Jung's empiricist stance that made him have to reject Hegel sight-unseen. The need to crush (and thus get rid of) the modern "doubt" is only the negative, defensive aspect. There is also a constructive or productive aspect, a wish to establish and celebrate something. Something was to be set up as being absolutely unquestionable, radically outside, above, or prior to cultural history and historical process, to consciousness and logos, to the human mind, something fundamentally Pre-... and absolutely privileged: primordial. Exempt from human thinking, from being a result of reflections, a product of culture. Something truly untouched and pure, an irreducible Other and vis-à-vis of consciousness. Something that is "behind" what is going on in life. A pure origin.

In Jung's psychology as well as in Archetypal Psychology this absolutely Pure and Pre-... appears in various guises. Jung time and again explicitly stated that what comes from the unconscious is "pure nature," unadulterated by any human processing. There are the archetypes as atemporal omnipresent consciousness-external dominants of consciousness. There is the idea of *Urerfahrung*. Jung entertains the

[83] A thinking that managed to start out from and end up with a *coniunctio oppositorum* so that semantics and syntax reflect each other perfectly: this is the sign of psychological "honesty" in the sense given.

idea of something "extramundane," to which we ought to relate. There is his concept of numinosity. Archetypal Psychology is explicitly defined as a "psychology with Gods." Jung's empiricism and immediatism reappears in it (in altered, much more subtle form) under the labels of "image-sense," "animal-certainty," and *aisthesis*. Refined as it is over against Jung's bulldozer-like overwhelmingness of *Urerfahrung*, Hillman's aestheticism nevertheless likewise proceeds from the assumption of absolutely "direct" experience, which also comes out in his decidedly anti-historical isolating sense of "eachness." He speaks of the inner "voices" to be listened to, of the "faces" that gaze at us from within the phenomena, and of "powers" we are lived by. He believes in something "pre-logical," "pre-dialectical." For him, too, the Gods and myths are eternal, fundamentally above historical time. He has in his scheme the "anima" as well as the "anima mundi" as a pure Other vis-à-vis our utterly "soulless" rationality and the "soulless" modern world.

What all this boils down to is an insistence on the logic of a *linear* relation and a *hierarchical* order. God, the Gods, the powers as dominants *rule*, the subject as "dumb fish" *receives*. The "voices" speak, we listen. The pure soul and the degenerated real world. The revelations from the unconscious and purely receptive consciousness. It is the linear and hierarchical order as we know it from the logical structure of religion and metaphysics, the relation between the absolute (in a metaphysical sense, beautifully reflected politically in absolutist monarchy) and the relative, between the metaphysical substance and the contingent, accidental—the psychological *Ancien Régime*.

What, by contrast, the "doubt" that Jung experienced so vividly, both biographically and culturally, "killed" is nothing else but this sense of any Pre-..., *Ur-*..., arche-..., *An-sich*, anything absolutely privileged and primordial, any Immediate, any absolute substance, anything exempt from human cultural productivity and above historical time. It is this very sense of linearity and hierarchy. The "doubt-that-killed-it" has pulled the floor out from under this thought structure, destroyed the precondition for this projecting a property of the mind out, for setting it up as existing outside and prior to it. But the achievement and gift of this destruction produced by "doubt" is that it forced and enabled man's world-relation to become uroboric. There is no extramundane other for the modern mind. This projection has been seen through. Absolute interiority. The mind knows that whatever it experiences, it may empirically be as unexpected and surprising as can be, is not anything truly primordial. In what it experiences, the mind only encounters (aspects of) itself. Experience happens *within* the mind's uroboric self-relation and self-knowledge. We are totally, on all sides, surrounded by soul. No fundamental Other. Nothing truly external. What we encounter is not "nature" but always already "culture."[84] The archetypes in particular and everything coming "from the unconscious" is sunken, sedimented cultural assets (in contrast to what the modern sciences discover, which amounts to truly new further-developments of the mind's self-understanding, self-reflection *in* the way physics, chemistry, and physiology force the mind to understand the *world*).

So we could also say that what the crushing of the "doubt" really boils down to is *the ideological translation of history (culture, human mind) into nature* (where "nature" means something pre-given and mind-external). It is ideological because the preconditions (and thus the justification) for such a projection (or extrajection) out of the mind and history into the status of an absolute "A priori" have in fact been destroyed. It had been perfectly legitimate during the time of myth as well as later during the age of religion and metaphysics in the sense of a *prima philosophia* to see the world and human existence in terms of a hierarchical world-order with a firm metaphysical *ground* and an extramundane and extratemporal Creator of the world and sustainer of it. This perceiving the soul's own contents or rather functions "out there" in the cosmos as entities and beings, as divine powers and as metaphysical "substance," was psychologically completely appropriate and fully backed up by the then prevailing status of consciousness reached and the actual mode of man's being-in-the-world. But once consciousness has come home to *itself*, once it has objectively seen through that which before had been experienced as cosmic powers, divine forces, and ontological beings are the result of its objectifications of its own thought structures extrajected out of the mind, once, that is to say, "doubt" has made all such apperception impossible, then one's personal clinging to the idea of a hierarchical order, of a linear vis-à-vis of consciousness as a passive receiver and the soul as pure nature

[84] In a most basic sense because it is linguistic.

and fundamental other, and one's belief in the immediacy of be it *Urerfahrung* or image-sense, is inevitably ideological. Ideology is the counterfactual giving out of subjective wishes as objective reality. It is a—structurally—metaphysical hypostasis that posits as actually existing what in truth is only sorely missed. It is the substantiation and objectification of subjective functions. Mystification, "fetishism."

It is clear that the refusal to be informed by and obedient to the already experienced "doubt" as the new truth of our situation is—seemingly paradoxically—a fundamental betrayal of the soul, paradoxically so since this refusal presents itself precisely as its opposite, as an explicit (and of course subjectively honest) programmatic intention of promoting the cause of the soul, of anima, of the anima mundi: of ensouling the world and truly finding oneself. It is a violation of the objectively already achieved awareness of the soul's uroboric interiority.

The deepest motivation was of a genuinely religious nature. For, as mentioned, the crushing of the modern status of consciousness which had been negatively attained by virtue of the "doubt-that-has-killed-it," the crushing that turned the human subject into a "dumb fish," has to be seen as a *sacrificium intellectus*, a notion to which we now, however, other than before, need to give its true religious meaning and depth. It was a sacrifice *ad majorem dei gloriam*, for still being able to stay in a stance of upward-looking to something numinous and absolute, ultimately for *having* something to worship, *having* a semantics. It was a self-castration structurally analogous to the self-castration of the *galli* in Antiquity, young men who in an ecstacy castrated themselves to honor Cybele, the Phrygian Great Mother goddess, following the model of Attis, her son and consort, but different from that self-castration in three points.

First, whereas the *galli*'s self-castration merely served, and once more celebrated and renewed, the glory of an already existing goddess, a goddess fully backed up by the internal syntax of the semantic image of her, the modern psychological self-castration served the purpose of a "primary" setting up of a relation of the human to some higher, divine forces under the *real* conditions of "doubt" and of "born man," that is, when there is no more any authorization of the semantic idea of divine forces by its own intrinsic syntax. Self-castration was the means, and the indispensable price that had to be paid, for the possibility of upholding the hierarchical "metaphysical" order in the first place *at a time* when it has become obsolete. Only through this self-castration was the possibility created of one's still being in possession of a semantic "truth," in possession of a sense of the eternal and divine, of "the sacred" and "the numinous," of "powers" and "voices" that deserve our "acts of humility and submission to their hints." Only the self-sacrifice of the subject *as intelligence* (which in the Jungian tradition IS in itself the real act of humility and submission, the only one feasible) established the *triumph* that consists in the stance of a psychology *with* a Self as God-image in the soul or of the stance of a psychology "*with* Gods." Immediate experience IS, metaphorically speaking, Jung's objectified version of *Annuntio vobis gaudium magnum: habemus Papam.*[85]

The (logical) self-castration produced, i.e., *was* the first-time production of, the (empirical) feeling of something absolutely overwhelming. There was not first something like the Phrygian Mother Goddess or, much later, the Christian Trinitarian God as culturally and cultically authorized and truly experienced reality[86] that demanded from us our humility and submission. The self-sacrifice was not a response to an experience of something overpowering. It was the other way around. In the modern situation in which Jungian psychology found itself and in which "doubt has killed it," the strategic stance[87] of humble submission and self-castration was the first thing; it was the method for a priori bestowing on ordinary dream images or fantasy experiences the aureole and numinous mystique of hints from the beyond, from voices and powers. "Numinosity" in Jungian psychology is a result and product of a (logical) fabrication. *Urerfahrung* is a construct: the systematic re-interpretation of (actual) experiences *as* primordial and *as* direct revelations of some "higher" significance and *as* overpowering. The virginally innocent directness

[85] With emphasis on "having," "possessing." Just as the Pope is the visible representative of the otherworldly Christ, so our symptoms and inner experiences ultimately point to something divine.

[86] The authorization lay in the fact that unborn man was in fact upward-looking and that these gods or goddesses were the semantic articulation of specific modes of this upward-looking. The semantic god-images were authenticated because they were animated from within themselves by this syntax of upward-looking.

[87] Instead of "strategic stance of ..." we could also say: the act of establishing the logic of ..., the decision to make this logic one's own.

and imagistic eachness assigned to phenomena, which finds its foundation in the idea of *the* imaginal with its timelessness, is the result of an abstraction.

Secondly, the sacrifice of the intellect differs from the self-castration in the context of the Phrygian Great Mother in that it is what Erich Neumann called an "upper castration" rather than a "lower" or literal one.

And thirdly, it differs in that it did not take the form of a literal ritual behavior in practical reality, but occurred already in the hidden recesses of the mind, as a general logical form, a purely epistemic or scientific-methodological construal of things on the syntactical level. This is why it *showed* itself (rather than disguised itself!) as Jung's empiricism in psychology, whose *intrinsic* religious aspect and significance becomes only indirectly manifest in the nearly fanatic affect with which he had to defend the claim that he was an empiricist against so much evidence to the contrary. It is an already fundamentally *sublated* sacrifice, fundamentally *sublated* religious act, a sacrifice as a general form of viewing events.

This again has two aspects. The first one we already touched upon above when we had to realize that Jung's crushing of the modern mind meant *logical*, not psychic or empirical, irrationalism. Jung, and the same applies to Hillman, did not literally cut out his intellect. His *sacrificium intellectus* was a logical, not literal, not empirical-practical sacrifice. What once upon a time had been a cultic or ritual act has in his case been "alchemically" evaporated and thus receded into the hidden syntax of psychology. The fact that the self-castration occurred in the fundamentally distilled form of a general syntax tells us that it is a sacrifice not of an object, a body organ as in the case of the *galli*, or, in Jung's case, a literal human faculty, namely *the* intellect or the human being's *capacity* to reason. Rather it is a sacrifice of the uroboric, self-reflective, dialectical *structure* or *logic* of consciousness achieved in modernity, the mind's self-contained interiority that objectively had already been realized. *If* there was to be the desired undialectical linear opposition (vis-à-vis) of ego and the unconscious, ego and Self, consciousness and overwhelming primordial experience (or, in Hillman's case, our direct vis-à-vis with "voices" or images in his sense of *aisthesis* = the stance of immediacy) then, as a matter of course, the uroboric self-relational structure of consciousness had to be eliminated.

The crushing of the modern "doubt"[88] IS the undoing of the uroboros as the new logical form of consciousness. It is this because this "doubt" is, negatively expressed, the undermining of the firm belief in the logical externality and independent objective existence of what is experienced, and, positively expressed, the first immediacy of the self-awareness of the *subject* as indispensable element in the production of experience: It is the awareness that it is the subject (the human mind) itself that has—maybe to a large extent unconsciously—*produced* what it consciously receives through its experience, produced even those experiences by which it may be overwhelmed. There is no Other as mysterious author.

So much on the first aspect. The second aspect is that the religiousness of the sacrifice has in itself semantically been completely negated and depleted. It is a religious sacrifice on that historical level of consciousness for which religion has already *in toto* become sublated, which means that where it is held on to it has logically but unwittingly turned into a nihilistic religion: a religion *of* nothing. There is in Jungian psychology no longer a specific deity to be worshiped or a specific creed, not any specific cult practice, no particular "meaning of life," in fact no concrete semantic content at all. It does not really matter anymore what name we use, whether God, or the Self, the god-image in the soul, or "archetypes," or even totally abstractly "the unconscious"—or, still more surprisingly, the merely scientific clinical names of symptoms, like "obsession" or "phobia," because according to Jung they, too, cannot help but confirm the general structure of "religious service." But *that* is precisely, though unadmittedly, the only thing that still really counts: namely that the abstract logical structure is retained of a linear relation to something overwhelming (no matter what), to something which is speechlessly venerated as "archetypal," "numinous," "sacred,"—*the empty form* of religion, the generalized methodological stance of upward-looking, the logic of "humility and submission," the blank "*That*" of higher meaning.

---

[88] The crushing of the modern doubt should by no means be confused with the *negation of the negation.* I argued against such a confusion—apropos of the particular topic of modern man's attitude towards nature—in the first pages of my "'Irrelevantification' or: On the Death of Nature, the Construction of 'the Archetype,' and the Birth of Man," in my *The Soul Always Thinks*, New Orleans, LA (Spring Journal Books) 2010, pp. 387–442.

"The mandala is the center," Jung said, advising us to circumambulate the center. "Later, everything points to the center" (*MDR* p. 196 f.). But Jung could never demonstrate such a center, and never say *what* this posited center is, what or who is in the center. When he tried to positively describe the center he could do no more than to use such *Leerbegriffe* (empty concepts) as "wholeness" or "the self." Mandala-drawing, circumambulating "the center," striving for "wholeness"—they *malgré lui* betray Jung's hidden nihilism: a practice of circling around nothing, an empty word, a mere suggestion of something. The Israelites who danced around the Golden Calf truly had a fulfilled center. There really was a Golden Calf that constituted a true center and made the circumambulation around it worthwhile and authentic. And the fact that they had been able to create this Golden Calf image in the first place was fully backed up by their psychology or the logic of their mode of being-in-the-world. But today?[89] The ego's idle circumambulation has the function of having to evoke the illusionary hope that where there is a circling movement there surely must also be a center. The circumambulation itself has become purely functional.

With big power-words like "wholeness" and "self" and "individuation" Jung posits something as positively existing which in itself has no content and cannot be documented: in this way he inadvertently (1) worships (2) Nothing. Therein lies the secret nihilism of Jung's project. What is "wholeness" other than the hypostatization of a totally *formalistic* abstraction? The whole talk of myths, of the Gods, of the imaginal boils down to a possession of a semantics that, however, is in itself hollow, the mere placeholder for one.[90] The zero-stage of a semantics. All this follows the

[89] In 1948 the art-historian Hans Sedlmayr published his influential *Verlust der Mitte* (1948, published in English in 1957 as *Art in Crisis: The Lost Center*, London: Hollis & Carter), and even if one may not want to accept his controversial anti-modernist evaluation, his analytical description of the phenomenology of 19th and 20th century art that shows the cultural loss of the center remains valid. We also remember the general attack on every sort of "centrism" by more recent "post-modern" philosophy and literary criticism.

[90] We merely have to contrast the Christian *Symbolum Apostolorum* (Apostles' Creed), which spells out specifically *what* is believed and thus concentrates on the semantics, with Jung's merely formal, content-less dictum, "I do not believe, I know," which focuses on the verb (the subjective act performed by the I) and the specific difference between believing and knowing.

logic expressed in Nietzsche's insight quoted above, "rather is Man willing to want *the nought* than *not* to want."

Whatever comes from the collective unconscious is viewed as (at least ultimately) being religious in this abstract, sublated, emptied-out sense. The very word *religio* means for Jung in the last analysis no more than the "careful observation" of our dreams and spontaneous fantasies. "What is the great Dream? It consists of the many small dreams and the many acts of humility and submission to their hints" (*Letters 2*, p. 591, to Read, 2 September 1960). Concrete images such as those occurring in our dreams and visions serve merely as a catalyst or as practice material by means of which the *functional* act of self-sacrifice can be performed ever anew, which in turn serves the purpose of erecting the structure of upward-looking, the sense of one's possessing (not something [logically] positive to look up to, a real Golden Calf, a real Truth, a real God, but merely) the vacuous *idea* of something positive.

Whereas Jung himself believed that his empiricism was the same truly scientific methodological stance as the one that prevails in modern science,[91] and whereas he was not really able to see through to the fact that it was for him much rather a synonym for religion in this diluted sense (*religio*, careful observation of pure "facts"), Archetypal Psychology is beyond that literal empiricism. However, it nevertheless precisely retained the basic structure achieved through the *sacrificium intellectus* in the religious sense, the structure of upward-looking. The fundamental sublatedness of its religion, and the nihilism inherent in its stance, become most apparent in its psychological "polytheism," on the one hand, which ultimately means that religiously "anything goes," and, of course, in the reduction of "the Gods" to metaphors, on the other hand. Again, it is the empty form of "religion," the methodological religious attitude *as such*, sort of *l'art pour l'art*, without any actual commitment. And because it somehow knows this, it does not call itself religion and has broken with Jung's more explicit "theology" (or, as I would prefer to say, his "theosophy"), calling itself imaginal psychology instead, *but* nonetheless a psychology "with Gods," a "polytheistic psychology." And as much as it does not take itself literally, but has an ironic and playful relation to itself as well as

[91] Although in another regard it was fundamentally different for him because it was an empiricism of *the soul*.

to its Gods as mere "metaphors," this playfulness is, however, *in itself* deadly serious! Semantically the Gods are no more than metaphors (not objects of belief and cult), but psychologically or syntactically the religious attitude survives.

The logic of the dictum so strongly endorsed by Jung, *Vocatus atque non vocatus deus aderit*, shows itself to be true here, too, here, namely at the time *post mortem dei*, to use Greg Mogenson's felicitous phrase.[92] Jungian psychology cannot offer us a god or a meaning, but only the irrevocably empty position of one, or the on principle unfulfillable striving for one, the *circumambulatio* around a center that by definition has to stay empty.[93] It does not set up a substance in the literal metaphysical sense, but it certainly provides the vague sense of one. We do not get full-fledged positivities, but nevertheless the empty form of positivity; no fulfilled semantics, but the empty form of semantics. This empty-form character is a tribute to modernity, to the absolute negativity inherent in the "doubt-that-has-killed-it" or, which is the same expressed from the point of view of the other side of the coin, to the uroboric status of consciousness. *Vocatus atque non vocatus*: you cannot escape from the "doubt," the absolute negativity, even if you crush it, crush the subjective mind, in order to simulate the situation of the fundamental Other. The negativity, once it happens to be the soul's real logical status, gets you one way or another. So despite the fact that the *sacrificium intellectus* that we find in Jung is a sacrifice of truly religious depth and significance *ad majorem dei gloriam*, what it ultimately strives to achieve has been fundamentally and unwittingly reduced to, "alchemically" evaporated into, the (secondarily semanticized) *syntactical form* of semantic contents (and the form of ideology[94] at that): that is, one that is "charged with the task of achieving what cannot be done by honest means."

In the last analysis it is itself the hypostatized "doubt" cunningly disguised as its lavishly decorated opposite.[95]

[92] Greg Mogenson, "Jungian Analysis *Post Mortem Dei*," in: *Spring Journal* Vol. 84, Fall 2010, pp. 207–270.

[93] "On principle" and "by definition" because psychology must not commit the "crime" of a literal metaphysical hypostasis. We can only have our own (irrevocably subjective) experiences. As to the emptiness we recall the already cited statement: "The goal is important only as an idea; the essential thing is the *opus* which leads to the goal: *that* is the goal of a lifetime" (*CW* 16 § 400).

[94] But of course, as we have seen, no more than a fundamentally empty form of ideology.

[95] The opposite: the wealth of archetypal symbols, mythological images, Hillman's polytheism *as a present reality*.

Part III.
Coda to *The Flight Into the Unconscious*

CHAPTER EIGHT

The Problem of "Mystification" in Jung

Concerning certain of his essential views about psychology and religion and his idea of our having "to dream the myth onwards," I have repeatedly charged Jung with "mystification." Leaving aside what I called Jung's "theosophy" (his speculations about Christian religion and the fate of the Godhead), which is another subject and of no concern for the present paper, Jung's "religious psychology," his insistence on "numinous experience" and "religious dreams" as a necessary part of the cure for neurosis and on the individuation of the individual through the experience of "the self" as a God-image in the soul have, I claimed, the character and status of a *simulation*.

This is a serious accusation that could be mistaken and unfair, perhaps based on a misreading or on false presuppositions. In numerous other papers I have argued my case in different contexts. But here I want to confront my view with Jung's own response to a similar charge that had from early on been raised against him and see whether and to what extent his defense of his position in view of this charge invalidates my own charge.

I. The justification for the religious dimension in psychology

In a paper published in 1929 as "Der Gegensatz Freud und Jung" ("The Freud-Jung Antithesis"), translated as "Freud and Jung:

Contrasts" (*CW* 4 §§ 768–784), Jung, after having made some other points, characterizes (§ 780) Freudian psychoanalysis as being only conscious of one half of all psychological reality, "namely of the fleshly bond leading back to father and mother or forward to the children that have sprung from our flesh—'incest' with the past and 'incest' with the future, the original sin of perpetuation of the 'family romance.'" Freud's exclusive horizon is "the sphere of the biological and of family relationships" (§ 781, transl. modif.). For Jung this is not merely a theoretical, but above all also a therapeutic deficit: Freudian psychology "points no way that leads beyond the inexorable cycle of biological events" (§ 780). In contrast to Freud Jung insists that there is a completely different, but equally important, if not more significant other side. This other dimension of the psychological and above all therapeutic issue comes out very clearly in the following statements.

> There is nothing that can free us from it [from "the original sin of perpetuating the 'family romance'"] ... except that opposite urge of life, the spirit. It is not the children of the flesh, but the "children of God," who know freedom. In Ernst Barlach's *The Dead Day*, the mother-daemon says apropos the tragic ending of the family romance: "The only strange thing is that man will not learn that his father is God." That is what Freud would never learn, and what all those who share his outlook refuse to learn or, at least, to which they never find the key. Theology does not make it easy for the seeker, because theology demands faith, and faith is a veritable gift of grace that nobody can make. *We moderns are faced with the necessity of experiencing the spirit again, that is to say, to have primordial experience* [*Urerfahrung*]. This is the only way to break through the magic circle of the biological. (§ 780, transl. modif., Jung's italics)

Because he holds this view, "I am," Jung says, "accused of mysticism" (§ 781).

The English word "mysticism" is ambiguous. As a neutrally descriptive term it can mean the mental world and attitudes of mystics, the experience of direct union with ultimate reality, etc. (in German *Mystik*). But it can also be a derogative term for unfounded beliefs in supersensible or mysterious powers or levels of reality (in German *Mystizismus*). *Mystik* relates to *Mystizismus* as does, e.g., psychology to psychologism. The suffix -ism implies something illegitimate. Jung has *Mystizismus* in this passage, but even in the English translation the combination of "mysticism" and "accusation" makes it clear that the second meaning of the English word is meant.

It can easily be seen why the reproach of mysticism might arise here. According to Jung, by exclusively focusing on the sphere of the biological and the family relationships Freud stays with that positive-factual level of reality that is empirically accessible and can legitimately be the object of scientific investigation. Jung, by contrast, clearly leaves the precincts of a positivistic science when he insists on "the spirit" as "that opposite urge of life," expressing himself in a decidedly religious diction ("children of the flesh" versus "children of God," "original sin") and by way of counter-attack accusing Freud of not wanting to learn the essential lesson that his father is God (whereby in order to express this accusation Jung avails himself of a piece of wisdom pronounced by a "mother-daemon" [!] in a modern poet's play). After having put his cards on the table in this way (as is necessary in a paper on the Freud-Jung antithesis), we can see what is at stake in the controversy between these two psychologists, but we also realize that although Jung in no way puts a smoke-screen up around his controversial tenets and thus does the exact opposite of *mystifying* his own position, with these particular views he nevertheless *for the scientifically minded public* obviously lays himself wide open to the charge of mysticism.

Precisely by showning his hand and squarely facing the charge of mysticism, Jung is able to take the bull by the horns and present his counter-argument as a defense against this accusation. He says:

> I do not, however, accept responsibility for the fact that man has, always and everywhere, quite naturally come up with religious functioning, and that therefore the human soul has from time immemorial been suffused and shot through with religious feelings and ideas. Whoever cannot see this aspect of the human soul is blind, and whoever chooses to explain it away, or to "enlighten" it away, has no sense of factual reality. (§ 781, transl. modif.)

In other words, Jung's described position, far from being a case of mysticism and mystification, is much rather a truly empirical, scientific one. Not he, Jung, gives (to speak with Kant) "the deceptive appearance of new lands" ("*neue Länder lügen*"!) where in reality there is nothing, or merely a fog-bank. Not he invents a supersensible dimension of reality, "the spirit" as the other pole of the world, the realm of gods and demons. No, the soul has produced these ideas and the corresponding deep feelings and needs. And to take them into account is the psychologist's scientific responsibility and the urgent therapeutic responsibility of the doctor faced with patients suffering from neuroses. Not he, Jung, is guilty of mysticism, but, conversely, those who deny the spirit are blind, indeed guilty of refusing to face up to reality, namely the reality of the *soul.* Their apperception of the very phenomena that they as psychologists are concerned with is fundamentally deficient. They a priori amputate a whole dimension inherent in that which they are called on to comprehend. They lack the full set of categories necessary to do justice to psychic reality.

Leaving completely aside in our context the issue of the Freud-Jung opposition as well as the question of the adequacy of Jung's Freud interpretation, but focusing only on Jung's justification of his own position, we can say that his point is well taken. I concur with his refutation of the charge of mysticism raised against him, *that* mysticism charge that was based on his openness to the religious dimension of the soul. It is perfectly legitimate to aim, as Jung did, for an "equal balance of the flesh and the spirit" (§ 783). It would, on the contrary, amount to an irresponsible curtailment, or, as I said, an amputation, if the whole dimension of the spirit and religion were excluded from psychology and if our psychological outlook were confined to the sphere of the biological and personalistic. The topics of initiation as man's "birth from the spirit" and, in general, of man's descent from divine parents are an irrenunciable part of psychic reality. And religious phenomena must not only have an acknowledged place in psychology as one particular aspect of all its diverse topics, i.e., within the semantics of psychology. The religious dimension must also be allowed to inform the whole conception and definition of soul and be included in the set of fundamental categories or perspectives that psychology works with. As a matter of course psychology must *liberate* the assessment of psychological phenomenology from the modern ideological and scientistic-positivistic straightjacket into which it is usually placed. It is required, as Jung says he prefers, "right away" "to call things by the names under which they have always been known" (§ 781), that is, to call things by their mythic and religious names, the names of gods, of spirits and of Spirit as such.

In general, science is wont to disregard the common vernacular names and instead to give artificial, newly coined names to phenomena, names mostly taken from Greek or Latin roots. Science prefers technical terms. But why is it, conversely, necessary in psychology to stick to the traditional names under which soul phenomena manifested themselves? Simply because the names are an indispensable part of the phenomena in question, nay, they *are* the very phenomena themselves. The names of soul phenomena—this is what is absolutely special about psychology—do not have behind them a positive substrate, a subsisting soul substance, *whose* mere designation or label they would be; there is not an external referent that they would merely *refer* to; the names of psychological phenomena (Zeus, God, angel, fairy, heaven and hell, soul, I, the unconscious, consciousness, faith, guilt, sin, mourning) are not the proper names *of* independently existing phenomena. Rather *they* are "the soul's" self-representation, self-expression, self-production. Psychology is, as it were, nothing but the study of "names," because those "names" are all that there is for psychology to study. The duality of and difference between name and phenomenon that prevails in everyday life and, in particular, in the sciences does not exist here. Psychology is that odd field of study that does not deal with positive realities, with substrates or substances. *Its* "substances" are the completely insubstantial, airy "names" invented by "the soul" and what they involve and imply.

Far from suggesting a form of illegitimate mysticism it is precisely the psychological virtue of Jung's approach that he goes on principle beyond the hard-core ideas of biological drives, "family romance," and "object relations." It is his virtue that—when he is at his best—he is capable of leaving behind any thinking in terms of positive-factual substrates or externally given referents and causes and seeing the soul *mystery* (something symbolic, a concern of the spirit and the religious soul) at work in the self-sufficient nothingnesses of mere names, fictions, images, comprehending these nothingnesses *as* the very "*substance*" that psychology is about. This ability to comprehend the "names" as self-sufficient, self-referential is the very point where the breakthrough from so-called psychology into psychology proper happens. It is its *sine qua non.*

II. The difference between the former and the present use of the same old religious "names"

Nevertheless, this result of our examination does not make my charge of "mystification" raised against certain aspects of Jung's thinking collapse into nothing. This is because my charge does not hinge on the "flesh-spirit," "biology-religion," "positivism-mythic meaning" opposition, on the question of whether or not religious symbols and feelings are to be taken seriously as authentic soul contents or whether they need to be reduced to some other positive-factual function by psychology, questions which were at stake in that earlier accusation and Jung's response to it. My charge takes issue with another problem and amounts to a critique that Jung was unaware of and did not even suspect, which also means that he could not respond to it, neither explicitly nor implicitly.

However, the fact that my critique refers to something that is *not* really the topic of the relevant passages in Jung's paper does not mean, as one might perhaps suppose, that we now would have to turn to other texts of Jung's in order to substantiate from them the charge of "mystification." It is on the contrary essential to see and demonstrate that the very defense (and, as I pointed out, the in itself convincing defense) Jung offered against the reproach of "mysticism" as understood by his psychoanalytic opponents contains traces of that thinking that gives rise to my accusation of a "mystification" in Jung. This indicates that my diagnosis of a mystification is really about a second-order or second-level "mysticism," one that is inherent, but hidden within Jung's argument (paradoxically that very argument with which he *successfully* defends himself against the first-level "mysticism" accusation), rather than being simply a completely other, additional mysticism (side by side with the already refuted first-sense mysticism).

Psychology, I said, is the study of nothing but "names." But this statement is only correct if and when the word "names" is expressive of a logic of identity, which is not always, indeed not usually the case.

Those "names" that are the subject-matter of psychology have to be self-sufficient and self-referential; they have to have "everything they need within themselves." The "name" in the narrower sense (as a linguistic sound cluster with a particular meaning) must itself be the very phenomenon "referred" to, "all there is," so to speak. Another, more psychological, way of putting it would be to say that the name must be the phenomenon's self-presentation, self-manifestation. It must be "the (not existing) soul's" speaking about itself. The moment, on the other hand, that there is a difference between name and phenomenon, the moment name and phenomenon are two separate entities and the name is *assigned* to an already given independent phenomenon we are no longer dealing with those "names" that psychology is about.

Looking from here at a sentence in Jung's text like "I have therefore preferred to call things by the names under which they have always been known" we notice that a logic of difference prevails in it. If Jung prefers one type of names over others for "things," he has a choice. In his thinking he is already in a situation in which name and phenomenon are two separate things. Others obviously prefer other names for the same things. So the names that Jung uses have their origin in his own subjective naming (assigning a name) and not in the things themselves as their inescapable self-presentation.

Now one might want to argue here that if his preference is to choose the names "under which things have always been known" Jung precisely avoids being the one who *assigns* a name to them according to his own taste. He lets the names be given to him. He listens to the already existing names. He is obedient. However, the same problem as before returns also with this argument. "Have always been known" entails a difference to "under what they are presently known." And choosing old, traditional names for phenomena does not turn these names into the phenomena's self-naming, unless one is dealing with historical phenomena and a historical psychology. But Jung is in the first place not concerned here with former times. *He* is talking about "us moderns" and wants to use the old names for present-day phenomena. He is seeking for a solution for today's psychological situation.

The extent to which he is aware of a fundamental difference, an unbridgeable gap, between former times and today in psychological regards comes out especially in this sentence of his: "Theology does not make it easy for those who are looking for the key, because theology demands faith, and faith is a veritable gift of grace that nobody can make." Actually, if Jung prefers the old names he ought to welcome theology and the Churches with open arms, because in them the inherited "old names" are still in use in a more or less unbroken continuous tradition, and thus with a certain legitimacy. In them the spirit of former ages juts into the modern world. The fact that Jung nevertheless needs to reject theology indicates that he is keenly aware of the fact that an attempt to *continue* the old tradition will psychologically not do today.

One reason for his rejection is his concern about those who seek. The need to seek is an expression of the modern predicament. Nobody needed to seek in traditional societies. But modernity is characterized by a loss, and that alone makes a seeking necessary. Those, by contrast, who in the modern world still uphold the old religious tradition and try to keep it alive do not need to *search* for any "key." For them nothing is missing. They always already have their place in that very spiritual reality (i.e., the insight that man's father is God) to which according to Jung truly modern man has not found the key.

A second reason is that Jung says theology "demands faith." This phrase either implies that the individual is supposed to "swallow" a belief system, force his mind to believe something that it is not naturally convinced of, or it implies that, as a veritable gift of grace, faith is an irrational and unpredictable happening. But in either case it is imposed or comes from outside upon the human mind, either from the will of the ego or from the will of God. As psychologists we do not have to be concerned here with the correct theological understanding of faith in its deepest sense, where the "gift of grace" idea has its rightful place. Our interest in this context, just as Jung's own interest in this paper of his, is the practical historical reality of religious faith. When we focus on faith in this sense (rather than on the subtleties of theology), it becomes immediately clear that the idea that faith is demanded and has to be imposed on consciousness is a decidedly modernist view, expressive of a situation in which religious faith has precisely been lost, a situation in which it is no longer the self-evident truth in which people live.

In former times, Christian faith had for centuries been a mass phenomenon, if I may say so. Theology did not have to demand it, nor was it for the majority of believers in any way "a veritable gift of grace." No, during those times it was, conversely, as Jung himself loved to cite, *quod semper et ubique et ab omnibus creditur* (what has always been and is believed everywhere and by everybody). It was the most normal and natural thing in the world. People were born into faith in God and Christ much the same way they were born into their mother tongue. The whole culture circled around and was permeated by a religious concern (Jung himself said: "suffused and shot through with religious feelings and ideas"). During the Middle Ages, numerous individuals felt driven to become monks or nuns, or to go as hermits into the wilds in order, as Jung once put it following Nietzsche, "to hum with the bears in honor of the Creator"[1]; masses were filled with pious passion. Theology did not have to make things easy for people to help them "find" the key (above all also for the simple fact that theology was a luxury for a few intellectuals only).

Jung himself time and again impressed on us that religion formerly used to be always antecedently given to the individual by his culture and was not based on personal experience or illumination. Just think of his repeated pointing to the explanation he was given for why the Elgonyi in Africa performed a certain ritual: "'That has always been done,' they said. It was impossible to obtain any explanation, and I realized that they actually knew only *that* they did it, not *what* they were doing" (*MDR* p. 266, transl. modif.). Neither theology (a "theory" about the meaning of this action) nor a gift of grace. Instead: an ancient custom that was alive and carried all its meaning and its fulfillment within *itself*, in the doing (logic of identity!).

Or, a second example for this Jungian insight, think of the following passage: Whereas for us "[t]he dogma of the trinity, the divine nature of the Redeemer, the Incarnation through the Holy Ghost, Christ's miraculous deeds and resurrection, are more conducive to doubt than to belief," "[t]his was not so in earlier centuries .... It needed no *sacrificium intellectus* to believe in miracles, and the report of the birth, life, death, and resurrection of the Redeemer could still

[1] *CW* 9i § 36, transl. modif. The Nietzsche reference is to *Zarathustra*, "Prologue, no. 2."

pass as biography" (*Letters 2*, p. 485, to Tanner, 12 Feb 1959). Faith came quite naturally. But "All this has radically changed in recent times ...," because "the object of belief is no longer inherently convincing." We have difficulties "in clinging on to our previous mythological tenets of belief. Nowadays they demand too much of the effort to believe" (*ibid.*). This passage makes the unbridgeable gap between modernity and "earlier centuries" explicit and thus at the same time reveals for us the unspoken background behind Jung's statement about theology "demanding" faith (which makes that effort necessary) and about faith being a gift of grace. Jung's statement is spoken from the point of view of *modern* consciousness subject to the logic of difference and to the feeling of loss.

This has immediate consequences for the topic of "names." In view of the historical gap (and Jung's full awareness of this gap), his preference "to call things by the names under which they have always been known" seems psychologically illicit. It amounts to a desire to adorn present-day phenomena in borrowed plumes, to a repristination. It is an attempt to create, *despite* the experienced historical gap, the impression of an unbroken continuity, the impression, furthermore, of our being able to *leap* across that great historical divide, much like (by Jung much despised) Kierkegaard wanted to leap into faith. While being on this bank of the river that separates us as moderns from the old world, Jung believes that we can and should take the names for the present-day phenomena from the other bank that we have left behind. Our apperception of today's psychic phenomena can a priori avail itself of given concepts and categories of the past as ready-mades. The logical bed for psychic events is always already made.

This would mean that psychology does no longer have to stick to the self-manifestation of phenomena. It does no longer have to listen to the names that "the soul" gives *today* to its phenomena of its own accord, to "the names" with which these phenomena come and present themselves to us *today*. It rather *knows* already from the outset what the right names must be: the old traditional names. To be sure, there has been a radical historical change, but nothing has really changed: "Our consciousness only imagines that it has lost its gods; in reality they are still there ..." (*Letters 2*, p. 594, 14 September 1960, to Serrano). This is a dogmatic presupposition.

There is, phenomenologically, nothing to indicate that the gods are still alive today. The phenomena do not present themselves as gods or their manifestation. Jung himself realized that "The gods have become diseases; Zeus no longer rules Olympus but rather the solar plexus ..." (*CW* 13 § 37). The psychologically true *name* of psychic phenomena is thus, in this case, "disease" and not god. "Diseases" call modern rational science and treatment methods onto the scene; "gods," by contrast, would demand religious service, ritual, priests. The point of what Jung in fact *said* (but not meant!) is that the whole aspect of the divine, *the very category of "gods,"* has disappeared. This loss is the gap that fundamentally divides us from former ages. With what justification then does Jung nevertheless insist on the name "gods," quite apart from the absurd pretense of a connection in substance, or at least a comparability, between modern problems in the solar plexus and the god Zeus? Jung contradicts himself. He does not abide by his own insight. With his "The gods have become diseases" he openly admits the historical divide, but at the same time he *smuggles* the idea of an unbroken continuity into his admission: "*the gods* have become ...." What once upon a time appeared as gods, *that same thing* now appears as diseases. It is merely a costume change.

But no, it is not *the gods* who have become neurotic diseases. The latter are an entirely new and different modern phenomenon that did not exist in former times. They are not merely a new guise for something ancient. The "name" change represents a real change *of the phenomena*, because, as I said, the name, the "category," *is* the psychological phenomenon; the different name is the indicator of something truly new that requires to be seen on its own terms and in its own context, the context of its historical locus.

The belief in "the rediscovery of the gods as psychic factors, that is, as archetypes of the unconscious" (*CW* 9i § 50) is an ideological conception. The various "archetypes" are a set of abstract instruments (categories) of the modern scientific mind for the psychological typology of historical images and ideas (i.e., *contents*) and of perspectives of consciousness (i.e., mental *structures*), just as "thinking," "feeling," "sensation," and "intuition" are abstract categories of the typology of orientation *functions*. The archetypes are neither themselves psychic phenomena, let alone *factors* ("makers"), nor are the gods "rediscovered." Both views amount to mystifications.

The decisive question is what the source of "the names" used is. For psychology the source has to be, as indicated, the phenomenon itself. Psychology is committed and bound to the self-presentation of phenomena (logic of identity). But frequently, really-existing psychology and collective consciousness use other sources for the names it assigns to phenomena. Three cases can be distinguished.

1. Very often consciousness lags for a long time behind the actual psychological development. It is still completely under the spell of the previous psychological situation and thus has only outdated categories and names available as conceptual tools for trying to make sense of a completely new, already real psychological situation, which necessarily miscarries. Repurposing a formulation used by Jung in a very different context we can say its mode of apperception (the names it uses, has to use) is in this case "a hangover from the past, a *caput mortuum*" (*CW* 10 § 367). The best examples are of course present-day Churches and all those who interpret modern life in the traditional terms of religion, sin, God, salvation, transcendence, absolute meaning.

2. The opposite case is retrojection. Here, names taken from the *new* psychological situation (for which they are appropriate and authentic) are absolutized and on this basis the "names" and thus the phenomena of former ages are denounced as illusions, as "nothing but." The prime psychological example is of course Freud's denouncement of religion as an illusion. Here we clearly see how the modern truth of the obsolescence of religion, how the psychological phenomenon of the disappearance of the self-representation of psychological phenomena as religious, as manifestations of gods, etc., is retrojected into the past and codified for all times. This is unpsychological and an illegitimate dogmatic prejudice, an encroachment of a subjective ideological or dogmatic prejudgment upon psychology.

Insofar as we are truly psychologists we can determine whether a description is the self-presentation of the phenomenon described, or not. But apart from this particular distinction we have no way of distinguishing between illusion and the real, since everything we are dealing with has the character of mere name, idea, fantasy, statement, image, belief. All our veritable phenomena in psychology are "illusions." Here we may recall Jung's warning of "the saving delusion that *this* wisdom was good and *that* was bad," of "the artificial sundering of true and false wisdom" (*CW* 9i § 31) as well as his crucial statement that "... there are still people who believe that a psychoanalyst could be lied to by his patients. But this is quite impossible. Lies are fantasies. And we treat fantasies" (*CW* 4 § 300 fn., transl. modif.). That is our *métier*. So the question for psychology is not whether something is an illusion or "real," but whether each particular illusion in question is described on its own terms (under the name by which it presents itself of its own accord and wants to be called) or not.[2]

Freud's view of religion is of course only one small specimen from the powerful general modern trend that started with Ludwig Feuerbach and went on to Heidegger, Derrida and beyond, the trend to time and again retrojectively denounce religion and classical metaphysics as faulty on the basis of the absolutized modern logic of difference.

3. The third possible problematic source of "religious" names is the psychologist's personal wish or need. At first glance, Jung's using, for phenomena in our modern world, the names "under which they have always been known" could appear as a case of "hangover from the past." But it is clearly not. For Jung rejects tradition (the Churches, theology) as not helpful. Instead he opts, as we have heard, for an alleged "rediscovery of the gods," for an "again," in other words, for something decidedly new after the acknowledged disruption of the continuity of tradition, however something new that is precisely supposed to be the very old, the true origin: "We moderns are faced with the necessity of experiencing the spirit again, that is to say, to have primordial experience

---

[2] And, of course, whether it is "*my* fable, *my* truth." Is it really *rooted* in an individual or a society and thus psychologically real?

[*Urerfahrung*]." But experiences by "us moderns" are inevitably *modern* experiences, reflective of our own historical locus, and not primordial, not *Ur-*.[3] The primordiality of the so-called primordial experience, the claimed true origin that is experienced through them, neither comes as a hangover from the past nor is it inherent in the experience itself (as its self-presentation and as the psychologist's simple noting), but rather modern Jung's addition, his claim, his attribution, if not invention.

Jung needed to propagate this his entirely novel idea, to instil it in the public mind and thus make people slowly get used to it, precisely because it was not something already known or a self-evident part of everybody's experience. The real source of the "primordiality" and the "again" and the "re-" (in "rediscovery") is a subjective need in Jung for *the immediate presence of the gods (or God) today*, under, and precisely despite, the adverse conditions of modernity.[4] The phenomena of modern deep experience do not themselves present themselves as primordial. The primordiality is pinned on them by Jung. It is a modern theoretical construct—an ideological act of naming. Ideology is a belief system driven by personal (or group) *interests*, and a belief system that has the task of providing a seeming rational justification for these interests. By saying, "Our consciousness only imagines that it has lost its gods; in reality they are still there ...," Jung performs the

[3] The prefix "*Ur-*" in German suggests three related things: 1. First, sometimes even absolute beginning, first cause. For example, the German word for "Big Bang" is *Urknall*. *Urkirche* = primitive church. Freud's *Urhorde* = patriarchal horde. 2. Pristine, virginal purity, the original true form of something unadulterated by the distorting influence history or conscious reflection. And 3. extra-temporal, "eternal" model or prototype. Jung's *Urerfahrung* or *Urerlebnis*, while retaining the first meaning ("primitive," "origin") nevertheless above all evokes sense 2, whereas his *Urbild* (archetypal image) obviously mainly relies on the third meaning.

[4] The need for "God as 'primordial experience'" becomes evident as being a subjective, indeed an ego need, in his *MDR* report about how in the Basel cathedral visionary thought episode he managed at age 11 or 12 through manipulation to turn the real experience of the destruction of the God idea into its opposite, into an experience of the absolute certainty of a direct encounter with God. See my papers "Psychology as Anti-Philosophy: C. G. Jung," and "The Disenchantment Complex: C.G. Jung and the modern world," Chapters Two and Three of W.G., *The Flight Into the Unconscious. An Analysis of C.G. Jung's Psychology Project*, New Orleans, LA (Spring Journal Books) 2013.

exactly opposite move to the one Freud performed when he called religion as such an illusion: Jung claims that modern religiouslessness is the *real* illusion.[5] So it's tit for tat. Retrojection (Freud) and repristination (Jung) are inimical twins. But whereas the retrojecting thinkers at least take the names from the real present phenomena and are true to them (despite illegitimately extending the use of the names beyond the modern sphere to phenomena of all times), the repristinating thinker takes his names from his own wishful thinking (and only seemingly, as we have seen, from the past) and thus mystifies the real phenomena.

We have a clear example of this mystification in *CW* 10 § 864.

> The word "principle" comes from *prius*, that which is "first" or "in the beginning." The ultimate principle we can conceive of is God. Principles, when reduced to their ultimates, are simply aspects of God. Good and evil are principles of our ethical judgment, but, reduced to their ontological roots, they are "beginnings," aspects of God, names for God.

For a believer, this may be true. But for a modern thinker, this is an irresponsible ontotheological prejudice. The *logical* meaning of the word "principle" is *reductively* turned into an *ontological* claim of God as an existing reality. "Principles" are themselves by definition "ultimates," otherwise they would not be principles, *archai*, first beginnings. Jung pulls "God" out of the hat and in order to give him a place he has to undo the logical advance from the mythic idea of gods or God to "principles" and to castrate the latter (or let Saturn swallow his children). The present-day phenomena of the words good and evil and the corresponding feelings do by no stretch of the imagination present themselves as *Gottesnamen*. They present themselves as terms for issues of human morality. And on top of it, since Nietzsche we know that culturally we are already beyond good and evil.

---

[5] Quite apart from this, the only point of interest for the psychologist in this regard is the fact that modernity *imagines* that it has lost its god. This is the psychological phenomenon to be studied. "And we treat fantasies"! Whether they are "true" or not is psychologically neither here nor there.

We have sifted through four possible modes of naming according to the source from which the name comes in each case, one psychologically legitimate and three problematic, so that now we are ready to evaluate a few special arguments and cases.

III. The claim that there is a "gold ground" behind ordinary psychic reality

After refuting the accusation of being guilty of mysticism raised above all by the Freudians (with his argument: "I do not, however, accept responsibility for the fact that man has, always and everywhere, quite naturally come up with a religious functioning, and that therefore the human soul has from time immemorial been suffused and shot through with religious feelings and ideas"), and after charging his accusers of blindness, Jung goes a decisive step further and argues that it is paradoxically they who easily succumb to an unwitting, a kind of upside-down mysticism since they deny this essential aspect of reality. Speaking of the father-complex and the concept of the superego in the Freudian school, Jung states:

> This father-complex with its stubbornness and oversensitivity is a religious function misunderstood, a piece of mysticism that takes possession of the sphere of the biological and of family relationships. With his concept of the "superego," Freud makes a bashful attempt to imprint his time-honoured image of Jehovah upon psychological theory. One would do better to express such things clearly right away. I have therefore preferred to call things by the names under which they have always been known. (§ 781, transl. modif.)

In other words, his argument is that "the opposite urge" of psychic life, the religious dimension of the soul, does not simply disappear in the modern secularized world by being denied, but merely continues its work unseen. This, Jung suggests, leads to the possibility that seemingly quite sober, empirical, even materialistic concepts and constructs become unacknowledged carriers of religious feelings.

This is an interesting and sophisticated argument. But it is not very convincing. It may of course well be that Freud's general way of thinking was deeply influenced by the patterns of thought that expressed themselves in the religion of his forebears. The character of the religious tradition from which he comes may well have left, indeed is likely to have left, its stamp on his mindset. However, such a stamp—the *formal* patterns of thought, a specific logical infrastructure inherited from the past—does not ipso facto imply an actual *religious* impulse, let alone the active presence of the image of *God* in a concept like that of the superego. Here Jung jumps to a conclusion or succumbs to a *petitio principii.* He would have had to demonstrate concretely that and how in Freud's case it is in fact a religious force, a (conscious or unconscious) devotion to Jehovah, that manifests itself in the ideas of the superego and in his father-complex.

If we followed Jung's line of thinking here, we would by the same token have to say that the powerful modern ideas of human dignity, of the inalienable worth of each individual, of welfare and social justice, of charity and relief organizations like the Red Cross, which all undoubtedly are an outcome of the Christian tradition, were "a religious function misunderstood" and "a piece of mysticism that takes possession of" worldly affairs. But they are precisely *secular* feelings and movements. The very point here is that the once upon a time "*religious* function" became fully secularized, that is to say, it emancipated itself from its religious origin and from the whole former religious superstructure. It has, while retaining the formal pattern and direction of the original religious impulse, really left behind the time-honored God-image that once upon a time gave rise to it. It is that "former" impulse *without* its religious motivation and superstructure, and thus not the former impulse. Deprived of the entire religious dimension, it is therefore the exact opposite of a "hangover from the past, a *caput mortuum.*" Neither hangover nor dead. It is much rather something that is very much alive, a real present reality, and it is something truly new, precisely because it has *pushed off* from its own religious ancestry for the sake of a future all its own. It has become autonomous.

This change is structurally similar to what in the case of individuals is their maturation, their leaving father and mother in order to become self-determined and self-responsible adults in their own right.[6] Another analogy: The French Revolution brought the change from kings with divine majesty to presidents of republics and democracies, presidents

---

[6] See my "Irrelevantification. Or: On the Death of Nature, the Construction of 'the Archetype,' and the Birth of Man," chapter 16 of my *The Soul Always Thinks*. Collected English Papers, vol. 4, New Orleans, LA (Spring Journal Books) 2010, pp. 387–442.

who derive their authority solely from the people. This is a revolutionary reversal (authority from above, from Heaven, from God, versus authority from below, from human, all-too-human people; a situation of "a sovereign and his subjects" versus a situation of the former "subjects'" own sovereignty and self-rule). Phenomenally speaking, presidents are of course the successors of kings; they have more or less the same function. No matter whether king or president, there is a continuity of position, role, or office. In a way, presidents are still "kings" of sorts, however, kings *deprived* of their divine majesty, kings *minus* the title of supreme sovereign, *minus* the higher, mysterious aura, which means precisely that they are kings no longer. They are simply people like everybody else, who happen to hold a high office. *Psychologically* the "same" office has been removed from one system, syntax, logic (the religious-metaphysical logic of the *Ancien Régime*) and transplanted into a wholly different, indeed opposite logic, that of modern positivity.

In this context of *Ancien Régime* versus French Revolution we do well to remember Jung's statement, "It is the fateful misfortune of psychotherapy to have been born in an age of enlightenment ..." (*CW* § 370). Jung clearly fraternized in psychology with a psychological Ancien Régime, that is with the religious logic of the *Vorzeit* ("former ages," an allusion to Joseph Kleutgen's reactionary [neo-scholastic] works[7]). What he aims at amounts to a modern simulation of the logical stance of pre-modern metaphysics: *Vocatus atque non vocatus deus aderit.*

The autonomy, the logical independence, the "coming of age," of phenomena, is what Jung cannot accept. We have seen this already in connection with "good" and "evil," which in his thinking were not allowed to be, as modern moral and philosophical notions, released into their autonomy, but had to be tied back to their past origin in religion, namely as "names of God." By the same token, the quite sober, rational and secular philosophical term "principle" was remythologized or retheologized by Jung. As I repeatedly stressed, Jung was fully aware of the historical gap and the negation it involved. But what he apparently could not swallow was that the

[7] "Theology der Vorzeit" (1853–60 in 3 volumes, later edition in 5 volumes) and "Philosophie der Vorzeit" (1860–63).

negation was a full negation, namely one of the very *definition* of things. Truly modern phenomena have negated their own provenance, have made themselves independent of it by pushing off from *themselves* (away from what they used to be). They no longer define themselves in terms of their lineage, but instead *self-ground* themselves by giving themselves their *own* new, fresh origin, an origin that is no longer given by history, myth, and religion with their contingent concrete-empirical semantic or imaginal specificity, but is freely established by and grounded in a *universal* idea, in a concept, in *logos*. Furthermore, this negation and effacement of that very ancestral source and former identity from which they historical-factually have come is not a mistake or mere mishap, but rather, the very point of the soul's historical development.

Jung's life-purpose as psychologist appears to have been to counteract this development, to resupply present-day life in its depth—*pars pro toto* represented time and again by particular phenomena—with the old, already overcome religious dimension as its allegedly still valid ground, a ground, however, which it was modernity's very *raison d'être* to overcome and leave behind.

We have to add that Jung wanted to resupply modern life with this ground *not* in the sense of historical memory, in dedication to Mnemosyne, and thus as a *historical* presence, but precisely as a *present reality*! This is what makes his overarching tendency one of mystification. And of course, his resupplying *phenomena* with a religious tain[8] as their backing, comparable to the golden background of medieval paintings, had psychologically the purpose of preventing or undoing *his own* logical coming of age, or, less personalistically put: of undoing or denying the psychological intrinsic content and purpose of modernity, the "birth of *man*"[9] in general.

Jung offered no good reason why Freud's ideas, even though in an abstract-formal sense indebted to aspects of Jewish religion, could not be thoroughly secularized ones. Since Jung's imputing to parts of Freud's theory an unconscious and denied religious agenda is only

---

[8] The *Oxford English Dictionary* provides s.v. the definition from "1858 Simmonds *Dict. Trade*,": "*Tain*, a thin tinplate; tinfoil for mirrors."

[9] Wolfgang Giegerich, "The End of Meaning and the Birth of Man", chapter 9 of *The Soul Always Thinks*. Collected English Papers, vol. 4, New Orleans, LA (Spring Journal Books) 2010, pp. 189–283.

founded on Jung's dogmatic assumption (on his own need to see something religious behind everything) and not on the real self-presentation of the critiqued phenomena (not on their *own* "name"), his reproach of mysticism recoils on Jung himself. His interpretation here amounts to a mystification.

I now want to compare and contrast this example with another one that presents more or less the same and a yet crucially different argumentation. In *MDR* (p. 150) we find Jung's report of the impression he got of the personal significance that Freud's sexual theory had had for Freud.

> When he spoke of it, his tone became urgent, almost anxious, and all signs of his normally critical and skeptical manner vanished. A strange deeply moved expression came over his face, the cause of which I was at a loss to understand. I had a strong intuition that for him sexuality was a sort of *numinosum.*

However, (according to his view) Freud's theoretical conception of sexuality was seriously impaired by his materialistic outlook:

> Although, for Freud, sexuality was undoubtedly a *numinosum,* his terminology and theory seemed to define it exclusively as a biological function. (*MDR* p. 152)

Obviously, this is a very similar argument to the foregoing one: the actually prevailing religious emotion and significance was held down and rendered invisible by the one-sided naturalistic and positivistic world-view that on principle did not allow for what Jung called the "opposite urge" of the soul, but what was nevertheless precisely secretly present in this biologistically-conceived theory of sexuality. Although Jung does not use this word, the idea is clearly that "a piece of mysticism" has taken possession of Freud's theory of sexuality precisely because of the unacknowledged religious dimension it had for him.

Despite the prevailing similarity, my evaluation of *this* Jungian view of Freud has to be different from that of the former example. I cannot just like that dismiss it as a mystifying interpretation by Jung. Because here Jung's interpretation is not solely based on his personal prejudice about the religious dimension. It rather has a phenomenological base. I have, of course, no knowledge about whether Jung's personal impression of the tone, manner, and atmosphere when Freud spoke about sexuality was "correct." But this is also not necessary because I am not concerned here with the truth about Freud, but only with the immanent stringency of Jung's argument. His subjective perception (which is the only thing he, or anyone for that matter, could go by) in fact *showed* him that Freud, Jung's Freud, was to an uncalled-for degree deeply moved. This is part of the self-presentation of the phenomenon. Thus it manifested itself (in Jung's experience) as one that could rightly be interpreted as numinous. And so in this case we get a total phenomenon that displays a contradictory character: inside and secretly numinous, outside and "officially" (in the explicit terminology and theorizing) biologistic. Quite apart from whether Jung's assessment of a hidden and, as it were, upside-down[10] mysticism is "true" in an absolute sense, it is certainly valid,[11] being consistent with the phenomenology experienced by Jung. Jung is guided here by the two contradictory "names" (numinous and materialistic) that the phenomenon gives itself of its own accord. And in this instance, quite in contrast to the previous example, Jung's insistence on "express[ing] such things clearly right away" and "call[ling] things by the names under which they have always been known" is therefore in place.

Having described Jung's overarching interest as resupplying phenomena with a religious tain or gold ground (which was to give out via simulation the old metaphysical logic as a present reality), we can be put in mind of the essential psychological insight into the "psychological difference" and, along with this, of the general methodological principle in psychology of distinguishing between "empirical (or merely psychic) foreground" and "psychological background," as possibly best expressed in Jung's statement apropos a dream or vision that he once discussed: "... behind the impressions of the daily life—behind the scenes—another picture looms up, covered by a thin veil of actual facts."[12] To penetrate to

[10] A mysticism ostensibly appearing in its opposite, unwittingly lying hidden under the garment of a positivistic theory.

[11] Cf. "Whether or not the stories are 'true' is not the problem. The only question is whether what I tell is *my* fable, *my* truth" (*MDR* p. 3). Only God, if he were still alive, could know what was the absolute truth about the personal psychological significance of sexuality for Freud. So we can agree with Jung that the "truth" in this sense "is not the problem." But in this instance we can confirm that what Jung said about Freud indeed deserved the predicate "*my* fable, *my* truth."

[12] C.G. Jung, *The Visions Seminars*, Zürich (Spring Publ.) 1976, p. 8.

this other picture behind the thin veil of actual everyday-like facts is the task of the psychologist.

From here we could perhaps wish to argue that with his insistence on seeing behind "good" and "evil," behind "principles," behind the psychoanalytical superego and behind neurosis and all kinds of other modern phenomena, a divine mystery and therefore calling them "by the names under which they have always been known," namely their religious names, is anything but a mystification. It is much rather nothing else than the application of depth psychology's foremost methodological principle of penetrating from the common-sensical foreground to what is behind the scenes.

But this argument does not work. The two ideas, despite their *formal* similarity, are fundamentally different. The idea of the "other picture behind the thin veil of external facts" refers to the *interpretation* of *dreams* and similar psychic phenomena. "Interpretation" means that it is *only* concerned with our understanding, comprehension, with our getting an insight. It thus contains within itself a fundamental distancing of ourselves from that other picture, a departure, a leave-taking. And the "dreams" themselves are likewise, as (often vague) memories of what we experienced during the night, fundamentally departed. On two counts there is a *kenôsis*. That "other picture" is, as it were, logically underworldly, yonder, *without* immediate relevance or practical benefit for us. As such it is what soul-making tries to attain, soul-making as a purely *psychological* concern. Here we are *only* committed to Mnemosyne. The "benefit" that we hope to gain is nothing but the delight of insight, insight as a value and end in itself and as its own satisfaction.

By contrast, Jung's whole commitment to "the numinous," his interest in resupplying phenomena with a mythic or religious tain or "gold ground" has the *external* aim of a practical gain for us as people, as individuals or as society at large: be it "the rescue of the world" (*CW* 10 § 536) from its going down the drain or our own "individuation" (individuation in Jung's special sense),[13] or be it our being cured from neurosis through the numinous,[14] our finding "meaning" and "the

[13] For Jung both aims are identical. The rescue of the world can only take place through the rescue of the individual's soul, that is, through his individuation.

[14] "But the fact is that the approach to the numinous is the real therapy, and inasmuch as you attain to the numinous experience you are released from the curse of pathology" (Letters 1, p. 377, to P.W. Martin, 20 August 45).

Self" or "God," our obtaining a high metaphysical status by having to play our roles "as actors in the divine drama of life" (*CW* 18 § 628) and even, so in Jung's late thinking, by having to serve as redeemers of God Himself from His abysmal unconsciousness. Instead of a *psychological* remembering of "the other picture," of myth and God in their departedness through our interpretative work, instead of our interiorizing of psychic material into itself, Jung's Restoration project is driven to achieve for "us moderns" an immediate presence of God and myth, thereby leaving psychology behind in favor of a *religious* commitment.

Because "present reality" of the religious dimension is indispensable for Jung and the Jungians, they cannot simply rest content with being confronted with all sorts of psychic phenomena whose "actual facts" and "impressions of daily life" still *have to be supplied* by them with "the other picture behind the scenes." As long as phenomena need to be *provided* with a religious, mythological gold ground, provided by the human psychologists through their own psychological *interpretation*, the "gold background" would appear to be the result of their methodical doing, their human activity of interpretation. They need something better: phenomena that relieve them of the necessity of any such subjective doing on their part by *coming with* the religious "gold background" from the outset on their own account. Jung and the Jungians need *certain particular* "actual facts," *special* empirical experiences, that, to be sure, appear within daily life, but nevertheless *within it* absolutely stand out from it. They must be factual events or experiences that by themselves precisely do *not* give the "impression of daily life" at all, do not seem to be ordinary phenomena, but from the outset appear precisely as the factual present reality of "the other picture," the mythic or religious tain. If there are indeed such empirical facts, then the religious dimension is proven to have a factual basis in ordinary reality and is not merely dependent on our seeing or interpreting the religious "gold ground" "into" or "behind" them for the first time. They would a priori *come* as religious experiences.

IV. The modern "myth" of religious meaning *as* a present reality

There are three main types of factual experience that in Jungian psychology are claimed to be factual religious experiences in this sense: 1. Jung's *primordial experience* [*Urerfahrung*]. 2. More generally but closely related to it, so-called "numinous experiences" at large. 3. Synchronistic events. In all three cases, there is believed to be an immediate presence of the numinous, a present reality of transcendence. And indeed, they are phenomenologically different from, for example, the Freudian "father complex" and the idea of the "superego," which clearly come as sober secular phenomena or concepts and only in Jung's subjective interpretation turn into a concealed appearance of the "time-honoured image of Jehovah." Synchronistic events are *positive-factually* mysterious. *Urerfahrungen* and "numinous experiences" quite naturally strike us as extraordinary, nonsecular, and loaded with religious or "higher meaning" significance. No interpretative addition on our part is needed. Paradoxically—and from now on I have to restrict my discussion to "primordial" and "numinous" experiences while postponing that of synchronicity for a while—*this* particular extraordinary, nonsecular quality *is* precisely quite obviously part of *the unusual* "impression of the daily life" that *they* give. In their case the surface empirical impression *is* itself that "other picture." In their case this "other picture" or the "gold ground" is not covered by a thin veil of actual facts and does not loom up behind the scenes.

But for this very reason, that is, because the religious dimension is their ordinary, "daily-life" impression, we as psychologists must not take these extraordinary phenomena at face value. We must not fall for the impression they give us and be seduced into believing in them. Intellectually this would be superstition and morally our consumption of them would be for our ego satisfaction. Precisely here the task arises for the psychologist to go behind *these* impressions of the daily life—behind the scenes—and penetrate to the other picture that looms up, covered by a thin veil of actual facts, namely (in this case) the veil of our emotions produced by our craving and induced by their suggestive power and our impressionability. Our task is to see through them.[15]

Whereas synchronistic occurrences are unambiguously positive-factual events, the situation is not so simple with "primordial experiences" and "the numinous." What we have to realize is that *Urerfahrung* and "numinosity" are modern *theoretical* concepts, constructs. *Urerfahrungen* were not both historically and during the 20th century well-known phenomena that were merely described and named by Jung. No, they are Jung's creative invention. No other school of psychotherapy felt induced by its experience of psychic life to record such phenomena. Nobody before Jung spoke of them.[16] And as we can see from the meagerness of examples in Jung's writings, he himself was not forced to coin this term by an overwhelming number of observations of *Urerfahrungen* in his therapeutic practice. Now that his *Red Book* has become available we also see that what is described therein hardly qualifies as primordial experiences in his sense, since, heavily based on his academic mythological and literary learning, they are rather modern and not "Ur-." The basis for Jung's term is not, as he wanted, his empiricism; it is not an empirical term. No, "*Urerfahrung*" is a noumenon, a product of his mind. The wish was father to the thought. Much the same applies to how Rudolf Otto's term "numinous" is used in psychology and to the Jungian term "numinous experience."

Now the interesting thing is that each idea is the opposite of itself. Both try to suggest something absolutely empirical, positive-factual. Real experience as present realities. However, they *are* themselves *intellectual* ideas, indeed, *programmatic* concepts, something demanded, a should and ought: "*We moderns are faced with the necessity of experiencing the spirit again, that is to say, to have primordial experience*

[15] For an example see my "Psychology as Anti-Philosophy: C.G. Jung" (chapter 2 in *The Flight Into the Unconscious*) where what Jung gives out as one of his main religious experiences is seen through as not truly being a religious experience at all.

[16] The *word* "Urerfahrung" does occur occasionally (e.g., once in Nietzsche, also in Oswald Spengler, at a later date in Adorno), but in a very different sense from Jung's, namely as "underlying or prototypical or core experience" and referring, in a similar way as the Platonic Idea, to a postulated abstract ideational essence that numerous real and less pure experiences have in common, i.e., sense 3 of the German prefex "*Ur-*" as elucidated above, rather than to an actual empirical experience. For example, "the human *Urerfahrung* of mortality, loss, separation."

[*Urerfahrung*]." In order to see the self-contradiction as which they exist we have to go a step further. I can have the program of getting a university degree. There is no self-contradiction in it because "getting a degree" is something that people can achieve through their own work. But *Urerfahrung* is similar to Jung's own critiqued idea of "a veritable gift of grace that nobody can make." The program of our having to gain primordial experience demands something that nobody can "make." First of all, experience happens or not, it comes, if it comes, of its own accord. And secondly, primordiality is all the more out of our intentionality and reach. Although primordial experience *is* an intellectual program, it disguises its having its origin in a modern theorizing mind as well as its program character and instead presents itself as something absolutely empirical that is available to everybody because it is allegedly in truth *ever-present* and in the depth always already real. That is what it suggests and what makes it self-contradictory, indeed, turns it into a "lie." It is a salvational promise.

So we get an intellectual concept that gives itself out as positive "fact." We get a modern myth *of* the positive-factual reality of the mythic, the religious gold ground. This is Jung's mystification.

Jung of course wants us to actually gain primordial and numinous experience. He offers Jungian analysis and dream work as well as active imagination as the road to it. But I submit that actually attaining such experience is not really the point. The real point is much rather, quite unwittingly, only the *myth* of numinous experience and *Urerfahrung*, the belief in it, the mystique of the idea of it. You only *think* that you go into Jungian analysis to actually get *Urerfahrung*, or the event of the experience of "the Self." In fact, though unwittingly, you go into analysis and study Jung's work as well as classical mythology merely in order to celebrate the *idea* of the numinous, to *dream* the *myth* of primordial archetypal experience onwards and to bask in this aura. It is *only* an intellectual game, a thoroughly modern game of entertaining the abstract idea of "the mythic" as a present reality in the mind—of course while (and by) making oneself believe that one was not at all interested in nothing more than the idea, the abstract concept in the mind. No, in fact one believes that one is precisely and only concerned with the real thing, the actual happening of an overwhelming numinous experience. But this experience usually does not happen at all and does not need to happen either. The *mystique* of the *abstract concepts* of "numinous experience," of "the Self," of *Urerfahrung* is what counts, not what they are the concepts of.[17] The belief in this promise is sufficient: self-sufficient, an end in itself. An actual fulfillment of the promise is unnecessary. It is only necessary that one believes and is enthusiastic about wanting the real experience.

As far as this area of Jungian psychology is concerned (there are of course other important areas and dimensions of Jungian psychology), it is not really *about* myths (real myths and real mythic experience), but *is* much rather *itself* the myth that it is seemingly about. Jung introduced his quite novel, previously unheard-of concepts of direct numinous experience, of the gods as still really present in the unconscious, of the Self, of *Urerfahrung* to an unprepared public. He propagated these ideas and his view that they are indispensably necessary, and first a few, and gradually more and more people, got used to them. And a number of them were enthralled by them.

In this connection we have to remember three things. The first is the *malleability* of modern individuals as described by Sonu Shamdasani, the fact that individuals "have been willing to adopt psychological concepts to view their lives (and that of others), in terms of a play of conditional reflexes, a desire to kill one's father and sleep with one's mother, a psychomachia between the good and the bad breast, a parade of dissociated alters, a quest for self-actualization through peak experiences or contorted twists through the hoola hoops of the symbolic, imaginary, and the real."[18] To this noninclusive list we have to add the ideas of the numinous, (Jungian) individuation, and "primordial experience." People not only adopt these abstract concepts when viewing their lives. They also try to enact them, to pretend to feel accordingly, to produce the feelings, experiences, and images demanded by the particular theory that they adopted and to stylize themselves in its spirit. In this sense psychological concepts become self-fulfilling prophecies. The invention of the concept of

[17] The mystique that it has results from the following contradiction: that it *is* an utterly abstract concept, but that it always already has obliterated its concept-character, presenting itself as something utterly real. The logic of this mystique follows the logic of the "commodity fetishism" according to Marx.

[18] Sonu Shamdasani, *Jung and the Making of Modern Psychology. The Dream of a Science*, Cambridge (Cambridge University Press) 2003, p. 11.

numinous experiences produces its own corroboration (of sorts), because before long there will be enough people who testify to having experienced the numinous.

The second point is about the psychological background for this malleability. It is modern man's straw-character. Through the loss in modernity of metaphysics and religion, modern man has lost his spiritual core and substance. He is not only uprooted, but in addition is also systematically becoming more and more hollowed out, hollowed out, for example, by television, this stultification machine, and the entertainment industry. (I am speaking about modern man as such, the concept of modern man, not about individuals in their diversity.) The emptiness and dryness of his straw-character makes modern man ready and eager to become inflamed, be it inflamed by "numinous experiences" or by Evangelists and other demagogues, by religious and political leaders, by gurus, by myth fetishism, exotic religions and religious craving (e.g., "shamanism"!), by drugs and so on. Apropos the straw nature of modern man we can also recall the following statement by Jung: "... I know from the work with my patients, as well as pupils [i.e., the Jungians!], how much the modern mind is in need of some guidance and how helpless people are in envisaging and dealing with the enormities the present time and still more the immediate future will present us with" (*Letters 2*, p. 498, to Werner Bruecher, 12 April 1959). The more vacuous modern man becomes inwardly (concerning a "spiritual" substance) and the less truly modern he is,[19] the more he may become apt to long for some doctrine or belief system as a psychological prop to lean on.

What I called the straw nature of modern man refers only to his inner psychological constitution, his inner "theoretical" foundation: his "metaphysical" stability, if I may say so. The same person that in this regard is without substance and inner solidity may (but may also not) be quite stable and competent in practical reality, in everyday life and social relations.

The third point is the mystique and fetish-character of the theoretical ideas offered by Jungian psychology as the very cure of modern man's metaphysical emptiness: the ideas of the numinous and

[19] Truly modern man does not need meaning, transcendence, and does not have any feeling of loss.

of primordial experience. Speaking once about certain Christian religious formulas that are taken over and repeated mindlessly, without thinking, Jung said: "One is being made unconscious again through them. Because one does not know what these words mean, and because one abandons oneself to the emotional impression. 'The blood of our Lord Jesus Christ'—this sounds so solemn and so beautifully like Sunday and so religious, so splendidly religious."[20] "Primordial experience," "process of individuation," "becoming Self," "numinosity": all these phrases, too, sound so solemn and so beautifully like Sunday and so religious, so splendidly religious, so seductive! Or maybe not so much like "Sunday" but rather like transcendence and absolute origin, unfathomable depth. They are power words, themselves, *as theoretical concepts*, filled with so-called numinosity (simply through the whole climate of the Jungian and New Age worlds with all their believers), that very numinosity which they insinuate and are supposed to be *about*. And this is why these abstract concepts bring their own fulfillment. As theoretical ideas they *are* themselves that numinosity and solemnity that they promise and preach. They provide the aura of the numinous, regardless of whether there is in actuality a substantial numinous experience or not. We could speak here, in analogy to "cloud computing," of "cloud experiencing," "cloud religiousness." Air bubbles and fictions *as fetishes*.

Now we have to be fair to Jung and acknowledge that he wanted anything but to offer a theory about the numinous depth of the soul which could serve as a prop for "spiritually" empty and unstable people (this is precisely why he rejected the faith demanded by theology) or which could be used as a fetish. He honestly believed in personal "primordial experiences" as actual occurrences, as realities, and he believed that *only* they could give the individual, under the conditions of modernity, "an indestructible foundation": "I know from experience that all coercion—be it suggestion, insinuation, or any other method of persuasion—ultimately proves to be nothing but an obstacle to the highest and most decisive experience of all, which is to be alone with his own self, or whatever else one chooses to call the objectivity of the psyche. The patient must be alone if he is to find out what it is that

[20] C.G. Jung, *Über Gefühle und den Schatten*. Winterthurer Fragestunden. Textbuch, Zürich and Düsseldorf 1999, p. 22. My translation.

supports him when he can no longer support himself. Only this experience gives him an indestructible foundation" (*CW* 12 § 32). In itself an admirable statement. However, Jung did not see two things.

First, he did not see that such a depth experience in the loneliness "with one's self" as he envisioned it could only happen as a kind of "veritable gift of grace that nobody can make," that is to say, it cannot be offered as a general goal of therapeutic psychology for ordinary patients and analysands and cannot serve as a valid answer to the "spiritual" predicament and inner substancelessness of modern man. But precisely this was Jung's fiction. He did not see that personal numinous experiences which really give an indestructible foundation are, if they happen at all,[21] something absolutely rare, isolated, and unpredictable in modernity, only for a very few "religiously" especially gifted individuals and, owing to the isolation and hidden inwardness of such experiences, of no relevance to the modern world at large; he furthermore did not see that psychotherapy and our own personal systematic attention to our dreams are certainly not the appropriate vessel for it. Just as according to Jung the Church "serves as a fortress to protect us against God and his Spirit" (*CW* 18 § 1534), so does the consulting room as well as our work with dreams. Psychology can only have the purpose of soul-making and psychological understanding, of interiorizing phenomena into themselves and releasing them into their truth. It must not want to provide a practical gain for individuals in their subjectivity, the practical benefit of their ultimately being guided to an experience that provides them with an indestructible spiritual foundation. Then psychology would

[21] Although culturally the metaphysical logic underlying religion is a thing of the past (our age is "so utterly deprived of gods and desacralized," *CW* 13 § 51, transl. modif.), we cannot be certain that this has to be the case for every single individual, or for a particular individual in all regards and at all times of his life. There are billions of people, and psychic life is unpredictable. All sorts of experiences are possible. It could well be possible that in the deepest subjectivity of the one or the other present-day person an authentic religious or mystic experience might occur that according to its logical character actually belongs to former ages. It would then be a *stray* experience within the modern context, a fluke of nature.—Also, as Jung pointed out, not all persons physically living today are psychologically rooted in the present time and up to the logic of modernity. Some may psychologically have their true place in the 19th century, some even further back in the Middle Ages, or, as Jung suggested, in some rare case even in the Stone Age. (If this is true, we could say that they represent the equivalent in the realm of actual human beings to what in the sphere of psychic contents Jung had called a "hangover from the past.")

misconstrue itself as Redeemer when in reality it can only have a very sober professional methodical task.

The second thing that Jung did not see is that by developing and propagating his theory of "primordial experience" *despite* the fact that this view of his had the character of a mere noumenon and a fiction *without* empirical-factual basis, he himself produced something that had to have that very effect of coming as mere "suggestion, insinuation, or ... persuasion" that he consciously rightly despised, i.e., the (to be sure, decidedly unwanted, but nevertheless inevitable) effect of becoming a fetish theory, a self-sufficient theoretical *myth* about primordial experience and the numinous.

On the other hand, after all the foregoing critical reflections, we have to acknowledge that without doubt in modern individual experience—both inside and outside analysis, in dreams, in visions, in schizophrenic delusions and so on—motifs of mythic proportion and character can appear and heightened emotions can be evoked by them. There are such experiences. They are real events and they have a substantial content. Where this is the case we are dealing with more than the mere mystique and empty aura of the *theory* or modern *myth* of numinosity and primordial experiences. Would we therefore not have to say that in them there is the empirical-factual basis that I insisted was lacking?

This question has to be denied. What we have here are subjective experiences, mental images, psychic events in people's consciousness. It has not been shown that experiences in which such motifs and emotions occur are experiences *of the spirit*, *of* "the Self" or "God," *of* something primordial. That this is the case is rather a "metaphysical" presupposition. The suggestion is clearly that personal experience or feeling is the experience or feeling *of* something substantial, *of* a real object. However, the *representation* of something mythic or spiritual in one's mind says nothing about a factual existence of "the spirit" and a present reality of mythic meaning. It is just a representation, an idea, an event in the psyche, and to take the presence of such an idea in a modern subject for the actual presence of the divine or transcendent is a serious fallacy. By the same token, we cannot conclude from a "numinous experience" that it is the experience of a *numen* or a numinous reality.

Here we can remember a relevant statement of Jung's. Reflecting on the word "archetype," Jung once said, "The word 'type' is, as we know, derived from τύπος, 'blow' or 'imprint'; thus an archetype presupposes an imprinter. ... The competence of psychology ... only goes so far as to establish ... whether for instance the imprint in the psyche can or cannot reasonably be termed a 'God-image.' Nothing positive or negative has thereby been asserted about the possible existence of God ..." (*CW* 12 § 15). In this argument we see the bungled logic of Jung's thinking in this matter. His last sentence does not make sense. If there is the idea of an imprint that presupposes an imprinter, then this already entails at least *syntactically* the metaphysical assertion of "God" (or some other imprinter), even if *semantically* the question is left undecided. And in addition, the competence of psychology does *not* go so far as to establish the "God-image"-character of "the imprint in the psyche." Because with the word "imprint" the metaphysical trespass has already happened, the substance-idea is already smuggled in.

But all that psychology can establish is that in the mind of modern human beings mythic or archetypal *images*, *ideas* and certain heightened emotions can emerge. There is only a psychic function, an event in consciousness, a production of mental contents or states. The imprint idea and insinuation of the realness of "meaning" is a mystification. By infering from a subjective, psychic event the idea that it is the experience *of* something, *of* a substance Jung commits what Kant called the subreption (*Erschleichung*) of an object where there is only a subjective function of the mind. Certainly, dreams and spontaneous visions are different from conscious imaginings, willful fantasizing. But there is nothing to prove that dream images of mythic figures are not just as much psychic productions, inventions (*produced* contents and *not experiences of* something) as are obvious concoctions of the consciously fantasizing mind.

By the same token, modern dream or visionary experiences are not proven to be "*primordial* experiences" merely because they indeed contain archaic-looking contents. These archaic-looking contents do not directly jut into our modern psyche from out of an ancient past or from a "primordial" depth of reality. Rather, they are thoroughly *modern* psychic *creations* of a modern *reflection* of ancient images by the psyche of modern man and within the context of modern life, in other words, modern fictions, just as modern history books present modern reconstructions of past ages and events and are not the intrusion or reappearance of the historical past itself into the consciousness of modern man, nor the representation of "*the* truth" about the past.

Actually occurring archetypal and numinous experiences do not therefore qualify ipso facto as the presence of religion. Religion in the time-honored sense was (the celebration of) the self-articulation of the self-representation of the irrepresentable inner logic and deepest truth of man's actual world-relation, world-experience at a given historical locus in imaginal and thus objectified form (gods, heaven, underworld, hell, etc.). As the self-representation of the innermost *truth* of lived life, life lived by a society or culture, it is fundamentally communal, public, and official. Just as there cannot be a private language, so there cannot be a private religion. But so-called numinous experiences today are fundamentally private, subjective experiences. That is to say, it is not merely that they happen in private individuals (and in their inner), but, more significant, they are also structurally only of personal relevance. In them the soul (if it is the soul) speaks only to the one individual concerned. These occurrences neither reflect the deepest truth of our historical locus, nor do they have a bearing on the community and on the further development of modern culture.

Furthermore, what comes as actual archetypal or numinous experience (in the narrower context of psychotherapy and in the wider context of an enthusiastic reception in the general public of Jung's ideas about primordial experiences, individuation, archetypes, and numinosity) is liable to the suspicion that it is something to which applies what we learned above about the malleability and suggestibility of people, their unconscious tendency to self-stylize according to a given theory. Such experience is not always truly as spontaneous as it is believed to be and cannot be used as empirical evidence. It is quite likely to be induced by conscious or unconscious longings on the part of individuals to produce in reality within themselves experiences that fulfill what the theory expects and makes them expect. Jungian theory, as all modern psychological theories, is a highly suggestive and seductive phenomenon. Quite apart from people's conscious longings, deep down Jungian theory exerts a certain totally unconscious pressure on the persons in an analytical process to deliver experiences and images of the type that the theory teaches should happen and that it thus in a sense demands. And it is not even only the explicit theory that has to be taken into account. Even for persons who had no previous contact with the theory, the mere atmosphere in the consulting room, the exposure to the reality of the analyst and thus to the mindset or belief prevailing in him or her, especially when it is noticeably inspired by his or her personal charisma and enthusiasm, may in receptive analysands on a deeply unconscious level create an aura and subliminally influence their fantasy productions.

One might here of course wish to object that according to the critical view presented all experiences of mystics of former ages would also appear to be declassed. But then one would overlook a fundamental difference. Just as in former times in private prayer the same official God was addressed who was worshiped in public Church teachings and ceremonies, so also was the mystic experience a, to be sure, factually private, inward experience, but nonetheless an experience *of* aspects or potentials of the same religious truths that in other ways were celebrated in the public official ceremonies. And this is also why very often mystic experiences were made public and in return enriched and deepened public religious life. The mystics never had a *fundamentally* private religion.

Nowadays, actually occurring numinous experiences may *simulate* experiences of the mystics, but they are not equivalents of their experiences. Despite their possibly similar abstract-formal appearance, they have a fundamentally different function and status. They are *only* psychic events, only subjective events, happenings and feelings that are logically enclosed in the individual who has them, but devoid of any religious backing, any authorizing reality of God. Numinous experiences do not entail a *knowing*. They are only the event of a feeling or sensation. But the case of the mystics of old was the exact opposite. In them the movement started out from the *knowledge* and *love* of the official God, the God who was known to be the real God, but then this knowledge and love were inwardized and intensified to a personal felt-experience of a mystic union *with this real Godhead*. Not the personal feeling as such was what counted, but (the personal feeling of) the experienced divine *reality*, the *objective* truth (that appeared in a subject). The further back we go in history, into medieval, ancient, archaic times, the less important personal feelings as psychic events become. Concerning modern so-called "numinous experiences" I would not even speak of a "mystic experience-lite." It is rather a former authentic mystic experience *stripped of* its ontological object and truth content. It is only the left-over subjective feeling, only an abstract(ed) substance-less half, the ego half. Fundamentally empty, nihilistic. It is subjective emotionality per se *with*, to be sure, a "religious" coloring and thus of a "noble," "spiritual" variety, but apart from this particular veneer it has the same logical status as other modern less noble feeling states, such as the "high" states of alcoholized soccer fans, drug addicts, rock festival crowds, "event" tourists. Ego-trips. Emotion and excitement for excitement's sake.[22] Surrogates. Subjective *substitutes* for the lost objective realness of God and the lost containment in a given faith, a consolation, indeed a pacifier, for the desacralization of the world.

Jung of course said about God: "I do not believe, I know." But first of all, "know" as used here in contrast to "believe" does not mean true knowing, but merely "having had *Urerfahrung*," so that we arrive at a point where the dog bites its tail. Secondly, if Jung had really *known* he could not have said what we heard from him above, "Nothing positive or negative has thereby been asserted about the possible existence of God ..." His is an idle, empty knowledge claim.

But on the other hand we must not overlook the fact that *subjectively* Jung definitely and honestly believed to be concerned with knowledge and truth and substantial ("metaphysical") realities, rather than with mere feelings. Jung did have a notion of truth. He had concrete archetypes as objective reals, as "facts" (as he thought). There existed for him a priori given contents, meanings. And Jung's prime concern was ultimately, as he said, with the Canonical God-image, not with just any image. "God is always locally valid, otherwise he would be ineffectual. The Western God-image is the valid one for me .... Only my intellect has anything to do with *purusha-atman* or Tao [here we could add: with Otto's *numen*], but not my living thraldom" (*Letters 2*, p. 33, to Neumann, 5 Jan. 52). But these ideas

[22] Of course, the excitement also seems to have a content. But this is only the way a log seems to be the content or substance of a fire: it exists only as fuel for the sake of being consumed, and thus as the enabling condition of the fire or the emotion, not as the in-itself essential content of mystic experience, namely the objective divine truth whose manifest *revelation* also happens to kindle a fire in the mystic as a mere side-effect.

lead already away from his emphasis on "primordial experience" (which was a theoretical concept of his, a myth of his) and take us to his later *theosophical* speculation about the nature of God himself.

In conclusion I come in all brevity to the postponed discussion of the third type of factual experiences that provide an empirical underpinning for "religious" experience or the experience of "transcendence" *as a present reality*, namely, synchronistic events. Synchronistic events are uncanny coincidences of an inner psychic, mental content and a corresponding outer physical occurrence, a coincidence that can neither be explained as mere chance event nor in terms of causality. It is clear that they are of a fundamentally different order from primordial and numinous experiences. The latter two types have to be seen either as a modern "myth" (in the pejorative sense of the word) in the intellect, abstract theoretical concepts that have a special mystique and thus appeal to certain suggestible persons, or, when they are actually occurring experiences, are merely subjective and without substantial content and thus in the last analysis typical modern ego-trips. Synchronistic events, by contrast, have the dignity of objective fact. They are something real. The theory of synchronicity begins with *empirical data* and not with a noumenon, a thought-thing. It is a theory about *real events* with an *objectively* mysterious, puzzling and disconcerting character, not with subjective experiences. Synchronistic events stand and fall with their objectivity-character.

However, there is no good reason why they should be seen as having a deeper-meaning quality and bringing the religious experience of transcendence. As is well known, in his attempt to comprehend them Jung felt induced to introduce the concept of the "psychoid." If we follow this hint of Jung's, we realize that synchronistic events involve the deeply unconscious level of the human *animal* in us or an even deeper level. "The deeper 'layers' of the psyche," Jung once said, "lose their individual uniqueness as they retreat farther and farther into darkness. 'Lower down,' that is to say as they approach the autonomous functional systems, they become increasingly collective until they are universalized and extinguished in the body's materiality, i.e., in chemical substances. The body's carbon is simply carbon" (*CW* 9i § 291). Synchronistic events impress us *in* our consciousness, to be sure, but they reach us and work *through* a subhuman and sub-soul, a fundamentally prelinguistic level. In contrast to the more familiar phenomenon of an *abaissement du niveau mental*, i.e., *our* consciousness's sinking to a lower psychic level, synchronistic events seem to amount to a *spontaneous* breakthrough at one point of a much, much lower purely *natural* level, a level at which we exist as a piece of nature beneath our being mind or soul and at which our nature is objectively connected with external nature at large through a kind of "sympathetic" oneness. These events are completely removed from that goal that Jung, as religious psychologist, had set for "us moderns" in that text that we started with: the experience of "the spirit," but also completely removed from anything religious and psychological, indeed even from what I call the "psychic" in contradistinction to "psychological" (which is precisely why Jung felt the need to coin the term "psychoid"). They affect us as miraculous (in contrast to "mysterious") because for us as subjects who experience them as a *factual* coincidence between inner and outer, inner and outer nevertheless *remain logically* absolutely disconnected (whereas in mysterious experiences there is at least an implicit, intuited, divined connection for us, even if we cannot grasp it yet[23]).

And here we must again do justice to Jung. It was not he who used synchronicity for the egoic purpose of providing an underpinning for "religious" or "transcendent" experience as a present reality. His synchronicity theory was quite sober and in this regard above board. It was only the Jungians who mystified and fetishized the *empirical-factually miraculous* phenomenon of synchronicity to satisfy their egoic craving for something supernatural-looking that came as a present reality.

---

[23] "Mysterious" suggests a mystery and thus something like a deep wisdom of intrinsic importance for the soul, whereas miracles are merely astounding: *dumb*founding. From here we could also see the fundamental difference between great art and synchronistic experiences, although in both something emerges from "deeper layers" of the psyche. In art it emerges as something symbolic in the widest sense and "makes sense" to the mind, reaches the mind, because it comes from the outset as a product of the mind, whereas synchronicity appears as the unbridgeable division between mind and physical fact, entirely meaningless fact.

Index

D

G

O

P

U

Kolibri 360 GmbH
Ferdinand-Jühlke-Straße 7
99095 Erfurt, Deutschland
produktsicherheit@kolibri360.de